Elizabeth Gaskell:
A *Reference Guide*

Robert L. Selig

G. K. HALL & CO., 70 LINCOLN STREET, BOSTON, MASS.

PR
4711
.S53
1977

Library of Congress Cataloging in Publication Data

Selig, Robert L
    Elizabeth Gaskell : a reference guide.

    (Reference guides in literature)
    Includes index.
    1. Gaskell, Elizabeth Cleghorn Stevenson, 1810-1865--
Bibliography. I. Title.
Z8324.6.S44 [PR4711]   016.823'8   76-30505
ISBN 0-8161-7813-5

This publication is printed on permanent/durable acid-free paper
MANUFACTURED IN THE UNITED STATES OF AMERICA

Contents

v

Introduction

The broad pattern of criticism of Elizabeth Cleghorn Gaskell over 128 years is one of rapid acceptance during her lifetime as a major novelist, a sharp fall after her death to a prolonged lower status as a charming semi-classic, and a fairly recent return toward major rank. In my opinion, the usually enthusiastic critics of her own time and the increasingly favorable critics of the past few years are closer to the truth than those intervening generations who tended to see her as the author of the wistfully comic but minor _Cranford_ and the kindly _Life of Charlotte Brontë_. Mrs. Gaskell ranks, I think, with George Eliot, Thomas Hardy, and Anthony Trollope as a novelist of provincial life who treated large human issues with honesty, insight, and art.

In some ways, the early critics were lucky in being ignorant of the facts of Elizabeth Gaskell's life (1810-1865), for they were unable to look for real-life models for her fiction--a futile guessing game that later dominated much of Gaskell criticism for more than sixty years. The early absence of knowledge about this at-first-anonymous author may be comically illustrated by the frequent inability of reviewers to spell her name correctly (_see_ 1853.B1, B4, B33; 1858.B6), by their underestimation of her age (_see_ 1865.B5, B12, B16, B21, B23, B28; 1866.B16), and by their belief that her maiden name was Stromkin (_see_ 1858.B1; 1865.B5, B6, B12, B21, B23, B28; 1866.B16). From 1867 to the mid-twentieth century most critics, because of her instructions to her family to withhold information from would-be biographers, knew little more than the basic facts about her. Consequently, commentators often treated the fiction as a quarry for biographical details (_see_, for example, Chadwick, 1910.A1). Since the biography by Hopkins (1952.A1) and, more recently, Chapple and Pollard's edition of Gaskell letters (1966.B3), there has been less temptation to confuse fact with fiction. The injunction against biographical criticism in twentieth-century critical theory has also had its effect.

The chief facts of Elizabeth Gaskell's life may be briefly summarized here. She was born in London as Elizabeth Stevenson, daughter of a former Unitarian minister. As a result of the early death of her mother, Elizabeth grew up in rural Knutsford, near Manchester. Her

marriage to the Rev. William Gaskell, a Unitarian minister of that
nearby city, made her a resident of Manchester, where, for more than
a decade, she lived the life of housewife and mother. A latecomer to
fiction, she published her first novel, Mary Barton, when she was
thirty-eight. Her early works tend to deal with Manchester's industrial problems, but her later fiction concentrates on a rural life
similar to that of her Knutsford upbringing.

Much valuable criticism of Elizabeth Gaskell's work appeared
during her lifetime and just after her death, yet most of this material has simply been neglected by scholars. The unsigned bibliography by Archie Stanton Whitfield in The Cambridge Bibliography of
English Literature (1966.B12) singles out only five entries from
1848 to 1866; Walter Savage Landor's short poem on Mary Barton in the
Eclectic Magazine (New York) (1849.B8); Émile Montégut's reviews of
Mary Barton, Ruth, and North and South in the Revue des Deux Mondes
(Paris) (1853.B62; 1855.B14); Edward Dicey's obituary on Mrs. Gaskell
in the Nation (New York) (1865.B33); Richard Monckton Milnes's
obituary on her in the Pall Mall Gazette (London) (1865.B35); and
W. R. Greg's Edinburgh Review piece on Mary Barton (1849.B6). Whitfield also mentions a supposed second essay on Mary Barton by Greg
in a later Edinburgh Review, but the piece was actually by Fitzjames
Stephen and contained only a passing reference to the Life of Charlotte Brontë (1857.B105). Out of the vast amount of largely unex-
plored criticism from 1848 to 1866, I here offer an alternative list
of twenty important items, most of them, I think, more insightful
than the above: Anon. on Mary Barton in Examiner (London) (1848.B3),
Anon. (perhaps William Howitt) on Mary Barton in Standard of Freedom
(London) (1848.B8), Anon. on Mary Barton in Atlas (London) (1848.B10),
Anon. on Ruth in Gentleman's Magazine (London) (1853.B11), Anon. on
Cranford in Examiner (London) (1853.B12), Anon. on Cranford in Non-
conformist (London) (1853.B19), Anon. on Ruth in Tait's Edinburgh
Magazine (1853.B54), George Henry Lewes (unsigned) on Ruth in Leader
(London) (1853.B59), George Henry Lewes (unsigned) on Ruth in West-
minster Review (London) (1853.B60), Anon. on North and South in
Examiner (London) (1855.B3), Anon. on The Life of Charlotte Brontë
in Spectator (London) (1857.B3), Anon. on The Life of Charlotte
Brontë in British Quarterly Review (London) (1857.B20), Anon. on The
Life of Charlotte Brontë in Manchester Guardian (1857.B25), Anon. on
Sylvia's Lovers in Examiner (London) (1863.B8, B9), Anon. on Sylvia's
Lovers and A Dark Night's Work in Nonconformist (London) (1863.B16),
Anon. on Sylvia's Lovers in Athenaeum (London) (1863.B23), Anon. on
Sylvia's Lovers in Morning Post (London) (1863.B30), Anon. on Wives
and Daughters in Spectator (London) (1866.B2), Anon. on Wives and
Daughters in Saturday Review (London) (1866.B23), and Henry James
(unsigned) on Wives and Daughters in Nation (New York) (1866.B26).
In general, the critics from 1848 to 1866 tended to put more emphasis
on moral questions than would a twentieth-century critic, yet they
also provided perceptive comments about the narrative technique,
structure, symbolic pattern, psychology, and the sociological implications of Mrs. Gaskell's works.

INTRODUCTION

Too much criticism on Elizabeth Gaskell from 1867 to 1946 tends
to freeze selected earlier opinions into dogma and, at the same time,
to respond to less and less of her work. Critic after critic tells
us that her writing was charming, feminine, true-to-life, various,
but also unintellectual and not well plotted. One group of critics
tells us that her only great work was Cranford, another group prefers
The Life of Charlotte Brontë, and still another Wives and Daughters,
but few feel called upon to respond intelligently to her whole body
of writings, unless, like Sir Adolphus William Ward (1906.B35-B42),
they are assigned to write introductions to her collected works.
Indeed, many of the most useful items on Mrs. Gaskell during this
period of her decline lie outside the realm of criticism: published
letters and memoirs of her contemporaries, biographical scraps, or
bibliographic details. One of the most interesting sequences of
material consists of what a cynic might call practical urban criticism: a debate in the Manchester newspapers from October 1913
through February 1914 about whether the city of Manchester should
pay for a Gaskell memorial museum in her old house. The City Council
decided against the memorial as a bad business proposition, but the
Manchester Guardian made up for its unfair attack on Mary Barton during Mrs. Gaskell's lifetime (1849.B4) by campaigning for the memorial
and then scolding the Council for refusing to sanction it (1913.B6,
B7, B12-14, B24, B47; 1914.B1, B4, B5, B7, B9-23, B25, B27-29, B34-40,
B44-49, B52-55). Among those scattered critical essays that have
something fresh to say in this period, one might single out two anonymous pieces: ". . . The Works of Mrs. Gaskell," Academy (London)
(1906.B11); and "The British Novel as an Institution," Edinburgh Review (1907.B2). Lord David Cecil's essay on Elizabeth Gaskell in
Early Victorian Novelists (1934.B1) is of particular interest, but as
much for its masculine bias as for positive critical virtues. Cecil
draws up a long list of Mrs. Gaskell's supposed limitations and then
labels them as all typically feminine.

The most important signs of a Gaskell revival shortly after the
Second World War were the Chiltern Library editions of her works,
with perceptive introductions by Lettice Cooper, Elizabeth Jenkins,
Margaret Lane, Rosamund Lehmann, and Elizabeth Bowen (1947.B3, B7,
B8; 1948.B14; 1951.B1). There were also some intelligent critical
responses to these editions, such as Naomi Lewis's suggestion, in
New Statesman and Nation (London) (1948.B15), that Elizabeth Gaskell's
two central qualities were impulsiveness and a gift for comedy. But
the Gaskell revival was hindered by F. R. Leavis's contemptuous dis-
missal of her in The Great Tradition (1948.B13), which may well have
discouraged a generation of graduate students from exploring her
works. Still, Angela Thirkell's chatty but insightful introduction
to yet another edition of Cranford (1951.B6) predicted that the
greatness of Wives and Daughters would one day "be rediscovered."
Detailed academic studies of Mrs. Gaskell began to appear--most
notably, Annette B. Hopkins's solid but pedestrian biography Elizabeth Gaskell: Her Life and Work (1952.A1) and Kathleen Tillotson's
excellent analysis of Mary Barton in Novels of the Eighteen-Forties
(1954.B7). The unacademic E. M. Forster, in a Sunday Times (London)

article, claimed greatness for Elizabeth Gaskell and declared Molly, of Wives and Daughters, his favorite nineteenth-century "heroine" (1957.B4). A similar claim for the greatness of Wives and Daughters was made by D. G. Klingopulos in From Dickens to Hardy (1958.B7), and a decade later Laurence Lerner, in his introduction to the Penguin Wives and Daughters (1969.B6), called it "the most neglected novel of its century."

The one hundredth anniversary of Elizabeth Gaskell's death stimulated some of the freshest work on her since the time just after her death. Most notably, Edgar Wright, in Mrs. Gaskell: the Basis for Reassessment (1965.A2), rejected a century of critical clichés about charm and femininity to explore the unity of her entire work in terms of her awareness of the interaction between character and environment. Somewhat less original than Wright, Arthur Pollard, in Mrs. Gaskell: Novelist and Biographer (1965.A1), nevertheless attempted to rebut the old charge that she could not portray "passion." John Lucas's fine essay on Mrs. Gaskell in Tradition and Tolerance in Nineteenth-Century Fiction (1966.B9) argued that her social novels are so honest that they suggest truths beyond their conscious theses. Margaret Ganz, in Elizabeth Gaskell: the Artist in Conflict (1969.A1), saw her humor as a means of transcending a conflict between impulse and convention. John Geoffrey Sharps, in Mrs. Gaskell's Observation and Invention (1970.A1), brought to the study of her work a scholarly minuteness and thoroughness usually reserved for giants such as Shakespeare. Barbara Hardy, in The Victorians (1970.B8), ranked Elizabeth Gaskell with George Eliot, a position that Mrs. Gaskell had not held as a novelist since the late 1860s. And, finally, the reawakened feminist movement of the 1970s turned its attention to Elizabeth Gaskell's works: for example, in Patricia Meyer Spacks's "Taking Care: Some Women Novelists," Novel (Providence) (1972.B14), and in Patricia Beer's Reader, I Married Him (1974.B5).

In 1975 and 1976, years that lie beyond the scope of this bibliography, the Gaskell revival continued in full force: W.[endy] A. Craik, Elizabeth Gaskell and the English Provincial Novel (London: Methuen & Co., 1975); Coral Lansbury, Elizabeth Gaskell: the Novel of Social Crisis (London: Elek, 1975); Winifred Gérin, Elizabeth Gaskell: a Biography (announced for publication by Oxford University Press for 1976). The interest in Mrs. Gaskell extended to the popular arts. In late 1975 Cranford was made into a musical by Joan Littlewood and John Wells at London's Theatre Workshop, and a dramatized version of North and South was shown on B.B.C. television in December of 1975. In England in the 1970s, Elizabeth Gaskell's books themselves were being revived and widely sold in paperback. She had again become a part of general British culture.

Three existing Gaskell bibliographies have been of particular use in the preparation of this research guide, but each also has distinct limitations. The bibliographies are Clark S. Northup's, at the back of Gerald DeWitt Sanders's Elizabeth Gaskell (1929.B6); A.[rchie]

Introduction

Stanton Whitfield's, at the back of his own <u>Mrs. Gaskell: Her Life and Work</u> (1929.A3); and Marjorie Taylor Davis's, recently done as a doctoral dissertation (1974.B6). Northup's work, considered standard by most authorities, is described by <u>The Cambridge Bibliography of English Literature</u> (1966.B12) as "very full" on secondary items, yet that description is misleading. Northup is reasonably "full" for 1867 to 1928 but surprisingly skimpy for the key years of 1848 to 1866--the period of response by Mrs. Gaskell's contemporaries. Whitfield has a similar paucity of early reviews. And Davis, though she provides the fullest annotations, does little more than relist the early items previously cited by Northup and Whitfield. For the period 1848 to 1866, Northup has 61 entries, Whitfield has 42, and Davis has 75. The present bibliography contains 367 items from this period, many of them major.

The previous Gaskell bibliographies share a second shortcoming, which this book has tried to correct. Northup and Whitfield over-rely on John Albert Green's <u>A Bibliographical Guide to the Gaskell Collection in the Moss Side Library</u> (1911.A2) without sufficient acknowledgement of their debt, and Davis takes over their indebtedness secondhand without, apparently, being aware of it. Green's guide was, in fact, a valuable pioneering effort, but it is full of inaccuracies that are reproduced by the later bibliographers. I have used Green sceptically and mainly as a check list during my work at the Gaskell Collection, which is now housed at the Manchester Central Library, to which I gratefully acknowledge my indebtedness. The collection contains hundreds of cuttings, from newspapers and periodicals, about Elizabeth Gaskell, and, although few cuttings go back before the beginnings of the collection in the 1890s, the librarians after Green have continued to accumulate material up to the present time. There is one basic problem, however, in using these Gaskell cuttings: often the page number has been clipped off, and at times the date, volume number, and even the name of the publication are missing. Sometimes the missing information is supplied by hand but not always correctly. There are a number of articles that were not, in fact, published in the place indicated. In short, this collection of secondary materials must be used with care, yet it is indispensable for any serious student of Mrs. Gaskell. The librarians at Manchester were particularly gracious and helpful to me in my efforts to use it.

This bibliography tries to be as inclusive as possible for the whole span of years covered but makes no foolhardy claim to be exhaustive. It does contain more than three times as many items as in any previous Gaskell bibliography. Some 44 per cent of its entries were previously undiscovered either by Northrup; Whitfield; Davis; by the standard annual bibliographies, such as those of the MLA or <u>Victorian Studies</u>; or by the collectors of Gaskell cuttings at the Manchester Central Library.

The annotations in this bibliography are abstracts of the original rather than expressions of my own opinion. Items that I was not able to see are marked with an asterisk and followed by a source. Whenever possible in such cases, an annotation is provided, based on that source. If the source seems to have been wrong about details of publication, the asterisked item is labeled "unlocatable." Abstracts from the Gaskell Collection that are so marked and labeled were taken from the cuttings themselves but not found in the indicated publication. Throughout the bibliography, items that are difficult to see, such as the early reviews or the introductions to scarce editions, receive particularly full abstracts. Books wholly on Mrs. Gaskell are abstracted in detail, and comments are also provided from selected reviews of these books. In two exceptional cases, a summary of reviews is given for books not primarily on Mrs. Gaskell: both are by Clement Shorter and deal with the Brontës (1896.B9 and 1908.B27), but they draw many significant comparisons with Elizabeth Gaskell's Life of Charlotte Brontë.

The organization of the bibliographic entries is chronological by year, with each year subdivided into alphabetically arranged sections: "A. Books," "B. Shorter Writings." A single, inclusive, alphabetized index covers the following categories: titles of Elizabeth Gaskell's works, titles of secondary works about her, authors of secondary works, and selected subject headings. Index references are to year, subdivision, and entry number.

Acknowledgments

I wish to express my gratitude to the following institutions for the use of their collections and for their generous help: British Library, Great Russell Street, London; British Newspaper Library, Colindale, London; Center for Research Libraries, Chicago; Chicago Public Library; Manchester Central Library; Newberry Library; New York Public Library; Purdue University Calumet Campus Library; Regenstein Library of the University of Chicago; University of London Library.

I should also like to thank the Purdue Research Foundation for an International Travel Grant that enabled me to pursue my bibliographic work in England.

I should further like to express my gratitude to Professor Carl R. Woodring of Columbia University for encouraging me to undertake this project in the first place.

List of Abbreviations

All abbreviations come from the "Master List and
Table of Abbreviations" in the 1973 MLA International
Bibliography of Books and Articles on the Modern
Languages and Literatures, I.

AQ   American Quarterly (Philadelphia)

AWR   The Anglo-Welsh Review (1968: Inkerrow, Worchestershire)

BJRL   Bulletin of the John Rylands Library (Manchester)

BNYPL   Bulletin of the New York Public Library

ContempR Contemporary Review (London)

CritQ   Critical Quarterly (Norwich and Hull)

DA   Dissertation Abstracts [superseded by DAI]
             (Ann Arbor, Michigan)

DAI   Dissertation Abstracts International [supersedes DA]
             (Ann Arbor, Michigan)

DUJ   Durham University Journal

EA   Etudes Anglaises (Paris)

EDH   Essays by Divers Hands (London)

EIC   Essays in Criticism (Oxford)

ELN   English Language Notes (Boulder, Colorado)

ESA   English Studies in Africa (Johannesburg)

HLQ   Huntington Library Quarterly (San Marino, California)

JPC   Journal of Popular Culture (Bowling Green, Ohio)

JRUL   Journal of the Rutgers University Library
            (New Brunswick, New Jersey)

LJ   Library Journal (New York)

ManR   Manchester Review

MLN   Modern Language Notes (1930: Baltimore)

MLQ   Modern Language Quarterly (Seattle)

MLR   Modern Language Review (Leeds)

MP   Modern Philology (Chicago)

NA   Nuova Antologia (Rome)

N & Q   Notes and Queries (London)

NCF   Nineteenth-Century Fiction (Berkeley and Los Angeles)

NEQ   New England Quarterly (1933: Portland, Maine)

PhQ   Philosophical Quarterly (Iowa City)

PULC   Princeton University Library Chronicle

QQ   Queen's Quarterly (Kingston, Ontario, Canada)

RES   Review of English Studies (Oxford)

RGB   Revue Générale Belge (Brussels)

SP   Studies in Philology (Chapel Hill, North Carolina)

SR   Sewanee Review (1900-1901: New York)

TLS   Times Literary Supplement (London)

VS   Victorian Studies (Bloomington, Indiana)

WHR   Western Humanities Review (Salt Lake City, Utah)

YR   Yale Review (New Haven)

Checklist of Works

I. FICTION AND BIOGRAPHY

"Life in Manchester: Libby Marsh's Three Eras," by Cotton Mather
    Mills, Esq., Howitt's Journal, I (5, 12, 19 June 1847), 310-13,
    334-36, 345-47

Mary Barton: a Tale of Manchester Life. London: Chapman & Hall,
    1848

"The Heart of John Middleton," Household Words, II (28 December
    1850), 325-34

The Moorland Cottage. London: Chapman & Hall, 1850

"The Old Nurse's Story," Household Words (Extra Christmas Number,
    1852), pp. 11-20

Cranford. London: Chapman & Hall, 1853

"My French Master," Household Words, VIII (17, 24 December 1853),
    361-65, 388-93

Ruth. A Novel. London: Chapman & Hall, 1853

Lizzie Leigh and Other Tales. London: Chapman & Hall, 1854

"Half a Life-Time Ago," Household Words, XII (6-20 October 1855),
    229-37, 253-57, 276-82

North and South. London: Chapman & Hall, 1855

The Life of Charlotte Brontë. London: Smith, Elder & Co., 1857

My Lady Ludlow. New York: Harper & Brothers, Publishers, 1858

Round the Sofa [includes "Round the Sofa," My Lady Ludlow, "An Accursed Race," "The Doom of the Griffiths," "Half a Life-Time Ago," "The Poor Clare," "The Half-Brothers"]. London: Sampson Low, Son & Co., 1859

Right at Last, and Other Tales. London: Sampson Low, Son & Co., 1860

Lois the Witch and Other Tales. Leipzig: Bernhard Tauchnitz, 1861

A Dark Night's Work. London: Smith, Elder & Co., 1863

Sylvia's Lovers. London: Smith, Elder & Co., 1863

Cousin Phillis. A Tale. New York: Harper & Brothers, Publishers, 1864

Wives and Daughters. An Every-Day Story. London: Smith, Elder & Co., 1886

Cranford. The Cage at Cranford. The Moorland Cottage. The Novels and Tales of Mrs. Gaskell, III. World's Classics, CX. London: Henry Frowde, Oxford University Press, 1907

II. LETTERS AND DIARIES

"My Diary." The Early Years of My Daughter Marianne. London: Privately Printed by Clement Shorter, 1923

Letters of Mrs. Gaskell and Charles Eliot Norton, 1855-1865. Edited by Jane Whitehill. London: Oxford University Press, Humphrey Milford, 1932

The Letters of Mrs. Gaskell. Edited by J. A. V. Chapple and Arthur Pollard. Manchester: University of Manchester Press, 1966

Writings about Elizabeth Gaskell, 1848-1974

1848 A   BOOKS – NONE

1848 B   SHORTER WRITINGS

1   ANON. "Fiction. Mary Barton,..." Critic (London), VII
    (15 November), 454-55.
       This novel has the unromantic subject of "steam chim-
    neys," trade "unions, and anti-corn-law leagues," yet "the
    author" has "discovered" in the "every-day life" of an in-
    dustrial city "the same passions" as in "the castles of
    the Norman barons." "The author draws town scenes with
    almost the skill of DICKENS, and his sketches of character
    are thoroughly life-like."

2   ANON. "Life in Manchester. Mary Barton,..." Literary
    Gazette (London), XXXVIII (28 October), 706-8. [Reprinted
    in London and Paris Observer (Paris) (19 November 1848),
    pp. 743-46.]
       "We are inclined to place Mary Barton foremost" among
    novels that describe working-class life. Though put in
    narrative form, the novel is clearly drawn from actuality.
    "This able performance" reproduces the "Lancashire dialect"
    and will give new insight about Manchester to general
    readers and its own citizens.

3   ANON. "Literary Examiner. Mary Barton,..." Examiner
    (London) (4 November), pp. 708-9.
       This novel has "unusual beauty," "merit," "plain and
    powerful interest," "a good and kind purpose," and a
    charming sincerity of style. The domestic detail shows
    that the author is a woman. In contrast to Disraeli's
    pretentious novels, this book gives an "ungilded" account
    of working-class hardships, is impartial between classes,
    and provides a "sense of what is due to the poor," along
    with human interest, "humour, pathos," and deeply moving
    tragedy. The writer's only fault is to be sometimes "com-
    monplace" or to deal with "questions" beyond her under-
    standing.

1848

4   ANON. "Literary Notices. Mary Barton," New Monthly Magazine
     (London), LXXXIV (November), 406.
          We have seldom read such an "earnest" and purposeful
     book as this or one with "more feeling," though it lacks
     Dickens's "humour" and "sly insights" or Anderson's
     "child-like simplicity." In spite of its "painful" sub-
     ject, the book is "almost sanctified by its wholesome
     truthfulness" and is brightened by its portrayal of Jem,
     the "gallant" workingman. But "the authoress...allows" the
     "discontented" John Barton "to utter communist sentiments
     without rebuking or correcting them" or showing that there
     "must be capitalists...." Nevertheless, the novel ends
     with a plea for "understanding" and "love...between" the
     "masters" and the suffering "men--the interests of the one
     being the interests of all."

5   ANON. "Literature. Mary Barton,..." Economist (London), VI
     (25 November), 1337-38.
          "This work" is truthful in its "appalling picture" of
     working-class suffering in Manchester and hence is "most
     depressing." Its portrayal of the "domestic virtues" and
     "industry" of "the miserable operatives" makes one wonder
     why the system victimizes good "men." We hope that Mary
     Barton will "inspire" readers "with the wish to" help the
     working poor, yet "we fear the author has but little hope,"
     as his only solution is to send "his hero and heroine...to
     Canada" in "voluntary banishment."

6   ANON. "Literature. Mary Barton,..." John Bull (London),
     XXVIII (4 November), 711.
          "... There are passages...of surpassing beauty and
     power" in this accurate story of factory working life. An
     especially "striking" narrative sequence is the one in
     which John Barton "confesses...to the father" of the man he
     has murdered. "This well-imagined and well-executed" book
     is "deeply and painfully instructive" about masters and
     men and should teach "a useful lesson."

7   ANON. "Literature. Mary Barton,..." Morning Post (London)
     (24 November), p. 6.
          "We heartily approve of the benevolent purpose" of this
     novel that shows the "good qualities" of "humble" Man-
     chester working people but does not "excuse" "their weak-
     ness" with "false sentimentality" nor "bring the rich into
     contempt...." Though the mistaken "views" of both sides
     are presented in "dialogue," "the author wishes manufac-
     turers to" display more understanding and "Christian sym-
     pathy" toward the "much neglected" operatives. Such

enlightenment on the part of employers would, we think, help allay dangerous working-class discontent.

8   ANON. "Literature. Mary Barton,..." Standard of Freedom (London), I (28 October), 12.
      "This will do. This is welcome. We have waited for it.... Here is a genuine book." We thank "the author for the good work which she (the style...betrays the sex) has accomplished. 'Mary Barton'...should be read by...all ranks, but especially...the highest and wealthiest.... We expect to hear it descried" by "both Whig and Tory," for the rich do not like to hear of "the monstrous inequalities in the social condition of God's human creatures.... The... publishing season will...produce...nothing as a whole, so good as 'Mary Barton'.... We can reveal" that the author "wrote a year ago, some clever stories in 'Howitt's Journal' under the assumed name of 'Cotton Mather Mills'." This novel's "plot" is "hacknied," but the subject of "starving...Manchester operatives" is handled masterfully in "the first volume,...by far the better half." Although Mary Barton "is not equal" artistically "to the best works of Fielding, Scott, Bulwer, Dickens, or Thackeray,...it is only second to their masterpieces; and we fully expect that the author's next work...will give her a position" unsurpassed by "any living" novelist.

9   ANON. "Literature. Mary Barton,..." Sun (London) (30 November), p. 3.
      Although "fictitious," this "admirable" book gives "a most graphic" and truthful "sketch of the habits and thoughts" of the working class. Yet it also "reveals" skillfully "the secret workings of the human heart, which are the same among all classes." The work makes us identify with both the "mirth of the factory-workers in" good times and their despair in bad. "The wrongs and the wrong-doings of both employers and employed are gently touched upon," without "malice." The "tragic incident" of the murder, the steady development of Mary's "character," and the trial scene are especially impressive elements in this "masterly novel."

10   ANON. "Literature. Reviews of New Books. Mary Barton,..." Atlas (London), XXIII (4 November), 722-23.
      "This work" presents a puzzling combination of "youthful" "freshness" and mature artistic self-confidence. "... In the bold outline and...the broad massive shadowing," the writer seems male, "but there is...woman in many of the details." Though the plot is a "stock" one, the

1848

(ANON.)
book's strength lies in the "reality" of its depiction of "a certain condition of society," along with its "distinctness" of characterization. Mary Barton herself is the least distinct, but Job Legh and his blind granddaughter are "worthy of Dickens." The women are generally more vivid than the men.

11   ANON. "Mary Barton," Athenaeum (London), no. 1095 (21 October), pp. 1050-51.
Perhaps "fiction" should not be used for exposing "social evils," yet Mary Barton's picture of working-class life has few equals for its "truth," force, and fairness. The author avoids melodrama, except in two places, where he uses "it with a master's hand." The book achieves a "very rare" if "painful interest" through its command of "character," "feelings," "motive," and "lifelike dialogue." The writer is skillful at "quaint and whimsical" scenes and has a fine ear for Lancashire dialect.

12   ANON. "Mary Barton,..." Britannia (London), IX (21 October), 684.
This book is a pleasant surprise, for it shows how workingmen are able to be content if they can provide for their family and how the poor help one another even in their misery. This is not a merely black picture of working-class life: Mary Wilson's "humble" character is excellently "drawn with the pen of a Christian," and there is "simple pathos" in the description of the Barton family on the death of the mother. The story of how John Barton is led to the murder of his employer's son is told "with great skill" and with no exaggeration of character. Although industrial conditions are presented in a balanced way, this book will "excite sympathy" for the factory workers.

13   ANON. "Reviews. Mary Barton,..." Inquirer (London), no. 332 (11 November), pp. 710-11.
"This work deserves a place beside the 'carol' of Dickens and the poetry of [Ebenezer] Elliott" as "an attempt to describe faithfully and simply the lives of the very poor.... Unlike most other" writers on "the poor," this novelist displays an "eloquent sympathy" for them that shows us how "little" "we know...of their...real greatness" and their "self-denying love" even in "wretchedness." Among other exquisite characterizations, we have the "good, honest" John Barton driven "desperate by hunger" and by his employer's thoughtlessness. This novel, which we "suspect"

is by a woman, will most impress "those who believe sin...
the worst error" and "good works the best evidence of...
faith."

1849 A BOOKS - NONE

1849 B SHORTER WRITINGS

1   ANON. "Literature," Sunday Times (London) (14 January), p. 3.
     "'Mary Barton' appears decidedly the novel of the day"
     and is praised by the Eclectic Review, which itself sup-
     ports "the rights of the people against those oppressive
     classes who...have styled themselves the upper,...important
     classes."

2   ANON. "Mary Barton,..." British Quarterly Review (London),
     IX (1 February), 117-36.
     Though this novel shows ability, it is a representative
     example of certain misguided notions about the conditions
     of the poor. The mill owners' reputations have been
     blackened by those who have a vested interest in opposing
     the cotton trade, and Mary Barton fails to set right these
     false charges. Through our own inquiries among Manchester
     workers and masters, we found the novel's depiction of in-
     dustrial misery to be "greatly exaggerated" and also "out
     of date." Most mill owners have learned that it is
     profitable to treat workers well.

3   ANON. "Mary Barton,..." Eclectic Review (London), n.s. XXV
     (January), 51-63.
     Mary Barton gives an "unbiassed human picture" of the
     plight of the working class in Manchester. Though it has
     a few beginner's "faults of construction," it shows "first-
     rate ability" and is more successful than any other novel
     in "years" in arousing a desire for social reform.

4   ANON. "Mary Barton,..." Manchester Guardian (28 February),
     p. 7.
     This is a well-told story, but, in misrepresenting the
     case of the men against the masters, the novel will do
     "mischief." Manchester workingmen are, in fact, well paid
     and well treated, and the author has been misled by
     propaganda of the anti-corn-law league.

5   B.[RADFORD], J. E. "Mary Barton," Christian Examiner
     (Boston), 4th ser. XI (March), 293-306. [On the 1 vol. ed.
     New York: Harper & Brothers, 1849.]

1849

(B.[RADFORD], J.E.)
This book's "intrinsic worth will ensure it a wide circulation, even in the...small type and double columns." More moving than Waverley, Mary Barton finds, within a world of machinery, unexpected "romance,...pathos," and even a rare "beauty of holiness," though the work is not explicitly "religious." "Still" its poverty-stricken readers will not be softened "towards the rich," though it will make the rich feel pity for "the poor." We know "that the author did not intend to" slight England's "magnificent charities."

6   [GREG, WILLIAM RATHBONE]. "Mary Barton," Edinburgh Review, LXXXIX (April), 402-35. [Reprinted in William Rathbone Greg. The Mistaken Aims and Attainable Ideals of the Artisan Class. London: Trübner & Co., 1876, pp. 111-173.]
Although the work shows great "promise" and "very high" "literary merit," it is marred both by "false philosophy" and "inaccurate descriptions" of Lancashire artisans, whose hatred toward "employers" it exaggerates, in spite of a few noble working-class exceptions. The supposedly intelligent John Barton fails to save for hard times in good, and the author slurs over the sufferings of employers in depressions and also their wisdom in saving during prosperity. Worst of all is the author's "fatally false idea" that the "poor" should depend on "the rich" rather than themselves for "relief" from social problems. The novel treats work as "a curse" instead of a blessing, ignores the manufacturers' many charities, and denies that their risk of capital entitles them to greater profits than their workers.

7   [KINGSLEY, CHARLES]. "Recent Novels," Fraser's Magazine (London), XXXIX (April), 429-32.
Pages out of Mary Barton should be placarded "on every wall" and "read aloud" from the "pulpit" until a so-called "Christian" "nation" repented of its "evil" and "the higher orders" became aware of the horrors of working-class life. Aside from the novelist's "talent," the book is important for "the facts" it presents, which show "why working men" are turning "Chartists and Communists." Let the public read "this extraordinary book" to learn why "kind" yet "poor men" grow desperate with hate, even against the Church and the Bible.

8   LANDOR, WALTER SAVAGE. "To the Author of Mary Barton," Eclectic Magazine (New York), XVII (June), 261. [Reprinted as "Epistle CCLXVIII: To the Author of Mary Barton," in

Walter Savage Landor. The Last Fruit Off an Old Tree.
London: Edward Moxon, 1853, pp. 481-82.]
[A poem, concluding with the following:] "... Thou
hast taught me at the fount of Truth, / That none confer
God's blessing but the poor, / None but the heavy-laden
reach His throne."

9   [TAYLOR, J. J.]. "Mary Barton," Prospective Review (London),
     V (month unknown), 36-57.
          This "poem in prose" deals with the "humble" and poor
     with remarkable skill for a first novel. Alice is worthy
     of Scott's Jenny Deans, the descriptions of death in hovels
     are "almost Dantesque," the domestic scenes have "Dutch"
     realism, and the "humour" is appealing. Some faults are a
     continual alternation of sad and happy scenes, and incon-
     sistent character development in both John and Mary Barton.
     Although the book attempts some balance between employers
     and men, it is overly harsh to Manchester's beneficent
     manufacturers.

10   W. E. "Mary Barton,..." Westminster and Foreign Quarterly
     Review (London), LI (April), 48-63.
          This "striking book" expresses our age's conviction that
     degrading poverty must be eliminated, although a later era
     must determine how. John Barton demonstrates the folly of
     not saving in good times for bad. His criminal attack on
     the son of a manufacturer is less "strange" than the
     "patience" with which most of the poor accept their suffer-
     ings. The characterization and the story telling are
     splendid. But the author is wrong in not studying "politi-
     cal economy," whose concepts would have averted all the
     tragedy.

11   WINSTANLEY, D. "Mary Barton. To the Editor,..." Manchester
     Guardian (7 March), p. 8.
          Your correspondent libels the author of Mary Barton, who
     has written out of "pure benevolence" and described an
     actual type of manufacturer. [Editor's reply:] Unfor-
     tunately the Carsons are shown as representative, and a
     worse flaw, overlooked by our reviewer, is the book's
     denial that the poor must help themselves.

1850

1850 A BOOKS - NONE

1850 B SHORTER WRITINGS

1   ANON. "Literary Examiner. Christmas Publications. The
    Moorland Cottage,..." Examiner (London) (21 December),
    pp. 813-14.
        The author's "advocacy" of "the oppressed and poor" is
    in the Christmas spirit. Her sensitive, "subtle," and
    Wordsworthian story of self-sacrifice avoids improbabili-
    ties and teaches unselfishness.

2   ANON. "Literary Notices," Britannia (London), XI (21 Decem-
    ber), 812.
        "The success of" Mary Barton "will be, if possible, in-
    creased by the slighter, but not less truthful, touches of"
    its author's Moorland Cottage.

3   ANON. "Literature. Christmas Books.... The Moorland
    Cottage,..." Morning Post (London) (23 December), p. 2.
        Much good may be done by the faithful "exhibition of"
    Maggie's noble qualities in this entertaining and edifying
    story of domestic life.

4   ANON. "Mary Barton's Christmas Book," Leader (London), I
    (21 December), 927-28.
        Moorland Cottage with its "close observation, delicate
    perception of character, truthfulness, and singularity of
    style is a great advance in art" over Mary Barton. "...
    The only fault we have to find with this delightful story"
    is its use of a deus ex machina at the end.

5   ANON. "The Moorland Cottage,..." Athenaeum (London), no. 1208
    (21 December), pp. 1337-38.
        This is a tale of "passion and feeling" "among" "every-
    day people" but not "of class-sufferings and class-inter-
    ests," as in Mary Barton. "Rarely has woman drawn a fairer
    study of self-sacrifice in woman than our authoress in
    Maggie Browne," and the wholesomely "moral" story has an
    unusually deep interest, in spite of a pardonable "touch of
    the Deus ex machina in the catastrophe...."

6   ANON. "The Moorland Cottage,..." Standard of Freedom (London),
    III (21 December), 11.
        This is "a very charming" and "beautiful...domestic"
    story, "such as few...but...the author of 'Mary Barton'
    could" write--"one teaching high principles, and awakening
    gentle emotions...."

7   ANON. "Publications Received. Books. <u>The Moorland</u>
       <u>Cottage</u>,..." <u>Spectator</u> (London), XXIII (21 December), 1217.
         This "skillfully-written story" has the "general"
       characteristics "of the juvenile tale," yet "its subject
       rather inclines to the novel."

8   ANON. "Reviews. <u>The Moorland Cottage</u>,..." <u>Guardian</u> (London),
       no. 262 (24 December), pp. 931-32.
         This "short" book "contains far more of character,...
       interest,...pathos,...humour, and a higher tone of teach-
       ing, than many an elaborate and pretentious novel." <u>The</u>
       <u>Moorland Cottage</u> "is almost as good" as the "splendid"
       <u>Mary Barton</u>, and the "gentle" meek Maggie "is a really
       poetical conception...."

9   EVANS, JOHN. "Rev. William Gaskell, M.A.," in <u>Lancashire</u>
       <u>Authors and Orators</u>. London: Houston & Stoneman,
       pp. 96-101.
         [A biographical sketch of Rev. Gaskell, cited by
       Northup (1929.B6) but with nothing on Gaskell.]

<u>1851 A BOOKS - NONE</u>

<u>1851 B SHORTER WRITINGS</u>

1   ANON. "Editor's Book Table. <u>The Moorland Cottage</u>,..."
       <u>Godey's Lady's Book</u> (Philadelphia), XLII (June), 392.
         This is "a domestic tale, familiarly written," instruc-
       tive and elevated in its moral "sentiments."

2   ANON. "Literary Notices," <u>Harper's New Monthly Magazine</u>
       (New York), II (March), 568.
         <u>The Moorland Cottage</u> is "a pleasing domestic story of
       exquisite beauty."

3   ANON. "Literary Notices. <u>The Moorland Cottage</u>,..." <u>Home</u>
       <u>Journal</u> (New York) (8 March), p. 2.
         "The numerous admirers of that unique and affecting
       picture of English manufacturing life, entitled 'Mary
       Barton', will hail" this "earnest, eloquent, and graphic"
       writer's "new work," which, though "intended for the young,"
       can be enjoyed by "all lovers of truth and nature...."

4   ANON. "<u>Moorland Cottage</u>,..." <u>Literary World</u> (New York), VIII
       (15 March), 215.
         "A very neat and elegant Boston edition" has appeared
       "of this popular tale."

1851

5   ANON. "New Novels," Ladies' Companion (London), III
        (1 February), 22.
        "Our readers" should "take" both "pleasure" and "pride"
        in The Moorland Cottage's "healthy and powerful and
        pathetic...story of Woman's love." The portrayal of
        "Woman's endurance and...generosity, claims honour, not
        merely for its own sake, but as illustrating a taste among
        English authors and readers, for works in which fancy and
        feeling...are harmonised by, virtue and reason."

6   ANON. "New Publications," Evening Post (New York) (27 March),
        p. 2.
        The Moorland Cottage, "a story of country life in
        England," is "related with an agreeable simplicity."

7   ANON. "New Publications. The Moorland Cottage,..." Daily
        Evening Transcript (Boston) (21 February), p. 2.
        "The author has acquired much reputation by her pictures
        of English rustic life, and a new work from her pen will
        command attention."

8   ANON. "Notices of New Books. The Moorland Cottage,..."
        United States Magazine and Democratic Review (New York),
        n.s. XXVIII (April), 372.
        "The great interest excited by the tale of Mary Barton,
        both in England and in this country, makes the announcement
        of a new work by the same author of importance. The pres-
        ent volume is of a similar character, but small...."

9   [HART, PROF. JOHN S.]. "Book Notices," Sartain's Union
        Magazine (Philadelphia), VIII (May), 346.
        The Moorland Cottage is "a tempting little story, by
        one of the very best of our recent novelists."

10   [WHEWELL, WILLIAM (?)]. "A Gossip about the Christmas Books,"
        Fraser's Magazine (London), XLIII (January), 42-43. [Re-
        printed in "The New English Books," North American Mis-
        cellany (Boston), I (22 February), 173-74.]
        The Moorland Cottage, a "strengthening little story by
        Mrs. Gaskill [sic]," is in some ways better than the "more
        ambitious Mary Barton." The new book, unlike the old, is
        free of "painful" "details," "dialect," and class-bound
        elements. "Gentle" Maggie Browne is a sweet and "touching"
        creation whose story illustrates "the beauty of" self-
        sacrifice. Near the close, however, the plot is marred by
        an "inartistic" and unconvincing "accident."

11   [WILLS, WILLIAM HENRY]. "Chips. A Disappearance," Household
        Words (London), III (21 June), 305-6.
          [On Gaskell's "Disappearances," Household Words, III
        (7 June 1851), 246-50.] "A correspondent gives the sequel
        of the 'disappearance' described in our pages": the boy
        took ship to America.

1852 A BOOKS - NONE

1852 B SHORTER WRITINGS

    1   GAUNT, JOHN and WILLIAM. "Chips. A Disappearance Cleared
        Up," Household Words (London), IV (21 February), 513-14.
          [On Gaskell's "Disappearances," Household Words, III
        (7 June 1851), 246-50.] According to a family unjustly
        suspected of murdering the missing boy, he enlisted in the
        East India Company "and died of cholera."

1853 A BOOKS - NONE

1853 B SHORTER WRITINGS

    1   ANON. "Anonymous Works," Boston Evening Transcript
        (19 September), p. 2.
          Among the major anonymous authors of our time is "Mrs.
        Gaskill [sic], who is looming up so fast and so high among
        the novelists of the day, as the author of 'Mary Barton',
        'Ruth', and very recently of 'Cranford'. She "is the wife
        of the Unitarian minister at Manchester, Eng."

    2   ANON. "Books and Their Authors," Sharpe's London Magazine,
        n.s. II (15 January), 125-26.
          Even though Ruth has "style," "tenderness," "power," and
        "delicious scenic descriptions," its moral is confused by
        a heroine too "childlike" to represent fallen women and
        by a "Gospel minister" guilty of a lie. Of the characters,
        Sally is "the most original," but the unfair portrayal of
        Bradshaw as a pharisee shows the author's tendency, as in
        Mary Barton, "to look at the wrong side of...'respectable
        persons'...." This "father of a family" is justified in
        protecting them from Ruth. In spite of the "talent" shown
        in the book, its far-too-painful subject should have been
        put into an "appeal to the matrons of England" and not into
        "a novel" to be dwelt on with "morbid fascination" and
        passed off as family reading.

1853

3   ANON. "Books. Ruth," Spectator (London), XXVI (15 January),
     61-62.
         Though some good writing is scattered through this book,
     it fails, as a whole, partly from a Dickens-like "straining
     and inflation" for effect and from overly long descriptions,
     but mainly from "the cant of philanthropy," which inac-
     curately shows "the poor" as "virtuous" and "the rich" as
     selfishly "hard." The attempt to portray Ruth as a Magda-
     lene is confused by having her win "wordly restoration"
     instead of "spiritual" redemption and by an unreal in-
     sistence on her innocence. The characters in the second
     half are striking but, except for the boring Sally and the
     "pharisaical" Bradshaw, are not true to life.

4   ANON. "Books on Our Table," Manchester Examiner and Times
     (2 February), p. 3.
         Ruth, "one of the most charming" novels "since...Mrs.
     Inchbald, Miss Austen, or Miss Edgeworth," is unsurpassed
     in loftiness, truth, beauty, and "courage" in facing its
     controversial topic. "Mrs. Gaskill [sic]"--we would be
     prudish to stick to her "incognito...any longer"--shows
     "versatility" in the variety of her excellent characteriza-
     tions, but the noble Ruth stands out among them. "There is
     more true philosophy in these volumes...than in three-
     fourths of the ethical mysteries which are scattered abroad
     in the modern world as...truth."

5   ANON. "Contemporary Literature," Bentley's Miscellany
     (London), XXXIII (3 February), 237-40.
         Ruth is a "joy," for it shows again "the genius of the
     authoress of 'Mary Barton'," though the new work is not
     "political" but rather religious. This story of fall and
     "atonement" illustrates the harm done to sinners by men's
     lack of "charity" and is "better than any sermon."

6   ANON. "Contemporary Literature of England," Westminster
     Review (London), n.s. IV (July), 273.
         Cranford is the author's chef-d'oeuvre, with "genius,"
     "wit," and "feeling" beyond any "male creature."

7   ANON. "Cranford,..." Literary World (New York), XIII
     (13 August), 39.
         If Ruth was "one of the best novels of...any...season,"
     Cranford was "a great favorite in" Household Words and
     "will doubtless continue to be one as a separate publica-
     tion."

8   ANON. "Editorial Notes. English Literature," Putnam's
     Monthly (New York), I (February), 233.
          Ruth is "one of those exciting fictions which depict the
     struggles and sorrows of the poorer classes of England...."

9   ANON. "England,..." New York Daily Times (15 February), p. 2.
          Gaskell is one of the many current "lady novelists"
     who, as a group, have outpublished men by "more than three
     to one.... Ladies are far more passionate and 'emotional'
     in their portrayal of character, and just now the taste of
     novel readers runs in that direction."

10   ANON. "A Good New Novel. Cranford,..." New York Daily Times
     (15 August), p. 2. [Reprinted as "Mrs. Gaskell and Her
     Sketches of Cranford," in Literary World (New York), XIII
     (3 September), 92.]
          This most delightful book "since...Miss Mitford's 'Our
     Village'" is "the work of a true woman," for "no man could
     have written it." Gaskell, who is rising to the highest
     ranks of literature, published Mary Barton anonymously in
     order not to offend "the old fogies" in her husband's
     congregation. Cranford is "her best work...because it is
     so easy, so unartificial, so exceedingly truthful," and
     "so quietly...satirical" about human "foibles" yet also
     a lesson that "the high and low have alike holiest
     virtues...."

11   ANON. "The Lady Novelists of Great Britain," Gentleman's
     Magazine (London), n.s. XL (July), 22-24.
          This "most striking of our English female novelists" is
     "able" in Ruth to convince us that her fallen woman has
     become a true "heroine." The novel shows the hypocrisy of
     a sexual double standard in thrusting erring women aside or
     driving them to deception, though the author should have
     made Ruth less simple-minded and more subject to sexual
     desire. We disagree with those readers who think that
     Ruth should have accepted her seducer's belated offer of
     marriage, for a woman that noble should not marry "such a
     man." One subtle touch is that Bradshaw, though personally
     repellent, is shown to be right in insisting that he should
     have been told the truth. Those who have "censured" this
     novel have "understood" it "least," for it uplifts us, as
     novels by women should.

12   ANON. "Literary Examiner. Cranford,..." Examiner (London)
     (23 July), 467-68. [Reprinted in Littell's Living Age
     (Boston), 2nd ser. II (10 September), 667.]

1853

(ANON.)
        All that we can say about Cranford is "read it." With-
out the "artifice" of the "formal descriptions of most
novels, this unpretending little" book evokes the reality
of its old-maid "heroines" and their commonplace lives.
It "is the most perfect...book of its kind...published for
many a day." The chief heroine, Matty, in spite of her
foibles, is most memorable for her "delightful" "goodness,"
and the narrator, Mary Smith, combines shrewdness and
"kindliness."

13   ANON. "Literary Examiner. Ruth,..." Examiner (London)
        (22 January), 51-53.
        This charming and moving book keeps a perfect "balance"
between "compassion" for Ruth and moral judgment of the un-
compassionate. The heroine is associated with the author's
evocation of nature, and "if Wordsworth had written in
prose he might have written this...." Ruth's essential
purity is convincing and so is the white lie of the
basically "good" minister, and the over-censorious reli-
giosity of Bradshaw, though perhaps this hypocrite should
not have been allowed to relent at the end. In this novel
even the insides of houses are evoked with the effect of
poetry.

14   ANON. "Literary Intelligence. Cranford," Daily Evening Trans-
        cript (Boston) (20 August), p. 1.
        Cranford, with its "latent and often exquisite satire,...
contains deep truth" beneath "a light and entertaining
guise."

15   ANON. "Literary Intelligence," Daily Evening Transcript
        (Boston) (6 August), p. 2.
        Cranford "has been published this day by the Harpers."
[A reprint follows of George Henry Lewes's anonymous review, "Mary Barton's New Work," Leader (London), IV
(2 July 1853), 644-45. See 1853.B58.]

16   ANON. "Literary Notes," Harper's New Monthly Magazine
        (New York), VII (September), 569.
        "This exquisite tale," Cranford, lacks the intensity "of
Mrs. Gaskell's former productions," yet it is "refined" in
its "humor" and masterful in its characterization. She is
"one of the best living writers of fiction."

17   ANON. "Literary Notices. Cranford Bridge [sic]. By the
        Authoress of Ruth," Britannia (London), XIV (13 August),
        531.

"We welcome this compact edition of that inimitable
sketch of the little country village, which so long graced
the pages of our excellent contemporary, Household Words.
Cranford Bridge [sic] is a fair pendant to Miss Mitford's
village."

18   ANON. "Literature. Cranford,..." John Bull (London), XXXIII
(25 June), 411.
     This tale of village "widows and spinsters afflicted
with that rare but dire complaint, androphobia...is not
likely to be surpassed" in its genre.

19   ANON. "Literature. Cranford,..." Nonconformist (London),
n.s. XIII (3 August), 625.
     We are amused that some readers who at first thought
Cranford "dull," "stupid," and "slow" in serialization
were converted into liking it by the "beautiful and pure"
heroine of Ruth. If Cranford resembles Miss Mitford's
sketches, Gaskell "has the higher genius" because of her
"deep intuition" into her living characters, such as the
"gentle" Matty. A writer who can give us "the moral
earnestness" of Mary Barton, the admirably plotted and
characterized Ruth, and the "imitation" of ordinary life
in Cranford "is capable" of a fiction that will "incorpor-
ate the life of the age in imperishable forms, and be at
once its drama and its epic."

20   ANON. "Literature. Cranford,..." Tait's Edinburgh Magazine,
n.s. XX (August), 503-4.
     These "chronicles" are "the most inimitable portraiture
of human nature female...that has ever been exhibited,"
particularly in the "lovable" Matty. "One regrets that
death has so much to do in this Paradise of old maids."
But "'births, deaths, and marriages' are the materials of
man's domestic history, and we have them all at Cranford
mingled with" lighter "elements of romance...."

21   ANON. "Literature and Music. Ruth,..." Sunday Times (London)
(20 February), p. 2.
     This novel, so disimilar from the admirable Mary Barton,
is the author's "most charming" and as "touching" a story
of female "sorrow in sin" as exists in fiction. Among the
other "healthy" morals, the Rev. Benson's momentous lie
shows that there can be no benefit in falsehood. Ruth's
"position toward the end of the novel is reminiscent of"
The Scarlet Letter's Hester, though some will consider
Ruth's death unnecessary, for it is "more in accordance
with actual life than with poetical justice."

1853

22   ANON. "Literature. Reviews of New Books. Ruth,..." Atlas
     (London), XXXI (5 February), 90.
          "Great sins are boldly confronted, things are called by
     their right names, and error" is "traced to ignorance" in
     this beautiful and "truthful" work. The writer's genius
     makes us share Ruth's sorrows but without morbidness. "A
     woman" with a "strong mind,...sound heart,...exquisite
     taste," and noble "Christian views" on forgiveness has here
     faced "questions that perhaps no man amongst us would have
     treated equally well."

23   ANON. "Literature. Ruth,..." John Bull (London), XXXIII
     (22 January), 59.
          "Fully equal to 'Mary Barton' in truthful" character
     portrayal, this book is "vastly superior" in emotional
     profundity. Ruth's repentant expiation of youthful "error"
     is admirably contrasted with the "selfish respectability"
     of "the money-dealer" who houses her. Ruth's refusal of
     her seducer's belated offer of marriage shows how her
     "virtue" and her "religion" have redeemed her nature.

24   ANON. "Literature. Ruth,..." Ladies' Companion (London),
     2nd ser. III (March), 162-64.
          In reply to critics of the novel's message of forgive-
     ness for fallen women, we say that "Mrs. Gaskell's aim" is
     Christian and "right," though the tale has some flaws, such
     as the pure Ruth's falling "too easily." Bradshaw's
     hypocrisy is portrayed with a skill "seldom" matched in
     "fiction." "... The real social difficulty of a position
     like Ruth's is" fittingly "left...unsettled" by having her
     reinstated only at death. "Such a novel is not for the
     day only," but "will live...to move the hearts and purify
     the conduct of many readers in times far off."

25   ANON. "Literature. Ruth.... London: Bentley [A mistake;
     Chapman & Hall was the publisher.]," Morning Post (London)
     (29 January), p. 3.
          "... The distressing themes from which the author has
     derived his inspiration...are as old as sin,...sorrow,...
     man's remorseless selfishness and woman's too ready
     faith...." Although this story of a young woman's "piti-
     less" punishment by society has a "commonplace" plot, it
     is ennobled by the writer's "genius" for characterization,
     pathos, and "style."

26   ANON. "Literature. Ruth,..." Nonconformist (London), n.s.
     XIII (26 January), 84-85.
          Although some may feel that "such subjects" should not
     be treated in fiction, "we are sure that the purest mind

will be strengthened in its purity by contact with the
delicate womanly instincts,...refined by religion, of the
author of" Ruth. The sight of a woman writer advocating
"tender pity" for "the sinner" is "rare and beautiful."

27 ANON. "Literature. Ruth,..." Observer (London) (23 January),
p. 7.
This outstanding but "sad" tale does not resolve the
mystery of why the "pure of heart" suffer "while the base"
go untouched. "There is, perhaps, over much religion in...
Ruth," but the narrative details, such as those of the
dressmakers, are "full of truth," and the work as a whole
excites "deep sympathy."

28 ANON. "Literature. Ruth,..." Sun (London) (12 February),
p. 3.
The "Christian" theme of this sweet but "sad tale" is
that punishment must benefit the sinner and not merely
chastise, though the book does not "mitigate the horror of"
a woman's fall from "virtue." The story is well told, but
"three volumes...are too long for it." The concluding
section, about Ruth's penitence and purification, "is, in
many respects, the best...."

29 ANON. "Miscellaneous Reviews. Cranford,..." Gentleman's
Magazine (London), n.s. XL (November), 494.
In this "delightful" story of "goodness" among commonplace people, Gaskell displays as much "wit" and "pathos"
as ever, though avoiding both tragedy and conventional
romance. Our only regret is the absence of religious
"differences" and "observations" in the town of Cranford.

30 ANON. "Miscellaneous Reviews. Ruth,..." Gentleman's Magazine
(London), n.s. XXXIX (February), 184-85.
This "very remarkable" novel, far more original than
Mary Barton, is a nearly perfect amalgam of fine pathos,
style, characterization, and evocation of scene. Any
reader who thinks that Ruth favors moral evil has a "perverted" "mind." Sally is as fine a comic creation as Topsy
in Uncle Tom's Cabin.

31 ANON. "New Publications. Ruth,..." Daily Evening Transcript
(Boston) (12 February), p. 2.
In Boston tomorrow Ruth will be published, which received a recommendation in the London Examiner not surprising for a work by such a promising writer.

1853

32   ANON. "New Publications. Ruth,..." Evening Post (New York)
      (23 February), p. 1.
          "... Readers who remember" Mary Barton, the "first"
      really successful working-class novel, "will" wish "to take
      up Ruth," with "a heroine of the same class in life."
      After she is cast off on account of her past, Ruth "behaves
      so as to compel respect for herself and kindness for her
      child."

33   ANON. "Notices of New Publications. Ruth,..." New York Daily
      Times (26 February), p. 3.
          The writer's Mary Barton made her as well known as
      Charles Kingsley for "compassionate" friendship "of the
      working classes." In Ruth she leaves the "town" for "a
      village" tale of a fallen woman's redemption, with a "moral
      ...as old as the parables of our Saviour." "Mrs. Haskell
      [sic] writes with" a "power and graphic effect" at times
      "rivalling...some of the finest passages of CURRER BELL."

34   ANON. "Notices of Recent Publications. Ruth,..." English
      Review (London), XIX (April), 193-94.
          "Scarcely equal...to" Mary Barton's "terrible" and
      "heart-rending" evocation of factory workers, Ruth's story
      of a fallen woman is both less original and less momentous.
      Yet the heroine is exquisitely characterized, and the
      "scene in which she meets her betrayer" years later is
      particularly memorable.

35   ANON. "Novels of the Season. Ruth,..." New Monthly Magazine
      (London), XCVII (February), 197-98.
          Unlike the old, pre-Scott novel, which amused in spite
      of deficiencies, Ruth is merely dismal and leaves the "un-
      pleasant sense of its being easier to commit error than to
      be purified thereof." It "is the most gloomy picture of
      the great 'inquisition' of the moral and intellectual
      world that we have ever seen depicted by artist's hand."
      In contrast to "our Saviour," the author does not allow
      her fallen woman to be absolved in life but, in a "ghastly
      conclusion," forces her to die.

36   ANON. "Our Lady Novelists," Britannia (London), XIV
      (29 January), 81.
          "We...protest against the unsoundness of the present
      crop of" women's "didactic novels, of which Ruth is one,"
      in presenting a "salad of sentiment." Ruth is especially
      offensive in attacking society's rational preventive tac-
      tic of "visiting the sins of" an errant mother on her
      child. The novel is all the more dangerous because of the
      author's descriptive skill and knowledge of human nature.

1853

37   ANON. "Publications Received. Books. Cranford,..."
      Spectator (London), XXVI (25 June), 614.
           This book has "some semblance to" Miss Mitford's Our
      Village, though Cranford had more "variety of story," if
      less detailed descriptions of its town. The work is a
      pleasant combination of "tale" and "descriptive essay."

38   ANON. "Recent Works of Fiction. Ruth,..." Prospective Review
      (London), IX (month unknown), 222-47.
           In their presentation of the moral essence of life,
      novels should avoid explicit didacticism, as Ruth succeeds
      in doing. Yet those, in the novel, who condemn Ruth are
      shown to be far more sinful than she is. We do find it a
      flaw that the Rev. Benson, a supposedly good Christian,
      should agree to the hiding of Ruth's past, yet this se-
      quence is redeemed by the lesson of the "wretchedness"
      that the deception causes. We find the portrayal of
      Ruth's innocence convincing and also see justification
      in her refusal of Bellingham's belated offer of mar-
      riage. "... We thank our author for directing public
      attention to a" painfully interesting "subject."

39   ANON. "Religious Novels of the Quarter," New Quarterly Review
      and Digest of Current Literature (London), II (month un-
      known), 172-74.
           If Ruth is partly "a religious novel," this "wholesome
      and tolerant" work portrays the effects of religion on
      specific minds instead of preaching "particular" "dogmas."
      Its "great lesson" is that "true piety...does good to all"
      and "hard self-righteousness" harms its perpetrator.

40   ANON. "Review of New Books. Cranford,..." Graham's Magazine
      (Philadelphia), XLIII (October), 447-48.
           Gaskell, "of Liverpool [sic]," well known for Mary
      Barton and Ruth, here gives us a work that is "genial"
      rather than "painful." Its style is part Addison and part
      Dickens, and its "kindly" "genius" in depicting "the human
      heart" will make the book "live."

41   ANON. "Review of New Books. Cranford,..." Peterson's Magazine
      (Philadelphia), XXIV (October), 215.
           "The author of 'Mary Barton' and 'Ruth' cannot write
      badly, even when, as now, she has almost nothing to write
      about." Cranford is as "graphic" and "interesting" as a
      book can be with "an almost total want of plot...."

42   ANON. "Review of New Books. Ruth,..." Graham's Magazine
      (Philadelphia), XLII (May), 636.

1853

(ANON.)
The "life-like" fidelity of this powerfully "tragic" work
is "almost painful." Its portrayal of "the purification
and exaltation of a character through suffering" deserves
"a permanent place in the literature of romance."

43   ANON. "Review of New Books. Ruth,..." Peterson's Magazine
      (Philadelphia), XXIII (April), 272-73.
      "The creation of" the beautiful character of "the
      heroine...is alone sufficient to stamp the author as among
      the first of living novelists." Ruth's noble refusal of
      the belated offer of marriage has "almost divine beauty....
      In any other novel the gentle, deformed pastor would have
      made the reputation of the book."

44   ANON. "Reviews. Cranford,..." Inquirer (London), no. 578
      (30 July), pp. 484-85.
      This story equals "the authoress's former works" in
      "pathos," "humour," and fine characterization. Its "moral"
      is that "a good innocent life" creates "friends," but we
      regret that there is less description of scenery than in
      the earlier books.

45   ANON. "Reviews. Ruth,..." Guardian (London), no. 374
      (2 February), pp. 82-83.
      Of novels in recent years, the "inexpressibly beautiful"
      Ruth is "inferior" only "to Mary Barton." Ruth's rejection
      of her seducer's delayed offer of marriage "because she sees
      his wickedness" is a fine and noble action. The description
      of nature's purifying effect "upon her mind and heart"
      reminds us of Wordsworth.

46   ANON. "Reviews. Ruth,..." Inquirer (London), no. 552
      (29 January), p. 66.
      Though less powerful than Mary Barton, Ruth "is superior
      in the drawing of minor characters. The author's genius is
      for profound sympathy with the lives of her characters
      rather than close analysis." She deals with the touchy
      subject of a seduced woman with honesty, charity, and
      purity in one of the "worthiest" of "modern novels."

47   ANON. "Ruth,..." Athenaeum (London), no. 1316 (15 January),
      pp. 76-78. [Reprinted in Littell's Living Age (Boston),
      XXXVI (19 March 1853), 543-45.]
      Although there is much beautiful, moving, and earnest
      writing in Ruth, which has finer pathos than Mrs. Inchbald's
      works, the book is morally flawed by having as good a man
      as the Rev. Benson shield Ruth by a lie.

48 ANON. "Ruth,..." Christian Observer (London), LIII (July),
498-500.
Though we have not "read through" all three "volumes,...
our attention" was "drawn to the last," and so we are
"giving our readers a seasonable warning against" the novel.
In Mary Barton the author "outrageously" employed "her very
considerable powers in the vindication of the lower classes
of society at the expense of the higher.... The object of"
Ruth is "to soften down undeniable crimes and to" condemn
those who do not grant "a plenary indulgence to" a fallen
woman. Such a teaching would undermine society, which must
maintain a separation "between the guilty and the" un-
fallen. The end, describing Ruth in isolated expiation,
is more fitting than those sections that show her re-
accepted into society.

49 ANON. "Ruth,..." Critic (London), XII (1 February), 69-70.
In Ruth Gaskell "has quitted" Manchester squalor for "a
country town," but the book is still full of "vice and
misery." One enjoys Ruth less for "its story" than for
its "admirable portraiture of character" and "very fine
descriptive passages." One flaw is Gaskell's "sentimental
insistence" upon the moral superiority of the rich over
the poor.

50 ANON. "Ruth," Eliza Cook's Journal (London), VIII
(26 February), 277-80.
In this "worthy" successor to the excellent Mary Barton,
Ruth's fall comes through "ignorance," and her "beautiful
story" teaches "charity for sinners."

*51 ANON. "Ruth," Literary Gazette (London) (22 January),
pp. 79-80.
Less satisfactory than Mary Barton, Ruth is "meagre,
improbable, and uninteresting, and the style laboured and
artificial." [Source: Marjorie Taylor Davis. "An Annotated Bibliography of Criticism on Elizabeth Cleghorn Gaskell, 1848-1973." Ph.D. dissertation, University of
Mississippi, 1974. See 1974.B6.]

52 ANON. "Ruth,..." Literary World (New York), XII (26 March),
250.
This sad and powerful novel provides a wholesome lesson
for both "pharisee" and "Magdalen" and teaches young women
to be kind to their fallen sisters.

53 ANON. "Ruth,..." Morning Advertiser (London) (12 January),
p. 6.

1853

(ANON.)
"The beautiful pure-hearted" heroine is clearly drawn
from life, and her trials as a seamstress remind one of
Hood's "Song of the Shirt." "There is an earnest terse-
ness, an absence of straining after effect, which invests
this writer's" narrative "with great solemnity and im-
pressiveness," but her religious convictions never obtrude.

54   ANON. "The Story of Ruth," Tait's Edinburgh Magazine, n.s. XX
      (April), 217-20.
      The work achieves interest by causing the reader to
      identify with the feelings of its characters, but "perhaps"
      it overuses this technique. As for the moral issue, Ruth's
      employer, Bradshaw, should have been told the truth, but
      the Bensons would have been wrong to proclaim her past
      publicly. Ruth, as the center of "interest," gives the
      book its "artistic excellence" and "unity," yet she is
      too sweet and innocent to be classed with "fallen women."
      Those who condemn her as hopeless have "a superstitious
      and exaggerated estimate of physical virginity...."

55   ANON. "Test of Popularity," Home Journal (New York)
      (26 March), p. 2.
      Ruth and Villette are tied for third after Henry Esmond
      and My Novel as being most in demand at Mudie's lending
      library in London.

56   [CHORLEY, HENRY F.]. "Cranford," Athenaeum (London), no. 1339
      (25 June), p. 765.
      Cranford's organization may have been achieved "by
      accident" during serialization, yet the book "is perfect"
      as "a picture of manners, motives, and feelings." Its
      lack of "romance" and "poetry" is made up for by rare
      kindliness and "humour." One possible flaw is Peter's
      return, but, after all, it resembles the close of The Vicar
      of Wakefield.

57   [CURTIS, GEORGE WILLIAM]. "Villette and Ruth," Putnam's
      Monthly (New York), I (May), 535-39.
      "More simple, more concentrated, more intense than
      Villette," Ruth makes us weep but is not sentimental. It
      is neither an indictment of society nor a hymn to things
      as they are. It is not told for mere entertainment nor
      for displaying "sins and wickedness, like 'Vanity Fair'....
      Its message is" Jesus' message--"let he who is without sin
      cast the first stone"--yet the book is not "a mere sermon"
      because of its moving "sympathy."

58 [LEWES, GEORGE HENRY]. "Mary Barton's New Work," <u>Leader</u>
    (London), IV (2 July), 644-45.
        In spite of early success, the author improves in each
    work, and "we think" that <u>Cranford</u> "will be more permanent
    than" her "others" because of its "delicate feminine ob-
    servation," "bright and genial humour," and "pathos."
    "Provincial life in its ineffable dullness moves before
    us," and "we enjoy every detail...as heartily as we should
    detest the reality."

59 _____. "Ruth,..." <u>Leader</u> (London), IV (22 January), 89-91.
        "The author of 'Mary Barton' has wisely done what very
    few authors see the wisdom of doing--opened a new mine,
    instead of working the old one." She has left the "social"
    and industrial problems of <u>Mary Barton</u> for the "moral
    problem" of "a beautiful soul" trying to adjust to "our
    semi-civilized condition." The book is unusually rich in
    "pathos," "love," "kindliness," "deep religious feeling,"
    and "fine observation." "The lessons are suggested, not
    preached...." We do advise that, in the "future," the
    author draw from personal "experience" rather than literary
    convention. One flaw is the boy's exaggerated shame over
    illegitimacy.

60 _____. "Ruth and <u>Villette</u>,..." <u>Westminster Review</u> (London),
    n.s. III (April), 474-85.
        Although fiction should not explicitly preach, its
    pattern should gratify our moral sense, and <u>Ruth</u> does so
    by its clear "feminine" insight into the nature of tempta-
    tion and rehabilitation. Yet the heroine's fall is pre-
    sented with so many "extenuating circumstances" that she
    is a special case difficult to judge harshly. One of the
    finest touches is Ruth's joy instead of shame in her il-
    legitimate child. But the story would be more instructive
    if Ruth were homelier and "less" "endowed" with "good
    qualities." The book has two morals: women must help
    other women back to self-respect, and one must reject
    conventional ideas and lies about sexual transgression.

61 [LUDLOW, JOHN MALCOLM FORBES]. <u>North British Review</u>
    (Edinburgh), XIX (May), 151-74.
        In this convincing yet dramatic story of the redemption
    of a seduced woman, Ruth's deathbed scene is worthy of
    Shakespeare's Ophelia. The book's moral is threefold:
    that the truth must be told under all circumstances, that
    children are a redeeming blessing even for fallen women,
    and that there is no philanthropic substitute for family
    love. The subplot is a flaw. To those who object that

1853

([LUDLOW, JOHN MALCOLM FORBES])
the book is not "pleasant," we reply that there is greater
obligation to be true to life, as Ruth is. The heroine's
refusal of marriage from her finally repentant seducer is
perhaps not morally justified. Ruth is more artistic and
far more universal than the class-bound Mary Barton. We
dislike most "women authors" as people, yet they are
writing our "best novels," for novelists must be emotional
rather than reasonable, though wives and mothers make better novelists than do emotionally inexperienced old maids.

62 MONTÉGUT, ÉMILE. "Les Romans de Mistress Gaskell," Revue des
Deux Mondes (Paris), XXIII (1 June), 894-926. [Reprinted
in Émile Montégut. "Mistress Gaskell. Mary Barton. Ruth,"
in Écrivains modernes de l'Angleterre. Paris: Librairie
Hachette et Cie., 1889. II, 3-64.]
Mary Barton is one of the best examples of the social-
reform novel characteristic of the nineteenth century. It
has a collective protagonist, concentrates on the subtler
miseries of the poor, and is less a novel than a mirror of
Manchester life. Christian in attitude, it advocates no
ideological program, and it shows that the English workers
are roused only by emotion, not theory. Ruth attacks the
hypocritical respectability of English society. The debate
of English critics about the Bensons' obviously justified
white lie illustrates British moral rigidity. Perhaps Ruth
is too long and a bit too forgiving toward English
hypocrisy.

1854 A BOOKS - NONE

1854 B SHORTER WRITINGS

1 ANON. "Literary Examiner. Select Library of Fiction. Mary
Barton.... Fifth edition," Examiner (London) (20 May),
pp. 309-10.
"Mr. Gaskell's lectures" in the appendix are an appropri-
ate "addition to a book" so successful at evoking "Lancashire life." Finer than any other recent popular novel,
this sweet and "unaffected" treatment of working-class life,
with its sympathetic call for "justice," will be influential
so long as the English poor are denied full justice.

2 GASKELL, REV. W.[ILLIAM]. Two Lectures on the Lancashire
Dialect. London: Chapman & Hall. [Reprinted as "Two
Lectures on the Lancashire Dialect," in Mary Barton. 5th
ed. Select Library of Fiction. London: Chapman & Hall,
1854. "Appendix," pp. 1-27.]

[The lectures, which do not mention Mary Barton by name, trace selected dialect words, including "clem," to Celtic, Anglo-Saxon, and Low German.]

3   [MARX, KARL]. "The English Middle Class," New York Tribune (1 August), p. 4.
      "The present splendid brotherhood of fiction writers in England, whose graphic and eloquent pages have issued to the world more political and social truths than have been uttered by all the professional politicians, publicists, and moralists put together, have described every section of the middle class from the 'highly genteel' annuitant and Fundholder who looked upon all sorts of business as vulgar, to the little shopkeeper and lawyer's clerk, and how have Dickens and Thackeray, Miss Brontë and Mrs. Gaskell painted them? As full of presumption, affectation, petty tyranny and ignorance; and the civilised world have confirmed their verdict with the damning epigram that it has fixed to this class 'that they are servile to those above and tyrannical to those beneath them'."

4   STOWE, HARRIET BEECHER. Sunny Memories of Foreign Lands. Boston: Phillips, Samson, & Co. New York: J. C. Derby. II, 41.
      At lunch in London, I met Gaskell, who "has a lovely, gentle face, and looks capable of all the pathos that her writings show. I promised her a visit when I go to Manchester."

1855 A BOOKS - NONE

1855 B SHORTER WRITINGS

1   ANON. Critic (London), XIV (1 October), 477.
      In Chapman & Hall's collection of Gaskell's "minor stories,...Lizzie Leigh is the longest and the best,...but all are interesting and" have "a good purpose."

2   ANON. "Flyleaves from a Circulating Library. Mrs. Gaskell's Novels," New Monthly Magazine (London), CV (December), 427-33. [Reprinted as "The Author of Mary Barton," in Eclectic Magazine (New York), XXXVII (February 1856), 259-63.]
      Gaskell demonstrated her capacity for "pathos" in Mary Barton, Ruth, and North and South, but in Cranford she subtly mixed "pathos" with humor.

1855

3   ANON. "Literary Examiner. North and South,..." Examiner
     (London) (21 April), pp. 244-45.
          Though many will think that this novel gives a fairer
     picture of the employer-employee relationship than Mary
     Barton, they will be wrong, for both books are evenhanded.
     North and South, reprinted from Household Words, "with...
     insertions that give greater finish to the story," is
     "worthy" of Gaskell's high reputation. Its moral for all
     groups and "classes" is "know one another." The theme is
     expressed both by the conflict between the "agricultural"
     South and the industrial North and by that between masters
     and men, for which Margaret serves as a unifying bridge of
     sympathy.

4   ANON. "Literary Notices. North and South,..." Godey's Lady's
     Book (Philadelphia), L (May), 469.
          "Lest the reader should suppose that this book" is about
     "the North and South of Mason's and Dixon's line," we will
     state that the incidents, which are graphically detailed,
     refer to the North and South of England."

5   ANON. "Literature. Miscellaneous," Atlas (London), no. 1518
     (16 June), p. 388.
          "The very pleasant Addisonian tale of Cranford...has
     just been reprinted...."

6   ANON. New Novels. North and South,..." Athenaeum (London),
     no. 1432 (7 April), p. 403.
          This tale will be one of the year's best because of its
     dialogue, humor, and characterization. But Gaskell's
     novelistic attempts to deal with moral dilemmas are unwise--
     as exampled by the lie that Margaret tells to save her
     brother--for they may undermine innocent readers, though
     Gaskell means well.

7   ANON. "New Novels. North and South," Spectator (London),
     XXVIII (31 March), 341-42.
          The author has "word power" but not that power of
     "genius and imagination" which enables a writer to illumin-
     ate "the spirit of things." When she is not giving harshly
     accurate descriptions of factories or small towns, she
     relies on "speculation" rather than observation, and, even
     at her best, lacks vitality, warmth, and drama. In North
     and South she sticks largely to what she knows, yet her
     weaknesses are still present. As representatives of the
     South, the Hales are simply not sufficiently typical.

8   ANON. "A Novel or Two," National Review (London), I
     (October), 336-50.
          North and South shows "much of the great power of its
     author" in the characterization, "but the plot is sadly
     disjointed...." The characters do not develop but jump
     from one state to another. The book is also "morbid" and
     "touched" with "false sentiment," a fault from which
     Cranford was wholly free.

9   ANON. "Our Library Table," Athenaeum (London), no. 1460
     (20 October), p. 1213.
          The stories in Lizzie Leigh and Other Tales have a high
     quality of "comedy" and of "deep and homely pathos," and
     "Mr. Harrison's Confessions" has humor as good as
     Cranford's.

10   ANON. "Our Library Table. Mrs. Gaskell's North and South,"
     Manchester Weekly Advertiser (14 April), p. 6.
          "Both in conception and execution," this is "the best"
     book of one of "the first of living English novelists."
     The work "aims...at reconciling two long-opposed sections
     of English society, by" showing "each the true worth...of
     the other": the industrialized North and the cultured
     South. The novel's serialization in Household Words "may
     retrieve" for the paper "some of the popularity which it
     lost, by being made the vehicle of that unjust and untrue
     caricature of manufacturing life,...Dickens's 'Hard Times'."
     The strike in North and South is not given "the undue
     prominence which" it had "in 'Mary Barton'."

11   ANON. "Review of New Books. North and South,..." Graham's
     Magazine (Philadelphia), XLVI (June), 576.
          A forthcoming work from Gaskell "excites something of
     the same pleasure that is experienced in the promise of a
     new volume from Thackeray or Miss Brontë," and North and
     South fulfills "this expectation." "The interest centres
     in Thornton and Margaret; and the representation of the
     influence which love exerts on the tough heart and hard
     business-head of the former, is done...with great knowledge
     of...passion. The novel is so good, that we wish the
     Harpers had issued it in a book, instead of pamphlet form."

12   ANON. "Reviews. North and South.... Second edition,..."
     Guardian (London), no. 507 (22 August), pp. 647-48.
          "Considerably" improved and "expanded" from Household
     Words, this "earnest" novel is one of the year's "best,"
     though not as good as Mary Barton or Ruth. The main "in-
     terest" is the way in which mutual love changes the northern

1855

(ANON.)
Thornton and the southern Margaret, yet the book's "true purpose" is to inculcate "a gentle feeling" toward rebellious and "misguided" workingmen who are open "to good influences."

13   [LEWES, GEORGE HENRY (?)]. "North and South,..." Leader (London), VI (14 April), 356.
The novel succeeds as a story, with superb "style" and "appreciation of character," but fails in presenting representative people from northern and southern England. The idealized Thornton contrasts with the reality that ignorance actually helps a manufacturer to succeed. The idealized Higgins contrasts with the reality that working people receive their wages "placidly" until "at the wrong time" they mutiny. Both "clergymen and women" really "should" avoid all labor-management issues.

14   MONTÉGUT, ÉMILE. "Le Roman des moeurs industrielles en Angleterre," Revue des Deux Mondes (Paris), XXV (1 October), 114-46. [Reprinted in Émile Montégut. "Mistress Gaskell. Nord et sud," in Écrivains modernes de l'Angleterre. Paris: Hachette et Cie., 1889. II, 67-129.]
Hale's resignation from the Church in North and South illustrates Gaskell's regard for the truth above all. Margaret, who at first hates the industrial North, learns to love it. Thornton could pass in any country as the perfect representative of the manufacturing class, and his mother is a bourgeois Valkyrie. The contrast between an angry working-class atheist and the sweetly pious working-class women is striking and effective. The author is moderate and impartial in dealing with masters and men, though she dislikes unions and strikes. She does not lapse into the sentimentality and vehemence of most women writers, such as Harriet Beecher Stowe.

15   [OLIPHANT, MARGARET]. "Modern Novelists--Great and Small," Blackwood's Edinburgh Magazine, LXXII (May), 559-60. [Reprinted in Littell's Living Age (Boston), 2nd ser. IX (16 June), 647-48.]
Though North and South is "extremely clever" and certainly "better and livelier than any of" Gaskell's "previous works," it suffers from the same flaw as 'Jane Eyre'. We cannot believe that" Gaskell's "lovely heroine" could love the "churlish" though "strong" Thornton. In Ruth Gaskell made a "blunder" in even attempting to portray a fallen woman.

1856 A BOOKS - NONE

1856 B SHORTER WRITINGS

1   ANON. "Lectures to Ladies on Practical Subjects. Cambridge:
     1855," Edinburgh Review, CIII (January), 151.
          A fine example of fiction's ennobling lesson is the
     "part of...'North and South'" that "portrays the" gradual
     "ascendency of Margaret over the radical and infidel
     weaver, Nicholas Higgins," with "humility" and "sympathy"
     on Margaret's part and the overcoming of "pride" on the
     part of Higgins.

2   [BALLANTYNE, THOMAS]. "Lancashire Strikes," Blackwood's
     Edinburgh Magazine, LXXXIX (January), 55.
          Gaskell has better "knowledge of Lancashire life" than
     any other modern novelist, and North and South accurately
     portrays workingmen's attitudes: "'It's th' masters as
     has made us sin, if th' union is a sin'."

3   [EVANS, MARY ANN (GEORGE ELIOT)]. "Silly Novels by Lady
     Novelists," Westminster Review (London), n.s. X (October),
     460.
          "... When a woman's talent is at zero, journalistic
     approbation is at the boiling pitch," but "if ever she
     reaches excellence, critical enthusiasm drops to the
     freezing point. Harriet Martineau, Currer Bell, and"
     Gaskell "have been treated as cavalierly as if they had
     been men."

*4   HEDOUIN, A. "Ruth," L'Athenaeum Français (31 May), 465-66.
          Ruth shows a gift for characterization and a forgiving
     spirit, though it is possibly overlong. [Source: Marjorie
     Taylor Davis. "An Annotated Bibliography of Criticism on
     Elizabeth Cleghorn Gaskell, 1848-1973." Ph.D. dissertation,
     University of Mississippi, 1974. See 1974.B6.]

1857 A BOOKS

1   SHEPHEARD, REV. H. A Vindication of the Clergy Daughters'
     School, and of the Rev. W. Carus Wilson, from the Remarks
     of "The Life of Charlotte Brontë." London: Kirkby Lon-
     dale, published by Robert Morphet, Printer, and by Seeley,
     Jackson & Halliday.
          This pamphlet vindicates Carus Wilson from Gaskell's
     charges by simple statement of "facts." Her "public
     retraction and apology, demanded by the solicitor of a

1857

(SHEPHEARD, REV. H.)
certain lady for a libel upon her character" in the Life
shows the suspect nature of Gaskell's "other statements."
The charges against the Rev. Wilson's school were based on
Miss Brontë's recollection from age ten, and Gaskell herself has made errors of fact. "The ultimate sufferers by
calumny are the unhappy authors of it themselves."

*2   WILSON, W. W. CARUS. A Refutation of the Statements in "The
Life of Charlotte Brontë" Regarding the Casterton Clergy
Daughters' School When at Cowan Bridge. Weston: Whereat.
[Source: Anon. "Our Library Table,..." Athenaeum
(London), no. 1547 (20 June 1857), p. 789: This "refuta-
tion" shows that Gaskell was too hasty in accepting Char-
lotte's own bitter "testimony" about the Cowan Bridge
School, which seems to have not been as bad as described
in Jane Eyre or the Life, but the pamphlet itself is too
full of self-serving testimonials.]

1857 B   SHORTER WRITINGS

1   ANON. "The Author of 'Jane Eyre'. The Life of Charlotte
Brontë,..." Evening Post (New York) (15 May), p. 1.
The book reveals that Charlotte's gloomy nature came
from her father's "diseased" mind, but it also shows her
"heroism" in facing her "trials." Gaskell has had a difficult "task" because many people in her narrative "are
still living," so that she has had "to throw a veil over
many things...." To say that she has met the expec-
tations aroused by "her subject, and her own reputation,
would be too high praise," but the biography is "sympathetic" and truthful.

2   ANON. "Biography. The Life of Charlotte Brontë,..." Weekly
Dispatch (London) (19 April), p. 6.
This "very sorrowful" biography enables us to better
understand Miss Brontë's novels. It "is executed with
great good taste, judgment and feeling, and" Gaskell's
"sketches of Haworth and its people are worthy of the
authoress of 'Ruth' and 'Cranford'."

3   ANON. "Books. Mrs. Gaskell's Life of Charlotte Brontë,"
Spectator Supplement. Spectator (London), XXX (4 April),
373-74. [Reprinted in Littell's Living Age (Boston), LIII
(16 May 1857), 392-96.]
In spite of Gaskell's handicap of probably having few
letters and supporting materials to work with, she

successfully evokes Charlotte as a woman of "character" as
well as "genius"--a person with "unconquerable will" but
also a martyr-like tendency toward self-sacrifice. This is
a classic biography of "the struggle of genius for recognition," but the emphasis is on the woman, not on the
authoress. The book is deeply tragic yet shows how
Charlotte won a "saint's victory" by her noble endurance.

4   ANON. "Charlotte Brontë," Boston Evening Transcript (2 June),
     p. 2.
        The Daily News (London) describes how people at Haworth
     are "eagerly" reading and criticizing Gaskell's life of
     Charlotte. "On all hands ready testimony is borne to" the
     book's "accuracy," including the account of the church
     riot over Rev. Redhead. A local bookseller "is now lend-
     ing" the Life at a shilling a volume "per week," and "pil-
     grims" are coming to Haworth to see places mentioned in
     it.

5   ANON. "Charlotte Brontë. The Ending of the Story of Her
     Life," Witness (Edinburgh) (18 April), p. 4.
        Gaskell's Life tells how Charlotte's father delayed her
     marriage and how she died shortly after she finally did
     marry.

6   ANON. "Charlotte Brontë. The Life of Charlotte Brontë,..."
     Eclectic Review (London), n.s. I (June), 630-42.
        Though we started Gaskell's book because of our interest
     in Charlotte's fiction, the tragic biography left us "un-
     able to think of anything but her life." Gaskell skill-
     fully evokes the environment and the people that shaped
     Charlotte.

7   ANON. "Charlotte Brontë," National Magazine (London), II
     (June), 76-78.
        This "careful and loving" biography "will do good, more
     good than many novels," for it shows how even a woman of
     genius was "cheerfully" and "deftly" able to perform "her
     home-duties." This "strange poem-picture" reveals a
     heroine and a "narrative" more memorable than even those
     in Charlotte's novels. Because of our fascination with
     the subject, we forget the high "excellence" of Gaskell's
     art in creating "not so much a book as a life...."

8   ANON. "Charlotte Brontë," Putnam's Monthly (New York), IX
     (June), 648-54.
        Gaskell's Life of Charlotte Brontë provides "the master
     key" to Charlotte's novels. "One hearty, religious, reso-
     lute woman comes to do womanly justice to another," with

1857

(ANON.)
"an exquisite appreciation of" the "subject." Gaskell "has written many a melancholy page, but she has never told a story more tragical than" this Life.

9 ANON. "Charlotte Brontë," Saturday Review (London), III (4 April), 313-14.
Gaskell's biography reveals that Charlotte created the passionate Rochester out of her imagination without a model, yet Gaskell does show the sources of many details in the novels. She skillfully brings out the "pathos" and "instructiveness" of Charlotte's life.

10 ANON. "Cranford,..." Weekly Dispatch (London) (17 June), p. 6.
This reprinted "gentle" chronicle of "pathetic trivialities" is unsurpassed in its touching presentation of "delicate" "human feelings." Though it lacks a "story," it contains enough for "a dozen." Yet its lightness contrasts with the power and deep emotions of the "marvelous" Mary Barton.

11 ANON. "'Currer Bell' and Her Sisters," Harper's Weekly (New York), I (16 May), 308.
[This summarizes the narrative of Gaskell's Life of Charlotte Brontë without mentioning either Gaskell or her book as the source.]

12 ANON. "Editorial Notes. Literary Intelligence and Gossip," Putnam's Monthly (New York), X (September), 411.
W. W. Carus Wilson's pamphlet defending his father's school against the charges in The Life of Charlotte Brontë makes us feel that both sides have some truth.

13 ANON. "Editor's Book Table. The Life of Charlotte Brontë,..." Independent (New York) (12 July), p. 8.
This biography is thrilling yet also awakens "a sympathy so keen and earnest as to be really painful.... To many the present year will be made more memorable by the publication of these volumes than by any other simply literary event to occur in it." The narrative has "exquisite naturalness and power," though apparently the author has been careless over certain controversial details.

14 ANON. "Editor's Table. Charlotte Brontë," Godey's Lady's Book (Philadelphia), LV (September), 274-75.
Gaskell, "herself a writer of great ability, and of much sounder mental conformation than Charlotte Brontë, has

32

lately given us the life of her unhappy friend." The
biography "will be widely read in our country" because of
"intrinsic merits" but also natural "curiosity about the
Brontës." Yet we warn our readers of "the unhealthy moral
conformation of both father and children...." They
neglected the Christian duty to cultivate "cheerfulness
and hopefulness."

15 ANON. "English Literature. Biography.... The Life of
Charlotte Brontë,..." Critic (London), XVI (15 April),
168-71. [Reprinted in "The Brontë Family," Boston Evening
Transcript (16 May), p. 1.]
Gaskell gives an ugly picture of the West Riding, the
Rev. Brontë, Emily, and Branwell. "... It is to be re-
gretted that" Gaskell "has not observed greater
reticence...."

16 ANON. "Foreign Literary Intelligence," Boston Evening Transcript (4 May), p. 2.
Gaskell's "'Life of Charlotte Brontë', and Charles
Kingsley's 'Two Years Ago', are the most successful books
of the season."

17 ANON. "History, Biography, Voyages, and Travels," Westminster
Review (London), n.s. XII (July), 294-96.
The Life of Charlotte Brontë shows that other things
besides formal education develop the character and intellect for a literary career. Charlotte's endurance in her
duties is inspiriting in these times of "collapsing
creeds." She was a saint of literature. Because of the
revelations of libel in the biography, we shall "say as
little as possible" about Gaskell's presentation of her
materials. Apart from these controversies, her worst mistake was to regard Branwell as a "ruined" "genius" when he
was simply a "worthless vagabond."

18 ANON. "A Lesson from a Woman's Life. Charlotte Brontë,"
Titan (Edinburgh), XXIV (January-June), 452-62.
Gaskell's "most graceful and satisfactory" biography
shows the connection between its heroine's life and the
rugged land of Yorkshire with its "shrewd" and humorous
dialect. Gaskell's account of Charlotte's stay at the
pensionnat in Brussels proves what we had already decided:
that its description in Villette was based on a key actual
experience. This "fascinating memoir" leaves us with un-
utterable sadness for this noble, gifted women who had to
struggle against many obstacles, and it "will win thousands"
of readers for Charlotte Brontë.

1857

19 ANON. "The Life of Charlotte Brontë,..." American Church
Monthly (New York), II (August), 113-27.
Miss Brontë, who proved that women have as much literary
genius as men, would need a Southey to do her full justice.
But Gaskell's overlong biography is rather "hasty and
crude," in spite of its splendid subject. Worst of all,
she "patronizes" Charlotte with an "apology" for her supposed "coarseness." Yet Gaskell's "descriptions of Yorkshire scenery and society" are "very clever and interesting."

20 ANON. "The Life of Charlotte Brontë,..." British Quarterly
Review (London), XXVI (1 July), 218-31.
It is a rare pleasure to read a life of a "remarkable
woman" by one who is herself a distinguished and "delightful" novelist. Gaskell's use of correspondence gives the
book "almost the charm of an autobiography," and it is "as
interesting as" a new Jane Eyre. This life shows that the
bad-tempered father was largely to blame for Charlotte's
vulnerability and lack of adequate religious faith. We do
wish that Gaskell had given more "extracts" from Charlotte's
juvenilia, for the one specimen provided is "startlingly
crude" in style compared with Jane Eyre. Southey's letter
advising Charlotte that women should not be writers was
obtuse and unfortunate. As for the story of Branwell's
debauches, Gaskell was foolish to blame a slandered woman
on the basis of a drunkard's word.

21 ANON. "The Life of Charlotte Brontë,..." Christian Observer
(London), LVII (July), 487-90.
Gaskell seems to have violated the Ninth Commandment
concerning both a slandered lady and the Cowan Bridge
School. Though the biographer seems to share Miss Brontë's
own faults, Gaskell "also is a writer of lively invention,
passion, power." But her "religious creed is, we...fear,...
of a very limited character" and far too rationalistic.

22 ANON. "The Life of Charlotte Brontë,..." Christian Re-
membrancer (London), XXXIV (July), 87-145. [Reprinted in
Littell's Living Age (Boston), 2nd ser. XIX (14 November
1857), 385-421.]
"... The interest of this remarkable biography"--"the
book of the season"--lies in "the contrast between" Charlotte's "outer" and "inner life." Though she lived a life
of "renunciation," her goals were unspiritual and "narrow,"
for she had a "masculine" "mind" in a weak female body.
Her devotion to her family kept her from properly judging
Emily's "pagan selfishness." Gaskell "has done her best...

to draw a faithful and true portrait of her friend" and
captures "the spirit of" the Brontës and of "wild" Yorkshire. Yet Gaskell's slanderous mistatements undermine
"our confidence" in her otherwise "thrilling" work, which
remains "a valuable addition to the world's experience."

*23   ANON. "The Life of Charlotte Brontë," Emerson's United States
      Magazine (New York), V (September), 269-81.
            Gaskell's life "of a woman of genius" is "written by
      another." Because Gaskell "could not fathom the depths of
      her friend," she sticks to day-to-day life. This approach
      is "natural, and to be expected from one who walks in the
      sunshine as does" Gaskell, "who covets life in its simpli-
      city and ease, not in its starry heights or savage
      grandeur." [Source: Marjorie Taylor Davis. "An Annotated
      Bibliography of Criticism on Elizabeth Cleghorn Gaskell,
      1848-1973." Ph.D. dissertation, University of Mississippi,
      1974. See 1974.B6.]

24   ANON. "The Life of Charlotte Brontë,..." Gentleman's Magazine
      (London), n.s. II (June), 688-94.
            The life story of Charlotte is as "interesting" as her
      novels but equally "melancholy."

25   ANON. "The Life of Charlotte Brontë,..." Manchester Guardian
      (7 May), p. 4.
            Gaskell's "beautiful" biography shows deep understanding
      of the northern England that produced Charlotte, though
      Gaskell's "quiet, humorous, and searching" study of "charac-
      ter" pays a just attention to heredity as well as environ-
      ment. The early sections are, in fact, a "valuable...con-
      tribution to provincial history." Those who call this
      biography "morbid" judge by false standards, for it is
      enchanting and stirring.

26   ANON. "The Life of Charlotte Brontë,..." New Quarterly Review
      and Digest of Current Literature (London), VI (month un-
      known), 222-28.
            Gaskell's account of the forbidding father and Emily and
      the sottish Branwell helps us understand Charlotte's novel-
      istic concentration on suppressed inward struggles and also
      her own constant tendency not to demand return for passion-
      ate love. Her life was a perpetual pattern of having to
      endure unpleasantness, but she emerged "pure and chastened."
      Gaskell's achievement in this "difficult task" is "very
      satisfactory," "very fairly executed, quite free from Bos-
      wellism." Minor faults are the overlong "introductory"
      section and a style occasionally too "feminine" and senti-
      mental.

1857

27   ANON. "The Life of Charlotte Brontë,..." New York Herald
       (20 May), p. 3.
              Gaskell, "herself an authoress of merit," gives us a
       story of Charlotte's lifelong "trials" that "will be read
       with deeper interest" and "sympathy...than any" other
       "episode in" history's "long list of literary struggles...."

28   ANON. "The Life of Charlotte Brontë," Times (London)
       (23 April), p. 10. [Reprinted in Anon., ed. Modern
       Literary Criticism. London: George Routledge & Sons,
       1867. I, 185-206.]
              This is a rare "portrait" of a literary genius by "a
       sister authoress gifted herself with superior powers" and
       one who describes her subject "with true womanly sympathy
       and eagerness." The biography reveals the wellspring of
       Charlotte's fiction and shows how her extraordinary gift
       arose in narrow circumstances.

29   ANON. "Literary," Boston Evening Transcript (1 May), p. 2.
              The Life of Charlotte Brontë is "the most interesting
       literary biography of the day...." Gaskell's book "is as
       significant as" Miss Brontë's novels. "It is, in fact, a
       psychological study and a vindication of what is highest
       and deepest in woman's nature," and "it will form a
       permanent addition to standard English female biography."

30   ANON. "Literary,..." Boston Evening Transcript (22 May), p. 2.
              "No English reprint, since Kingsley's last novel, has
       attracted so much attention as" Gaskell's "Life of Charlotte
       Brontë. It is so thorough and carefully elaborated a biog-
       raphy, embracing the surroundings and consciousness as well
       as the life-incidents of Charlotte, that it is quite a
       study of character;--painful--but attractive through its
       intensity and productiveness."

31   ANON. "Literary Examiner. The Life of Charlotte Brontë,..."
       Examiner (London) (11 April), pp. 228-29. [Reprinted in
       Littell's Living Age (Boston), 2nd ser. XVII (27 June 1857),
       777-80.]
              Because this biography deals with a recent life in-
       volving still living relations, Gaskell is forced to omit
       things and is also sometimes too swayed by friendship, so
       that she minimizes the mental unhealthiness of the Brontës
       in a way that is itself unhealthy. We wish that she
       had omitted those embarrassing letters expressing Char-
       lotte's inexperienced and emotional judgments on art and
       people. Yet we praise the book for its "loving sympathy"
       with its subject and its telling use of "anecdote" and
       detail.

32 ANON. "Literary Gossip," <u>Nonconformist</u> (London), n.s. XVII
    (29 April), 336.
        Gaskell's "interesting 'Life of Charlotte Brontë'...has
    already reached a second edition...."

33 ANON. "Literary," <u>Harper's Weekly</u> (New York), I (28 February),
    150.
        Gaskell, the "author of" many "capital and popular
    novels, has written the Life of Miss Charlotte Brontë...."

34 ANON. "Literary," <u>Harper's Weekly</u> (New York), I (21 March),
    182.
        Gaskell's <u>Life of Charlotte Brontë</u> "will possess
    special interest in a portrait of the subject of the
    memoir which is promised with it."

35 ANON. "Literary," <u>Harper's Weekly</u> (New York), I (27 June),
    406.
        Gaskell's "<u>Life of Charlotte Brontë</u> has caused a pretty
    hubbub," by offending the founder of the Cowan Bridge
    School, Patrick Brontë too, and a woman supposedly involved
    with Branwell, to whom the author has had to make "a hu-
    miliating" public "apology" for her "shameful" imputations
    about this lady.

36 ANON. "Literary Intelligence," <u>Boston Evening Transcript</u>
    (25 May), p. 2.
        "... We agree with a London critic that, as a piece of
    literary art," Gaskell's biography of Charlotte Brontë is
    the finest "life of a woman written by a woman...." Gas-
    kell's "skill and tact" have "made" Charlotte "a heroine
    of sorrow, faith and moral beauty.... It is the book of
    the day--the companion in boudoir and study, and the sub-
    ject of conversation in all spheres."

37 ANON. "Literary Intelligence," <u>Publishers' Circular</u> (London),
    XX (1 September), 373.
        Maria S. Cummins's <u>Mabel Vaughan</u> "will possess the addi-
    tional interest of a Preface" by Gaskell, who is "so well
    versed in the life of England," just as Miss Cummins is
    versed in that of America.

38 ANON. "Literary Notes," <u>Court Journal</u> (London), n.s. no. 487
    (18 July), p. 487.
        "The squabble concerning the mis-statements in" Gas-
    kell's <u>Life of Charlotte Brontë</u> "still continues. A pam-
    phlet is the last addition to this controversial and un-
    profitable literature, which is a refutation of the charges

1857

(ANON.)
made against the Casterton Clergy Daughters' School. It
is a pity that these mis-statements have found place in a
biography which would otherwise have been a valuable one."

39   ANON. "Literary Notices. The Life of Charlotte Brontë,..."
Godey's Lady's Book (Philadelphia), LV (July), 85.
This biography has "a deep and melancholy interest for
the thousands of readers who were the sincere and enthusiastic admirers of the works" of Charlotte Brontë.

40   ANON. "Literary Notices. Life of Charlotte Brontë,..."
Graham's Illustrated Magazine (Philadelphia), LI (July),
85.
We have read this book "with the deepest, though at
times, the most painful interest, yet feel that its effect
on most minds must be...highly beneficial...." We should
like "every lady-reader in the country" to read it and
also would-be writers in order to learn how much will can
triumph over obstacles. Gaskell is splendidly qualified
to appreciate Charlotte and has created a well-written
biography.

41   ANON. "Literary Notices. The Life of Charlotte Brontë,..."
Knickerbocker (New York), XLIX (June), 621-22.
This biography provides "an enduring record" of the
"renowned" Miss Brontë.

42   ANON. "Literary Notices. The Life of Charlotte Brontë,..."
Russell's Magazine (Charleston, South Carolina), I (July),
378-80.
This "extraordinary" and tragic biography combines "con-
scientiousness," "sympathy," and "womanly appreciation and
insight into character.... It reveals the existence of
social conditions, fearful to contemplate, and of individual suffering no less fearful." Gaskell's anecdotes of
the district lead us to conclude "that the systematic
Devil, who is the hero of 'Wuthering Heights', is a life-
like portrait of an original not a whit exaggerated."

43   ANON. "The Literary World: Its Sayings and Doings," Critic
(London), XVI (1 June), 240.
The Life of Charlotte Brontë should be withdrawn until
its passages libeling an innocent lady are removed. [A
letter follows from W. W. Carus Wilson protesting the
book's charges against his father's school and saying that
Gaskell's Life has offended even Patrick Brontë.]

44   ANON. "Literature. Description of Keighley and Haworth,"
      Leeds Mercury (30 April), p. 4.
           Gaskell's "fascinating though sad biography of Charlotte
      Brontë" contains "a graphic description of Keighley and
      Haworth."

45   ANON. "Literature. The Life of Charlotte Brontë,..." Court
      Circular (London), III (25 April), 2.
           If materials are probably "somewhat scanty" for a life
      of Miss Brontë, one could not tell from Gaskell's "inter-
      esting" and affectionate biography. Gaskell shows that
      Charlotte's life "divided into two parallel currents"--
      writer and "woman"--"not impossible, perhaps, but difficult
      to be reconciled."

46   ANON. "Literature. The Life of Charlotte Brontë,..." Daily
      News (London) (4 April), p. 2.
           This account of Charlotte's struggle to express her
      "genius" against adversity is the saddest we know. It is
      splendidly and "artistically" organized and displays "ex-
      traordinary" "courage" in criticizing living persons,
      though possibly overstepping "good taste." Gaskell
      graphically evokes the Yorkshire of the Brontës. "Let
      those who would know more, who would know all that can be
      told, and ought to be told, hasten to read this history
      which a woman of kindred genius has fearlessly and truth-
      fully written of Charlotte Brontë."

47   ANON. "Literature.... The Life of Charlotte Brontë,..."
      Economist (London), XV (18 April), 425-26.
           This is "the life of a truly great and noble woman,
      written by one who has sufficient moral sympathy to under-
      stand her character, and sufficient intellectual insight
      to appreciate her genius." The book is of "special inter-
      est for female readers" as a refutation of "the assumption"
      of incompatability between womanly duties and genius.
      Gaskell "has wisely endeavoured," wherever possible, "to
      make the subject of her memoir tell her own tale."

48   ANON. "Literature. The Life of Charlotte Brontë,..."
      Observer (London) (12 April), p. 5.
           Charlotte's life "presents few salient features for the
      biographer to dwell upon, and therefore the extraordinary
      charm which" Gaskell "has thrown over the narrative is all
      the more striking." Because Charlotte left "no clue" about
      "the inner workings of her wonderful intellect," the "merit"
      and "success" of Gaskell is "all the more surprising in
      presenting such an attractive work to the public upon such

1857

(ANON)
a comparatively barren subject." She "has raised herself
fully to the level of" the gifted Charlotte.

49   ANON. "Literature. The Life of Charlotte Brontë,..." Press
      (London), V (4 April), 339-41. [Reprinted in Littell's
      Living Age (Boston), 2nd ser. XVII (16 May 1857), 385-402.]
           This "pathetic" story of literary success and premature
      death is done "full justice" by Gaskell, "one of Charlotte's
      few female friends." Apart from their sympathy for one
      another, their writings show some resemblance of mind.
      Gaskell "does not attempt to criticize" Charlotte's "works"
      or "character" but lets "facts...speak for themselves."
      The ruggedness of Haworth and its people helps explain the
      "masculine" roughness of Charlotte's books, which quality
      Gaskell eloquently but unnecessarily defends.

50   ANON. "Literature. The Life of Charlotte Brontë,..." Sun
      (London) (1 May), p. 3.
           "The names" of both Miss Brontë and Mrs. Gaskell "will at
      once excite the interest...of a large circle of readers"
      for this book. It shows that Charlotte's "spirit of self-
      sacrifice" for her "family" exceeded even her "wonderful
      powers of intellect." Gaskell "writes...with that true
      feeling and correct judgment that distinguish the biographer
      no less than the subject of the memoirs." "Though" Gaskell
      "scarcely ever alludes to the fact, it is impossible...to
      forget that she is also one of the foremost of our writers."

51   ANON. "Mrs. Gaskell's Life of Charlotte Brontë," Boston
      Evening Transcript (20 June), p. 2.
           "This work has brought the authoress into an unfortunate
      affair. The unnecessary reference to an alleged private
      fact in Branwell's unhappy career turns out...to be a
      wretched lie." Gaskell's "excuse is, that she has been
      deceived; but...she had no right to parade" the story "in
      the manner she did." She has been forced to make a "hu-
      miliating apology" in the Times (London), and London's
      Critic urges that the Life be withdrawn until the offending
      statements can be expunged.

52   ANON. "Mrs. Gaskell's Life of Charlotte Brontë," Manchester
      Weekly Examiner and Times. Supplement (25 April), p. 3.
           "A sister genius and a loving friend" of Charlotte's has
      written a beautiful, "faithful," and arduously researched
      biography of her. "With almost religious care," Gaskell
      "abstains from comment whenever" Charlotte's "letters" can
      speak for themselves. "No one can read these volumes with-
      out rising from them sadder and perhaps wiser...."

53   ANON. "Mrs. Gaskell's Life of Charlotte Brontë (second
      notice)," Manchester Weekly Examiner and Times. Supplement
      (2 May), p. 3.
         Gaskell's accounts of Emily and Anne are "second in in-
      terest" only to the subject of Charlotte herself. Gaskell's
      book "is worthy to stand...with Carlyle's 'Life of Ster-
      ling'.... The apparent demerits of" Gaskell's work "are
      really evidences of discernment and judgment,--that she has
      wisely resisted many opportunities for exercising her well-
      known talents for narrative" in order to insert Charlotte's
      own "words." We are also consoled by the thought that, in
      Gaskell's research in Yorkshire, London, and Brussels, "she
      will have retained a rich store of materiel" for use in her
      own later novels.

54   ANON. "Mrs. Gaskell's Recantation. The Biographer of Char-
      lotte Brontë Taken to Task. Good Advice to Authors,"
      Evening Post (New York) (30 June), p. 1. [Reprinted in
      Littell's Living Age (Boston), 2nd ser. XVIII (19 September
      1857), 721-23.]
         Gaskell's highly "interesting" biography is marred by a
      slander that she has been forced publicly to disown. She
      "is a woman of real genius" with "humane and benevolent
      views," but she should never have made untrue moral allega-
      tions against "a woman and a mother." Just as Gaskell
      writes novels about those oppressed by "social arrangements,"
      she told in the Life of a "clever" young man led to his
      death by the woman he loves. The gift of weighing factual
      "evidence" does "not come by nature to every person who has
      either a warm heart or a strong imagination." Yet, even if
      Gaskell's false statements had been true, her own Ruth
      shows the cruelty of public exposure of a sinner who may
      be repentant.

55   ANON. "The Mystery of Jane Eyre," New York Daily Times
      (15 May), p. 2.
         "No other living author could have done so well" in
      writing a Life of Charlotte Brontë, for Gaskell has both an
      affectionate "knowledge" of her subject and "natural
      genius." Perhaps some of the opening description of York-
      shire might be shortened and Charlotte's letters put in an
      appendix. Yet Gaskell is excellent at developing "the
      character of her subject" and "has presented us with a
      piece of family and individual history...more fascinating
      than any romance." It is a "moral" and "religious" "tonic"
      that "will become a permanent" and classic "addition to...
      English literature."

1857

56   ANON. "New Books. The Life of Charlotte Brontë,..." Ladies'
     Treasury (London), I (May), 55.
         "Some critics" who have read Gaskell's biography now
     believe that Charlotte never really experienced love but
     wrote of it only out of intuition and imagination. Yet we
     think that she must have known "actual love," probably
     before Gaskell met her.

57   ANON. "New Publications. Life of Charlotte Brontë,..."
     New York Observer (28 May), p. 174.
         "Whatever may be thought of" Charlotte Brontë's works,
     Gaskell's biography of her is "one of the most interesting
     ...of its class in the English language."

58   ANON. "New Publications. The Life of Charlotte Brontë,..."
     New York Observer (2 July), p. 214.
         "More interesting than any of her novels is this memoir
     of the remarkable woman whose works of fiction produced so
     much excitement in literary circles a few short years ago."
     Gaskell has satisfied the widespread curiosity about Char-
     lotte Brontë and created a "thrilling" book.

59   ANON. "New Publications. Charlotte Brontë. The Life of
     Charlotte Brontë,..." New York Daily Tribune (21 April),
     p. 6.
         Gaskell's book has much "of the somber fascination" of
     Charlotte's novels. Gaskell "has acquited herself with
     fidelity to the truth, with commendable frankness...where
     publicity was allowable, but with a modest reserve" about
     "private" matters. Her biography is "more touching in its
     truthful simplicity than the mimic pathos of romance."

60   ANON. "New York Literary Correspondence," Ladies' Repository
     (Cincinnati), XVII (June), 372.
         Gaskell's Life of Charlotte Brontë, a work "as interest-
     ing as any of" Miss Brontë's novels, presents "an evidently
     faithful and tolerably minute analysis of the mental
     progress and struggles of two of the most remarkable women
     of the age"--Charlotte and Emily.

61   ANON. "Notices to Correspondents. The Cowan-Bridge [sic]
     School Controversy," Halifax Guardian (25 July), p. 8.
         "We are compelled to close our columns to this in-
     terminable...controversy," which we now sum up ourselves.
     Actual "hardships" existed at the school in Charlotte's
     time but "were remedied as soon as" the Rev. Wilson learned
     of them. She heightened the "wrongs" in Jane Eyre, and
     Gaskell, "in that spirit of hero-worship with which modern

biographers are infected, accepted the exaggerated caricature for the reality...."

62   ANON. "Notices of New Books. The Life of Charlotte Brontë,
      ..." Southern Literary Messenger (Richmond, Virginia),
      n.s. III (June), 473-77.
         "These remarkable volumes" present a story unsurpassed
      "in literary history" for both "interest" and "pain," as
      it "moves on with the deep and certain horror of a Greek
      tragedy."

63   ANON. "Novel Proceedings in an English Church," Boston
      Evening Transcript (9 May), Supplement, p. 1.
         The account in Gaskell's Life of Charlotte Brontë of
      the church riot at Haworth reveals "what manner of humor
      was possessed by the parishioners...."

64   ANON. "Our Book Table. The Life of Charlotte Brontë,..."
      United States Democratic Review (New York), n.s. XL
      (August), 191.
         Gaskell has "the zeal of a congenial and admiring"
      biographer, "and though we think that Charlotte Brontë's
      French exercises, with the marginal criticism of M. Heger,
      ...might have been advantageously omitted, still their
      introduction" shows "evidence of minute fidelity."

65   ANON. "Our Library Table. The Life of Charlotte Brontë,..."
      Ladies' Companion (London), XI (May), 266-68.
         "This is one of the most remarkable and painfully in-
      teresting books it has ever been our duty to notice--the
      life of one woman of genius, written by another of kindred
      mind" with "straightforwardness," "vigour," care, and
      skill. It shows "what a noble, true, and tender woman
      Charlotte Brontë was...."

66   ANON. "Our Weekly Gossip," Athenaeum (London), no. 1545
      (6 June), p. 727.
         We recommended The Life of Charlotte Brontë because we
      believed in its accuracy, which, in fact, it lacked, as
      Gaskell's apology shows in this issue. The book "must" be
      revised before "it can be further circulated."

67   ANON. "Personal. Mrs. Gaskell's Life of Charlotte Brontë,"
      Evening Post (New York) (4 September), p. 2.
         "The errors into which" Gaskell "has fallen in her"
      book "are almost unparalleled in biographical literature."
      They include the now retracted charges against a lady sup-
      posedly involved with Branwell and insulting inaccuracies
      about the Brontës' father.

1857

68 ANON. "The Professor,..." Evening Post (New York) (1 July),
    p. 1.
    Gaskell's "memoirs of Charlotte Brontë have been before
    the American public scarcely six weeks, and the sad satis-
    faction which they gave us is not yet passed away."

69 ANON. "The Professor," Manchester Examiner and Times
    (31 July), p. 4. [Reprinted as "Literature. The Pro-
    fessor," in Manchester Weekly Examiner and Times (1 August
    1857), Supplement, p. 3.]
    For "those who have read" Gaskell's "memoir, 'The Pro-
    fessor' will throw...additional light on the...remarkable"
    Charlotte.

70 ANON. "Recent Publications," National Magazine (New York),
    XI (July), 94.
    Gaskell "has acquired considerable reputation as" a
    novelist, but, with her skillful Life of Charlotte Brontë,
    "she has won for herself a high place among the best biog-
    raphers of the age. Her style is marked by vivacity and
    conciseness."

71 ANON. "The Life of Charlotte Brontë,..." Home Journal
    (New York) (23 May), p. 2.
    "The life of one woman of genius written by another is
    not an everyday treat.... The History of the Brontë
    family would be the more correct designation of the first
    of these two volumes," for it deals with all the Brontës--
    "a strange family, living in a strange place, and among
    strange people." The biography is harder to put down than
    even Jane Eyre, Shirley, or Villette.

72 ANON. "Review of New Books. The Life of Charlotte Brontë,
    ..." Peterson's Magazine (Philadelphia), XXXII (July), 76.
    "The author of 'Ruth' and 'Mary Barton' was" uniquely
    "fitted to write the life of the author of 'Jane Eyre'."
    This "sad" history is "naturally, yet eloquently told."

73 ANON. "Reviews. The Life of Charlotte Brontë,..." Athenaeum
    (London), no. 1536 (4 April), pp. 427-29.
    "As a work of Art, we do not recollect a life of a woman
    by a woman so well executed." Most remarkable is the way
    that it evokes the rough Yorkshire society of the past and
    relates it to the qualities of Charlotte's fiction. This
    gentle, sad biography is "a labour of love."

74 ANON. "Reviews. The Life of Charlotte Brontë,..." Guardian
    (London), no. 596 (6 May), pp. 359-60.

We think that the "High Church curates" made fun of in
Shirley reacted with "good taste" and good humor, though
Gaskell "calls it obtuseness." Gaskell had a "difficult"
"task" in this life because of the "strangeness" and "re-
serve" of her subject. Unlike Lockhart's biography of
Scott, her book, though "most interesting," does not "admit us into the penetralia of" Charlotte's "mind." Yet
the "peculiar texture" of "the feminine mind" and also
"of its creations...must...be measured by a standard of
its own."

75   ANON. "Reviews. Life of Charlotte Brontë,..." Inquirer
      (London), no. 773 (25 April), p. 260.
         This work reconciles "the authoress and the woman" and
      teaches patience better than most sermons. Gaskell "has
      been honest and true,...generous and tender," and her
      biography "may take its place" beside Mary Barton and
      Carlyle's life of Sterling.

76   ANON. "Reviews. Life of Charlotte Brontë.... Jane Eyre:
      An Autobiography," Weekly Times (London) (24 May), p. 3.
         The school described in Gaskell's Life, and in Jane
      Eyre, "has gained a literary notoriety" comparable to
      Dickens's Dotheboys Hall. Although "things have" now
      "been cleaned" up at the Cowan Bridge School, the change
      does not justify the past conditions described by the
      biographer.

77   ANON. "Reviews of New Books. The Life of Charlotte Brontë,
      ..." Englishwoman's Review (London), I (18 April), 2.
         This biography "gives an interesting résumé of" Char-
      lotte's "whole life, almost day by day," with perhaps
      over-much detail, though "we have little else to" complain
      of. Gaskell's "style is clear and vigorous, and her com-
      position here far more faultless than in 'Ruth' and some
      of her tales." However, she "might have" prudently sup-
      pressed references to the "eccentricities" of the "still
      living" Rev. Brontë and also to the "well-intentioned
      minister" who ran the Cowan Bridge School.

78   ANON. "Reviews and Notices. The Life of Charlotte Brontë....
      Second Edition," English Churchman (London), XV (28 May,
      4 June, 11 June), 517-18, 533-35, 559-60. [The second
      installment includes a reprint of the Newton and Robinson
      advertisement in the Times (London) (30 May 1857), p. 5.
      See 1857.B95.]
         "Dr. Johnson was scarcely more fortunate in his biog-
      rapher than" Charlotte "has been in having the authoress of

1857

(ANON.)
'Mary Barton'" to write this "interesting and instructive"
biography. Gaskell, though a friend, does not "omit or
gloss over" anything. As "the wife of a Socinian minister,"
Gaskell "may be supposed to have some prejudices against an
establishment conducted upon those ultra-Protestant principles with which Mr. Carus Wilson is so notoriously identified." The Life "will make many read Miss Brontë's works
who have not read them before" and others reread them in
"the new light" of Gaskell's narrative, though "we" can
never "be reconciled to certain passages in Jane Eyre, especially as the work of a...daughter of an English Clergyman." Gaskell's apology in the Times (London) over the
Branwell matter shows that she should have verified her
facts before publishing.

79   ANON. "Tangled Talk. Mrs. Gaskell's Life of Charlotte
      Brontë," Tait's Edinburgh Magazine, n.s. XXIV (May), 292-95.
         Charlotte's ability to convey our own "conscientious"
      character through her fiction "is the rarest of all quali-
      ties" among novelists, "and I am not sure that I know any"
      other, "except" Gaskell, "who put so much of it into her
      writing as Charlotte" has. Two "obvious" "instances of
      merit" in modern fiction are Jane Eyre and Mary Barton.

80   ANON. "Vindication of Charlotte Brontë," Halifax Guardian
      (23 May), p. 7. [Reprinted in Thomas James Wise and John
      Alexander Symington, eds. The Brontës: Their Lives,
      Friendships and Correspondence. IV. The Shakespeare Head
      Brontë. Oxford: Shakespeare Head Press, published by Basil
      Blackwell. Appendix I, 297-314; Clement [K.] Shorter, ed.
      The Brontës: Life and Letters. New York: Charles Scrib-
      ner's Sons. II, Appendix VIII, 447-62. See 1932.B22 and
      1908.B27. Nicholls's letter also appeared without comment
      in Leed's Mercury (23 May 1857), p. 6; Manchester Daily
      Examiner and Times (22 May 1857), p. 4; Manchester Guardian
      (22 May 1857), p. 4.]
         We did not print "the letters" darkening Charlotte's
      noble "memory," but "we willingly" insert the Rev.
      Nicholls's "vindication of" her. [A letter by A. Nicholls
      follows:] Wilson's defense of his father's school in
      Charlotte's day quotes praises from a later time and loca-
      tion and ignores the facts that the school was supported
      by public contributions and that the food was poorly
      cooked.

81   BALDWIN, SARAH. "The Cowan Bridge School Controversy....
      To the Readers [advertisement],..." Halifax Guardian

(1 August), p. 6. [Reprinted in Wise and Symington, eds. The Brontës. IV, Appendix I, 297-314; Shorter, ed. The Brontës: Life and Letters. II, Appendix VIII, 447-62. See 1932.B22 and 1908.B27.]

The editor's "summing up" was wrong in assuming "that 'there were certain hardships' at the school...."

82 _____. "'Jane Eyre' and the Cowan Bridge School. To the Editors,..." Halifax Guardian (13 June), p. 6. [Reprinted in Wise and Symington, eds. The Brontës. IV, Appendix I, 297-314; Shorter, ed. The Brontës: Life and Letters. II, Appendix VIII, 447-62. See 1932.B22 and 1908.B27.]

It is unjust for you to print letters by the Rev. Nicholls and not by the Rev. Wilson, so, as an old pupil at Cowan Bridge, I wish to defend the school and its founder against willful misrepresentation.

83 _____. "'Jane Eyre' and the Cowan Bridge School. To the Editor,..." Halifax Guardian (11 July), p. 7. [Reprinted in Wise and Symington, eds. The Brontës. IV, Appendix I, 297-314; Shorter, ed. The Brontës: Life and Letters. II, Appendix VIII, 447-62. See 1932.B22 and 1908.B27.]

In spite of the Rev. Nicholls's sneers about my not having been at the school at the same time as Charlotte, I can attest to the nobility of the Rev. Wilson's character. In any case, I went to the school only "about a year after she left." The Rev. W. W. Carus Wilson has received over three hundred letters refuting Jane Eyre and The Life of Charlotte Brontë.

84 BAYNE, PETER. "Ellis, Acton, and Currer Bell," in Essays in Biography and Criticism. Boston: Gould and Lincoln. I, 424.

Gaskell's "most interesting and valuable biography of" Charlotte Brontë shows that Charlotte's fiction was more insightful about love and marriage than she was in her private opinions.

85 A Cowan Bridge Pupil in the School's Early Years. "Charlotte Brontë. To the Editor,..." Manchester Daily Examiner and Times (15 June), p. 4.

"A Lover of Truth" is mistaken in thinking that she upholds Gaskell's charges, for Gaskell did not merely talk of "spoiled porridge" but portrayed the school and its founder as vile, which charges I, a former pupil, reject.

86 [DALLAS, ENEAS SWEETLAND]. "Currer Bell," Blackwood's Edinburgh Magazine, LXXXII (July), 77-94.

1857

([DALLAS, ENEAS SWEETLAND])
Gaskell's Life of Charlotte Brontë is spoiled by gossip
about scandals and a catty way of dealing with personalities. Gaskell is patronisingly "apologetic" about Charlotte, though we think less of Charlotte as a writer than
does Gaskell. Women, in general, are handicapped as
novelists because of their difficulty in depicting men.
Gaskell draws a very harsh portrait of Patrick Brontë, yet
his strengths and virtues must have something to do with
his children's talent, and he seems to have been the model
for both Rochester and Heathcliff. Emily "had powers
greater than either of her sisters," but Gaskell, "who
probably was never troubled in her life with a doubt as to
her own excellent qualities," is unable to do "justice to"
Emily's despairing genius, which produced, in Wuthering
Heights, our age's "nearest approach...to...Greek tragedy."

87   DEARDEN, WILLIAM. [Letter to editor], in Thomas James Wise
and John Alexander Symington, eds. The Brontës: Their
Lives, Friendships and Correspondence. I. The Shakespeare
Head Brontë. Oxford: Shakespeare Head Press, published by
Basil Blackwell, 46-52; Clement [K.] Shorter, ed. The
Brontës: Life and Letters. New York: Charles Scribner's
Sons. I, 55-61. See 1932.B22 and 1908.B27.
[Both Wise and Shorter identify the letter as first ap-
pearing in the Examiner (Halifax?) (July 1857), which I
have been unable to see. The letter was partially reprinted
in "Personal. Mrs. Gaskell's Life of Charlotte Brontë,"
Evening Post (New York) (4 September 1857), p. 2, and identified as first appearing in the Daily News (London).]
Gaskell, in her Life, has violated the "sacred" trust of
a biographer by painting the Rev. Patrick Brontë in a false
and "unfavourable" light based on "ignorant country gossip."
"'I did not know,' said the venerable old man, a few weeks
ago, 'that I had an enemy in the world; much less one who
would traduce me before my death'."

88   E. S. "'Jane Eyre' and Charlotte Brontë. To the Editor,..."
Times (London) (3 June), p. 10.
Shepheard's letter exaggerates what Gaskell said in the
Life of Charlotte Brontë about the Rev. Wilson's school.
She mentioned Wilson's good points and was fair to the
school.

89   [HUNT, THOMAS]. "Mrs. Gaskell's Life of Charlotte Brontë...
(first notice)," Leader (London), VIII (11 April), 353-54.
Charlotte's life is "written by a congenial hand, a
fellow artist, and a friend...whose powers of portrait-

painting have already been established by her own novels."
Gaskell "was of living writers the one best fitted to
describe" the real Charlotte.

90 _____. "Mrs. Gaskell's Life of Charlotte Brontë...(second
notice)," Leader (London), VIII (18 April), 376-77.
"Even" Gaskell's "graphic power...falls short" in
describing Charlotte's face, which was appealing if
irregular.

91 KNICK [pseud.]. "New York, July 9, 1857. Literary. Dear
Transcript,..." Boston Evening Transcript (10 July), p. 2.
A debate over "literary ethics" has been going on in the
British and American press" concerning Gaskell's "free comments" in The Life of Charlotte Brontë. Apparently "publicity and delicacy" are "incompatible in women." Gaskell
"is evidently a well meaning and gifted writer--but the
freedom with which she exposes family affairs and private
sayings and doings...must astonish" lovers of justice and
propriety. Yet her book "forms a positive contribution to
our psychological knowledge--a new anatomy both of melancholy and of character."

92 A Lover of Truth. "Charlotte Brontë. To the Editor,..."
Manchester Daily Examiner and Times (5 June), p. 4.
Mr. Wilson and the "Rev. H. Shephard [sic]" are "unjust"
in suggesting that present conditions at the Cowan Bridge
School are the same as in Charlotte's time. "I was a
school fellow of Charlotte Brontë" and can testify that
Charlotte's and Gaskell's charges are accurate.

93 NATHANIEL, SIR [pseud.]. "Notes on Note-Worthies of Divers
Orders, Either Sex, and Every Age.... Charlotte Brontë,"
New Monthly Magazine (London), CXI (July), 317-35.
Gaskell, the "loving and beloved biographer" of Charlotte
and herself "the genial author of 'Cranford'," emphasizes
Charlotte's constitutional pessimism. Our interest in
Charlotte's fiction is "enhanced" by this biography.

94 NEWTON and ROBINSON. "Erratum. Charlotte Brontë. To the
Editor [advertisement],..." Times (London) (5 June), p. 12.
There was a minor misprint in our advertisement in the
May 30th issue.

95 _____. "Life of Charlotte Brontë. To the Editor [advertise-
ment],..." Times (London) (30 May), p. 5. [Also published
as "Correspondence. Life of Charlotte Brontë. To the
Editor,..." Critic (London), XVI (1 June 1857), 257;

1857

(NEWTON and ROBINSON)
"Advertisement," Athenaeum (London), no. 1545 (6 June
1857), p. 726. Reprinted in Wise and Symington, eds. The
Brontës. IV, 223; Shorter, ed. The Brontës: Life and
Letters. I, 322-23. See 1932.B22 and 1908.B27.]
[Gaskell's solicitor, William Shaen:] "I am instructed
to retract every statement" in The Life of Charlotte Brontë
reflecting on an unnamed widow. [The widow's solicitors,
Newton and Robinson:] "We accept the apology...."

96   NICHOLLS, A. B. "Charlotte Brontë. To the Editor,..."
Halifax Guardian (6 June), p. 7. [Also published in Leeds
Mercury (9 June 1857), p. 4; Manchester Daily Examiner and
Times (1 June 1857), p. 4. Reprinted in Wise and Symington,
eds. The Brontës. IV, Appendix I, 297-314; Shorter, ed.
The Brontës: Life and Letters. II, Appendix VIII, 447-62.
See 1932.B22 and 1908.B27.]
"If Mr. Wilson's friends had confined themselves to a
legitimate review of" Gaskell's "work, I should never have
written a line on this subject, but when they attacked the
dead" with "vile" anonymous "slander...(actually sending
a copy to Mr. Brontë)," I had to challenge their assertions.

97   _____. "The Cowan Bridge Controversy. To the Editor [adver-
tisement],..." Halifax Guardian (8 August), p. 3. [Re-
printed in Wise and Symington, eds. The Brontës. IV,
Appendix I, 297-314; Shorter, ed. The Brontës: Life and
Letters. II, Appendix VIII, 447-62. See 1932.B22 and
1908.B27.]
According to Mr. Wilson's dates, Mrs. Baldwin "went to
Cowan Bridge seven years...after C. Brontë left," and according to Mrs. Baldwin's own words, "about a year after
she left...." Such testimony is "worthless."

98   _____. "'Jane Eyre' and Cowan Bridge School. To the Editor,
..." Halifax Guardian (4 July), p. 7. [Reprinted in Wise
and Symington, eds. The Brontës. IV, Appendix I, 297-314;
Shorter, ed. The Brontës: Life and Letters. II, Appendix
VIII, 447-62. See 1932.B22 and 1908.B27.]
Though Mrs. Baldwin "was not" at the school when Charlotte was, a lady who was Charlotte's schoolmate declares
that 'I would rather see a child of mine in its grave than
subjected to the treatment I endured'" at Cowan Bridge.

99   _____. "'Jane Eyre' and the Cowan Bridge School. To the
Editor,..." Halifax Guardian (18 July), p. 3. [Reprinted
in Wise and Symington, eds. The Brontës. IV, Appendix I,
297-314; Shorter, ed. The Brontës: Life and Letters. II,
Appendix VIII, 447-62. See 1932.B22 and 1908.B27.]

All of the "testimony" produced by Mr. Wilson's friends is "misleading" and irrelevant. I have nothing to say against the school as it is now--only against the way it was during Charlotte's time.

100   A Railway Auditor. "End of the Brontë Correspondence. A Suggestion. To the Editor,..." <u>Manchester Daily Examiner and Times</u> (7 July), p. 4.
        It would benefit both the "most useful minister" the Rev. W. Carus Wilson and the "talented" and famous Gaskell if references to Cowan Bridge were pruned in the new edition of <u>The Life of Charlotte Brontë</u>.

101   [ROSCOE, WILLIAM CALDWELL]. "Miss Brontë," <u>National Review</u> (London), V (July), 127-64.
        Gaskell's biography is "unjust" in blaming critics for not being kinder to Charlotte's books because of her unhappy life, and Gaskell also unwisely violates the privacy of living persons. Though her narration is skillful and "absorbing," she substitutes unqualified enthusiasm for reasoned judgments about her subject. She exaggerates the roughness of Yorkshire people, which, in any case, cannot explain the over-singularity of Charlotte's character. Gaskell needlessly condescends about Charlotte's supposed coarseness, for Charlotte wrote plainly of harsh realities, though Gaskell's novels soften them.

102   SHEPHEARD, H. "'Jane Eyre' and Charlotte Brontë. To the Editor,..." <u>Times</u> (London) (27 May), p. 12. [Also published in <u>Manchester Examiner and Times</u> (28 May 1857), p. 4.]
        In March 1856 Gaskell was shown through the school at Casterton, was very favorably impressed, and ought to have said so in her book, which, however unintentionally, has done real damage to the school's reputation.

103   _____. "To the Editor,..." <u>Manchester Weekly Examiner and Times</u> (6 June), p. 3.
        [A letter from Daniel Stone is printed and rebutted. Stone's letter:] Was not the Cowan Bridge School improved as a result of Charlotte's charges, and did not a former teacher drown herself as a result of hardships there? [Shepheard's reply:] The teacher did not drown herself because of neglect by Wilson and anyway had long since left the school. No changes were "made" or will be "made" because "of the unprincipled attacks in 'Jane Eyre' or" Gaskell's "book."

1857

104   SKELTON, JOHN [SHIRLEY]. "Charlotte Brontë," Fraser's Magazine
      (London), LV (May), 569-82.
            Gaskell "has done her work well" and, in "simple, di-
      rect" narrative, vividly evokes the "people" and land of
      Yorkshire. She depicts Charlotte's character with "tact,"
      "understanding," and "tenderness," though occasionally
      Gaskell rages at those who wronged Charlotte. The "re-
      markable letters" are "excellently selected" and extracted.
      "We are thankful that" Charlotte's biography "should have
      been written by the" author of Ruth, who was uniquely
      qualified to pay tribute to "the most remarkable woman of
      her age."

105   [STEPHEN, FITZJAMES]. "The License of Modern Novelists,..."
      Edinburgh Review, CVI (July), 153-56. [Reprinted as "The
      Life of Charlotte Brontë,..." in Littell's Living Age
      (Boston), 2nd ser. XVIII (19 September 1857), 712-14.]
            Gaskell, in her Life of Charlotte Brontë, writes her
      opening episodes "like a novel" and so distorts the plain
      facts. She has also insulted living persons with calumny
      and false charges which the threat of legal proceedings
      have forced her to withdraw. She was wrong in believing
      that it was the job of a writer and "romancer" to try
      alleged yet doubtful offenses before "the bar of public
      opinion."

106   [SWEAT, MRS. M. J.]. "The Life of Charlotte Brontë.... The
      Brontë Novels,..." North American Review (Boston), LXXXV
      (October), 295-329.
            Gaskell's biography gives us "a key to Currer Bell's
      fictions," for "the atmosphere of the novels" permeates the
      Life. Because some of the people involved in the Life are
      still alive, Gaskell "had a very delicate and...difficult
      task...." The biography shows that women can write and
      also fulfill their household duties. "The charge of coarse-
      ness has occasionally" been leveled against Charlotte, "but
      after" Gaskell's "vindication" of her, the charge "must take
      rank with those suggestions which recommend a 'Shakespeare
      for the use of private families' and a mantilla for the
      Venus de' Medici."

107   VERAX [pseud.]. "Charlotte Brontë. To the Editor,..." Times
      (London) (29 April), p. 9.
            "Hundreds" of former students, along with their "parents"
      and "teachers," refute the charges in Gaskell's Life of bad
      food and ill treatment at the Cowan Bridge School.

108   W. "The Brontës [letter to editor]," Boston Evening Transcript (27 May), p. 2.
"... Everyone who has read" Gaskell's "touching life of
Charlotte Brontë is only made thereby so much the more
eager to learn all that can be known of her and" her "extraordinary family." The public will be interested in a
forthcoming Boston edition of the poems of the Brontë
sisters.

109   WILSON, W. W. CARUS. "The Charlotte Brontë Controversy;
Positively the Last. To the Editor,..." Manchester Daily
Examiner and Times (13 July), p. 2.
"In answer to...'A RAILWAY AUDITOR'." I should say that
"in...a correspondence with" Gaskell, "I have found her
most willing to rectify the injustice she has done my
father and his institutions; and her third edition will be
a work...which none can cavil at but all extoll."

110   _____. "Charlotte Brontë. To the Editor,..." Manchester
Guardian (11 May), p. 4. [Also published, with minor vari-
ations, in Leeds Mercury (16 May 1857); Manchester Daily
Examiner and Times (18 May 1857), p. 4. Reprinted in Wise
and Symington, eds. The Brontës. IV, Appendix I, 297-314;
Shorter, ed. The Brontës: Life and Letters. II, Appendix
VIII, 447-62. See 1932.B22 and 1908.B27.]
"... The following, taken out of a review,...is an ample
answer to the statements in the 'Life of Charlotte Brontë',
regarding my father's charitable institutions." [Passages
are quoted from "the lady who was the superintendent...in
1824," defending Wilson and his school against the charges
in Jane Eyre and the Life.]

111   _____. "Charlotte Brontë. To the Editor,..." Leeds Mercury
(20 May), Supplement, p. 12. [Also published in Leeds
Mercury (28 May 1857), p. 3; Manchester Examiner and Times
(27 May 1857), p. 4; Manchester Guardian (28 May 1857),
p. 4. Reprinted in Wise and Symington, eds. The Brontës.
IV, Appendix I, 297-314; Shorter, ed. The Brontës: Life
and Letters. II, Appendix VIII, 447-62. See 1932.B22 and
1908.B27.]
In my previous letter I published only part of the lady
superintendent's letter. Now let me cite the following
from her: though the doctor criticized the "baked rice
pudding," the ingredients were wholesome. My father should
be believed more than a nine-year-old child.

112   _____. "Charlotte Brontë. To the Editor,..." Leeds Mercury
(4 June), p. 1. [Also published in Manchester Examiner and
Times (4 June 1857), p. 4.]

1857

(WILSON, W. W. CARUS)
Mr. Nicholls, in his letter in the June 9th Leeds Mercury, is "welcome" to one case of "burnt pudding" and a
few cases of "wet feet," but his major charges about the
school are all false.

113   . "The Cowan Bridge School. To the Editor,..." Halifax
Guardian (18 July), p. 3. [Reprinted in Wise and Symington,
eds. The Brontës. IV, Appendix I, 297-314; Shorter, ed.
The Brontës: Life and Letters. II, Appendix VIII, 447-62.
See 1932.B22 and 1908.B27.]
"... In a correspondence I have had with" Gaskell, "I
have found her most willing to rectify the injury she has
done to my father and his institutions, and I believe her
third edition will be a work which none can cavil at, but
all extol. I gladly do her justice in saying that I am
sure she only desires to elicit truth. I do think she is
more to blame than C. Brontë for having too much endorsed
as facts the exaggerated fictions of 'Jane Eyre'."

114   . "'Jane Eyre'. To the Editor,..." Daily News (London)
(24 April), p. 2. [Reprinted in Wise and Symington, eds.
The Brontës. IV, Appendix I, 297-314; Shorter, ed. The
Brontës: Life and Letters. II, Appendix VIII, 447-62.
See 1932.B22 and 1908.B27.]
Concerning Gaskell's Life of Charlotte Brontë, "now one
of the most popular works of the day," I must assert that
the "statements" about the Cowan Bridge School are "un-
founded."

1858 A   BOOKS - NONE

1858 B   SHORTER WRITINGS

1   ALLIBONE, S.[AMUEL] AUSTIN. A Critical Dictionary of English
Literature and British and American Authors. Philadelphia:
J. B. Lippincott Co. [Reprinted in 1872.] S. v.
"Gaskell, Mrs., formerly Miss Stromkin [the source of
the incorrect maiden name in many of Gaskell's obituaries
in 1865]." This author has won "considerable popularity."

2   ANON. "Literary," Harper's Weekly (New York), II (2 January),
p. 6.
Gaskell's Life of Charlotte Brontë "was the leading
biographical work of the year, but was a sad mistake in the
author, though it sold remarkably well." Gaskell "quarreled with pretty much everyone concerned, and after trying

to revise and reform the book by erasures and new editions,
gave it up in despair, and submitted to be universally con-
demned." Gaskell "writes admirable novels and is therefore
a poor historian of facts."

3   ANON. "Literary," Harper's Weekly (New York), II (30 October),
     694.
          My Lady Ludlow sustains "the reputation" of Gaskell's
     earlier novels, which "converted the most rigid people in
     Manchester into diligent novel-readers." Even "those who
     had denounced" "fiction" as ungodly admitted "that, if all
     novels were like" hers, "novel reading would not be a sin."
     Gaskell's "insight" into "the human heart" and into the re-
     lationship of "rich and poor" makes this "delightful" story
     appealing to Americans in spite of its English setting.

4   ANON. "Literary Notices. My Lady Ludlow,..." Graham's Illus-
     trated Magazine (Philadelphia), LIII (December), 568.
          "We have not read this work, but have heard it, like
     the Andes, very highly spoken of, and therefore commend it
     to all our friends."

5   ANON. "Review of New Books. My Lady Ludlow,..." Peterson's
     Magazine (Philadelphia), XXXIV (December), 449.
          "A charming story, by a favorite author, which we recom-
     mend to our fair readers."

6   JEAFFRESON, J. CORDY. "L. E. [sic] Gaskill [sic]," in Novels
     and Novelists from Elizabeth to Victoria. London: Hurst &
     Blackett. II, 351-53.
          "We" lack adequate "space to express...our deep grati-
     tude to" Gaskell "for...rousing us in moments of selfish-
     ness or apathy to a healthy sympathy with the desolate and
     distressed." Her novels are "of the very highest order,"
     for they display "a tender heart, a lively imagination,
     rare moral courage, high aspirations," and "startling force
     of diction." The only fault in her Life of Charlotte Brontë
     is that Gaskell uses too many letters, instead of "relying
     more on her own unusual gift of nervous and skilful narra-
     tion." The attacks on the biography by the followers of
     the Rev. Carus Wilson are singularly unconvincing.

7   T. H. New York Times (11 October), p. 2; "Visit to Haworth.
     The Brontë Family," Littell's Living Age (Boston), 3rd ser.
     III (6 November 1858), 474-75. [Reprinted from Scotsman
     (Edinburgh) (9 October 1858).]
          Haworth people are angry at the way that they were por-
     trayed in Gaskell's Life of Charlotte Brontë.

1859

1859 A BOOKS - NONE

1859 B SHORTER WRITINGS

  1   ANON. "Literary Examiner. Round the Sofa,..." Examiner
      (London) (26 March), p. 197.
         In one of these two volumes, Gaskell's "popular story of
      My Lady Ludlow" is "reprinted from the Household Words."
      In the other, some of her "choice" "shorter stories" are
      reprinted.

  2   ANON. "Literary Women of the Nineteenth Century," English-
      woman's Domestic Magazine (London), VII (December), 341-43.
         Gaskell's book on Charlotte Brontë "displays considerable
      talent, and ranks with Southey's 'Biography of Kirke White'
      or Milne's 'Life of Keats'."

  3   ANON. "Publications Received. Round About [sic] the Sofa.
      By the Author of 'Mary Barton', 'Life of Charlotte Brontë',
      ..." Spectator (London), XXXII (19 March), 330.
         These forceful stories of "incident" and "passion"
      illustrate "national or provincial manners," but some do
      not have a pleasing subject.

  4   ANON. "Round the Sofa," Saturday Review (London), VII
      (25 June), 782-83.
         These reprinted stories make a wholly shapeless book of
      reused materials. Gaskell suffers from the disadvantages
      of serial publication. She has never been good at the con-
      struction of plots that hold the reader's interest. Her
      best works, such as Cranford, are plotless and show off her
      compensatory talents of "humour," moving characterization,
      "irony," "taste," "style, and observation." But her most
      successful works, unlike Jane Austen's, are essentially
      static. One wishes that Lady Ludlow were more central in
      the present volume, for she has fine possibilities for "de-
      velopment." The "invincible" "old maid" Miss Galindo is
      a most amusing portrait.

  5   GREEN, HENRY. Knutsford. Its Traditions and History: with
      Reminiscences, Anecdotes and Notices of the Neighborhood.
      London: Smith, Elder & Co. 2nd ed. Manchester: Charles
      Simms & Co., pp. 114, 119-30.
         Gaskell's fiction, and most notably Cranford, reflects
      the manners and mores of Knutsford with "good-natured
      humour and kindliness of spirit."

6   [GREG, WILLIAM RATHBONE]. "The False Morality of Lady Novel-
     ists," National Review (London), VIII (January), 144-67.
     [Reprinted in William Rathbone Greg. Literary and Social
     Judgments. London: Trübner & Co., 1877, pp. 102-42.]
          The flaw in Gaskell's Ruth, otherwise "a most beautiful
     and touching tale," is that the author presents her heroine
     as essentially innocent in spite of the circumstances of
     her seduction and yet later gives in "to the world's" con-
     ventional "estimate" of Ruth's "sin." Gaskell should have
     either made Ruth an "ordinary" sinner or a saint without
     the taint of sin.

7   [MORLEY, HENRY]. "Chips. Character Murder," Household Words
     (London), XIX (8 January), 139-40.
          [On Gaskell's "Disappearances," Household Words, III
     (7 June 1851), 246-50.] Although the town meeting in North
     Shields proved that the vanished man--John Margetts--had
     died in the East India Company, no reparations have been
     made to the family unjustly accused of his murder.

1860 A BOOKS - NONE

1860 B SHORTER WRITINGS

1   ANON. "Brief Notices. The Life of Charlotte Brontë....
     New Edition,..." Eclectic Review (London), n.s. III (April),
     434-35.
          The spirit of this biography is the same as that of
     Jane Eyre. To understand Charlotte's fiction, one must
     read this life, which is "a monument of the sympathy and
     ability of" Gaskell, as well as of the sad "genius" of
     Miss Brontë.

2   M. M. "Novels of the Day: Their Writers and Readers,"
     Fraser's Magazine (London), LXII (August), 209-10.
          "That the quietest scenes and the most commonplace char-
     acters can be so described as to be both pathetic and
     amusing, without the introduction of any overstrained or
     improbable incident, has...seldom" been "more effectually"
     demonstrated "than in" Gaskell's Cranford or Longfellow's
     Kavanagh, both of which are "less known than they deserve
     to be."

3   [ROBERTSON, JAMES CRAIGIE]. "Scenes of Clerical Life, Adam
     Bede, and The Mill on the Floss,..." Quarterly Review
     (London), CVIII (October), 470.

1860

([ROBERTSON, JAMES CRAIGIE])
"Unsparing revelations" in Gaskell's Life of Charlotte
Brontë show that the element of male corruption, recognized
in Jane Eyre by the Quarterly Review, came from the "de-
praved" influence of Branwell on poor Charlotte.

1861 A BOOKS - NONE

1861 B SHORTER WRITINGS

*1 DE MOUY, CHARLES. "Romanciers anglais contemporains: Mistress
Gaskell," Revue Européenne (Paris), XVII (month unknown),
138-64.
"Two centers of heat and light illuminate" Gaskell's
"work: the sensitivity of the woman and the faith of the
Christian." If Mary Barton is artistically immature, the
calmer North and South has less excitement. Ruth "takes
the character and almost the form of a poem"; Cranford and
later works are "genre" pieces. The English, unlike the
French, refuse to be unserious in novels, and Gaskell is
one of their important novelists. [Source: Marjorie
Taylor Davis. "An Annotated Bibliography of Criticism on
Elizabeth Gaskell, 1848-1973," Ph.D. dissertation, University of Mississippi, 1974. See 1974.B6.]

1863 A BOOKS - NONE

1863 B SHORTER WRITINGS

1 ANON. "Belles Lettres," Westminster Review (London), n.s.
XXIII (April), 622-33.
Sylvia's Lovers "is very beautifully told," with "humour," "sympathy," and charm, and, if "some" may prefer
"two volumes" to "three," most will want the story to go
on as long as possible.

2 ANON. "Belles Lettres," Westminster Review (London), n.s.
XXIV (July), 304-7.
Although A Dark Night's Work has a disappointingly
"flat" beginning, the later part, dealing with nemesis and
dread, shows Gaskell's "peculiar power."

3 ANON. "The Book of the Month. Sylvia's Lovers,..." Englishwoman's Domestic Magazine (London), n.s. VI (April),
281-82.
People have been wondering what became of the author of
Mary Barton, Ruth, Cranford, and North and South. Sylvia's

Lovers lacks the humor of the delightful Cranford and the
power of Mary Barton, but Gaskell still writes "well and
still has kept" her faith. She still has weaknesses of
illogicality and narrowness, but she has "gained in
subtlety." Gaskell seems to like characters with tempers.

4 ANON. "The Books of the Week," New York Times (23 March),
     p. 2.
     Gaskell "never trifles with her readers...." Sylvia's
Lovers "is an earnest and faithful study of life among the
great middle classes--elaborated, perhaps, with something
of a pre-Raphaelite minuteness, but redeemed from the
possible charge of heaviness by a plot of great interest,
admitting much development of character and turning on the
complications arising from an ill-assorted marriage."

5 ANON. "Books of the Week. A Dark Night's Work,..." New York
     Times (26 May), p. 2.
     "... With every new book," Gaskell gets better at
"simplicity of plot and structure" in her fiction. "A
Dark Night's Work forms a remarkable contrast to Sylvia's
Lovers" and "has all the severity of purpose of an ancient
Greek tragedy.... Restricted space gives strength and dis-
tinctness" to Gaskell's story of nemesis.

6 ANON. "A Dark Night's Work,..." Athenaeum (London), no. 1857
     (30 May), p. 708.
     Though this story was "wearying" as a serial, it has a
"delicate quiet interest" "when read as a whole." But the
girl's dull eighteen years of self-sacrifice are dragged
on for too long, so that we have a sense of nightmare rather
than sympathy with her. "We like" this unhealthy story
"less than anything" else Gaskell "has yet written."

7 ANON. "A Dark Night's Work,..." John Bull (London), XLIII
     (30 May), 348.
     This powerful story is "almost" "too painful." Gas-
kell's "mournful tales" have a "soft beauty" and "delicate
shading" that will not appeal to lovers of "sensation
novels."

8 ANON. "Literary Examiner. Sylvia's Lovers,..." Examiner
     (London) (28 March), p. 197.
     "This is a novel to be read slowly, as one reads a poem.
Its plot is...such...as Crabbe might have chosen," for "it
deals...with the truest poetry of life" among simple and
unfashionable people." Gaskell "has never written with
more care than in this" masterful "novel." The skillful

1863

(ANON.)

use of "Yorkshire dialect...gives...a Doric simplicity to
the whole idyll." The relentless "fate of a Greek tragedy"
is replaced in the novel by the "iniquity of law," epitomized by the press-gang.

9   ANON. "Literary Examiner. Sylvia's Lovers...(second notice),"
    Examiner (London) (11 April), p. 231.
        In the scene in which both Sylvia's mother and Philip
    advise that she buy grey "duffel for a cloak" but "she
    willfully...buys the scarlet," "Philip himself" is "the
    grey duffel that does not please the maiden's fancy," and
    "the scarlet is Charley Kinraid...." Gaskell "does not
    describe either the trial or the execution" of Daniel
    Robson yet subtly conveys "the tragedy" that happens off-
    stage. "The end of the book is like the burden of some
    true-hearted old ballad tale," but "the graceful and shrewd
    humour of...Cranford lives again in the first half...."

10 ANON. "Literary Intelligence.... In Fiction...." Publishers'
    Circular (London), XXVI (2 March), 108.
        Gaskell, "so long silent, publishes a new novel, en-
    titled Sylvia's Lovers, the scene of which introduces us to
    a kind of life almost new to novel-readers--...a town on
    the coast of Yorkshire, chiefly devoted to whaling expedi-
    tions...."

11 ANON. "Literary Notes," New York Illustrated News (30 May),
    p. 66.
        Sylvia's Lovers deals with "rough North country folk"
    and displays "the abundant humor and cordial sympathy with
    all things human which are the great charms of" Gaskell's
    "works."

12 ANON. "Literary Notices," Harper's New Monthly Magazine
    (New York), XXVII (June), 129.
        Sylvia's Lovers "is a story of humble life" most notable
    for the characterization of the heroine. A Dark Night's
    Work, a story of a guilty secret, "is of a more ambitious
    character." These two works "are among" the "best" of one
    of "the foremost novelists of" our time.

13 ANON. "Literary Notices. Sylvia's Lovers,..." Godey's Lady's
    Book and Magazine (Philadelphia), LXVI (June), 586.
        Gaskell "is not a sensation writer, but there is sterling
    merit in her productions." In this novel the "main inci-
    dents" derive from the unjust working of a late-eighteenth-
    century press gang in Yorkshire.

14   ANON. "Literature and Art. Sylvia's Lovers,..." Weekly
      Dispatch (London) (15 March), p. 6.
          The novel is a remarkable combination of historical
      facts and imaginary art. This story of Sylvia's loss of
      her true love through the lying treachery of the man who
      persuades her to marry him is "the best the author has
      produced." Particularly fine is the "death-bed" scene
      between Sylvia and her broken husband.

15   ANON. "Literature. Mrs. Gaskell's New Novel," Manchester
      Daily Examiner and Times (14 April), p. 3.
          Some will find Sylvia's Lovers Gaskell's finest novel,
      but those expecting a book like her previous ones will be
      disappointed. We in Manchester are proud of Gaskell, but
      we would have liked her story better if Philip's "character
      had not been blackened to such an awful extent by" his "act
      of...designing cruelty." Gaskell's talent for portraying
      "passionate feeling" shows when Kinraid returns to find
      Sylvia married to Philip, and "from this point to the
      close...the writing intensifies.... Is it a fault or a
      merit that the book deals only with personages in the lower
      ranks of life?"

16   ANON. "Literature. Mrs. Gaskell's New Novels," Nonconformist
      (London), n.s. XXIII (6 May), p. 356.
          Gaskell "has fully established her...place in the first
      rank of female novelists.... She has never" learned "the
      secret of" spell-binding plot, "but her tales are always
      marked by a sustained power and a skillful employment of
      character and incidents...." Sylvia's Lovers is, "in some
      ways,...more elaborate and artistic than any of her former
      productions," but, unlike them, it has no "distinct moral
      or social purpose," though it does have an implied moral
      point. The "graphic" depiction "of the violent doings of
      the press gang...may serve to remind us of the advances we
      have made in our own generation in the enjoyment of real
      freedom." The book's "general effect is painful" because,
      with the minor exceptions of Hestor Rose "and the generous
      brothers Foster," there are no really admirable characters.
      Gaskell makes a moral mistake in "awakening our" sympathies
      for the despicably behaving Philip. "... A blank is
      caused by the absence of all religious purpose and motive,"
      for Alice Rose's religion is too "sour," "narrow," and
      "forbidding" to be any help. A Dark Night's Work is as
      good as Sylvia's Lovers and just as depressing.

17   ANON. "Literature. Sylvia's Lovers,..." Daily News (London)
      (3 April), p. 2.

1863

(ANON.)
Although Gaskell has "narrative" skill and "vigour in description," she "would" need "almost superhuman powers to" interest us in the "series of dreary images and comfortless events" of this novel. The picture of an ignorant "family" in a "barren" and poor Yorkshire arouses neither "pleasure" nor interest. Sylvia is "beautiful" but a mere "human animal." Even a hanging and an impressment do not arouse our interest. We might have felt sympathy for Philip if he weren't so "hang-dog." When Kinraid returns and Sylvia agrees with him that her husband is a "'damned scoundrel'" in spite of his helping her during "years of happy domesticity and the birth of a child," "we must confess to a slight feeling of disgust."

18   ANON. "Literature. Sylvia's Lovers,..." Morning Advertiser (London) (26 February), p. 3.
"We do not hesitate...in placing" Gaskell "in the foremost rank of living writers." Her "style is unaffected, yet nervous, and invested with a simple pathos entirely captivating.... Like a well-composed...panoramic picture, the scenes widen as they role on,...revealing the author's high purpose--the inculcation of sound morality, and the... virtues necessary...in every-day life."

19   ANON. "Literature. Sylvia's Lovers,..." Morning Herald (London) (6 April), p. 7.
Gaskell "stands in the very first rank of living novelists...." Charlotte Brontë founded a school of fiction which thinks less of the plot than the characterization, does not shrink from moral questions, and is completely honest. Gaskell belongs to this tradition.

20   ANON. "Literature. Sylvia's Lovers,..." Sun (London) (27 February), pp. 2-3.
Philip "is a masterpiece of" characterization because of Gaskell's "lifelike delineation" of "his virtues" and "vices." "The point on which the story turns is as skillful in design as was ever introduced into a picture of real life...." The description, at the end, of the ocean's ever-recurring roar "is a symbol of the story": life's events are "transitory,...but" man's "ruling passions... can never change" so long as he "walks the earth as a sinful and suffering being.... There is more pathos in this story...and more unexpressed but comprehended sentiment" than in any of Gaskell's earlier novels.

21   ANON. "Magazine Day. Cornhill," Sun (London (2 November),
      p. 1.
           "'Cousin Phillis' begins a new tale, that is so far very
      interesting, and contains some well-defined characters. It
      has also the novelty of a heroine in a pinafore."

22   ANON. "The Monthly Mirror of Fact and Rumour," National
      Magazine (London), XIV (May), 48.
           Though there is much excellence in Sylvia's Lovers,
      there is also "a chill something, a harshness, a want of
      femininity [sic]...in the heroine; a something unlovable
      and repellent...."

23   ANON. "New Novels. Sylvia's Lovers,..." Athenaeum (London),
      no. 1844 (28 February), p. 291.
           Except for the difficulty of reading its Yorkshire dia-
      lect, this is, artistically, the finest of Gaskell's works
      to date. The relationship of Sylvia to her soon-to-be-
      impressed sailor lover is both movingly and convincingly
      portrayed. The book's one weakness comes from Gaskell's
      unwillingness to play out in full scenes the trial and
      execution of Daniel Robson. But the gradual development
      of sympathy for Philip, Sylvia's betrayer, is "true" and
      "powerful."

24   ANON. "Notices of New Books. A Dark Night's Work,..."
      Observer (London) (10 May), p. 7.
           This is "another of" Gaskell's "delightful tales" with
      "characters" that are plainly "careful studies from human
      nature." Gaskell "is one of our most refined lady authors;
      her style is fresh, pure, and natural."

25   ANON. "Notices of New Books. Sylvia's Lovers,..." Observer
      (London) (1 March), p. 7.
           "The hardships of the pressgang law are well depicted,...
      and the domestic scenes of country low life are decidedly
      good and true to nature. But the continued use of the
      common dialect of the northeastern shore of England is both
      useless and fatiguing."

26   ANON. "Review of Current Literature. Sylvia's Lovers,..."
      Reader (London), I (28 February), 207-8.
           We find that the reaction of contemporary fiction against
      "eighteenth century gentility" is somewhat "regressive" and
      that too great an emphasis is placed on low life. Still,
      Gaskell's new book "is one of the very best" fictional at-
      tempts to deal with the poor. Though it has less "vigorous
      colouring" than Adam Bede, Sylvia's Lovers has a plot

1863

(ANON.)
>superior to George Eliot's. Unlike the less artistic Mary
>Barton, Sylvia's Lovers avoids both contemporary politics
>and the artificial introduction of "gentility." What is
>lacking in Gaskell's tragic story is a central figure "ex-
>celling, not necessarily in virtue, but in energy," "ele-
>vation," and "strength." Philip is so inadequate that
>even "the stock novel character" Kinraid would have made a
>better central protagonist. "The delineation of indi-
>vidual character is not the forte of our author, but she
>has wisely chosen a subject" that displays "her almost un-
>equalled power of painting the character of a class" and
>of conveying "universal" "emotions."

27   ANON. "Review of New Books. A Dark Nights's Work,..."
>Peterson's Magazine (Philadelphia), XLIII (June), 473.
>"Like everything" that Gaskell "writes, this story, for
>it is hardly a novel, exhibits considerable power."

28   ANON. "Review of New Books. Sylvia's Lovers,..." Peterson's
>Magazine (Philadelphia), XLIII (May), 400.
>"... With the very greatest pleasure,...we welcome"
>Gaskell "back to the field of fiction, from which "for many
>years she has been unaccountably silent." Her Ruth was one
>of the finest tragic "tales of the day," and Cranford was
>worthy of Jane Austen. "But we shall be surprised if
>'Sylvia's Lovers' does not come to be considered the most
>artistic" of her tales. The racy North-country dialogue
>is "like the salt breeze of the coast where it is spoken."

29   ANON. "Sylvia's Lovers,..." John Bull (London), XLIII
>(7 March), 156.
>This "tale of marvellous beauty" gains for Gaskell "a
>high place among living novelists." The book's deeply
>moving study of "low life" on the "north-east coast" shows
>that the strength of British character resides in such
>people and not in city dwellers.

30   ANON. "Sylvia's Lovers," Morning Post (London) (26 March),
>p. 3.
>Gaskell "does not...rank with the" greatest of living
>writers, yet "she has maintained a high position among
>second-rate novelists...." She makes up for her lack of
>genius by applying those talents she does possess: "a
>clear perception of truth, keen...observation,...a remark-
>able faculty" for "local" color, for style, and for con-
>sistency of method. Gaskell "is deficient in imagination,
>...warmth,...vitality,...cannot portray emotion satisfac-
>torily," fails to concentrate on a central character, and

seems "uninterested" in plot. "... Her realism is of the
pre-Raphaelite order, ugly and flat, though it will bear
minute examination.... 'Sylvia's Lovers' is in some
respects the best of the author's works.... It is...tire-
some...to get through, and yet, when read," it leaves one
feeling "satisfied with it.... The first volume...is
rather tedious," yet the second surprises one by its sudden
interest, though the conclusion is "overstrained."

31 ANON. "Sylvia's Lovers.... A Dark Night's Work,..." Guardian
(London), no. 921 (29 July), pp. 718-19.
    "As is not always the case" with Gaskell, the "merits"
of Sylvia's Lovers are "of a peculiarly feminine kind."
The first part "moves...somewhat tardily," but "the interest" grows "warmer" as Kinraid and the repellent Philip
become rivals for Sylvia's love. Toward the end, the
writing becomes "dramatic," "highly wrought," "pathetic,"
and "tragic." A Dark Night's Work is a "far slighter tale"
but handled with considerable "artistic skill.... In
several parts" Gaskell "shows liking for the Church, which
we little expected to find in her pages."

32 ANON. "Sylvia's Lovers," Saturday Review (London), XV
(4 April), 446-47.
    If Gaskell's previous works had not raised our expecta-
tions too high, we would consider Sylvia's Lovers "a fairly
good book," in spite of its uninteresting plot development.
Unfortunately, Gaskell's characterizations of the lesser
figures are more vividly realized than her portrayal of
Sylvia herself. Perhaps the last third of the novel, with
the return of Kinraid and other "unexpected" ironies "of
fate" is the best.

33 ANON. "Three One-volume Novels.... [including] A Dark Night's
Work,..." Reader (London), I (9 May), 451.
    Though this book "is marked by the same finish of charac-
ter and extreme melancholy as the rest of" Gaskell's
"works," it would be "better if the first half...had been
lengthened, and the last half omitted...." Yet it is "a
great concession" for Gaskell to allow her heroine a happy
marriage after "twenty years" of misery caused by her
"father's errors." Gaskell used to kill off only secondary
characters, but "now" "she makes her principal characters
so miserable that it would be a charity" to kill them off
too.

34 ESPINASSE, FRANCIS. In The Imperial Dictionary of Universal
Biography. London. William Mackenzie. S.v. "Gaskell,
Mrs. Elizabeth C."

1863

(ESPINASSE, FRANCIS)
Gaskell is "one of the most distinguished of living English lady novelists."

1864 A BOOKS - NONE

1864 B SHORTER WRITINGS

1   ANON. "Belles Lettres," Westminster Review (London), n.s. XXV (April), 622.
     This "cheap edition of Sylvia's Lovers should obtain deserved popularity," though the illustrations are poor.

2   ANON. "Literary Examiner. Christmas Books for the Young," Examiner (London) (24 December), p. 823.
     Gaskell's Cranford, in a new reprint, is "a perfect little study of life by a woman of true independent genius" and is "thoroughly amusing, distinctly individual," an enduring contribution to our literature.

3   ANON. "Literary Notices. Cousin Phillis," Godey's Lady's Book and Magazine (Philadelphia), LXIX (August), 177.
     This "story" is "quietly and well told, with culminating interest."

4   ANON. "Notices of New Books. Cranford,..." Observer (London) (4 December), p. 7.
     "Every person who has read" Gaskell's many "truthful and pleasant tales...must be acquainted with" her "power and ability...and will welcome...the present...edition of... Cranford."

5   ANON. "Review of New Books. Cousin Phillis,..." Peterson's Magazine (Philadelphia), XLVI (August), 147.
     "Said to be by the author of 'The Story of Elizabeth' [a mistake], but, though almost Pre-Raphaelitish, hardly so good."

1865 A BOOKS

1   DRUMMOND, JAMES. The Holiness of Sorrow. A Sermon, Preached in Cross Street Chapel, Manchester, on Sunday, November 19, 1865, on the Occasion of the Sudden Death of Mrs. Gaskell. Manchester: Guardian Steam Printing Press.
     Gaskell's "life was joyous to the last; and for her such a departure is blessed.... The genial humour and exquisite pathos" of her fiction remain with us.

1865 B SHORTER WRITINGS

1   ANON. "Correspondence. London," Round Table (New York),
    n.s. I (9 December), 224.
        Gaskell is greatly missed. Cranford is "incomparably
    the best" of her fictional works. She will "be remembered
    longest" for The Life of Charlotte Brontë."

2   ANON. Court Circular and Court News (London), [Court Circu-
    lar:] XVI [Court News: X] (18 November), 1098.
        The death of Gaskell, "one of our most popular writers,"
    is a "loss" to "literature."

3   ANON. "Death of Mrs. Gaskell," Manchester Daily Examiner and
    Times (14 November), p. 5.
        Death has come to "the popular authoress" Gaskell, whose
    "earliest and best-known work" was Mary Barton.

4   ANON. "Death of Mrs. Gaskell," Manchester Guardian
    (14 November), p. 5.
        Gaskell, who has just died, had four daughters and was
    useful as "a minister's wife" for "years before" she "be-
    came known as" a writer, but this delay matured her work.
    "Her greatest" book "is her life of Charlotte Brontë, un-
    paralleled since Boswell's Johnson."

5   ANON. "Death of Mrs. Gaskell," Morning Advertiser (London)
    (14 November), p. 3.
        The late Gaskell's "maiden name was Stromkin [sic]."
    She "was born about 1822 [sic]...."

6   ANON. "Death of Mrs. Gaskell," Public Opinion (London), VIII
    (18 November), 546.
        The late Gaskell's maiden name was "Stromkin [sic]."

7   ANON. "Death of Mrs. Gaskell," Sun (London) (14 November),
    p. 2.
        The late Gaskell's most popular works were Mary Barton
    and Ruth, "of at least equal merit." Gaskell "was born
    early in the present century."

8   ANON. "Death of Mrs. Gaskell," Times (London) (15 November),
    p. 12. [Reprinted from Globe (London).]
        "... Besides being loved and esteemed by a large circle
    of friends," the late Gaskell "was also one of the most
    popular writers of the day."

1865

9 ANON. "Deaths of Distinguished Persons. Mrs. Gaskell,"
Observer (London) (19 November), p. 7.
The late Gaskell "was favourably distinguished as a
writer of fiction." She "was born early in the present
century."

10 ANON. "Dr. Marigold's Prescriptions," Round Table (New York,
n.s. I (30 December), 274.
"It is...whispered that one of these papers in the
Christmas number of All the Year Round is the last work
ever penned by" Gaskell.

11 ANON. "Home News," Guardian (London), no. 1041 (15 November),
p. 1141.
The late Gaskell was known for Mary Barton and Cranford,
"one of the choicest and purest pieces of modern humouris-
tic writing." Her Life of Charlotte Brontë, though "com-
posed under great difficulties," has won "a permanent place"
in our literature.

12 ANON. "Literary, Artistic and Scientific Gossip," Queen
(London), XXXVIII (18 November), 347.
The late Gaskell "was born about 1822 [sic], and her
maiden name was Stromkin [sic]." Her Mary Barton "depicted
the struggles of the working cotton-spinner with...poverty,
and gave many forcible illustrations of the evil of
strikes." Her Ruth, published in "1850 [sic]," "advocated"
Christian charity for fallen women.

13 ANON. "Literary Intelligence," Publishers' Circular (London),
XXVIII (15 November), 653-54.
The late Gaskell was "43 [sic]," and her "maiden name
was Stromkin [sic]." Her Mary Barton unfairly took the
side of the workers over the masters, her Ruth was "somewhat gloomy," but Cranford was "charming." Sylvia's Lovers
was a "beautiful story," but her "most enduring" work, in
spite of its "original defects," is her Life of Charlotte
Brontë.

14 ANON. "Literature and Art. The Cornhill Magazine,..."
Weekly Dispatch (London) (3 December), p. 6.
"'Wives and Daughters' is as charming as ever, and nearly
ended, Cynthia being married at last, and Molly on the road
to it."

15 ANON. "Literature and Literary Gossip," Court Journal
(London), no. 1922 (18 November), p. 1229.

The late Gaskell's novels, which include Mary Barton and North and South, had the "stamp of truth," "force," and a "high moral and religious tone."

16   ANON. "Literature. Literary Notes," Nation (New York), I (14 December), 750.
      Gaskell was a prolific novelist, "considering that her death took place at the early age of forty-three [sic] and that her first book was published" in "1848." Though she made her reputation with Mary Barton, a tale of industrial life, her Wives and Daughters, "now near completion in the 'Cornhill Magazine', develops powers of conferring interest on scenes of ordinary life...at least equal to" those of Jane Austen.

17   ANON. "Miscellanea," Reader (London), VI (18 November), 572.
      The late Gaskell "was one of the earliest contributors to our pages, and her last contribution to The Reader was a review of Torrens's 'Lancashire Lesson' in the spring of the present year. She was born in the early part of the present century, and was between fifty and sixty...." Among her many works, "perhaps her best novel" was Ruth. She "could paint English life in its truest colours," and so her works will "descend to posterity as a study both of genteel and manufacturing life of the reign of Queen Victoria, of which no other writer has given so vivid a picture."

18   ANON. "Mrs. Gaskell," Athenaeum (London), no. 1986 (18 November), pp. 689-90.
      "If not the most popular," Gaskell was "the most powerful and finished female novelist of an epoch singularly rich in female novelists." Mary Barton was her first success; Ruth was "powerful," "though based on a mistake"; Cranford is comparable to Jane Austen's works; North and South is "prejudiced," though well-meaning; and Wives and Daughters is "excellent."

19   ANON. "Mrs. Gaskell," Examiner (London) (18 November), p. 726. [Reprinted in Littell's Living Age (Boston), 3rd ser. XXXI (16 December 1865), 520.]
      The late Gaskell "united to rarest literary ability all the best and highest gifts of a very noble woman." The "pathos,...gentle humour,...delicate perception,...wide sympathy," and "sweet moralities" of her fiction will endure, for she combined "genius" with painstaking craft. In her personal life, she helped "many young authors" but also mill workers, and she made her home a center of culture.

1865

20   ANON. "Mrs. Gaskell," Saturday Review (London), XX
      (18 November), 638-39. [Reprinted in Littell's Living Age
      (Boston), 3rd ser. XXXI (16 December 1865), 518-20.]
          Though not a "unique" or "extraordinarily original"
      writer, the late Gaskell deserved her success. She some-
      times had impulsive and "onesided" "social views," but her
      work got better when she gave up "didactic" fiction. Mary
      Barton will be "forgotten" when Cranford and Sylvia's
      Lovers are still read.

21   ANON. "Necrology," Churchman (London), XXIII (16 November),
      314.
          The late Gaskell's "maiden name was Stromkin [sic],"
      and she "was born about 1822 [sic]."

22   ANON. "News of the Week," Spectator (London), XXXVIII
      (18 November), 1273.
          The late Gaskell's finest work was Cranford, unless
      Wives and Daughters "surpasses it." Mary Barton is "a
      tale of great power." The Life of Charlotte Brontë is
      memorable in spite of "grave defects."

23   ANON. "Obituary. Death of Mrs. Gaskell," Nonconformist
      (London), n.s. XXV (15 November), 926.
          The late Gaskell's "maiden name was Stromkin [sic],"
      and she "was born about 1822 [sic]." Her Ruth advocates
      Christian "charity" as opposed to unforgiving religion.

24   ANON. "Obituary of Eminent Persons. Mrs. Gaskell," Illus-
      trated London News, XLVII (18 November), 499.
          The late Gaskell was "a novelist and writer of much
      talent and deserved popularity."

25   ANON. "Obituary. Mrs. Elizabeth Gaskell,..." Press (London),
      XIII (18 November), 1117.
          The late Gaskell "was born early in the present century"
      and published a number of memorable books.

26   ANON. "Obituary. Mrs. Gaskell," Inquirer (London), XXIV
      (18 November), 742-43.
          The late Gaskell "lived the honoured and useful life of
      a minister's wife for many years before her name became
      known as an authoress," but those years helped to mature
      "the powers" that gave her a "high...place among modern
      novelists and biographers.... Her greatest work...is her
      'Life of Charlotte Brontë'...."

27 ANON. "Obituary. Mrs. Gaskell, the Authoress," New York
Times (11 December), p. 2.
"We believe" that the late Gaskell "was about fifty
[actually fifty-five].... Both in this country and her
own," her novels "were esteemed for" their ability to analyze "character" and "their earnestness in pointing out...
social" ills. Gaskell's works will endure because of their
literary power and their teachings about "individual duty."
"... Throughout the late war, she was a firm sympathizer
with our struggles for Union and freedom."

28 ANON. "Obituary. Mrs. Gaskell," St. James's Chronicle
(London), no. 16,622 (18 November), p. 734.
The late Gaskell's "maiden name was Stromkin [sic],"
and she "was born about 1822 [sic]...."

29 ANON. "Personal," Round Table (New York), n.s. I (9 December),
220.
The late Gaskell's first novel, Mary Barton, "attracted
considerable attention" because of its working-class subject" and also because of "an appreciative [sic] article
in the 'Edinburgh Review'." "Her age is variously stated"
as either forty-three or "between fifty and sixty."

30 ANON. "Personal," Round Table (New York), n.s. I (30 December), 271.
"The last thing that" Gaskell "wrote was a little story
for the Christmas number of 'All the Year Round',..." to
be reprinted here in a later issue.

31 ANON. "Sudden Death of Mrs. Gaskell," Manchester Courier and
Lancashire General Advertiser (14 November), p. 3.
The late Gaskell was "one of the most original and
popular writers of the day." Mary Barton "was an admirable"
portrait of Lancashire working-class life, "thoroughly
appreciated by the business men of" Manchester. Gaskell
"was a thorough student of" human "nature" and "a thorough
woman," whose lighter work pleases by its "wit." Her
"tale" now appearing in Cornhill is her "best" "for purity
of style and intensity of interest."

32 ANON. "Summary. Literature," Saint James's Chronicle
(London), no. 16,622 (18 November), p. 722.
The late Gaskell wrote Cranford "and other delightful
stories of domestic interest."

33 [DICEY, EDWARD]. "Mrs. Gaskell," Nation (New York), I
(7 December), 716-17.

1865

([DICEY, EDWARD])
Gaskell's works were widely read in the United States,
and "she was in many ways a representative English writer
of the highest class...." Sir Edward Bulwer once told me
that "'the only thing'" that he "'ever knew about Manchester was that Mary Barton was born there'.... 'Ruth'
was comparatively a failure" because Gaskell's "mind" was
too pure "to describe a Magdalene." Cranford and North and
South were "clever" but "lacked any central interest," and
Sylvia's Lovers was "marred" by Gaskell's "inability to"
portray "passion of the highest order." The controversial
Life of Charlotte Brontë was "the cleverest...of all her
writings," and Wives and Daughters was as "popular" as any
of her novels except Mary Barton. In contrast to Carlyle
and Ruskin, Gaskell wrote with "grand simplicity."

34   [HERFORD, MRS. CHARLES (MARY JANE ROBARDS)]. "The Late Mrs.
     Gaskell," Unitarian Herald (Manchester), V (17 November),
     366-67. [Reprinted in Inquirer (London), XXIV (18 Novem-
     ber 1865), 742-43; Manchester City News (18 November 1865),
     p. 3; Manchester Guardian (17 November 1865), p. 2.]
     Gaskell "steadily and consistently objected to her time
     being considered as belonging in any way to her husband's
     congregation," but, out of her own kindness and choice,
     she helped the poor and troubled in the community. Through
     this work, she gained her "sympathetic understanding" of
     the "manufacturing poor," which she displays in her fiction.
     Some think The Life of Charlotte Brontë her finest work,
     but others prefer Cranford. "The necessity of perfect
     quiet and retirement while she" wrote fiction took "her
     a good deal from home...."

35   [HOUGHTON, RICHARD MONCKTON MILNES, LORD]. "Occasional Notes,"
     Pall Mall Gazette (London), II (14 November), 10. [Re-
     printed in Inquirer (London), XXIV (18 November 1865),
     742-43; Manchester Courier and Lancashire General Adver-
     tiser (15 November 1865), according to Davis (1974.B6);
     Manchester Daily Examiner and Times (15 November 1865),
     p. 3; Manchester Guardian (15 November 1865), p. 3.]
     Gaskell has "passed away in the midst of that domestic
     life out of which her literary talent grew and flourished."
     Her Cranford "is the purest...humouristic description...
     since...Lamb, and the pathos of 'Sylvia's Lovers' bears
     comparison with" "Enoch Arden." Her offending of people
     still alive in her Life of Charlotte Brontë was "an error
     of judgment" discordant "with the usual" tolerant "spirit
     of her writings.... Her books will be studied in years to
     come, both for their...style and incident, and as a

faithful picture of good English life and sound English manners, beyond the accidents of class or fashion...."

36 KRINITZ, ELSIE [CAMILLE SELDEN]. "Charlotte Brontë et la vie morale en Angleterre," in L'Esprit des femmes de notre temps. Paris: Charpentier, p. 135.
   If one wishes to learn about Charlotte's education at Brussels, one will find, in Gaskell's biography, everything desirable to know, and even some things that are not.

37 MASSON, DAVID [D.]. "Mrs. Gaskell," Macmillan's Magazine (London), XIII (December), 153-56. [Reprinted in Littell's Living Age (Boston), 3rd ser. XXXII (6 January 1866), 23-26; Manchester Guardian (4 December 1865), p. 3.]
   "Because" Gaskell's "private life was full, she wrote only when she felt like writing." A gentle sadness fills all her books. She turned to fiction late, and so her work was never immature, but it lacked the youthful intensity of passion. She was very sensitive to criticism, yet her controversial Life of Charlotte Brontë was her "ablest" literary work, "almost unequalled" "as a biography." In her novels "passion...lay out of her domain...." North and South and Cranford lacked "sustained interest" of plot, but Wives and Daughters won back all her public. She never wrote a word that would not make her readers better persons. Her reputation will survive as an important and very English writer, if not among the very greatest.

1866 A BOOKS - NONE

1866 B SHORTER WRITINGS

1 ANON. "Announcements," Round Table (New York), III (6 January), 7.
   "... Harper Brothers will soon publish...'Mothers and Daughters' [sic], a novel, by the late" Gaskell.

2 ANON. "Books. Wives and Daughters," Spectator (London), XXXIX (17 March), 299-301.
   This book is the author's "best," except for Cranford, and, of the two, Wives and Daughters has greater scope and complexity, though it is "somewhat less perfectly worked out." It is closer to Jane Austen than to Mary Barton or Ruth, and, although Gaskell lacks Austen's formalistic perfection, Gaskell has more "intensity" and "depth of character." The book's heroine and hero are too vaguely drawn, but the other characterizations are splendid, particularly the very different yet subtly similar Cynthia

1866

(ANON.)
and Clare Kirkpatrick. If the book lacks an exciting plot and remains incomplete because of Gaskell's death, it will nevertheless "take a permanent and...high place in... English fiction."

3   ANON. "Charlotte Brontë," Englishwoman's Domestic Magazine (London), 3rd ser. II (May), 136-46.
Gaskell quotes from Charlotte's juvenile "letter to the editor of one of the little magazines" got up by the Brontë children but doesn't seem to appreciate "the purity of its language" nor "the fervour of its imagination." Yet we recommend this generally "admirable" Life of Charlotte Brontë.

4   ANON. "Editor's Table. One Book of the Late Mrs. Gaskell," Godey's Lady's Book and Magazine (Philadelphia), LXII (February), 186.
Gaskell died "in the prime of her genius," but she "left one book--Cranford, which will" remain immortal "while the language lives."

5   ANON. "Four New Novels," Boston Evening Transcript (5 February), p. 2.
"... Harpers have published" Gaskell's "'Wives and Daughters', the last, the best, the most popular and the most extensively read of her works." When it was serialized in the Cornhill and reprinted in American journals, "the eagerness of those who followed the course of the story for each new installment,...was almost as great as that of the readers of 'Our Mutual Friend'...."

6   ANON. "Literary," Harper's Weekly (New York), X (24 February), 115.
Gaskell's Wives and Daughters is out in book form. "During its serialization, its authorship was for some time unknown," so the "interest it excited" was a tribute to her "talent." Its greatest "excellence is the way it shows the interaction of its characters" and reveals their "mixed motives." It will rank "among the best" "novels" of our time.

7   ANON. "Literary Notices. Wives and Daughters,..." Godey's Lady's Book and Magazine (Philadelphia), LXXII (April), 372.
"This story is the last that we shall ever have from the pen of" Gaskell.

8   ANON. "Literary Notices. Wives and Daughters,..." Harper's
     New Monthly Magazine (New York), XXXII (March), 527.
         "Of the four great female novelists of" our day--
     "Charlotte Brontë, Marian Evans, Miss Mulock, and Mrs.
     Gaskell--it is hard to say" which is the greatest, though
     none of them surpass Gaskell in range. This last novel,
     "even unfinished, is, the best of her works," with her
     widest "range of" characters and her most skillful "plot,"
     but also with her usual "sweetness" and style. She
     "will hold a place among the classic writers of English
     fiction long after the 'Sensation Novelists' of the day
     are forgotten."

9   ANON. "Literary Table. Wives and Daughters,..." Round Table
     (New York), III (24 February), 116-17.
         "... Only George Eliot could excell" Gaskell in the
     treatment of a domestic subject such as this. Molly is a
     splendid and lovable heroine, and the next finest charac-
     terization is that of Cynthia, which subtly shows her to
     be "a coquette" and yet is completely fair to her. In
     Gaskell's "previous novels," though they are good, "there
     is less variety in subject and tone." Mary Barton has
     "great intensity"; North and South and Cranford "are
     striking pictures of...commonplace scenes and people; but
     in the present novel these elements are fused into one...."

10   ANON. "Literature and Literary Gossip," Court Journal
     (London), no. 1929 (6 January), p. 18.
         "As a whole, we consider" Wives and Daughters "inferior
     to its predecessor, 'Cousin Phillis', which, perhaps, is
     the most touching fiction" Gaskell "ever gave to the
     public."

11   ANON. "Literature. Magazines, etc.," Atlas (London), XLI
     (13 January), 5.
         "... It now appears, to the sad disappointment of
     scores of thousands of readers," that Gaskell "left her
     delightful tale in the 'Cornhill' uncompleted." Yet Wives
     and Daughters "was nearing" its end, "and the clue to the
     close was becoming in every chapter more clearly indicated."

12   ANON. "Magazine Day. Cornhill," Sun (London) (1 January),
     p. 2.
         "The numerous readers who for some time past have dwelt
     with interest upon the story of 'Wives and Daughters' will
     be shocked and distressed to find in this installment that
     they can never read" the "conclusion" of this delightful
     work. Gaskell "has long been a favorite among novel

1866

(ANON.)
readers, and she has always had something good to teach by
her works, and something which led upward and onward in
the race of life."

13   ANON. "The Magazines," Press (London), XIV (6 January), 19.
Gaskell's "death left 'Wives and Daughters' with but
one chapter unwritten."

14   ANON. "The Magazines for January," Guardian (London),
no. 1048 (3 January), p. 21.
"Readers of" the Cornhill "will...look with a mournful
interest to what ought to have been the conclusion of"
Gaskell's "story, 'Wives and Daughters'....'"

15   ANON. "Mrs. Gaskell," Christian Freeman (London), X
(November), 255-56.
On this anniversary of Gaskell's death, we remember her
religion, her philanthropic work, and her novels. "She
might have won fame in any other class of fiction, but it"
is "to her honour that she choose to" show "the beauty" in
"humble life."

16   ANON. "Mrs. Gaskell," Englishwoman's Domestic Magazine
(London), II (March), 90-93.
The late Gaskell, Charlotte Brontë's biographer, needs a
biographer herself, for we know little about her, except
that she was supposedly born in "about 1822 [sic]" and that
"her maiden name was Stromkin [sic]." We have not gone out
of our way to research the facts of her life, for her books
lack the stamp of a singular personality, and she herself
was best at describing the inner lives of apparently ordinary people and revealing their hidden nobility. In her
fiction, her Unitarianism seems to have helped her to be
firm of conviction and yet tolerant, though, regrettably,
she lapsed from fairness in her life of Charlotte. Mary
Barton has a "clever plot" but lacks the "colour" of Gaskell's "exquisite" Cousin Phillis. Gaskell tried to paint
"souls" rather than "characters," so her people remain
rather dim.

17   ANON. "Mrs. Gaskell's Last Novel," Manchester Examiner and
Times (27 February), p. 3.
The late Gaskell was "one of the greatest novelists of
our times--one of the greatest female novelists of all
times." Like Jane Austen, Gaskell was "a character
painter," but her characters are more "refined" and her
stories "more poetical" than Miss Austen's. Although

Gaskell avoids open preaching, her novels all convey a moral message about actual life. This quality "is most of all apparent in this last and greatest of her works, 'Wives and Daughters'," which portrays "goodness" exquisitely, and delicately satirizes viciousness.

18   ANON. "Music and the Drama. Lyceum," Athenaeum (London), no. 2030 (22 September), pp. 376-77.
       Dion Boucicault's The Long Strike, based "partly" on Mary Barton and "partly on" Lizzie Leigh, simplifies Gaskell's themes for the sake of theatrical intensity.

19   ANON. "New Publications.... Wives and Daughters," New York Times (26 February), p. 4.
       "No writer of our day has taken a stronger hold on the sympathies of the public than" the late Gaskell, and "Wives and Daughters...is unquestionably her best work. It shows in every line a delicate perception of character, a latent sense of true humor,...and a power of conferring interest on the ordinary affairs of life that are the prerogatives of genius alone."

20   ANON. "Obituary. Elizabeth Cleghorn Gaskell," Annual Register [for 1865] (London) (1866), p. 194.
       The late Gaskell was "one of the most admired and successful of that group of female writers of fiction whose productions form one of the marked features of modern literature." Her "best known" tale was Mary Barton.

21   ANON. "Obituary Memoirs. Mrs. Gaskell," Gentleman's Magazine (London), 4th ser. I (February), 279-80.
       The late Gaskell's finest work is, perhaps, her Life of Charlotte Brontë, in spite of the controversy it aroused. Gaskell was renowned for her books but also was admired for her private life and her benevolent activities.

22   ANON. "Recent Novels: Wives and Daughters,..." Manchester Guardian (1 May), p. 7.
       We "doubt" that Wives and Daughters will rank with Mary Barton or North and South. In this, her final work--as well as in "'Sylvia's Lovers', 'Cranworth' [sic], 'A Dark Night's Work'"--she was deflected away from her unique talent of portraying Lancashire life and led to emulate other writers: Charlotte Brontë, Trollope, Dickens, and Jane Austen. Though the plot of Wives and Daughters is deficient, the characterization is excellent, resembling Trollope's rather than Jane Austen's or George Eliot's.

1866

23 ANON. "Wives and Daughters," Saturday Review (London), XXI
(24 March), 360-61.
Gaskell's death is even more shocking than that of
Thackeray, for it came when she "was within a few pages"
of completing her "crowning work." Gaskell illustrates the
advantage that women novelists have over male writers
through a feminine capacity for empathy with the inner
lives of others, including men, as in her subtly complex
portrayal of Squire Hamley. She does not exaggerate,
not even in her comic "masterpiece"--the character Clare
Gibson. Gaskell may be compared with Jane Austen but
surpasses her through "pathos" and "refinement." George
Eliot, in many ways comparable to Gaskell, creates characters with more "vigorous individuality" and "tragic
grandeur," but Gaskell excels Eliot in tranquil sympathy
for fellow human beings.

24 [CHORLEY, HENRY FOTHERGILL]. "New Novels. Wives and
Daughters," Athenaeum (London), no. 2001 (3 March),
pp. 295-96.
"There has been no such" "everyday" novel "as this since
Jane Austen," though Gaskell's book has some surface similarities to Miss Bremer's A Diary. The portrayal of the
coquettish Cynthia is even better than that of the "shallow"
Clare, though perhaps Molly is too good to be true. We
reviewed Gaskell's first novel, and, if she sometimes "lost
her literary way" later through enthusiasm for reform,
Wives and Daughters shows her high achievement as a story-
teller.

25 [GREENWOOD, FREDERICK]. [Editorial note appended to the unfinished installment of Wives and Daughters], Cornhill
Magazine (London), XIII (January), 11-15.
"What promised to be the crowning work of a life is a
memorial of death," though the book was almost finished at
Gaskell's sudden passing. Her superb final works--
Sylvia's Lovers, Cousin Phillis, and Wives and Daughters--
have a kind serenity that makes them surpass her earlier
novels and rank with "the finest of our time." Gaskell
was, as her books reveal, "a wise good woman."

26 [JAMES, HENRY]. "Wives and Daughters," Nation (New York), II
(22 February), 246-47. [Reprinted as "Mrs. Gaskell," in
Henry James. Notes and Reviews. Cambridge, Massachusetts:
Dunster House Bookshop, 1921, pp. 153-59.]
This is one of "a score" of our "works of fiction" that
will outlive our time and is "the best of" Gaskell's "own
tales," excepting the lesser yet "classic" Cranford. Wives

and Daughters "is also one of the best novels of its kind,"
and "so delicately, so elaborately, so artistically, so
truthfully, and heartily is the story wrought out that" it
seems like actuality rather than fiction, with its skillfully concealed "literary artifice." Gaskell's "genius"
sprang from her "affections, her feelings, her associations" rather than her intellect, but rather than value
"her intellect less," we value "her character the more."
Throughout her career "she displayed...a minimum of head,"
as, for example, in her "indiscretions" and lack "of critical power" in her nevertheless "very readable and delightful" Life of Charlotte Brontë. Molly Gibson "commands a
slighter degree of interest than the companion figure of
Cynthia Kirkpatrick," about whom Gaskell "leaves the reader
to draw his conclusions," a method that "shows" Gaskell's
"weakness" yet "also" "her wisdom" in presenting a character with "infinite revelations of human nature." The
"simple and honest" Roger "is hardly interesting enough in
juxtaposition with his vivid sweethearts," yet Doctor
Gibson and Squire Hamley "are as forcibly drawn as" by "a
wise masculine hand...."

1867 A BOOKS - NONE

1867 B SHORTER WRITINGS

  1 ANON. "The Spirit of Fiction," All the Year Round XVIII
         (27 July), 119.
            George Eliot and Gaskell "would make the opposite use of
         the same materials," for novels depend less on the subject
         than on the writer's interpretation of it.

  2 ANON. "The Works of Mrs. Gaskell," British Quarterly Review
         (London), XLV (1 April), 399-429. [Reprinted in Eclectic
         Magazine (New York), n.s. VI (July 1867), 1-19; Littell's
         Living Age (Boston), 4th ser. V (27 April 1867), 237-52.]
            Gaskell's "wholesome" books always do "some good," and,
         if others surpassed her in "poetry," learning, style, and
         "passion," she was second to none as a storyteller. Like
         a good Christian "peacemaker," she preached "Patience with
         the Poor." The one flaw in Mary Barton is that John Barton
         "goes unpunished" by "human justice," and so the book
         might have encouraged hotheaded unionists. North and South
         shows a deepened knowledge of master and men; the kindly
         and humorous Cranford bears many rereadings; but we like
         Ruth "least" of all her novels, largely because we believe
         that "the world is right in its social strictures against

1867

(ANON.)
wanton women" and that Ruth is too "special" a "case."
Gaskell's Life of Charlotte Brontë remains a classic, in
spite of its indiscretions and its tendency to apologize
for the Brontës' own flaws.

3   BELLOC, MME LOUISE SW.[ANTON]. "Elizabeth Gaskell et ses
ouvrages," in Cousine Phillis, L'Oeuvre d'une nuit de mai,
Les Héros du fossoyeur. By Mrs. Gaskell. Translated by
E. D. Forgues. Paris: Librairie de L. Hachette et Cie.,
pp. 1-30.
Both Gaskell and her works have an English gaiety that
finds humor in contrasts but without any unkindness or
bitterness, and her compassionate Christian faith was
wholly opposed to Puritan strictness. Her Mary Barton
made a great sensation, and the workers read it avidly,
but some manufacturers accused her of communism, though,
in fact, she wished to teach mutual understanding. Ruth
told a beautiful story of expiation and redemption; North
and South was a response to critics who accused her of
taking one side on the industrial question; but in Cranford
Gaskell turned to her most personal source of inspiration--
Knutsford, though this book failed in France because we
do not appreciate slow and subtle development in fiction.
Lady Ludlow is like a painting by Chardin, The Life of
Charlotte Brontë is touching, Sylvia's Lovers develops a
moral point with great art, and Cousin Phillis is a delicate eclogue. Each of Gaskell's works shows artistic
progress over the last, but Wives and Daughters is her
masterpiece, with her most profound characterizations.
Molly is the finest of her many portrayals of good, modest
feminine nature. Gaskell's works divide into two periods:
the first, one of social purpose, and the second, one of a
calm, smiling world.

4   HERFORD, BROOKE. Travers Madge: A Memoir. London: Hamilton, Adams & Co. Manchester: Johnson & Rawson. Norwich:
Fletcher & Son, pp. 63-65.
Madge edited the Sunday School Penny Magazine "for Sunday scholars and little children," and he published a number of "beautiful" stories "for children" by Gaskell, who
was "always a willing helper of Travers in all his good
work...."

1868 A   BOOKS - NONE

1868 B   SHORTER WRITINGS

1   ANON. "Brook Street Chapel, Knutsford. The Burial Place of
        Mrs. Gaskell," Christian Freeman (London), XII (August),
        120-21.
            "... Under the cross nearest the west end of the Chapel
        lie the remains of the late" Gaskell, "the well known
        authoress...."

2   [GARLAND, F. A.]. "Jane Eyre's School," Belgravia (London),
        IV (April), 237-43.
            On the basis of my experience as a "drawing-teacher at
        the School for Clergymen's Daughters at Casterton" some
        twenty-five years ago, I am convinced that Charlotte
        Brontë's portrayal of the school was grossly unfair. [This
        is followed by an anonymous letter from a student who was
        at the school in 1829, found it "Spartan" then, and heard
        that it was worse when Charlotte was there in 1827.]

1869 A   BOOKS - NONE

1869 B   SHORTER WRITINGS

1   ANON. "Mrs. Gaskell," Christian Freeman (London), XIII
        (April), 57 and 59.
            One of Gaskell's former Sunday-school pupils at Knuts-
        ford tells us that many of them date their "first religious
        impressions from her kind, earnest, and intelligent instruc-
        tion...." Gaskell's realistic portrayal in her fiction of
        the "domestic life" of the poor is based on the time that
        she "spent...visiting and instructing" them. Her
        Wives and Daughters is "a perfect picture of the every-day
        life of mankind," and she is loved in America as well as
        in England.

2   ROBINSON, HENRY CRABB. Diary, Reminiscences and Correspond-
        ence. Selected and edited by Thomas Sadler. Boston:
        Fields, Osgood, & Co. II, 390.
            [Letter of (Edward) Quillinan to Henry Crabb Robinson,
        14 October 1849:] Gaskell, "the author of 'Mary Barton',
        was,...for some weeks, in that neighborhood and I got Mr.
        Wordsworth to meet her and her husband.... She is a very
        pleasing, interesting person."

1870

1870 A   BOOKS - NONE

1870 B   SHORTER WRITINGS

    1   [CHORLEY, HENRY FOTHERGILL]. "A Memoir of Jane Austen. By
        J. E. Austen-Leigh. The Life of Mary Russell Mitford. Ed.
        by A. G. L'Estrange," Quarterly Review (London), CXXVIII
        (January), 204.
            Only one novelist rivaled Jane Austen in "finish and
        excellence," and that was Gaskell, whose Cranford and Wives
        and Daughters deserve to rank with Mansfield Park and
        Persuasion.

1871 A   BOOKS - NONE

1871 B   SHORTER WRITINGS

    1   ANON. "The Author of 'Jane Eyre'," Literary Budget (London),
        I (13 May), 113.
            Gaskell, "in her 'Life of Charlotte Brontë', gives" an
        "interesting" description of Charlotte's physical appear-
        ance.

    2   ANON. In Chambers's Encyclopaedia. S.v. "Gaskell, Mrs.
        Elizabeth C."
            Mary Barton and Ruth are "the best examples" of her
        novels, which have "remarkable dramatic power" and "very
        graphic" descriptions.

    3   SPAULDING, WILLIAM. The History of English Literature; with
        an Outline of the Origin and Growth of the English Language,
        Illustrated by Extracts: for the Use of Schools and of
        Private Students. 11th rev. ed. Edinburgh: Oliver &
        Boyd. London: Simkin, Marshall, & Co., p. 415.
            "The strange life of" the Brontës "has been narrated,
        with all the interest of romance, by" Gaskell, "who, her-
        self a novelist, did for her native Lancashire what Char-
        lotte Brontë did for Yorkshire."

1872 A   BOOKS - NONE

1872 B   SHORTER WRITINGS

    1   [HAMLEY, W. G.]. "Old Maids," Blackwood's Edinburgh Magazine,
        CXII (July), 96-97.
            Gaskell, "in her incomparable Cranford," subjects to
        "tender ridicule" the "scruples of caste" of "poor" but

"genteel" ladies, which prevent them from marrying anyone they like and condemn them to spinsterhood.

2   HOLLAND, SIR HENRY. Recollections of Past Life. 2nd ed. London: Longmans, Green, & Co., p. 7.
    "My cousin," Gaskell, "who knew Sandlebridge well, has pictured the place by some short but very descriptive touches in one or two of her novels."

3   LAROUSSE, PIERRE. Grand dictionnaire universel du XIXe siècle française. Paris: Larousse. S.v. "Gaskell, Mrs. Elizabeth Cleghorn."
    Gaskell, one of England's most distinguished women of letters, was a literary realist who depicted working-class conditions. Her tales with morals became popular in France through translations.

4   MASKELL, WILLIAM. "The Mystery of Owen Parfitt," in Odds and Ends. London: James Toovey, pp. 77-78.
    [On Gaskell's "Disappearances," Household Words (London), III (7 June 1851), 246-50.] "Some twenty years ago a contributor to 'Household Words'...gave...a garbled variation of the" disappearance "of Owen Parfitt."

1873 A   BOOKS - NONE

1873 B   SHORTER WRITINGS

1   ANON. "Books Received," Publishers' Circular (London), XXXVI (16 July), 477.
    Gaskell's Life of Charlotte Brontë, "one of the best biographies written in modern times, has been reissued...."

2   ANON. "Books Received.... My Lady Ludlow,..." Publishers' Circular (London), XXXVI (17 November), 829.
    We do not need to recommend Gaskell's short tales, for "they are...well known.... My Lady Ludlow,...the most powerful and longest," is one "which our rising writers would do well to study."

3   ANON. "Mrs. Gaskell," Christian Freeman and Record of Unitarian Worthies (London), XVII (December?), 124-25.
    Gaskell "had a natural enthusiasm,...which rendered her works the more interesting, but perhaps led her sometimes to be inconsiderate in her expressions of opinion upon actions and individuals." The Life of Charlotte Brontë may be even more famous than Gaskell's fiction, but Wives and Daughters is "a beautiful domestic tale." She

1873

(ANON.)
"wrote some of the purest and truest works of fiction in
the language...."

4   HEWLETT, HENRY G., comp. Henry Fothergill Chorley: Auto-
biography, Memoir, and Letters. London: Richard Bentley &
Son. II, 104 and 254.
Chorley wrote the reviews in the Athenaeum for Gaskell's
Cranford and for Wives and Daughters.

1874 A   BOOKS - NONE

1874 B   SHORTER WRITINGS

1   FLETCHER, MRS. [ELIZA DAWSON]. Autobiography of Mrs. Fletcher
of Edinburgh, with Selections from Her Letters and Other
Family Memorials, Compiled and Arranged by the Survivor of
her Family [Lady Richardson]. Carlyle: C. Thurnam &
Sons, for private circulation only, pp. 237, 246, 254, 255.
W. E. Forster brought us "a novel then just published,
'Mary Barton'," and, though neither he nor we knew who the
author was, "we were at once struck by its power and pathos,
and it was with infinite pleasure I heard that it was
written by" Gaskell, the daughter of a woman I had
"revered."

2   FORSTER, JOHN. The Life of Charles Dickens. London:
Chapman & Hall. II, 423 and 438; III, 3.
Dickens had "a high admiration" for Gaskell's "powers."
She was present at his dinner in honor of the publication
of David Copperfield. He thought her "charming."

3   S.[MITH], G.[EORGE] B.[ARNETT]. "Mrs. Gaskell and Her
Novels," Cornhill Magazine (London), XXIX (February),
191-212. [Reprinted in Eclectic Magazine (New York),
n.s. XIX (April 1874), 468-83; Every Saturday (Boston),
n.s. I (28 February 1874), 233-41; Littell's Living Age
(Boston), 5th ser. V (28 March 1874), 787-801.]
Gaskell was both a womanly woman and a woman with a
career. Though she had less "genius" than Charlotte
Brontë and less power of characterization than either
Charlotte or George Eliot, Gaskell surpassed them both in
"range." The murder trial in Mary Barton is even better
than the trial of Hetty Sorel in Adam Bede. Gaskell was
attracted to misery more than to joy. The tragic Sylvia's
Lovers shows a "maturing" of "powers." Wives and Daughters
is "the best of all her novels" in its "human affection,"

"humour," and characterization. "She wrote first for the sake of truth, and secondly for posterity." In her fiction, she recreated faithfully the actual world around her.

1875 A BOOKS - NONE

1875 B SHORTER WRITINGS

1   DOBSON, AUSTIN. The Civil Service Handbook of English Literature. London: Lockwood & Co. New edition. Revised with new chapters, and extended to the present time, by W. Hall Griffin. New York: Longmans, Green, & Co., 1897, p. 207.
    Gaskell's Life of Charlotte Brontë, "bating some inaccuracies,...is a model of a biography." Her Cousin Phillis is a "beautiful cabinet-picture," and her "unfinished" Wives and Daughters is the "most charming of modern novels of everyday life,...with sweet, truthful, and pure domestic pictures...."

1876 A BOOKS - NONE

1876 B SHORTER WRITINGS

1   [GLEAVE, JOHN J.]. "Haworth and the Brontë Family,..." Craven Pioneer (Skipton) (19 February), p. 4.
    Although we took a literary tour of Haworth Parsonage, it would be "supererogation to describe the interior" because Gaskell has already described it in her Life of Charlotte Brontë.

2   MacDERMID, THOMAS WRIGHT. The Life of T. Wright of Manchester, the Prison Philanthropist. With a preface by the Earl of Shaftesbury, K.G. Manchester: John Heywood. London: Simpkin, Marshall, & Co., pp. 38-39, 71.
    "The gifted authoress of 'Mary Barton'," Gaskell, gave her "practical sympathy" to Wright in his work of aiding discharged convicts, and she supplemented "with a liberal hand the deficiencies of his own scanty treasury" and helped to find "openings in social life for" his protégés.

3   REID, T.[HOMAS] WEMYSS. "Charlotte Brontë: a Monograph," Macmillan's Magazine (London), XXXIV (September and October), 385-401, 481-99; XXXV (November), 1-18. [Reprinted in Eclectic Magazine (New York), n.s. XXIV (December 1876), 699-715; n.s. XXV (January and February 1877), 83-97, 192-212. Also reprinted in Littell's Living Age (Boston), 5th

1876

(REID, T.[HOMAS] WEMYSS)
ser. XV (23 September 1876), 801-16; 5th ser. XVI
(4 November and 9 December 1876), 289-306, 611-27. Published in book form as Charlotte Brontë: a Monograph.
New York: Scribner, Armstrong & Co., 1877.]
    Gaskell's Life of Charlotte Brontë, though "written with
admirable skill," was handicapped by so many involved
people still being alive, and Gaskell also began with the
preconception that Charlotte's character was more per-
sistently gloomy than it really was. "Readers of" this
lively "biography know that" Patrick Brontë "was an eccentric man, but the full measure of his eccentricity and
waywardness has never yet been revealed to the world."
Gaskell "has given us some idea of" the Brontës' "juvenile"
writings, but she "paid exclusive attention to Charlotte's
productions." Gaskell was inaccurate in identifying Branwell's downfall as the major sorrow of Charlotte's life and
the stimulus of her fiction, for the key experience was the
stay in Brussels.

1877 A BOOKS - NONE

1877 B SHORTER WRITINGS

*1 "A Correspondent Writes," Manchester Guardian (21 October).
        [On Gaskell's use of dialect.] [Unlocatable. Source:
    Gaskell cuttings, Manchester Central Library.]

2 KINGSLEY, CHARLES. Charles Kingsley. His Letters and Memories
    of His Life. Edited by his wife. London: Henry S. King &
    Co., I, 370; II, 24-25.
        [Letter from Kingsley to Gaskell, 25 July 1853:] Ruth,
    unjustly called immoral, has "beauty and righteousness."
    [Letter from Kingsley to Gaskell, 14 May 1857 (Reprinted
    as "How Charles Kingsley Changed His Mind," Brontë Society
    Transactions (Shipley), XII, part 62 [1952], 124.):] Your
    admirable Life of Charlotte Brontë shows me that I "mis-
    judged Miss Brontë's works" as "coarse." Though I seldom
    read any fiction but "yours...and Thackeray's," I shall now
    re-read Charlotte's books "carefully and lovingly."

3 POLE, WILLIAM, ed. The Life of Sir William Fairbairn, Bart.,
    Partly Written by Himself. London: Longmans, Green & Co.
    Reprint. With new introduction by A. E. Musson. Newton
    Abbot, Devon: David & Charles, 1970, pp. 451, 460-62.
        [Letter from Gaskell to Fairbairn, June 1857:] Your
    praise of my Life of Charlotte Brontë was "one little drop

of sweet honey" among so much criticism. Someone has suggested that I use the following as "a preface" to the third
edition: "'If anybody is displeased with any statement in
this book, they are requested to believe it withdrawn, and
my deep regret expressed for its insertion, as truth is
too expensive an article to be laid before the British
public'. But for the future I intend to confine myself to
lies (i.e. fiction). It is safer."

4   SWINBURNE, ALGERNON CHARLES. A Note on Charlotte Brontë.
     London: Chatto & Windus, pp. 28-31, 60.
        The splendid "first two-thirds of" The Mill on the Floss
     owes a "palpable and weighty and direct obligation...to"
     Gaskell's "beautiful story of 'The Moorland Cottage'...."
     Both heroines are named Maggie and have the same "single-
     ness of heart and simplicity of spirit." Gaskell's Maggie
     is "gentler" but "less high-thoughted and high-reaching"
     than George Eliot's.

1878 A BOOKS - NONE

1878 B SHORTER WRITINGS

1   ADAMS, W.[ILLIAM DAVENPORT]. Dictionary of English Literature.
     Being a Comprehensive Guide to English Authors and Their
     Works. London, Paris, and New York: Cassell, Petter, &
     Galpin, S.v.
        "Gaskell, Mrs., neé Promkin [sic], novelist (b. 1811
     [sic], d. 1865)...."

2   BIBBY, R. E. "[no. 352] Mary Barton and Greenheys Fields
     [reply to nos. 250, 259, 274, 289, and 321]," [Manchester]
     City News Notes and Queries, I (22 June), 88-89.
        Two of the old farmhouses in the area are still stand-
     ing, and a nearby cottage was "the residence of" the "power-
     loom weaver" who is "said to have" been the model for Job
     Legh, though Gaskell seems to have relocated his house in
     Mary Barton to make it more depressing.

3   BURY, JAMES. "[no. 259] Mary Barton and Greenheys Fields
     [reply to no. 250]," [Manchester] City News Notes and
     Queries, I (11 May), 36-37.
        The site of Greenheys Fields lies along a lane that runs
     into "Chester Road," but the fields are now covered by the
     Moss Side "dwellings," and Gaskell was wrong in describing
     a "want of wood" in the fields.

1878

4   C. J. W. "[no. 289] Mary Barton and Greenheys Fields [reply
    to nos. 250, 259, and 274]," [Manchester] City News Notes
    and Queries, I (23 May), 51.
        Mr. Bury made a few minor errors and left out some local
    history in his account of Greenheys Fields.

5   CLARKE, CHARLES COWDEN and MARY. Recollections of Writers.
    New York: Charles Scribner's Sons, pp. 92-93, 336.
        We found Gaskell "a charming, brilliant-complexioned,
    but quiet-mannered woman; thoroughly unaffected, thoroughly
    attractive--so modest that she blushed like a girl when we
    hazarded some expression of our ardent admiration of her
    'Mary Barton'...." She was "full of enthusiasm on general
    subjects of humanity and benevolence" and looked much
    younger than her actual age.

6   J. T. S. "[no. 274] Mary Barton and Greenheys Fields [reply
    to nos. 250 and 259]," [Manchester] City News Notes and
    Queries, I (18 May), 45.
        James Bury made minor errors about the streets and land-
    marks near Greenheys Fields.

7   MINTO, W.[ILLIAM]. "Mrs. Gaskell's Novels," Fortnightly
    Review (London), n.s. XXIV (1 September), 355-69.
        Mary Barton was probably suggested by Sybil, but Gaskell,
    unlike Disraeli, knew the poor from direct observation.
    She advocated mutual understanding between masters and men,
    but Disraeli, "perhaps" understanding human nature better,
    emphasized "inevitable" class antagonisms. W. R. Greg, in
    attacking Mary Barton, failed to understand that its basic
    purpose was not to preach to workingmen but to inform the
    general public about working-class attitudes. North and
    South, Ruth, and even the humorous Cranford all have this
    quality of seeking understanding for a misjudged social
    group. Gaskell ranks below Dickens and Thackeray, has a
    less intense style than Charlotte Brontë, but Gaskell's
    fiction succeeds "perfectly" in its modest and "homely"
    aims. Her two best constructed novels are Sylvia's Lovers
    and Wives and Daughters, the last of which is also her most
    mature. Gaskell influenced the early works of George Eliot.

8   SURGE, W. "[no. 250] Mary Barton and Greenheys Fields,"
    [Manchester] City News Notes and Queries, I (4 May), 30.
        I should like information about Greenheys Fields and
    their surroundings, as described in Mary Barton.

9   _____. "[no. 321] Mary Barton and the Greenheys Fields [reply
       to nos. 259, 274, and 289]," [Manchester] City News Notes
       and Queries, I (8 June), 71-72.
           The area has changed sadly since Mary Barton.

1879 A   BOOKS - NONE

1879 B   SHORTER WRITINGS

1   ANON. "Contemporary Literary Chronicles.... Essays, Novels,
       and Poetry & c," Contemporary Review (London), XXXIV
       (December), 204-5.
           We love Gaskell more than any other novelist. She is
       more pleasant than the bitter Mrs. Oliphant or the later
       George Eliot, who has left behind the sweetness of the "Sad
       Fortunes of the Rev. Amos Barton." If Hardy were a woman,
       he might have equaled some of Gaskell's "happy" fiction
       but not Cranford. Cranford and Wives and Daughters shall
       endure when all of George Eliot's works after Silas Marner
       have been forgotten.

2   BIBLIOS [pseud.]. "[no. 1,343] Mrs. Gaskell," [Manchester]
       City News Notes and Queries, II (25 October), 247.
           Is George Rivers correct, in his Ninth Catalogue of
       Second-hand Books, in attributing a work called America,
       North and South (London, 1863) to Gaskell--"the White
       Republican of Fraser's Magazine"? [The work is not by
       Gaskell, and it takes the Confederate side in the American
       Civil War.]

3   GRUNDY, FRANCIS H. Pictures of the Past. London: Griffith &
       Farran, pp. 73-93.
           Gaskell's comments on Branwell in her Life of Charlotte
       Brontë heaped "unnecessary scandal" on this man who "was
       at least as talented as" any of the other Brontës and who
       was not the "social demon" that Gaskell portrayed.

4   H. "Mr. Nicholls: Charlotte Brontë," N & Q, 5th ser. XII
       (26 July), 65.
           Gaskell's "interesting" and "melancholy" Life of Char-
       lotte Brontë is inaccurate in saying that Mr. Brontë
       tutored the family of the Rev. Mr. Tighe, "my grand-uncle,"
       who did, however, serve as Brontë's teacher and admire his
       "ability."

5   KEEGAN, P. QUIN. "Mrs. Crowe's and Mrs. Gaskell's Novels,"
       Victoria Magazine (London), XXXIII (May), 42, 44-53.

1879

(KEEGAN, P. QUIN)
Gaskell began with novels about the working class, but her later non-industrial works, such as Cranford and Sylvia's Lovers, "are more womanly" than her earlier ones on account of a "freshness," "minuteness," insight, "discrimination," and a "profound knowledge of household existence."

6   MASSON, FLORA. In Encyclopaedia Britannica. A Dictionary of Arts, Sciences, and General Literature. 9th ed. S.v. "Mrs. Gaskell, Elizabeth Cleghorn."
Though Gaskell was "one of the most distinguished of England's women novelists," her "life was" both "thoroughly literary and domestic.... Most of what she wrote was founded on observation and experience," as in Cranford and Mary Barton, the one work for which she "will be" most "remembered." "Perhaps the two best of" Gaskell's "productions...are the exquisitely humorous Cranford and" the idyllic Cousin Phillis. "Even in its uncompleted state," Wives and Daughters is "almost faultless," with "a quiet restful beauty." The Life of Charlotte Brontë is a biography "written with the consummate skill of the novelist."

7   XIPHIAS [pseud.]. "[no. 971] Haworth and Charlotte Brontë," [Manchester] City News Notes and Queries, II (19 April), 85-86.
The "abuse" that "assailed" Gaskell "for her fearless exposure of the evils resulting from the blundering benevolence at Cowan Bridge School" makes me think of "Carlyle's adjuration: 'O beloved brother blockheads of mankind! let us close those wide mouths of ours; let us cease shrieking and begin considering'."

1880 A   BOOKS - NONE

1880 B   SHORTER WRITINGS

1   ANON. "Mrs. Gaskell. A Biographical Sketch," Manchester City News (3 January), p. 6.
"The ninth edition of the Encyclopaedia Britannica... contains the most complete account of the life of the distinguished novelist, the late" Gaskell, yet "published."

2   BROWN, E. K. "[no. 1,644] Mrs. Gaskell [reply to nos. 1,606 and 1,616]," [Manchester] City News Notes and Queries, III (28 March), 68.

Henry Irving gave a public reading of Gaskell's "The Crooked Branch" and not, as J. B. claimed, "The Ghost in the Garden Room."

3   DICKENS, CHARLES. The Letters of Charles Dickens. Edited by Georgina Hogarth and Mamie Dickens. London: Chapman & Hall. 2nd ed. London: Chapman & Hall, 1880. I: 216, 269-70, 292, 293, 301, 355, 360, 381.
    [See The Letters of Charles Dickens. Edited by Walter Dexter. 3 vols. Bloomsbury: Nonesuch Press, 1938 (1938.B2), for a much fuller selection of Dickens's letters to Gaskell.]

4   J. B. "[no. 1,616] Mrs. Gaskell [reply to no. 1,606]," [Manchester] City News Notes and Queries, III (6 March), 54.
    The tale that Henry Irving read in public was Gaskell's "The Ghost in the Garden Room," from the Christmas number of All the Year Round (London), 1859.

5   WADE, RICHARD. The Rise of Nonconformity in Manchester: with a Brief Sketch of the History of Cross Street Chapel. Manchester: Unitarian Herald printing office, Johnson & Rawson. London: Smart & Allen, pp. 52-53.
    The Rev. William Gaskell's "gifted wife was one of the three greatest female novelists of the century, and...her writings are among the enduring works in our language."

6   X. L. C. R. "[no. 1,606] Mrs. Gaskell," [Manchester] City News Notes and Queries, III (28 February), 49.
    Which tale of Gaskell's was read on Ash Wednesday by Henry Irving "to the costermongers of the East End of London?"

1881 A   BOOKS - NONE

1881 B   SHORTER WRITINGS

*1   BAYNE, PETER. Two Great Englishwomen, Mrs. Browning and Charlotte Brontë, with an Essay on Poetry. London: James Clarke & Co., pp. 160-70.
     Gaskell's Life of Charlotte Brontë is "an acknowledged masterpiece," and Grundy's defense of Branwell leaves "the impression of a much worse man than we derive from" Gaskell's "biography." [Source: Marjorie Taylor Davis. "An Annotated Bibliography of Criticism on Elizabeth Cleghorn Gaskell, 1848-1973." Ph.D. dissertation, University of Mississippi, 1974. See 1974.B6.]

1881

2   MORLEY, HENRY. Of English Literature in the Reign of Victoria,
     with a Glance at the Past. Tauchnitz edition, MM. Leipzig:
     Bernhard Tauchnitz, pp. 389–91.
          Mary Barton was "a tale of factory life" that blended
     "pathos," "humour," and "a keen feminine perception of
     character." Cranford, for all its "playful humour," "makes
     us feel that souls may be heroic and poetic" even in "the
     narrowest surroundings."

3   THIRLWALL, CONNOP, Late Lord Bishop of St. David's. Letters
     to a Friend. Edited by the Very Rev. Arthur Penrhyn
     Stanley, D.D. London: Richard Bentley & Sons, pp. 42, 43,
     55.
          [Letter of 24 November 1865:] "Alas! what an irreparable
     loss have all intelligent novel-readers suffered" by Gas-
     kell's death. "I am trembling lest she should have left...
     'Wives and Daughters', which she had been writing for the
     Cornhill, unfinished. I did not know who was the author
     until I saw the report of her death; but it appeared to me
     one of the most delightful specimens of the still-life
     novels that I have ever read." [Letter of 5 January 1866:]
     "I mourn deeply over the loss of" Gaskell. "To 'Wives and
     Daughters' it is irreparable,..." for "there was matter
     left for another volume."

1882 A BOOKS - NONE

1882 B SHORTER WRITINGS

1   ANON. "Mrs. Gaskell's Novels," Literary World (Boston) XIII
     (1 July), 216-17.
          Although Gaskell's novels have "a deservedly high repu-
     tation," she is best known for her Life of Charlotte Brontë.
     Mary Barton, North and South, and Ruth are all notable for
     approaching fresh subjects for fiction, but each of the
     three is too long and slow moving. Cranford is the favorite
     of those readers who like humor and graceful style but "can
     do without plot," yet Gaskell's masterpiece is the tragic
     Sylvia's Lovers. Wives and Daughters "shows something of
     a falling off in power."

1883 A   BOOKS - NONE

1883 B   SHORTER WRITINGS

*1   ANON. New York Times (August).
        "'Mary Barton', the book with which" Gaskell "made her
    reputation in 1848 has been published in the Harper Frank-
    lin Square series. If the records are to be credited, this
    talented woman is now in her seventy-third year, and still
    retains her mental freshness and vigor." [Unlocatable.
    Source: Gaskell cuttings, Manchester Central Library.]

2   J. B. S. "A Pilgrimage to Haworth. Wycollar Hall and the
    Homes of the Brontës," [Manchester] City News Notes and
    Queries, V (8 December), 173-76.
        Gaskell, in her Life of Charlotte Brontë, quotes Char-
    lotte's letter about the "sapient young Irishman" who
    proposed and was rejected for marriage, but Gaskell does
    not mention that the disappointed man died "a few months"
    later. His name was Pryce, which Gaskell misread from his
    tombstone as Bryce.

3   LEYLAND, FRANCIS A. [Letter to editor], Athenaeum (London),
    no. 2908 (21 July), p. 79.
        It is regretable that Swinburne, in reviewing Miss
    Robinson's Emily Brontë, intensifies the slanders against
    Branwell by Gaskell. In spite of some "irregularities"
    in Branwell's life, one must remember that the Brontë sis-
    ters and their father were "staid" and also that Charlotte
    never intended Branwell's troubles to be made public.

4   ROBINSON, A. MARY F. [née DUCLAUX]. Emily Brontë. The Famous
    Women Series. Boston: Roberts Brothers, pp. 21, 23,
    29-30, 33, 48, 100, 152-54.
        As Gaskell tells us, Mr. Brontë cut up his wife's dress.
    Who can say if the marriage was happy? As we also learn
    from Gaskell, the Cowan Bridge School was a dreadful place.

1884 A   BOOKS - NONE

1884 B   SHORTER WRITINGS

1   ANON. "Books Received...Cranford and Other Tales,..."
    Publishers' Circular (London), XLVII (16 June), 574.
        This collection "of really healthy and attractive fic-
    tion," including Cranford, "will have a charm for all ages"
    and be ideal for a family "summer outing."

1884

2   ANON. "Funeral of the Rev. William Gaskell," Manchester
    Guardian (19 June), p. 8.
        The late Rev. William Gaskell was buried Saturday in
    Knutsford, next to his wife.

3   ANON. "Literary Gossip," Athenaeum (London), no. 2955
    (14 June), p. 76.
        The Rev. William Gaskell, Unitarian Pastor and husband
    of "the author of 'Mary Barton', 'Ruth', and other popular
    works," is dead.

4   ANON. "Obituary. The Late Rev. William Gaskell, M.A.,"
    Inquirer (London) (21 June), pp. 400-402.
        "We take the following notes, written by one of his
    oldest and most attached friends, from the Manchester
    Guardian, omitting only a few extracts from Mr. Gaskell's
    addresses which appeared at the time in our own columns."

*5 ANON. "The Rev. W. Gaskell's Literature Class," Manchester
    Guardian (12 January).
        [Unlocatable. Source: Catherine Margaret Ellen Halls.
    "Bibliography of Elizabeth C. Gaskell." Diploma in
    librarianship dissertation, University of London, 1957.
    See 1957.B5.]

6   AXON, W.[ILLIAM] E. A. "Knutsford and Its Associations,..."
    Manchester Guardian (19 June), p. 8.
        Standing by the grave in Knutsford of the late Gaskell
    for the funeral of her husband reminds one that she im-
    mortalized the town in such works as Cranford and "The
    Squire's Story."

7   _____. "Obituary. William Gaskell," Academy (London), XXV
    (21 June), 439.
        The late William Gaskell was buried beside his famous
    wife, the author of Mary Barton, Cranford, and "'Wives and
    Mothers' [sic]." This Unitarian minister married Miss
    Elizabeth Stevenson in 1832, and the husband's "scholarly
    activities put both husband and wife in the center of a
    cultural circle."

8   GREVILLE, HENRY. Leaves from the Diary of Henry Greville.
    Edited by Viscountess Enfield. London: Smith, Elder & Co.
    II, 392-93.
        [21 October 1856:] "Yesterday...Mr. and Mrs. Gaskell
    dined here. The latter is the authoress of 'Mary Barton',
    'Ruth' and 'Cranford', and other excellent novels. She is
    remarkably pleasing, unaffected, and easy in her manners
    with a melodious" speaking "voice."

9   NICOLL, HENRY J. <u>Landmarks of English Literature</u>. New York:
     D. Appleton & Co., p. 394.
       "Charlotte Brontë's life was written with admirable
     literary skill and taste by her friend," Gaskell, "herself
     a novelist of high merit" and the author of <u>Mary Barton</u>,
     <u>Ruth</u>, and "'Crauford' [<u>sic</u>]."

1885 A BOOKS - NONE

1885 B SHORTER WRITINGS

1   EVANS, MARY ANN [GEORGE ELIOT]. <u>George Eliot's Life as Re-</u>
     <u>lated in her Letters and Journals</u>. Edited by J.[ohn]
     W.[alter] Cross. Edinburgh and London: William Blackwood
     & Sons. I: 304-5; II: 111-12, 140-41, 146-47.
       [Letter from Mary Ann Evans to Mrs. Peter Taylor,
     1 February 1853:] Though "its style was a great refresh-
     ment to me,.... 'Ruth', with all its merits, will not be
     an enduring or classical fiction--will it?" Gaskell "seems
     ...constantly misled by a love of sharp contrasts--of
     dramatic effects.... But how pretty and graphic are the
     touches of description!" With her "rich humour" and "sly
     satire," Gaskell "has certainly a charming mind and one
     cannot help loving her as one reads her books." [Letter
     from Mary Ann Evans to Major Blackwood, 6 June 1859:]
     Gaskell wrote to me that she was flattered to be "sus-
     pected" of having written <u>Adam Bede</u>. [Letter from Mary Ann
     Evans to Miss Sara Hennell, 11 November 1859:] Gaskell has
     praised <u>Adam Bede</u> in "a very beautiful letter--beautiful in
     feeling" with "very sweet and noble words." [Letter from
     Mary Ann Evans to Madame Bodichon, 5 December 1859:]
     Gaskell wrote to me that she "'earnestly, fully, and
     humbly' admired <u>Scenes of Clerical Life</u> and <u>Adam Bede</u> and
     that she 'never read anything so complete and beautiful in
     fiction'...."

2   MÉRIMÉE, PROSPER. [Letters mentioning Gaskell, in Gabrielle
     Paul Othenin de Cléron, comte d'Haussonville. <u>Etudes</u>
     <u>biographiques et littéraires</u>. Prosper Mérimée. Hugh
     <u>Eliot</u>. Paris: Calmann Lévy, pp. 54, 56, 63. [The same
     letters appear in Prosper Mérimée. <u>Correspondance générale</u>.
     Edited by Maurice Parturier. 2nd series. Toulouse:
     Édouard Privat, 1953. I, 357, 440-42, 453-55.]
       [Letter from Prosper Mérimée to Mrs. William Senior,
     26 September 1854:] I shall read <u>Ruth</u>, as you asked,
     though I fear that it will sadden me. [Letter from Prosper
     Mérimée to Mrs. William Senior, 5 March 1855:] I have read

1885

(MÉRIMÉE, PROSPER)
Ruth with all the attention that it deserves. I think that
the enslavement of women is worse in England than anywhere
else, for there it is rare for them to be able to take
lovers. [Letter of Prosper Mérimée to Mrs. William Senior,
23 March 1855:] I have read Ruth and have met its author.
Although unhappy endings make me miserable, I recognize
the novelist's abundant natural talent. The characterization is excellent, but Ruth is portrayed as far more unhappy than necessary. Gaskell tells me that the book has
been publicly burnt--an action worthy of your Puritans.

3 O'MEARA, KATHLEEN. "Madame Mohl, Her Salon and Her Friends,"
Atlantic Monthly (Boston), LV (January, February, March,
April), 67-79, 169-84, 318-30, 477-90. [Reprinted as
Madame Mohl: Her Salon and Friends. A Study of Social
Life in Paris. Boston: Roberts Brothers, 1886. Published
in French as Un salon à Paris: Madame Mohl et ses intimes.
Librairie Plon. Paris: E. Plon, Nourrit et Cie., 1886.]
    Gaskell, Madame Mohl's "best friend...in England" and
"perhaps anywhere," "wanted to meet M. de Tocqueville, and
Madame Mohl...appealed to Ampère to help...gratify this
wish."

1886 A BOOKS - NONE

1886 B SHORTER WRITINGS

1 ANON. "Mementoes of Charlotte Brontë," Manchester [City News]
Notes and Queries, VI (6 March), 184.
    Sold at Saltaire, "among other mementoes" that used to
belong to Mrs. Peter Binns, a sister of Martha Brown, the
Brontës' servant, was an autographed copy of The Life of
Charlotte Brontë, for 24s.

2 LEYLAND, FRANCIS A. The Brontë Family. With Special Reference to Patrick Branwell Brontë. London: Hurst & Blackett.
Reprint New York: Haskell House, 1971. I: 181-83; II:
73-74, 106-12, 123-24, 139-44, and numerous other references
to Gaskell.
    Though Gaskell portrays Branwell as a debased opium ad-
dict, she herself admits to having tried the drug. In
general, she exaggerates Branwell's faults. Gaskell was
misled about Branwell's relationship to Mrs. Robinson by
his own wild assertions in his letters and to his sisters.

3   M. H. R.   "Mrs. Gaskell's Features," N & Q, 7th ser. I
    (5 June), 445.
       In a letter by Madame Mohl printed in Madame Mohl: Her
    Salon and Friends, Gaskell's nose is misdescribed as
    "little" and "turned up" and her eyes as "blue," "round,
    full and wide open," but Gaskell's nose, in fact, was
    "well formed" and "high," and her eyes were "grey" and
    "small."

1887 A   BOOKS - NONE

1887 B   SHORTER WRITINGS

1   ANON.   "The Old Saloon. The Literature of the Last Fifty
    Years," Blackwood's Edinburgh Magazine, CXLI (June), 758.
       Because of a "frankness of revelation new to the time,"
    Gaskell's Life of Charlotte Brontë created public interest
    in all the Brontës. Yet, though Gaskell's own novels are
    "worthy" of attention, she survives only in "a sort of
    secondary classical rank" and "has fallen into...respectful
    oblivion." Her fiction reflects a "society" with "purer"
    and "better manners" than our own.

2   BIRRELL, AUGUSTINE. Life of Charlotte Brontë. Great Writers.
    London: Walter Scott, pp. 5, 141-42.
       Charlotte Brontë's life "has been written once for all
    by" Gaskell; "but as no criticism of Miss Brontë's novels
    is possible apart from the story of her life, I have at-
    tempted" a "biographical sketch." Gaskell was "herself a
    novelist of rare excellence and rich in the quality Currer
    Bell was most deficient in, true humour and playfulness....
    Cardinal Newman...has given evidence of his familiarity
    with the works of" Gaskell, "but I should fear his judgment
    upon" Charlotte's novels.

3   SIMPSON, M.[ARY] C.[HARLOTTE] M.[AIR]. Letters and Recollec-
    tions of Julius and Mary Mohl. London: Kegal Paul, Trench
    & Co., pp. 126-27, 163-64, 167, 183-84, 201-2, 217-18, 219.
       In 1855 Madame Mohl first met Gaskell, whom she came to
    love and respect deeply. Gaskell often stayed at Madame
    Mohl's and composed "the greater part of 'Wives and
    Daughters'" there, "standing up before the mantlepiece,
    which she used as a desk...." [Letter from Madame Mohl to
    Gaskell, 28 December 1864:] "I have this very evening read
    the last number of the Cornhill, and am as pleased as ever.
    The Hamleys are delightful, and Mrs. Gibson!--oh, the
    tricks are delicious; but I am not up to Cynthia yet. Molly

1887

(SIMPSON, M.[ARY] C.[HARLOTTE] M.[AIR])
is the best heroine you have had yet. Every one says it's
the best thing you ever did. Don't hurry it up at the
last; that's a rock you must not split on."

4   TOLLEMACHE, [HON.] B.[EATRIX] L. "Correspondence. King Knut
and Knutsford," Academy (London), n.s. XXXI (14 May), 346.
Gaskell is buried at Knutsford, and she "depicted" the
town in her fiction.

1888 A   BOOKS - NONE

1888 B   SHORTER WRITINGS

1   Editor. "[no. 5,081] Brontë or Prunty [reply to no. 5,073],"
Manchester [City News] Notes and Queries, VII (25 August),
235-36.
Gaskell was wrong in thinking that Patrick Brontë changed
his name from "Prunty," though it is possible that it
could have been "Brunty" or "Branty."

2   LETHERBROW, E. "[no. 5,073] Notes. Brontë or Prunty,"
Manchester [City News] Notes and Queries, VII (18 August),
23.
Gaskell, in her Life of Charlotte Brontë, was mistaken
in describing Rev. Patrick Brontë as having "regular Greek
features." His features were strongly "Celtic," as a
"photograph in my possession" shows.

3   STUART, J. A. ERSKINE. The Brontë Country: Its Topography,
Antiquities, and History. London: Longmans, Green & Co.,
pp. 85-90 and numerous incidental references to The Life
of Charlotte Brontë.
Gaskell's biography of Charlotte gives a "most un-
pleasant impression of" the town of Cowan Bridge, but "it
is, in reality, a comfortable hamlet of whitewashed cot-
tages, situated among lovely pastures, and overshadowed by
splendidly foliaged trees.... It is an infinitely more
cheerful place than lonely, heathery Haworth...."

1889 A   BOOKS - NONE

1889 B   SHORTER WRITINGS

1   CINQBARS [pseud.]. "Gaskell: Gascoign," N & Q, 7th ser. VIII
(28 December), 509-10.

"A relative of" Gaskell's told me that "the name is...
a corruption of Gascoign. The Milnes-Gaskells of Wenlock
Abbey and Wakefield spelled" their name Gaskell as "far
back as 1600." [See 1890.B1.]

2 HOWITT, MARY. Mary Howitt. An Autobiography. Edited by
Margaret Howitt. London: Wm. Isbister. II: 28, 59, 65,
66, 115, 116.
    My husband urged Gaskell "to use her pen for the public
benefit," and so she wrote Mary Barton, "the first volume
of which was sent in MS. to my husband, stating this to be
the result of his advice. We were both delighted with it,
and a few months later" Gaskell "came up to London, and
to our house, with the work completed." A rich silk manufacturer, who "is a fat, jolly Conservative," "thinks 'Mary
Barton' a dangerous, bad book."

1890 A BOOKS - NONE

1890 B SHORTER WRITINGS

1 BARDSLEY, C. W. "Gaskell: Gascoigne [reply to 7th ser. VIII,
509]," N & Q, 7th ser. IX (8 February), 115.
    "There is no connection between" Gaskell and Gascoigne.
The Gaskells are named after some Yorkshire place, "probably" near Sedburgh, for "the North English" gill means
"narrow ravine." There were Gasegills, Gaysegills, and
Gasegyls in 1379 in Yorkshire. In Furness and other parts
of Lancashire the name changed to Gaitskell. [See
1889.B1.]

2 BRIDELL-FOX, E. F. "Memories. Elizabeth C. Gaskell," Girl's
Own Paper (London), XI (19 July), 660.
    The "second" time I met Gaskell, I was reading Mary
Barton when she came in with a "bright face," "radiant
smile, and clear blue eyes," so I had to put down the
novel "at its most thrilling point" "to make the author
welcome." At a party lionizing her, Gaskell came away from
the others and instead talked to me and another young girl,
as "the hostess...in vain brought up one great notability
after another to be introduced to the now famous authoress."

*3 CAINE, HALL. In Celebrities of the Century: Being a Dic-
tionary of Men and Women of the Nineteenth Century. Edited
by L. C. Sanders. New and rev. ed. London: Cassell.
S.v. "Gaskell, Elizabeth Cleghorn."

1890

(CAINE, HALL)
[Source: Clark S. Northup. "Bibliography," in Eliza-beth Gaskell. By Gerald DeWitt Sanders. New Haven: Yale University Press, for Cornell University. London: Humphrey Milford, Oxford University Press, 1929. See 1929.B6.]

4   GORDAN, ALEXANDER. In The Dictionary of National Biography. S.v. "Gaskell, William."
    The Rev. Gaskell married Elizabeth Cleghorn Stevenson in 1832. In 1854 his Two Lectures on the Lancashire Dia-lect were "appended to" the fifth edition of Mrs. Gaskell's Mary Barton.

5   PICKFORD, JOHN. "Gaskell: Gascoign [reply to 7th ser. VIII, 509; IX, 115]," N & Q, 7th ser. IX (8 March), 193.
    In Aberford, Yorkshire, Gascoign is pronounced Gaskin, and "Gaskell is sometimes changed" to Gaitskill. [See 1889.B1, 1890.B1, 1890.B6.]

6   RATCLIFFE. THOMAS. "Gaskell: Gascoign [reply to 7th ser. VIII, 509; IX, 115]," N & Q, 7th ser. IX (8 March), 193.
    "... The Common pronunciation of Gascoign is Gaskell or Gaskill," though present Gaskells and Gascoigns are unre-lated. [See 1889.B1, 1890.B1, 1890.B5.]

7   STOWE, HARRIET BEECHER. Life of Harriet Beecher Stowe. Com-piled from Her Letters and Journals. Edited by Charles Edward Stowe. Boston and New York: Houghton Mifflin & Co., p. 312. [Mrs. Stowe's letter about Gaskell is re-printed in Harriet Beecher Stowe. Life and Letters of Harriet Beecher Stowe. Edited by Annie Fields. Boston and New York: Houghton, Mifflin & Co., Riverside Press, Cambridge, 1897, p. 235.]
    [Letter of Mrs. Stowe to her daughters, June 1857:] At Manchester I "found the Rev. Mr. Gaskell waiting to welcome me in the station." Mrs. Gaskell "seems lovely at home, where besides being a writer she proves herself to be a first-class housekeeper, and performs all the duties of a minister's wife."

8   WARD, SIR ADOLPHUS WILLIAM. In The Dictionary of National Biography. S.v. "Gaskell, Elizabeth Cleghorn."
    Mary Barton "made" Gaskell "famous," but The Moorland Cottage showed her "first traces" of "delicate" "humour." Ruth is a better book than Mary Barton and may have in-fluenced Hard Times. The humorous Cranford gave Gaskell "literary immortality," yet North and South is "still more

important" and shows an "advance" in construction, except
for flaws caused by serialization. The controversial Life
of Charlotte Brontë is a skillful and powerful biography.
Sylvia's Lovers is a "vivid" and "pathetic" story based on
historical research, though the concluding section is marred
by "coincidences." The idyllic little Cousin Phillis is
Gaskell's "most perfect" book. Wives and Daughters "is a
masterpiece" of playfulness, "pathos," and truthful "characterization," though with some flaws of "construction."

1891 A   BOOKS - NONE

1891 B   SHORTER WRITINGS

1   ANON. [Editorial] Manchester Guardian (29 September), p. 5.
    Mary Barton, still Gaskell's most popular book, identi-
    fies her with Manchester. Although we are sad that the
    Greenheys Fields, described at the novel's opening, have
    disappeared, we are glad for the improvement of the de-
    plorable conditions of the workers, which Gaskell described
    truthfully. Although her "later writings" gained in
    maturity and "depth," Mary Barton was her social message
    to her readers.

2   BETTANY, G. T. "Biographical Introduction," in Mary Barton.
    The Minerva Library of Famous Books. London: Ward, Lock,
    Bowden, & Co., pp. v-xxiii.
    Although Gaskell was below "the intellectual level" of
    Goethe, Manzoni, Hugo, Scott, and Dickens, she, like them,
    left, in Mary Barton, a book that records in a memorable
    way a time of "upheaval." "... Like most works of genius,"
    Mary Barton "had to go through the usual mortifying rebuffs
    from publishers...." Many consider Wives and Daughters
    Gaskell's finest work. Her life "could scarcely be ex-
    celled" "for purity and benevolence."

3   E. V. T. "Mrs. Gaskell's Father," Athenaeum (London), No.
    3333 (12 September), 352.
    Bettany's introduction to the Minerva Library edition of
    Mary Barton creates the false impression that Gaskell's
    father was "a 'rolling-stone' kind of person." Actually,
    he achieved high distinction as a magazine writer, editor,
    and "historical" researcher. Finally, he served as Keeper
    of the Records of the Treasury.

4   GRISWOLD, W.[ILLIAM] M.[cCRILLIS]. A Descriptive List of
    British Novels. Cambridge, Massachusetts: W. M. Griswold,

1891

(GRISWOLD, W.[ILLIAM] M.[cCRILLIS])
pp. 363-64, 476, 488, 498, 502, 552f., 610.
[Quotes selected reviews of Gaskell's novels.]

5 HELD, ADOLF. Zwei Buecher sozialen Geschichte Englands.
From the literary remains of A. H. hrsg. von G. F. Knapp.
Leipzig: Duncker & Humbolt.
[Although this work is cited by Northup (1929.B6), the
only Gaskell references are to Peter Gaskell, author of
The Manufacturing Population of England.]

6 REID, T.[HOMAS] WEMYSS. The Life, Letters and Friendships of
Richard Monckton-Milnes, First Lord Houghton. New York:
Cassell Publishing Co. I: 476, 481.
Milnes had suggested that he might obtain a pension for
Charlotte Brontë, "but" Gaskell's "womanly intuition sug-
gested another mode of giving the desired aid"--a pension
for Charlotte's husband based on his work as a clergyman.
Gaskell was pleased that Milnes liked her controversial
Ruth.

7 RITCHIE, [MRS.] ANNE THACKERAY [later Lady Ritchie].
"Preface," in Cranford. London and New York: Macmillan &
Co., pp. v-xxiv.
I remember reading the story of Captain Brown in Household Words and showing it to my father, who "told me the
writer's name." Gaskell's comedy has been justly compared
to Lamb's, but only Jane Austen's "very sweetest heroines"
"are worthy" of Cranford. Gaskell was a born storyteller,
for I can remember, as a child, hearing her tell wonderful
ghost stories. Mary Barton, though about social problems,
is alive and not abstract. Even her light work in Cranford
has "deeper echoes" than Jane Austen because of Gaskell's
nineteenth-century capacity for "sentiment."

1892 A   BOOKS - NONE

1892 B   SHORTER WRITINGS

1 ANON. "A New Edition of Cranford," Critic (New York), n.s.
XVII (6 February), 83.
In this, "one of the happiest of...resurrections of
half-forgotten books,...the peculiarities of the better
half of humanity" are "touched upon with a" rare knowledge
and deftness. The work is not "vulgarly realistic" but
rather "delightfully unreal," though there are touches of
"verisimilitude" that give Gaskell's "dolls" a "strange
hold on our affections."

2   ANON. "Tales of Three Villages [includes a review of new
       edition of Cranford]," Atlantic Monthly (Boston), LXX
       (July), 130-33.
         Gaskell "never reached Miss Mitford's craft in mere
       writing, and almost all" of Gaskell's "books have" some
       "clumsiness of form,...but her talent is so much richer,
       deeper, more comprehensive, that a really kind heart is
       ready to grant Miss Mitford" her technical "superiority."
       Because of Gaskell's extraordinary range, great disagree-
       ment exists as to which are her finest works. We have "a
       particular affection for My Lady Ludlow," for, though the
       work is marred by clumsy organization, Gaskell's portrait
       of "an exquisite old" aristocratic woman is as good as any-
       thing else she ever did. Cousin Phillis is "charming" but
       "grows dim...beside the blended humor and pathos and sweet
       reasonableness of Cranford."

3   BOASE, FREDERIC. Modern English Biography. Truro: Nether-
       ton & Worth. S.v. "Gaskell, Elizabeth Cleghorn."
         Gaskell wrote Mary Barton, which has been "translated
       into many languages"; Ruth; North and South; The Life of
       Charlotte Brontë; Sylvia's Lovers; "and 14 other books."

4   DICKENS, CHARLES. Letters of Charles Dickens to Wilkie
       Collins. Edited by Laurence Hutton. New York: Harper &
       Brothers, pp. 28-29.
         [Letter dated 4 April 1855:] Gaskell has been insisting
       that "her proofs" not be edited, not "'even by Mr.
       Dickens.' That immortal creature had gone over" North and
       South "with great pains--had of course taken out the
       stiflings--hard-plungings, lungeings [sic], and other con-
       vulsions--and had also taken out her weakenings and
       damagings of her own effects." Later she will see that
       I was right.

5   JEWSBURY, GERALDINE ENSOR. Selections from the Letters of
       Geraldine Ensor Jewsbury to Jane Welsh Carlyle. Edited by
       Mrs. [Alexander] Ireland. London and New York: Longman,
       Green, & Co., pp. 383-84.
         [Letter dated Sunday, December 1850:] "The people here
       are beginning mildly to be pained for Mr. 'Mary Barton'
       [Gaskell's husband]. And one lady said to me the other
       day, 'I don't think authoresses ought ever to marry', and
       then proceeded to eulogise Mr. Gaskell." Yet "I have a
       notion that if one could get at the 'Mary Barton' that is
       the kernel of Mrs. Gaskell, one would like her, but I never
       have done so yet. Have you?"

1892

6   KIRK, JOHN FOSTER. A Supplement to Allibone's Critical Dic-
     tionary of English Literature and British and American
     Authors. Philadelphia: J. B. Lippincott. S.v. "Gaskell,
     Mrs. Elizabeth Cleghorn."
          Gaskell's name, incorrectly given in volume I, was not
     Stromkin but Stevenson.

7   KIRKLAND, E.[LIZABETH] S.[TANSBURY]. A Short History of
     English Literature for Young People. Chicago: A. C.
     McClurg & Co., pp. 314-15.
          Gaskell "was one of the most distinguished of England's
     women novelists." Her Mary Barton "has always held its
     place as a standard work of fiction," though Cranford,
     North and South, and Wives and Daughters "are generally
     considered" her "best...novels," and her Life of Charlotte
     Brontë "is as interesting as a novel...."

8   OLIPHANT, MRS. [MARGARET] and F.[RANCIS] R.[OMANO]. The
     Victorian Age of English Literature. London: Percival &
     Co. I, 325-29. [Published in the United States as Mrs.
     [Margaret] Oliphant. The Victorian Age of English Litera-
     ture. New York: Dodd, Mead & Co., 1892.]
          Though Gaskell showed compassion for the poor--if not
     the rich--in Mary Barton, she betrayed her own class by
     her ruthless exposure of the private secrets of the Brontë
     family in her Life of Charlotte Brontë. Yet Gaskell's
     Wives and Daughters "was in many respects an almost perfect
     example of the" finest in English fiction during the
     period.

9   STEPHEN, [SIR] LESLIE. "Charlotte Brontë," in Hours in a
     Library. Rev. ed. London: Smith, Elder & Co. III:
     7-8, 9-13.
          Gaskell's "touching biography" is, "with certain minor
     faults,...still one of the most pathetic records of a
     melancholy life in our literature." Yet Mr. Wemyss Reid
     "virtually accuses" Gaskell "of unintentionally substi-
     tuting a fiction for a biography." Probably she "did in
     fact err by carrying into the earlier period the gloom of
     later years," but surely she and not Wemyss Reid is cor-
     rect in portraying Charlotte as an exceptionally gloomy
     woman. Wemyss Reid's few examples of Charlotte's humor
     hardly show Gaskell to be wrong, for if "Charlotte had al-
     ways been at her worst, she would have been mad.... The
     doctrine that the people of Haworth were really commonplace
     mortals may be accepted with a similar reserve."

10   STUART, J. A. ERSKINE. <u>The Literary Shrines of Yorkshire:</u>
      <u>the Literary Pilgrim in the Dales</u>. London: Longmans,
      Green & Co., pp. 107-10.
          <u>Sylvia's Lovers</u> "gives a vivid picture of Old Whitby,"
      and Gaskell is "at her best" in her description of "the
      return of a Greenland whaler to Whitby."

11   WALFORD, MRS. L.[UCY] B.[ETHIA] [née COLQUHOUN]. "Elizabeth
      Gaskell," in <u>Twelve English Authoresses</u>. London and
      New York: Longmans, Green, & Co., pp. 155-65.
          Gaskell's first novel, <u>Mary Barton</u>, is "the outcome of
      a mature mind, albeit of a young author." <u>Cranford</u> is
      Gaskell's "masterpiece of...still life." <u>Wives and</u>
      <u>Daughters</u> is inferior to her other works, for here she
      departs from her true specialty, "humble life." Her <u>Life</u>
      <u>of Charlotte Brontë</u> is "brilliant" as an "artistic composi-
      tion" but unreliable as biography. Gaskell "died in 1857
      [<u>sic</u>]...."

1893 A BOOKS - NONE

1893 B SHORTER WRITINGS

1   ANON. In <u>La Grande encyclopédie: inventaire raisonné des</u>
      <u>sciences, des lettres et des arts, par une société de</u>
      <u>savants et de gens de lettres</u>. S.v. "Gaskell, Elizabeth
      Cleghorn."
          <u>Mary Barton</u> is a touching history of the miserable lives
      of workers in the cotton factories. In addition to her
      many novels and her <u>Life of Charlotte Brontë</u>, Gaskell
      engaged in extensive charitable work.

2   COLERIDGE, CHRISTABEL. "Molly Gibson," in <u>Great Characters</u>
      <u>of Fiction</u>. Edited by M. E. Townsend. London: Wells,
      Gardner, Darton, & Co., pp. 211-18.
          In her portrayal of Molly Gibson, Gaskell shows "a
      finer perception and deeper insight" than Jane Austen,
      "and the atmosphere is no longer that of genteel comedy."
      In Jane Austen "the memory of Clare's early struggles
      would have been deprived of the tragical touch which makes
      us tolerate her after all." And Jane Austen would not
      "have recognised that Cynthia could be at once honest and
      untruthful," "shallow" and yet loving toward Molly.

3   HAMILTON, CATHERINE J.[ANE]. "Mrs. Gaskell," in <u>Women</u>
      <u>Writers: Their Works and Ways</u>. London: Ward, Lock, &
      Bowden. II: 166-89.

1893

    (HAMILTON, CATHERINE J.[ANE])
       Gaskell, as a writer, has "very little in common" with
    Charlotte Brontë, "except sincerity and earnestness."
    She was less "passionate," less self-centered, more "ob-
    jective," with "wider and broader" "sympathies." Cranford
    is a comic classic. Gaskell's male characters, as in North
    and South, are well depicted. "In Wives and Daughters she
    accomplished the...difficult task of making" an "every-day
    story...as interesting as a romance.... For purity of
    tone, earnestness of spirit, depth of pathos, and lightness
    of touch," Gaskell is unsurpassed "in fiction."

4   MONKHOUSE, [WILLIAM] COSMO. Life of Leigh Hunt. London:
    Walter Scott, pp. 207, 208, 228.
       Hunt "made many new acquaintances among the younger
    generation of literary men and women, the most distinguished
    of whom were Dickens, Thackeray," Gaskell, "and the Brown-
    ings." In his "The Religion of the Heart," Hunt wrote that
    he never missed any works of Gaskell, "whose 'Mary Barton'
    gave me emotions that required more and more the considera-
    tion of the good which it must do."

5   NIGHTINGALE, REV. B. Lancashire Nonconformity: or, Sketches,
    Historical and Descriptive of the Congregational and Old
    Presbyterian Churches in the Country, V: The Churches of
    Manchester. Manchester: Oldham, Ashton, & Co. London and
    Bristol: John Heywood, pp. 47, 106.
       Gaskell's father was both tutor in the classics at the
    Manchester Academy and minister of the Dob Lane Chapel,
    Falsworth. There are plaques to both Gaskell and her
    husband in the Cross Street Chapel.

6   WRIGHT, DR. WILLIAM. The Brontës in Ireland, or Facts
    Stranger than Fiction. London: Hodder & Stoughton,
    pp. vii, 2-3, 204.
       Gaskell's Life of Charlotte Brontë "is an exquisite
    tribute from a gifted hand laid on a sister's grave, but"
    Gaskell's "dreary moorlands and dismal surroundings are as
    inadequate to account for the Brontë genius as the general
    picture of suppressed sadness is unwarranted...."

1894 A BOOKS - NONE

1894 B SHORTER WRITINGS

1   ANON. "Books. Mrs. Gaskell's Collected Works," Spectator
    (London), LXXIII (17 November), 698-700.

This eight-volume "pocket edition" is "too large" for a "pocket" and "too small" for "a library." Gaskell was "a good novelist, though not one of the greatest," and her books tend to be too drawn out. Her treatment of comedy and tragedy is closest to that of George Eliot, and even though Gaskell has less intensity, she has her own individual "picturesqueness" and "force." Cranford will be "her chief title to enduring fame." Though the editor of Cornhill praised her later works over her earlier ones, there is much to be said for her "northern stories," with "their grasp of human passion" and "local" color. Gaskell belongs "in the front" of "second"-rank "favorites," such as Charlotte Brontë and Charles Reade.

2   GRAY, MAXWELL [pseud.]. "The Human Novel as Exemplified by Mrs. Gaskell," Atalanta (London), VII (June), 606-9.
    Gaskell "truly and skilfully depicts humanity." After the greatest of English novelists, Thackeray, comes Gaskell, in the same rank as George Eliot, Jane Austen, and Charlotte Brontë. In Cranford, Gaskell makes the dull reality of the town sparkle by her "minute" "perception," "delicacy, and subtlety of...humour." Perhaps the "gloom" of much of her fiction accounts "for the slight estimation in comparison with her merits in which" this writer "is held." Wives and Daughters is her "most popular work," but Mary Barton and Ruth are both excessively "depressing." Yet Gaskell is able to be much more sympathetic about her characters' weaknesses than is the stern George Eliot. Gaskell's "genius was slow to develop," and Dickens was a bad influence on her early work. Perhaps the explanation of why "so much" of her "work" fell "beneath what it ought to have been" is that her household duties as a woman "prevented" her from fully "developing her mental and artistic power."

3   HAMILTON, CATHERINE JANE. "Letters to the Editor. Mrs. Gaskell's Collected Works," Spectator (London), LXXIII (1 December), 778.
    Your reviewer was wrong in thinking that Gaskell was influenced by George Eliot. It was "the other way" around, as George Eliot herself acknowledged.

4   KING, BOLTON. [Introductory note to] Joseph Mazzini. "The Question of the Exiles," in Essays by Joseph Mazzini. Translated by Thomas Okey. London: J. M. Dent & Co., p. 228.
    Agostini Ruffini "is said to be 'Sperano' in" Gaskell's Round the Sofa.

1894

5   RUSSELL, PERCY. A Guide to British and American Novels.
    London: Digby, Long & Co., pp. 9, 13, 159-60.
        Mary Barton and Ruth are notable as "realistic" por-
    trayals "of the working poor." Wives and Daughters is "a
    great novel" because it builds up "entrancing interest"
    out of "ordinary" "English life."

1895 A   BOOKS - NONE

1895 B   SHORTER WRITINGS

1   ANON. "Account of the Opening of the Brontë Museum at
    Haworth, May 18th, 1895 [Report of the remarks of the Rev.
    J. T. Slugg]," Brontë Society Transactions (Bradford), I,
    part III (December), 30.
        Because the Haworth "residents" "were civilised," they
    would not attack the museum with stones, but they lacked
    enthusiasm for it, partly because of Gaskell's Life of
    Charlotte Brontë, which Haworth people said was "crammed
    full of mistatements."

2   ANON. "Books and Bookmen," Manchester Guardian (17 August),
    p. 9.
        Axon's bibliography of Gaskell's writings, privately
    printed from the papers of the Manchester Literary Club,
    proves "the lasting popularity of our great Manchester
    novelist." Mary Barton has the most new editions, followed
    by Cranford and The Life of Charlotte Brontë. Wives and
    Daughters and Ruth are tied for next place, and after them
    and also tied are Sylvia's Lovers and North and South.

3   BIERBAUM, FRIEDRICH JULIUS. History of the English Language
    and Literature. 3rd ed., rev. New York: B. Westermann
    & Co. Heidelberg: George Weiss, p. 220.
        "Uniting fine imagination and deep feeling with a
    delicate and playful humour," Gaskell "depicts the life of
    happy, modest society and the sufferings of the working
    classes."

4   HOMPES, [MISS] MAT. "Mrs. Gaskell," Gentleman's Magazine
    (London), CCLXXIX (August), 124-38. [Reprinted in Living
    Age (Boston), CVI (7 September 1895), 623-33.]
        Almost nothing has been revealed of Gaskell's life,
    though "she was a noble woman" as well as "a great novel-
    ist." Mary Barton shows that she knew the details of the
    lives of the Manchester poor. Ruth, though inferior in
    "style and power" to all her other major works, gains

importance from its "courage" in dealing with the theme of
a fallen woman. The delightful Cranford portrays "Knutsford as" Gaskell "knew it some seventy years ago." North
and South, unlike Mary Barton, takes the "side" of the
masters rather than the men but is chiefly interesting for
the story of Mr. Hale's resignation from the ministry for
conscience's sake. The controversial Life of Charlotte
Brontë, Sylvia's Lovers, and Cousin Phillis are all fine,
but Wives and Daughters "is almost perfect" in "its ease
and grace."

5 HOWITT, MARGARET. "Stray Notes from Mrs. Gaskell," Good Words
   (London), XXXVI (September), 604-13.
        Gaskell's letters, from which we give a few extracts un-
   published till now, bring us "face to face with" her "and
   into the very centre of Knutsford." She was a "gifted and
   diffident woman." Her novels and private activities contributed "to the vast mental and moral improvement which
   has been wrought in Manchester during the last forty
   years."

6 [MACLOED, DONALD], ed. "Stray Notes about Mrs. Gaskell,"
   Good Words (London), XXXVI (October), slip bound in before
   p. 649.
        We apologize for publishing "extracts" of Gaskell's
   letters without the permission of her daughters, for they,
   at their mother's request, "have consistently" refused
   such permission to all.

7 PAYNE, [REV.] GEORGE A. "Knutsford in Fiction," Gentleman's
   Magazine (London), CCLXXIX (November), 507-14.
        Knutsford is the model for "Cranford," "Duncombe" in
   "Mr. Harrison's Confessions," "Holingford" in Wives and
   Daughters, "Eltham" in Cousin Phillis, "Hamely" in A Dark
   Night's Work, and "Banford" in "The Squire's Story."
   Though Gaskell did not "consciously" copy Knutsford in her
   fiction, the town worked its way into her imagination.

8 _____. "Mrs. Gaskell's Short Stories," Light on the Way
   (Manchester), III (October), 214-16.
        Gaskell wrote "a large number of short stories, many...
   well worth reading."

9 REID, SIR [THOMAS] WEMYSS. "Address [read by Mr. W. S.
   Cameron] at the Opening of the Brontë Museum at Haworth,
   May 18th, 1895," Brontë Society Transactions (Bradford), I,
   part III (December), 22-25.

1895

    (REID, SIR [THOMAS] WEMYSS)
       "Thanks to the heart and the brain of another great
woman," Gaskell, "we have been enabled to see" Charlotte's
"life as it really was." That sad yet glowing life, as
told by Gaskell, "has made the name of Charlotte Brontë a
cherished one in thousands of households."

10   TOLLEMACHE, [HON.] BEATRIX L. "Cranford Souvenirs," Temple
Bar (London), CV (August), pp. 536-39. [Reprinted in
Living Age (Boston), CVI (31 August 1895), 575-76, and in
(Hon.) Beatrix L. Tollemache. Cranford Souvenirs and Other
Sketches. London: Rivingtons, 1900, pp. 1-7.]
       Although "I never met" Gaskell, I knew the model for
her Captain Brown in Cranford--Captain Hill of the Cheshire
Yeomanry. According to Knutsford people, Peter Leigh was
"the original of Miss Matty's lover." According to my
mother, "the garden party" at the beginning of Wives and
Daughters was just like my grandmother's "parties at
Tatton."

1896 A BOOKS - NONE

1896 B SHORTER WRITINGS

1   BROWN, ALICE. "Latter-Day Cranford," Atlantic Monthly
(Boston), LXXVII (April), 526-34.
       "The present Knutsford" is not identical to Gaskell's
Cranford, yet there are "links of similitude." Although
her working-class fiction performed an admirable service,
Cranford will "be loved so long as there smiles and tears
in this April world."

2   BUTLER, SAMUEL, ed. Life and Letters of Dr. Samuel Butler,
Headmaster of Shrewsbury School...and Afterwards Bishop of
Lichfield. London: John Murray. I, 90-99.
       The Rev. W. Maskell traces Gaskell's account of a dis-
appearance, in Household Words, to an anecdote originally
told by Dr. Butler many years before.

3   COLTON, ARTHUR W. "Charlotte Brontë," Citizen (Philadelphia),
I (January), 253-56.
       "No part of" Gaskell's Life of Charlotte Brontë "is more
curiously interesting than the picture of these children
who talked politics in pinafores, with Tory principles,
and wrote tales for private entertainment." It seems evi-
dent that Gaskell "had unconsciously too much of a weather
eye on Jane Eyre and Lucy Snowe and the public expectation

to be thoroughly trusted" in her gloomy portrayal of the Brontës, but "we will agree to forgive her...."

4   COWDEN-CLARKE, [MRS.] MARY. My Long Life. An Autobiographic Sketch. 2nd ed. London: T. Fisher Unwin, pp. 123-24.
    [The gist of the passage is the same as in 1878.B5, although there are extensive verbal changes.]

5   G.[ILDER], J.[EANNETTE] L. "A Book and Its Story. Mrs. Gaskell and Her Life of Charlotte Brontë," Critic (New York), n.s. XVIII (16 May), 353-55.
    Clement K. Shorter, in The Woman at Home, "whets the public's interest in his forthcoming...'Charlotte Brontë and Her Circle' by" describing how Gaskell wrote her great life of Charlotte, which "gave" to "the woman, not the author," the public esteem that she "has held for nearly forty years."

6   HARE, AUGUSTUS J. C. The Story of My Life. London: George Allen. II: 224-27; III: 117-23.
    It was "a great pleasure" to be a friend of Gaskell, whom "everybody liked." I was "struck" by "her kindness, but" also by "her extreme courtesy and deference to her own daughters." Gaskell was deeply convinced of the reality of ghosts.

7   KEYWORTH, REV. THOMAS. "Morton Village in Jane Eyre," Brontë Society Transactions (Bradford), I, part IV (December), 7-19, plus "a note" on 18-20.
    We would be helped in solving problems of fact about Charlotte Brontë "if names could be put in the place of initials throughout" Gaskell's Life and if the recipients of the letters were identified. [Note:] "Shorter's great book" does just as I suggested with initials and recipients of letters.

8   SAINTSBURY, GEORGE. A History of Nineteenth Century Literature (1780-1895). London and New York: Macmillan & Co., p. 335.
    Mary Barton, for "its vivid picture of Manchester life," is "nearly" Gaskell's "best book." Though she "never wrote anything bad,...it may be doubted whether anything but Cranford will retain permanent rank."

9   SHORTER, CLEMENT K. Charlotte Brontë and Her Circle. New York: Dodd, Mead & Co., pp. 1-26, and see the index for further references.
    Gaskell's Life of Charlotte Brontë is the most widely read of all biographies. Her novelistic "gifts were

1896

(SHORTER, CLEMENT K.)
employed upon a romance of real life," yet she was remarkably "conscientious" as a biographer. For all the controversy over the Cowan Bridge School passages, her
"description was substantially correct," but, on the Mrs.
Robinson matter, Gaskell was singularly reckless in accepting Branwell's account. [Most reviewers agreed that
Shorter's work supplemented but did not replace Gaskell's
classic Life of Charlotte Brontë. See, for example, Anon.
"The Brontë Circle," Nation (New York), LXIII (24 December
1896), 478-79; Anon. "The Brontës. Some Further Account of
Mr. Shorter's Book," New York Times Saturday Review of Books
and Art (21 November 1896), p. 7; Anon. "Charlotte Brontë
and Her Circle,..." Athenaeum (London), no. 3602 (7 November 1896), 634-35; Anon. "Charlotte Brontë: New Light on
the Woman and the Genius," New York Daily Tribune (18 October 1896), section 3, part 2; Anon. "Charlotte Brontë,"
Spectator (London), LXXVII (7 November 1896), 644-45;
Alice Meynell, "Charlotte Brontë and Her Circle," Bookman
(London), XI (November 1896), 34-37; Sir T.(homas) Wemyss
Reid. "Charlotte Brontë and Her Circle," Nineteenth Century (London), XL (November 1896), 772-76; (Butler Wood).
"Charlotte Brontë and Her Circle,..." Brontë Society Trans-
actions (Bradford), I, part IV (December 1896), 28-33.]

10   . "Mrs. Gaskell and Charlotte Brontë," Bookman
(New York), III (June), 313-24. [Reprinted in The Woman
at Home (London), IV (May 1896), 681-91.]
    Gaskell's Life of Charlotte Brontë is the most widely
read English biography, ranking with Boswell's Johnson and
Lockhart's Scott. The letters that I possess to Charlotte's friends from Gaskell reveal her as even more charming and humane than in her fiction. She obtained letters
of Charlotte's from George Smith and his editors at Smith &
Elder, and, most importantly, from Ellen Nussey. I have
been preparing a new collection of Charlotte's letters and
papers.

11   WARD, [SIR] A.[DOLPHUS] W.[ILLIAM]. "Mrs. Gaskell," in
English Prose. Edited by [Sir] Henry Craik. New York:
Macmillan Co. London: Macmillan & Co. V: Nineteenth
Century, 523-24.
    Gaskell was "a classic author of English prose" but
lived "in a period of transition." In Mary Barton, she
"asserted the right of treating serious social problems
sentimentally--a woman's right if ever there was one...."
Her so-called "late manner" appears as early as Cranford,
which "will always be treasured" as a miniature of the

early 1800s. After her "masterpiece," The Life of Charlotte Brontë, Gaskell developed a fictional "style...un-
alienably her own," and among her later works Sylvia's
Lovers is the most intense, Wives and Daughters the most
tranquilly humorous, and Cousin Phillis the most perfect.

12   WARNER, CHARLES DUDLEY, ET AL., eds. [Biographical and
     critical note preceding extracts from Cranford in] Library
     of the World's Best Literature. New York: International
     Society. XV, 6205-6. [Revised by John W. Cunliffe and
     Ashley H. Thorndike. New York: Columbia University Press,
     1917.]
          Critics find Gaskell's fiction equal to that of Jane
     Austen and Charlotte Brontë. Gaskell's chief merit is as
     a faithful recorder of her "native" region at a particular
     time in the past.

13   WOODPARK, ARTHUR, and ISABELLA BANKS. "[no. 7,701] Portrait
     of Mrs. Gaskell [replies to no. 7,695]," Manchester City
     News [Notes and Queries] (26 December), p. 2.
          [Two separate replies telling where published descrip-
     tions and portraits of Gaskell can be found.]

1897 A   BOOKS - NONE

1897 B   SHORTER WRITINGS

1   ANON. "An Appreciation of Mrs. Gaskell," New Saturday
     (London), II (16 January), 74-75.
          Though Gaskell lacked Charlotte Brontë's "fire,"
     Gaskell had her own equally fine qualities: a wider range
     than Charlotte, more human sympathy, and a "profounder"
     and "more balanced" philosophy. Wives and Daughters con-
     tains Gaskell's subtlest characterizations. Sylvia's
     Lovers has the inexorability of a tragedy of Aeschylus.
     The dark and relentless "Crooked Branch" "is, in our
     opinion, the most powerful and poignant" of Gaskell's
     writings.

2   ANON. "Books and Bookman," Manchester Guardian (20 November),
     p. 5.
          "A correspondent writes" about little-known verses by
     Gaskell first published in Blackwoods in January of 1837.

3   ANON. In Chambers's Encyclopaedia. S.v. "Gaskell, Mrs."
     [Cf. Edith Clara Batho. In Chambers's Encyclopaedia. 1950
     ed. S.v. "Gaskell, Elizabeth Cleghorn," which is largely
     the same article as in 1897.]

1897

(ANON.)
Gaskell's novels "have permanently enriched English literature and almost lifted the authoress into a rank represented alone by Jane Austen, Charlotte Brontë, and George Eliot."

4   ANON. "Preface," in Mary Barton: a Tale of Manchester Factory Life Fifty Years Ago [abridged] Penny Popular Novels, the Masterpiece Library, edited by W. T. Stead, IX. London: Review of Reviews Office, opposite p. 2.
Gaskell's "wide and deep" masterpiece has...long been established as a general favorite, especially among the great masses of the toiling population with whose life it specially deals...."

*5   AXON, W.[ILLIAM] E. A. "Mrs. Gaskell's First Appearance in Print," Temperance Star (Manchester) (December), pp. 136-38.
[Source: John Albert Green. A Bibliographic Guide to the Gaskell Collection in the Moss Side Library. Manchester: Reference Library, King St.; Moss Side Library, Bradshaw St., 1911. See 1911.A2.]

6   BAYLEY, ADA ELLEN [EDNA LYALL]. "Mrs. Gaskell," in Women Novelists of Queen Victoria's Reign. A Book of Appreciations. By Mrs. [Margaret] Oliphant [neé Wilson] et al. London: Hurst & Blackett, pp. 119-45.
We feel "more love and gratitude" toward Gaskell than toward any other Victorian novelist because of her "broad human" "sympathy" and "a mind as delicately pure as a child's," yet "free from...prudery." Her greatest work is Cranford, unsurpassed in "Victorian literature" "for humour," "pathos," and characterization. Though many admire Sylvia's Lovers, "we infinitely prefer" Wives and Daughters. Gaskell was a woman first and a writer second, and she never neglected her domestic duties.

7   BIRCHENOUGH, ALBERT A. "Knutsford in the Thirties," Cheshire Notes and Queries [reprinted from Stockport Advertiser] (Stockport), II, 121-22.
[Although cited by Northup (1929.B6), this article on Gaskell's town does not mention Gaskell.]

8   CORY, WILLIAM. Extracts from the Letters and Journals of William Cory, Author of "Ionica." Edited by Francis Warre Cornish. Oxford: printed for the subscribers by Horace Hart, p. 560.
[Letter to Miss Jane Bartrum, 20 October 1891:] Charlotte Brontë "was not nearly so good or wise as" Gaskell

"or Juliana [Ewing] or perhaps Christina [Rossetti], but"
Charlotte "told us all about her eager passionate life."

9   C. S. C. "Editorial Note," in Mary Barton. Stead's Penny
    Library of Famous Books, no. 137. London: George Newnes,
    opposite p. 3.
        Gaskell's "sympathies" with the Manchester working class
    "provoked some little objections," yet she did not fall
    into the "error" of making all workingmen heroes and all
    employers villains, for she "saw with the eyes of an ex-
    ceedingly feminine heart...."

10 [DABBS, GEORGE]. "Alfred, Lord Tennyson--a Memoir. By His
    Son," Quarterly Review (London), CLXXXVI (October), 513-14.
        Gaskell, "who was struck by" Samuel Bamford's love of
    Tennyson's poetry, got Tennyson to send the humbly grateful
    Bamford an inscribed copy of Tennyson's poems.

*11 E. P. "Woman's Interests," Philadelphia Ledger (3 November),
    p. 11.
        [Describes Gaskell's house and recalls The Life of
    Charlotte Brontë.] [Source: Marjorie Taylor Davis. "An
    Annotated Bibliography of Criticism on Elizabeth Cleghorn
    Gaskell, 1848-1973." Ph.D. dissertation, University of
    Mississippi, 1974. See 1974.B6.]

12 GOSSE, EDMUND. A Short History of English Literature. Short
    Histories of the Literatures of the World, III. London:
    William Heinemann. Reprint. London: William Heinemann,
    1923, pp. 356-57. [The passage is repeated in Edmund Gosse.
    English Literature: an Illustrated Record. New York:
    Macmillan Co. London: Macmillan & Co., 1903-4. IV, 284-
    88.]
        Gaskell was much better than Charlotte Brontë at "the
    art of building a consistent plot." Gaskell wrote "one or
    two short books which are technically faultless, and might
    be taken as types of the novel form," yet "the recognition
    of her delicate and many-sided genius has never been quite
    universal.... Her work has not the personal interest of
    Thackeray's, nor the intense unity and compression of
    Charlotte Brontë's." Gaskell "suffers from having done
    well too many things."

*13 GRAHAM, RICHARD D. The Masters of Victorian Literature, 1837-
    1897, London: Thin, pp. 81-85, 232.
        [Source: Clark S. Northup. "A Bibliography," in
    Elizabeth Gaskell. By Gerald DeWitt Sanders. New Haven:
    Yale University Press, for Cornell University. London:

1897

(GRAHAM, RICHARD D.)
Humphrey Milford, Oxford University Press, 1929, pp. 165-267. See 1929.B6.]

14   LESLIE, MARION. "Mrs. Gaskell's House and Its Memories," The Woman at Home. Annie S. Swan's Magazine (London), V (June), 761-70.
Gaskell never had a study to write in and was often interrupted in composing by domestic problems, but sometimes she "rose early and wrote...before breakfast." Her daughters have maintained the Plymouth Grove house as it was, and it is filled with letters and mementos of Gaskell and her famous friends.

15   PAUL, HERBERT. "The Apotheosis of the Novel Under Queen Victoria," Nineteenth Century (London), XLI (May), 778-79. [Reprinted as Herbert Paul. "The Victorian Novel," in Men and Letters. London and New York: John Lane, the Bodley Head, 1901, pp. 134-36.]
Though she lacked the "power" and "range" of Dickens, Thackeray, George Eliot, or Charlotte Brontë, Gaskell was "one of the most charming" of all English novelists. She succeeded with two distinct subjects: social reform and "domestic" "life." In spite of the virtues of a number of her novels, most readers prefer Cranford's "still life," which is as perfect as Jane Austen's fiction in conveying the atmosphere of small-town life. Gaskell's "finest character" may be Mr. Gibson in Wives and Daughters.

16   SHORTER, CLEMENT [K.]. Victorian Literature. Sixty Years of Books and Bookmen. London: James Bowden, pp. 70-71.
"Next to Charlotte Brontë and George Eliot the most distinguished woman novelist of the era is" Gaskell. Her "two books...certain to secure immortality are 'Cranford'... and 'The Life of Charlotte Brontë'...."

17   TAYLOR, JOHN. "Charlotte Brontë. A Story of Sorrow, Heroism, and Victory," Methodist Monthly (London), n.s. VI (January), 2-8.
Before Charlotte Brontë, Haworth was best known as the home of William Grimshaw, whom Gaskell in her Life of Charlotte Brontë describes as whipping "loiterers" into church, though Gaskell adds that Grimshaw is still "held in reverence" in Haworth.

*18   TOOLEY, SARAH A. "Miss Gaskell and Miss Julia Gaskell," in "Ladies of Manchester," The Woman at Home. Annie S. Swan's Magazine (London), V (March), 488-89.

[Source: Marjorie Taylor Davis. "An Annotated Bibliography of Criticism on Elizabeth Cleghorn Gaskell, 1848-1973." Ph.D. dissertation, University of Mississippi, 1974. See 1974.B6.]

19 TRAIL, H. D. Social England: A Record of the Progress of the People. New York: G. P. Putnam's Sons. London: Cassell & Co. VI, 6, 281, 283.
Gaskell, along with Reade and Kingsley, ranks after Dickens, Thackeray, Charlotte Brontë, and George Eliot as one who, "without exactly attaining classic" status, comes very close to "greatness." Gaskell's Sylvia's Lovers, "finer than" the "more famous" Mary Barton, "is one of the most powerful and moving stories in...English fiction."

20 WALKER, HUGH. The Age of Tennyson. London: George Bell & Sons, pp. 106-8.
Gaskell's Life of Charlotte Brontë is almost one of "the best biographies in the language." Though Gaskell lacks the "genius" of George Sand and George Eliot and the "poetry" of Charlotte Brontë, Gaskell is "the most feminine" of important Victorian women novelists. "... She stands midway between Thackeray and Dickens, who are emphatically men of genius, and writers like Trollope who, with abundant talent and exhaustless industry, have no genius whatever."

1898 A BOOKS - NONE

1898 B SHORTER WRITINGS

1 AINSWORTH, M. "The Labour Movement in Fiction. Mary Barton, ..." National Home-Reading Union Magazine. The General Course (London), IX (7 April), 103-5.
Gaskell herself would have admitted that many employers were much friendlier toward their workers than were her Carsons. Also, employers were harder hit by the "depression" than Mary Barton shows. Yet Mary Barton is essentially "an appeal" for mutual "sympathy" between masters and men, and, in any case, North and South makes up for any onesideness in the earlier book.

2 ANON. "Memorial to Mrs. Gaskell at Knutsford," Manchester Guardian (26 February), p. 7.
The memorial contains a bas-relief of Gaskell by Cavaliere Achille D'Orsi, and "lovers of" her "writings owe a debt of gratitude to Mr. R. L. Watt for his timely gift of so fitting a memorial."

1898

3 COLLEY, T. "Gleanings and Jottings in Knutsford," Cheshire
Notes and Queries [reprinted from Stockport Advertiser]
(Stockport), III, 61-64.
Gaskell, who is buried outside Knutsford's Unitarian
Chapel under a "stonecross upon three steps," put numerous
references to the town in her fiction.

4 HERFORD, BROOKE, D.D. "Preface," in Cranford. London: Walter
Scott, pp. v-viii. [This appears to be the same as Herford's "Preface" in Cranford. Boston: J. Knight Co.,
1891, which I have not seen.]
Knutsford people of Gaskell's time were a little upset
at being personally depicted in her Cranford, but now they
are proud of her portrayal of their town.

5 HOLLAND, BERNARD, ed. Letters of Mary Sibylla Holland,
Selected and Edited by Her Son. 2nd ed. London: Edward
Arnold, p. 21.
"It was sometimes...alleged" that Mary and Lucy Holland,
my father's aunts, had "served as the models of Miss Matty
and her sister" in Gaskell's Cranford.

6 NICOLL, DR. W.[ILLIAM] ROBERTSON. "The Brontë Sisters. Notes
of an Address Delivered at Haworth,...April 10th, 1897,..."
Brontë Society Transactions (Bradford), I, part VIII
(March), 20-23.
It would have been more "consonant" with the "highest
feeling" if Gaskell had left secret the private lives of
the Brontës, yet I admire her Life of Charlotte Brontë so
much that I cannot wish it unwritten.

7 NICOLL, [DR. WILLIAM] ROBERTSON. "Introduction," in Cranford,
...with Which Is Included the Moorland Cottage. London:
Ward, Lock & Co., pp. vii-xii.
The book reprint of Cranford in June 1853 did not have
a "rapid sale," and it was "two years" until a second edition came out, but the book was praised by "competent
judges."

8 SAINTSBURY, GEORGE. A Short History of English Literature.
London: Macmillan & Co. Reprint. New York: Macmillan
Co., 1929, pp. 749-50.
Mary Barton's faithful picture of lower-class life de-
served its "success," but Ruth was "theatrical." Cranford
owes much to Jane Austen, but its "amiable sympathy" is
"less potent" than Miss Austen's "slightly merciless
satire."

9   SCRUTON, WILLIAM. "Reminiscences of the Late Miss Ellen
    Nussey," Brontë Society Transactions (Bradford), I, part
    VIII (March), 23-42.
        Miss Nussey was angered by a New Times article on The
    Life of Charlotte Brontë called "The Brontë Girls, or the
    Daughters of Doom," which described Patrick Brontë as a
    brute, and she blamed Gaskell for creating a false im-
    pression. Although Miss Nussey's letters from Charlotte
    were the main source for Gaskell's book and although Miss
    Nussey was promised a perusal of the manuscript, she com-
    plained that she was "barely" given even time to go through
    it.

10 SHARP, R.[OBERT] FARQUHARSON. A Dictionary of English Authors:
    Biographical and Bibliographical.... 2nd ed., with list of
    errata. London: George Redway, S.v. "Gaskell, Mrs. Eliza-
    beth Cleghorn."
        Gaskell was intimate with William and Mary Howitt and
    with Dickens.

11 SHORTER, CLEMENT K. "New Light on the Brontës. An Address
    Delivered at Haworth on April 10th, 1897,..." Brontë Society
    Transactions (Bradford), I, part VIII (March), 10-19.
        The impression of the Brontës given by Gaskell's "beauti-
    ful biography" can be altered only in lesser details, though
    "...sooner or later, I hope to re-edit" her book. Even more
    than the Brontës' own works, Gaskell's Life made the public
    enthusiastic about the Brontës.

12 SIMPSON, M.[ARY] C.[HARLOTTE] M.[AIR]. Many Memories of Many
    People. London: Edward Arnold, p. 120.
        Gaskell "was most womanly and attractive; the expression
    of her countenance was lovely, and her manner very pre-
    possessing.... She never wrote anything better than her
    last unfinished work, 'Wives and Daughters'."

13 TAVARÉ, FRED L. "[no. 2,295] Notes and Queries. Mary Barton
    [reply to no. 2,123]," Manchester Weekly Times (26 August),
    p. 5.
        Although the catalogue of "The Relics of Olde Manchester
    and Salford" at the Royal Jubilee Exhibition, at Old Traf-
    ford, identifies the "Mary Barton Farm" as Birchhall Farm,
    W. E. A. Axon, at the opening of the Moss Side Free Library,
    declared that the Greenheys Fields had been on the site of
    the present library.

1899

1899 B   SHORTER WRITINGS

1   ANON. "Chronicle and Comment," Bookman (New York), X
        (October), 111-13.
            Because the English copyright runs out this year, there
        are "likely to be a number of" new editions of Gaskell's
        vastly popular Life of Charlotte Brontë, which "will be
        remembered long after Wives and Daughters...and even
        Cranford...."

2   ANON. "Fifth Annual Meeting of the Brontë Society," Brontë
        Society Transactions (Bradford), II, part IX (April), 14.
            The Rev. Canon Louther-Clarke "proposed a vote of thanks
        to Mr. W. E. B. Priestly" for the "gift" to "each member"
        of Scruton's Thornton and the Brontës, which corrects the
        injustice done to Patrick Brontë by Gaskell, as demon-
        strated by the investigations of Mr. Yates of Dewsbury.

3   AXON, WILLIAM E. [A.]. Echoes of Old Lancashire. London:
        William Andrews & Co., pp. 14-21.
            Edward Higgins, the Knutsford highwayman mentioned by
        De Quincey in "Murder as a Fine Art," became the basis of
        Gaskell's sketch, "The Squire's Tale."

4   BARDSLEY, [REV. CANON, VICAR OF HUDDERSFIELD]. "Charlotte
        Brontë. A Paper Read at Huddersfield,...on January 14th,
        1899," Brontë Society Transactions (Bradford), II, part IX
        (April), 34.
            My father told me of Mr. Brontë's "tears" over Gaskell's
        "aspersions on his domestic character" and her exaggerations
        of his "eccentricities." Though Gaskell was a "genius,"
        her Life of Charlotte Brontë remained exaggerated even
        after the worst errors were removed from later editions.

5   BROWNING, ELIZABETH BARRETT. The Letters of Elizabeth
        Barrett Browning. Edited with biographical additions by
        Frederic C. Kenyon. New York: Macmillan Co. London:
        Macmillan & Co. I: 471-72; II: 139, 141-42, 259.
            [Letter to Mrs. Mitford, 13 December 1850:] "For 'Mary
        Barton' I am a little, little disappointed," for though it
        has "power and truth," the novel is "so tedious every now
        and then, and besides I want more beauty...--these class
        books must always be defective as works of art.... The
        style of the book is slovenly...." [Letter to Mrs. Martin,
        5 October (1853):] The admirable "'Ruth' is a great ad-
        vance on 'Mary Barton'." [Letter to Mrs. Jameson, 9 April

(1857):] Gaskell "is coming, whom I am sure to like and love," as "I know" from "her letters" and "her books."

6 CASH, SARAH. "Knutsford Parish Church. A Few Stray Glean-ings," Cheshire Notes and Queries [reprinted from Stockport Advertiser] (Stockport), IV, 148-51.
    [This article, though cited by Northup (1929.B6), does not mention Gaskell.

7 CROSS, WILBUR L. The Development of the English Novel. New York: Macmillan Co. Rev. ed. New York: Macmillan Co. London: Macmillan & Co., 1905, pp. 194-95, 234-38, 244.
    In Gaskell's industrial novels, she "was wise enough to offer no final solution...beyond trying to inspire employer and employee with the spirit of her own reasonableness." In the tradition of Maria Edgeworth, Gaskell's fiction reaches its culmination in Cranford. This writer, in her analysis of ethical motives, was moving toward the psycho-logical novel perfected by George Eliot, though Gaskell lacked George Eliot's intellectual "breadth."

8 LINTON, MRS. [ELIZABETH] LYNN. My Literary Life. London: Hodder & Stoughton, pp. 92-93.
    I met Gaskell, a "sweet" and "beautiful" woman, only once, yet "her manner" toward "me," a literary beginner, was so "perfect" that "I have always loved and cherished her memory...."

9 LOW, FRANCIS H. "Mrs. Gaskell's Short Tales," Fortnightly Review (London), n.s. LXVI (1 October), 633-43.
    Gaskell's short stories would, by themselves, make the reputation of a lesser writer, but they have lacked due recognition because of unevenness of quality. Although they do not obey "modern" "rules" for the short story, such works as her "Mr. Harrison's Confessions" are worthy of Lamb's comedy, and her idyllic Cousin Phillis equals the finest works of Hawthorne and Mérimée. By avoiding facile moral judgments, Gaskell achieves a Shakespearean quality unmatched by "any other woman writer."

10 LUCAS, E.[DWARD] V. "Introduction," in Cranford. The Little Library. London: Methuen & Co., pp. vii-xliv.
    Wives and Daughters is, "psychologically," Gaskell's "finest work in fiction, although in actual writing Cran-ford is, I think, its superior." Cranford is "autumnal," for even Mary Smith has "an old head" on her young "shoulders." Cranford was surely "written without

1899

(LUCAS, E.[DWARD] V.)

painstaking artifice," "came trippingly off the pen and
taxed the mind but little." Gaskell wrote best when she
was least "conscious" as a "literary artist." "Lamb sought
for oddity in human nature," but Gaskell "was far more
interested in the norm."

11   PAYNE, REV. GEORGE A. "A Memorial to Mrs. Gaskell,..."
Sketch (London) (1 March), p. 344.

The memorials to Gaskell include the Gaskell collection
at Manchester's Moss Side Library, a bas-relief and bust
at Knutsford, numerous articles in periodicals, and new
editions of her works.

12   REID, SIR T.[HOMAS] WEMYSS. "The Brontës. An Address Delivered...at Halifax, on January 15th, 1898," Brontë Society
Transactions (Bradford), II, part IX (April), 12.

"I can recall quite vividly the day, more than forty
years ago, when I read The Times review of" Gaskell's
"noble memoir of Charlotte Brontë; and I still seem to feel
the thrill of exultation with which I followed the bewitch-
ing story to the end."

13   TAVARÉ, FRED L. "Heath House, Knutsford," Cheshire Notes and
Queries [reprinted from Stockport Advertiser] (Stockport),
IV, 153-55.

The rumors of a highwayman in Cranford were based on
Edward Higgins of Heath House, but, although Mrs. Ritchie
in her "preface" describes a "secret passage in the house,"
the passage no longer exists. Gravestones of the Higgins
family can be seen in Knutsford churchyard.

14   [TENNYSON, HALLAM]. Alfred, Lord Tennyson. A Memoir by His
Son. New York: Macmillan Co. London: Macmillan & Co.
I: 283-86.

[Contains two of Gaskell's letters to John Forster and
one from Samuel Bamford to Tennyson--all related to Gaskell's success in getting Tennyson to send Bamford an inscribed copy of Tennyson's poems.]

15   TERHUNE, MARY VIRGINIA HAWES [MARION HARLAND]. Charlotte
Brontë at Home. New York and London: G. P. Putnam's Sons,
the Knickerbocker Press, pp. 11-12, 18, 38, 39, 45-46, 48,
54, 58, 76, 85, 97, 101, 107, 144, 158-59, 175-78, 194,
198, 209-10, 222-23, 233-34, 259, 263, 272, 285.

Gaskell's controversial account of the Cowan Bridge
School in her Life of Charlotte Brontë probably contains
much truth, but Gaskell was misled on the Mrs. Robinson
matter by Branwell's disturbed fantasies.

1900 A BOOKS

1   PAYNE, REV. GEORGE A. <u>Mrs. Gaskell and Knutsford</u>. With an
     introduction by Ada Ellen Bayly [Edna Lyall]. Manchester:
     Clarkson & Griffiths. London: Gay & Bird. 2nd ed. Man-
     chester: Clarkson & Griffiths. London: Mackie & Co.,
     1905.
          Gaskell's imagination transformed her materials, yet,
     to understand Gaskell and her works, one must visit Knuts-
     ford, which contributed much to <u>Cranford</u>. Gaskell was
     aware of human "follies" but also was aware of "the good
     qualities inherent in every individual." [Reviews of
     Payne's book included the following: Anon. "Books of the
     Week," <u>Manchester Guardian</u> (8 January 1901), p. 7 (In spite
     of Payne's disclaimer, this highly "conjectural" memoir is
     too uncritical of the assumption that Cranford is merely
     Knutsford.). Anon. "<u>Mrs. Gaskell and Knutsford</u>,..."
     <u>Academy</u> (London), LX (23 February 1901), 164 (We disagree
     with Payne's argument that Cranford is not equivalent to
     Knutsford, yet he has written "a pleasant little book.").
     Anon. "<u>Mrs. Gaskell and Knutsford</u>," <u>Bookman</u> (London), XIX
     (February 1901), 160 (In the absence of a "real biography,"
     this "booklet" is "pleasant" and "sympathetic."). Anon.
     "New Books," <u>Manchester Guardian</u> (19 December 1905), p. 5
     (The second edition of Payne's "pleasant little book" adds
     new arguments to his attempt to identify Cranford with
     Knutsford.). Anon. "Short Notices," <u>Inquirer</u> (London),
     LIX (15 December 1900), 802 (This is "an attractive book.").
     Charles Roper. "<u>Mrs. Gaskell and Knutsford</u>," <u>Inquirer</u>
     (London), LX (19 January 1901), 36 (Payne's "most assiduous"
     book "does not...run to death the theory that" Gaskell's
     fiction is literally based on Knutsford.). W. Burnett
     Tracy. "Mrs. Gaskell and Knutsford," <u>Lancashire Faces and</u>
     <u>Places</u> (Manchester), n.s. I (May 1901), 69-71 ("... This
     little book is altogether acceptable because it is so
     entirely sympathetic.").]

1900 B SHORTER WRITINGS

1   ANON. "Books of the Day," <u>Morning Post</u> (London) (24 May),
     p. 2.
          Gaskell's <u>Life of Charlotte Brontë</u> "forms an admirable"
     addendum to the Haworth edition of the Brontes.

2   ANON. "Book Reviews. The Brontë Annals," <u>Public Opinion</u>
     (New York), XXVIII (28 June), 824.

1900

(ANON.)
Shorter's annotations to the Haworth edition of The Life
of Charlotte Brontë supplement Gaskell, who was "compelled
to reticences" in her "conscientious and painstaking effort
to interpret Charlotte Brontë to her own age."

3   ANON. "Charlotte Brontë. Mrs. Gaskell's Biography of Her,
with Notes and Other New Matter from Mr. Shorter," New York
Times Saturday Review of Books and Art (16 June), p. 388.
Gaskell's Life of Charlotte Brontë is "the most valuable
of all the volumes in the Haworth edition" of the Brontës.
Shorter bases his edition of Gaskell's work on her third
edition, whose changes, he claims, improved the work,
though they also avoided libel suits. "Had" the Brontës
"written nothing or even had they produced much poorer work,
their memoir" by Gaskell "would still take high rank among
the few great masterpieces of biography in the language."

*4   ANON. [Reference to Gaskell] Household Words (26 May), p. 2.
[Source: John Albert Green. A Bibliographic Guide to
the Gaskell Collection in the Moss Side Library. Manchester: Reference Library, King St.; Moss Side Library,
Bradshaw St., 1911. See 1911.A2.]

5   ANON. "The Life of Charlotte Brontë,..." Athenaeum (London),
no. 3798 (11 August), pp. 177-78.
Gaskell's "judicious and affectionate" biography remains
the essential work on the Brontës. She did not understand the greater genius, Emily, and even with Charlotte
stuck to day-to-day life rather than examining the sources
of her genius. On the whole, Shorter does a good job of
editing and leaves Gaskell's portrait of Charlotte unchanged
in its essentials.

6   ANON. "The Life of Charlotte Brontë,..." London Quarterly
Review, n.s. IV (July), 177.
Shorter is the best possible editor of Gaskell's book,
for, instead of rewriting it, he merely corrects and adds.

7   ANON. "The Literary Week," Academy (London), LIX (29 September), 252.
E. V. Lucas's introduction to the Methuen Little Library
edition of Cranford points out cogently that Gaskell's con-
centration on "the norm" contrasts with Lamb's love for
eccentricity.

8   ANON. "Minor Books and New Editions," Glasgow Herald (10 May),
p. 11.

Gaskell's Life of Charlotte Brontë, reissued in the Haworth edition, "has won a place in our literature as secure, though not as lofty, as the great masterpieces of Boswell and Lockhart."

9 ANON. "New Editions," Guardian (London), LV, part I (9 May), 676.
 The Haworth reissue of Gaskell's Life of Charlotte Brontë, annotated by Shorter, will become "the standard edition."

10 ANON. "New Editions. The Life of Charlotte Brontë...Haworth Edition,..." Literary World (Boston), XXXI (1 September), 38.
 Gaskell's "standard life of Charlotte Brontë...left little to be added, and for that little we are mainly indebted to Mr. Shorter...."

11 ANON. "New Leaves,..." Outlook (London), V (12 May), 47.
 Except for printing a letter of Charlotte's about Balzac out of sequence, Shorter has done an excellent job of editing Gaskell's Life of Charlotte Brontë. The author of Ruth "understood the charms of quietness" and so was "ideally" suited to be Charlotte's biographer. The painful parts are "relieved by" Gaskell's "sanity."

12 ANON. "New Novels," Manchester Guardian (7 November), p. 3.
 In both Dent's Temple Classics edition of Cranford and Methuen's Little Library edition, "the old misprint of 'cold loin' for 'cold lion'" is perpetuated.

13 ANON. "Notes of the Day," Literature [published by Times (London)], VII (13 October), 266.
 Mrs. Tollemache's Cranford Souvenirs throws "pleasant light on Knutsford, the model of" Gaskell's "town," and E. V. Lucas's introduction to Methuen's Little Library edition of Cranford is also "pleasant."

14 ANON. "Notes," SR, VIII (October), 309-10.
 Gaskell's Life of Charlotte Brontë, reissued in the Haworth edition, is "one of the masterpieces" of "sympathetic biography" of "our century."

15 ANON. "Reviews. The Great Sisters. The Life of Charlotte Brontë,..." Academy (London), LIX (4 August), 87-88.
 Shorter's emendations to Gaskell's "noble" work clarify it yet leave it intact as a "classic." Gaskell describes the Brontës' lives and surroundings "with a quiet... strength...and insight."

1900

16   ANON. "Some Books of the Week," Spectator (London), LXXXIV
      (12 May), 678.
         It is no disgrace to Gaskell that her Life of Charlotte
      Brontë, now more than forty years old, needs "annotation,"
      and Shorter's emendations increase its "interest."

17   ANON. "Some New Editions," American Monthly Review of Re-
      views (New York), XXII (December), 769.
         Shorter's introduction and notes to the Haworth edition
      of Gaskell's "famous Life of Charlotte Brontë" are very
      useful.

18   AXON, WILLIAM E. A. N & Q, 9th ser. V (9 June), 449-51.
         The reissue by Shorter of Gaskell's great biography of
      Charlotte Brontë reminds one of Charlotte's connection with
      Manchester, including her several visits to Gaskell's
      house.

19   CASH, SARAH. "Knutsford and Its Surroundings Some Sixty Years
      Ago," Cheshire Notes and Queries [reprinted from Stockport
      Advertiser] (Stockport), V, 220-28.
         A lady similar to those in Cranford was scared away from
      the old church fields by a snake.

20   COLLEY, T. "Gleanings and Jottings in Knutsford," Cheshire
      Notes and Queries [reprinted from Stockport Advertiser]
      (Stockport), V, 159-64.
         Captain Hill, the model for Captain Brown in Cranford,
      died a natural death, in contrast to Brown. There are
      many other probable actual models for Gaskell's fictional
      characters.

21   GILDER, JEANNETTE L. "Books and Writers. A New Light on
      Charlotte Brontë," Harper's Bazar (New York), XXXIII
      (16 June), 434-35.
         Shorter has chosen to annotate the third edition of
      The Life of Charlotte Brontë as "the one generally ac-
      cepted." Gaskell "was...a wise choice as...biographer" for
      she was acquainted with both Charlotte and her fiction and
      was herself a skillful novelist. Gaskell's Life is largely
      responsible for the public's present affection for the
      Brontës.

22   G.[OLLANEZ], I.[SRAEL]. [Note at end of text] In Cranford.
      London: J. M. Dent & Co., Aldine House, p. 271 [an un-
      numbered page].
         "'Cranford' is a picture of life in Knutsford...."

23   [JOHNSON, LIONEL P.]. "Charlotte Brontë and Her Champion.
      The Life of Charlotte Brontë,..." Daily Chronicle Clerken-
      well News and Evening Chronicle (London) (23 June), p. 3.
      [Reprinted as "Charlotte Brontë and Her Champion," in Post
      Liminium: Essays and Critical Papers by Lionel Johnson.
      Edited by Thomas Whittemore. London: Elkin Mathews, 1911,
      pp. 42-50.]
           Gaskell wrote The Life of Charlotte Brontë "with a Bos-
      wellian industry," with high "art," and with truthfulness,
      but Shorter's edition provides a very useful updating. The
      most valuable "fresh" materials are the "pathetic" letters
      of Mr. Brontë to Gaskell asking her to do the biography
      and then adding that "if all else...failed," he would have
      to try to write it himself. Gaskell did not know Charlotte
      intimately but "discerned the truth by an unerring intui-
      tion." The "biography is a veritable interpretation" that
      illuminates the apparant contrast between the "parson's"
      retiring "daughter" and the author of the bold novels. All
      later works on the Brontës, even the most "brilliant," "are
      as nothing beside" Gaskell's Life.

24   LAMB, T. A. "John Bright or Cranford," N & Q, 9th ser. VI
      (8 December), 445.
           A saying of John Bright, quoted in the current Anglo-
      Saxon Review by Sir Wemyss Reid, also appears in Cranford:
      Gaskell's ladies "observe" that it does not matter how they
      dress "at Cranford, where everybody knows us" nor away from
      Cranford, "where nobody knows us." [See 1901.B5, 1901.B8.]

25   PAYNE, REV. G.[EORGE] A. "Literature. Mrs. Gaskell and
      Knutsford," Manchester Herald (6 and 13 January), p. 2.
           Gaskell transformed Knutsford through her imagination
      into her fictional towns. Wives and Daughters is very sug-
      gestive of Knutsford. "Mr. Harrison's Confessions" "al-
      most" excells Cranford. "Passages" in My Lady Ludlow
      remind us of Cranford.

26   SEGRÉ, CARLO. "Carlotta Brontë," NA, 4th ser. CL (16 Novem-
      ber), 244-61.
           The Life of Charlotte Brontë, reissued in the Haworth
      edition and splendidly annotated by Shorter, was one of
      the most noteworthy books to come out of England in the
      last fifty years. It was Gaskell's finest literary hour,
      and it remains the supreme authority on the Brontës.

27   SHIPMAN, CAROLYN. "An Old Friend in a New Dress," Critic
      (New Rochelle, New York), XXXVI (May), 415-16.

1900

(SHIPMAN, CAROLYN)
Among other new materials in this annotated edition of
The Life of Charlotte Brontë, Shorter refutes Gaskell's
story of Mr. Brontë's destruction of his wife's dress.

*28   SHORTER, CLEMENT K.   "Introduction," in The Life of Charlotte
Brontë.   Haworth Edition.   London: Smith, Elder & Co.
[Source: Clark S. Northup.   "A Bibliography," in
Elizabeth Gaskell.   By Gerald DeWitt Sanders.   New Haven:
Yale University Press, for Cornell University.   London:
Humphrey Milford, Oxford University Press, 1929.   See
1929.B6.]

29   _____.   "Mrs. Gaskell's Charlotte Brontë.   To the Editor,..."
Outlook (London), V (19 May), 499.
Contrary to what your reviewer says, I did not mix up
the two letters of Charlotte Brontë's mentioning Balzac,
though I did allow them to remain in Gaskell's order in my
edition of her Life of Charlotte Brontë.   This order was
probably based on a muddle originally created by George
Henry Lewes.   [See 1900.B11.]

30   TORRANCE, LOUISE M.   "A Cranford Evening and Entertainment,
in Which the Characters of Mrs. Gaskell's Famous Book Acted
Scenes from It," Puritan (New York), VIII (August), 513-20.
[The same article appeared in Munsey's Magazine (New York),
XXIII (5 August 1900), 627-34.]
We put on a dramatized version of Gaskell's Cranford to
raise money for our favorite charity.

1901 A   BOOKS - NONE

1901 B   SHORTER WRITINGS

1   AINGER, ALFRED.   In The Dictionary of National Biography.
XXII: Supplement.   S.v.   "Du Maurier, George Louis
Palmella Busson."
Du Maurier based his illustrations for Sylvia's Lovers
on Henry Keene's "sketches" of Whitby because they looked
right, though Du Maurier did not know that Gaskell had
actually modeled her seaport on Whitby.

*2   ANON.   "Elizabeth Gaskell," in The World's Great Women
Novelists.   Philadelphia: The Booklover's Library,
pp. 97-100.
[Source: Marjorie Taylor Davis.   "An Annotated Bibliography of Criticism on Elizabeth Cleghorn Gaskell, 1848-

1973." Ph.D. dissertation, University of Mississippi, 1974. See 1974.B6.]

3 FLETCHER, J.[OSEPH] S.[MITH]. Picturesque Yorkshire. London: J. M. Dent & Co. III, part XVII, 339.

Gaskell used Whitby as the model for "Monkshaven in her charming novel Sylvia's Lovers, and used the old-world material of press-gangs, whaling ships, and North Sea life with great effect."

4 HENNEMAN, JOHN BELL. "The Brontë Sisters," SR, IX (April), 220-34.

"The total impression left by" Gaskell's Life of Charlotte Brontë--"the worthy tribute of one noble woman to another spiritually akin--is nowhere altered, but merely strengthened and confirmed by the fresh material" in Shorter's Haworth edition. Through the Life, Gaskell "achieved an immortality." She stands in a "splendid line of women writers of fiction extending through the" nineteenth "century: Maria Edgeworth, Jane Austen, the Brontës," Gaskell, George Eliot, and Mrs. Humphry Ward.

5 LAWSON, RICHARD. "John Bright or Cranford [reply to 9th ser. VI, 445]," N & Q, 9th ser. VII (2 February), 93.

Neither Bright nor Gaskell originated the quoted saying about its not mattering how one dressed. In the Kaleidoscope (22 March 1825), the saying was attributed to a then long-dead "Liverpool gentleman." [See 1900.B24, 1901.B8.]

6 LAYARD, GEORGE SOMES. Mrs. Lynn Linton. Her Life, Letters, and Opinions. London: Methuen & Co., pp. 75, 326-27.

[Mrs. Lynn Linton in letter to Mrs. Gedge, 17 January 1897:] I should like to write on Gaskell for my contribution to the Queen's Jubilee collection of essays on dead authoresses. I prefer Gaskell over George Eliot, Charlotte Brontë, Mrs. Craik, and Harriet Martineau because Gaskell was a "sweet" woman who was nice to me on our one meeting and who later defended me against others.

7 [MEYNELL, MRS. WILFRED]. "Woman in Literature," Gentlewoman (London) XXII (5 January), 30.

Among distinguished women writers of the 1840s, Gaskell "was an author of fine," not "great" "talent." Her male characters are drawn conventionally, but "her portraits of women" are "keen."

8 WELLFORD, R. "John Bright or Cranford [reply to 9th ser. VI, 445; VII, 93]," N & Q, 9th ser. VII (23 February), 154.

1901

(WELLFORD, R.)
In the Newcastle Chronicle (2 February 1901), the
Gaskell-Bright saying about its not mattering what clothes
one wore is attributed to a Mrs. Orde (misspelled Ord) who
"died in 1842." [See 1900.B24, 1901.B5.]

1902 A BOOKS - NONE

1902 B SHORTER WRITINGS

*1 ANON. "A Very Dainty Cranford," Literary World (Boston?)
    (17 October), p. 275.
        [On a pocket edition of Cranford.] [Unlocatable.
    Source: Gaskell Cuttings: Manchester Central Library.]

2   CHAMPNEYS, BASIL. "Mrs. Gaskell's Novels," Pilot (London), V
    (28 June), 672-73; VI (5 July), 11-12.
        Though Gaskell's works have never been neglected, they
    have been underrated because of their seemingly artless
    ease. Her greatest works "dispensed entirely" with a
    social "purpose," allowed her "humour" full play, and stuck
    to "ordinary experience: Cousin Phillis, Cranford, and
    Wives and Daughters. The last of these three "is the best
    purely domestic novel in the English language...." Dis-
    playing a rare insight into the factor of human heredity,
    Wives and Daughters is "a criticism of life" and a "master-
    piece," though her only one, and it establishes "her right
    to rank as a 'classic'."

3   COMPTON, EDWARD. "Preface," in Scenes from Cranford. Ar-
    ranged for Dramatic Performance. By Beatrice Hatch.
    London: Alexander Moring, the De La More Press, pp. 5-6.
    [Also published in London by Grant Richards, 1902.]
        Cranford today is more popular "than ever."

4   IRVINE, WILLIAM FERGUSSON, ed. A History of the Family of
    Mobberly and Knutsford in the County of Chester. With Some
    Account of the Family of Upholland and Denton in the County
    of Lancaster. From Materials Collected by the Late Edgar
    Swinton Holland. Edinburgh: privately printed at the
    Ballantine Press, pp. 62, 69, 76-79, 88.
        When the young Gaskell was sent to live with her aunt,
    "Mrs. Lumb was not in good circumstances, and lived in a
    modest house on the heath surrounded by an old-fashioned
    garden," but Elizabeth "spent a happy childhood" there.

5   MORTIMER, JOHN. "Lancashire Novelists. Mrs. Gaskell,"
     <u>Manchester Quarterly</u> [published in <u>Papers of the Manchester
     Literary Club</u>], XXI (July), 195-228.
         Gaskell's Knutsford background is reflected in her comic
     fiction, such as <u>Cranford</u>, and her Manchester experiences
     find expression in her darker works, such as <u>Mary Barton</u>,
     but the Knutsford "experience" was the more enduring one in
     her work. Gaskell's marriage to a distinguished Unitarian
     minister broadened the scope of her knowledge and experi-
     ence. She was a "perfect" "wife and mother" yet also en-
     gaged in benevolent work among the poor. Her two most
     lasting works are <u>The Life of Charlotte Brontë</u> and <u>Cranford</u>.

6   PALMER, WILLIAM T.[HOMAS]. "Over Sands," in <u>Lake Country
     Rambles</u>. London: Chatto & Windus, pp. 90-118.
         [The chapter contains no reference to Gaskell, although
     cited by Northup (1929.B6), but it does describe the locale
     of "The Sexton's Hero."]

7   SIMONDS, WILLIAM EDWARD. <u>A Student's History of English
     Literature</u>. Boston: Houghton Mifflin & Co., Riverside
     Press, pp. 425-26.
         Gaskell's <u>Cranford</u> is "purely realistic." Some of her
     "other tales...had a decided influence upon the early work
     of George Eliot and are among the first belonging to...the
     so-called psychological novel."

8   S.[MITH], [MRS.] E.[LIZABETH], ed. <u>George Smith: A Memoir,
     with Some Pages of Autobiography</u>. London: privately
     printed [by Elizabeth Smith], p. 28. [In section reprinted
     from Sidney Lee's memoir on George Smith in the first
     volume of the Supplement to the <u>Dictionary of National
     Biography</u> (1901).]
         Although Smith warned Gaskell of "the possible conse-
     quences" of the Mrs. Robinson passages in <u>The Life of Char-
     lotte Brontë</u>, Gaskell left them in. She "was travelling
     in France" with her whereabouts "unknown" when a libel suit
     was threatened, so Smith, after his own investigation,
     "withdrew the book" in order to remove the offending ma-
     terial from "later editions." Sir James Stephen negotiated
     with Smith on Mrs. Robinson's behalf.

9   STANBERY, KATHERINE S. [Photograph] <u>Photo-Miniature</u>
     (New York), III (February), opposite 487.
         [Cited by Green (1911.A2) as a "painting" of Lady Glen-
     mire of <u>Cranford</u>, this is actually a photograph of a posed
     model.]

1903

1903 A BOOKS

1   GREEN, J.[OHN] A.[LBERT]. A Hand-list of the Gaskell Collec-
    tion in the Public Library, Moss Side, Manchester. Man-
    chester: the Library.
        [The twelve-page list includes bibliographies, works by
    Gaskell, works about Gaskell, miscellaneous materials, and
    works by Gaskell's husband.]
        [Reviews of Green's hand-list included the following:
    Anon. "Literary News and Notes," Manchester City News
    (5 September 1903), p. 2 (The hand-list cites Gaskell's
    "delightful" short stories. There is no place more ap-
    propriate than Manchester for the Gaskell collection, un-
    less perhaps Knutsford.). Anon. Sphere (London), XV
    (3 October 1903), p. 22 (The list is useful, but Manches-
    ter's collection of its "greatest" writer lacks the
    separate edition of "The Sexton's Hero" and a first edi-
    tion of Sylvia's Lovers, and Green misdescribes Round the
    Sofa as in three volumes rather than two.). A Man of Kent.
    "Rambling Remarks," British Weekly (London), XXXIV
    (10 September 1903), 529 (The list is "very good" but is
    incomplete both on Gaskell's "works" and on secondary
    materials.).]

1903 B SHORTER WRITINGS

1   ADAMS, W.[ILLIAM] E. Memoirs of a Social Atom. London:
    Hutchinson & Co., pp. 390-91.
        As a student of the Rev. William Gaskell, "husband of
    the famous novelist," I can testify that he was a splendid
    teacher of literature.

2   ANON. "Introduction," in Cranford and Mary Barton. London:
    Blackie & Son, pp. i-iv.
        Gaskell's "husband became her constant adviser in her
    literary work." Cranford, "in many ways her finest work,"
    "rivals Jane Austen," and Cousin Phillis is "one of"
    Gaskell's "most perfect" books.

*3 ANON. Manchester Guardian (27 December).
        [Reply to Lockwood Kipling in T. P.'s Weekly (London),
    who said that Manchester was still awaiting its novelist:]
    What about Gaskell? [Unlocatable. Source: Gaskell
    Cuttings, Manchester Central Library.]

4   ANON. "Memorial Notices. Edna Lyall," Manchester Guardian
    (10 February), p. 12.

Ada Ellen Bayly (Edna Lyall) "considered" Gaskell "her favourite writer of fiction" and thought that her best works were <u>Cranford</u> and <u>Wives and Daughters</u>.

5   ANON. "Under Protection. The Ballad of the Oldham Weaver," <u>Manchester Guardian</u> (28 December), p. 4.
     "In her affecting story of 'Mary Barton'," Gaskell quotes the whole of the Lancashire song of "The Oldham Weaver."

6   CROFTON, HENRY THOMAS. <u>Old Moss Side</u>. Manchester: the [Manchester] <u>City News</u> offices, pp. 18-22, 36.
     In spite of a number of other claimed models, Pepperhill Farm was, "beyond all doubt," the original for "Mary Barton's Farm."

7   GISSING, GEORGE. <u>Charles Dickens: A Critical Study</u>. London: Gresham Publishing Co., p. 243 [first published in London by Blackie, 1898].
     "For the purposes of fiction," "the working-class" is "still awaiting its portrayer." Gaskell "essayed the theme very faithfully, and with some success; but it was not her best work."

8   GRANT, JOSHUA. "May-day at Cranford," <u>Treasury</u> (London), I (May), 720-29.
     Some in Knutsford still remember Gaskell and her family, and customs described in her <u>Cranford</u> still survive in the village.

9   JAMES, HENRY. <u>William Whetmore Story and His Friends: from Letters, Diaries, and Recollections</u>. Boston: Houghton Mifflin & Co. I: 352-59, 361, 362, 364-65, 368; II: 84-85.
     Gaskell's <u>Cranford</u>, <u>Sylvia's Lovers</u>, and <u>Wives and Daughters</u> are "admirable things which time has consecrated." Gaskell's letters show what a charming friend she was and how "she read all poetry into almost any friendship." In one letter, written at Whitby, where she was researching <u>Sylvia's Lovers</u>, "she mentions that Hawthorne was at the same time on the same coast, at Redcar, ten miles off, engaged in finishing 'Transformation', the subject of which she sketches as she has heard it narrated.... 'For all of which, somehow'," Gaskell says, "'you like Donatello better!'... For all of which...we like her" too.

10 LANMAN, C. R. "Orange Eating Once More. To the Editor,..." <u>Nation</u> (New York), LXXXVI (16 April), 310-11.
     The saying that "the only way to eat an orange" is "to lock yourself in your room and eat it" comes from Gaskell's <u>Cranford</u>.

1903

11 LEEDS, G. E. "'Lois the Witch' [reply to 9th ser. XII, 89],"
    N & Q, 9th ser. XII (15 August), 134.
        The story is by Gaskell and is reprinted in Cranford and
    Other Tales in the Smith & Elder pocket edition of her
    works. [See 1903.B14.]

12 MORLEY, JOHN [M.P.]. "Mr. John Morley. Great Free-Trade Hall
    Meeting,..." Manchester Guardian (20 October), p. 6. [Re-
    printed as Report of the Annual Meeting of the National
    Reform Union, October 19, 1903. Speeches by Right Hon.
    John Morley, M.P....and Others. Manchester and London:
    Reddish, printed at Guardian General Printing Works, for
    the National Reform Union, Manchester, p. 20.]
        [At William E. A. Axon's suggestion, Morley changed the
    reference below from Ruth to North and South, but Axon
    thought that Mary Barton would have been an even more ap-
    propriate reference.] In order to learn about the evils
    of protection, one "should read Disraeli's 'Sybil' and"
    Gaskell's "novel called 'Ruth',...two most interesting and
    agreeable fictions."

13 STREET, G. S. "The Provincial Mind," Quarterly Review
    (London), CXCVII (April), 526.
        Cranford is one of the clearest illustrations of the
    fact that a "writer on provincial themes" need not be "pro-
    vincial," for Gaskell's book displays "an all-embracing
    humanity."

14 R. B. P. "'Lois the Witch'," N & Q, 9th ser. XII (1 August),
    89.
        "Who wrote" this "powerful story"? [See 1903.B11.]

15 T. W. "Wives and Daughters," N & Q, 9th ser. XII (5 Septem-
    ber), 188.
        What magazine published Wives and Daughters? [The
    answer given by the editors: Cornhill (London), August,
    1864, to January, 1866.]

1904 A BOOKS - NONE

1904 B SHORTER WRITINGS

1 CAZAMIAN, LOUIS. "Mrs. Gaskell: l'interventionnisme
   chrétien," in Le Roman social en Angleterre (1830-1850).
   Dickens, Disraeli, Mrs. Gaskell, Kingsley. 2nd ed. Paris:
   Société Nouvelle de Librairie et d'Édition. Translated by
   Martin Fido as The Social Novel in England 1830-1850.

Dickens, Disraeli, Mrs. Gaskell, Kingsley. London and
Boston: Routledge & Kegan Paul, 1973, pp. 117, 166, 211-31,
232, 235, 239, 264-65, 292-95.
  Mary Barton and, to a lesser extent, North and South
"remain" Gaskell's "greatest achievement," in spite of the
sympathetic penetration of The Life of Charlotte Brontë and
the near rivaling, in Wives and Daughters, of the art of
George Eliot for novelistic artistry. Mary Barton is emotional, sensitive, and intuitive rather than the result of
a conscious "social philosophy." Through illustration instead of preaching, the book "proposes compassionate inter-
ventionism based on a religious ideal of human brotherhood."
Gaskell, like Disraeli, fears unions, yet she presents an
excuse for the workers' behavior in the cold and thought-
less behavior of their employers. In spite of its greater
timidity, North and South, like Mary Barton, "demonstrates"
Gaskell's "familiarity with the workers."

2   COWARD, T. A. Picturesque Cheshire. 2nd ed. London and
Manchester: Sherratt & Hughes, pp. 18, 79-82, 85-87.
[1st ed. was published in 1903.]
  Gaskell, who portrayed both Manchester and Knutsford in
her fiction, is buried outside the Unitarian Chapel of
Knutsford.

3   [DENT, J. M.]. "Forwards," in Cranford. Series of English
Idylls. London: J. M. Dent & Co. New York: E. P.
Dutton & Co., pp. xi-xv. [Reprinted in Cranford. Everyman's Library. London: Dent. New York: Dutton, 1906;
(slightly abridged and signed) in Cranford. Everyman's
Library. London: Dent. New York: Dutton, 1954.]
  It is too bad that Gaskell, born in Chelsea, did not
grow up in London, for she might have "left us a book of
London idylls" instead of her idylls of Knutsford. In Gaskell's London, "the heroism and the beauty would have been
no less, even if the suffering might have been greater"
than in Cranford. In spite of some resemblance to Lamb,
Cranford is far too feminine in laughing at "women's
oddities" and in describing their "tenderness" for Lamb to
have written it. And Gaskell's men are all seen through
the deference of women's eyes.

4   FARADAY, F. J. "Correspondence. Greenheys Fields and Mary
Barton," Manchester Guardian (14 November), p. 5.
  "Pepper Hill Farm and the old 'Cinder Walk'...across
the Coffin Bridge that spanned the Corn Brook" are definitely identified as Gaskell's models for Mary Barton's
opening scene in a letter to me, which I enclose, from
her husband.

5   GARNETT, DR. R.[ICHARD]. "The Place of Charlotte Brontë in
     Nineteenth Century Fiction," Brontë Society Transactions
     (Bradford), II, part XIV (February), 211-12.
        Gaskell, along with Charlotte Brontë, ranks as one of
     the great Victorian novelists, and her "classical biography"
     of Charlotte shows Gaskell's versatility. "All her books
     are masterly, but no two are alike...."

6   GORDAN, ALEXANDER. "William Stevenson, 1792-1796," in
     Historical Account of Dob Lane Chapel, Failsworth, and Its
     Schools. Manchester: H. Rawson & Co., pp. 46-47.
        William Stevenson's "resignation of his connection with
     Manchester Academy and with Dob Lane was due to scruples
     in regard to a paid ministry...." His daughter, Gaskell,
     had "literary power and pathos" that made her loved
     throughout Lancashire.

7   GREEN, J.[OHN] A.[LBERT]. "Gaskell Collection at Moss Side
     Library [Paper read by Green at Liverpool Central Refer-
     ence Library]," Manchester City News (20 February), p. 2.
        The collection, started by W.[illiam] E. A. Axon, was
     made part of the Moss Side Library at its opening in 1897.
     In 1895 Axon compiled "a privately printed Gaskell
     Bibliography."

8   KNIGHT, WILLIAM. Retrospects. New York: Charles Scribner's
     Sons, pp. 271-72.
        [Prints a letter from Gaskell dated 28 October 1852,
     describing having dinner with Mrs. Wordsworth and listening
     to her reminisce about her husband.]

9   MOULTON, CHARLES WELLS, ed. "Elizabeth Cleghorn Gaskell,
     1810-1865," in The Library of Literary Criticism of English
     and American Authors. Buffalo, New York: Moulton Publish-
     ing Co. VI, 427-34, and see index for other references to
     Gaskell.
        [This item gives extracts from selected secondary
     material on Gaskell.]

10   NICOLL, W.[ILLIAM] ROBERTSON. In Chambers's Cyclopaedia of
     English Literature. New ed. London and Edinburgh: W. & R.
     Chambers. Philadelphia: J. B. Lippincott Co. S.v. "Mrs.
     Gaskell, Elizabeth Cleghorn."
        The "tender" and "autumnal" Cranford is Gaskell's "most
     enduring" book, and her Life of Charlotte Brontë, though it
     offended "living people," has been "confirmed" in "its
     substantial truth" by recent scholarship. Sylvia's Lovers
     "is perhaps the least satisfactory of" Gaskell's "novels,"

and <u>Wives and Daughters</u> is her "fullest and ripest."
"Though not a writer of the first rank, she succeeded more
than most in measuring her powers and in achieving her am-
bitions." Gaskell's village novels are "more successful"
than her industrial ones.

11 RODGERS, JOSEPH. "Mrs. Gaskell's <u>Sylvia's Lovers</u>," <u>N & Q</u>,
    10th ser. I (5 March), 187-88.
       Gaskell studied Whitby for the locale of <u>Sylvia's Lovers</u>,
    and her chief informant was Mr. Corney, proprietor of a
    "confectioner's shop," whom she thanked by an inscribed
    copy of her novel.

*12 [TOUT, MRS.]. <u>Manchester High School Magazine</u> (April).
    [On Knutsford as Cranford.] [Source: John Albert Green.
    <u>A Bibliographical Guide to the Gaskell Collection in the
    Moss Side Library</u>. Manchester: Reference Library, King
    St.; Moss Side Library, Bradshaw St., 1911. <u>See</u> 1911.A2.]

1905 A   BOOKS - NONE

1905 B   SHORTER WRITINGS

1 ANON. "Miscellaneous. Notes on Books, & C.," <u>N & Q</u>, 10th
   ser. IV (21 October), 331.
      Routledge's "New Universal Library" has reprinted <u>Cran-
   ford</u> and <u>Sylvia's Lovers</u>, two "unequalled" novels, "of
   which the world will not soon tire." We hope to see all
   of Gaskell's works reprinted in this series.

2 ANON. "Miscellany," <u>Manchester Guardian</u> (14 November), p. 5.
      A sketch of the Pepper Hill Farm, the model for the one
   in the opening passage of Gaskell's <u>Mary Barton</u>, is owned
   by the Whitworth Art Gallery, and the artist has suggested
   that a plaque be erected at the farm. There is a Mary
   Barton Street in Manchester but nothing else to commemorate
   Gaskell.

3 ANON. "Miscellany," <u>Manchester Guardian</u> (15 November), p. 5.
      Mary Barton Street is not named after Gaskell but after
   the wife of the man who owned the property. Also, at a
   cottage near Pepper Hill Farm, a "powerloom weaver" lived
   who was the original for Job "Leigh [<u>sic</u>]."

4 ANON. "Miscellany," <u>Manchester Guardian</u> (24 November), p. 5.
      The name of Mary Barton Street is now shortened to
   Barton Street.

1905

5   ANON. "The Realms of Gold. The Independent Minister [a quo-
      tation from Gaskell's Cousin Phillis, preceded by a biog-
      raphical note]," Daily News (London) (1 April), p. 5.
           Cranford, "the work by which" Gaskell's "name will al-
      ways live," immortalized Knutsford. Cousin Phillis is a
      "beautiful little idyll," and Gaskell's Life of Charlotte
      Brontë is a "classic."

6   ANON. "Social Movements as Reflected in Novels. Mary Bar-
      ton,..." National Home Reading Union. General Course
      Magazine. (London), XVII (7 September), 18-21.
           "Although 'Mary Barton' has not the gracefulness and
      the delicious sunny humour of" Gaskell's "later" books,
      "it is, in many ways, the most powerful" and "popular."
      "More nearly than any other book," Mary Barton reconciles
      the claims of art and social "purpose."

7   DILWYN. "[no. 10,716] Mrs. Gaskell's 'Milton'," Manchester
      City News [Notes and Queries] (9 December), p. 2.
           What is "the real name of the place called 'Milton' by"
      Gaskell in North and South?

8   HOMPES, [MISS] M.[AT]. "Mrs. Gaskell. Part I--Personal,"
      Students' Magazine. Organ of Manchester [Municipal]
      Evening School of Commerce, I (January and February),
      20-21, 36-37.
           Gaskell was a much admired novelist but also "a noble
      woman, who led an active, self-sacrificing life." Though
      she, as wife of the Rev. William Gaskell, insisted "that
      no congregation has the right to usurp the time of a minis-
      ter's wife," she did extensive benevolent work and showed
      an intuitive rapport with the working girls whom she
      taught. She was gifted at telling impromptu stories, par-
      ticularly ghost stories. In her later years Gaskell knew
      that she had heart disease but did not worry about it,
      though her friends did.

9   _____. "Mrs. Gaskell. Part II--Literary Work. Mary Barton,"
      Students' Magazine. Organ of Manchester Municipal Evening
      School of Commerce, I (May), 68-69.
           Mary Barton "was written...on irregular scraps of paper."
      After one publisher turned it down promptly, it was kept
      by Chapman & Hall for "a whole twelve months without" their
      "even sending an acknowledgement", but at last they bought
      the copyright for £100. Gaskell "wrote for Lancashire
      people; she pleaded the cause of the poor, and they did not
      find too many advocates in her day."

10   REID, [SIR] T.[HOMAS] WEMYSS. <u>Memoirs of Thomas Wemyss Reid</u>,
      <u>1842-1885</u>. Edited by Stuart J. Reid. London: Cassell &
      Co., pp. 231-41.
          Ellen Nussey "expressed regret that" Gaskell "had not
      done justice to Charlotte's life and character.... To me
      this was rank heresy," but Miss Nussey asked me to write a
      book setting Gaskell straight and offered to provide me
      with "letters" and "documents." Instead I wrote three
      articles on the Brontës for <u>Macmillan's Magazine</u> but later
      expanded them into a book.

11   SAMPSON, MARTIN W. "Introduction: Biographical Sketch. The
      Novel of Cranford," in <u>Cranford</u>. Macmillan's Pocket Ameri-
      can and English Classics. New York: Macmillan Co. London:
      Macmillan & Co., pp. vii-xviii.
          American students of Gaskell's work should bear in mind
      that she, in her advocacy of the poor, was one whose re-
      ligious faith lay outside "the Established Church" and was
      therefore "regarded as" an outsider. Although <u>Mary Barton</u>
      was her most popular work during Gaskell's lifetime, today
      the favorite is <u>Cranford</u>, which "is delicate and feminine
      without the least trace of triviality or false sentiment."
      This "little classic" portrays a "life that is real and
      cheerful and healthy," and the book shows "that under the
      ridiculous may lie the lovable."

12   WILLET, B. W. "Introduction," in <u>The Life of Charlotte Brontë</u>.
      Notes by Temple Scott and B. W. Willet. Edinburgh: John
      Grant, pp. xi-xvi.
          We have used the first edition, because, as Mary Taylor
      said, "libellous or not," it was "true."

<u>1906 A BOOKS - NONE</u>

<u>1906 B SHORTER WRITINGS</u>

1   ANON. "Bookland. <u>North and South</u> (Knutsford edition),..."
     <u>Manchester Evening News</u> (20 October), p. 6.
         This is a "fine work of fiction" because Gaskell, out
     of the knowledge gained from her affectionate domestic life,
     understood "the best" in human nature. She knew more about
     industrial realities than Dickens did.

2   ANON. "Books. Mrs. Gaskell and Her Work," <u>Spectator</u>
     (London), XCVII (29 September), 437-38.
         Women have dominated the English novel since the early
     nineteenth century, and Gaskell is "not the least" among

1906

(ANON.)
these female novelists. Until this edition Gaskell's work
as a whole has not been available. Cousin Phillis is
idyllic though a bit flawed by the "jerkiness" of the
writing, a fault which Gaskell overcame only in her two
finest books, Cranford and Wives and Daughters, the last
of which is "her masterpiece."

3   ANON. "Comment on Current Books. Works of Mrs. Gaskell,"
Outlook (New York), LXXXIV (17 November), 683.
Although the "old-time refinement" of Cranford is well
known, "it is doubtful...whether" Gaskell "is known by any
other of her stories, and yet several of them are" indeed
"worth reading." Although Ward, in his introductions to
the Knutsford edition, "overstates, in some respects, the
value of" Gaskell's "work," much of her fiction still has
charm.

4   ANON. "Literature. Minor Books and New Editions," Glasgow
Herald (8 November), p. 10.
"The most notable" of the miscellaneous works in volume
five of the Knutsford edition is My Lady Ludlow.

5   ANON. "Literature. Minor Books and New Editions," Glasgow
Herald (15 November), p. 10.
"The sixth volume of the 'Knutsford Edition'" includes
Sylvia's Lovers, "next to 'Cranford' the most notable of
the novels."

6   ANON. "May Day at Knutsford," Faces and Places (Manchester),
n.s. V (May), 171.
Apart from its ancient history, Knutsford has "modern"
interest as "the resting-place" of Gaskell.

7   ANON. "Minor Books and New Editions," Glasgow Herald
(20 September), p. 10.
"... The precise place of" Gaskell "in English literature still remains in some respects...debatable," though it
is, "in any case, a unique one." If she lacked the "intensity" of Charlotte Brontë and the intellectual "range"
and "imagination" of George Eliot, Gaskell surpassed them
both "in breadth of human sympathy" and "patient realism."
She was "one of the greatest" of "humanitarian novelists."

8   ANON. "Minor Books and New Editions," Glasgow Herald
(1 November), p. 10.
In North and South, just republished in the Knutsford
edition, we find a "less zealous" companion to Mary Barton,

yet Ward's introduction "acquits" Gaskell of trying to "balance" her previous criticism of employers "by showing what could" be said in their favor.

9   ANON. "Minor Books and New Editions," Glasgow Herald (13 December), p. 12.
         The final "volume of the Knutsford edition...contains Wives and Daughters," which is, "as the introduction states, 'the most artistically perfect of all'" Gaskell's "'productions'."

10   ANON. "Mrs. Gaskell's Novels," Yorkshire Weekly Post (Leeds) (29 September), p. 4.
         The Knutsford edition is an important "literary event," particularly "for North-country folk." Gaskell was more serene than the "enigmatical" Charlotte Brontë and the intellectual George Eliot. It is too bad that this edition does not include The Life of Charlotte Brontë. Cranford "remains" Gaskell's "most popular" book, and Wives and Daughters is "the deepest and best."

11   ANON. "Mrs. Gaskell. The Works of Mrs. Gaskell,..." Academy (London), LXXI (24 November), 519-20.
         Gaskell deserves to be known by her "more serious" novels as well as by her comic masterpiece Cranford, so "we welcome" the Knutsford edition. Gaskell always wrote in "a seeing-beauty spirit," yet she could also face ugliness and evil. Her sense of humor, Gaskell's greatest quality, gave her a more "balanced insight" into her characters than we find in the bitter George Eliot, the individualistic Brontës, the grotesque Dickens, the brilliant Disraeli, the laborious Trollope, or the sneering Thackeray. Gaskell expresses "the quiet beauty of Victorian life" and what was "highest and noblest" in it, including its sense of family.

12   ANON. National Home Reading Union (London), XVIII (November), 60.
         As J.[ohn] A.[lbert] Green has pointed out to us, we were wrong on page 22 of our September issue about Mary Barton's being published in 1844; it was written from 1845-47 and published in 1848.

13   ANON. "New Editions," Guardian (London), LXI, part II (19 September), 1526.
         The first volume of Gaskell's works in the Knutsford edition, Mary Barton and Other Tales, has a "neat and convenient" format and "clear and good" print.

1906

14   ANON. "New Editions," Guardian (London), LXI, part II
     (26 September), 1563.
          "We have already called attention to the great merit of"
     the Knutsford edition of Gaskell's works, now in its
     second volume with Cranford and Other Tales.

15   ANON. "New Editions," Guardian (London), LXI, part II
     (10 October), 1058.
          "Volume III of the 'Knutsford' edition of" Gaskell's
     "works comprises Ruth and several short pieces in one or
     two of which--notably in 'Cumberland Sheep-shearers'--
     the writer's charm makes itself felt not less than in the
     more sustained efforts...."

16   ANON. "Some New Editions. Mrs. Gaskell Sympathetically
     Edited,..." New York Times Saturday Review of Books
     (15 December), p. 878.
          Readers who are not "literary specialists" know Gaskell
     only for Mary Barton and The Life of Charlotte Brontë and
     neglect the many other fine novels and stories "with a not
     too-intruding moral point.... No one interested in the
     early Victorian novel" can "deny that her force in letters,
     plaintive and gentle though it was, demands some permanent
     recognition and record," such as is provided by the Knuts-
     ford edition.

17   ANON. "Some Social Movements as Reflected in Novels. North
     and South,..." National Home Reading Union. General Course
     Magazine (London), XVIII (September), 22--24.
          Gaskell was shocked by the contrast between happy little
     Knutsford and the misery of Manchester in difficult eco-
     nomic times. Mary Barton, with its plea for "patience and
     sympathy" for the working poor, shares ideas with Lord
     Shaftesbury, Bright, Cobden, Carlyle, Maurice, Kingsley,
     and "the more thoughtful of the Chartists." Yet Gaskell
     wished to be "a peacemaker," and her North and South
     strives for full impartiality between capital and labor.

18   AXON, WILLIAM E. A. "Mrs. Gaskell," Bookman (London), XXXI
     (November), 75-78.
          Ward's introductions to the Knutsford edition of Gas-
     kell's works make up, in part, for the lack of a biography
     on her. Gaskell's social-problem novels are memorable, and
     her Cranford is delightful.

19   BENJAMIN, LEWIS S. [LEWIS MELVILLE]. "Mrs. Gaskell," in
     Victorian Novelists. London: Archibald Constable & Co.,
     pp. 204-23.

In spite of Gaskell's moving social sympathy in Mary Barton, most of its characters are "lay figures", and its plot is melodramatic. North and South is more objective about capital and labor and has better construction and characterization. Wives and Daughters "makes up for a certain weakness of construction by...excellent characterization." Sylvia's Lovers, a tale of a great wrong redeemed by expiation, has been underrated. Cranford is Gaskell's one "masterpiece."

20 [COLERIDGE, MARY ELIZABETH]. "Mrs. Gaskell," TLS (14 September), 312-13. [Reprinted almost in entirety in Mary E.(lizabeth) Coleridge. "Mrs. Gaskell," in Gathered Leaves from the Prose of Mary E. Coleridge. London: Constable. New York: E. P. Dutton & Co., 1910, pp. 186-93.]
    The Knutsford edition is disappointing on account of its overly "thin" paper, the absence of The Life of Charlotte Brontë, and a lack of new information in the introductions. Less poetic than Charlotte Brontë and less "analytical" than George Eliot, Gaskell surpassed them both in her "special graces of womanhood" and her "innate gift of story-telling." Her "Christian...compassion," more than that of any other English writer, is comparable to the quality in Tolstoy's novels. Her choice of "an assassin" for a central figure in Mary Barton was "more daring" than that of any other Victorian novelist. We could not have told from Mary Barton that Gaskell would write the "enchanting" portrait of spinsterhood in Cranford, the equally fine My Lady Ludlow, and the splendid portrayal of a doctor in Wives and Daughters. Gaskell's "old maids," such as Miss Galindo, "are as inexhaustable as Rembrandt's Jews."

21 DAWSON, A. P. "Letters to the Editor. Mrs. Gaskell's Novels," Spectator (London), XCVII (6 October), 490.
    The reviewer of the Knutsford edition is mistaken in thinking that Gaskell's works have been largely out of print. Smith & Elder put out an eight-volume pocket edition, and there are many editions of individual works.

22 HARRISON, ALICE B. "A Romance of the Cheshire Cheese," Century (New York), n.s. L (September), 709.
    [A fictional character is talking:] Cranford, Boswell's Johnson, and Alice in Wonderland are my three favorite books. "When I spend an hour in the genteel society of Cranford, I come back to actualities as reluctantly as one comes into the glare of mid-day after a morning in an old attic."

1906

23   H.[ERFORD], C. H.   "Mrs. Gaskell," Manchester Guardian
      (4 September), p. 5.
          Though Gaskell is usually ranked below George Eliot,
      this Knutsford edition is a sign of Gaskell's surviving
      high reputation. She wrote about the working classes with
      more "intimate sympathy" than either Dickens or Disraeli.
      Of interest in Ward's introduction is the letter from
      Gaskell to W. R. Greg's daughter apologizing excessively
      for Mary Barton, in view of Greg's criticism.

24   JONES, DORA M.   "Mrs. Gaskell and Her Books," African Monthly
      (Capetown), I (December), 31-38.
          Gaskell's finest works are Cranford, Cousin Phillis,
      and Wives and Daughters. Her "work as a novelist falls
      into two divisions": social-problem novels, admirable but
      artistically immature, and novels in which she "let herself
      go" and avoided didactic social issues.

25   NEWCOMER, ALPHONSO GERALD. English Literature. Chicago:
      Scott, Foresman & Co., pp. 334, 335, 406.
          "Among the popular writers of the middle of the century
      ...may be noted" Gaskell, "the author of various realistic
      tales, not unlike Maria Edgeworth's, several of which,"
      including Mary Barton and Cranford, "have become fairly
      classic."

26   RITCHIE, MRS. [ANNE THACKERAY, later LADY RITCHIE].   "Black-
      stick Papers. No. 11. Mrs. Gaskell," Cornhill Magazine
      (London), n.s. XXI (December), 757-66. [Reprinted as "The
      Author of Cranford," in Putnam's Monthly (New York), I
      (December 1906), 345-52; also reprinted in Blackstick
      Papers. London: Smith, Elder & Co., 1908, pp. 222-46.]
          Gaskell was gifted at friendship, full of "good sense,"
      "bright intuitions," and had "extraordinary ability" in
      everything she did. She sent a "motherly letter" of in-
      vitation on the death of my father. Wives and Daughters
      was her "most mature and lovable" book. One of her daugh-
      ters said that Gaskell wrote an outline of her novels in
      advance and then "kept to her plans." Unlike George Eliot
      or Mrs. Oliphant, who hold themselves at a distance from
      their characters, Gaskell identifies closely with hers.
      She "poured" into her fiction what she had experienced and
      observed. Her Life of Charlotte Brontë will endure be-
      cause it recreates the "landscape" and "atmosphere" of
      Miss Brontë's life. Gaskell wrote "to make people happier"
      but also "to teach the truth."

27 SAMPSON, GEORGE. "Books of the Day. A Herald of Labour. Mary Barton and Cranford, in the Knutsford Edition,..." Daily Chronicle The Clerkenwell News and Evening Chronicle (London) (22 September), p. 3.

An historian researching the rise of the machine operative could find "important material" about "how he lived and...worked" in Gaskell's fiction. Readers of Cranford knew that she was tender hearted, so it "is no wonder that" in the struggle "between capital and labour she cast herself whole-heartedly upon the side that suffered." Apart from Gaskell's social "indignation," she had a "peculiar penetrating simplicity" as "a story-teller, though" she does not belong in "the first rank of novelists, and scarcely even in the second." Yet in the sweet, gentle Cranford, Gaskell "can challenge all her rivals and beat them."

28 SECCOMBE, THOMAS, and W. ROBERTSON NICOLL. The Bookman Illustrated History of English Literature. London: Hodder & Stoughton. II, 492.

Cranford had "very little plot,...no serious purpose, and none of the melodramatic shadow...of Mary Barton...and ...Ruth,...but the milieu of Cranford exactly suited" Gaskell's "peculiar faculty." Her Life of Charlotte Brontë is a classic, and her Sylvia's Lovers shows "an enhanced ripeness of humour and maturity of style. And these qualities are even more manifest in...Wives and Daughters."

29 SHORTER, CLEMENT K. Charlotte Brontë and Her Sisters. London: Hodder & Stoughton, pp. vii, 13, 26, 28, 35, 36, 99–100, 109, 110, 139, 165, 176, 177, 179–81, 190, 199, 214, 215–17, 232, 242–43.

It is "in a measure true" that Gaskell "wrote the only life of Charlotte that everyone should read,...but much new material has been published since" Gaskell "wrote." She was prejudiced against the Rev. Nicholls by Ellen Nussey's biased account of him. Gaskell's "beautiful" biography has been read by some "who have never read the" Brontë "novels."

30 _____. "Introduction," in Mary Barton. The Novels and Tales of Mrs. Gaskell, I. World's Classics, LXXXVI. London: Henry Frowde, Oxford University Press, pp. v–ix.

Gaskell "expressed deep regret when she learned that living members of the Ashton family had been pained" by the resemblance of the murder of young Carson to that of Thomas Ashton.

1906

31 SHORTER, CLEMENT [K.]. "Introduction," in Ruth. The Novels
and Tales of Mrs. Gaskell, II. The World's Classics,
LXXXVIII. London: Henry Frowde, Oxford University Press,
pp. v-ix.
The willingness of Charlotte Brontë to delay the publication of Villette until Ruth came out contrasts "with
to-day, when books by well-known writers jostle one another
ruthlessly." Gaskell is less passionate but saner than
Villette. George Eliot's belief that Ruth, though good,
would not endure as a classic shows that she "had no
special distinction as a critic."

32 SICHEL, EDITH. The Life and Letters of Alfred Ainger.
New York: E. P. Dutton & Co., pp. 279-80.
[Letter from George Du Maurier to Alfred Ainger, early
1896:] When you are at Whitby tell your nieces "to walk
along the cliffs, westward from the Spa, through fields
and over stiles till they reach Sylvia Robson's cottage
(of course they know their Sylvia's Lovers by heart)...."

33 SIMONDS, WILLIAM EDWARD. "Introduction," in Cranford.
Standard English Classics. Boston: Ginn & Co., pp. ix-
xxiii.
Gaskell's earlier novels, except for Cranford, tend to
be sad, but her later work is more "cheerful" and done
"with a lighter touch." She is possibly underestimated as
a writer at present. Cranford is a series of "sketches"
rather than a novel, but it has an "essential unity"
provided by recurring references. The "confessions" of
the narrator, not identified until chapter fourteen as
Mary Smith, remind one of The Essays of Elia. Gaskell was
influenced by Jane Austen, Maria Edgeworth, and particularly by Mary Russell Mitford, though an element of Dickens
was always present.

34 TOLLEMACHE, LIONEL ARTHUR. "Letter to the Editor. Lady
Cumnor in Wives and Daughters," Spectator (London), XCVII
(6 October), 490.
The model for Lady Cumnor was the mother-in-law of my
own mother-in-law, the first Lady Egerton of Tatton.

35 WARD, [SIR] A.[DOLPHUS] W.[ILLIAM]. "Editor's Preface.
Biographical Introduction. Introduction," in Mary Barton
and Other Tales. The Knutsford Edition, I. New York:
G. P. Putnam's Sons. London: Smith, Elder, & Co.,
pp. xi-lxxvii.
"In the introductions it has been sought to avoid an
expository kind of criticism of which few authors have ever

stood less in need...." Gaskell "never dwelt in extremes" as a writer. She began as one of the most important didactic writers on social questions, but her finest work resulted when she left didacticism. Her "distinctive quality...is her sweet serenity of soul." In her preface to Mary Barton, Gaskell disclaimed "knowledge" of economics, but she had, in fact, "read Adam Smith." Mary Barton's "ethical" message is deeply moving: Gaskell never "surpassed" the book "in mere power of narrative."

36 _____. "Introduction,..." in Cranford and Other Tales. The Knutsford Edition, II. New York: G. P. Putnam's Sons. London: Smith, Elder, & Co., pp. vii-xxxiv.
    Cranford is still the most popular of Gaskell's "works," though Cranford's "pathos" is excelled by that in Mary Barton, and Cranford's "humour" by that in Wives and Daughters. Cranford is a cross between a "short tale" and an "essay." The closest precursers of Gaskell's "sympathetic humour" are the novels of Miss Edgeworth, Galt's Annals of the Parish, and the poetry of Crabbe. Gaskell once told George Smith of a plan to write a "Cranford Abroad" and to "'send Miss Pole'" into foreign parts "'to write letters to Miss Matty'."

37 _____. "Introduction,..." in My Lady Ludlow and Other Tales. The Knutsford Edition, V. London: Smith, Elder, Co. New York: G. P. Putnam's Sons, pp. xi-xxvii.
    The interest of this collection of tales lies in its diversity. Gaskell's use of a frame story has a special interest because of its Edinburgh setting. My Lady Ludlow is almost one of Gaskell's major stories but is marred by having too much crammed into short space.

38 _____. "Introduction,..." in North and South. The Knutsford Edition, IV. New York: G. P. Putnam's Sons. London: Smith, Elder, & Co., pp. ix-xxvi.
    North and South is "one of the finest of modern English fictions." Gaskell's happy domestic life "helped to mature her in the knowledge of men's and women's hearts." She was now "wiser" about industrial relations than in Mary Barton, but also working conditions had improved since the earlier novel. We have also the theme of the conflict between the manufacturing North and the rural South. But Gaskell had too much "humour" and "serenity" ever to have shared the prejudice of Margaret against the North. North and South has an "almost faultless" "construction" and one of the most charming heroines in fiction.

39   WARD, [SIR] A.[DOLPHUS] W.[ILLIAM]. "Introduction,..." in
      Ruth. The Knutsford Edition, III. London: Smith, Elder &
      Co. New York: G. P. Putnam's Son, pp. ix-xxxii.
          Though the novel, which may have owed some of its pathos
      to Crabbe's "Ruth" in Tales of the Hall, shocked many, its
      treatment of a seduced woman was eloquently defended by a
      number of eminent Victorians. In spite of flaws of plot,
      the novel's handling of character and setting is splendid.
      The conclusion is justified by Gaskell's didactic purpose.

40   _____. "Introduction,..." in Sylvia's Lovers, etc. The
      Knutsford Edition, VI. London: Smith, Elder, Co.
      New York: G. P. Putnam's Sons, pp. xi-xxxiii.
          Less "popular" than Cranford, Sylvia's Lovers is never-
      theless "one of the most fascinating of" Gaskell's novels,
      and she took great pains with it, even rewriting the scene
      in which Kinraid returns after Sylvia's marriage. Yet the
      second half of the novel is a disappointment. The portrait
      of Whitby is memorable. The old and hated system of im-
      pressment is central to the novel, which may have been in-
      fluenced by Crabbe's "Ruth" in Tales of the Hall. Gaskell's
      one mistake, of having "the counsel for the defence" make
      "a speech for the prisoner," Daniel, which would not have
      been permitted, was eliminated in later editions. Most
      memorable is the story's insight into the human heart.

41   _____. "Introduction,..." in Wives and Daughters. The Knuts-
      ford Edition, VIII. New York: G. P. Putnam's Sons.
      London: Smith, Elder, & Co., pp. xi-xxx.
          Wives and Daughters is "the most artistically perfect"
      of Gaskell's works, and, in it, we see her "genius" "fully
      developed." Wives and Daughters has the "humour" and
      "pathos" of earlier books plus the "irony" of Sylvia's
      Lovers and Cousin Phillis. Tentative titles were "Molly
      and Cynthia" and "Mr. Gibson's Daughters" before the less
      appropriate Wives and Daughters was settled upon. When
      Gaskell feared that the serialization "'was getting'" too
      "'long'," she toyed with the idea of not concluding the
      Molly-Roger "'love-story'" till another novel. "Molly...is
      perhaps the loveliest conception" in Gaskell's fiction, the
      "fascinating" and "irresistible" Cynthia is unique among
      Gaskell's characters, and the comic figure Clare might have
      been "envied" by Thackeray. The plot of Wives and Daugh-
      ters is better constructed than that of any other of the
      writer's novels.

42   _____. "Prefatory Note. Introduction,..." in Cousin Phillis
      and Other Tales. The Knutsford Edition, VII. New York:

G. P. Putnam's Sons. London: Smith, Elder, & Co.,
pp. xi-xliii.
     Of all of Gaskell's "shorter stories," <u>Cousin Phillis</u>
"most nearly" approaches "literary perfection." All the
characters except the intruder Holdsworth have the "homely
charm" of "simplicity," and particularly Phillis herself.
The inconclusive ending is an artistic virtue. The writer's
"Lois the Witch" has the quality of classic tragedy, with
"fate" playing a major role. Gaskell and her husband had
been present at a "country-house" in Essex, when their
"magistrate" "host" saved an accused witch.

1907 A BOOKS - NONE

1907 B SHORTER WRITINGS

1   ANON. "Bookmarker's Notes," <u>Manchester City News</u> (2 March),
     p. 2.
          Shorter points out in his "introduction" to "a new
     edition" of <u>Cranford</u> that Dickens made Gaskell alter a
     reference from "Boz" to Hood.

2   ANON. "The British Novel as an Institution. The Works of
     Mrs. Gaskell,..." <u>Edinburgh Review</u>, CCVI (July), 110-27.
          The English novel--at present judged on aesthetic and
     mimetic grounds--until recently was also judged by its
     "moral" fitness for the young. "The two writers" who
     "best" epitomize "the English novel at its full develop-
     ment" are Trollope and Gaskell. Gaskell's early novels
     are clearly didactic, with the exception of her charming
     and famous <u>Cranford</u>. <u>North and South</u>, with its moral
     judgments of industrial and love problems, shows "the
     English novel at its best and most typical development."
     Although <u>Cousin Phillis</u> is another exception as a touching
     idyll, <u>Sylvia's Lovers</u> shows Gaskell's ability to make
     fair judgments about passion. Even her humorous master-
     piece <u>Wives and Daughters</u> warns young readers of the dan-
     gers of heartless flirtation through its portrayal of the
     delightful but unreliable Cynthia. With the exception of
     Hardy, who has tried to depict life without moral didac-
     ticism, most English novelists still work within the same
     moral tradition as Gaskell.

3   ANON. "Clergy Favor <u>Mary Barton</u>," <u>New York Times</u> (24 June),
     p. 4.
          Clergymen protest the London County Council's banning of
     <u>Mary Barton</u> and argue that any "child" "intelligent enough"

1907

(ANON.)
    to "select" it would also have the discrimination to bene-
    fit from it.

4   ANON. "Cranford Once More," Manchester City News (7 December),
     p. 4.
         Gaskell's works have "a special appeal" for "us in
     Northern England," and her "literary legacy...cannot be too
     highly estimated." Her Cranford is sweet and good.

5   ANON. "Gaskell Memorial at Knutsford," Daily Dispatch
     (Manchester) (29 March), p. 7.
         "One of the literary events of the year is" the opening
     of Knutsford's seventy-foot-high Memorial Tower in honor
     of Gaskell, "the distinguished woman novelist."

6   ANON. "The Literary Week [Editorial]," Academy (London),
     LXXII (22 June), 595.
         The London County Council's discussion of banning Mary
     Barton from elementary schools is ridiculous. The book is
     "scarcely a classic" and need not be required reading, but
     it "is an excellent standard novel" that should be read if
     the children's parents approve. If Mary Barton is immoral,
     so are the Holy Scriptures.

7   ANON. "London County Council.... Mrs. Gaskell's Mary Barton,"
     Times (London) (19 June), p. 8.
         "The Education Committee" recommended that Gaskell's
     Mary Barton "be removed from the" school "requisition list"
     and from all "public elementary school libraries" as un-
     suitable for young boys and girls. The Rev. Stewart Headlam
     defended the book as "one of the finest classical novels in
     the English language," but "the recommendation of the com-
     mittee was adopted."

*8   ANON. Manchester City News (2 March).
         [A "Knutsford correspondent" writes:] In contradiction
     to your contention that a copy of Cranford cannot be found
     in Knutsford, I found it at two "stationers" and "two branch
     circulation libraries." The town has a "Cranford Avenue,...
     a 'Cranford Cafe'," its school "children" "act scenes from"
     Cranford, and picture postcards show where Gaskell's grave
     is. [Unlocatable. Source: Gaskell Cuttings, Manchester
     Central Library.]

9   ANON. "Mary Barton Banned. Not Fit for Children of Fourteen,"
     Manchester Evening Chronicle (19 June), p. 5.

The recommendation of the Education Committee of the
London County Council to ban Mary Barton from public elementary schools, though opposed by the Rev. Stewart Headlam,
was "adopted."

10   ANON. "Mary Barton as a School Book," Yorkshire Post (Leeds)
      (9 May), p. 6.
         By a vote of fourteen to ten, "Mary Barton was taken off
      the list of school literary books by the London Education
      Committee yesterday...." It was charged that the story's
      riots "are too exciting for children, that it suggests
      trade unionism, and that it has reference to immorality,"
      but some speakers seemed, in fact, to believe that "London
      street children live in dreams of idyllic purity and happi-
      ness." The Rev. Stewart Headlam defended the book by saying
      that "children who had to lead the lives of working people's
      children were the better for reading in beautiful language
      about the things with which they are...very familiar."

11   ANON. "Memorial to Mrs. Gaskell at Knutsford," Cheshire Notes
      and Queries [reprinted from Stockport Advertiser] (Stock-
      port), n.s. VII, 198-200.
         Knutsford's tourist trade owes a great deal to Gaskell's
      writings, yet the town has done "little to show...its ap-
      preciation of the gifted writer." R. H. Watt's new Gaskell
      Memorial Tower is, at last, a fitting tribute.

12   ANON. "Memorial to Mrs. Gaskell at Knutsford," Knutsford and
      Northwich Advertiser and East and Mid Cheshire Gazette
      (22 March), p. 4.
         The Gaskell Memorial Tower, "designed and built by R. H.
      Watt," is an impressive and appropriate tribute to Gaskell.

13   ANON. "Mrs. Gaskell and Mary Barton," T. P.'s Weekly (London),
      IX (28 June), 804.
         Concerning the London County Council's banning of Mary
      Barton from elementary schools, one must ask "what did that
      most moral writer" Gaskell "do that she should be condemned
      thus?" Mary Barton "couldn't harm even a fourteen-year-old
      girl.... The foolishness and banality of much modern fic-
      tion are infinitely more injurious than anything in" Gas-
      kell's honest description of factory life.

14   ANON. "Mrs. Gaskell. Memorial Tower at Knutsford. Opening
      by Vice-Chancellor Hopkinson," Knutsford Guardian
      (30 March), p. 6.
         Many speeches were made at the opening of the Gaskell
      Memorial Tower praising Gaskell and her works of literature.

1907

15   ANON. "Notes," Nation (New York), LXXX (7 March), 221.
"None of our English novelists has been more pleasantly
and adequately presented than" Gaskell "in the Knutsford
edition...."

16   ANON. In Nouveau Larousse illustré: dictionnaire universel
encyclopédique. S.v. "Gaskell, Elizabeth Cleghorn."
Gaskell's novels belong to the realistic and humanitarian school of Dickens and George Eliot. Gaskell is
capable of a gentle mockery, and her pity for the poor
keeps her social-problem novels from becoming too dry.

17   ANON. "The Office Window," Daily Chronicle Clerkenwell News
and Evening Chronicle (London) (9 May), p. 4. [Reprinted
as "Mary Barton Banned," in Manchester Evening News
(9 May 1907), p. 3.]
The banning of Mary Barton from "school libraries" by
the Education Committee of the London County Council re-
vives the "controversy" of 1848, when opponents "declared"
the book socially unsettling. This renowned novel by "a
London woman...is now pronounced unfit for the boys and
girls of London."

18   ANON. "Opening of the Gaskell Memorial Tower. Knutsford
Honors the Author of Cranford. Some Appreciations of Mrs.
Gaskell," Knutsford and Northwich Advertiser and East and
Mid Cheshire Gazette (29 March), p. 8.
"The Gaskell Memorial Tower was opened...by the Vice-
Chancellor of the Manchester University, Principal Hopkin-
son," and many eulogies to Gaskell were delivered.

19   ANON. "Popular Novel Banned," Daily Chronicle Clerkenwell
News and Evening Chronicle (London) (19 June), p. 5.
"The latest pose of the Moderate majority" on the London
County Council "is that of censor," for "the Education
Committee recommended that" Mary Barton be banned from ele-
mentary schools. The Rev. Stewart Headlam said that such
a ban would make the Council look "ridiculous." "Mr.
Taylor made a very feeble defence" of his committee's ac-
tion, and six of his party "deserted him on the vote," yet
the recommendation carried.

20   ANON. "Supplement. The Gaskell Memorial at Knutsford,"
Knutsford and Northwich Advertiser (22 March), a single
inserted sheet.
[Cited by Green (1911.A2), this item contains nothing
but two pictures.]

21   ANON. "Topics of the Week," <u>New York Times Saturday Review</u>
      <u>of Books</u> (29 June), p. 416.
         It is absurd that the London County Council has found
      Gaskell's <u>Mary Barton</u> "not fit for general reading," for
      it "is one of the finest and sweetest stories in the
      language."

22   CASH, SARAH. "Mrs. Gaskell and Knutsford," <u>Manchester City</u>
      <u>News</u> (23 February), p. 8.
         The woman who dressed the sick cow in a flannel jacket,
      as portrayed in <u>Cranford</u>, "was a relative of" mine, and
      the model for Dr. Hoggins was "my grandmother's doctor."

23   GREEN, JOHN ALBERT. <u>Catalogue of the Gleave Brontë Collection</u>
      <u>at the Moss Side Free Library, Manchester</u>. Manchester:
      the Moss Side Free Library.
         [Contains a number of secondary items referring to
      Gaskell.]

24   JOHNSON, R.[EGINALD] BRIMLEY. "Introduction," in <u>Cranford</u>.
      London: Chatto & Windus, pp. ix-xx. [Reprinted in
      R.(eginald) Brimley Johnson. <u>The Women Novelists</u>. London:
      W. Collins Sons & Co., 1918, pp. 152-63.]
         Gaskell "must always be remembered as authoress of
      <u>Cranford</u>, which has startling similarities to the work of
      Jane Austen and excells her in pathos." Gaskell was "the
      Apologist of Gentility." She "is frankly feminine, and not
      superior to the small details of parochial gossip." In
      spite of an apparent formlessness, <u>Cranford</u> is actually
      "composed with an almost perfect sense of dramatic unity"
      around the character of Matty.

25   LEIRION [pseud.]. "Cranford [reply to 10th ser. VII, 188,
      235]," <u>N & Q</u>, 10th ser. VII (6 April), 273.
         "The story of Sidi Nouman and Aminê," alluded to in
      <u>Cranford</u>, can be found in Edward Forster's translation of
      <u>The Arabian Nights</u>. [<u>See</u> 1907.B37, 1907.B41.]

26   MAGNUS, LAURIE. <u>How to Read English Literature. II: Dryden</u>
      <u>to Meredith</u>. London: George Routledge & Sons. New York:
      E. P. Dutton & Co., p. 276.
         Gaskell was the "author of <u>Cranford</u>, the tenderest study
      of a society composed chiefly of maiden ladies, and author,
      too, of a life of her more brilliant contemporary Charlotte
      Brontë."

27   A Man of Kent. "Rambling Remarks. Mrs. Gaskell Once More,"
      <u>British Weekly</u> (London), XLII (25 April), 61.

1907

(A Man of Kent)
"Like other recent writers on" Gaskell, Paul Elmer More
in the Nation (New York) does not recognize the flaws in
Sylvia's Lovers. Sylvia is a bad "specimen of womanhood"
and also "unreal," particularly in the concluding section.

28 M. G. "New Books. Mrs. Gaskell," Manchester Guardian
(10 January), p. 5.
Wives and Daughters, the last volume of the Knutsford
edition, was Gaskell's "most perfect novel." Ward's introductions are the most important criticisms yet written on
Gaskell's works, for they unite "intimacy" with a discrimi-
nating "temper." This writer "made literature not out of
literature but out of life." She saw both rural and industrial England as valid ways of life.

29 M.[ORE], P.[AUL] E.[LMER]. "Mrs. Gaskell," Nation (New York),
LXXXIV (11 April), 331-33. [Reprinted as "Literary News
and Reviews. The New Edition of Mrs. Gaskell,..." in
Evening Post (New York) (13 April 1907), Saturday Supplement, p. 6; also reprinted in Paul Elmer More. Shelburne
Essays. 5th ser. New York and London: G. P. Putnam's
Sons, the Knickerbocker Press, 1908, pp. 66-85.]
"There is...nothing recondite in either the beauties or
the limitations of" Gaskell's "genius." Though many readers know Cranford and "some" Wives and Daughters, her
other works are also very worthwhile: Ruth, with its
"pathos"; Mary Barton and North and South, with their
"deeper pity"; My Lady Ludlow, with its "mingled satire
and regret"; and those "riper" books, Sylvia's Lovers, with
its "humble tragedy," and "the flawless...Cousin Phillis."
Unlike later writers such as Gissing, Gaskell preached
reconciliation between rich and poor.

30 PANCOAST, HENRY S. An Introduction to English Literature.
3rd ed., enlarged. New York: Henry Holt & Co., p. 557.
Gaskell's Cranford "is a masterly study of the little
world of English provincial life." She "is further remembered for" works, such as Mary Barton, that are "of a
more tragic and powerful order than the quaint and pathetic
...Cranford."

31 PAYNE, [REV.] GEORGE A. "Cranford: Mrs. Gaskell's Connection
with Knutsford," Manchester City News (16 February), p. 2.
Gaskell was married in the Parish Church, because marriage could not be performed "in Nonconformist chapels
until 1836." She wished to be buried at Knutsford largely
because so many of her family were buried there.

32 SHORTER, CLEMENT [K.]. "Introduction," in Cranford. The Cage
    at Cranford. The Moorland Cottage. The Novels and Tales
    of Mrs. Gaskell, III. The World's Classics, CX. London:
    Henry Frowde, Oxford University Press, pp. v-xiii.
        "The Cage at Cranford," a late work, "is equal, if not
    superior to certain of the other sketches" in the original
    Cranford. Gaskell's Cranford is a town rather than the com-
    munity of a half dozen houses in Miss Mitford's Our Village.
    In contrast to Jane Austen's and George Eliot's "tart"
    "humour," Gaskell's comedy is "entirely kindly"--a quality
    unique among women novelists.

33 _____. "A Literary Letter," Sphere (London), XXX (20 July),
    68.
        Brook Street Chapel, of Knutsford, "depicted" in Ruth
    as the Rev. Benson's chapel, remains unchanged to this day.

34 _____. "Lord Acton's List of the Hundred Best Books," in
    Immortal Memories. London: Hodder & Stoughton, p. 270.
        [Shorter includes Cranford among the twenty-five best
    works of fiction in his own list of one hundred books "for
    English boys and girls just growing into manhood and woman-
    hood, or for those who have had no educational advantage in
    early years."]

35 _____. Sphere (London), XXIX (13 April), 46.
        "The Cage at Cranford" appears for the first time in
    book form in the World's Classics edition of Cranford.

36 THOMAS, REV. E. L. H., ed. Illustrations of Cross Street
    Chapel: the First Home of Nonconformity in Manchester,
    with Short Descriptive Notes. Manchester: H. Rawson & Co.,
    n. pag.
        [Contains photographs of a memorial tablet to Mrs.
    Gaskell and one to her husband.]

37 T. J. H. "Cranford," N & Q, 10th ser. VII (9 March), 188.
        "What is the allusion...in chap. iv of 'Cranford'" to
    "Aminé at her grains of rice after her previous feast with
    the Ghoul?" [Editor's answer: It apparently refers "to
    the second tale in the 'Arabian Nights'," though pomegranate
    seeds are mentioned there rather than rice grains.] [See
    1907.B25, 1907.B41.]

38 TOZIER, JOSEPHINE. "A Day in Cranford," Putnam's Monthly
    (New Rochelle, New York), II (September), 643-54.
        I made a pilgrimage to Knutsford in honor of "the lovable
    spirit, the gentle genius, whose amiable wit" gave us

1907

(TOZIER, JOSEPHINE)
Cranford, which "shall...endure while English literature
lasts."

39 Whitby Visitor. "Sylvia's Lovers. To the Editor,..."
Standard (London) (12 July), p. 10.
Readers of Sylvia's Lovers will "regret that the old
shop of Bridge Street, Monkshaven (Whitby), the scene of
much of the novel," is to be torn down "for harbour
improvements."

40 WROOT, H. E. "The Late Rev. A. B. Nicholls," Brontë Society
Transactions (Bradford), IV, part xvi (March), 16-17.
Mr. Nicholls's "implicit disapproval" of Gaskell's Life
of Charlotte Brontë came from his belief that she under-
valued Patrick Brontë and not from "any supposed slight to
himself."

41 YARDLEY, E. "Cranford [reply to 10th ser. VII, 188]," N & Q,
10th ser. VII (23 March), 235.
The Cranford allusion "is to 'Sidi Nouman'," a "later"
story from The Arabian Nights, probably not in Lane's
translation. Aminé eats some rice grains and then meets
"a female ghoul." [See 1907.B25, 1907.B37.]

1908 A BOOKS - NONE

1908 B SHORTER WRITINGS

1 ANON. In Brockhaus' Konversations-Lexikon. Leipzig: F. A.
Brockhaus. S.v. "Gaskell, Elizabeth Cleghorn."
Gaskell was observant, skilled at characterization, and
had a noble style. Her gentle humor is revealed in
Cranford, Cousin Phillis, and even in her social-problem
novels. Her style is particularly impressive in her Life
of Charlotte Brontë.

2 ANON. "A Brontë Link Severed," Manchester City News
(31 October), p. 6.
Miss Julia Gaskell's death focuses "the attention of all
who love literature on her house," a literary shrine as "the
home" of her mother, Mrs. Gaskell. Charlotte Brontë particularly liked Julia as a child for her "fine little
nature," much like her mother's.

3 ANON. Christian Life and Unitarian Herald (London), XXXIV
(5 December), 649.

[Cited by Northup (1929.B6), this article reports on Julia Gaskell's will but does not mention Mrs. Gaskell.]

4   ANON. "Cousin Phillis," Bookman (London), XXXV (November), 98.

    To those who know only the autumnal Cranford, the youthful, lyrical Cousin Phillis will come as a surprise in this reprint forty-five years after its original appearance.

5   ANON. "Cousin Phillis,..." Outlook (London), XXII (21 November), xv.

    The drawings in this new edition of Gaskell's book match the "dainty simplicity" of the story.

6   ANON. "The Late Miss Julia Gaskell," Christian Life (London), XXXIV (14 November), 611-12.

    In a memorial service for Miss Gaskell at the Lower Mosley-Street Schools, Mr. Smith "described her as" coming from a great line of religious dissenters, with a distinguished Unitarian minister for a father and the "gifted" Mrs. Gaskell for a mother.

7   ANON. "Literary Club," Manchester City News (31 October), p. 3.

    The club's president referred to the death of Julia Gaskell, daughter of the famous novelist.

8   ANON. Manchester City News (14 April), p. 2.

    Although Gaskell's wish that no biography be done of her has been up till now adhered to by her family, it appears "that Shorter will have the help of the daughters in preparing" a memoir of Gaskell for the "English Men of Letters series."

*9   ANON. "Mary Barton Defended. Mrs. Gaskell. 'The Literary Genius of Manchester'," Rochdale Observer (February).

    The Rev. Dr. Horton said that, far from banning Mary Barton, as the London County Council did, he would teach it, along with Gaskell's North and South, to show, through the works of Manchester's "literary genius," why residents "love" the city "with a tender homely passion." [Unlocatable. Source: Gaskell Cuttings, Manchester Central Library.]

*10 ANON. "Memories of Plymouth Grove," Woman's World (Chicago) (29 October).

1908

(ANON.)
[Source: Catherine Margaret Ellen Halls. "Bibliography
of Elizabeth C. Gaskell." Diploma in librarianship dissertation, University of London, 1957. See 1957.B5.]

11 ANON. "Miscellany," Manchester Guardian (28 October), p. 5.
"The Brook Street Chapel at Knutsford, where Miss Julia
Gaskell was buried yesterday," has many similarities to the
chapel described by her mother in Ruth.

*12 ANON. "Miss Gaskell's Will," Morning Leader (London)
(14 November).
"Miss Julia Bradford Gaskell,...youngest daughter of Mrs.
Gaskell, the well-known authoress,...left estate valued at
£28,737 gross and £28,300 net." [Unlocatable. Source:
Gaskell Cuttings, Manchester Central Library.]

13 ANON. "Miss Julia Gaskell [Editorial]," Manchester Guardian
(26 October), p. 6.
We deeply regret the loss to Manchester culture by the
death of Miss Julia Gaskell, Mrs. Gaskell's daughter.

14 ANON. "Mrs. Gaskell's 'Life'," T. P.'s Weekly (London), XI
(12 June), 746.
May Sinclair's introduction to this new edition of The
Life of Charlotte Brontë "pays a well-deserved tribute to
this wonderful book."

*15 ANON. "Mrs. Gaskell and Charles Dickens. Literary Assoc.,"
Manchester Guardian (October).
[Unlocatable. Source: Gaskell Cuttings, Manchester
Central Library.]

16 ANON. "Obituary. Miss Julia Gaskell," Inquirer (London),
n.s. no. 566 (31 October), pp. 694-95.
Like her mother, Julia died suddenly, but, unlike Mrs.
Gaskell, whose "strength had failed" and who "left her
last and best book 'Wives and Daughters' unfinished, Miss
Gaskell seemed in good health."

17 AXON, WILLIAM E. A. "'The Heart of John Middleton' [reply to
10th ser. IX, 430]," N & Q, 10th ser. IX (20 June), 493.
This "short story"--"not a novel"--was published by
Gaskell in Household Words (28 December 1856) and was "reprinted with 'Lizzie Leigh' in 1855." "The Heart" is "one
of" Gaskell's "finest" short stories. [See 1908.B25.]

18 BURNHAM, ARCHIBALD MOWBRAY. "Humanitarian Fiction from 1830
      to 1880." Master's thesis, University of Chicago,
      pp. 147-59.
         Gaskell's portrayal of the working-class poor in Mary
      Barton is intuitively "feminine," emphasizes their good
      qualities, and "ends...with a picture of ideal labor
      conditions."

19 CUMMINS, AGNES. "'Pleasure Digging His Own Grave'," N & Q,
      10th ser. X (1 August), 89.
         An engraving with the above name was mentioned in The
      Moorland Cottage as "by a German artist.... Who was he"
      and "where" can "the picture...be found?"

20 HORNE, CHARLES F. The Technique of the Novel: the Elements
      of the Art, Their Evolution and Present Use. New York and
      London: Harper & Brothers, p. 186.
         "Professor Cross has pointed out the genesis of the
      psychological novel in" Gaskell's fiction, but she did not
      have "an immediate influence in introducing psychological
      analysis into the general technique of the novel." [See
      1899.B7.]

21 LEHMANN, R.[UDOLPH] C., M.P., ed. Memories of Half a Century:
      A Record of Friendships. London: Smith, Elder & Co.,
      p. 248.
         [A letter from Frederick Lehmann to Nina Lehmann, 23
      January 1864:] I "talked a good deal to" Gaskell, "the
      authoress."

22 LORNA [pseud.]. "The Woman's World.... The Late Miss Julia
      Gaskell," British Weekly (London), XLV (20 October), 97.
         Julia Gaskell's mother, Mrs. Gaskell, wrote "her books
      in the dining-room," and would break off, when necessary,
      to tend to the children. "The only part of" her "work
      which was done in stricter privacy was that which she
      wrote early in the morning before breakfast. She suf-
      fered from insomnia, and was accustomed to rise early.
      All her" writing "was done before luncheon."

23 A Man of Kent. "Rambling Remarks: Julia Gaskell," British
      Weekly (London), XLV (29 October), 101.
         Julia Gaskell has died in the house at Plymouth Grove
      which, with her sister, she kept as a literary shrine to
      the memory of her mother, Mrs. Gaskell.

24 [MARSHALL, REV. T. L.]. "Notes of an Octogenarian Minister,"
      Christian Life (London), XXXIV (5 December), 647.

1908

([MARSHALL, REV. T. L.])
A recent anecdote in the Guardian (London) told how
"three eminent writers" picked Cranford as "the most perfect novel in...English." I knew Gaskell at "the height
of her fame, and of her sweet matronly beauty...."

25 PEET, W. H. "'The Heart of John Middleton'," N & Q, 10th
ser. IX (30 May), 430.
Who wrote the 1851 "novel [sic]" called "The Heart of
John Middleton?" [See 1908.B17.]

*26 SECCOMBE, THOMAS. "Preface," in Cousin Phillis. London:
George Bell & Sons.
[Source: Clark S. Northup. "A Bibliography," in
Elizabeth Gaskell. By Gerald DeWitt Sanders. New Haven:
Yale University Press, for Cornell University. London:
Humphrey Milford, Oxford University Press, 1929. See
1929.B6.]

27 SHORTER, CLEMENT [K.]. The Brontës: Life and Letters.
New York: Charles Scribner's Sons, see index for references
to Gaskell.
[Most of Shorter's comments about the letters and documents merely reproduce what he said in Charlotte Brontë and
Her Circle (1896.B9).] [Reviewers of Shorter's new Brontë
work tended to divide between those who complained that it
was inferior as literature to Gaskell's Life and those who
praised Shorter for providing a useful supplement to Gas-
kell. See, for example, the following reviews that pre-
ferred Gaskell's Life to Shorter: Anon. Athenaeum
(London), no. 4227 (31 October 1908), 535-36; Anon. Con-
temporary Review (London), XCIV (November 1908), 17; Anon.
Spectator (London), CI (19 December 1908), 1058-59; C. H.
H.(erford). Manchester Guardian (22 October 1908), p. 5.
For examples of pro-Shorter reviews, see the following:
Sir William Robertson Nicoll (Claudius Clear). British
Weekly (London), XLV (29 October 1908), 101; Thomas
Seccombe. Bookman (London), XXXV (December 1908), 152-53.]

28 _____. "Introduction," in North and South. The Novels and
Tales of Mrs. Gaskell, IV. World's Classics, CLIV. London:
Henry Frowde, Oxford University Press, pp. v-vii.
In addition to the themes of industrial conflict and the
conflict between northern and southern England, North and
South's opening section deals with the subject of religious
"questionings."

29 _____. "A Literary Letter.... Julia Gaskell," _Sphere_
(London), XXXV (7 November), x.
Now that Gaskell is gaining a "recognition that was never
hers" during her lifetime or since, it is sad that one of
her daughters has died before full recognition is achieved.

30 SINCLAIR, MAY. "Introduction," in _The Life of Charlotte
Brontë_. Everyman's Library. London: J. M. Dent & Co.
New York: E. P. Dutton & Co., pp. vii-xv.
"No woman who ever wrote was ever so self-effaced as"
Gaskell, the biographer, though her _Wives and Daughters_ and
Cranford are full of her own fascinating personality. _The
Life of Charlotte Brontë_ has the rightness, power, and ob-
jective vision of a great classical tragedy.

31 SMITH, REV. A. COBDEN. _Miss Julia Gaskell, 1846-1908: A
Memorial Address Delivered to the Congregation of the Lower
Mosley Street Sunday School, Manchester, on Sunday Evening,
1st November, 1908._ Manchester: H. Rawson & Co., p. 7.
Julia's mother, Mrs. Gaskell, was associated with the
Sunday School from "about 1832" till her death, and she
found time to teach the girls even during periods when she
was writing her famous novels.

32 STODDART, ANNA M., ed. _Life and Letters of Hannah E. Pipe_.
Edinburgh and London: William Blackwood & Sons, pp. 10-11.
Gaskell wrote _Mary Barton_ "to assert, with all her fine
sympathy and tact, the needs and calls of the cotton
operatives."

33 WALKER, HENRY. "Literary Pilgrimages...Cranford," _Millgate
Monthly_ (Manchester), IV (October), 54-57.
Interest was aroused in the delightful Knutsford by the
publication of _Cranford_, and the town is still little
changed since Gaskell's day.

34 WINKWORTH, SUSANNA and CATHERINE. _Memorials of Two Sisters,
Susanna and Catherine Winkworth_. Edited by Margaret J.
Shaen. London: Longmans, Green, & Co., pp. 23-26, 29-33,
39, 43, 49-50, 55, 98-101, 103-4, 112-15, 122, 132-34, 170.
We became friends with Mrs. Gaskell before she was
famous. She learned much about English literature through
her husband. We were "struck" by her genius, noble appearance, and presence. Emily guessed her authorship of the
anonymous _Mary Barton_.

1909

1909 A   BOOKS - NONE

1909 B   SHORTER WRITINGS

1   ANON. "Miscellaneous. Notes on Books, & C.," N & Q, 10th
    ser. XII (7 August), 119.
        North and South, "one of the books which have a permanent
    hold on readers, has been reissued in the 'World's Clas-
    sics'.... A modern reader...wonders at the sermonizing" of
    the heroine, yet one must remember that Gaskell "lived in
    an exceptionally serious circle." Nevertheless Margaret is
    "one of the most attractive of girls, and, fortunately, not
    perfect."

2   CANBY, HENRY SEIDEL. The Short Story in English. New York:
    Henry Holt & Co., pp. 265, 272-73, 274, 282, 322.
        Because of looseness of technique, Gaskell, like Dickens,
    Thackeray, Eliot, and Trollope, did not write what we,
    nowadays, call a short story, but she, like them, was moving
    toward the form. "Cousin Phillis," her one exception, "is
    a genuine short story, for the gentle artist of Cranford
    has made the serene, yet tragic Phillis emerge as the one
    sum and expression of the whole story." Although the work
    could be cut, cutting would make it "lose...much in over-
    tones."

3   CRAIK, GEORGE LILLIE. Manual of English Literature. London:
    J. M. Dent & Sons. New York: E. P. Dutton & Co., p. 348.
        Gaskell's "Cranford,...a very humorous and tender pre-
    sentation of the lives of provincial old ladies,...presents
    only one phase of the various work of" an "original" writer
    of fiction.

4   J. B. M. "Going A-Maying. The Lancashire and Cheshire
    Revels," Manchester City News (1 May), p. 5.
        [Photograph of Knutsford, with the caption "Knutsford
    (Mrs. Gaskell's 'Cranford') where a great maypole dance
    takes place," but the text itself has no reference to
    Gaskell.]

5   KELLNER, LEON. Die englische Literatur im Zeitalter der
    Königin Viktoria. Leipzig: Bernhard Tauchnitz, pp. 11,
    33, 48, 54, 243, 249, 366-68.
        Mary Barton was a great success less from its art than
    from its subject of industrial strife, of which Gaskell had
    intimate knowledge. Gaskell's My Lady Ludlow is an under-
    valued portrait of an aristocratic lady of the old school.

6   MAGNUS, LAURIE. <u>English Literature in the Nineteenth Century</u>.
     <u>An Essay in Criticism</u>. London: A. Melrose, pp. 253-54.
           Though <u>Mary Barton</u> was praised in its time "as a pathe-
     tic picture of working-class life" and though <u>Sylvia's</u>
     <u>Lovers</u> is "a moving tale of urban and rural characters,"
     Gaskell "is chiefly remembered" today for her "simple,
     humorous" <u>Cranford</u> and her <u>Life of Charlotte Brontë</u>.

*7   PAYNE, [REV.] GEORGE A. "Mrs. Gaskell and Knutsford," <u>Trans-</u>
     <u>actions Burnley Literary and Scientific Club</u>, XXVII, 75-77.
     ["Abstract of a paper read" on 19 October 1909.]
     [Source: Clark S. Northup. "A Bibliography," in <u>Elizabeth</u>
     <u>Gaskell</u>. By Gerald DeWitt Sanders. New Haven: Yale Uni-
     versity Press, for Cornell University. London: Humphrey
     Milford, Oxford University Press, 1929. <u>See</u> 1929.B6.]

8   SHORTER, CLEMENT K. "Introduction," in <u>Sylvia's Lovers</u>. The
     Novels and Tales of Mrs. Gaskell, V. The World's Classics,
     CLVI. London: Henry Frowde, Oxford University Press,
     pp. v-x.
           Gaskell researched the historic Whitby as the basis for
     Monkshaven in her novel. In 1793, as a result of an actual
     riot against a press-gang, "an old man named Atkinson" was
     hung for inciting the rioting sailors. Gaskell drew upon
     Admiralty documents, "the Calendar of felons," and "a
     letter from a woman friend" who remembered a case of re-
     sistance to the press-gang at Hull. Out of spare documents,
     Gaskell recreated an era, in this, her "highest and best"
     novel. It is characteristic of her period that she accepts
     "so passively" those "cruel laws" that condemn Daniel
     Robson to death, but this attitude is the only flaw in the
     novel.

<u>1910 A BOOKS</u>

1   CHADWICK, MRS. [ESTHER ALICE] ELLIS H. <u>Mrs. Gaskell: Haunts</u>,
     <u>Homes, and Stories</u>. London: Sir Isaac Pitman & Sons.
           This book is intended to supplement what is known of
     Gaskell's life, which unfortunately has been limited by
     her wish to have no biography done of her. "All" of Gas-
     kell's "novels are founded on fact, and,...except in
     <u>Sylvia's Lovers</u>, those facts came out of her own life, or
     the lives of her relatives and friends...." "One of"
     Gaskell's "daughters said that her mother was the best
     housekeeper and cook she had ever known...." Gaskell "was
     always more successful with her heroines than with her
     heroes because she could draw from her own life, and she

1910

(CHADWICK, MRS. [ESTHER ALICE] ELLIS H.)
  had the constant companionship of her own daughters...."
  Gaskell, though a Unitarian, learned a sympathy for the
  Church of England services through attending them at Avon-
  bank School. The marriage of Mr. and Mrs. Gaskell was a
  happy one, yet "in all" of her works, there is no "description of a wedding." She, like most Unitarian women, "always dressed very plainly." Gaskell's harsh judgment of
  the Rev. Patrick Brontë must be understood in the framework
  of an implied comparison with her own husband, who devoted
  much time to their children, and her harsh portrayal of
  Haworth as "wild" is clearly in contrast to Knutsford.
  She "might have lived longer if she had been content to
  do less work and had lived more quietly...."
  [Reviews of Chadwick's book included the following,
  along with replying letters to the editor: Anon. "The
  Author of Cranford," Guardian (London), LXV, part II
  (16 September 1910), 1255 (Mrs. Chadwick's writing has a
  heavy touch, yet her book is thorough, and "she has had the
  cooperation of" Gaskell's "surviving daughter and other
  relatives...." We admire Gaskell's works but think her
  success "too sudden" and "popular" for us to be sure of
  her "ultimate worth."). Anon. "Books. Mrs. Gaskell,"
  Spectator (London), CV (17 September 1910), 431 (This is a
  worthy effort to commemorate Gaskell's centenary.). Anon.
  "Current Literature,..." Daily Telegraph (London) (16 September 1910), p. 4 (Though Gaskell is a fine and underrated
  writer, Mrs. Chadwick's book on her is "scrappy" and "repetitious."). Anon. "The Gaskell Centenary," World (London)
  no. 1894 (18 October 1910), supplement, p. vi (We doubt
  that Gaskell's works, except for Cranford, will "be counted
  among the great works of the nineteenth century," and Mrs.
  Chadwick's book, though timely, is not a great "biography."). Anon. "Literature,..." Athenaeum (London), no.
  4327 (1 October 1910), pp. 381-82 (Mrs. Chadwick was handicapped by Gaskell's wish to have no biography, yet, although there are useful tidbits in this miscellany, Gaskell's "genius" deserves better than this trivial book.).
  Anon. "Literature. The Author of Cranford,..." Nation
  (New York), XCIV (18 January 1912), 61 (Reprinted in
  Evening Post [New York] [20 January 1912], Saturday supplement, p. 8.) (It would have been better if Gaskell's injunction had been obeyed, for this book is marred by "mala-
  droit phrases" and is an utter failure as a biography.).
  Anon. "Literature," Glasgow Herald (29 September 1910),
  p. 10 (Although Mrs. Chadwick's "enthusiasm" is admirable,
  her method of mingling facts with fiction is fundamentally
  unsound.). Anon. "Mrs. Gaskell: A Biographical Sketch,"

Illustrated London News (24 September 1910), p. 470 (Mrs. Chadwick has given us "a sympathetic portrait," based on "much painstaking research."). Anon. "Mrs. Gaskell," Bookshelf (London), IV (September 1910), 501-2 (Mrs. Chadwick's book is an "essential" work done with great "diligence."). Anon. "Mrs. Gaskell," CONTEMPR XCIX (May 1911), Literary Supplement, 2-15 (This is a loving and sound treatment of the works and life of "one of the most charming writers of the last century."). Anon. "Mrs. Gaskell," Publishers' Circular (London), n.s. XLII (24 September 1910), 371 (Mrs. Chadwick's wordy book disappoints us somewhat, though she does appreciate Gaskell.). Anon. "New Books. Biographical Guesswork," Manchester Guardian (26 September 1910), p. 5 (This "gossipy volume" incorrectly "assumes" that Gaskell lacked imagination and that all her characters can "be identified" with actual people. Mrs. Chadwick also "has a fatal facility for inaccuracy."). Anon. "New Cheaper Edition,..." Christian Life and Unitarian Herald (London), XXXIX (26 April 1913), 194 (Mrs. Chadwick's book "needed a great deal of correction but has" now "been brought up to date."). Anon. "Notices of Books,..." Bookseller (London), n.s. XCI (23 September 1910), 1207 ("Mrs. Chadwick has done her work with singular completeness." Gaskell's "seven or eight novels...ensure her a place among the half dozen great novelists of the Victorian era, with Thackeray, Dickens, George Eliot, the Brontë sisters, and Anthony Trollope."). Anon. "Reviews and Views,..." Christian Life and Unitarian Herald (London), XXXVI (15 October 1910), 524 (Gaskell's works will continue to "live," but Mrs. Chadwick's book is careless and wordy.). Anon. "Today's Literary Centenary," Daily Graphic (London) (29 September 1910), p. 5 (Gaskell was "one of the most gifted writers and...most charming personalities of the nineteenth century," but Mrs. Chadwick's book on her is "disjointed," though it does contain some valuable information.). Anon. "The Treasury Book of the Month. Mrs. Gaskell,..." Treasury (London), VI (October 1910), 55-61 (Mrs. Chadwick has put together what is "almost an autobiography" of Gaskell.). William E. A. Axon. "The Homes and Haunts of Mrs. Gaskell," Bookman (London), XXXIX (October 1910), 44 (Mrs. Chadwick's book contains errors, and she goes too far in identifying actual people with fictional characters, yet she does appreciate Gaskell's high merit.). (Mrs.) R. B. B.(elloc). "Mrs. Gaskell," Morning Post (London) (29 September 1910), p. 2 (As one who knew Gaskell, I have been asked to review this attempt to get around her prohibition of a biography. "It is disconcerting to" see passages from her fiction used as supposed

(CHADWICK, MRS. [ESTHER ALICE] ELLIS H.)
biography.). E.(sther) A.(lice) (Mrs. Ellis H.) Chadwick.
"Mrs. Gaskell. To the Editor,..." Manchester Guardian
(30 September 1910), p. 4 (Your review of my book on 26
September 1910 harped on supposed minor inaccuracies, but,
on most of the points, you, and not I, were wrong.).
M.(argaret) E. Gaskell. "Mrs. Gaskell's Life" (letter to
editor), Guardian (London), LXV, part II (30 September
1910), 1337 ("Instead of my having 'co-operated' with Mrs.
Chadwick in writing the book, I have urged her most
earnestly, on the...three occasions when I have seen her,
to respect my mother's wish that no biography should be
written...."). (Helen Melville). "Mrs. Gaskell,..." TLS
(29 September 1910), 349 (Reprinted in Irish Times [Dublin]
[29 September 1910], p. 7.) (With her "sense of humour"
and distaste for "publicity," Mrs. Gaskell would have
laughed at Mrs. Chadwick's book, and Miss Gaskell disclaims
having cooperated in the writing of it. In spite of the
loose Victorian structure of Gaskell's novels, they are
still read, for they present a world that we can all
recognize.). Sir William Robertson Nicoll (Claudius Clear).
"The Correspondence of Claudius Clear. Mrs. Gaskell,"
British Weekly (London), XLVIII (15 September 1910), 573
(Gaskell was "a considerable artist" but not "a writer of
the first order." Some of Mrs. Chadwick's identifications
or real-life models are convincing, but she goes too far.).
Thomas Seccombe. "Literature. A Book of the Day. Elizabeth Gaskell, 1810-1865,..." Daily News (London) (15 September 1910), p. 3 (Mrs. Chadwick has had to make "bricks
without straw," and the result is a "modest" narrative
based on the fiction and the "localities," though with
some minor errors.). Clement K. Shorter. "Books of the
Day. The First Biography of a Famous English Novelist,"
Daily Chronicle (London) (15 September 1910), p. 6 (If
someone had written a life of Gaskell as great as her own
Life of Charlotte Brontë, Gaskell's own reputation would
stand much higher today than it does. In the absence of
a real biography, one must encourage such "compilations as
Mrs. Chadwick's, though she makes many mistakes....").
C.(lement) K. S.(horter). "A Literary Letter: the First
Life of Mrs. Gaskell,..." Sphere (London), XLII (17 September 1910), 272 (Mrs. Chadwick's book is "brimful of information" and "opportune.").]

1910 B SHORTER WRITINGS

1   ANDREWS, LOUISE. "Old Cranford," New England Magazine
    (Boston), n.s. XLIII (November-December), 345-51.
        Knutsford, the model of Cranford, still reminds one of
    Gaskell's delightful book.

2   ANON. "The Art of Mrs. Gaskell," Nation (London), VII
    (10 September), 832-33.
        "People who have not succeeded in getting through 'Ruth',
    'Mary Barton', or 'Wives and Daughters', have loved 'Cran-
    ford'." Most critics rate Cousin Phillis next. Gaskell is
    a "novelist of the passing mood or feeling, detached from
    its profounder groundwork," for she does not show "es-
    sential" human "nature." If she had stuck to her strength
    and avoided elaborate plots, she would have written more
    first-rate books.

3   ANON. Athenaeum (London), no. 4339 (24 December), 792.
        Sylvia's Lovers, in a new edition introduced by Thomas
    Seccombe, is a "delightful" book "for thoughtful readers."

4   ANON. Athenaeum (London), no. 4323 (3 September), 264.
        We are surprised at Shorter's suggestion, in the World's
    Classics edition of Wives and Daughters, that Mr. and Mrs.
    Gibson are comparable to Mr. and Mrs. Bennett in Pride and
    Prejudice.

5   ANON. "The Author of Cranford. The Centenary of Mrs. Gaskell,
    the Novelist," Manchester Evening Chronicle (31 August),
    p. 2. [Reprinted in (Manchester) Sunday Chronicle
    (4 September 1910), p. 14.]
        The centenary of Gaskell, best known for Cranford, is
    getting considerable attention.

6   ANON. "Bookmarker's Notes," Manchester City News (13 August),
    p. 2.
        Gaskell's centenary "has been commemorated" by the
    World's Classics edition of her works. Mrs. Frederick
    Greenwood once said that, in spite of Gaskell's wide repu-
    tation, she "never had her due share of honour and reward
    among the geniuses of the nineteenth century."

7   ANON. Book Monthly (London), VIII (October), between 32-33.
        [Incorrectly cited by Northup (1929.B6) as a review of
    Chadwick (1910.A1), this item is a picture of Gaskell with
    the following caption: Gaskell, "whose centenary--Septem-
    ber 29, 1910--has been duly and honourably celebrated, in

1910

part by a biography of her, which Mrs. Ellis H. Chadwick
has published with Pitman and Sons."]

8   ANON. "A Book to Read. The Gaskell Centenary," Yorkshire
Weekly Post (Leeds) (1 October), p. 6.
We in the North are "especially interested" in Gaskell's
centenary, for she "belongs to us by reasons of birth" and
on account of her Life of Charlotte Brontë. "The world
might never have known" the Brontës "but for" the biographer's "genius" and "sympathy." Mrs. Chadwick's centenary
book on Gaskell is repetitious and overlong, but admirers
of Gaskell and the Brontës will like it anyway. It is
pleasant these days to see so many reprints of Gaskell's
novels.

9   ANON. "The Brontë Family. Their Association with Manchester.
A Permanent Memorial Suggested," Manchester Guardian
(21 February), p. 8.
Among the many tributes to Gaskell at "the annual meeting of the Brontë Society" at the Athenaeum, Manchester,
Mr. Derwent Simpson proposed that the Plymouth Grove house
"should be preserved for posterity," and Mrs. L. Grindon
suggested a statue in Manchester to Gaskell and Charlotte
Brontë.

10   ANON. "The Brontës and Manchester. Society's Celebrations,"
Manchester Courier (21 February), p. 11.
In 1851 Charlotte Brontë stayed at Gaskell's Plymouth
Grove house, which "was probably built in the early nine-
teenth century"--it is said by a "rich" but "paralyzed
bachelor" who "found...amusement in designing houses."
"The interior" of Gaskell's house is "unique and ingenious."

11   ANON. "Casual Comment," Dial (Chicago), XLIX (16 September),
172.
Gaskell's "'Cranford' and in lesser degree 'Mary Barton'
still have their admiring readers," though the writer's
imaginative powers were less than Charlotte Brontë's and
Gaskell's "quiet realism" is inferior to that of Jane Austen. Yet Gaskell's Life of Charlotte Brontë is a classic.

12   ANON. "Centenary of Birth of Mrs. Gaskell," Publishers' Circular (London), n.s. XLII (1 October), 401.
Macmillan is "marking the hundredth anniversary of" Gaskell's birth by publishing "a centenary edition of her
works [a mistake]." Most critics agree that "she was a
great writer, a woman of genius," but we found Wives and
Daughters hard going. Even in the case of her famous Life

<u>of Charlotte Brontë</u>, one wonders whether the book is imaginative literature or accurate biography.

13 ANON. "The Centenary of Mrs. Gaskell," <u>American Review of Reviews</u> (New York), XLII (November), 607-8.
    Gaskell's centenary has been celebrated by a number of magazine articles.

14 ANON. "The Centenary of Mrs. Gaskell," <u>Bookseller</u> (London), n.s. no. 88 (2 September), p. 1116.
    "... The life and character of Lancashire and Cheshire fifty or sixty years ago" are portrayed in Gaskell's works of fiction "with such inimitable skill" that they still "appear almost regularly" in new editions. "... The pure and healthy tone of everything she wrote, set a standard of excellence" that "has not always been followed" by subsequent novelists. Gaskell's "work...always...reached so high a plane that the absence of actual genius, if indeed it was absent, was hardly noted by the novel readers of her own time or of the present day."

15 ANON. "Centenary of Mrs. Gaskell [advertisement]," <u>Inquirer</u> (London), n.s. no. 665 (24 September), p. 613.
    "... An illustrated lecture will be given in the Essex Church School room, by the Rev. Frank K. Freeston, on 'The Authoress of <u>Cranford</u>'. All lovers of" Gaskell "are invited to attend."

16 ANON. "The Centenary of Mrs. Gaskell," <u>Inquirer</u> (London), n.s. no. 666 (1 October), p. 644.
    Last Thursday's "<u>Manchester Guardian</u> devoted special attention to" Gaskell's centenary.

17 ANON. "Centenary of Mrs. Gaskell, the Novelist," <u>Liverpool Daily Post and Mercury</u> (29 September), p. 9.
    [Five pictures appear on the same page under the heading "Gaskell Centenary--Associations with Knutsford."] Gaskell's Unitarian background provided her with a strong intellectual and moral tradition. In her happy marriage with the Rev. William Gaskell, she concentrated for eight years on being a wife and mother, but, when she began to succeed as a writer, her husband encouraged her at it. Dickens's influence seems to have "liberated" Gaskell's "delicate sense of humour." She had a great "capacity for friendship" and "talked" and "wrote as she felt," for her nature was "translucent," "radiant," and optimistic.

1910

18   ANON. "The Centenary of Mrs. Gaskell," Review of Reviews
      (London), XLII (October), 352-53.
          A number of articles in the September magazines deal
      with Gaskell's centenary.

19   ANON. "Centenary of Mrs. Gaskell's Birth: Scenes in Knuts-
      ford, Her Early Home, and the Original of Cranford,"
      Illustrated London News (24 September), p. 464.
          Gaskell, famous for many books, is best known for
      Cranford, which was modeled on Knutsford.

20   ANON. "Charlotte Brontë. Her Visits to Manchester," Manches-
      ter City News (26 February), p. 2.
          An address at the annual meeting of the Brontë Society,
      held this year in Manchester, emphasized the close friend-
      ship of Charlotte Brontë and Gaskell.

21   ANON. "Charlotte Brontë and Manchester [Editorial]," Manches-
      ter Guardian (21 February), p. 6.
          It is appropriate that the Brontë Society has met this
      year in Gaskell's Manchester, for her Life of Charlotte
      Brontë is largely responsible for the enduring fame of
      the Brontës.

22   ANON. "Cranford," Knutsford and Northwich Advertiser and East
      and Mid Cheshire Gazette (30 September), p. 4.
          "... Knutsford is still essentially 'Cranfordian'," and
      it has honored Gaskell by place names and by the Gaskell
      Memorial Tower.

23   ANON. "Dickens' Appreciation of Mrs. Gaskell," Millgate
      Monthly (Manchester), VI (October), 43.
          Lewis Melville, honoring Gaskell in the Nineteenth
      Century, points out that Dickens admired her fiction.

24   ANON. "Edward Memorial. What is Manchester Going To Do?
      Miss Gaskell's Idea--Money for the Sick Nursing of the
      Poor," Manchester Evening Chronicle (10 August), p. 3.
          Miss Margaret E. Gaskell, in her fund raising for a
      nursing institution, carries on the tradition of her famous
      mother, Mrs. Gaskell, who worked with Florence Nightingale
      in the development of "the Queen Victoria Jubilee Insti-
      tution for Nurses."

25   ANON. "Garratt Hall Interesting Manchester Relic," Manchester
      Evening News (23 April), p. 3.
          [Though included in the Gaskell Cuttings at Manchester
      Central Library, this item describes Garratt Hall, "shortly

to be demolished," but does not refer to Gaskell, who did,
however, mention Garratt Hall in her "Disappearances,"
Household Words (London), III (7 June 1851), 246-50.]

26 ANON. "The Gaskell Centenary," Daily News (London) (29 September), p. 2.
      We honor "the celebrated authoress of 'Cranford'" by
publishing photographs of Gaskell and her Chelsea birthplace.

27 ANON. "The Gaskell Centenary," Manchester City News
(3 September), p. 2.
      "... Mrs. Ellis H. Chadwick discovered the place of"
Gaskell's birth through a study of "the rate books" and
"an old print of Lindsey Row," Chelsea.

28 ANON. "The Gaskell Centenary," Manchester City News
(10 September), p. 2.
      As "the magazines and journals" are "honouring" Gaskell,
we should like to assert that her fame does not rest on
personal charm and goodness but on the "comic spirit" in
"her best writing"--Cranford and, above all, Wives and
Daughters.

29 ANON. "The Gaskell Centenary [Editorial]," Manchester
Courier (29 September), p. 6.
      The Gaskell centenary has been used as a welcome "occa-
sion" "to do homage once more to the genius of one of the"
unquestionably "great Victorian writers."

30 ANON. "The Gaskell Centenary," Manchester Evening Chronicle
(29 September), p. 2.
      "Those who delight in the faithful and vivid portrayal
of rural and domestic life still find in" Gaskell's "work
a peculiar charm."

31 ANON. "The Gaskell Centenary," Manchester Evening News
(28 September), p. 6.
      [Cited by Green (1911.A2) as "Mrs. Gaskell: an Appre-
ciation," this item consists of nothing but photographs.]

32 ANON. "The Gaskell Centenary [Editorial]," Manchester
Guardian (29 September), p. 6.
      In spite of Gaskell's splendid personal qualities, her
fame, more and more, will rest on the "comic" urbanity and
lucidity "of her best writing." When she wrote about industrial questions, she was limited to the attitudes of
her time, but "her comedy" remains ageless "in 'Cranford'
and perhaps especially in 'Wives and Daughters'."

1910

33   ANON. "The Gaskell Centenary. Dickens's Admiration for the Famous Lady Novelist. Her Friendship with Charlotte Brontë," <u>Manchester Evening Chronicle</u> (31 August), p. 2.
       Gaskell's <u>Cranford</u> is her one truly great novel.

34   ANON. "The Gaskell Centenary Exhibition," <u>Manchester Guardian</u> (29 September), p. 4.
       "A representative selection" from the Gaskell Collection, "founded fourteen years ago, has been placed on view at the King-Street Reference Library." Green's catalogue to the exhibition is "a useful addition to literary bibliography."

35   ANON. "The Gaskell Centenary. A Guide for Gaskell Students," <u>Rochdale Observer</u> (1 October), Literary Supplement, p. 8.
       Because of Gaskell's increasing reputation as a novelist, her centenary has been of "some importance" in Manchester "literary circles." J. A. Green has provided "an excellent bibliographical guide to the Gaskell Collection,...temporarily" moved from the Moss Side Library to the King-Street Reference Library.

36   ANON. "The Gaskell Centenary," <u>Yorkshire Weekly Post</u> (Leeds) (1 October), p. 3.
       [Five photographs with captions, including "the Lawn, Holybourne, where the novelist died suddenly."]

37   ANON. "Gaskelliana. Manchester Memories," <u>Manchester City News</u> (10 September), p. 2.
       There are many Gaskell centenary pieces in the September magazines, and we ourselves have received many letters from Gaskell scholars about details in our centenary article of last week.

38   ANON. "Gaskell Treasures at King-Street," <u>Manchester City News</u> (24 September), p. 2.
       The King-Street Library is displaying a Gaskell collection of "410 items, together with portraits and a book of cuttings," and J. A. Green has prepared "a bibliographical guide" of the display.

39   ANON. "The Gentle Radiance of Mrs. Gaskell's Enduring Fame," <u>Current Literature</u> (New York), XLIX (November), 560–62.
       In our period of literature in revolt, <u>Cranford</u> seems a "sweet" echo from a "pastoral" "golden" age, yet Gaskell, in <u>Mary Barton</u>, was "one of the first heralds of collectivism." Nevertheless, her reputation will continue to rest on <u>Cranford</u> and <u>Cousin Phillis</u>.

40 ANON. "Harper's Weekly Advertiser. The Celebrated Brontë
    Books," Harper's Weekly (New York), LIV (22 October), 27.
    Gaskell's "skilful" Life of Charlotte Brontë helped to
    convince the public that "the Brontë books must be books
    of genius, because the Brontës are so interesting and
    their story is so tragic."

41 ANON. "History and Biography. Mrs. Gaskell," Bookshelf
    (London), IV (November), 524.
    Numerous eulogies in the press have honored Gaskell on
    her centenary, and Mrs. Chadwick's book on Gaskell has been
    much praised.

42 ANON. "Introduction. Mrs. Gaskell. Cranford," in Cranford.
    New York and Boston: H. M. Caldwell Co., pp. vii-xli.
    Cranford is Gaskell's "most perfect and distinguished
    work," with "more delicacy, more atmosphere,...more style"
    than the others. In terms of its psychological perception,
    Wives and Daughters is Gaskell's "finest work" of "fiction,"
    but Cranford's style is "superior."

43 ANON. "Ladies' Letter. Mrs. Gaskell's Centenary," Knutsford
    and Northwich Advertiser and East and Mid Cheshire Gazette
    (9 September), p. 9.
    Gaskell is being honored on her centenary by many
    articles in the periodicals.

44 ANON. "Lest We Forget! Rev. William Gaskell, M.A., 1805-
    1884," Unitarian Monthly (Manchester), VII (September), 97.
    The Rev. William Gaskell "married Elizabeth Cleghorn
    Stevenson, who became famous as" the author of Mary Barton,
    Cranford, and The Life of Charlotte Brontë.

45 ANON. "A Literary Centenary," Graphic (London) (3 September),
    p. 356.
    "The discovery of" Gaskell's "birthplace lies with Mrs.
    Sarah Tooley."

46 ANON. "Literary Notes," Inquirer (London), n.s. no. 666
    (1 October), p. 641.
    "The Cornhill for October will contain a special article
    on" Gaskell "by the Master of Peterhouse."

47 ANON. "Literary Notes," Outlook (London), XXVI (1 October),
    473.
    "We doubt" that Gaskell's "fame has ever been commensurate
    to her worth. She has never been boomed like the Brontës
    nor exalted to the immortals like Jane Austen. George

1910

(ANON.)
Eliot's reputation has fallen under an eclipse, but she
would still probably be placed higher" than Gaskell "in a
list of English women novelists. Yet in our estimation
none of these writers has written anything quite as perfect
as Cranford, and the best of" Gaskell's "other works will
bear comparison with the best of theirs."

*48   ANON. "Literary and Scientific Society. Mrs. Gaskell's
Centenary," Radcliffe Guardian (ca. 17 November). [Reprint
of talk on Gaskell.]
[Source: Catherine Margaret Ellen Halls. "Bibliography
of Elizabeth C. Gaskell," Diploma in librarianship dissertation, University of London, 1957. See 1957.B5.]

*49   ANON. Literary World (Boston) (13 September), p. 284.
[On Gaskell and Charlotte Brontë.] [Source: Gaskell
Cuttings, Manchester Central Library.]

50   ANON. "Local Notes," Knutsford and Northwich Advertiser and
East and Mid Cheshire Gazette (6 May), p. 5.
The Gaskell centenary was celebrated on Saturday by
"the Lancashire Authors' Association."

51   ANON. "Local Notes. Cranford," Knutsford and Northwich and
East and Mid Cheshire Gazette (13 May), p. 6.
Although "nothing is at present settled, the Gaskell
centenary will doubtless" be observed in both London and
Manchester. In spite of competition from "rapid and sen-
sational fiction," Gaskell's works still sell, and she
ranks along with Jane Austen, the Brontës, and George Eliot.

52   ANON. "Lower Mosley-Street Schools, Manchester. Annual Reunion. A Link with Mary Barton," in Inquirer (London),
n.s. no. 634 (19 February), pp. 124-25.
The "former caretakers of the old school, Mr. and Mrs.
Smethurst" were honored on "their golden wedding" anniversary, and Rev. A. Cobden Smith pointed out that "Mrs.
Smethurst had been a member of" Gaskell's "class" and had
"received" a presentation copy from her of Mary Barton's
first edition.

53   ANON. Manchester Courier (27 September), p. 6.
Knutsford is still like Cranford and has adopted the
name on "gate posts," a café, and a street, and the town
also now has a Gaskell Memorial Tower.

54 ANON. Manchester Courier (14 October), p. 6.
        Silverdale "was a favorite haunt of" Gaskell's, and she
    wrote My Lady Ludlow there and "part of 'Mary Barton'."

55 ANON. "Manchester Literary Club," Manchester City News
        (29 October), p. 3.
        A number of speakers gave "short papers" at the club in
    honor of Gaskell's centenary.

56 ANON. "Manchester Literary Club," Manchester Guardian
        (26 October), p. 4.
        The club's meeting "was devoted to the reading of short
    papers on" Gaskell "in commemoration of" her centenary.

57 ANON. "Manchester Notes," Manchester City News (7 May), p. 8.
        "The Brontë Society has just issued a full report" of
    their meeting in Manchester with "Richmond's portrait of"
    Gaskell as "an interesting frontispiece."

58 ANON. "Miscellany," Manchester Guardian (22 February), p. 7.
        Charlotte Brontë's description of Gaskell's house,
    quoted by Bishop Welldon, reminds one how delightfully
    rural Plymouth Grove was in those days.

59 ANON. "Mrs. Gaskell. Centenary of the Author of Cranford,"
        Daily Dispatch (Manchester) (29 September), p. 4.
        Gaskell's treatment of social problems in her fiction
    suggests that she would have made a good "journalist" to-
    day. Gaskell's industrial novels were "good, but not the
    true gold," and the world has forgotten them, yet Cranford
    "will continue to live,...down through the generations."

60 ANON. "Mrs. Gaskell Centenary Celebration at Knutsford.
        Lancashire Author's [sic] Visit Knutsford," Knutsford and
        Northwich Advertiser and East and Mid Cheshire Gazette
        (6 May), p. 5.
        The Lancashire Authors' Association held a meeting at
    Knutsford in honor of Gaskell's centenary.

61 ANON. "Mrs. Gaskell and Knutsford," Knutsford and Northwich
        Advertiser and East and Mid Cheshire Gazette (9 September),
        p. 4.
        "A most interesting article" on Gaskell appears in this
    week's Great Thoughts, from which we quote a passage on
    her Knutsford background.

62 ANON. "Mrs. Gaskell: Lancashire Admirers at Knutsford,"
        Manchester Guardian (2 May), p. 5.

1910

(ANON.)
    At the meeting of Lancashire Authors' Association in
Knutsford, the Rev. G. A. Payne hailed Gaskell as "a woman
of great genius."

*63   ANON. "Mrs. Gaskell's Centenary," <u>Philadelphia Press</u>
    (24 September), p. 6.
    [A "brief" account of Gaskell's "life and works."]
    [Source: Marjorie Taylor Davis. "An Annotated Bibliog-
    raphy of Criticism on Elizabeth Cleghorn Gaskell, 1848-
    1973." Ph.D. dissertation, University of Mississippi, 1974.
    <u>See</u> 1974.B6.]

64   ANON. "Mrs. Gaskell (Writer and Philanthropist)," <u>Unitarian</u>
    <u>Monthly</u> (Manchester), VII (April), 37.
        Gaskell combined a life of philanthropic work for "the
    poor" with a career of writing "famous" novels.

65   ANON. "The New Books of the Month. Classic Reprints. <u>Cran-</u>
    <u>ford</u>,..." <u>Book News Monthly</u> (Philadelphia), XXIX (October),
    135.
        This "neat library edition" of <u>Cranford</u> commemorates
    Gaskell's centenary.

66   ANON. "News Notes," <u>Bookman</u> (London), XXXVIII (September),
    231.
        "We are greatly indebted to" Mrs. Gaskell's "daughter,
    Miss M. E. Gaskell, for the interest she has taken in this
    preparation of this number" and for the pictures that she
    has allowed us "to reproduce."

67   ANON. "Notes and Jottings. The Inspiration of Mrs. Gaskell's
    Early Works," <u>Inquirer</u> (London), n.s. no. 667 (8 October),
    p. 663.
        [Summarizes points from (Sir) A.(dolphus) W.(illiam)
    Ward. "In Memoriam: Elizabeth Cleghorn Gaskell," <u>Cornhill</u>
    <u>Magazine</u> (London), n.s. XXIX (October), 457-66. <u>See</u>
    1910.B136.]

68   ANON. "Notes of the Week," <u>Inquirer</u> (London), n.s. no. 665
    (24 September), p. 615.
        Although literary archeologists have "ransacked" Gas-
    kell's books for real-life counterparts, "great novelists
    are not photographers": Gaskell "used" her memories as
    "the vehicles" for conveying "her vision of life."

69   ANON. "Notes of the Week," <u>Inquirer</u> (London), n.s. no. 665
    (24 September), p. 616.

We "call...attention" to the Rev. F. K. Freeston's free
lecture on Gaskell at the Essex Church, Kensington.

70   ANON. "Our London Dispatch.... The Centenary of Mrs. Gaskell," Daily Dispatch (Manchester) (18 August), p. 4.
      There are no specific plans yet in London for cele-
brating Gaskell's centenary, yet Londoners like her books
more and more, as reprints by London publishers show.

*71   ANON. "Pioneer Women. Mrs. Gaskell, the Novelist. The In-
fluence of Mary Barton," Cooperative News (Manchester)
(1 October).
      [On Gaskell's career as writer.] [Source: Gaskell
Cuttings, Manchester Central Library.]

72   ANON. "Review of the Year. 1910 at Home and Abroad,"
Knutsford and Northwich Advertiser and East and Mid Cheshire Gazette (30 September), p. 9.
      "Centenaries of celebrities were few in number, the
principal being that of" Gaskell "on September 20th [sic].
..."

73   ANON. "Scenes from Cranford. Charming Play at Wilmslow,"
Knutsford and Northwich Advertiser and East and Mid Cheshire Gazette (28 October), p. 6.
      Amid all the recent "tributes" to Gaskell, one should
point out that, for women readers, she is superior even to
Dickens. Appropriately, a musical drama based on "her best
book, 'Cranford'," was given by the Wilmslow Girls' Club
to raise "funds."

74   ANON. "Sixteenth Annual Meeting of the Brontë Society,"
Brontë Society Transactions (Bradford), IV, part XX (March),
141-43.
      Many tributes were paid to Gaskell at the meeting, in-
cluding Derwent Simpson's proposal that her Plymouth Grove
house "be preserved" as a shrine and Miss L. Grindon's suggestion that Manchester erect a statue of Gaskell and Charlotte Brontë. Vice-Chancellor Hopkins of the University of
Manchester said that the bust of Gaskell in its library
was a "treasured possession."

75   ANON. "Sylvia's Lovers," Athenaeum (London), no. 4339
(24 December), p. 792.
      As Thomas Seccombe "justly remarks" in his introduction
to this new edition, Gaskell's "novels are perenially
fresh."

1910

*76   ANON. <u>Unitarian Monthly</u> (Manchester), VII (October), 114.
[On Gaskell's centenary.] [Source: Clark S. Northup.
"A Bibliography," in <u>Elizabeth Gaskell</u>. By Gerald DeWitt
Sanders. New Haven: Yale University Press, for Cornell
University. London: Humphrey Milford, Oxford University
Press, 1929. <u>See</u> 1929.B6.]

77   ANON. "The Women's Guild," <u>Manchester and Salford Co-operative Herald</u> (October), p. 196.
    A large group from the guild was taken on a Gaskell tour
of Knutsford by the Rev. George A. Payne.

78   AXON, WILLIAM E. A. "The Centenary of Mrs. Gaskell," <u>Millgate
Monthly</u> (Manchester), V (September), 778-81.
    "One of the most famous novelists of the Victorian
period," Gaskell was good at both long and short fiction.
Her humor deepened in her later works, which remained
"ethical" but were no longer didactic.

79   _____. "Mrs. Gaskell and G. F. Watts's 'Good Samaritan',"
<u>Manchester Guardian</u> (30 September), p. 5.
    The Manchester Art Gallery's ownership of George
Frederick Watts's portrait of Thomas Wright as "The Good
Samaritan" reminds us that Gaskell helped arrange for the
painting to be made.

*80   _____. "Mrs. Gaskell's Ghost Stories," <u>Millgate Monthly</u>
(Manchester), V (September). [Reprinted in <u>Inquirer and
Christian Life</u> (London) (12 November 1910).]
    [Source: Gaskell Cuttings, Manchester Central Library;
John Albert Green. <u>A Bibliographical Guide to the Gaskell
Collection in the Moss Side Library</u>. Manchester: Refer-
ence Library, King St.; Moss Side Library, Bradshaw St.,
1911. <u>See</u> 1911.A2.]

81   _____. "The Rev. William Gaskell's Temperance Rhymes,"
<u>Alliance News and Temperance Reformer</u> (Manchester), LVII
(22 September), 604.
    For Gaskell's centenary, the Manchester Reference
Library is displaying "an interesting exhibition," including a copy of her husband's <u>Temperance Rhymes</u>, three
of which we reprint.

82   BENJAMIN, LEWIS S. [LEWIS MELVILLE]. "The Centenary of Mrs.
Gaskell," <u>Nineteenth Century and After</u> (London), LXVII
(September), 467-82.
    The absence of a full biography of Gaskell is no great
regret, for her life was uneventful. The truth is that

Gaskell, except for Cousin Phillis and Cranford, "was an indifferent novelist." Mary Barton, North and South, and Ruth "attracted" "attention" because of extraneous social reasons, yet these books are spoiled by melodrama, sentimentality, and "wooden" characterization and dialogue. The characters in Wives and Daughters are convincing, but the story itself is dull: Molly is admirable, but the others, including Cynthia, Dr. Gibson, and the Hamleys "are profoundly uninteresting." Sylvia's Lovers, in spite of faults, is Gaskell's best long novel, but her only masterpiece is the relatively short Cranford.

83   BLUNDELL, A. W. "Mrs. Gaskell, 1810-1910," Christian Freeman and Sunday School Monthly (London), LIV (November), 244-47.
      Much has been written about the centenary of Gaskell, who was in the great tradition of English Dissent and of Unitarianism.

84   BONE, FLORENCE. "The Story of Mrs. Gaskell," Great Thoughts (London), 6th ser. VIII (10 September), 376-78. [Reprinted, abridged, in Christian Life and Unitarian Herald (London), XXXVI (24 September 1910), 483.]
      Gaskell loved Knutsford yet "her happiest years were spent" married in Manchester. She was a great conversationalist but retiring in a crowd. Gaskell "made Manchester richer than all its gaunt mills and...looms...."

85   BRADLEY, JONAS. "Notes and Queries. The Rev. Patrick Brontë and His Pistol," Yorkshire Weekly Post (Leeds) (15 October), p. 13.
      Gaskell's Life of Charlotte Brontë told an "alarmist" story about Mr. Brontë and his pistol, which Gaskell changed in her 1860 edition. As Leyland's The Brontë Family (1886.B2) shows, Mr. Brontë, during the Luddite troubles, had fallen into the habit of firing his pistol "to renew the charge."

86   CAUTLEY, C. HOLMES. "Old Haworth Folk Who Knew the Brontës," Cornhill Magazine (London), n.s. XXIX (July), 76-84.
      [Though referred to by Green (1911.A2) as containing "references to" Gaskell, this item does not mention her.]

87   CHAPMAN, EDWARD MORTIMER. English Literature in Account with Religion, 1800-1900. London: Constable & Co. Boston: Houghton Mifflin Co., pp. 295, 330-31.
      Although Gaskell was a popular author in her time, these days her works, with the exception of Cranford, are more "praised by critics than read" by the public.

1910

*88 CLAYTON, JAMES. "The Gaskell Centenary" [A "paper...read at
Radcliffe, November 17, 1910," a "typed copy" of which is
in the Moss Side Library.]
[Source: John Albert Green. A Bibliographical Guide
to the Gaskell Collection in the Moss Side Library. Manchester: Reference Library, King St.; Moss Side Library,
Bradshaw St., 1911. See 1911.A2.]

89 C.[LAYTON?], J.[AMES?]. "Recollections of Mrs. Gaskell,"
Christian Life and Unitarian Herald (London), XXXVI
(October), 496.
I was one of the boys who had Gaskell as a teacher at
the Lower Mosley Street School. "... Her playful manner...
was a...joy" and "comfort to lads pinched by poverty." She
"excelled" at teaching reading and at using games for in-
struction. She also "told tales" and read to us in a
"clear" and "expressive" "voice." Gaskell "was indulgent
and painstaking with all of us...and brightened our lives
with her affectionate regard and hope...."

90 _____. "A Wise, Good Woman. Centenary of Elizabeth Cleghorn
Gaskell," Scottish Co-operator (Glasgow) (30 September),
p. 2.
"As a novelist," Gaskell "stands among the great names
of the Victorian era.... There is no healthier writer of
fiction in the English language...."

91 COBLENTZ, H. E. "Preface.... Introduction.... Explanatory
Notes.... Questions and Suggestions," in Cranford.
Boston: Houghton Mifflin Co., Riverside Press, pp. v-xxvii,
249-79.
Gaskell's "novels" tend to be "underestimated even when
they are compared with the great masterpieces of fiction."
"Strictly speaking, Cranford is not a novel," for it lacks
"complex organization," though the sketches do have a certain unity. The book concludes with "Mr. Peter as the
grand Aga of Cranford, the conqueror of the Cranford Ama-
zons, and restorer of peace between the warring factions
of the aristocracy...."

92 COUSIN, JOHN W. A Short Biographical Dictionary of English
Literature. London: J. M. Dent & Sons. New York: E. P.
Dutton & Co. S.v. "Gaskell, Elizabeth Cleghorn." [Article
reprinted in D. C. Browning. Everyman's Dictionary of
Literary Biography English and American. Compiled after
John W. Cousin. London: J. M. Dent & Sons. New York:
E. P. Dutton & Co., 1958.]
Gaskell "had some of the characteristics of Miss Austen,
..." Gaskell is less perfect but deeper.

93   DARTON, F. J. HARVEY. "The Two Nations. Gaskell's centenary,"
     Morning Leader (London) (29 September), p. 4.
          Gaskell is "unworshipped," with "no...shrine, no cult,
     not even a standard biography. Few books have taken a
     stronger hold upon the English mind than" hers; "few
     authors reveal themselves less in their writings than
     she.... And yet" Gaskell "wrote books which not merely
     are great in themselves, but portray England itself with
     a breadth and sincerity surpassed nowhere in Victorian
     fiction." Cranford "was an epitome of English tradition
     and English gentility, in the best sense, just as 'Mary
     Barton' was an epitome of the solid strength and dignity
     of the English poor."

94   F.[REESTON], [REV.] F.[RANK] K. "Life, Religion, and Affairs.
     The Centenary of Mrs. Gaskell," Inquirer (London), n.s. no.
     665 (24 September), pp. 618-19.
          Gaskell "was imbued with the fine spirit and true
     quality of cultured Nonconformity," of which she gave a
     memorable portrait in Mr. Benson of Ruth.

95   HAMILTON, C.[ATHERINE] J.[ANE]. "The Centenary of Mrs.
     Gaskell," Guardian (London), LXV, part II (23 September),
     1297.
          "Some" of the "pathetic touches about the childhood of
     Molly" in Gaskell's splendid Wives and Daughters seem to
     reflect her own childhood. Gaskell was "beautiful" but
     "small." She was delightfully "bright and cheery." In
     her philanthropic work, she once stopped a near "stampede"
     of five hundred "wild and undisciplined" Irishwomen in a
     sewing school "by standing...at the door and shaking hands
     with each...."

96   H.[ERFORD], C. H. "Mrs. Gaskell's Power. The Rise of Her
     Fame," Manchester Guardian (29 September), p. 5.
          Gaskell's fame need not be "revived" because she has
     retained her popularity through the years by her "classic"
     "lucidity," her realistic portrayal of the working poor,
     and, above all, her "humanity" and "humour."

97   HEY, MARGARET. "Notes and Queries. The Rev. Patrick Brontë
     and His Pistol," Yorkshire Weekly Post (Leeds) (15 October),
     p. 13.
          "As the widow of" a "parishioner of...Patrick Brontë, I
     resent" any perpetuation of Gaskell's slurs against him in
     her Life of Charlotte Brontë.

1910

98   HILL, J. ARTHUR. "Mrs. Gaskell. To-day's Centenary of the
      Brontës' Biographer," Daily Chronicle (London) (29 Septem-
      ber), p. 4.
          Gaskell was an excellent novelist, and her Life of
      Charlotte Brontë will endure. But I knew the Brontës and
      can attest that Gaskell made many mistakes about Yorkshire.

99   [HOMPES, MISS MAT]. "Mrs. Gaskell and Her Social Work Among
      the Poor," Inquirer (London), n.s. no. 667 (8 October),
      p. 656.
          While two continents are praising Gaskell, let us in
      Manchester praise her "genius" "for good works."

100   JENKINS, HOWARD M. "The Real Cranford," Girl's Own Paper
      (London), XXXII (October), 42-43. [Originally published
      anonymously in The Girl's Realm (London), IV (March 1902),
      434-36.]
          Knutsford is full of reminiscences of Gaskell's fiction
      and not only of Cranford but also Wives and Daughters and
      "The Squire's Tale."

101   J. F. C. "Notes and Queries. The Rev. Patrick Brontë,"
      Yorkshire Weekly Post (Leeds) (8 October), p. 13.
          The reference to Patrick Brontë in last week's article
      on Gaskell is puzzling. Even if he had "alcoholic tenden-
      cies," why should he fire his pistol in the morning? "Did
      the sparrows bother him?"

*102 J. H. "Manchester and Charlotte Brontë," Co-operative News
      (Manchester) (26 February).
          ["With reference to" Gaskell.] [Source: John Albert
      Green. A Bibliographical Guide to the Gaskell Collection
      in Moss Side Library. Manchester: Reference Library,
      King St.; Moss Side Library, Bradshaw St., 1911. See
      1911.A2.]

103   J. M. W. "Mrs. Gaskell. An Appreciation," Manchester Evening
      News (28 September), p. 2.
          Gaskell lacked the "power" and "range" of George Eliot
      and George Sand but had her own "delicate charm," "sensi-
      bility," and lyricism. "Several" of her "stories" show
      "genius." The great virtue of Gaskell's novels is their
      lovingly exact depiction of the humble and obscure.

104   MACMILLAN, FREDERICK. "Mrs. Gaskell's Works. A New Thackeray
      Edition," Publishers' Circular (London), n.s. XLII (22
      October), 606.

Publishers' Circular was mistaken in saying that Macmillan's intended to publish an edition of Gaskell's works.
The Circular was perhaps thinking of our announced "Centenary Edition" of Thackeray.

105   A Man of Kent. "Rambling Remarks. Mrs. Gaskell," British
      Weekly (London), XLIII (11 August), 463.
          We prefer Wives and Daughters to Sylvia's Lovers, each
      reprinted in the World's Classics series, yet we find both
      "delightful."

106   MASSON, FLORA. "The Gaskell Centenary. The Novelist's
      Career," Manchester Guardian (29 September), p. 4.
          Gaskell's middle name came from Mrs. Cleghorn (mother
      or wife of James Cleghorn), who had been kind to the
      Stevensons in their "early married days at Saughton and
      Edinburgh." Gaskell "was very proud of her father's
      memory, and used often to talk of him long after he was
      dead...." Her marriage meant that she did not have
      to depend on her writing for income, but her duties as
      mother, minister's wife, and philanthropist often came
      "between" Gaskell and her fiction.

107   M.[ATZ], B. W. "Mrs. Gaskell and Charles Dickens," Dickensian
      (London), VI (October), 266–67.
          In spite of some editorial quarrels with Gaskell,
      Dickens admired her work. "There was distinction in every-
      thing she wrote," and Cranford "is destined to live for
      all time, whilst 'Mary Barton' and 'North and South' may be
      classed amongst the best in literature...."

108   MELVILLE, HELEN. "Mrs. Gaskell and Cranford," Chambers's
      Journal (London), 6th ser. XIII (17 September), 667–69.
          Gaskell's "fame" and "popularity" are still high but
      rest primarily on Cranford.

109   M. N. "[no. 13,410] Mrs. Gaskell," Manchester City News
      [Notes and Queries] (1 October), p. 2.
          Who was the actual model for Gaskell's "Lois the Witch,"
      which "is probably founded on fact?"

110   MONTGOMERY, K.[ATHLEEN] [and] L.[ETITIA]. "Elizabeth Cleghorn
      Gaskell," Fortnightly Review (London), n.s. LXXXVIII
      (1 September), 450–63.
          Mrs. Gaskell received a wider education than was usual
      for a girl, and her marriage to the Rev. William Gaskell
      was itself a broadening experience. She is as good as Poe
      at horror stories. In her novels she combines a female

1910

(MONTGOMERY, K.[ATHLEEN] [and] L.[ETITIA])
"insight into detail" with "a masculine" moral "tolerance."
A Middlesex library has banned Ruth as immoral, just as it
had been criticized in Gaskell's lifetime.

111   _____. "An Italian Town Amid English Fields," Lady's Realm
(London), XXVIII (July), 321-25.
Memories of Cranford still remain in Knutsford, a town
with an ancient history.

112   MORTIMER, JOHN. "Mrs. Gaskell and Christmas. A Budget of
Good Stories--Grave and Gay," Manchester City News
(24 December), p. 5.
Gaskell's stories that explicitly deal with Christmas
include The Moorland Cottage, "Half a Lifetime Ago," "The
Old Nurse's Story," and "Christmas Storms and Sunshine."
Cranford is in the Christmas spirit.

113   NICHOLSON, ALBERT. "Heaton Park Exhibition," Manchester City
News (15 October), p. 6.
A drawing of the Greenheys Fields farmhouse described in
Mary Barton and also portraits of Mrs. Gaskell and her hus-
band loaned by Miss Gaskell appear "at the 'Old Manchester
and Salford Exhibition' at Heaton Park."

114   Old Mancunian. "Pepper Hill Farm," Manchester City News
(24 September), p. 2.
A tablet should be erected at Pepper Hill Farm in honor
of its description by Gaskell in Mary Barton.

115   PAYNE, REV. GEORGE A. "Gaskell Centenary," Manchester City
News (10 September), p. 2.
Most "cultured people" have "read at least one" of
Gaskell's novels, and her popularity has been increasing
with inexpensive reprints. Cousin Phillis, rather than
Cranford, is now considered by critics to be her "most
perfect" work. Gaskell, as a "woman" and "model" wife and
mother, was even greater than Gaskell the writer.

116   _____. "Gaskell Centennial," Christian Life and Unitarian
Herald (London), XXXVI (24 September), 484.
Full public honor to Gaskell has been deferred for too
long, but her centennial has brought a "flood" of writings
about her. Gaskell ranks with George Eliot and Charlotte
Brontë and "is much more pleasing than the...stilted...
Jane Austen."

117   [REID, STUART]. "Mrs. Gaskell [Editorial]," Standard
      (London) (29 September), p. 6.
         Gaskell's husband "was perhaps the only critic to whose
      judgment she was inclined to defer." Her "place in English
      letters" is "secure" with Cranford, Sylvia's Lovers, Wives
      and Daughters, and The Life of Charlotte Brontë.

118   ROBERTS, W. J. "The Cranford of Mrs. Gaskell. In Commemora-
      tion of the One Hundredth Anniversary of the Birth of
      Elizabeth Cleghorn Gaskell," Book News Monthly (Philadel-
      phia), XXIX (September), 21-28.
         Gaskell's works, and most notably Cranford, "still...
      charm those who...take pleasure in the study of all that
      was quaint, picturesque and, possibly, narrow in the
      middle-class lives of the early Victorian days."

119   SARGISSON, REV. C.[ONRAD] S. "An Afternoon at 'Cranford',"
      Wesleyan Methodist Magazine (London), CXXXIII (September),
      665-71.
         Knutsford still "comes fully up to the expectations of
      the diligent reader and lover" of Gaskell's fiction. "Let
      the reader take Cranford and Wives and Daughters as his
      guidebooks, not neglecting to read also Ruth, Cousin
      Phillis, Mr. Harrison's Confessions, and some of the
      shorter tales...."

120   _____. "The Centenary of Elizabeth Cleghorn Gaskell,"
      Sphere (London), XLII (24 September), 295.
         [Many photographs plus "a chronology" of Gaskell's
      "life and works."]

121   _____. "Mrs. Gaskell's Early Surroundings, and Their In-
      fluence on Her Writings," Bookman (London), XXXVIII
      (September), 245-50.
         Visitors still leave flowers on Gaskell's grave in
      memory of her fiction, which presents Knutsford through a
      golden glow of memory, though she actually was happier as
      a married adult in Manchester.

122   SECCOMBE, THOMAS. "Introduction," in Sylvia's Lovers.
      London: G. Bell & Sons, pp. ix-xlvii.
         Gaskell achieved unsurpassed excellence within "the
      normal type of English novel"--in Mary Barton, North and
      South, Sylvia's Lovers, and Wives and Daughters. Unlike
      such giants as Scott, Dickens, and Thackeray, she subor-
      dinated her own personality to the development of her
      subjects. Philip, in Sylvia's Lovers, is "the most com-
      plicated character-study" Gaskell "ever attempted" and is

1910

(SECCOMBE, THOMAS)
greatly superior to George Eliot's Tito in Romola. Above
all, the tragic love story in Sylvia's Lovers is handled
superbly. Gaskell avoids narrative comment in dealing with
moral problems, even in the case of Philip's treachery.
This fine book ranks with Adam Bede as an intensely English
novel. "Sylvia's Lovers is the greatest if not the most
perfect of" Gaskell's "books," with her "strongest" "plot,"
which, however, takes her beyond her powers at the end.

123 _____. "The Reader. Elizabeth Cleghorn Gaskell, 1810-1865,"
Bookman (London), XXXVIII (September), 237-44.
[Largely repeats the material in Seccombe's prefaces to
editions of Gaskell's novels.] I predict "that the memory
of" Gaskell's "fame will have risen considerably by 2010."

124 SHORTER, CLEMENT [K.]. "The Centenary of Mrs. Gaskell,"
Glasgow Herald (29 September), p. 11.
Though Gaskell was born in Chelsea, grew up in Knutsford,
and lived most of her life in Manchester, she was half
Scotch, for her father was "born in Berwick." She "is
the only woman novelist of first-rate importance" who was
a mother, and "she was, in fact," "adored" by her daughters,
but perhaps this "domestic" characteristic has harmed her
literary reputation. "Alone among...English novelists,"
Gaskell's work had "perfect geniality."

125 _____. In The Encyclopaedia Britannica. 11th ed. S.v.
"Gaskell, Elizabeth Cleghorn."
Gaskell "has enjoyed an ever gaining popularity since
her death." Apart from the many editions of Cranford and
The Life of Charlotte Brontë, "the many volumes of novels
and stories seemed of less secure permanence until the"
expiration "of their copyrights revealed...that a dozen
publishers thought them worth reprinting."

126 _____. "Introduction," in Wives and Daughters. The Novels
and Tales of Mrs. Gaskell, VI. The World's Classics,
CLVII. Henry Frowde, Oxford University Press, pp. v-xii.
Although Wives and Daughters was not quite finished, it
is much more complete than The Mystery of Edwin Drood or
St. Ives. Apparently, one of Gaskell's daughters provided
"suggestions from her mother's conversation" that enabled
Frederick Greenwood to write the concluding note in the
Cornhill. "Molly's character contains very much of" Gaskell's "in her early years." The greatest creation in the
novel is Mrs. Gibson, who is parallel to Mrs. Bennet in
Pride and Prejudice. Gaskell "has yet to receive...just...
praise from a generation other than her own."

127 _____. "A Literary Letter," Sphere (London), XLII (10 September), 252.

It is nice to have centenary appreciations of Gaskell, but why in the August periodicals when her birthday was September 29th? In general, the recent articles on her lack critical perspicacity. Ward's biography of her in The Dictionary of National Biography had "at least a dozen errors," which he has "repeated in his new...edition of" Gaskell's "novels."

128 _____. "A Literary Letter," Sphere (London), XLIII (5 November), ii.

Gaskell is going to have "a great revival."

129 _____. "A Little-Known Home of Mrs. Gaskell," Sphere (London), XLIII (8 October), 36.

Gaskell loved to stay in Silverdale, and she wrote "part of Ruth" there and also "part of Mary Barton."

130 _____. Sphere (London), XLIII (22 October), vi.

George Eliot was wrong when she predicted that Gaskell would not "last."

131 SWINDELLS, T. "Life-Story of Mrs. Gaskell, Novelist Who Added to Manchester's Fame: Her Pictures of City Life,..." Manchester Evening Chronicle (9 December), p. 2.

Gaskell's reputation will continue to grow. She was never "more popular than" she is today.

132 _____. "Garratt Hall: A Relic of Old Manchester To Be Demolished," Manchester Guardian (9 February), p. 5.

[Though included in the Gaskell Cuttings, Manchester Central Library, this item does not refer to Gaskell, but she did mention Garratt Hall in her "Disappearances," Household Words (London), III (7 June 1851), 246-50.]

133 TOOLEY, SARAH A. "The Centenary of Mrs. Gaskell," Cornhill Magazine (London), n.s. XXIX (September), 315-25.

Gaskell was right in believing that her future fame would rest on Cranford. The Rev. G. A. Payne gave me a guided tour of Knutsford, which is still full of echoes of Cranford. Gaskell modestly excluded from The Life of Charlotte Brontë Charlotte's letters praising Gaskell's own fiction. She wrote after breakfast, though she "never had a study" and would go on talking to the children and servants as she wrote.

1910

134 TOOLEY, SARAH A. "The Centenary of Mrs. Gaskell's Birth:
the Friend of Charlotte Brontë and the Creator of Cranford.
Illustrated from a Unique Collection of Pictures in the
Possession of Her Daughter Miss Gaskell," Graphic (London)
(1 October), supplement, 4 pages.
[Though this item consists largely of pictures, an un-
titled article by Mrs. Tooley appears on p. 4 of supplement.] Mrs. Gaskell is best known for Cranford. Miss
Gaskell's home at 84, Plymouth Grove, Manchester, remains
a "shrine" to her mother's "memory."

135 WALKER, HUGH. The Literature of the Victorian Era. Cambridge:
University Press, pp. 650-51, 658, 710, 724-28, 738, 1034.
Gaskell's best fiction is humorous, and Cranford "stands
on a wholly different plane from the rest of her works"--
even from the charming Wives and Daughters and Cousin
Phillis. "Had she written several stories of the quality
of Cranford," Gaskell would "have ranked among the greatest
of English novelists. As it is," she belongs "high in the
second rank."

136 WARD, [SIR] A.[DOLPHUS] W.[ILLIAM]. "In Memoriam: Elizabeth
Cleghorn Gaskell," Cornhill Magazine (London), n.s. XXIX
(October), 457-66.
Cranford and The Life of Charlotte Brontë are recognized
classics. Sylvia's Lovers, though outside of Gaskell's
usual "locality" and period, is a Christian tale "with the
directness...of...Greek tragedy." Cousin Phillis is a perfectly executed prose "idyll," and Wives and Daughters is
the greatest of Gaskell's novels. Her fiction reflects a
mid-Victorian social reformism yet also the rest from
social concerns of the later Victorian period.

137 WARNER, CHARLES DUDLEY, ET AL., eds. Warner's Dictionary of
Authors Ancient and Modern. Akron, Ohio: Werner Co.
S.v. "Gaskell, Elizabeth Cleghorn."
Gaskell's "best" works are Mary Barton, Sylvia's Lovers,
Cousin Phillis, The Life of Charlotte Brontë, and the
"classic" Cranford.

138 WELLDON, [RT. REV.] J. E. C. "The Brontë Family at Manchester," Cornhill Magazine (London), n.s. XXVIII (April),
494-501.
Gaskell connects the Brontës with Manchester.

139 _____. "The Brontë Family in Relation to Manchester. An
Address...at the Annual Meeting held in Manchester,...
February 19th, 1910," Brontë Society Transactions (Brad-
ford), IV, part XX (March), 144-50.

Charlotte Brontë visited Gaskell in Manchester, and Charlotte's letters show how much she valued Gaskell's friendship.

140 WHITMORE, CLARA H. <u>Woman's Work in English Fiction: from the Restoration to the Mid-Victorian Period</u>. New York and London: G. P. Putnam's Sons, Knickerbocker Press, pp. 274-92.

Gaskell was "one of the most feminine" of "writers." The women in <u>Mary Barton</u> possess great "strength of character.... There is hardly a story of" Gaskell's "which is not adorned by the friendship of the heroine for some other woman...." <u>Wives and Daughters</u> is her finest long novel, though <u>Cranford</u> will always have a unique place in literature. Gaskell influenced George Eliot, who, in spite of her "intellectual power," had less hope about life than Gaskell, a person filled with characteristically Unitarian optimism.

*141 WILSON, REV. J. MaCARTNEY. <u>Presbyterian Messenger</u> (London).

[Centenary article on Gaskell.] [Source: Esther Alice (Mrs. Ellis H.) Chadwick. "The Gaskell Collection at Manchester," <u>Bookman</u> (London), XLI (October 1911), 45-46. <u>See</u> review under 1911.A2.]

142 X. "The History of Garratt Hall [letter to Editor]," <u>Manchester Guardian</u> (16 February), p. 3.

The article on the disappearance of a master of Garratt Hall that appeared in <u>Household Words</u> "was written by our greatest Manchester novelist," Gaskell, and "I believe I know" where she got the story. But "in the course of a not inconsiderable amount of investigation I have not met with a scrap of evidence to support it."

<u>1911 A BOOKS</u>

1 CHADWICK, ESTHER ALICE [MRS. ELLIS H.]. "Introduction.... Calendar of Principal Events in Mrs. Gaskell's Life," in [Selections from] <u>Mrs. Gaskell</u>. Regent Library. London: Herbert & Daniel, pp. ix-xxxiv, and other scattered critical comments. [Republished in Chicago: F. G. Browne & Co., 1913.]

<u>Mary Barton</u> is, "in some ways," Gaskell's "best" novel "because of" its "intense feeling." Gaskell's other two best known works are <u>Cranford</u> and <u>The Life of Charlotte Brontë</u>, but all her novels "deserve to be much better known," and <u>Wives and Daughters</u> is, on the whole, her

1911

(CHADWICK, ESTHER ALICE [MRS. ELLIS H.])
masterpiece. [Chadwick's "Selections" from Gaskell were
largely ignored by reviewers, but the following contemptuous
notice is worth citing: Anon. Sphere (London) XLVIII
(17 February 1912), 216 (The Regent's Library's Selections
from Mrs. Gaskell is "an outrage," for novelists should be
reprinted whole.).]

2   GREEN, JOHN ALBERT. A Bibliographical Guide to the Gaskell
Collection in the Moss Side Library Manchester: Reference
Library, King St.; Moss Side Library, Bradshaw St.
[This guide to the collection (now housed in the Manchester Central Library and brought up to date) includes
primary and secondary Gaskell material, autographs, manuscripts, pictures, works by Gaskell's husband, and miscellaneous items.]
[Reviews of the bibliography included the following:
Anon. "A Gaskell Bibliography," Millgate Monthly (Manchester), VI (September 1911), 750-51 (Green's bibliography
shows that the Gaskell Collection "has been much extended.")
Anon. "Miscellaneous Publications," Yorkshire Post (Leeds)
(1 November 1911), p. 5 (This bibliography will interest
readers of Gaskell's books.). Anon. "New Books," Manchester Guardian (21 July 1911), p. 5 (Green's bibliography
will be "a valuable" tool "for the literary historian.").
Anon. "The Observatory," Manchester City News (29 July
1911), p. 6 (Green's guide to the collection is well done,
but it is too bad that the library does not have more
manuscripts and autographs of Gaskell's.). Esther Alice
(Mrs. Ellis H.) Chadwick. "The Gaskell Collection at Manchester," Bookman (London), XLI (October 1911), 45-46.
(This is an "invaluable" bibliography, but it shows that
some important Gaskell items are missing from the collection.) C.[lement] K. S.[horter]. Sphere (London), XLVI
(19 August 1911), p. 212 (Green has "prepared a valuable
guide.").]

1911 B   SHORTER WRITINGS

1   ANON. "Annual Meeting," Brontë Society Transactions (Bradford),
IV, part XXI (4 February), 201-3.
The sixteenth annual meeting of the society was held in
Manchester in honor of the centenary of Gaskell, "Charlotte
Brontë's eminent biographer."

2   ANON. "A Letter of Rev. Patrick Brontë," Christian Life
(London), XXXVII (25 March), 140.

Miss Gaskell has given to the Moss Side Library a letter from the Rev. Patrick Brontë to Mrs. Gaskell's husband that refers to her work on The Life of Charlotte Brontë.

*3   ANON. "'Lizzie Leigh' Sold as a Dickens Item," Americana (New York), no. 6 (December), pp. 1208-9.
        [Source: Catherine Margaret Ellen Halls. "Bibliography of Elizabeth C. Gaskell." Diploma in librarianship dissertation, University of London, 1957. See 1957.B5.]

4   ANON. "Manchester: Lower Mosley-Street," Inquirer (London), n.s. no. 680 (7 January), p. 14.
        J. A. Green gave a "lantern lecture" on Gaskell, and the Rev. A. Cobden Smith's "centenary address" on Gaskell "and Lower Mosley-Street" has been published in the Sunday School Quarterly (London) for January.

5   ANON. "New Books of the Month. Classic Reprints. Sylvia's Lovers,..." Books News Monthly (Philadelphia), XXIX (May), 626.
        This new edition of "one of" Gaskell's "lesser known stories" has an "interesting" introduction by Thomas Seccombe.

6   AXON, W.[ILLIAM] E. A. "Mrs. Gaskell, Thomas Wright, and G. F. Watts's 'Good Samaritan',..." Papers of the Manchester Literary Club, XXXVII, 417-19.
        Watts's portrait of Thomas Wright as "The Good Samaritan," in the Manchester Art Gallery, reminds us of the help that Gaskell gave to Wright in his efforts to rehabilitate convicts.

7   _____. "News for Bibliophiles," Nation (New York), XCII (15 June), 600.
        The italicized phrase in Gaskell's "The Crooked Branch"--"It's dairy and it might have been arable"--was taken, as Ward pointed out "in the Knutsford edition," from "a dear friend who occasionally" made notes of the racy talk of farm families. This lady's notes were privately and posthumously printed as Country Conversations (1881) but without her name--Miss Tollet.

8   BAILEY, ELMER JAMES. "Studies in English Masterpieces.... Mrs. Gaskell's Cranford," American Education (Albany, New York), X (April), 537-38. [Reprinted as Outlines of English Masterpieces. No. 17. Albany, New York: American Education Co., 1911.]

1911

(BAILEY, ELMER JAMES)
[The reprint is cited by Northup (1929.B6), but the item is merely a chapter-by-chapter outline of the events in Cranford.]

9 CHADWICK, ESTHER ALICE [MRS. ELLIS H.]. "Introduction," in Sylvia's Lovers. Everyman's Library. London: J. M. Dent & Sons. New York: E. P. Dutton, vii-xiii.

All of Gaskell's "novels except Sylvia's Lovers were based on her own actual experience of life, or on that of her relatives and friends, and the scenes are laid in places where she lived at one time or another." But Sylvia's Lovers is based on careful historical research. The writing spanned three years, and Gaskell took "greater pains with it than any of her other stories, and even re-wrote some of the latter portion," "contrary to her usual custom."

10 COOK, E. T. The Life of John Ruskin. New York: Macmillan Co. London: George Allen & Co. I: 440; II: 73.

Ruskin, who admired Gaskell's fiction, visited her in Manchester. He also wrote to her of his extreme distress, the first time that he read Cranford, over Captain Brown's death.

11 GOODWIN, UNAM. "The Fireside Reading Circle. Cranford,..." National Home Reading Union. Young People's Magazine (London), XXIII (December), 36-38.

In spite of the simplicity of the book, "...a child is not able to see all the humour and the pathos of the Cranford ladies with their little pretences and their large generosities.... Nearly all the characters" have "something to admire in" them, "except Mrs. Jamieson, her lazy butler, and her greedy dog."

12 HARRISON, FREDERIC. Autobiographic Memoirs. London: Macmillan & Co. I: 275.

I lent a diary of "my general impressions of the manufacturing world" to Gaskell, "the author of Ruth, who was good enough to read the Ms. and told me that it had much interested her."

13 LARTER, C. E. "Wives and Daughters,..." National Home Reading Union. General Course Magazine (London), XXIII (December), 70-72.

Gaskell's "genius...shows itself in 'Wives and Daughters'." Although Molly Gibson is "tender-natured," like her creator, Molly lacks her creator's "sense of humour."

1911

Gaskell is "the Jane Austen of the nineteenth century,"
but Gaskell's characters have "far more depth." Cynthia
is the writer's "most complex character," whose sincerity,
in spite of her flaws, is shown by her continuing "affection" for Molly.

14   MORIER, RT. HON. SIR ROBERT. Memoirs and Letters of the Right
      Hon. Sir Robert Morier, G.C.B., from 1836-1876. Edited by
      Mrs. Rosslyn Wemyss. London: Edward Arnold. I: 80.
           [Letter to his mother, summer 1849:] Gaskell "is so ex-
      ceedingly human--not one speck of literary dust soils her...
      femininity"--and she "is thoroughly unaffected.... Her
      strength lies, as I think you can see in her book, in a
      certain truth and reality, an earnestness of character
      more than in any brilliancy of genius."

15   MORTIMER, JOHN. "Concerning the Mary Barton Fields," Manches-
      ter Quarterly (January) [published in Papers of the Man-
      chester Literary Club], XXXVII, 1-8.
           The Greenheys Fields, along with the Pepper Hill Farm,
      described in pastoral beauty at the opening of Mary Barton,
      have been destroyed in present-day Manchester, except for
      a small "recreation ground" and a "tract of park land."
      Gaskell ends her novel with a description of a lovely rural
      farmhouse in America, which returns us to the opening image
      of Greenheys Fields.

16   PAYNE, [REV.] G.[EORGE] A. "Writers on Mrs. Gaskell," Papers
      of the Manchester Literary Club, XXXVII, 413-17.
           Much good criticism has been written about Gaskell, but
      Lewis Benjamin's [Lewis Melville] centenary article is
      "incompetent." [See 1910.B82.]

17   SHORTER, CLEMENT [K.]. "Introduction," in Cousin Phillis and
      Other Tales, etc. The Novels and Tales of Mrs. Gaskell,
      VII. The World's Classics, CLXVIII. London: Henry
      Frowde, Oxford University Press, pp. vii-xviii. [Reprinted
      as "Preface," in Cousin Phillis. Compiled by Rikicki Sato.
      Tokyo: Daito Shobo, 1933, unnumbered pages preceding p. 1.]
           Gaskell wrote five remarkable novels...and the incom-
      parable Cranford, the most popular book of the Victorian
      era, excepting only the novels of...Dickens.... Cousin
      Phillis is one of the best short stories ever written...."

18   SMITH, [REV.] G.[EORGE] A. "Mrs. Gaskell and Lower Mosley
      Street," Sunday School Quarterly (London), II (January),
      156-61.

1911

(SMITH, [REV.] G.[EORGE] A.)
There are those still alive who remember with gratitude
Gaskell's "kindly and unselfish labours" as teacher in the
Lower Mosley Street Schools. She insisted that her work
for the Sunday school was not done as the obligation of a
minister's wife but out "of her own choice and desire."

19   TUELL, ANNIE KIMBALL. "Mrs. Gaskell," CONTEMPR C (November),
      681-92. [Reprinted in Living Age (Boston), CCLXXI
      (2 December 1911), 528-36; in A Victorian at Bay. Boston:
      Marshall Jones, 1932, pp. 61-80, with omission of original
      first paragraph.]
      Gaskell deserved to be better remembered than she was
      on her centenary. She still seems "alive" and even
      "modern," for all of her "quaintness of style and taste."
      Because the reviews of her period judged novels by whether
      they liked the characters, Gaskell had a resulting tendency
      to make her heroines too good, and she also accepted re-
      viewers' encouragement to be didactic. Gaskell's greatest
      quality was her gentle sense of humor. Her evocation of
      place almost approaches that of Hardy, though her portrayal
      of nature is pleasant and consoling. Of all unfinished
      novels, Wives and Daughters is the one whose ending I
      should most like to have.

20   WOOD, BUTLER. "Some Bibliographical Notes on the Brontë
      Literature,..." Brontë Society Transactions (Bradford), IV,
      part XXI (March), 189.
      Gaskell's Life of Charlotte Brontë not only "takes first
      place" among Brontë biographies but also ranks among the
      world's "great" biographies.

1912 A   BOOKS - NONE

1912 B   SHORTER WRITINGS

1   ANON. "Bookmarker's Notes," Manchester City News (4 May),
     p. 2.
     "A valuable donation" has been made to the Moss Side
     Library's Gaskell Collection, which contains "probably the
     largest number of books, pamphlets, magazine articles, and
     pictures" about Gaskell "to be found anywhere."

2   ANON. "Mrs. Gaskell's Characters," Manchester City News
     (2 March), p. 3.
     Miss J. Taylor, in a paper on Gaskell's books read at
     the Manchester School of Technology, said that "none of"

Gaskell's "characters are wholly good or wholly bad"--not even Molly Gibson, who can be "petulant."

3   CHADWICK, [ESTHER ALICE] MRS. ELLIS H. "Mrs. Gaskell's Birth-place," Bookman (London), XLIII (December), 160-63.
      I demonstrated from the "rate books" that a house still standing in Chelsea was the one in which Gaskell was born, and I found confirming evidence from an old Chelsea directory.

4   DICKENS, CHARLES. Charles Dickens as Editor. Being Letters Written By Him to William Henry Wills, His Sub-editor. Edited by R.[udolph] C. Lehmann. New York: Sturgis & Walton Co., pp. 20, 23, 42-43, 93, 122, 126, 134-35, 137, 141-46, 151, 155, 176, 242, 266, 318, 321-25.
      [The book contains numerous letters from Dickens to Wills complaining about editorial quarrels with Gaskell.]

5   GOSSE, EDMUND. Portraits and Sketches. London: William Heinemann, pp. 39-40.
      In Florence in 1863 Swinburne spent much of his time with Gaskell, whom he described as that "'dear, brilliant, ingenious creature'."

6   HAMILTON, MARGARET. "The Women of Mrs. Gaskell," Everyman (London), I (22 November), 174.
      Gaskell was "a genius," and her "masterpiece" Sylvia's Lovers portrays a tragic character in an "everyday" setting. Sylvia's one moment of "eloquent wrath" is all the more impressive for being rare in this "natural, unaffected" woman. In Cranford Gaskell achieves subtle comedy with "simple" women. None of today's writers "has mastered" Gaskell's "art" of creating "a simple woman strong enough to dominate the stage."

7   HARDY, A. K. "News for Bibliophiles," Nation (New York), XCV (29 August), 188.
      Contrary to Ward in his introduction to volume V of the Knutsford edition of Gaskell's works, "The Manchester Marriage" was first published in Household Words (London) and not in Littell's Living Age (Boston), which reprinted it.

8   HOLLIDAY, CARL. English Fiction from the Fifth to the Twentieth Century. New York: Century Co., pp. 324, 342-44, 350-51.
      Gaskell is now best known for Cranford, but her fame during her lifetime rested more on her social-problem

1912

(HOLLIDAY, CARL)
  novels <u>Mary Barton</u> and <u>North and South</u>, with their truthful
  portrayals of industrial conditions. Her <u>Cranford</u> showed
  "humanity" in a "hidden" spinster's "corner." The writer's
  other fiction is "now almost forgotten," but <u>Ruth</u> is still
  worth reading "as a psychological study." Many later
  writers rebelled against the domestic and civilized tradition represented by Gaskell's fiction.

9   LANG, ANDREW. <u>History of English Literature from "Beowulf"</u>
    <u>to Swinburne</u>. New York: Longmans, Greene & Co. London:
    Longmans & Co., p. 41.
      Among "minor novelists" was Gaskell, whose treatment of
    "strikes and grimy" working-class "lives" opened up "a new
    theme for fiction."

10 [LARTER, C. E.?]. "General Literature. About Some of Mrs.
    Gaskell's Other Novels," <u>National Home Reading Union.</u>
    <u>General Course Magazine</u> (London), XXIII (May), 173-76.
      <u>Wives and Daughters</u> is a "perfect" picture of a "paro-
    chial" little "country town," yet Gaskell, in <u>North and</u>
    <u>South</u> and <u>Mary Barton</u>, also described the industrial work-
    ing class "with charm and vitality."

11 MARSH, GEORGE L. "<u>Cranford</u>,..." in <u>A Teacher's Manual for the</u>
    <u>Study of English Classics</u>. Chicago and New York: Scott,
    Foresman & Co., pp. 212-14.
      [Though cited by Northup (1929.B6), this item consists
    merely of "study" questions.]

12 MORLEY, HENRY. <u>A First Sketch of English Literature: New</u>
    <u>and Enlarged Edition, Bringing the Work Down to the Deaths</u>
    <u>of Swinburne and Meredith</u>. London: Cassell & Co.,
    pp. 1069-70.
      [This item merely repeats the passage in <u>Of English</u>
    <u>Literature in the Reign of Victoria, with a Glance at the</u>
    <u>Past</u>. Tauchnitz edition, MM. Leipzig: Bernhard Tauch-
    nitz, 1881, pp. 389-91. <u>See</u> 1881.B2.]

13 SECCOMBE, THOMAS. "Introduction," in <u>Mary Barton</u>. Everyman's
    Library. London and Toronto: J. M. Dent. New York:
    E. P. Dutton & Co., pp. vii-xiv. [Reprinted as "<u>Mary</u>
    <u>Barton</u>," in <u>Modern English Essays</u>. Edited by Ernest Rhys.
    New York: Dutton. IV, 196-207.
      "<u>Mary Barton</u> remains unrivalled" in the knowledge and
    "power of the plea that it makes for the poor.... In the
    history of ideas, <u>Mary Barton</u> will always occupy a noble
    place as the starting point and rallying-cry of a new

generation of Humanitarians...." The book's art consists
of simplicity, "limpid dialogue," and the self-effacement
of the author to her larger "purpose."

14 _____. "Preface," in Wives and Daughters. London: Herbert &
Daniel, pp. v-xx.
     Wives and Daughters is "one of the most perfect and pro-
foundly interesting English novels ever written." Though
it contains very little psychological "analysis," "it has
the true greatness of simplicity in the delineation of
English character...." Gaskell's gift was for domestic
fiction, for she was a very feminine writer. "... The
characters of both Cynthia and Molly are so good that the
characters of Cynthia's father and Molly's mother are known
by induction." The novel's style is not memorable, and
the plot has some "padding" toward the close.

15 SINCLAIR, MAY. The Three Brontës. Boston and New York:
Houghton Mifflin Co., Riverside Press, pp. xii, 4-6, 33,
38, 43, 44, 46-47, 52, 64, 101-2, 108, 133, 163, 193,
276-79.
     Gaskell was too "hard" on Mr. Brontë and was unfair to
Branwell, but her motive was to vindicate Charlotte by The
Life of Charlotte Brontë. "In her very indiscretions,"
Gaskell was "incorruptibly and profoundly true" to
Charlotte.

1913 A BOOKS - NONE

1913 B SHORTER WRITINGS

1 ANON. "Daughter of Famous Cheshire Novelist Buried at 'Cranford'," Daily Sketch (30 October), p. 1.
     "Miss Margaret E. Gaskell,...daughter of" Mrs. Gaskell,
"the famous mid-Victorian novelist, and authoress of 'Cranford', was buried at Knutsford yesterday.... Many distinguished literary people were present."

2 ANON. "Death of Miss Gaskell. Daughter of the Authoress of
Cranford,..." Manchester Evening News (27 October), p. 6.
     Miss Gaskell, dead at 76, "was the last survivor but
one of a large family of daughters." Her mother's "best
known work was 'Cranford'."

3 ANON. "The Death of Miss Gaskell," Guardian (London), LXVIII,
part II (31 October), 1354.

1913

(ANON.)
The "youngest daughter of" Mrs. Gaskell has died.
Miss Gaskell "was a Unitarian of the older school represented by Dr. Martineau, and of a truly devout mind, in
reality not far from the Catholic Faith." [See 1913.B27,
1913.B31.]

4 ANON. "Death of Miss M. E. Gaskell," Glasgow Herald (28 October), p. 9.
The "second daughter" of Gaskell, "the famous novelist,"
has "died at the home, still hers, where her mother had
entertained" the famous.

5 ANON. "Deaths. Gaskell [paid announcement]," Times (London)
(28 October), p. 1.
Miss Margaret Emily Gaskell, "second daughter of the
late Rev. William and Mrs. Gaskell," has died.

6 ANON. "The Gaskell Family. Unanimous Desire for a Memorial
Statue Suggested. Views of Representative Citizens,"
Daily Dispatch (Manchester) (31 October), p. 4.
The following objections have been made to the proposal
for a Gaskell memorial at 84, Plymouth Grove: the house
is "rather far from the centre of the city," the Moss Side
Library collection already is a memorial, and a simple
statue would be better.

7 ANON. "Gaskell Memorial. Proposal to Secure Noted House.
Literary Relic. Manchester's Indebtedness to the Dead,"
Daily Dispatch (Manchester) (28 October), p. 3.
B. E. M. writes to suggest that 84, Plymouth-Grove,
should be made into a Gaskell memorial.

8 ANON. "Indication of Houses of Historical Interest by the
L.C.C.," N & Q, 11th ser. VII (29 March), 260.
A plaque commemorating Gaskell's birthplace has been
"affixed" to no. 93, Cheyne Walk, Chelsea.

*9 ANON. "Judge Mellor and the Late Miss Gaskell," Manchester
Guardian (29 October).
[Unlocatable. Source: Gaskell Cuttings, Manchester
Central Library.]

10 ANON. "The Late Miss Gaskell. Representative Gathering at
Yesterday's Funeral," Daily Dispatch (Manchester)
(30 October), p. 3.
"The profound feeling of respect which Manchester enter-
tains for the Gaskell family" was "shown by the large
gathering of representative citizens" at Miss M. E.
Gaskell's funeral.

*11   ANON. "A Link with the Brontës," Daily Mail (London)
       (28 October).
          We print "the portrait of Miss Margaret Emily (Meta) Gas-
       kell, second daughter of Mrs. Gaskell, friend of Charlotte
       Brontë and authoress of 'Cranford'...." Miss Gaskell has
       just died. [Unlocatable. Source: Gaskell Cuttings,
       Manchester Central Library.]

12   ANON. "Literary," Manchester City News (1 November), p. 7.
          Mr. George Butterworth reminisced at the Literary Club
       about the late Miss M. E. Gaskell, and there was also a
       discussion about "a permanent memorial to the" Gaskells in
       Manchester.

13   ANON. "Manchester and the Late Miss Gaskell. The House in
       Plymouth Grove," Manchester Guardian (29 December), p. 8.
          A motion will be made "before the City Council" on
       January 7th to turn the Plymouth Grove house into a "Gas-
       kell Museum," but "the Finance Committee" will oppose the
       proposal.

14   ANON. "Mementoes of Mrs. Gaskell," Manchester City News
       (13 December), p. 12.
          The Gaskell family's "collection of antique furniture,
       china, pictures, books," etc. will go on sale at an
       auction.

15   ANON. "Miss Gaskell," Daily Dispatch (Manchester)
       (28 October), p. 2.
          Miss Gaskell was a link with the great Victorians.
       Charlotte Brontë sent Mrs. Gaskell Ruskin's Stones of
       Venice and hoped that it would "please" her and Meta.

16   ANON. "Miss Gaskell [Editorial]," Manchester Guardian
       (27 October), p. 8.
          The late Meta Gaskell, who knew many of the illustrious
       Victorians, continued to live in her mother's and father's
       house.

17   ANON. "Miss Gaskell," Manchester Guardian (27 October),
       p. 16.
          We regretfully note the death of Miss Margaret E.
       Gaskell, daughter of "the famous novelist.... In looks,"
       Meta "bore some resemblance to her mother...." Miss Gas-
       kell carried out her mother's request not to cooperate
       with would-be biographers "with a staunchness unequalled
       in any of the similar cases in modern literary history."

1913

18   ANON. "Miss Gaskell," Times (London) (28 October), p. 11.
         In "obedience" to her mother's wishes, the late Miss
      Margaret Gaskell "declined all requests to assist in the
      preparation of a biography of Mrs. Gaskell."

19   ANON. "Miss Gaskell's Bequests," Inquirer (London), n.s. no.
      830 (22 November), p. 748.
         The late Miss Gaskell has left the Richmond portrait of
      her mother to the National Portrait Gallery.

20   ANON. "Miss Gaskell's Death. Daughter of a Famous Novelist,"
      Daily Chronicle (London) (28 October), p. 4.
         Mrs. Gaskell's daughter, the late Miss Gaskell, was a
      link with a great period of Victorian literature.

21   ANON. "Miss Meta Gaskell," Spectator (London), CXI (1 Novem-
      ber), 704-5.
         The death of Meta Gaskell, daughter of "the famous
      author of Cranford, brings sorrow to many."

22   ANON. "Mr. R. H. Watt," Manchester Guardian (15 March), p. 8.
         Mr. Watt, who died yesterday as a result of a fall from
      his trap, built the Gaskell Memorial Tower.

23   ANON. "Mrs. Gaskell's Birthplace," Manchester Guardian
      (15 March), p. 10.
         "A bronze tablet is to be placed...on the house in
      Cheyne Walk, Chelsea, where" Gaskell "was born."

24   ANON. "Mrs. Gaskell's Memory. Memorial Scheme Finds Favour.
      Museum of Relics. Manchester's Poor Share in Literature,"
      Daily Dispatch (Manchester) (29 October), p. 3.
         "Widespread approval" by important citizens is being
      given to the proposal that 84, Plymouth-Grove, be made a
      memorial to Gaskell.

25   ANON. "Notes of the Week," Inquirer (London), n.s. no. 827
      (1 November), p. 692.
         So long as the late Miss M. E. Gaskell "lived in" Mrs.
      Gaskell's old house, "the spirit which created 'Cranford'
      and 'Wives and Daughters' and challenged the apathy of
      middle-class comfort in the social ideals of 'Mary Barton'
      and 'North and South' seemed to be still in our midst."

26   ANON. "A Rare Example [Editorial]," Daily Chronicle (London)
      (28 October), p. 6.
         "The daughter of the authoress of 'Cranford'," the late
      Miss M. E. Gaskell was herself a remarkable person who had
      known the great Victorians.

27   ANON. "What Lancashire Thinks,..." Guardian (London), LXVIII,
       part II (14 November), 1437.
          "The correspondent who" objected "to my remark that the
       late Miss Gaskell,...a Unitarian of the older school," was
       "not far from the Catholic faith," ought to reread his New
       Testament. [See 1913.B3, 1913.B31.]

28   ANON. "Worthy Daughter of Famous Mother. The Late Miss
       Gaskell. Touching Tribute by Leading Citizens," Manchester
       City News (1 November), p. 7.
          Apart from the high position that came naturally as the
       daughter of a famous novelist, the late Miss Margaret Gas-
       kell was revered in her own right. [The article is fol-
       lowed by excerpts from letters by Charles Hughes reminiscing
       about Mrs. Gaskell and by Rt. Rev. J. E. C. Welldon praising
       Miss Gaskell.]

29   FITZGERALD, PERCY. Memories of Charles Dickens. Bristol:
       J. W. Arrowsmith. London: Simpkin, Marshall, Hamilton,
       Kent & Co., pp. 132, 153.
          Gaskell was almost the equal of Jane Austen. Dickens
       "admired the beautiful finish and delicacy of" Gaskell's
       "work," though she frequently quarreled with him over his
       editorial suggestions.

30   H.[ERFORD], C. H. "Memorial Notices. Miss Gaskell," Inquirer
       (London), n.s. no. 827 (1 November), pp. 698-99.
          Meta Gaskell's mother was a famous writer--"the literary
       comrade, if not precisely the compeer of Dickens, Thackeray,
       and Ruskin." Miss Gaskell carried on in her mother's tra-
       dition of benevolent work and interest in the arts.

31   KELLY, E. E. "Correspondence. Christians, Catholics and
       Orthodox," Guardian (London), LXVIII, part II (7 November),
       1381.
          I object to your reference to a late Unitarian lady
       [Gaskell's daughter] as having been 'in reality not far
       from the Catholic faith'.... The creed of Athanasius"
       seems much "more definite than" that "of Unitarians," even
       "'the older school'." [See 1913.B3, 1913.B27.]

32   NORTON, SARA, and M. A. DeWOLFE HOWE. Letters of Charles
       Eliot Norton, with Biographical Comment by His Daughter
       Sara Norton and M. A. DeWolfe Howe. Boston and New York:
       Houghton Mifflin Co., Riverside Press, I: 154-56, 167-69,
       171-74, 201-2, 204-6, 238-41, 304.
          [There are many references to Norton's close friendship
       with Gaskell and his warm admiration of her work.]

1913

33 PROTHERO, JOHN K. "Masterpiece for the Week: <u>Sylvia's
    Lovers</u>,..." <u>Everyman</u> (London), I (14 March), 694, 696.
        Gaskell was a "genius of domesticity," but, in <u>Sylvia's
    Lovers</u>, she created a splendid novel out of the "materials"
    of "history." Gaskell rose "to supreme heights" in "the
    closing scene of the book," in which "Sylvia's repentance
    comes too late."

34 RALLI, AUGUSTUS. "Charlotte Brontë," <u>Fortnightly Review</u>
    (London), n.s. XCIV (1 September), 524-38.
        The recent "publication in the <u>Times</u> [London] of Char-
    lotte Brontë's four letters to Professor Heger has not
    altered" the essentials of Gaskell's interpretation of
    Charlotte in <u>The Life of Charlotte Brontë</u> as a brooding
    and morbid person.

35 RITCHIE, LADY [MRS. ANNE THACKERAY]. <u>A Discourse on Modern
    Sibyls</u>. The English Association Pamphlet, no. 24. Oxford:
    Horace Hart, pp. 2, 5, 6-7, 8-9.
        [Lady Ritchie's Presidential Address was read by Ernest
    G. von Glehn at the Annual General Meeting, 10 January
    1913:] Gaskell "and Mrs. Oliphant were my torch-bearers
    in youth as afterwards." Gaskell "became the people she
    wrote about." Whether she wrote of Charlotte Brontë, Molly
    Gibson, or Clare Gibson, Gaskell "saw with" the "eyes" of
    the characters that she was describing. <u>Cranford</u> "reveals
    the mighty secret of kindness allied to gentle fun."

36 SAINTSBURY, GEORGE. <u>The English Novel</u>. London: J. M. Dent &
    Sons. New York: E. P. Dutton & Co., pp. 253-55.
        Gaskell's novels convey considerable "power" and
    "pleasure," but they are unsuccessful as artistic works.
    For example, her characters in <u>Cranford</u> are "mere types,"
    and <u>North and South</u>, in spite of a good beginning, does not
    hang together. Gaskell's "means were, perhaps, greater
    than those of most of her brother-and-sister novelists, but
    she set them to loose ends, to ends too high for her, to
    ends not worth achieving; and thus produced...flawed and
    unsatisfactory work."

37 SANFORD, MARTHA COBB. "'What Does It Signify How We Dress?'
    The Latest Fashions in Cranford Seventy Years Ago,"
    <u>Woman's Home Companion</u> (New York), XL (March), 14-15.
        [An informal essay about clothes in <u>Cranford</u>, with many
    direct quotations from the novel.]

38 SECCOMBE, THOMAS. "Report of an Address by Mr. Thomas Sec-
    combe, M.A., entitled 'The Place of the Brontës among Women

1913

Novelists of the Last Century'. Reprinted...[from]
Huddersfield Daily Examiner," _Brontë Society Transactions_
(Bradford), V, part XXIII (April), 8-12.
  Charlotte Brontë and Gaskell belong in the second rank
of distinguished novelists, just below Fielding, Scott,
Dickens, and Meredith.

39 SHORTER, CLEMENT [K.]. "Introduction," in _Lizzie Leigh. The_
Grey Woman. And Other Tales. The Novels and Tales of
Mrs. Gaskell, VIII. The World's Classics, CLXXV. London:
Henry Frowde, Oxford University Press, pp. vii-xiv.
  Gaskell was a "very fine...short story writer and...
essayist," and her short works are superior to those of
Dickens and Thackeray.

40 _____. "Introduction," in _Round the Sofa_. The Novels and
Tales of Mrs. Gaskell, IX. The World's Classics, CXC.
London: Humphrey Milford, Oxford University Press,
pp. vii-xiv.
  The frame narrative for _Round the Sofa_ was "invented for
...book-publication, for five of the six pieces had appeared serially in _Household Words_ [London]." Lady Ludlow
is supposed to be based on Lady Jane Stanley. I have been
unable to discover if "The Half Brothers" was first published in a periodical, but Ward is wrong in assigning it
to the _Dublin University Magazine_ (1858), for the anonymous
story with that name in the magazine is certainly not by
Gaskell.

41 _____. "A Literary Letter. The Late Miss 'Meta' Gaskell,"
Sphere (London), LX (8 November), 154.
  As Meta wrote me, "'you will so well understand that in
our eyes'" Gaskell "'was just a (perfect) _mother_ rather
than a writer'." Meta "did not like Mrs. Chadwick's life
of her mother [1910.A1]" and "sent me some 150 corrections"
of the book. Meta was ready to assist me in my wish to
write "a little book biographical and critical" about Gaskell, and Meta gave me a very large number of letters
written to her mother, including one from Patrick Brontë.

42 _____. "Serial Issue of Two Stories," _N & Q_, 11th ser. VIII
(27 September), 247.
  I wish "information" about where, if at all, Gaskell's
"The Half Brothers" "was first serialized." Ward is wrong
in identifying it with "The Half Brothers" by another
anonymous author in _Dublin University Magazine_ (November
1858).

1913

43 S.[HORTER], C.[LEMENT] K. Sphere (London), LIII (7 June), 272.
    Sir Alfred Comyn Lyall's "sister married a Mr. Holland,
    a member of the family to which" Gaskell "belonged." I
    have talked with him about her.

44 _____. Sphere (London), LV (29 December), 320.
    Percy Fitzgerald, in his book on Dickens [1913.B29],
    shows "no perception that" Gaskell "is now acknowledged to
    be entitled to a place among our great novelists."

45 SPIELMANN, MARION H. "Charlotte Brontë's 'Tragedy'. The Lost
    Letters. Dr. Heger's Gift to the British Nation. Text and
    Translation," Times (London) (29 July), 9-11. [Reprinted
    in Brontë Society Transactions (Bradford), V, part XXIV
    (April 1914), 49-75.]
    "... Small unimportant portions of three of these
    letters" appear in Gaskell's Life of Charlotte Brontë, but,
    on account of "the biographer's peculiar purpose,...garbled
    in a manner rare in a frankly and candidly conceived nar-
    rative." Gaskell's "first extract...consists of two dif-
    ferent letters pieced together" to "give the impression of
    one;...scraps of sentences are interwoven in such a way as
    to avoid the appearance of the selection and the careful
    suppression of passages, and even the real significance"
    is "thus ingeniously and successfully concealed." Her
    second abstract is also "a skillful patchwork."

46 WEBB, W. T., and J. A. ALDIS. A Handbook of English Litera-
    ture. London: John Bale, Sons & Danielsson, p. 83.
    Gaskell has "a special claim to be regarded as" a clas-
    sic novelist, along with Trollope, Reade, Meredith, and
    Hardy. Mary Barton gives "a striking picture of" class
    war, Wives and Daughters is "admirable," but "the exqui-
    sitely humorous and sympathetic" Cranford is Gaskell's
    "masterpiece."

47 WELLDON, [RT. REV.] J. E. C. "The Late Miss Gaskell. To the
    Editor,..." Manchester Guardian (31 October), p. 3.
    Cannot the Plymouth Grove house "be preserved as a
    memorial" to the Gaskell family?

48 WOOD, BUTLER. "The Connection of Charlotte Brontë with the
    Lake District. Being the Substance of a Lecture Delivered
    before the Kendal Literary and Philosophical Society in
    1911," Brontë Society Transactions (Bradford), V, part
    XXIII (April), 13-24.
    Though Gaskell's charges against the Cowan Bridge School
    in her Life of Charlotte Brontë were contested by relations

of the Rev. W. Carus Wilson and particularly by his son-in-law, Rev. H. Shepheard, Wilson's temperament actually made him unfit to run a school, however well he meant. His fierce eccentricities are confirmed by his own published stories.

1914 A BOOKS

1   GREEN, JOHN ALBERT. Catalogue of an Exhibition of Books and Autographs Illustrating the Life and Work of Mrs. E. C. Gaskell Held at the Manchester Reference Library in March and April 1914. Manchester: Reference Library, Picca-dilly: Moss Side Library, Bradshaw St.
    [The catalogue serves as a supplement to Green's 1911 Bibliographical Guide (1911.A2) and contains bibliography, holograph materials, pictures, and works by Gaskell, in-cluding first editions.]
    [The following review noted items of particular interest in the Catalogue, all of which had been previously men-tioned in the 1911 Guide: Anon. Manchester City News (4 April 1914), p. 8 (The exhibit includes the manuscript of "Crowley Castle" and a few assorted letters.).]

1914 B SHORTER WRITINGS

1   ANON. "City Council. Foregone Conclusions. The Gaskell House," Manchester City News (7 February), p. 9.
    There was pathos in Councilor Derwent Simpson's "plea" to "blank" faces that the city purchase, or accept as a gift, Gaskell's old house for the honor of literature. Then the Council rejected his appeal.

2   ANON. "An Edition of Cranford," Manchester Guardian (28 November), p. 4.
    "A capital little edition of 'Cranford' is edited by Mrs. E. V. Lucas," and E. H. New's "illustrations recover something of the spirit of the story."

3   ANON. "Editorial Notes. Death of Miss Gaskell," Brontë Society Transactions (Bradford), V, part XXIV (April), 78.
    Miss Margaret ("Meta") E. Gaskell died on October 26, 1913. She was often mentioned in Mrs. Gaskell's letters.

4   ANON. "Gaskell Collection. Decision of Libraries Committee," Manchester Evening News (28 January), p. 4.

1914

(ANON.)
"The Libraries Committee of the Manchester Corporation...
regretfully decided not to recommend the purchase of the
Gaskell collection, nor to accept administration" of it.

5   ANON. "The Gaskell House [Editorial]," Manchester Guardian
(3 February), p. 8.
"If the Libraries and Art Gallery Committees really reflect" the opinions of the majority in Manchester, the
Gaskell memorial proposal will probably be killed tomorrow
by the City Council. The memorial would have given "pleasure" to "those who love" Gaskell's "books. To the argument
that it is not 'practical,' we answer that one earns money
through the practicalities of commerce precisely in order
to enjoy the happiness obtainable from music, from books,
from pictures, from the play and sparkle of the human
spirit...." The city will be sorry later.

6   ANON. "Gaskell Manuscripts at the Manchester Reference
Library," Manchester Guardian (17 March), p. 11.
Gaskell's manuscripts and first editions can be seen in
the Gaskell exhibit at the Manchester Reference Library's
temporary home at Piccadilly.

7   ANON. "The Gaskell Memorial. Books and Manuscripts,"
Manchester Guardian (2 February), p. 11.
"The Libraries Committee" of the city corporation has
refused to recommend the purchase or administration of "the
Gaskell property," but it is exploring whether "certain"
specific "books and manuscripts" of Gaskell's might be
purchased.

*8   ANON. "Gaskell Memorial as Council Chamber," Daily News
(London) (20 April).
"The Knutsford Council has accepted the offer by Mrs.
Watt of a portion of the Gaskell Memorial Tower and King's
Coffee House for use as a Council Chamber." [Unlocatable.
Source: Gaskell Cuttings, Manchester Central Library.]

9   ANON. "The Gaskell Memorial. Council Decline Councillor
Simpson's Proposal," Manchester Guardian (5 February),
p. 12.
Mr. Simpson, in moving that the Gaskell house be made a
city memorial, reminded the council that Gaskell's name
would be remembered "centuries hence" when most other Manchester names have been forgotten. Mr. Wood, in opposing
the motion, said that Manchester loved literature but that
84, Plymouth Grove, was an example of ugly Victorian

architecture and that a Gaskell memorial should be collected
in an already existing public hall. Simpson's motion was
defeated.

10   ANON. "The Gaskell Memorial. Further Progress of the Scheme.
Support by Bishop Knox and Judge Parry," Manchester Guardian
(31 January), p. 11.
       Judge Parry and Bishop Knox, along with others, have
pledged donations for a Gaskell memorial at 84, Plymouth
Grove. Although the Finance Committee of the City Council
has refused to approve purchase of the house, all that
would be needed, if it is accepted as a gift, is "upkeep."

11   ANON. "The Gaskell Memorial," Manchester Guardian (29 January),
p. 8.
       The Libraries Committee of the Manchester City Council
has "decided regretfully not to recommend the purchase of
the Gaskell collection nor to accept administration of the
same in the event of the corporation having the option of
controlling it."

12   ANON. "The Gaskell Memorial," Manchester Guardian
(12 February), p. 11.
       A private citizen, whose name we cannot disclose, has
offered to buy the Gaskell house and to donate it to the
public or to a group of "trustees."

13   ANON. "Gaskell Memorial. Present Stage of Negotiations,"
Manchester Evening News (30 April), p. 5.
       Negotiations are under way by private parties to buy
and maintain the Gaskell house, "but a difficulty has
arisen regarding the question of terms."

14   ANON. "A Gaskell Memorial for Manchester. Progress of the
Scheme. The Committee and Subscriptions," Manchester
Guardian (30 January), p. 11.
       A private committee of citizens is obtaining pledges
toward a proposed £2,000 to be given to the City Council for
purchase and annual expenses of a Gaskell memorial at 84,
Plymouth Grove. Mr. Simpson's proposal yesterday that the
Art Gallery Committee agree to administer the house as a
museum if citizens provided the money was rejected by a
single vote, with many abstentions, but purchase of some of
the house's contents was tentatively approved.

15   ANON. "The Gaskell Sale," Manchester City News (7 February),
p. 2.
       Beginning on Monday the Gaskell collection of 84, Ply-
mouth Grove, will go on "sale by auction."

1914

16   ANON. "The Gaskell Sale. Public Interest in the Library,"
     Manchester Guardian (18 February), p. 11.
          The "melancholy" act of auctioning off Gaskell relics
     "was brought to an end yesterday." Among the items sold
     were some autographed editions of Gaskell's books, "four
     volumes of manuscript music" copied in her own hand, a
     number of Brontë books, and assorted first editions by
     various authors.

17   ANON. "The Gaskell Shrine [Editorial]," Manchester City News
     (7 February), p. 7.
          For all "our sympathy" concerning Gaskell's memory, we
     feel that the City Council made the right decision in not
     buying her house, for it would have been a poor "business
     proposition." In any case, the shrine should be at
     Knutsford.

18   ANON. "The Home of the Gaskells," Manchester Evening News
     (3 January), p. 3. [With photograph of 84, Plymouth Grove.]
          "On Wednesday the City Council will be asked to purchase
     this building as a memorial to" Gaskell. "The price asked
     is £1,500."

19   ANON. "The Home of the Gaskells [Editorial]," Manchester
     Guardian (2 January), p. 6.
          Although "it is quite right for a Corporation Finance
     Committee to take a strictly financial view of any pro-
     posal," we still favor "Dr. Derwent Simpson's proposal for
     a Gaskell museum" at 84, Plymouth Grove.

20   ANON. "The Home of the Gaskells. Proposal that the City
     Should Purchase. The Finance Committee View," Manchester
     Guardian (2 January), p. 6.
          On Wednesday the City Council will take up the proposal
     of Councilor H. Derwent Simpson that the city buy the
     Plymouth Grove house and turn it into a Gaskell museum,
     but the Finance Committee advises against the proposal.

21   ANON. "Manchester Council. Mrs. Gaskell's House. Proposal
     Deferred," Manchester Guardian (8 January), p. 9.
          "Mr. Derwent Simpson asked" permission "to withdraw
     his motion suggesting the purchase of" Gaskell's house,
     "so that he might submit a full...scheme at the next meet-
     ing." Though a "majority" voted against delay, Mr. Simpson
     achieved it "by simply declining to move the resolution."

22   ANON. "The Memory of Mrs. Gaskell," Manchester Evening News
     (7 January), p. 6.

By a parliamentary maneuver Mr. Simpson obtained a delay till next meeting of a vote on his proposal to make Gaskell's house a city museum--a plan opposed as too vague by the Finance Committee.

23 ANON. "Mrs. Gaskell. Mr. Derwent Simpson and City Memorial," Manchester Guardian (26 January), p. 11.
    Mr. Simpson writes to say that he placed a proposal on the agenda of the City Council for February 4th that 84, Plymouth Grove, be preserved or acquired as a Gaskell museum. The executors now say that they will sell it for £750 plus an annual rent of £50, excluding the property around it.

24 ANON. "Mrs. Gaskell's House," Manchester Guardian (3 March).
    [Unlocatable. Source: Gaskell Cuttings, Manchester Central Library.]

25 ANON. "Mrs. Gaskell's House. Should It Be Bought by the Corporation?" Manchester Evening News (7 January).
    Councilor Simpson, to "cries of 'no'," tried to postpone his motion that the city buy Gaskell's house, yet he then achieved a delay by a parliamentary maneuver. [Unlocatable. Source: Gaskell Cuttings, Manchester Central Library.]

26 ANON. "Mrs. Gaskell's London Home," Manchester Guardian (13 April), p. 6.
    The London County Council has placed a tablet at 93, Cheyne Park, Chelsea, commemorating Gaskell's birthplace and "has issued a little booklet" about it.

27 ANON. "The Proposed Gaskell Memorial: Mrs. Gaskell's Drawing-Room," Manchester Guardian (6 January), p. 11.
    [Photograph of Gaskell's "Drawing-room."]

28 ANON. "The Proposed Manchester Memorial," Manchester Courier (3 January), p. 9.
    The Corporation is considering making Gaskell's house "a public museum" "because of 'the distinction conferred on Manchester by the great writer'."

29 ANON. "The Proposed Purchase of Mrs. Gaskell's House by the Manchester Corporation," Manchester Guardian (3 January), p. 7.
    "It is proposed that the house in Plymouth Grove,... where" Gaskell, "the novelist, lived and wrote most of her books, should be purchased by the Corporation and preserved as a memorial."

1914

30   BALL, M. B. "Mrs. Gaskell and Manchester. To the Editor,..."
     Manchester Guardian (7 January), p. 9.
          Stanley Withers is wrong in thinking that "the whole of"
     Gaskell's "works were written at Plymouth Grove," for
     "Sylvia's Lovers and at least one" other work "were written
     at" Silverdale.

31   CHADWICK, [ESTHER ALICE] MRS. ELLIS H. In the Footsteps of
     the Brontës. London: Sir Isaac Pitman & Sons, see index
     for numerous references to Gaskell. [Reprinted in New York:
     Haskell House, 1971.]
          "The old inhabitants of Haworth have always resented the
     account which" Gaskell "gave of the village in" The Life of
     Charlotte Brontë, and, "in some respects," Gaskell "failed
     to appreciate much that is worthy...in the place and in
     the villagers." The writer gets so many details wrong in
     her account of the Brontë sisters at the Cowan Bridge
     School that it is hard to believe in the justice of her
     charges. "The Rev. A. B. Nicholls has proved that" she
     "greatly underestimated the amount" of Charlotte's juveni-
     lia. Gaskell certainly saw Charlotte's letters to M. Heger
     and intentionally concealed "the real drift of the corre-
     spondence." Branwell was not always "the drunken wretch
     that" Gaskell portrayed. In spite of her disapproval
     of Emily, Sylvia's Lovers owes much to Wuthering Heights.

32   _____. "Introduction," in North and South. Everyman's
     Library. London: J. M. Dent & Sons. New York: E. P.
     Dutton & Co., pp. vii-xiv.
          Gaskell considered North and South her "favorite" among
     her novels but thought that Cranford would be her one im-
     mortal work. North and South is well plotted and "the
     first of her novels in which she handles her characters
     with perfect ease."

33   DOWDEN, EDWARD. Letters of Edward Dowden and His Correspond-
     ents. Edited by Elizabeth D. and Hilda M. Dowden. London:
     J. M. Dent & Sons. New York: E. P. Dutton & Co., pp. 290,
     378.
          [Letter of Dowden's to son Richard, 26 June 1899:] "I
     am glad to hear that you are interested in" Gaskell's "'Life
     of Currer Bell'. There is a great mass now of Brontë lit-
     erature, but" Gaskell's "book remains the most interesting."
     [Extract from diary, 2 June 1912:] In preparing a lecture
     that I gave on the "dangers" and "horrors" "of our material
     civilization," I consulted Gaskell's Mary Barton and North
     and South.

34   GLEAVE, JOSEPH. "Proposed Gaskell Memorial. To the Editor,
      ..." Manchester Guardian (10 January), p. 11.
          "All lovers of pure literature" are indebted "to you"
      and the others who have supported a Gaskell memorial. "We
      had in" Gaskell "not only a great novelist but a great
      biographer...."

35   GOLDSCHMIDT, H. J. [Deputy-Chairman of Finance Committee of
      Corporation of Manchester City Council]. "Report of the
      Finance Committee on Councilor Simpson's Notice of Motion
      Involving Capital Expenditure, Standing Order No. 69 (11),"
      in [Documents of] The Corporation of Manchester City Coun-
      cil [for 1913]. Manchester: Corporation, pp. 1447-48.
          [Report dated 24 December 1913:] Because of the cost
      annual charges, repairs, and administration, and in the
      absence of a specific "decision" concerning "the use" to
      which the house "would be put," the Finance Committee is
      unable to recommend the purchase of the Gaskell property.

36   HADFIELD, A. "Proposed Gaskell Memorial. To the Editor,..."
      Manchester Guardian (31 January), p. 11.
          "If need be, let us raise the money privately" to secure
      the Gaskell house as a "memorial.... Think of the number-
      less institutions the late Miss Gaskells were ever ready
      to help...."

37   HUGHES, CHARLES. "The Proposed Purchase of Miss Gaskell's
      House. To the Editor,..." Manchester Guardian (2 February),
      p. 11.
          I favor a Gaskell memorial but think that the Plymouth
      Grove house with most of the things auctioned off "will
      soon be an empty shell. Who will go to a Manchester
      suburb, which has no other attractions, to see the house
      where" Gaskell "lived" but "about which she did not
      write?" It would be far better to create "a Gaskell Room"
      with "relics" of her "in the coming Reference Library."

38   HUMPHRIES, EDWIN E. "Proposed Gaskell Memorial. To the
      Editor,..." Manchester Guardian (8 January), p. 9.
          "The rate payers of Manchester" do not appreciate the
      wish expressed in your newspaper "that the city buy and
      maintain the Gaskell home. Let books be her monument, or
      let her admirers" pay for the memorial themselves.

39   LARMUTH, GEORGE H. & SONS. Catalogue Re the Late Miss M. E.
      Gaskell, 84, Plymouth Grove, Manchester...To Be Sold by
      Auction by Messrs George H. Larmuth & Sons. On the
      Premises as Above Commencing on Monday, February 9th, 1914,

1914

(LARMUTH, GEORGE H. & SONS)
and Tuesday, Wednesday, Thursday, Friday, and Following
Monday, 16 February. Manchester: George H. Larmuth & Sons.
[This provides an account of the Gaskell home as kept
intact by Gaskell's daughters until the death of Meta in
1913.]

40 _____. [Advertisement], Manchester Guardian (7 February),
p. 18.
"Many admirers of" Gaskell's "works will have an oppor-
tunity of acquiring some personal memento of this famous
authoress. To the literary public the books, of which
there are many rare volumes and first editions, will appeal. To the collectors of china, old furniture, pictures,
prints, & c., the contents of this house will also prove
attractive."

41 LEVY, RAZEL E. Z. "Mrs. Gaskell's Mary Barton [Prize Essay],"
Everyman (London), III (9 January), 429-30.
Mary Barton "is not typical of" Gaskell's later and
better-known humorous vein, yet its "record of woe" contains
small foreshadowings of her later comedy. The book is old-
fashioned in its undisguised intrusive narrative comments
and "leisurely" style. Yet it has a good plot and forms
an artistic whole around John Barton's "thought": "'...
rich and poor; why are they so separate?'" Mary Barton is
most valuable as "an imaginative record" of the condition
of "the working classes" in hard times, supplementing the
studies of "historians, economists, and philosophers."

42 London County Council. Mrs. Gaskell, No. 93, Cheyne Walk,
Chelsea, S.W. Indication of Houses of Historical Interest
in London, part XXXIV, no. 1665. London: Jas. Truscott &
Son, for London County Council, pp. 6-8.
Gaskell had only two "residences in London: no. 93,
Cheyne Walk, where she was born, and no. 3, Beaufort Row,
where her father moved" soon after her birth. "From an
examination of the structure" of 93, Cheyne Walk, "it
seemed probable that" it had "been demolished and a new
house erected," but Mrs. Chadwick showed that, though the
house had been "altered from time to time," it remained
"substantially identical with" Gaskell's birthplace. No. 3,
Beaufort Row has, on the other hand, "been demolished."

43 MACDONALD, FREDERIKA. The Secret of Charlotte Brontë. Followed by Some Reminiscences of the Real Monsieur and Madame
Heger. London and Edinburgh: T. C. & E. C. Jack, pp. 3-4,
7-8, 10, 17, 36-37, 117-18.

1914

Although Gaskell dealt with the other parts of Charlotte's life with considerable "skill" and exactness, Gaskell was inaccurate about the Brussels episode. "I do not think that" she "actually believed her own assertions that Charlotte had no romantic feelings for M. Heger." Gaskell's motives "may have been" admirable, but she created a false impression about the central event of Charlotte's life.

44 S.[HORTER], C.[LEMENT] K. "The Preservation of Mrs. Gaskell's House for Manchester," Sphere (London), LVI (17 January), 74.
     As for the cost of the proposal, "many such" public "memorials" "are self-supporting" by means of the admission charge. In addition to having written an "immortal" biography of Charlotte Brontë, Gaskell is "one of the very great novelists of the Victorian era whose fame is only now becoming fully recognized." Manchester ought to honor her.

45 SIMPSON, H. DERWENT. "Miss Gaskell's House. Uses to which Manchester Might Put the Property. To the Editor,..." Manchester Guardian (5 January), p. 9.
     There is some misunderstanding of my proposal, for the £1,500 to purchase the Plymouth Grove house also will purchase enough land for "recreational purposes" and two "semi-detached houses" that could be used for the "school for the semi-blind" desired by the Educational Committee.

46 _____. "Proposed Gaskell Memorial. Details of the Possible Collection. To the Editor,..." Manchester Guardian (6 January), p. 11.
     The museum could be filled with "a very interesting and valuable permanent collection of paintings, plate, furniture, books, memorabilia, and letters connected with" Mrs. Gaskell, who honored a Manchester that should honor her. Furthermore, Miss M. E. Gaskell gave either £500 or £1,000 "to the Corporation towards the purchase of the Recreation Ground in Plymouth Grove."

47 _____. "The Proposed Gaskell Memorial. To the Editor,..." Manchester Guardian (3 February), p. 11.
     Over £150 have already been pledged toward the Gaskell memorial by private citizens. Several Americans have told me that "any city in the United States...would be glad to acquire" the memorial to Gaskell "even at twelve times the cost."

1914

48   SIMPSON, H. DERWENT. "The Proposed Purchase of Miss Gaskell's
       House. To the Editor,..." Manchester Guardian (2 February),
       p. 11.
            "Mr. J. L. Patton, High Master of the Manchester Grammar
       School," has pledged a donation for the Gaskell fund and
       hopes that "the house will be left as much as possible
       just as it is...."

49   TATHAM, WORTHING & CO. "The Gaskell Sale. To the Editor,..."
       Manchester Guardian (21 February), p. 11.
            In order to correct a "misconception," "we are in-
       structed by the executors to say that" the Gaskell auction,
       "after the distribution of" many "things to public insti-
       tutions," was "in accordance with Miss Gaskell's wishes"
       and "that her family" receives none of the proceeds.

50   WALKER, HUGH. "The Short Story in English," in Selected
       English Short Stories (Nineteenth Century). The World's
       Classics, CXCIII. London: Humphrey Milford, Oxford Uni-
       versity Press, pp. xxviii.
            [Gaskell's "The Squire's Story" is reprinted on pp. 207-
       224.] Among novelists whose short stories were not worthy
       to be included in this collection, "why is it that the
       female absentees so much outnumber the male? Except" for
       Gaskell, "not one of our first-rate women novelists ap-
       pears. Have women disdained the art, or is there something
       in its conditions which renders it less perfectly adapted
       to their genius than the novel?"

51   WELLDON, [RT. REV.] J. E. C. "Miss Gaskell," Cornhill Maga-
       zine (London), n.s. XXXVI (January), 32-35.
            At Miss M. E. Gaskell's funeral, "an old friend of"
       Meta's father "remarked to me that he doubted" that Mrs.
       Gaskell "would have achieved all her notable success in
       literature but for her husband." Meta wrote of her
       mother that "'Mamma's last days had been full of loving
       thought and tender help for others. She was so sweet,
       and dear, and noble beyond words'."

52   _____. "Proposed Gaskell Memorial. Bishop Welldon's Appeal.
       To the Editor,..." Manchester Guardian (7 January), p. 9.
            If the Gaskell house were bought and kept by the city as
       a memorial, "it would be a valuable acquisition to the
       higher life of the city."

53   _____. "The Proposed Purchase of Miss Gaskell's House. To
       the Editor,..." Manchester Guardian (2 February), p. 11.

If the Gaskell house could be bought as a memorial "wholly, or mainly by private contributions" without costing anything to "the ratepayers," the matter would be removed from "politics."

54 WITHERS, STANLEY. "To the Editor,..." Manchester Guardian (6 January), p. 11.
     "Practically the whole of" Gaskell's "literary work was done here," "and it would be a reproach to the intelligence and judgment of Manchester" if it did not honor its most distinguished writer by making her house a public museum.

55 WOOLRICH, GEORGE. "Proposed Gaskell Memorial. To the Editor, ..." Manchester Guardian (15 January), p. 11.
     The Rev. William Gaskell's own distinction is still another reason why Manchester must "not fail to discharge its obligation" to set up a Gaskell memorial.

1915 A BOOKS - NONE

1915 B SHORTER WRITINGS

*1 ANON. "Kingsley and Charlotte Brontë," Christian Science Monitor (Boston) (23 October).
     [Gaskell's biography of Charlotte Brontë changed Kingsley's opinion of Charlotte from unfavorable to favorable. Source: Gaskell Cuttings, Manchester Central Library.]

*2 ANON. "Mrs. Gaskell Visits Charlotte Brontë," Christian Science Monitor (4 November). [Reprints Gaskell's letter describing her visit to Charlotte Brontë.]
     [Source: Gaskell Cuttings, Manchester Central Library.]

3 ERSKINE, MRS. STEUART, ed. Anna Jameson. Letters and Friendships (1812-1860). London: T. Fisher Unwin, pp. 14, 292-300, 321, 337.
     Although Gaskell and Anna Jameson were close friends who exchanged many letters, Anna's expressed dislike of The Life of Charlotte Brontë caused a temporary coolness on Gaskell's part.

4 A Man of Kent. "Rambling Remarks. Mr. Shorter's Edition of Mrs. Gaskell," British Weekly (London), LIX (11 November), 115.
     Shorter's scholarship and his introductions in the Gaskell World's Classics edition are generally admirable, but

1915

(A Man of Kent)
he is wrong and unhistorical in calling Cotton Mather,
mentioned in "Lois the Witch," "'a cruel ruffian'."

5   SHORTER, CLEMENT [K.]. "Introduction," in Right at Last and
Other Tales, Etc. The Novels and Tales of Mrs. Gaskell, X.
The World's Classics, CCIII. London: Humphrey Milford,
Oxford University Press, pp. vii-xiv.
Of the four generally workmanlike stories in Right at
Last, the most noteworthy is the "thrilling, poignant"
"Lois the Witch," a powerful treatment of "a subject almost
too terrible for modern romance"--the persecution of sup-
posed witches by the Puritans in New England.

6   _____. "A Literary Letter. Mrs. Gaskell and Charlotte
Brontë," Sphere (London), LXIII (2 October), 24. [Re-
printed in Brontë Society Transactions (Bradford), V, part
XXVI (April 1916), 144-49.]
Gaskell's great Life ensures that she and Charlotte
Brontë will always be remembered together. In an "unpub-
lished" batch of Gaskell's letters, I have found a few with
references to Charlotte, which I here print.

1916 A   BOOKS - NONE

1916 B   SHORTER WRITINGS

1   ANON. "Note. An Interesting Gaskell Letter," Manchester City
News [Notes and Queries] (5 February), p. 2.
With the permission of Mr. Barnes of Palace Square, Manchester, we print "a letter from" Gaskell "to John Forster,
...begging him to ask Tennyson for a copy of his works to
give to Samuel Bamford, the weaver poet."

2   GREEN, JOHN ALBERT. Brontë Collection, Public Library, Moss
Side, Manchester: List of Additions, 1907-1916. Manches-
ter: Reference Library, Piccadilly; Public Library, Moss
Side, pp. 1-24.
[The list contains some items about Gaskell.]

3   IRWIN, MRS. SURTEES. "Cranford" in War Time. To Be Sold for
Benefit of Red Cross Hospital and Hospital Supply Guild,
Knutsford. N.p., [ca. 1916], n. pag.
[For sale at Clarke School, Northampton, Mass.] Knuts-
ford, though changed by war industries, still has much to
remind one of Gaskell's Cranford.

4   WARD, SIR A.[DOLPHUS] W.[ILLIAM]. "The Political and Social
    Novel: ...Mrs. Gaskell,..." in The Nineteenth Century.
    The Cambridge History of English Literature, edited by Sir
    A.[dolphus] W.[illiam] Ward and A. R. Waller, XIII, part II.
    Cambridge: University Press. New York: G. P. Putnam's
    Sons, 1917, pp. 371-81.
        Hostile critics did not realize that Gaskell's descrip-
    tion in Mary Barton of working-class sufferings expressed
    the aroused conscience of the country, yet, in North and
    South, she showed that she could see the point of view
    of masters as well as workers. Gaskell wrote for Dickens
    but rarely fell under the influence of his "manner," for
    she had a pure "style" all her own. Cranford's inter-
    mingling of "pathos" and "humour" is unique, North and
    South is "one of the finest" of Gaskell's novels, and her
    Life of Charlotte Brontë is a great biography in spite of
    "cavils" against it. Except "for a certain lengthiness"
    and a flawed ending, Sylvia's Lovers is "a perfect" his-
    torical novel, full of "infinite pity" and worthy to be
    ranked with The Heart of Midlothian. Cousin Phillis is
    "one of the loveliest" idylls ever written, and Wives and
    Daughters remains "one of the most exquisite examples in
    English fiction of the pure novel of character."

1917 A   BOOKS - NONE

1917 B   SHORTER WRITINGS

1   GOSSE, EDMUND. The Life of Algernon Charles Swinburne.
    New York: Macmillan Co., p. 104.
        "Swinburne stayed some weeks in Florence, where he
    visited pictures in the delightful company of" Gaskell.

2   GRETTON, M. STURGE. "Women Novelists," Queen (London), CXLII
    (3 November), 620-21.
        Though she did not have the perfection of Jane Austen,
    Gaskell had great emotional depth and surpassed Miss Austen
    in "pages" of Cousin Phillis, Sylvia's Lovers, and Wives
    and Daughters. She was influenced by Crabbe. Gaskell's
    compassion and even tearfulness were largely the result of
    a general Victorian "idealism." She was a philanthropist
    but, above all, a mother, "housewife," and a person talented
    at social intercourse. Her "width of intellectual sympathy"
    was typical of well-off Unitarians or Quakers of Gaskell's
    time.

1917

*3   HAWTHORNE, HILDEGARDE. "Mrs. Gaskell's Masterpiece," St.
      Nicholas (New York), XLV (November), 74-76.
           [A schoolchild's essay on Cranford. Source: Marjorie
      Taylor Davis. "An Annotated Bibliography of Criticism on
      Elizabeth Cleghorn Gaskell, 1848-1973." Ph.D. dissertation,
      University of Mississippi, 1974. See 1974.B6.]

4   HOLLAND, BERNARD [HENRY]. The Lancashire Hollands. London:
      John Murray, p. 300.
           Gaskell's "uncle, Dr. Peter Holland, and his family can
      be recognised among the characters in her stories.... The
      two" Browning sisters "in Wives and Daughters are the
      images of two" spinster "daughters of Peter Holland,...and
      the two old sisters in Cranford...also" resemble them
      strongly.

5   McNULTY, J. H. "Thoughts on Re-reading The Pickwick Papers,"
      Dickensian (London), XIII (February), 38-39.
           "In that delightful novel 'Cranford', there is a charm-
      ing literary conversation on the merits of Pickwick."

6   MILLER, EDWIN L. English Literature. An Introduction and
      Guide to the Best English Books. A Handbook for Schools
      and Readers. Philadelphia and London: J. B. Lippincott
      Co., pp. 47, 502.
           Gaskell's "fame...rests mainly on 'Cranford', a novel"
      that "depicts almost perfectly a society in which vivid
      passion, forcible incident, and absorbing motives have
      passed by for the principal personages, and have not yet
      arrived for the secondary characters."

7   RANKIN, THOMAS E., and WILFORD M. AIKIN. English Literature.
      New York: Macmillan Co., pp. 17, 181, 258, 266.
           One "minor novelist," Gaskell, "who wrote a biography of
      Charlotte Brontë, has delighted the gay and the serious
      alike with her Cranford, a pleasing story of village life."
      Gaskell's Cousin Phillis "is one of the best...examples of"
      a "novelette" that falls "between" the border of "the novel
      and the short-story."

8   WARD, MRS. HUMPHRY. "Some Thoughts on Charlotte Brontë. An
      Address Delivered...to the Brontë Society,...March 3,
      1917," in Charlotte Brontë 1816-1916: A Centenary Memorial
      Prepared by the Brontë Society. Edited by Butler Wood.
      London: T. Fisher Unwin, pp. 17, 18.
           Gaskell's "account," in her Life of Charlotte Brontë, of
      the suffering of the Brontë sisters during their "appalling
      year at the Cowan Bridge School...has never been sub-
      stantially shaken."

9   WELLDON, RT. REV. BISHOP [J. E. C.]. "Centenary Address at
     Haworth," in Charlotte Brontë 1816-1916: A Centenary
     Memorial Prepared by the Brontë Society. Edited by Butler
     Wood. London: T. Fisher Unwin, pp. 65-66, 71.
          The death of "Meta" Gaskell, daughter of Charlotte
     Brontë's biographer, has cut off a living link between the
     Brontës and the present. I disagree with those who think
     that Gaskell's Life of Charlotte Brontë exaggerated Miss
     Brontë's gloom.

1918 A BOOKS - NONE

1918 B SHORTER WRITINGS

1   BATES, HERBERT. English Literature. New York: Longman's,
     Green & Co., p. 482.
          Gaskell "wrote a novel called Mary Barton that showed
     rebellion against things as they were, pointing out the
     hardships of the laborers in the manufacturing towns," but
     "she is best known...for Cranford, a picture of life in an
     uneventful village" that outdoes "Trollope's work in...
     warmth" and "tenderness." Cranford is as genial as Dickens
     "yet never exaggerates."

2   CHADWICK, ESTHER ALICE [MRS. ELLIS H.]. "Patrick Branwell
     Brontë, June 24, 1817-September 28, 1848: a Vindication,"
     Nineteenth Century and After (London), LXXXIV (August),
     296-311.
          The evidence of Branwell's poems and the testimony of
     his friends indicate that Gaskell was unfair to him in her
     Life of Charlotte Brontë. The falling out between Branwell
     and Charlotte may be partly blamed on Charlotte's own bad
     temper. In defense of Gaskell's charges against Mrs.
     Robinson, one can say that Charlotte's now published letters
     are "more libellous" than anything in Gaskell's book.

3   FOLLETT, WILSON. The Modern Novel. A Study of the Purpose
     and the Meaning of Fiction. New York: Alfred A. Knopf,
     pp. 123-24.
          Gaskell's Mary Barton was "the most powerful" and remains
     "the most readable" of all those mid-Victorian social pro-
     test novels that "are the fictional counterparts of the
     Chartist movement." Her North and South shows greater ob-
     jectivity than Mary Barton in suggesting that both manage-
     ment and labor need forgiveness. It is too bad that, be-
     cause of the popularity of the admirable Cranford, Gaskell's
     didactic fiction is not better known.

4 GLOVER, T. R. "Correspondence. Some Speculations on Cranford.
   To the Editor,..." TLS (30 August), 405.
       There are many literary and historical allusions in
   Cranford that suggest the dates of key events: for example,
   the reference to Pickwick Papers, which sets the date for
   Captain Brown's death as 1836 or 1837.

5 LEY, J.[AMES] W.[ILLIAM] T.[HOMAS]. The Dickens Circle: a
   Narrative of the Novelist's Friendships. London: Chapman &
   Hall, pp. 322-24.
       Gaskell was "on good, though not intimate terms with
   Dickens," who admired her fiction in spite of her resistance
   to his editorial suggestions. In any case, Gaskell, as an
   established novelist in her own right, was entitled to
   literary independence.

6 MOODY, WILLIAM VAUGHN, and ROBERT MORSS LOVETT. A History of
   English Literature. Rev. ed. New York: Charles Scribner's
   Sons, pp. 415-16. [1st ed. New York: Charles Scribner's
   Sons, 1902.]
       Gaskell's Mary Barton and North and South treat indus-
   trial problems "with great skill." Cranford, "her best-
   known book," consists "of realistic observation, developed
   in a somewhat fantastic setting."

7 NICOLL, SIR WILLIAM ROBERTSON [CLAUDIUS CLEAR]. "The Correspondence of Claudius Clear. Mary Barton: a Tale for the
   Times," British Weekly (London), LXIII (31 January), 333.
       Gaskell's growing "reputation" rests on Wives and Daugh-
   ters, her "best" book; Cranford; and Mary Barton, which will
   probably endure the "longest" because of its unsurpassed
   "record" of "the feelings of a starving people provoked to
   a rebellion."

8 S.[HORTER], C.[LEMENT] K. "A Literary Letter: a Visit to
   Hampshire Literary Shrines," Sphere (London), LXXIII
   (25 May), 148.
       The plainness of Gaskell's "country home" in Hampshire
   makes one wonder why she picked a house so far from the
   "pleasant" 84, Plymouth Grove. I here publish, for the
   first time in "entirety," a letter of Meta Gaskell to Ellen
   Nussey describing Mrs. Gaskell's death. [The letter includes the following passage:] "When we had all come in
   we had tea, and then were sitting round the fire in the
   drawingroom, so cozily and happily (darling Mama talking
   and planning a most kind plan of lending the house to Lady
   Crompton, who was very much broken down) when quite suddenly, without a moment's warning, in the middle of a sentence she fell forwards--dead."

9   WHITEFORD, ROBERT NAYLOR. Motives in English Fiction.
New York and London: G. P. Putnam's Sons, Knickerbocker
Press, pp. 218, 291-94, 296, 322-24.
Gaskell's Moorland Cottage and, even more so, Cranford
owe something to Mary Russell Mitford's Our Village, though
The Moorland Cottage also shows the influence of Harriet
Martineau's Deerbrook. Gaskell's Mr. Thornton in North and
South is indebted to Charlotte Brontë's Mr. Moore in
Shirley.

1919 A BOOKS - NONE

1919 B SHORTER WRITINGS

1   ANON. Athenaeum (London), no. 4667 (10 October), p. 1005.
Shorter's reissue of The Life of Charlotte Brontë, in
the World's Classics series, is particularly valuable for
its inclusion of "an unpublished letter by" Gaskell "which
gives an even more vivid picture...of the Brontës" and
their tragedy "than any...in her book. The letter is a
masterpiece of quick and passionate apprehension...."

2   ANON. "A Day in 'Cranford'. Literary Societies' Pilgrimage,"
Manchester City News (19 July), p. 2.
Last Saturday the Poetical Society, the Manchester
Shakespeare Society, and the Bolton Shakespeare Society
were given a tour of Knutsford, Gaskell's "Cranford," by
the Rev. George A. Payne.

3   ANON. "Some Books of the Week," Spectator (London), CXXIII
(20 September), 378.
Gaskell's masterful Life of Charlotte Brontë has been
reprinted in the World's Classics series.

4   CHADWICK, ESTHER ALICE [MRS. ELLIS H.]. "Emily Brontë,"
Nineteenth Century and After (London), LXXXVI (October),
677-87.
Gaskell's "assurance," in The Life of Charlotte Brontë,
that "Shirley Keeldar was modelled on Emily" helps correct
the usually gloomy picture of Emily Brontë, who was the
most "good-hearted" and domestically capable of the sisters.
Although Gaskell could not learn from Ellen Nussey of
Emily's true "views of religion," Emily was, in fact, religious in a non-sectarian way.

5   CROTCH, W. WALTER. The Secret of Dickens. 2nd rev. ed.
London: Chapman & Hall, pp. 71, 81-82, 84-88, 98, 131,
172-73.

1919

(CROTCH, W. WALTER)
Dickens was the chief literary influence upon the works of Gaskell, who, like him, "enlarged the narrow sympathies" of the Victorian "age." "She was one of the great artists of the Nineteenth Century...." Both Gaskell and Dickens helped to soften public attitudes toward the poor.

*6   MARKERT, GOTTFRIED. "Mrs. Gaskells Romantechnik." Ph.D. dissertation, University of Leipzig.
[Source: Richard D. Altick and William R. Matthews. Guide to Doctoral Dissertations in Victorian Literature 1886-1958. Urbana, Illinois: University of Illinois Press, 1960. See 1960.B1.]

7   PATTON, JULIA. The English Village: A Literary Study, 1750-1850. New York: Macmillan Co., pp. 4, 6, 40, 135, 215-16.
Gaskell "made her industrial novel Mary Barton the story of a manufacturing city, while in Cranford she drew the picture of an untroubled village life.... In her North and South the village appeared as the antithesis of the town in beauty and peacefulness...." Sylvia's Lovers and Ruth both are set in villages and center around "individual lives," though larger social issues enter into both novels.

8   SANSOM, MARGARET BEST. "Mrs. Gaskell's Place as a Novelist," QQ, XXVII (July), 93-100.
It is too bad that Cranford, though justly one of the "best loved" works in English fiction, tends to be the only book of Gaskell's still widely read. Cousin Phillis and Wives and Daughters are, as Gosse has said, "'technically faultless'," and Ruth foreshadows the "psychological novel." Cranford has survived the others by literary accident, because its idyllically unrealistic portrayal of village life has broad "appeal." Unlike George Eliot, the self-effacing Gaskell has the art of seeming artless. Her awareness of the human complexity of good and evil and her avoidance of absolute villains put her closer to the great male novelists than to women writers.

9   SHORTER, CLEMENT [K.]. "Introduction," in The Life of Charlotte Brontë. The Novels and Tales of Mrs. Gaskell, XI. The World's Classics, CCIV. London: Humphrey Milford, Oxford University Press, pp. v-xiv.
This "is one of the best biographies" in English, because Gaskell combined sympathetic insight into Charlotte with a novelistic "power," though Charlotte's father and husband resented the portrayals of themselves. This edition is a reprint of the third edition, from which materials

were removed that had been threatened with libel suits by
Mrs. Robinson and Carus Wilson, both of whom Gaskell was
unjust to. Gaskell's three main sources for the childhood
of the Brontës were Ellen Nussey, Mary Taylor, and Margaret
Wooler.

1920 A BOOKS - NONE

1920 B SHORTER WRITINGS

1   ANON. "Introduction," in Cranford [This edition contains only
    the first half of the text.] Blackie's English Texts.
    London: Blackie & Son, unnumbered page.
        The "favorites" among Gaskell's books are Sylvia's Lovers
    and Wives and Daughters.

2   COURTNEY, C. J. "The Charms of Mrs. Gaskell [in shorthand],"
    Reporters' Journal (London), LIV (March), 38.
        "No writer in English literature, perhaps, has suffered
    more at the hands of her critics than" Gaskell, who has
    been "made the object of bitter and unworthy diatribes....
    Yet...she was greater...than all" her "critics." Gaskell
    portrayed the poor, not according to a theory of reform,
    but from observation. She is a "realistic" novelist who is
    "shrewd," "tolerant," "humorous," and stresses the emo-
    tional life, though she lacks the intellect and "artistic
    power" of the greatest "writers of her time." The amusing
    Cranford "is her highest achievement in fiction." But her
    other works will continue to be referred to as a record of
    social history. Gaskell's "works are understood by the
    common people" because they present "commonplace men and
    women and things in eloquent" language that reveals the
    inner spirit.

3   ELTON, OLIVER. A Survey of English Literature 1780-1880.
    New York: Macmillan Co. IV: 283, 284, 288, 297-304,
    383-84.
        Gaskell "was the first writer of any real gift who
    described, as an inhabitant and from within, both the black
    country and also some of the green country upon its fringe."
    She was best at "charitable," though unintellectual, humor;
    "idyllic or domestic" scenes; and "pathos," which is, how-
    ever, sometimes marred by "an undertone of feminine preach-
    ing." Though she frequently overreaches her talent with a
    striving for "tragic effects," she at times "surprises us
    with something that seemed beyond her strength." "Lois
    the Witch" shows a real "tragic gift," Sylvia's Lovers is

1920

(ELTON, OLIVER)
Gaskell's "most solid and admirable" long novel, and
Cousin Phillis is her most perfect short work.

4   RUSSELL, FRANCES THERESA. Satire in the Victorian Novel.
New York: Macmillan Co., pp. 45, 49, 84, 92, 130, 157,
183, 191, 195, 205, 216, 247, 270, 278-79, 285, 287, 306.
Gaskell's satire never directly attacks the institution
of the church itself, though she may attack individual
clergymen. Gaskell, Disraeli, Reade, and George Eliot are
the only important Victorian satirical novelists who re-
frain from attacking education. Gaskell's satire has a
"lack of flourish" yet a "deft sureness of...touch."

*5   SCHMIDT, ELIZABETH. "Mrs. Gaskell als Vorläuferin von George
Eliot." Ph.D. dissertation, University of Jena.
[Source: Clark S. Northup. "A Bibliography," in
Elizabeth Gaskell. By Gerald DeWitt Sanders. New Haven:
Yale University Press, for Cornell University. London:
Humphrey Milford, Oxford University Press, 1929. See
1929.B6.]

6   THORNDIKE, ASHLEY H. Literature in a Changing Age. New York:
Macmillan Co., pp. 82, 107-13, 197.
Gaskell's conventionally plotted Mary Barton "is extraordinary for the convincing truthfulness of its pictures
of factory life and for the sincerity and fervor of its
emotions." Even John Barton, though drawn by despair to
"murder," is portrayed sympathetically.

1921 A   BOOKS - NONE

1921 B   SHORTER WRITINGS

1   BIRKHEAD, EDITH. The Tale of Terror. A Story of the Gothic
Romance. London: Constable & Co., pp. 192-93.
Gaskell's "supernatural tales" were "based directly on
tradition. She was always attracted by the subject of
witchcraft, and she had collected a store of 'creepy'
legends...." In Gaskell's best tale of terror, "The
Nurse's Story," "the carefully disposed tableau of ghosts
...is too definite and distinct, but the conception of...
the dead child outside the manor...and luring away the
living is delicately wrought."

2   HARMON, ALICE IRENE. "The Social Attitude of Charles Kingsley
and Mrs. Gaskell." M.A. thesis, University of Chicago.

Although Kingsley and Gaskell, as Christians, both criticize classical economists, Kingsley advocates Christian socialism and Gaskell Christian love.

3   HATFIELD, C. W. "Suppressed Passages. A Collation of the Earlier and Later Editions of Mrs. Gaskell's Life of Charlotte Brontë," Brontë Society Transactions (Shipley), VI, part XXXI, 50-64.

Most of Gaskell's major changes were from the second to the third edition and included passages offensive to Brontë servants, to Mr. Brontë, to the Rev. Carus Wilson (though these cuts were limited to a few sentences and phrases), to local people, and to Mrs. Robinson.

4   HEPPLE, NORMAN. "Commentary. A Brief Memoir of Mrs. Gaskell. The Scene of the Story. Questions and Literary Exercises," in Cranford. King's Treasuries of Literature. New York: E. P. Dutton & Co. London and Toronto: J. M. Dent & Sons, pp. 275-88.

Gaskell "seemed to write best of friends, scenes, and experiences she had actually known...." In Cranford she "gives us...extraordinarily little direct description of the...town itself," though we do get a sense of its reality, but in "Mr. Harrison's Confessions" she provides some vivid physical details concerning the town.

1922 A   BOOKS - NONE

1922 B   SHORTER WRITINGS

1   BOAS, MRS. FREDERICK. "Introduction," in Cranford. Abridged and edited for schools by Mrs. Frederick Boas. London: Macmillan & Co., pp. ix-xiii.

Cranford appeals to children because, though it deals with "elderly people," it shows them "through the eyes of" young Mary Smith. Probably the reason why church and parish life play almost no role in Cranford is that Gaskell was Unitarian. Although the women in the book are famous, the male characters are also fine.

2   BRIGHOUSE, HAROLD. [Preface], in Followers. A 'Cranford' Sketch [a play based on Gaskell's Cranford]. Repertory Plays, no. 21. London and Glasgow: Cowans & Gray. Boston: LaRoy Phillips, unnumbered page.

Gaskell "is an excellent author to steal from," but it is difficult to translate her subtleties to the stage.

1922

3   LANCASTER, J. T. "Bibliography: Gaskell," N & Q, 12 ser. XI
     (7 October), 289.
         "The Half-Brothers," "like other stories in 'Round the
     Sofa'," probably first appeared in a periodical but where?
     It is not the same as "The Half-Brothers" that appeared in
     the Dublin University Magazine (November 1858) but was not
     by Gaskell.

4   SADLEIR, MICHAEL. Excursion in Victorian Bibliography.
     London: Chaundy & Cox, pp. 201-13.
         [A description of first editions of Gaskell's works.]

*5   SANDERS, GERALD D. [eWITT]. "The Works of Mrs. Gaskell."
     Ph.D. dissertation, Cornell University.
         [Source: Richard D. Altick and William R. Matthews.
     Guide to Doctoral Dissertations in Victorian Literature
     1886-1958. Urbana, Illinois: University of Illinois Press,
     1960. See 1960.B1.]

6   S.[HORTER], C.[LEMENT] K. "A Literary Letter. Mrs. Gaskell's
     Diary," Sphere (London), LXXXVIII (4 March), 258.
         "Thirty years ago we all" thought George Eliot our
     "greatest" novelist and dismissed Gaskell's Cranford as "a
     pretty book" and Mary Barton as a moral tract, but we did
     not realize Gaskell's achievement in "preserving for us a
     vanishing" world. "In another generation," she "will be-
     come an acknowledged classic." Her descendants have
     allowed me to make public her 1831 "diary" written when
     Marianne was born.

7   WALKER, JANIE ROXBURGH [MRS. HUGH WALKER]. Stories of the
     Victorian Writers. Cambridge: University Press. [Reprint.
     Freeport, New York: Books for Libraries, 1968, pp. 93-101.]
         Gaskell "would take her place amongst the great English
     writers" if she had "written more novels" like Cranford,
     her "best" work of fiction. She never wrote an "ill-
     natured word."

8   WHITFIELD, A.[RCHIE] STANTON. "Elizabeth Cleghorn Gaskell,"
     N & Q, 12th ser. X (22 April), 309.
         I am looking for "unpublished letters" and other
     materials on Gaskell.

1923 A BOOKS - NONE

1923 B SHORTER WRITINGS

1   ANON. In <u>Larousse universel en deux volumes</u>. S.v. "Gaskell,
     Elizabeth Cleghorn."
          Gaskell movingly and truthfully portrayed the life and
     customs of the working class in <u>Mary Barton</u> but is known
     also for <u>Cranford</u>.

2   ANON. "Life, Letters, and the Arts. A <u>Cranford</u> Play and Some
     Others," <u>Living Age</u> (Boston), CCCXVIII (18 August), 331-32.
          <u>Come through a Cranford Door</u>, a play based on Gaskell's
     <u>Cranford</u> and written by Frank Lind and Irene Ross, "was
     presented at the New Theatre in London, in aid of the
     Society for the Prevention of Cruelty to Animals." Although
     the novel lacks "the clash of vigorous wills" usually neces-
     sary to drama, the adaptation retains "most of the memorable
     incidents" and is true to the characterizations.

3   ANON. "Life, Letters, and the Arts. Mrs. Gaskell's Diary,"
     <u>Living Age</u> (Boston), CCXVIII (4 August), 236.
          Gaskell "was just the sort of person whose diary is sure
     to make good reading." She "is revealed by the diary as a
     curiously modern parent. She is not above reading books on
     the education of children, she avoids the old Victorian
     habit of extreme severity, and she also reveals some of the
     qualms that affect modern parenthood...."

4   ANON. "New Books and Reprints. Literary. <u>My Diary. The
     Early Years of My Daughter Marianne</u>,..." <u>TLS</u> (29 July),
     506.
          "Lovers of" Gaskell will perhaps value the book not, as
     Shorter says, for its contribution to child psychology, but
     for its light on "that very lovable woman.... It is touch-
     ing and charming to study" the behavior of Gaskell's chil-
     dren "through such eyes and such a heart as those of their
     mother."

5   BALD, MARJORY A. <u>Women-Writers of the Nineteenth Century</u>.
     Cambridge: University Press, pp. v-vi, 25, 45, 47-48, 52,
     54, 57-58, 78, 100-61, 166, 191, 230, 276, 278, 280-81,
     283.
          One reason why Gaskell "is often forgotten is that she
     was a normal woman" who "never allowed her genius" to in-
     terfere with her being "a wife,...mother,...friend and
     succourer of many." Gaskell's "humour," an expression of
     her "exuberance," is used in such works as <u>Wives and</u>

1923

(BALD, MARJORY A.)
Daughters as a means to "interpretative insight." "Nearly all" of Gaskell's women characters find "their true life in the atmosphere of family affection," and she most "valued" woman's quality of peacemaker. If Disraeli's fiction emphasized "the romance of machinery," Gaskell's industrial novels concentrated on "the human power which mastered machinery." In Cranford she was able to laugh sympathetically rather than bitterly at "class prejudice" and to show sympathy for aristocratic characters. Her fiction is moral but not moralistic, and, though her work has religious implications, the religion grew less and less explicit as her art developed. "Just because" Gaskell "was so little restricted by self-consciousness, she represented her sex more adequately than any other woman writer of her generation."

6   DOBSON, AUSTIN. "Incognita [1866]," in The Complete Poetical Works of Austin Dobson. Edited by Alban Dobson. London: Humphrey Milford, Oxford University Press, pp. 270-73.
[This poem, describing a conversation on a train with a beautiful young girl, includes the following lines about Gaskell:] "She thought 'Wives and Daughters' 'so jolly'; / Had I read it? She knew when I had, / Like the rest, I should dote upon 'Molly'; / And 'poor Mrs. Gaskell--how sad!'"

7   FEHR, BERHARD, ed. Die englische Literatur des 19 und 20 Jahrhunderts. Ein Handbuch der Literaturwissenshaft. Edited by Oskar Walzel. Wildpark-Potsdam and Berlin-Neubabelberg: Akademische Verlags Gesellschaft Athenaion MBH, pp. 157, 158.
Gaskell, who came up against Chartism in Manchester, wrote a social-problem novel about working class sufferings, Mary Barton, which nevertheless also had artistic structure. Her North and South gives a sympathetic portrayal of the problems of the factory owners.

8   [HUXLEY, LEONARD]. "Four Friends...Mrs. Gaskell," in The House of Smith Elder. London: printed for private circulation by William Clowes & Sons, pp. 73-81.
The letters from the friendship of Gaskell and George Smith, which began with her writing of The Life of Charlotte Brontë, show "business...tempered by a frequent personal and humourous touch." Gaskell gave part of her Brontë manuscript to George Smith and William S. Williams for pre-publication advice. Smith, afraid of libel, warned her "not to indicate so clearly the lady supposed to be

concerned in Branwell's undoing," but Gaskell retained the charges. When "a libel action was threatened" by Mrs. Robinson's lawyers, Gaskell was on the continent and un-reachable, so Smith, on his own, hired "detectives" to find out how legally defensible Gaskell's charges were and de-cided that they could not be sustained in court. He re-solved "to withdraw the edition, destroy all existing copies,...publish a new edition without the libel," and also place a retraction in the Times (London). When Gas-kell returned she mildly rebuked Smith for not having warned her about the libel, yet he refrained from reminding her that he had. Later she realized how gently Smith had behaved and felt deeply indebted to him. Before Wives and Daughters came out in the Cornhill, she begged Smith to leave her name out of announcements of the serial in order to save her from "criticisms, suggestions, and questions."

*9   RIDLEY, H. M. "Great Friendships: Charlotte Brontë and Mrs. Gaskell," Canadian Magazine (Toronto), LX (March), 445-50.
       Although Charlotte Brontë was "intensely subjective" in temperament and Gaskell was "objective," Gaskell, in her "greatest book," The Life of Charlotte Brontë, assumed Charlotte's point of view. [Source: Marjorie Taylor Davis. "An Annotated Bibliography of Criticism on Elizabeth Cleg-horn Gaskell, 1848-1973." Ph.D. dissertation, University of Mississippi, 1974. See 1974.B6.]

10   SHORTER, CLEMENT [K.]. "Introductory," in My Diary. The Early Years of My Daughter Marianne. By Elizabeth Cleghorn Gaskell. London: privately printed by Clement [K.] Shorter, pp. 3-4.
       "More than twenty years" ago, George Macmillan agreed "that I should write a life of" Gaskell "for the 'English Men of Letters' series," but "I spent so much time...col-lecting documents that when I" was ready to write, Mac-millan's declined to publish. I put the work aside, and then Mrs. Chadwick came out with her book on Gaskell. "My material" on Gaskell "includes first editions of all" her "books," much "pamphlet literature," and many of her "un-published" "letters." This diary of hers has been privately issued in a limited edition with the permission of Gaskell's grandson (Brian Holland) and his sister.

1924 A BOOKS

1   DULLEMEN, JOHANNA JACOBA VAN. Mrs. Gaskell: Novelist and Biographer. Academisch Proefschrift ter Verkrijing van den

1924

(DULLEMEN, JOHANNA JACOBA VAN)
Graad van Doctor in de Letteren en Wijsbegeerte aan de Universiteit van Amsterdam, op Gezag van den Rector-Magnificus, Dr. R. C. Boer, Hoogleeraar in de Faculteit der Letteren en Wijsbegeerte, in het Openbaar te Verdedigen in de Aula der Universiteit op Donderdag 10 April te 3 Uur door Johanna Jacoba van Dullemen geboren te 's Hertogenbosch. Amsterdam: H. J. Paris.

Gaskell's unhappiness at her father's remarriage and the disappearance of her brother "changed" her from a child into a woman and gave her that sympathy for mental suffering that she revealed later in her fiction. Though a Unitarian with deep conviction in her faith, she found the artistic beauty of the Anglican Church attractive. "It is my impression that Mr. Gaskell as a husband and father was not always the most sympathetic and devoted of men." Mrs. Gaskell's fiction is concerned with the question of whether women should be educated, but, though she admired "intellectual qualities in a woman," she emphasized the duties of marriage and motherhood. In her characterization, Gaskell sometimes fails to "show much development," as, for example, in the cases of Margaret Hale and Molly Gibson, and she does not handle plots well. In her later work, Gaskell's "pathos become more delicate," as in the fine Wives and Daughters, her greatest novel. In her Life of Charlotte Brontë, Gaskell "did not reach the heights and depths of" Charlotte's "nature," for Gaskell did not understand impassioned love. She had a narrower intellect than George Eliot but a "happier" nature, and Gaskell had an objectivity that Charlotte Brontë lacked. Gaskell's character "was not complicated, she was simple and frank," and she gave this quality of simple openness to everything that she wrote.

1924 B SHORTER WRITINGS

1   ABERCROMBIE, LASCELLES. "The Brontës Today. An Address... Delivered...March 8th, 1924," Brontë Society Transactions (Shipley), VI, part XXXIV, 185.
The Brontës "had the advantage of being presented from the first in a work which itself showed, in the nicety and vigour of its detail, and in the order of its design, a most unusual genius"--Gaskell's Life of Charlotte Bronte.

2   BIDWELL, ALICE TOWNSEND, and ISABELLE DENISON ROSENSTIEL. The Places of English Literature. A Literary Guide to the British Isles. Boston: Stratford Co., p. 134.

Gaskell's works include <u>Cranford</u>, <u>The Life of Charlotte Brontë</u>, and <u>Mary Barton</u>.

3 CAZAMIAN, LOUIS. "Époque moderne et contemporaine (1660–1914)," in <u>Historie de la littérature anglaise</u>. By É.[mile] LeGouis and Louis Cazamian. Paris: Librairie Hachette, pp. 984, 1084–85, 1136. [Translated by Helen Douglas Irvine from rev. ed., with additions by Raymond Las Vergnas and bibliography by Donald Davie and Pierre LeGouis, as <u>A History of English Literature</u>. London: J. M. Dent. New York: Macmillan Co., 1964.]
   Gaskell's "originality" "lies in...combining...a manifest purpose with a descriptive realism" that is "supple and free." In such works as <u>Mary Barton</u> and <u>North and South</u>, she gets at the deep "psychological" aspects of social problems. In Gaskell's works she accurately portrays characters from all social classes. <u>Cranford</u>'s "mingling of sly satire, humour, and emotion" is "dear to all English hearts" and provided a "model" for George Eliot's early fiction.

4 HATFIELD, C. W. "The Case for Branwell Brontë," <u>TLS</u> (1 May), p. 268.
   [This item is listed in Northup (1929.B6) but contains no reference to Gaskell.]

5 _____. "Correspondence. The Case for Branwell Brontë," <u>TLS</u> (15 May), p. 304.
   Alice Law, in her <u>Patrick Branwell Brontë</u>, is mistaken in thinking that Charlotte was not sure who wrote <u>Wuthering Heights</u> and in concluding that Branwell wrote it. Charlotte spoke to Gaskell about "'Emily--poor Emily'" and her "'pangs of disappointment'" over unfavorable reviews of her novel.

*6 HUMPHREY, GRACE. "In Quaint Old Cranford: Elizabeth Gaskell," in <u>The Story of the Elizabeths</u>. Philadelphia: Penn Publishing Co.
   [Source: Catherine Margaret Ellen Halls. "Bibliography of Elizabeth C. Gaskell." Diploma in librarianship dissertation, University of London, 1957. <u>See</u> 1957.B5.]

7 LAW, ALICE. [Letters to Editor], <u>TLS</u> (8 May), p. 286; (22 May), p. 322; (5 June), p. 356.
   [These items are cited by Northup (1929.B6) but contain no references to Gaskell.]

1925

1925 A   BOOKS - NONE

1925 B   SHORTER WRITINGS

1   ANON. "Literature. New Novels," Glasgow Herald (10 December),
    p. 8.
         The republication by John Murray of the Knutsford edi-
    tion of Gaskell is now complete in "handsome and inexpen-
    sive" volumes.

2   ANON. "Mrs. Gaskell's Ruth. A Story of Sin and Redemption,"
    Manchester City News (12 September), p. 2.
         The Rev. H. H. Johnson, in an address on Gaskell's Ruth
    at Cross Street Chapel, declared its heroine "one of the
    very greatest womanly creations in literature" and said
    that Gaskell had still not been justly honored as a writer.

3   ANON. In The New International Encyclopaedia. 2nd ed.
    New York: Dodd, Mead & Co. S.v. "Gaskell, Elizabeth
    Cleghorn."
         Gaskell's "usual aim was to combine instruction with
    pleasure. Her first novel and several others depict the
    habits, thoughts, privations, and struggles of the indus-
    trial poor," but "her classic...is the delightfully and
    delicately humorous Cranford...."

4   MACY, JOHN. The Story of the World's Literature. New York:
    Boni & Liveright, pp. 360-61.
         Gaskell's Mary Barton "is a faithful picture of the poor,
    written without Carlyle's indignant thunder or Dickens's
    sentimental influence." The book's very quietness seems to
    have allowed "its greatness" to be "forgotten." Perhaps
    readers dislike accurate portrayals of the poor, but the
    same readers love the people in Cranford--a work in which
    "nothing happens and everything happens."

5   OSBORN, E. E. "The Tragical Comedies of Gentle Lives. The
    Genius of Mrs. Gaskell," John O'London's Weekly, XIV
    (19 December), 468-69.
         Although some "young people" find Gaskell's "stories
    tedious and goody-good," she understood "human nature" at
    least "as well as any of the modern novelists." Her fiction
    is given great value by her truthfulness, but it is lucky
    that Gaskell did not stick to her first intent of describing
    only the lives of the Manchester poor, for, though "all"
    her fiction "will be read...as long as Miss Austen's,"
    Gaskell's Cranford will outlive even the English language.

6 QUILLER-COUCH, SIR ARTHUR THOMAS. Charles Dickens and Other
   Victorians. Cambridge: University Press, pp. 179, 199-218.
      Cranford remains a popular gift book in a way similar to
   the Rubáiyát of Omar Khayyám. Yet it is too bad that Gaskell's other books, including her great biography of Charlotte Brontë, are not more widely read. In spite of some
   flaws, Gaskell's works always have "the best literary
   breeding." Her masterpiece is Cousin Phillis, as pastoral
   as Theocritus and Virgil and yet wholly English. Eventually Gaskell's "genius" must receive its full recognition.

7 ROBERTS, R. ELLIS. "Mrs. Gaskell," Guardian (London), LXXX,
   part II (11 December), 1075.
      The lack of a biography on Gaskell, though in accordance
   with her wishes, helps explain the present "comparative
   neglect" of her novels, for readers need the illumination
   provided by a knowledge of her particular background and
   "environment." Gaskell "is the first, and has in many
   ways remained the greatest, of middle class authors" who
   dealt with the problems of capitalism. She was able to
   be "fair" to the arguments of the manufacturers, yet her
   Mary Barton is "an indictment" of the sins of "property,"
   though Gaskell lacked Ruskin's prophetic intuition that
   perhaps "the whole system" is "a gross mistake." Her
   loyalty to her husband kept her from openly attacking the
   way of life in Manchester, but her Cranford, Cousin Phillis, and Wives and Daughters were a release from the
   "great burden" of the industrial north.

8 S.[TRANG], H.[ERBERT]. "Introduction," in Cranford. Herbert
   Strang's Library. London: Humphrey Milford, Oxford
   University Press, pp. v-vi.
      Cranford "is not a complete, continuous story, with ex-
   citing incidents and situations,...but a series of pen pictures drawn by a hand that was as kindly as skillful." The
   work assures Gaskell "a permanent rank among English
   writers."

9 WEYGANDT, CORNELIUS. A Century of the English Novel.
   New York: Century Co., pp. 143, 145-46, 272, 440.
      "One hesitates to speak of other books of" Gaskell, "for
   none of them is of a class with" the kindly humor of
   Cranford.

1926

1926 A   BOOKS - NONE

1926 B   SHORTER WRITINGS

1   COMPTON, J.   "Introduction [and prefatory notes to selections
     from Mary Barton, North and South, Cranford, and Sylvia's
     Lovers]," in The Austen-Gaskell Book. Scenes from the
     Works of Jane Austen and Mrs. Gaskell. London: G. Bell &
     Sons, pp. ix, xi-xiv, 93, 122, 133, 208.
         Gaskell and Jane Austen "belong to the company of great
     English writers whom one can never know well enough."
     Gaskell was gifted at both comedy and tragedy and had a
     wider range of interests than Jane Austen. Gaskell's
     "greatest" novel is Sylvia's Lovers.

2   F. R.   "Early Strike Vocabulary," N & Q, CL (29 May), 389.
         The strikers' vocabulary in North and South, different
     at times from "modern" usage, employs "knobstick" for
     "blackleg" and "turn-out" for "strike." Were these "North-
     country words" or from the common vocabulary of Gaskell's
     day?

3   JANSONIUS, HERMAN.   Some Aspects of Business Life in Early
     Victorian Fiction [Ph.D. dissertation, University of
     Amsterdam]. Purmerend: J. Muusses, pp. 18, 19, 28, 30-32,
     37, 45, 48, 53-54, 57-58, 61, 62, 74, 89, 96-99, 198.
         In Mary Barton Gaskell describes the "immigration into
     the industrial towns" from the country. Thornton, in North
     and South, is "the most elaborate...literary" portrait of
     an industrial businessman in the Victorian novel. He is
     less "unjust" than "unfeeling" in his treatment of his men
     at the beginning. Through the mouth of Job Legh in Mary
     Barton, Gaskell criticizes "political economy" for its lack
     of humanity. Foreign competition is blamed for industrial
     troubles in both Mary Barton and North and South, although
     Higgins does not believe the argument. Mr. Thornton's
     financial troubles in North and South are blamed on "a
     strike" and "a fall in the prices of raw materials," but
     Gaskell's financial details do not hang together. Like
     Dickens and Charlotte Brontë, Gaskell despised the working-
     class "leaders" from London, in spite of her sympathy for
     the working class itself.

*4   KATOW, MAUF.   "A Study on Mrs. Gaskell [in Japanese]," Japan
     Jurisprudential Magazine (Tokyo), XXIII, nos. 10 and 12.
         [Source: A.(rchie) Stanton Whitfield. "Appendix III.
     Biographical and Critical Notices, Essays and Apprecia-
     tions," in Mrs. Gaskell: Her Life and Work. London:
     George Routledge & Sons, pp. 237-253. See 1929.A3.]

5   READ, HERBERT. "Charlotte and Emily Brontë," in Reason and
     Romanticism: Essays in Literary Criticism. London:
     Faber & Gwyer, pp. 160, 167, 168, 172, 174, 178.
          Gaskell's "rather picturesque description" in The Life
     of Charlotte Brontë of Patrick Brontë's "passionate nature
     has been discredited in some of its details, but enough
     remains of authentic evidence to evoke for us a grim
     puritanical mask, expressing, even while it repressed, the
     fires beneath." About the charge of Charlotte's supposed
     "coarseness," "even Gaskell, who by no means shared all the
     prudery of her age, thought it necessary to apologize for
     this lapse on the part of her heroine...."

6   WOOD, BUTLER. "Charlotte Brontë on Her Contemporaries. Mrs.
     Gaskell," Brontë Society Transactions (Shipley), VII, part
     XXXVI, 8-10.
          Although Gaskell's Cranford "has now an assured place in
     English literature," her masterpiece is The Life of Char-
     lotte Brontë, "one of the finest biographies in our lan-
     guage." Charlotte thought her "a good" and "great woman,"
     with "the most genuine talent."

1927 A   BOOKS - NONE

1927 B   SHORTER WRITINGS

1   BAILLIE, DR. J. B. "Religion and the Brontës," Brontë Society
     Transactions (Shipley), VII, part XXXVII, 60.
          Gaskell's Life of Charlotte Brontë is "full and inform-
     ing," though "rather dull," but it "contains hardly a hint
     and certainly no clear indication that any one of" the
     Brontës "was touched by the issues raised by the newly
     awakened religious life around them."

2   DRINKWATER, JOHN. "Patrick Branwell Brontë and His 'Horace',"
     in A Book for Bookmen: Being Edited Manuscripts and Mar-
     ginalia with Essays on Several Occasions. New York:
     George H. Doran, pp. 44, 46, 51, 53.
          Gaskell unjustly disparages Branwell Brontë's ability
     as a painter in her Life of Charlotte Brontë. "Loving
     Charlotte as she did," Gaskell, as might be expected, "did
     not like what she knew of Branwell--she never met him--but
     her affection at least did not sharpen what was, perhaps,
     no great natural acumen as an art critic."

*3   ROBINSON, HENRY CRABB. The Correspondence of Henry Crabb
     Robinson with the Wordsworth Circle (1808-1866), the

1927

(ROBINSON, HENRY CRABB)
Greater Part Now for the First Time Printed from the Ori-
ginals in Dr. Williams's Library, London, Chronologically
Arranged and Edited with Introduction, Notes and Index.
Edited by Edith Julia Morley. 2 vols. Oxford: Clarendon
Press, see index for references to Gaskell.
[Source: John Geoffrey Sharps. Mrs. Gaskell's Obser-
vation and Invention: a Study of Her Non-biographic Works.
Fontwell, Sussex: Linden Press, 1970. See 1970.A1.]

4   VOOYS, SIJNA DE. The Psychological Element in the English
Sociological Novel of the Nineteenth Century [Ph.D. dissertation, University of Amsterdam]. Amsterdam: H. J. Paris.
[Reprint. New York: Haskell House, 1966, pp. 39, 50-55.]
"The great novelists of" the Victorian era--Dickens,
Kingsley, Gaskell, and George Eliot--"are all influenced
more or less by Carlyle...in their sociological novels."
In Mary Barton Gaskell sees things from the workers' view-
point and in North and South from the viewpoint of the em-
ployers, but each novel advocates a solution of Christian
good will on both sides, though the reconciliation of Mr.
Carson and John Barton is unconvincing.

1928 A   BOOKS - NONE

1928 B   SHORTER WRITINGS

1   GRABO, CARL H.   The Technique of the Novel.   New York:
Charles Scribner's Sons, pp. 241-42.
In contrast to Kingsley's ill-constructed "pseudo-novels"
of "social commentary" and preaching, Gaskell's Mary Barton
and North and South are more successful than his at making
"the social background" an "intrinsic" element of the
story.   Furthermore, Gaskell's plots are "adequately de-
signed," and her characters" are "sufficiently real" and
also plausibly "motivated by the forces of their environment."   Yet even in Gaskell's works, "the blending of"
purpose and art is incomplete, for we remember her "pictures of mill life" long after we have forgotten her plot.

2   JOHNSTON, JOSEPHINE.   "The Sociological Significance of the
Novels of Mrs. Gaskell," Journal of Social Forces (Chapel
Hill, North Carolina), VII (December), 224-27.
Gaskell's novelistic portrayals of "the evils" of the
"factory system" gave impetus to reform.   She was "an
earnest social worker, a liberalist, a dissenter, a humanitarian, and a prophetess of distinctly modern social

methods." Mary Barton, North and South, and Ruth are of
particular sociological significance. In both Gaskell's
own philanthropic work and her depiction of those who help
the poor, she anticipated the technique of the modern
"social worker," and in A Dark Night's Work she even "foreshadows" the modern "parole system."

*3   WOLLWEBER, KAROLA. Der soziale Roman der Mrs. Gaskell [Ph.D.
     dissertation, Giessen]. Mainz: Georg Aug Walters
     Druckerei.
        [Source: Margaret Ganz. "Bibliography," in Elizabeth
     Gaskell: The Artist in Conflict. New York: Twayne
     Publishers, pp. 293-308. See 1969.A1.]

1929 A BOOKS

1   PAYNE, [REV.] GEORGE A. Mrs. Gaskell: a Brief Biography.
     Manchester: Sherratt & Hughes.
        Marianne Gaskell, who married Edward Thurston Holland,
     "was the longest lived" of Gaskell's children and died on
     September 17th, 1920, at eighty-six. In spite of W. E. A.
     Axon's noting, in 1892, of the misprint of "cold loin" for
     "lion" in editions of Cranford, the error reappears in
     A. & C. Black's edition of 1929. Gaskell "was no narrow
     denominationalist," "her religion was the religion of
     doing good," and "she was opposed to bigotry and narrow-
     mindedness." [Payne's book received the following review:
     Anon. "Some Books of the Week," Spectator (London), CXLIV
     (8 February 1930), 200 (The "revival of interest in" Gas-
     kell's "charming stories" justifies Payne's "very slight
     memoir."). For an additional review of Payne, see Anon.
     TLS, under 1930.A1.]

2   SANDERS, GERALD DeWITT. Elizabeth Gaskell. With a Bibliog-
     raphy by Clark S. Northup. New Haven: Yale University
     Press, for Cornell University. London: Humphrey Milford,
     Oxford University Press.
        This is "a study of" Gaskell's "works" rather than "a
     Life." Gaskell, as an unknown, found it difficult to get
     Mary Barton published, for novels about social problems
     were not yet popular, though the book later influenced
     both Hard Times and Felix Holt. "John Barton is the most
     powerfully conceived of the characters" in her first
     novel. Cranford, the most popular of her works, "depends
     for interest upon location, characterization, and incident
     rather than plot" and thus established "a type of narra-
     tive half way between the informal essay and the novel."

Ruth, "an example of Christianity as it should be applied to life," may have influenced Tess of the D'Urbervilles. "Love" is the dominant theme of the essentially optimistic North and South, which deals only secondarily with the social problems of factory life. In the great Life of Charlotte Brontë, Gaskell employed the tactic of letting Charlotte's own letters speak for themselves as much as possible. Gaskell's charges against the Cowan Bridge School seem to have been justified but not those against Mrs. Robinson. Cousin Phillis is Gaskell's "best short story," and Sylvia's Lovers is better constructed than any previous novel of hers, with the press gang at the center, though the work has minor flaws. With the "almost perfect" Wives and Daughters, she had developed from "social reformer... to...sheer novelist" and had lifted herself "to a level with" Jane Austen, Thackeray, and Dickens. Gaskell was one of the most skillful users of dialect among novelists in our language, and her example "went very far to establish the use of dialect in realistic fiction." [For a description of Northup's bibliography, see 1929.B6.]
  [Reviews of Sanders's book included the following: Anon. "Critic's Commentary,..." Time and Tide (London), XI (2 May 1930) ("This sober work of scholarship," though based on the limited materials available, is a first step toward a full biography and is far superior to last year's "remarkably bad attempt.") (See 1929.A3). James R. Foster. "Elizabeth Gaskell,..." MLN, XLV (November 1930), 476-77 (Though limited in scope, this is an "authentic and dependable" study.). Richard E. Russell. "Literary History and Criticism," London Mercury, XXIII (January 1931), 294 (Sanders's book is "careful and competent" but written in an "unattractive academic style."). For an additional review of Sanders, see Anon. TLS, under 1930.A1.]

3 WHITFIELD, A.[RCHIE] STANTON. Mrs. Gaskell: Her Life and Work. London: George Routledge & Sons.
      Gaskell's fiction frequently reflects the actual details of her life, as, for example, the echoes of her father's death that can be found in "My French Master." Her marriage was fortunate and happy. Perhaps her closest friend was Madame Mohl. In spite of Gaskell's literary successes, she attended to her feminine duties, and she was a good woman out of natural warmheartedness rather than prudent calculation. In her industrial novels, Gaskell truthfully describes the sufferings of the working classes, yet she ignores the fact that the industrial revolution enabled them to participate more fully "in knowledge, religion, and culture." In any case, Mary Barton warns the

workers against resorting to "violence," for Gaskell wished
a reconciliation between "masters and men." Her Life
of Charlotte Brontë is a great book because of its evocation
of the very atmosphere of the Brontës' way of life.
Sylvia's Lovers is a remarkable blending of tragedy and
history, except for its melodramatic ending. Wives and
Daughters, a great recreation of a vanished rural age, surpasses Jane Austen in the range of its characterizations.
Gaskell's best short story is Cousin Phillis, and almost as
impressive are her weird tales, such as "Lois the Witch"
and "The Crooked Branch." In spite of her lack of literary
artifice, her honest and warm-hearted fiction is more
highly regarded and more widely read today than ever. [Ap-
pendix III, pp. 237-53, contains a bibliography of more
than 350 secondary items on Gaskell, but the annotations
are sparse and fragmentary, and many mistakes result from
an overreliance on Green's bibliography (1911.A2).]
      [Reviews of Whitfield's book included the following:
Anon. "Critic's Commentary,..." Time and Tide (London), X
(5 July 1929), 822 ("This biography and critical study" appears to owe its method to Philip Guedalla's "cross-section
historical" approach.). Anon. "New Books and Reprints....
Biography,..." TLS (25 July 1929), p. 593 (This study "of
the author of one of the outstanding biographies" in the
language and the creator of "the subtle and delightful
'Cranford'" is valuable for its scholarship but not for its
"presentation of" Gaskell's "life and character.").
V.(ictoria) Sackville-West. "Reviews. Mrs. Gaskell,..."
Nation and Athenaeum (London), XLV (20 July 1929), 539
(Gaskell "appears to have been a woman of great charm, intelligence, and sensibility...." Whitfield appreciates her,
but his "style...is sometimes arch...and sentimental.").
Gilbert Thomas. Spectator (London), CXLIII (6 July 1929),
24 (Gaskell was as personally delightful as her books, and,
though her character was superficially Victorian, she "was
essentially opposed to complacency." Whitfield's book on
Gaskell is somewhat flawed by being too short and by being
written in a flippant style.).]

1929 B   SHORTER WRITINGS

  1   CHARLETON, H. T.   [No. 27,121. Reply to no. 27,114], Manches-
       ter City News [Notes and Queries] (24 August), p. 2.
          The World's Classics edition of Gaskell includes "The
       Cage at Cranford" and The Moorland Cottage. [A similar
       reply from (Rev.) G.(eorge) A. Payne was also printed in
       this item:] "All" of Gaskell's "stories" appear in the
       World's Classics edition.

1929

2   DEVONSHIRE, MARION GLADYS. The English Novel in France, 1830-
     1870. London: University of London Press. [Reprint.
     London: Frank Cass & Co., 1967, pp. 351-55.]
          Gaskell "enjoyed" an equivocal "reputation" in France,
     where her novels dealing with social problems were read
     primarily by those interested in the social history of
     England.

3   HERFORD, C. H. "Literary Manchester," in The Soul of Manches-
     ter. Edited by W. H. Brindley. [Manchester:] Manchester
     University Press, pp. 126, 135-36.
          "Of far greater merit...than any previous study of Man-
     chester character was that achieved by" Gaskell "in 'Mary
     Barton'" and, "with less distinction but more art, in 'North
     and South'." The fact that she was not a native yet was "a
     resident" made her "qualified both by intimacy and by de-
     tachment" to write insightfully about the city.

4   HUGHES, T. CANN. [no. 27,114] "Gaskell Queries," Manchester
     City News [Notes and Queries] (17 August), p. 2.
          Have the various pieces missing from the Smith, Elder
     "Pocket Edition" of Gaskell's works been "reprinted" else-
     where?

5   LANGBRIDGE, ROSAMUND. Charlotte Brontë: a Psychological
     Study. London: William Heinemann, pp. 3-4, 7, 19-20, 21,
     23, 31, 32, 41, 52, 53, 64, 65-66, 69, 71-73, 87, 90, 101,
     124-26, 131, 136, 199-201, 203, 209, 217, 223, 241-42, 243,
     245, 253.
          Gaskell started "the foolish fashion of canonising Char-
     lotte" for her suffering. In The Life of Charlotte Brontë,
     Gaskell probably softened her criticisms of the Cowan Bridge
     School because she "had the usual feminine weakness for the
     clergy." The writer did not understand that the Brontë sis-
     ters' dislike of children stemmed from "their own unhappy
     childhood." "The tradition that" Gaskell's hagiographic
     and "biased Life...is a classic" has misled those who argue
     that Charlotte was not in love with M. Heger. Even in the
     case of such hypocritic clergymen as Patrick Brontë, A. B.
     Nicholls, or Carus Wilson, the genteel Gaskell felt com-
     pelled to mute her criticisms. Because of her own Vic-
     torian limitations, she could not "know that Charlotte's own
     powers of psychology were extremely incomplete," and Gas-
     kell sentimentalized Charlotte's "lifeless" marriage to
     the Rev. Nicholls.

6   NORTHUP, CLARK S. "A Bibliography," in Elizabeth Gaskell. By
     Gerald DeWitt Sanders. New Haven: Yale University Press,

for Cornell University. London: Humphrey Milford, Oxford
University Press, pp. 165-267.
[Northup's bibliography contains 479 items on primary
materials, 394 on secondary materials, and an index. Among
the secondary items are a number of inaccuracies taken over
from Green (1911.A2), and only a small percentage of secondary items are annotated and then only briefly. See also
1929.A2.]

7 REYNOLDS, GEORGE F. English Literature in Fact and Story:
Being a Brief Account of Its Writers and Their Backgrounds.
New York: Century Co., pp. 273, 330, 331.
Gaskell is remembered for Mary Barton, "on industrial
life"; Cranford, "a pleasantly placid account of quaintly
genteel feminine" village "society"; and her "excellent"
and "sympathetic biography of Charlotte Brontë."

8 RICHMOND, THOMAS (Chairman), R. CALVERLY (Treasurer), and
J. C. LACEY (Secretary) [Committee for a memorial to Gaskell
at Silverdale]. "Letters to the Editor. Mrs. Gaskell and
Silverdale,..." Manchester Guardian (15 April), p. 18.
We are raising money to carry out "a scheme" started by
the late Sir Norman Rae to erect a "village hall" in Silverdale in honor of Gaskell, who wrote most of her best work
at Gibraltar Tower.

9 SIMPSON, CHARLES. Emily Brontë. London: Country Life.
New York: Charles Scribner & Sons, pp. 19-20, 22, 202,
205.
Branwell's portrait of the Brontës, described by Gaskell
and purchased by the National Portrait Gallery, contains
"the only unquestioned" representation "of Emily now known
to exist."

10 WAGENKNECHT, EDWARD. The Man Charles Dickens: a Victorian
Portrait. Boston: Houghton Mifflin Co., Riverside Press,
p. 220. [Rev. ed. published at Norman, Oklahoma: University of Oklahoma Press, 1966.]
"Sometimes" Dickens "ran into a writer" such as Gaskell
"or Miss Martineau who refused to allow him to take" editorial "liberties, and then it was a case of Greek meeting
Greek. I think Dickens sensed that he had met his match in
these ladies but he behaved well toward both of them....
Still, I imagine he was glad there weren't many like them."

1930

1930 A BOOKS

   1   HALDANE, ELIZABETH. Mrs. Gaskell and Her Friends. London:
       Hodder & Stoughton.
         "This book endeavours to study" Gaskell "in relation to
       the friends who were intertwined with her life." Compared
       with Jane Austen, Gaskell is a "minor" writer. Typically
       Victorian, she exhibited the complexities of the age: she
       was a realist, was married to a minister, but also had a
       romantic liking for tales of "ghosts and murderers." Ele-
       ments of "rebellion" lay beneath her placid "exterior,"
       yet she also had a strong "regard for family." She knew
       sorrows, but her life was basically a contented one. "One
       thing she did learn as an only child...was not to be afraid
       of expressing her opinion." "All" of Gaskell's "tales that
       count are drawn very closely from real life." Cranford is
       her best work. Her "place" in literature "is high, but not
       among the highest" because of her lack of "passion" and of
       a firm sense of construction. Charlotte Brontë correctly
       perceived that Gaskell was not completely able to be her
       "'own woman'" as a writer because of her ties to family
       and church. Yet she "was as near the ideal biographer as
       any that could be found" for Charlotte, though "a man
       might have" understood Emily better. Gaskell was wrong
       to attack Mrs. Robinson without having her facts sure but
       was essentially right about the Cowan Bridge School. She
       wrote a number of fine short stories, including the re-
       markable ghost tale "The Old Nurse's Story" and the Haw-
       thorne-like "Lois the Witch," yet too much of her short
       fiction gives "a feeling of hurry." Sylvia's Lovers "is
       well planned," except for the melodramatic ending, and
       Gaskell's description of the riot shows "an almost mascu-
       line power." The touchingly simple Cousin Phillis is un-
       surpassed among the author's works. She "was not a model
       letter-writer," for she lacked either "great matter" or a
       great style, but her letters are humorous and admirable.
       An unusually large advance from Smith enabled Gaskell to
       take her time with Wives and Daughters and to make it her
       best full-length novel, comparable to Middlemarch as a
       portrait of "rural life." Gaskell lacks George Eliot's
       philosophic mind but equals her in humor if not in subtlety
       of characterization. Gaskell was not a feminist, though
       there was an element of sexual rebellion in her. Her fic-
       tion "is clear and straightforward," though "not profound,"
       and is rare in its good-natured tolerance.
        [Reviews of Miss Haldane's book included the following:
       Anon. "Biography," Saturday Review of Literature (New
       York), VII (11 July 1931), 963 ("... It is pleasant...to

come upon the quiet and calm of" this "thoughtful life of" Gaskell, though Miss Haldane shows that Gaskell also was a bit of a "rebel."). Anon. "Elizabeth Gaskell,..." Listener (London), IV (3 December 1930), Supplement, xii (Gaskell "represented a fine type of womanhood," but, perhaps because her "life was uneventful,...we do not get a very deep impression" of her "from this book," which is mainly valuable for excerpts about other Victorians from Gaskell's letters.). Anon. "Mrs. Gaskell," TLS (4 December 1930), 1035 (Miss Haldane's book is "a biography of real merit," superior to the studies by Sanders and by Payne on account of its more detailed research.) (See 1929.A2 and 1929.A1). C. H. H.(erford). "Books of the Day. Mrs. Gaskell,..." Manchester Guardian (4 December 1930), p. 5 (This biography has "proportion and dignity" and presents Gaskell's "Victorian limitations" sympathetically and without "irony."). V.(ictoria) Sackville-West. "Four Victorian Women,..." Listener (London), IV (24 December 1930), 1066 (Gaskell was aware of the conflict between a set feminine role and being an artist. She "was more serious in her writings than in her life," yet "she could appreciate" women who refused to conform, though she was too "warm" and "feminine" to follow their example.). Cecilia Townsend. "Dear Mrs. Gaskell,..." Spectator (London), CXLV (22 November 1930), 797 (Although Gaskell's literary rank is "uncertain," her works are "immortal" as social history. Miss Haldane's "charming" study shows that Gaskell was a delightful person.). W. H. "Friend to Charlotte,..." Time and Tide (London), XI (20 December 1930), 1611 (Because Gaskell, "for all her charming gifts," "will be chiefly" remembered as Charlotte Brontë's biographer, Miss Haldane's book is most valuable for its newly published letters of Gaskell's about Charlotte and also about Florence Nightingale.).]

1930 B SHORTER WRITINGS

1   ANON. In Enciclopedia universal ilustrada europeo-americana. Barcelona: Hijos de J. Espasa [ca. 1930]. S.v. "Gaskell, Elizabeth Cleghorn."

   Gaskell was one of the finest of English storytellers, and her greatest work is Mary Barton.

2   ANON. "Recent Brontë Literature," Brontë Society Transactions (Shipley), VII, part XL, 238-42.

   Emily Brontë by Charles Simpson provides a welcome corrective to Gaskell's emphasis on gloom in The Life of

1930

(ANON.)
Charlotte Brontë, and Rosamund Langbridge's Charlotte
Brontë: a Psychological Study uses psychoanalysis to at-
tack Gaskell's portrait of Charlotte as a "family martyr."

3   BENJAMIN, LEWIS S. [LEWIS MELVILLE], and REGINALD HARGREAVES.
    [Introductory note to] "Curious If True," in Great English
    Short Stories. New York: Blue Ribbon Books, p. 466.
        Gaskell's Cranford "was at once acclaimed a masterpiece
    of humoristic literature."

4   CARLOS [pseud.]. "Mrs. Gaskell: Associations with Knutsford
    and Manchester," Manchester City News (4 October), p. 7.
        Gaskell filled her fiction with "anecdotes" of actual
    people. Her work displays "splendid" descriptive powers,
    deep "human sympathy," and sweetness, and, although "imagi-
    nation" is not Gaskell's strong point, this lack is made up
    for by her social conscience.

5   PAYNE, REV. GEORGE A. "'Charlotte Brontë's Biographer'. An
    Address Given...January 25th, 1930," Brontë Society Trans-
    actions (Shipley), VII, part XL, 227-37.
        The three greatest Victorian women novelists--Charlotte
    Brontë, Gaskell, and George Eliot--were interested in one
    another, but Gaskell and Charlotte were particularly close
    friends. Gaskell's arduously researched biography of Char-
    lotte is a great book in spite of a few indiscretions, and
    Charlotte and Gaskell were "right" about "the character" of
    the Rev. William Carus Wilson.

6   SHEPPARD, ALFRED TRESSIDER. The Art and Practice of Historical
    Fiction. London: Humphrey Toulmin, p. 273.
        Gaskell "wrote one memorable strictly historical novel,"
    Sylvia's Lovers, in which "the press gang plays a notable
    part."

1931 A   BOOKS - NONE

1931 B   SHORTER WRITINGS

1   ANON. "In Manchester. By Staff Correspondents. A Gaskell
    Sunday," Manchester Guardian (17 September), p. 11.
        In commemoration of the centenary of Mrs. Gaskell's
    arrival in Manchester "as the wife of" the Rev. William
    Gaskell, a service will be held September 27th by the Rev.
    C. W. Townsend at Cross Street Unitarian Chapel, and Mr.
    Henry Brown will address the congregation on "The Manches-
    ter life and influence of Mrs. Gaskell, the novelist."

2   ANON. "Kingsley and the Gaskells. An Interesting Link,"
    Manchester City News (21 February), p. 7.
        Mr. W. Henry Brown gave a "lantern lecture on Charles
    Kingsley at Cross-Street Chapel" and described how Kingsley
    defended Gaskell from attacks against Ruth and her Brontë
    biography. The Gaskells were also associated with two
    other Christian Socialists--F. D. Maurice and Tom Hughes.

3   ANON. "A Memorial Tablet," Manchester Guardian (8 June),
    p. 11.
        The Manchester Corporation has put up a tablet to Gaskell
    on her old Plymouth Grove house.

4   ANON. "Mrs. Gaskell's Home. A Manchester Memorial," Manches-
    ter City News (7 February), p. 8.
        If the present "owner" of 18 [formerly 84] Plymouth Grove
    agrees, a plaque honoring Gaskell will be put up outside
    the house by the Manchester Town Hall Committee.

5   C. R. "A Gaskell Memorial [letter to the Editor]," Manchester
    City News (21 February), p. 5.
        Why is there no "Gaskell Society to acquire" Gaskell's
    "house in Knutsford for" a permanent memorial?

6   DOTTIN, PAUL. La Littérature anglaise. Paris: Librairie
    Armand Colin, p. 147.
        Gaskell is the most feminine of novelists. Her Mary
    Barton dealt with industrial miseries, but she was best at
    novels of provincial and family life, and, in her master-
    piece, Cranford, she shows, with a malice worthy of Jane
    Austen, the vain agitation of a little village.

7   HATFIELD, C. W. "Letter from the Rev. Patrick Brontë, on the
    Death of His Wife," Brontë Society Transactions (Shipley),
    VII, part XLI, 284-89.
        Gaskell, for her Life of Charlotte Brontë, was misin-
    formed by Mr. Brontë about the date of the arrival of Aunt
    Elizabeth Branwell at Haworth, as she actually came before
    Mrs. Brontë died. Gaskell was also misled by a servant
    about Patrick Brontë's supposedly eccentric behavior.

8   HOPKINS, A.[NNETTE] B. "Liberalism in the Social Teachings of
    Mrs. Gaskell," Social Service Review (Chicago), V (March),
    57-73.
        Gaskell's "liberal" teaching about social "problems" are
    still relevant today, particularly because of their wise
    "tolerance." Her denial, in Mary Barton, of any "knowledge
    of political economy" may have been because, like Ruskin

1931

(HOPKINS, A.[NETTE] B.)
and Carlyle, "she could not accept the" dogmas of classical
economics. Gaskell's portrayals "of industrial problems"
are the most "reliable" of those of any Victorian novelist.

9   PRIESTLEY, J. B. The English Novel. Benn's Essex Library.
     London: Ernest Benn, pp. 85-88.
          Gaskell was "perhaps the most gracious figure" among
     English novelists, but she lacked "Jane Austen's perfection
     of art" and "the Brontës' flashes of genius," and no single
     work of Gaskell's does full justice to her talent. The
     "humorous" and "idyllic" Cranford is "her most famous book,"
     but the "rural" pastel Cousin Phillis is "perhaps her best."
     "With a little more sheer creative power, unifying her work
     and giving her character-drawing a sharper edge, she would
     have been the greatest woman novelist we have had."

*10   STEPHENSON, HAROLD WILLIAM. Unitarian Hymn-Writers. London:
      Lindsey Press.
          "In her husband" Gaskell "found a wise and able critic
      in whom she placed complete reliance. If Charles Dickens
      wished to enliven with purple patches work that had passed
      Mr. Gaskell's critical examination, he met with nothing but
      firm resistence." [Source: quoted in Anon. Dickensian
      (London), XXVIII (June 1932), 240.]

1932 A   BOOKS - NONE

1932 B   SHORTER WRITINGS

1   ANON. "Annotated Books. Public Library," Manchester Guardian
     (21 July), p. 11.
          The Manchester Corporation Libraries Committee has re-
     ceived a bequest from the late Miss Gertrude Wright of the
     following books signed and annotated by Gaskell: Lois the
     Witch and Other Tales, Mary Barton (1856 ed.), The Life of
     Charlotte Brontë (1860 ed.).

2   ANON. "Letters of Mrs. Gaskell and Charles Eliot Norton,..."
     Bookman (New York), LXXV (December), 886.
          "The author of Cranford and what might be called the
     first proletarian novel, Mary Barton, had a genius for
     correspondence." Gaskell's letters are "delightful," for
     "she was excited by everything she saw or heard of."

3   ANON. "A Delightful Friendship. Letters of Mrs. Gaskell and
     Charles Eliot Norton,..." Saturday Review of Literature
     (New York), IX (10 December), 304.

Gaskell's letters in this "pleasing memento" are "full of underlinings, ejaculations, inquiries, family gossip, and occasional reference to public events."

4 ANON. "Letters of Mrs. Gaskell,..." TLS (6 October), 767.
Gaskell's "bountiful and beauty-loving nature was not satisfied by the life she shared so gallantly and devotedly with" the sober Rev. Gaskell, and so her friendship, formed in Europe, with Charles Eliot Norton served a need, though it had to be carried on by letters. Gaskell's correspondence in Letters of Mrs. Gaskell and Charles Eliot Norton conveys the "flavour of the period."

*5 ANON. "Mrs. Gaskell's Wedding Bells Echo. 'Cranford' Tribute to Authoress," N[orth?] C[heshire?] [Herald?] (26 August).
The bells of Knutsford's parish church will be rung Tuesday to celebrate what would be Gaskell's hundredth wedding anniversary, an "idea" suggested "by Mr. Thomas Beswick,...of the local Council." [Unlocatable. Source: Gaskell Cuttings, Manchester Central Library.]

6 BAKER, ERNEST A., and JAMES PACKMAN. A Guide to the Best Fiction: English and American Including Translations from Foreign Languages. New and enlarged ed. [first published in 1903 and rewritten in 1913] London: George Routledge & Sons, p. 194.
Mary Barton "draws some beautiful types of intrinsic" working-class "nobility and fortitude," Cousin Phillis is an "affecting" love idyll, but Cranford is "by far" Gaskell's "finest" work of fiction. The aristocratic title character of My Lady Ludlow "is one of" Gaskell's finest. "The sufferings of" the "whale-fishers" in Sylvia's Lovers are "reminiscent" of the Cotton Famine of 1862-63. Wives and Daughters is a great achievement because of its depiction of a wide diversity of human nature.

7 BENSON, E.[DWARD] F. Charlotte Brontë. London: Longmans, Green & Co., see index for numerous references to Gaskell.
Gaskell, in her Life of Charlotte Brontë, "produced an admirable book which will always rank high for its technical excellence," but Gaskell softened too many of the negative traits of Charlotte's character and was sometimes careless about verifying her information.

8 _____. "A Page out of Cranford. Letters of Mrs. Gaskell and Charles Eliot Norton,..." Spectator (London), CXLIX (15 October), 485.

1932

(BENSON, E.[DWARD] F.)
These letters reveal Gaskell's "tranquil" "charm," but
they also show that she was capable of an amusing petty
stinginess over trifles and could express ideas about
America that remind one of her own Miss Matty.

9   BOWEN, ELIZABETH. English Novelists. London: William
Collins, pp. 36-37. [Reprinted as "English Novelists," in
Romance of English Literature. Edited by W. J. Turner.
New York: Hastings House, 1944, pp. 258-59.]
"In my heart I prefer" Gaskell to George Eliot, who is
more of a major writer. Gaskell's "reaction to the injustices" of "industrial England" "was of the heart, but was
ruled by her steady head: unlike Dickens, she never over-
painted.... Happy in her own life as a woman, she was,"
as, for example, in Ruth, "keenly aware of injustices done
to her sex in the name of morality." Gaskell's Cranford,
in contrast with Jane Austen's Emma, shows small-town peace
threatened by "vibrations from Drumble" [Manchester].

10 BRADBY, G. F. The Brontës and Other Essays. London: Oxford
University Press, Humphrey Milford, pp. 15-16, 38-41,
43-47, 49.
Gaskell, in her Life of Charlotte Brontë, accepts a number of obviously apocryphal stories about Patrick Brontë
and also believes Branwell's story about Mrs. Robinson.
Gaskell was a lady "not given to suspicion."

11 BROCKBANK, JAMES. "Mrs. Gaskell and Silverdale," Manchester
Quarterly [published in Papers of the Manchester Literary
Club], LVIII, 271-82.
Gaskell loved to get away from Manchester by vacationing
at Silverdale. She lived at many places during her life,
and she based her fiction on her experience of these places.
Her love of Silverdale, and more broadly of Lakeland, was
a general "influence" on her writings. One of Gaskell's
finest short stories, "The Sexton's Hero," was written at
Silverdale, and her description of the place in her letters
is worthy of Shakespeare. Silverdale also "figures" in
Alice Wilson's deathbed "ramblings" in Mary Barton and as
Abermouth in Ruth.

12 BROWN, W.[ILLIAM] HENRY. "Mrs. Gaskell: a Manchester Influence," Manchester Quarterly [published in Papers of the
Manchester Literary Club], LVIII, 13-26. [Reprinted as
pamphlet in Manchester: Sherratt & Hughes, 1933.]
Gaskell was one of our most notable "Manchester resi-
dents." Here she learned about the problems of the poor

and also was subjected to laissez faire theories of the Manchester school of economics, however much she may have resisted them. Working people appreciated the portrayal of industrial problems in Mary Barton, but factory owners did not. Gaskell contributed six articles to Kingsley's and Maurice's Christian Socialist. Her later, non-industrial novels have been highly praised.

13   COLLINS, NORMAN. The Facts of Fiction. London: Victor Gollancz, pp. 166, 174, 177.
　　　Gaskell was one of "the best of the second-best" novelists of the Victorian era, but her Life of Charlotte Brontë is a classic.

14   DE SÉLINCOURT, ERNEST. In Enciclopedia italiana di scienze, lettere, ed arti. S.v. "Gaskell, Elizabeth Cleghorn."
　　　Mary Barton is sympathetic toward the workers in the industrial crisis of 1842; North and South is more objective and better constructed; Cranford is a humorous, lucid classic; Gaskell's Brontë biography is a masterpiece, with vivacity and creative spirit; but many consider Gaskell's later books her best.

15   FFRENCH, YVONNE. "Letters of Mrs. Gaskell and Charles Eliot Norton,..." London Mercury, XXVII (November), 85-86.
　　　Gaskell's letters are "altogether sprightly. Whether on the sofa racked with neuralgia, or flustered by a houseful of visitors she seems to have been able to keep up a perpetual rattle of information, always cheerful, on occasion coy, and never malicious."

16   LOVETT, ROBERT MORSS, and HELEN SARD HUGHES. The History of the Novel in England. Boston: Houghton Mifflin Co., Riverside Press, pp. 183, 240-43, 247.
　　　Gaskell's Mary Barton and North and South contributed to "better understanding" of the working classes by "the privileged classes." Ruth makes a "striking departure from" Victorian conventionality when the heroine refuses the seducer's belated offer of marriage.

17   McLAUGHLIN, FLORENCE CATHERINE. "Mrs. Gaskell's Accomplishment as a Novelist in Her First Three Novels." M.A. thesis, University of Pittsburgh, 1932. [Abstracted in University of Pittsburgh Bulletin, XXVIII, 395-96.]
　　　As art, Mary Barton, North and South, and Ruth are weakened by Gaskell's humanitarian attempts to go beyond her observation, and she is best at domestic and rural scenes.

1932

18   SOUTHRON, JANE SPENCE. "The Communion of Two Eminent Victorian
Minds,..." New York Times Book Review (25 December), p. 9.
    Gaskell's correspondence in Letters of Mrs. Gaskell and
Charles Eliot Norton reveals her "as the kindly, humorous
and generous woman who saw so deeply into the human heart
that she was able to make a 'Cranford'."

19   WELBY, T. EARLE. "The Bookshelf. Mrs. Gaskell's Letters,..."
Bookman (London), LXXXIII (November), 120.
    "The charm and exuberance of" Gaskell's "nature come out
in innumerable passages" in Letters of Mrs. Gaskell and
Charles Eliot Norton. She "flows on nearly always very
vivacious, often exclamatory, seldom without a certain
shrewdness in even the blandest of her social observations."

20   WHITEHILL, JANE. "Introduction," in Letters of Mrs. Gaskell
and Charles Eliot Norton, 1855-1865. London: Oxford University Press, Humphrey Milford, pp. vii-xxix.
    Gaskell's horizons were far wider than those of Knuts-
ford, but she did share some of its traditional serenity.
Her talk was "delightful," but she also was a splendid
listener. Gaskell's high-serious and rather rigid husband
"must have" often felt "bewildered affection," without understanding, for his society-loving wife. In Rome Norton
gave Gaskell "a Tauchnitz edition of The Life of Charlotte
Brontë," the first version that she had seen in print, and
"it is now among the Norton books in the Harvard College
Library." Norton kept "all" of Gaskell's letters to him.
The attacks on her Brontë biography hurt her "so deeply"
that for a time she planned, through Norton's help, to
publish only in the United States, though she eventually
dropped this "idea." Gaskell wrote to Norton that their
days together in Italy had been the happiest of her life.
her life.

21   WHITFIELD, A.[RCHIE] STANTON. "Introduction," in The Sexton's
Hero and Other Tales. 3rd ed. Tokyo: Hokuseido Press,
pp. i-xiii.
    Gaskell "was the earliest of our first-rate women
writers" to become proficient at the short story. Looser
than most modern short stories, Gaskell's some thirty works
of short fiction have "diverse" "themes" but tend toward
"an air of spectral mournfulness." A scene in "The Heart
of John Middleton" foreshadows the one in North and South
in which Margaret protects Thornton from the mob's stones
and gets struck herself. "Half a Lifetime Ago" has a Silas
Marner-like "pathos," Gaskell's ghost stories are as effective as Poe's, the tragedy of "Lois the Witch" is worthy of

Hardy, and a number of her other tales have the qualities of those of Hawthorne.

22   WISE, THOMAS JAMES, and JOHN ALEXANDER SYMINGTON, eds. "Friendship with Mrs. Gaskell" and "Mrs. Gaskell's Biography," in The Brontës: Their Lives, Friendships, and Correspondence. The Shakespeare Head Brontë. Oxford: Shakespeare Head Press, published by Basil Blackwell. IV, 61-91, 186-246, and see index for numerous other references to Gaskell.

Both Gaskell and Charlotte Brontë wholly admired the novels of the other. Gaskell "has of late obtained a far greater reputation in literature than could have been anticipated by her contemporaries...." The Life of Charlotte Brontë was successful because of the writer's narrative talents as a novelist but also her conscientious research. She had been a friend of Charlotte's but not an intimate friend. In spite of the resulting controversy and Gaskell's withdrawal of questioned passages, she was "fairly correct" both about Mrs. Robinson and the Cowan Bridge School. Gaskell's portrayal of Charlotte was not, as some have charged, too gloomy.

1933 A   BOOKS - NONE

1933 B   SHORTER WRITINGS

1   ANON. "The Gaskell Collection of Letters," BJRL, XVII (July), 193-94.

Executors of the late Miss M. E. Gaskell have given "upwards of three hundred letters" from famous Victorians to Mrs. Gaskell to the Rylands Collection of English manuscripts.

2   BENSON, E.[DWARD] F. "Archbishop Benson and the Brontës. To the Editor,..." Times (London) (20 September), p. 11.

[Benson prints an "extract from a book of jottings by" his "father," Archbishop Benson, "dated January 25, 1858":] Gaskell "was very hasty and inaccurate in the steps she took to gain information, and never consulted Mr. Nicholls or old Mr. Brontë, as the latter himself told me. They never saw" The Life of Charlotte Brontë "till it was in print."

3   _____. "Charlotte Brontë. To the Editor,..." Times (London) (26 September), p. 15.

Miss Haldane's book on Gaskell prints a letter from Patrick Brontë to William Dearden complaining about

1933

(BENSON, E.[DWARD] F.)
mistatements in The Life of Charlotte Brontë. Also, Mrs.
Lowndes, in her letter to the Times, is wrong in thinking
that her mother and Gaskell were at Charlotte Brontë's
wedding, for "the only guests" were Miss Wooler and Miss
Nussey.

4   CHEW, SAMUEL C.   "Letters of Mrs. Gaskell and Charles Eliot
Norton," YR, XXII (June), 835-38.
These letters "give us pleasant glimpses of" Gaskell's
"busy life in England,...but they have to do...with the
small intimacies of daily life rather than with the larger
world of literature and the arts."

5   CUNLIFFE, J.[OHN] W.[ILLIAM].   Pictured Story of English Literature: from Its Beginning to the Present Day.   New York and
London: D. Appleton-Century Co., pp. 317-18.
In spite of the controversy over Mary Barton and in spite
of Gaskell's offer of "a solatium" to the manufacturers by
North and South, her portrayal of industrial conditions is
accurate.   Her Life of Charlotte Brontë is admirably
discreet "compared with...some modern" biographies, but it
was attacked in its time for its "personal revelations."
Gaskell's only uncontroversial book is her beloved Cranford.

6   ELIOT, T. S.   [Review of Letters of Mrs. Gaskell and Charles
Eliot Norton], NEQ, VI (September), 627-28.
"This is not a book for admirers of Norton so much as
for admirers of" Gaskell.   The important point about their
meeting in Rome was that "neither" "was a European."   Gaskell "was married to an earnest, conscientious, somewhat
humorless Unitarian pastor" from Manchester who tended to
avoid vacations, but Gaskell, "who bore him...children,"
served him, and even "sacrificed herself" to him, "was entitled to take a holiday."   Both she and Norton were Uni-
tarians, but "Norton was a Unitarian of a type unfamiliar
to" her, for "he was rich, good, and cultivated."   Gaskell
"had a sense of humor, timid and fluttering as it was; she
had an unsatisfied love of beauty, gaiety, and civiliza-
tion; she profited by" her introduction to Italian art;
and "her later correspondence with Norton must have been
a relief from the labors of slaving to provide for the old
age of Mr. Gaskell."   Mrs. Gaskell "was not George Sand;
but the best of her writing is perhaps more permanently
readable, for she is among those English (and American)
writers who have known how to make a literary virtue out
of provinciality--and, in her case, simple goodness."

7 HALDANE, ELIZABETH S. "Charlotte Brontë. The Accuracy of Mrs. Gaskell's Life. A Visit to Haworth...To the Editor, ..." Times (London) (23 September), p. 11.
  Mr. Benson's account, in his letter to the Times, of Patrick Brontë's criticism of Gaskell's Brontë biography does not agree with published evidence that shows Mr. Brontë's approval of the book.

8 HATFIELD, C. W., and [MRS.] C. MABEL EDGERLEY. "The Reverend Patrick Brontë and Mrs. E. C. Gaskell. Sources of Biographer's Information," Brontë Society Transactions (Shipley), VIII, parts XLIII-XLIV, 83-100, 125-38.
  "In collecting material for her 'Life of Charlotte Brontë'," Gaskell "accepted as true many slanderous" and spiteful stories about Mr. Brontë based on "village gossip" and the lies of a "discharged" Brontë "day-nurse." Mr. Brontë's requests for withdrawal of the "fabrications" were so kind and mild that they disprove the charges of his having an "ungovernable temper." We here print in full for the first time eighteen letters from Mr. Brontë to Gaskell and her husband, which were given to the University of Manchester libraries by Miss M. E. Gaskell in 1913.

9 LOWNDES, MARIE BELLOC. "Charlotte Brontë. The Accuracy of Mrs. Gaskell's Life. A Visit to Haworth. To the Editor, ..." Times (London) (23 September), p. 11.
  "In 1856 my mother, then Miss Bessie Parkes,...accompanied" Gaskell "to Haworth, where they stayed three nights." Gaskell "spent the whole day making notes, asking questions of Mr. Brontë and making careful notes of his replies. Mr. Nicholls was terribly moved, for seeing" her "recalled to him his wedding day, at which she and Mr. Gaskell had been among a handful of guests [a mistake]."

10 _____. "Charlotte Brontë. To the Editor,..." Times (London) (28 September), p. 11.
  "Mr. Benson misquotes me," for "I wrote" that Mrs. Gaskell and her husband were at Charlotte Brontë's wedding [they were not]--not Mrs. Gaskell and my mother--and my statement is confirmed by Ward's article on Gaskell in the Dictionary of National Biography.

11 PARRISH, M.[ORRIS] L.[ONGSTRETH]. "Mrs. Gaskell," in Victorian Lady Novelists: George Eliot, Mrs. Gaskell, the Brontë Sisters. First Editions in the Library at Dormy House, Pine Valley, New Jersey, Described with Notes. London: Constable & Co. [Reprint. New York: Burt Franklin, 1969, pp. 54-75.]

1933

(PARRISH, M.[ORRIS] L.[ONGSTRETH])
Besides its first editions, this collection includes an important letter from Gaskell to M. Emil Souvestre and one from Patrick Brontë to Miss Nussey. The collection also includes the oddity of a pirated American edition of Lizzie Leigh, which the publisher labeled as by Dickens. The copy of Cranford contains a hand-written inscription from Gaskell to her husband.

12   SCHNURER, CLARA. "Mrs. Gaskell's Fiction." Ph.D. dissertation, University of Pittsburgh, 1932. [Abstracted in University of Pittsburgh Bulletin, XXIX, 206-13.]
Gaskell's "achievement" rests "not upon her manipulation of plot...but...her choice of themes,...her treatment of setting to reveal character," and her "insight into" both "individuals" and "classes."

1934 A BOOKS - NONE

1934 B SHORTER WRITINGS

1   CECIL, [LORD] DAVID. Early Victorian Novelists: Essays in Revaluation. London: Constable. Indianapolis and New York: Bobbs-Merrill Co., 1935, pp. 25, 133, 158, 163, 179, 182, 207-50, 273, 292, 293, 295, 298, 302-4, 306, 307, 309, 336.
"The outstanding fact about" Gaskell "is her femininity." Compared with other Victorian women novelists, "she was a dove" among "eagles." "As Trollope was the typical Victorian man," Gaskell was the quintessential Victorian female: "gentle, domestic, tactful, unintellectual, prone to tears, easily shocked." Her fiction is limited by her womanly qualities: she cannot handle ideas, cannot deal with harsh passions, and cannot go beyond the placidity of average attitudes. Yet, though a "minor" novelist, Gaskell "has her own special merits." She uses "detail" like a miniaturist, has an unconscious "feminine" subtlety in analyzing people, and an appealing unsophistication. She is perceptive about polite society but does "not understand" the poor except as a benevolent visitor among them. At her best, in Wives and Daughters, she surpasses Trollope's realism. Though Gaskell prefers Molly, "would we not sacrifice twenty Mollys for a single Cynthia," a "complex flirt" who is a "masterpiece" of characterization and "unique" in Gaskell's "work" and also "in Victorian fiction?" Gaskell had "twenty times the talent of most novelists," but she was not as successful as she should have been, for she often

wrote "outside" of her "range" and was too careless in technique. Her didactic novels are all failures.

2 CROSSLAND, JOHN R. "Introduction," in Pride and Prejudice,... Jane Eyre,...Cranford. London and Glasgow: Collins' Clear-type Press, pp. xi-xx.

We are offering together "three" enduring "classics" of our literature, which "will provide, in this age of exotic and neurotic fiction, a pleasant backwater." Gaskell clearly relishes "the innocuous peccadilloes of the spinsters of" Cranford. If Jane Austen "wrote and stood aloof" and Charlotte Brontë "throbbed" with "fire," Gaskell "wrote and chuckled."

3 CUNLIFFE, JOHN W.[ILLIAM]. Leaders of the Victorian Revolution. New York and London: Appleton-Century Co., pp. 22, 103-5, 110, 113-15.

Gaskell's fine biography of Charlotte Brontë "has perhaps" drawn "attention" away "from" Gaskell's "own novels," which are "gentler" than those of the Brontë sisters.

*4 GERNSHEIMER, JOSEPHINE. "Mrs. Gaskell's Novels: Their Reception in Various Periodicals, 1848-1910." M.A. thesis, Columbia University.

[The thesis gives "some excerpts from reviews."] [Source: Marjorie Taylor Davis. "An annotated Bibliography of Criticism on Elizabeth Gaskell, 1848-1973." Ph.D. dissertation, University of Mississippi, 1974. See 1974.B6.]

5 HARDY, THOMAS J. Books on the Shelf. London: Philip Allan. [Reprint. Freeport, New York: Books for Library Press, 1970, pp. 207-8.]

Gaskell's "Cranford is regional and so too, in point of identification, are her factory stories; but her dominating interest in both is class rather than locality."

6 MASEFIELD, [MRS.] MURIEL [AGNES]. "The Life of Elizabeth Cleghorn Gaskell" and "Mrs. Gaskell's Novels," in Women Novelists from Fanny Burney to George Eliot. London: Ivor Nicholson & Watson, pp. 161-90.

Richmond's "charming" portrait suggests that Gaskell had "a sweet and happy nature." She is the only woman novelist included in this book "who was both a wife and mother," and the demands of domestic duty may explain why Gaskell achieved "real art" in only a few works. Though her writing was made "lovable" by her domestic experiences, Ruth showed her courage in braving conventional morality, but "she suffered" when accused of being immoral. Her

1934

(MASEFIELD, [MRS.] MURIEL [AGNES])
"best work," <u>Wives and Daughters</u>, was written under unusual conditions of ease and leisure, with the most generous literary contract of her career. Gaskell's finest works are those that are not propagandistic: <u>Cranford</u>, <u>Cousin Phillis</u>, <u>Sylvia's Lovers</u>, and <u>Wives and Daughters</u>. <u>Mary Barton</u>, <u>Ruth</u>, and <u>North and South</u> are mainly of historical interest. <u>Cranford</u> has the limitations of "a <u>genre</u> piece"; the tragic <u>Sylvia's Lovers</u>, though almost great, is marred by a pietistic ending; <u>Cousin Phillis</u> contains Gaskell's finest prose; but <u>Wives and Daughters</u> is her masterpiece. Cynthia's complexity is made skillfully "convincing," and the uncomplex but truly "nice" Molly is a creation of some "genius."

1935 A BOOKS - NONE

1935 B SHORTER WRITINGS

1   ANON. "Letters to Mrs. Gaskell. What Some Eminent Contemporaries Thought of Her Novels. Publication for the First Time," <u>Manchester Guardian</u> (4 February), p. 11.
     An article by Mr. R. D. Waller gives a selection from the John Rylands Library collection of letters to Gaskell from "eminent Victorians."

2   ANON. "Memorabilia," <u>N & Q</u>, CLXIX (30 November), 379.
     The Gaskell collection at the John Rylands Library is of particular interest for its "many letters of Dickens."

3   ANON. "Mrs. Browning on Marriage. Charming Letters to Mrs. Gaskell. Rylands Library Publication," <u>Yorkshire Post</u> (4 February), p. 4.
     "The latest Bulletin of the John Rylands Library" prints many letters, from its collection, addressed to Gaskell "by celebrated contemporaries."

4   ANON. "Mrs. Gaskell's Letters for Rylands Library," <u>Daily Dispatch</u> (Manchester) (4 February), p. 7.
     "A collection of letters" to Gaskell, "from Victorian celebrities, has been deposited in the John Rylands Library" and "edited by Ross D. Waller."

5   BENSLY, EDWARD, and A. FRANCIS STEUART. "Rizpah [reply to CLXIX, 333]," <u>N & Q</u>, CLXIX (23 November), 373-74.
     Tennyson's poem was based on a story related in a "penny magazine" named <u>Old Brighton</u>, and "in one of" Gaskell's

"novels, she refers to this story as that of 'the poor Rizpah'."

6 CRUSE, AMY. The Victorians and Their Reading. Boston and New York: Houghton Mifflin Co., pp. 36, 65, 66, 92, 115, 116, 123-24, 127, 143-44, 176, 189, 190, 217-18, 220, 228-29, 260, 266, 267, 270-72, 277-79, 281-82, 349-50, 355, 366, 420.

Gaskell, "the wife of a Unitarian minister, wrote in 1842 that she was 'taking a course of Newman's sermons'." Gaskell's novels illustrated the popularity of "sermon reading" in the Victorian period. In Mary Barton she describes workingmen who read Newton's Principia. Cynthia at her boarding school in Wives and Daughters learned to recite Byron's "The Prisoner of Chillon" but "preferred Johnnie Gilpin." The Victorians ranked Gaskell after "Dickens, Thackeray, Charlotte Brontë, and George Eliot,... in a lower class" with Trollope and Kingsley--"not of the greatest, but certainly of the great." Among Victorians who loved Cranford were Mr. and Mrs. Burne-Jones. "Cardinal Newman thought Sylvia's Lovers the best of all" Gaskell's "stories."

7 HOWE, SUSANNE. Geraldine Jewsbury. Her Life and Errors. London: George Allen & Unwin, pp. 12, 38-39, 55-56, 65, 69, 111, 121, 128, 130, 133, 200.

The Jewsburys lived in Greenheys, and the "Mary Barton" fields "were visible from" their door. The Gaskells lived in a larger house nearby, so near the Jewsburys that Jane Carlyle could easily stroll over to breakfast with the Gaskells when the Carlyles stayed with the Jewsburys. Geraldine Jewsbury, like Jane Carlyle, was prejudiced against Gaskell's Unitarianism. "The soil" in the neighborhood "was so clayey that" Gaskell's "children grew up scarcely knowing what cowslips looked like."

8 LeGOUIS, ÉMILE. A Short History of English Literature. Translated by V. F. Boyson and J. Coulson. Oxford: Clarendon Press, p. 330.

"Social problems" "were almost" Gaskell's "sole concern." Mary Barton, North and South, and Ruth all express sympathy for "victims" of society, but Cranford is the work of a splendid "humorist."

9 OSGOOD, CHARLES GROSVENOR. The Voice of England: a History of English Literature. New York and London: Harper & Brothers Publishers, pp. 456, 475, 509-10, 578-79.

1935

(OSGOOD, CHARLES GROSVENOR)
Gaskell's most enduring works are her "idyllic" and "domestic" tales, Cranford and Cousin Phillis. The Life of Charlotte Brontë is a "great" biography, in spite of the controversy it aroused.

10 WALLER, ROSS D. "Correspondence. Articles by Mrs. Gaskell," TLS (25 July), p. 477.
I have located the following articles of Gaskell's, mentioned in my edition of letters to her in the BJRL of January 1935: "The Last Generation in England," Sartain's Union Magazine (Philadelphia), V (July 1849), 45-48; "Martha Preston," Sartain's Union Magazine (Philadelphia), VI (February 1850), 133-38.

11 WALLER, ROSS D., ed. "Letters Addressed to Mrs. Gaskell by Celebrated Contemporaries. Now in the Possession of the John Rylands Library," BJRL, XIX (January), 102-69.
In spite of Gaskell's wish that materials for a biography be suppressed, much material exists still untapped. On the death of her last surviving daughter, the John Rylands Library was given many letters to Gaskell by famous people, a large number of which were hitherto unpublished. Though "gracious and noble," Gaskell did not stimulate most of her correspondents to "spontaneous self-expression." There are letters praising Mary Barton from Samuel Bamford, Maria Edgeworth, and Thomas Carlyle. There are letters from such "radical politicians and social reformers" as Lord Shaftesbury, Cobden, and Florence Nightingale. The many letters from literary celebrities include those from the Howitts, Godwin, Leigh Hunt, Landor, Matthew Arnold, George Henry Lewes, Mrs. Browning, Ruskin, and Rossetti. Among Gaskell's French correspondents, de Circourt and Guizot both complained of her unproductivity since The Life of Charlotte Brontë.

12 WROOT, HERBERT E. "Sources of Charlotte Brontë's Novels: Persons and Places," Brontë Society Transactions (Shipley), VIII, supplementary part IV, 7-214.
[This is a reprint, with amplifications and corrections, of the study printed by the Brontë Society as volume III of its publications, 1902-1906. The references to Gaskell are mainly citations from The Life of Charlotte Brontë, along with Shorter's annotations, in support of attempted real-life identifications of Charlotte Brontë's characters and settings.]

1936 A BOOKS - NONE

1936 B SHORTER WRITINGS

*1 ANON. "More about 'Cranford'. Forgotten Stories by Mrs.
    Gaskell. Brandy a 'Lady's Drink'. From Our Own Correspond-
    ent," Sunday Times (London) (24 February).
         Ross D. Waller, in the BJRL, has been led, by a letter
    from Mary Howitt to Gaskell, to the discovery of two of
    Gaskell's "forgotten" but worthy "pieces." [Unlocatable.
    Source: Gaskell Cuttings, Manchester Central Library.]

2   ANON. "Peeps at Dickens. Pen Pictures from Contemporary
    Sources.... A Dinner Party at Devonshire Terrace,"
    Dickensian (London), XXXIII (December), 39-40.
         Gaskell, in a letter dated May 13, 1849, describes "the
    party" to which she was invited by Dickens "to celebrate
    the start of David Copperfield."

3   E.[DGERLEY], [MRS.] C. M.[ABEL]. "Book Reviews. Some Recent
    Publications," Brontë Society Transactions (Shipley), IX,
    part XLVI, 48-51.
         "In reviewing books on the Brontës, one is struck with
    the fact that the basis of all of them is" Gaskell's "Life
    of Charlotte Brontë." In spite of our age's increase in
    knowledge and decrease in discretion, Gaskell's biography,
    even with its few errors, is still the great and standard
    work on the Brontës. "We do not agree" with Mrs. Masefield
    in her Women Novelists "that Mr. Brontë was displeased with"
    Gaskell's book. "At first...he was extremely pleased,"
    later "made little protest," and greeted her "most
    cordially, not long before he died."

4   MOORE, VIRGINIA. The Life and Eager Death of Emily Brontë.
    A Biography. London: Rich & Cowan, pp. ix, 128, 144, 258,
    287.
         "I have paid especial and respectful attention to"
    Gaskell's "facts, not her opinions," in The Life of
    Charlotte Brontë.

5   PRAMPOLINI, GIACOMO. Storia universale della letteratura.
    Turin: Unione Tipografico. III, part II, 625-26.
         Gaskell's social-problem novels--Mary Barton, North and
    South, and Ruth--have more artistic subtlety than those of
    Disraeli. Her portrayal of a small English town in Cran-
    ford is delightfully humorous.

1936

6   SIMISON, BARBARA DAMON.   In British Authors of The Nineteenth
     Century.   Edited by Stanley J. Kunitz and Howard Haycraft.
     New York: H. W. Wilson Co. S.v. "Gaskell, Elizabeth
     Cleghorn Stevenson."
         In Gaskell's early novels, Mary Barton, North and South,
     and Ruth, "the moral is all too obvious.... When she pays
     less attention to" a moral, as "in Cranford and Wives and
     Daughters, she ranks high as a novelist." Her strengths
     are "humor" and "realism." Although her Life of Charlotte
     Brontë aroused great controversy, it places Gaskell among
     the greatest of biographers.

7   UTTER, ROBERT PALFREY, and GWENDOLYN BRIDGES NEEDHAM.
     Pamela's Daughters. New York: Macmillan Co., pp. 49,
     252-53, 345-46, 357, 360, 363, 365.
         The prudish Pamela stereotype of femininity cannot be
     "found in any approach to entirety in the works of Trol-
     lope," Gaskell, "or George Eliot," though some of the at-
     tributes appear in their essentially realistic portrayals
     of women. Although Cranford portrays "a whole village of
     old maids," "there is hardly a stock trait in the whole
     village," for the characterization is unsurpassed in "fine-
     ness" by even Jane Austen. Gaskell's Mary Barton and Ruth
     illustrate that for working girls the only training avail-
     able "is apprenticeship," and the only possibility of escape
     from their class is "marriage."

8   WALLER, ROSS D. "Mrs. Gaskell," BJRL, XX (January), 25-27.
         From a clue in letters to Gaskell in BJRL (January 1935),
     I have discovered "The Last Generation in England" and
     "Martha Preston" in Sartain's Union Magazine (Philadelphia)
     of July 1849 and February 1850, respectively.

9   WRIGHT, THOMAS. The Life of Charles Dickens. New York:
     Charles Scribner's Sons, pp. 159, 215-16, 223, 224-25,
     317-18.
         "Dickens's intimate friends Forster, William Johnson
     Fox, and" Gaskell "were Unitarians." In Dickens's "haste
     to" remove the reference to himself in Cranford, he got
     the name of a Hood poem wrong--"Miss Kelmansegg and Her
     Golden Leg" for "Miss Kelmansegg and Her Precious Leg."
     Gaskell "wrote to say that she enjoyed" Dickens's Christmas
     stories "The Child's Story" and "Poor Relations,...and her
     encomiums gave him the liveliest pleasure." Her "Ruth
     stirred Dickens more than any other of her books."

1937 A BOOKS - NONE

1937 B SHORTER WRITINGS

1   BAKER, ERNEST A. "Mrs. Gaskell and Other Women Novelists,"
    in The History of the English Novel. VIII: From the
    Brontës to Meredith: Romanticism in the English Novel.
    London: H. F. & G. Witherby, pp. 81-111.
        Although in her finest works--Cranford, My Lady Ludlow,
    "My French Master," Wives and Daughters, and Cousin Phillis--
    Gaskell gives the impression of being the equal of Jane
    Austen, actually Gaskell is not, because she showed only
    "intermittant" artistic control. She has some of the
    romanticism of the Brontës, a didacticism similar to George
    Eliot's, and a tendency to draw upon her own experiences in
    a transparent way. Her social novels Mary Barton and Ruth
    are greatly inferior to her non-sociological fiction.
    and even North and South is now mainly of "historical"
    interest. Gaskell was not particularly good at plots.
    Cousin Phillis is a rare achievement for her because "the
    humour and the pathos are not put in different compart-
    ments." Cynthia Kirkpatrick is Gaskell's "most delicate
    and delectable creation," and Wives and Daughters deserves
    comparison with Trollope's novels.

2   BEARD, PAUL. "Introduction," in The Cage at Cranford and Other
    Stories. London: Thomas Nelson & Sons, pp. 7-22.
        Gaskell's short stories survive through their "integrity,"
    in spite of "a certain naiveté of form." She combined the
    writing of fiction with her many other "duties" as "a wife
    and mother." She was a "moral" and didactic writer, who,
    like other Victorians, makes "extraneous comments" that jar
    the contemporary reader, but, at least, she makes us feel
    the "sweetness and strength" of a world dominated by the
    moral certainties of her age. Gaskell remains much closer
    than Dickens to the "true feelings" of "men and women,"
    partly because of her" deliciously temperate sense of
    humour." Her weakness for "happy" endings reflected
    the "Victorian" belief that "virtue" would ultimately re-
    ceive material reward, yet she went against this complacent
    convention in Cousin Phillis. Gaskell represents "Vic-
    torianism's first stirrings of awareness of its own hubris."
    Gaskell "is most completely an artist" in the humorous ele-
    ments in her fiction.

3   E.[DGERLEY], [MRS.] C. M.[ABEL]. "The Late Bishop Welldon,"
    Brontë Society Transactions (Shipley), IX, part XLVII, 131.

1937

(E.[DGERLEY], [MRS.] C. M.[ABEL])
For thirteen years as "Dean of Manchester," Bishop
Welldon "was on intimate terms with the" Gaskell daughters
"and heard much of" Gaskell "and her relations with Charlotte Brontë."

4   FOX, ARTHUR W.   "The Rev. William Gaskell, M.A.," Manchester
Quarterly [published in Papers of the Manchester Literary
Club], LXIII, 275-79.
The handsome and delightful Rev. William Gaskell lived
an "almost ideally happy life" till the sorrow of Mrs.
Gaskell's "early death." Many stories are told of his
youthful love of mischievous "pranks." He was able to
hold his own in the conversations at his wife's literary
and social salons. He was deeply interested in the Manchester poor, and he was a great preacher. Although the
Rev. Gaskell's ministerial duties left him in Manchester
while his wife often traveled, the rumor that she "'neglected him'" is "absurd." Mr. Gaskell deserves to be
remembered in his own right and not merely as Elizabeth
Gaskell's "husband."

5   MULLER, HERBERT J.   Modern Fiction. A Study of Values.
New York and London: Funk & Wagnall's Co., pp. 136, 186,
323, 325, 326.
In spite of the "feminine Declaration of Independence"
in Virginia Woolf's A Room of One's Own, the "gentle folk"
of Mrs. Woolf's own fiction are "framed in a beautiful
little picture in a cloistered gallery" and have the same
"charm" and "limitation" as the characters in Gaskell's
Cranford. The characters of both Mrs. Woolf and Gaskell
never have "an emotion that cannot be wrapped up in a
pocket-handkerchief." Most contemporary women novelists
are "modern-dress" Gaskells, and she was a "busy housewife,
mother, and soft-eyed model of Victorian womanhood who was
restricted by her utter femininity."

6   PRAZ, MARIO.   Storia della letteratura inglese. Florence:
G. C. Sansoni, p. 312.
Through Gaskell's portrayal of industrial conflict in
Mary Barton and North and South and of ethical problems in
Ruth, she urges the duty of charity and mutual sympathy.
Her most enduring work is Cranford, a delicately humorous
portrait of the social preoccupations of a small village.
Unlike a writer such as Sterne, Gaskell in Cranford con-
centrates exclusively on comedy and pathos and omits all
intermediate emotions.

7   WHITE, W. BERTRAM. The Miracle of Haworth: a Brontë Study.
     London: University of London Press, pp. 2, 8, 21, 24–28,
     34, 37, 151, 152, 221, 239, 297, 310, 316, 333–34, 336,
     340, 341.
          Gaskell's "otherwise excellent" Brontë biography is un-
     fair to Patrick Brontë. To someone who was herself pros-
     perous, such as Gaskell, Haworth may have seemed humble,
     particularly in contrast with Charlotte's literary fame.
     The proximity of the gravestones to the vicarage, empha-
     sized by Gaskell, is typical of most English vicarages.

1938 A BOOKS – NONE

1938 B SHORTER WRITINGS

1   BATHO, EDITH, and BONAMY DOBRÉE. The Victorians and After,
     1830–1914. With a Chapter on the Economic Background by
     Guy Chapman. London: Cressett Press, pp. 80, 86, 88–90,
     109, 117, 150–52, 183, 274, 290, 291.
          Hostile critics of Gaskell's Mary Barton and North and
     South accused her of having "wrong theories" about indus-
     trial questions. "Perhaps" she did, "but her facts were
     right." The delightfully comic Cranford is Gaskell's only
     book still widely read, for the others "are dull in long
     stretches" in spite of their virtues. Some readers "would
     plead for Wives and Daughters or Cousin Phillis," but Gas-
     kell's greatest work was clearly her Life of Charlotte
     Brontë.

2   DICKENS, CHARLES. The Letters of Charles Dickens. Edited by
     Walter Dexter. Bloomsbury: Nonesuch Press. II: 202,
     359, 380, 457, and see index for numerous other references
     to Gaskell.
          [To Gaskell, 31 January 1850:] "If you could and would
     prefer to speak to me" about your writing for Household
     Words, I should come to see you in Manchester. "My unaf-
     fected and great admiration of" Mary Barton "makes me very
     earnest in all relating to you." [To Gaskell, 25 November
     1851:] "MY DEAR SCHERAZADE,--for I am sure your powers of
     narrative can never be exhausted in a single night, but
     must be good for at least a thousand nights and one." [To
     Gaskell, 25 February 1852:] "O, what a lazy woman you are,
     and where IS that article!" [To Gaskell, 13 April 1853:]
     "I have joyfully sent the Cranford last received to the
     printers.... I receive you...(if Mr. Gaskell will allow
     me to say so) with open arms.... You shall collect Cran-
     ford when you please, and publish where you please. My

1938

(DICKENS, CHARLES)
  dear friends Ruth and Mary Barton, I can put no limitations
  on. Their visits are too like those of angels."

3   HOPKINS, ANNETTE B.   "Mrs. Gaskell in France 1849-1890," PMLA,
    LIII (June), 545-74.
    There were many more editions of Gaskell's works in
    France and considerably more French criticism of them than
    is indicated in Devonshire's The English Novel in France
    [1929.B2]. "About four-fifths of" Gaskell's "entire work
    was translated, including practically all of her important
    writings." In general, French critics did not appreciate
    Cranford, gave most attention to The Life of Charlotte
    Brontë, were impressed by the early social-problem novels,
    but had little to say about Gaskell's "humor." She
    tended to be admired in France by conservative opponents
    of Naturalism. Gaskell's books were, apparently, "far...
    more widely read" in France than those of George Eliot.

4   MADLE, HERBERT.   Die Maschine und der technische Fortschritt
    in der englischen Literatur des 19, und 20 Jahrhunderts.
    Breslau: Verlag Priebatchs Buchandlung, pp. 14-15, 45.
    North and South deals more subtly than Mary Barton with
    the anguish of hand workers faced with the rise of the
    machine, for in the later novel Gaskell also indicates the
    grandeur and power of machinery.

5   ROBINSON, HENRY CRABB.   Henry Crabb Robinson on Books and
    Their Writers. Edited by Edith J. Morley. London: J. M.
    Dent & Sons. II: 685, 688, 722-23, 768.
    [Diary, 22 April 1849:] On meeting Gaskell, I found her
    "a woman of agreeable manners, with a hale, florid complex-
    ion, with nothing literary about her appearance. She
    pleased me." [Diary, 28 April 1849:] "I like Gaskell "the
    more the more I see her...." [Diary, 6 January 1849:]
    Mary Barton "is a book I would rather recommend others to
    read than read myself," though "it is...very good...and edi-
    fying.... The first volume consists of painful pictures of
    poverty--the poverty of the worthy--but with no relief by
    any touch of imagination.... The moral tendency is far
    better than the artistic merit." [Diary, 16 February
    1853:] "... Ruth I could not finish; but I have no doubt
    that she as well as her child dies.... The assignable
    fault, if any, might be an excess of repentence; yet there
    is no cant certainly...." [Diary, 23 May 1857:] I
    "talked" with Sir James Stephen about Gaskell's "attack"
    in the Brontë biography on Mrs. Robinson, "of whom Sir
    James gives a very high character." Gaskell "is incapable

of having intended to slander a virtuous woman," but she
will probably have to make an apology.

1939 A BOOKS - NONE

1939 B SHORTER WRITINGS

1 ANON. "A Famous Knutsford Chapel. Next Month's Celebration
of Its 250th Anniversary,..." Manchester Guardian
(11 April), p. 11.
"The 250th anniversary of the...Brook Street Chapel,
Knutsford, will be celebrated on May 20th with a meeting in
Knutsford Town Hall.... Literary associations...have
brought thousands of pilgrims to pay their tribute to the
author of 'Cranford' and 'Wives and Daughters'."

2 O'CLAIR, ROBERT M. "Mr. and Mrs. Victorian [High-school prize
literary article]," Scholastic (Pittsburgh), XXXIV (6 May),
29-E.
Trollope and Gaskell "would have made an ideal married
couple--he, with his great long beard, and she, probably
rather retiring, and fully conscious of her proper place in
the scheme of things." Both novelists should be revived
and read for "the amusingly normal and accurate picture
that they give of Victorian life." Gaskell is the most
feminine of Victorian women novelists.

1940 A BOOKS - NONE

1940 B SHORTER WRITINGS

1 EDGERLEY, [MRS.] C. MABEL. "Ellen Nussey," Brontë Society
Transactions (Shipley), X, part L, 3.
Stung by misrepresentations about Charlotte Brontë in
Sharpe's Magazine (London) of June 1855, Ellen Nussey asked
Gaskell to "write a refutation" and provided Charlotte's
letters for Gaskell to work with. But Ellen disliked the
resulting Life of Charlotte Brontë because of its treatment
of Branwell and of Mr. Brontë.

2 _____. "Tabitha Aykroyd," Brontë Society Transactions (Shipley), X, part LI, 62-68.
Although Gaskell, in her Brontë biography, emphasized
Tabby's Yorkshire "dialect" and "character," Tabitha Aykroyd's "relations tell me she was not rough, but intelligent
and refined."

1940

3 HATFIELD, C. W. "Charlotte Brontë and Hartley Coleridge 1840,"
Brontë Society Transactions (Shipley), X, part L, 15–24.
In The Life of Charlotte Brontë, Gaskell mistakenly con-
cluded that Charlotte sent the manuscript of a story to
Wordsworth "'in the summer of 1840'." Actually, the manu-
script was sent to Hartley Coleridge.

4 HENKIN, LEO J. Darwinism in the English Novel, 1860–1910.
The Impact of Evolution on Victorian Fiction. New York:
Corporate Press, p. 37.
Roger Hamley, in Gaskell's Wives and Daughters, is sup-
posed to be based on "the character and experiences of
Charles Darwin," though "somewhat romanticized."

5 MARRIOTT, SIR JOHN. English History in English Fiction.
London and Glasgow: Blackie & Sons, pp. 293.
Gaskell, "as a novelist," was as good as Kingsley and
Disraeli and far more knowledgeable than they were about
conditions in the industrialized north. Though Cranford is
artistically comparable to the works of Jane Austen, Gas-
kell's Mary Barton, North and South, and even Sylvia's
Lovers are more notable than it as sources of history.
Gaskell's social novels can all be described by a sentence
from Carlyle: "All battle is misunderstanding."

*6 MICKLEWRIGHT, F. H. A. "The Religion of Mrs. Gaskell," Modern
Churchman (Knaresborough) (June), pp. 12–17.
[Source: Catherine Margaret Ellen Halls. "Bibliography
of Elizabeth C. Gaskell." Diploma in librarianship dissertation, University of London, 1957. See 1957.B5.]

7 RUDMAN, HARRY WILLIAM. Italian Nationalism and English Letters: Figures of the Risorgimento and Victorian Men of
Letters. New York: Columbia University Press. London:
George Allen & Unwin, pp. 220–21, 313.
The Italian man of letters and supporter of the Risorgimento Angostino Ruffini "appears in" Gaskell's "Round the
Sofa...as Mr. Sperano, an Italian exile in Edinburgh who had
been banished even from France and now was teaching Italian
with meek diligence."

*8 THÉRIVE, ANDRÉ. "Introduction," in Cranford. Translated by
Jeanne Bourret. Paris: Sorlot.
[Source: Catherine Margaret Ellen Halls. "Bibliography
of Elizabeth C. Gaskell." Diploma in librarianship dissertation, University of London, 1957. See 1957.B5.]

1941 A BOOKS - NONE

1941 B SHORTER WRITINGS

1   BATES, H.[ERBERT] E. The Modern Short Story. Boston: the
     Writer, pp. 35, 36, 56, 102-3.
          Gaskell, a "rather self-effacing figure," was "the only
     potentially important short-story writer" of mid-Victorian
     England, but she concentrated on "the rather ponderous
     literary" form of the three-volume novel. She is also the
     only Victorian writer, except for the poets, to describe
     the "English countryside."

2   BENTLEY, PHYLLIS. The English Regional Novel. London:
     George Allen & Unwin, p. 18.
          Gaskell "wrote two admirably regional novels about in-
     dustrial Lancashire: Mary Barton...and North and South."
     The latter "is still very readable" and is notable for
     Thornton, a "'granite' northern" character. Mary Barton is
     made "rather heavy going" by its excessive number of deaths,
     but the book is important for its portrayal of Lancashire
     "workpeople" and their "dialect."

3   BRUNER, DAVID KINKAID. "Family Life in Early Victorian Prose
     Fiction." Ph.D. dissertation, University of Illinois.
          Gaskell was one of the most prominent of the novelists
     of the period to criticize the Victorian faith in the male-
     dominated family, whose function was to guard respectability
     in social, economic, intellectual, and sexual matters. Gas-
     kell's Ruth shows the dependency and helplessness of women
     in such a society. She criticized the tyranny of society
     over individuals.

4   HOUSE, HUMPHRY. The Dickens World. London: Oxford University
     Press, pp. 108, 199, 204, 217.
          "It has been said that Dickens was a good deal influenced
     by Mary Barton in writing Hard Times; it might even be added
     that he was influenced by" Gaskell "herself--it is impos-
     sible that he should have known her without being half in
     love--for his editorial letters about her work show an af-
     fectionate care abnormal even for him. But there was never
     any question of a conscious and deliberate imitation of
     her...."

5   MILFORD, H. J. "Correspondence. Mrs. Gaskell," New Statesman
     and Nation (London), n.s. XXI (28 June), 652.
          Pritchett, in this publication's columns, "says that"
     North and South "'is dead'," yet "it has been continuously

(MILFORD, H. J.)
on sale in The World's Classics since 1908 and still sells
some hundreds of copies a year." [Editor's note:] "Another
correspondent writes" that Gaskell "was not...'Low-church'"
but Unitarian.

6   PRITCHETT, V. S. "Current Literature. Books in General,"
     New Statesman and Nation (London), n.s. XXI (21 June), 630.
          Lord David Cecil's criticism of Gaskell for writing "be-
     yond" her "range" in her didactic novels imposes our world
     view on the Victorians, who generally wrote didactically
     and emphasized the idea of "responsibility," just as we em-
     phasize "self-sufficiency" and "guilt." Our preference for
     hedonistic Cynthia over the worthy Molly is a mere cultural
     bias, as is our objection to Gaskell's melodrama, which ac-
     curately expresses "the Victorian mind." If "all" of Gas-
     kell's "books, except Cranford," are "too long, North and
     South successfully portrays the emotions" of such repre-
     sentative figures of the industrial north as Thornton and
     his "fierce" yet "yielding" mother. Margaret is a con-
     vincing characterization of a "prim young woman...freezing
     up in a hostile environment." Cranford limits itself to
     "impecunious" gentility, but Wives and Daughters depicts
     the "whole" range of rural society. Gaskell's dialect is
     always accurate whatever class she portrays.

7   RATCHFORD, FANNIE ELIZABETH. The Brontës' Web of Childhood.
     New York: Columbia University Press, pp. ix, x, xi, xiii,
     xiv, 221.
          Gaskell's Life of Charlotte Brontë "holds its place
     after eighty-three years as one of the most popular biog-
     raphies in the language," and "later research has added
     little of essential value or interest." But Gaskell did
     not understand the importance of the Brontë juvenilia.

8   ROBERTS, W. WRIGHT. "English Autograph Letters in the John
     Rylands Library," BJRL, XXV (August), 129.
          The John Rylands Gaskell collection provides a valuable
     "quarry" of letters to Gaskell from distinguished
     Victorians.

9   SAMPSON, GEORGE. The Concise Cambridge History of English
     Literature. Cambridge: University Press. New York:
     Macmillan Co., pp. 781-83.
          The "powerful and disturbing" Mary Barton "is the first
     'labour' novel," which, in spite of flaws, nobly illuminates
     the shocking conditions of the Victorian working class. In
     spite of Gaskell's "contact with Dickens," her own "creative

gift" kept her from any "imitation" of him. In Gaskell's "hands the social novel developed into a form...which she made entirely her own," for "she knew instinctively how to subdue controversial matter to the service of art...." Though less memorable than her quaint characters in Cranford, Gaskell's working-class figures successfully sum up the workers of an entire era.

*10 WAIDE, HELEN. "The Reception of Mrs. Gaskell's Life of Charlotte Brontë." M.A. thesis, Columbia University.
      [Source: Catherine Margaret Ellen Halls. "Bibliography of Elizabeth C. Gaskell." Diploma in Librarianship dissertation, University of London, 1957. See 1957.B5.]

1942 A BOOKS - NONE

1942 B SHORTER WRITINGS

1 EDGERLEY, [MRS.] C. MABEL. "The Rev. Arthur Bell Nicholls," Brontë Society Transactions (Shipley), X, part LII, 95-101.
      Charlotte Brontë's "friend," Gaskell, "dearly loved a romance, but had her misgivings" about Charlotte's impending marriage to the Rev. Nicholls, whom Gaskell thought "stern and bigoted, exacting and law-giving." She "feared he would not approve of such friends as Unitarians for his wife." It is lucky for posterity that Ellen Nussey disobeyed Nicholl's injunction to burn Charlotte's letters to her, for, without them, Gaskell could not have written her great biography.

2 GEROULD, GORDON HALL. The Patterns of English and American Fiction. A History. Boston: Little, Brown & Co., pp. 281, 307-12, 314-15, 335, 372, 465.
      Gaskell, with Trollope and Thackeray, was "the third great mid-Victorian novelist of manners," though, like Jane Austen before, Gaskell's "scope was narrower than theirs." She has been underrated until recently "because of a failure" on the part of critics "to discriminate between her work and the commonplace fiction which it superficially resembles." Mary Barton convincingly portrays characters from all classes, Cranford is loved but insufficiently admired for its narrative artistry, Sylvia's Lovers is well constructed yet "too studied" in its characterization, Cousin Phillis is "simple and lovely," and Wives and Daughters is Gaskell's "masterpiece." "No single novel gives a better objective representation of the Victorian world" than does Wives and Daughters.

1942

3   HAINES, HELEN E. What's in a Novel. New York: Columbia Uni-
    versity Press, pp. 83, 89-90.
        Gaskell's "courageous novels...recorded miseries of in-
    dustrial oppression in Lancashire cotton mills during the
    'hungry forties'," but, like the novels of Dickens and of
    Kingsley, Gaskell's "are not proletarian...in the strict
    meaning of the term," for she does not advocate class
    warfare.

4   TREVELYAN, G. M. Illustrated English Social History. IV:
    The Nineteenth Century. London: Longmans, Green & Co.
    [Reprint, London: Longmans, Green & Co., 1952, p. 27.]
        Some of the fund-holders, "who enjoyed incomes secured
    on the national credit," lived "inactive, respectable lives
    on their small, carefully treasured investments," like Gas-
    kell's "innocent ladies" in Cranford. Gaskell, in Sylvia's
    Lovers, "throws much light on the ways of the press-gang,
    and on the English whalers of the Greenland and Arctic
    Seas."

5   WAGENKNECHT, EDWARD. Cavalcade of the English from Elizabeth
    to George VI. New York: Henry Holt & Co., pp. 182, 251-60,
    304, 316, 399, 597-98.
        Gaskell's ghost, horror, and crime stories appealed to
    the readers of Household Words and All the Year Round, yet
    she herself seems to have had a temperamental affinity for
    such themes. Because Gaskell's "proper range" was "domes-
    tic," her Cranford, Sylvia's Lovers, Wives and Daughters,
    and Cousin Phillis are superior to her "didactic" novels
    about social problems, Mary Barton, North and South, and
    Ruth. Gaskell "was not a great novelist" yet made a "con-
    siderable" contribution "to the English novel."

1943 A   BOOKS - NONE

1943 B   SHORTER WRITINGS

1   ANON. "Obituary. Mr. Jonas Bradley," Brontë Society Trans-
    actions (Shipley), X, part LIII, 173-74.
        The late member of the Brontë Society Jonas Bradley
    "maintained that" Gaskell "had done an injustice to the
    Rev. Patrick Brontë in her portrait of him" in her Brontë
    biography. "'I've talked to those who knew him,'" said
    Bradley, and "'he was not a fierce old monster'."

2   ENTWISTLE, WILLIAM J., and ERIC GILLET. The Literature of
    England, A.D. 500-1942: a Survey of British Literature

from the Beginnings to the Present Day. London: Longmans, Green & Co., p. 142.

In Mary Barton, North and South, and Sylvia's Lovers, Gaskell "shows greatness" in portraying "classes and communities" under stress, "but her plots are not remarkable, nor does she develop arresting characters." As sheer literature, Cranford is Gaskell's best work, with a "cunningly negligent style."

3 F. P. "The Good and the Clever," N & Q, CLXXXV (18 December), 376.

Alice Meynell noticed an absurd triple negative in a comment on Charlotte Brontë by Harriet Martineau, which Gaskell quoted in her Brontë biography "with no consciousness of anything amiss."

4 GRUBB, GERALD G. "Dickens' Editorial Methods," SP, XL (January), 85, 92-98.

Gaskell was uncomfortable with the short length required by Household Words and "was inclined to rebel against Dickens' editorial methods." Yet, in spite of their editorial quarrels, he retained her as "a valuable contributor" by a mixture of firmness and tact. She may even have learned her lesson by realizing that he and not she had been right about the problems involved in North and South. Even later, however, he remained anxious about Gaskell's "seeming inability to work steadily at her task."

5 HOPEWELL, DONALD G. "The Brontë Society. Its Past, Its Present and Its Future," Brontë Society Transactions (Shipley), X, part LIII, 139-43.

Gaskell "brought to her task" as Brontë biographer "many admirable qualities: unflagging energy, boundless enthusiasm, literary skill and charm, dramatic power, the true sympathy of a clear and beautiful mind, and, above all, a passionate determination to secure for her friend real justice." But Gaskell "had the defects of her qualities" too: "enthusiasm" without "discretion," a "dramatic sense that led to exaggeration," and a "sympathy" that made her too uncritical of what she was told. "The result was a masterpiece...that created as many problems as it solved."

6 OFFOR, DR. RICHARD. "The Brontës--Their Relation to the History and Politics of Their Time," Brontë Society Transactions (Shipley), X, part LIII, 150-60.

Gaskell, in her Brontë biography, shows how Charlotte researched the period of the Luddite riots by reading old issues of the Leeds Mercury. Charlotte, in Shirley, "was

1943

(OFFOR, DR. RICHARD)
not as outspoken as her friend and biographer" Gaskell "in
Mary Barton."

1944 A   BOOKS - NONE

1944 B   SHORTER WRITINGS

1   ANON. "'Cold Loin' at Cranford," TLS (22 January), 48.
        [Editor:] Out of the many replies to the Dean of Lich-
     field's "inquiry" about the misprint "cold loin" in Cran-
     ford, we have selected the following: [Sir Humphrey Mil-
     ford:] The mistake was noted in the Nation (New York)
     (1892), by W. E. Axon in his Gaskell bibliography (1895),
     and by Clement Shorter in the World's Classics edition
     (1907). The error originated in the 1864 edition. [Pro-
     fessor R. J. A. Berry:] The mistake was corrected in
     Dent's the King's Treasuries edition (1920) and in the Mac-
     millan edition (1905), which even has a picture of a "pud-
     ding in the mould of a lion." [Rev. George A. Payne:] I
     believe that the mistake "began...in the cheap edition" of
     1855. [See 1944.B3.]

2   EDGERLEY, [MRS.] C. MABEL. "Mary Taylor, the Friend of Char-
     lotte Brontë," Brontë Society Transactions (Shipley), X,
     part LIV, 220.
        When Gaskell sent Mary Taylor a copy of The Life of
     Charlotte Brontë in 1857, "Mary considered that the 'Life'
     did not go beyond the facts. Indeed, it was not so gloomy
     as the truth. She commented that women were not justified
     in sacrificing themselves for others."

3   IREMONGER, VERY REV. F. A. [Dean of Lichfield]. "'Cold Loin'
     at Cranford," TLS (15 January), 36.
        "In each of...three editions of 'Cranford'" that I have
     checked, from 1891 on, "'cold loin'" in the meal in chapter
     xiv seems to be a printer's mistake for "'cold lion'." Can
     anyone tell me if this mistake appeared in earlier editions?
     [See 1944.B1.]

4   THOMAS, GILBERT. "Mrs. Gaskell and George Eliot: a Study in
     Contrast," Chambers's Journal (London), 8th ser. XIII
     (December), 631-34. [Reprinted as "Mrs. Gaskell and George
     Eliot," in Builders and Makers: Occasional Studies.
     London: Epworth Press, 1944, pp. 164-72.]
        Gaskell has been misunderstood by being associated almost
     solely with Cranford, for, though "Victorian, in certain

respects," she was also a "hater of complacency" and a true "rebel," yet without doctrinaire bitterness. "... She had a firmer hold upon herself, and a truer grasp of the social problem, than Dickens...or...Disraeli." The fact that "some of" the "domestic revelations" of her Life of Char-lotte Brontë shocked the Victorians is a demonstration of her "honesty." Because Gaskell came from a less rigid "in-tellectual tradition" than George Eliot and could be "gay" as well as serious, Gaskell seems far more current today than George Eliot.

1945 A BOOKS - NONE

1945 B SHORTER WRITINGS

1 HINKLEY, LAURA L. The Brontës: Charlotte and Emily.
New York: Hastings House, pp. 10, 11, 85, 98, 118, 146-47, 169, 172, 204, 206, 243-44, 273, 279, 315-16, 319.
Gaskell discretely suppressed, in her Brontë biography, what Charlotte's letters to M. Heger revealed. Gaskell's account of Mrs. Robinson seems to have been based on Bran-well's distortion of a "harmless flirtation."

2 MALCOLM-HAYES, MARIAN V. "Notes on the Gaskell Collection in the Central Library," Memoirs and Proceedings of the Man-chester Literary and Philosophical Society, 1945-46, LXXXVII, 149-74.
The collection was begun by W. E. Axon and built by J. A. Green. After a full bibliographical guide of the collection came out in 1910, important additions were made, in 1914 following Miss M. E. Gaskell's death, and from 1911-1922 through gifts of American editions from David Hutcheson, yet no recent catalogue has been made. Some of Gaskell's memorabilia, such as her music books and family atlas, were acquired after the 1910 catalogue was made.

3 OLSEN, THOMAS. "The Weary Are at Rest. A Reconsideration of Branwell Brontë," Brontë Society Transactions (Shipley), X, part LV, 270, 271, 275, 277.
One wonders why biographers "now" deny the "authenticity" of Gaskell's portraits of the Rev. Patrick Brontë and of Branwell's love affair in her Life of Charlotte Brontë. She "had no axe to grind,...no reason to seek anything but the truth.... As a shrewd, penetrating writer, her in-clination was to show things as they are," even if they of-fended the man who had asked her to do the biography, Mr. Brontë.

1945

4   POPE-HENNESSY, UNA. Charles Dickens, 1812-1870. London:
     Chatto & Windus, pp. 272, 276, 277, 304, 396.
         The first issue of Household Words began, after the
     "editorial word," with "the first chapter of Lizzie Lee
     [sic] by" Gaskell, "a short and dismal serial opening with
     a Christmas corpse, and this an Easter number!" Gaskell
     "never learnt to accept" Dickens's "rulings and was in-
     furiated when North and South was cut."

5   WATT, HOMER A., and WILLIAM W. A Dictionary of English
     Literature. College Outline Series. New York: Barnes &
     Noble. S.v. "Gaskell, Elizabeth Cleghorn."
         Cranford combines Goldsmith's "rural felicity," Jane
     Austen's "satire," and the quiet "realism" of Mary Russell
     Mitford. Gaskell's industrial novels show a closer knowl-
     edge of the conditions of the poor than do the works of
     Dickens or Disraeli.

1946 A BOOKS - NONE

1946 B SHORTER WRITINGS

1   ANON. [Prefatory note], in A Cameo from Cranford. By Agnes
     Adam. Glasgow: William MacClellan [1946], on verso of
     front cover. "The more mechanized the times become, the
     greater our nostalgia for the horse-and-cab days, the
     lavender and lace charm of Victorian times."
         This "adaptation of" Gaskell's "famous classic" succeeds
     in capturing "the delicate qualities of the original."

2   ANON. "Education: Cowan Bridge College [a reprint of the
     prospectus of the Cowan Bridge School, from 'a Country
     Newspaper, August 1824]," Brontë Society Transactions
     (Shipley), XI, part LVI, 20-22.
         [See also 1946.B7 and 1953.B6.]

3   BULLET, GERARD. "An Early Victorian Novelist.... On Mrs.
     Gaskell Author of Cranford," Listener (London), XXXVI
     (21 November), 721-22.
         Gaskell's "most famous and popular" book, Cranford, re-
     captures her "childhood" memories of Knutsford. In Manches-
     ter, just "seven or eight minutes' walk from William Gas-
     kell's chapel," a section called "Little Ireland" had
     "hovels" with an average of twenty living in each and "only
     one privy" for the entire area. Mary Barton is flawed ar-
     tistically but is still a moving social protest against
     such conditions. Ruth is "much better" than Mary Barton,

for in Ruth the characters exist in their own right, as well as to illustrate a theme, though the ending is "melodrama-tic," just as the much greater Sylvia's Lovers is marred by its conclusion. Cousin Phillis "is a little masterpiece of self-effacing art," and Wives and Daughters showed that Gaskell was, "at last, an uncontestably major novelist.... The Cranford vogue did not begin till after her death," and that work's popularity now regrettably "obscures" Gaskell's "other work."

4   HINKLEY, LAURA L. Ladies of Literature. New York: Hastings House, pp. 159, 167-70.
    "The best and, on the whole, most intimate of the friends Charlotte" Brontë "owed to her books was" the suc-cessful novelist Gaskell, who "might have been surprised" to know that posterity would remember her mainly as Charlotte's biographer.

5   HOBMAN, MRS. D. L. "Art or Life. A Woman's Problem," Hibbert Journal (London), XCIV (April), 258-62.
    There were basic differences between Gaskell, "artist and wife," and the spinsterish writer Charlotte Brontë. Gaskell had a happier family life, was far more sympathetic to the poor, was more sensitive to criticism, and was much more sociable than the semi-recluse Charlotte. Charlotte's solitude did give her a definite imaginative power but left her far less interested than Gaskell "in the outside world," even though Gaskell's best novels are not those that deal with broad social questions. Did Gaskell's domestic "duties...enrich...her mind," or did they prevent her from developing greater "power in her work"? The answer to the question is complex, for perhaps she derived her fullest "satisfaction" from those very domestic "duties" that tended to conflict with her writing.

6   HOPKINS, ANNETTE B. "Dickens and Mrs. Gaskell," HLQ, IX (August), 357-85.
    In her earliest work for Dickens, Gaskell did submit, "apparently without question," to his editorial changes, but by Cranford she was resentful of them, and by 1852 she was refusing to let him alter her short stories. In their most bitter quarrel, that over North and South, the problem was that the work, "by its very nature, was unsuitable for serialization on the Dickens pattern." Though Dickens later still wanted Gaskell as a contributor, she published Sylvia's Lovers "in book form only" and also began con-tributing to Cornhill, whose monthly format suited her art better than Dickens's weekly installments. Dickens, though

1946

(HOPKINS, ANNETTE B.)
"a great novelist, did not have the temperament for a reliable critic," and Gaskell came "to realize that she" was
"a sounder critic of her work than" he.

7 NEYDHAME, F. [Introductory note to] "Cowan Bridge College. A
New Song," Brontë Society Transactions (Shipley), XI, part
LVI, 23-28.
A satirical poem has been found attacking the Cowan
Bridge School. [The poem, perhaps from the period 1825-
1833, ends:] "And his pockets well-crammed with simoniacal
gold, / He'll a school keep at last with the Devil." [See
also 1946.B2 and 1953.B6.]

8 SADLEIR, MICHAEL. "An English Memory," PULC, VIII (November),
2-5.
"The day when" Morris L. Parrish "bought the fine copy
of Cranford presented by" Gaskell "to her husband was a day
to remember. Radiating excitement," Parrish "carried...
about in his pocket" the "spotless...copy so preciously inscribed" and kept "pulling it out, gloating, displaying and
stroking it."

9 STEBBINS, LUCY POATE. "Elizabeth Gaskell," in A Victorian
Album: Some Lady Novelists of the Period. New York:
Columbia University Press. London: Secker & Warburg,
pp. ix, 95-128.
Gaskell "was perhaps the most limpid character in letters: her life explains her works; her books reveal the
woman." Her "prime motive in writing was...pleasure...in
self-expression," which came easily, followed by a "touching desire to establish harmony between people and classes
who hated each other.... Her chief ethical preoccupation
was with the lie...." Only Mary Barton, of her social
novels, remains of interest today, and Gaskell's best work
was built from idealized memories of a rural childhood
that was often actually "lonely." Gaskell probably liked
writing less than "housekeeping," in which "results are
speedy and nervous tension finds a quick relief"; she
"trained her maids" well; and it was probably her choice
to write in the dining room, in close touch with her household. "A subdued morbid strain in" Gaskell was "relieved"
by "writing macabre tales." She lacked "staying power" for
the long Victorian novel; her short Cousin Phillis is "exquisite"; and Wives and Daughters is her "most nearly perfect" long work, comparable to Jane Austen's Mansfield Park.
Cynthia "is very like Lady Cecilia in Miss Edgeworth's
Helen" but surpasses her model.

10 WEIR, EDITH M. "Cowan Bridge: New Light from Old Documents," Brontë Society Transactions (Shipley), XI, part XVI, 16-19.
In the controversy over the Cowan Bridge School aroused by Gaskell's Life of Charlotte Brontë, Mrs. A. H. Harben (née Evans), the model for Miss Temple in Jane Eyre, seems to have been the most moderate of W. Carus Wilson's "witnesses." She concedes that the school, though not guilty of actual mistreatment of students, may have been, like other similar schools, too austere for the "young" and "delicate."

1947 A BOOKS - NONE

1947 B SHORTER WRITINGS

1 ANDREWS, W. L. "Ups and Downs of Celebrity: a Brontë Investigation," Brontë Society Transactions (Shipley), XI, part LVII, 82.
Gaskell's "'Life' must have given a sharp new impetus to curiosity about the Brontës after the first phase of interest had declined, but their fame was not yet established beyond challenge."

2 ANON. "Mrs. Gaskell's Manifesto," TLS (30 August), 438.
Gaskell's message of tolerant Christianity, which emerged in the same period as the hostile message of Marx and Engels, is far more relevant today than the proto-fascism of Carlyle and Kingsley. Though Gaskell was didactic, she was "better than George Eliot" at controlling her "purpose" by artistry and "a tolerant humour." In Mary Barton, Gaskell "understands the Chartists but is not convinced by them or" their opponents. The Chiltern Library's republication of Mary Barton, to be followed by other novels of Gaskell's, is "welcome." Even better than Gaskell's didactic novels are Cranford and Wives and Daughters, which have a "precision," "clarity of style," and "shrewdness" of characterization comparable to Jane Austen's, though less subtle yet more tender. Perhaps Gaskell's biography of the long-suffering Charlotte Brontë purged Gaskell's later fiction of morbidness. Her charm gives her a place in English fiction "below the first rank but elect in her sphere."

3 COOPER, LETTICE. "Introduction," in Mary Barton. The Chiltern Library. London: John Lehmann, pp. v-x.
Gaskell, who saw at first hand the plight of the Manchester poor, expressed her own nostalgia for rural life by

1947

(COOPER, LETTICE)
the green field at the beginning of Mary Barton, by old
Alice's reveries, and by the garden and orchard at the end.
John Barton is a tragic figure led by his sense of injustice
to commit a murder that goes against his own moral standards. The book emphasizes the willingness of the poor to
help one another in their troubles. Gaskell "is too good
a novelist to write propaganda." All the telling criticism
of the employers is put into the mouths of individual
characters.

4   DIGEON, AURÉLIEN. Histoire illustrée de la littérature
anglaise. Paris: Didier, p. 307.
Gaskell's Life of Charlotte Brontë remains essential as
a first-hand account. Mary Barton, North and South, and
Ruth are important for understanding the social history of
the English poor. Wives and Daughters, however, is a
satirical portrait of the middle class, with marvellous
humor, and so is Gaskell's masterpiece Cranford.

5   DILLON, ALFRED E. "The Brontës: a Manchester Appraisal,"
ManR, IV (Summer), 353-54.
Gaskell's Life of Charlotte Brontë, which "has the
double appeal of subject and author," was written in Manchester at 84, Plymouth Grove. This house, occasionally
visited by Charlotte, "should be named Gaskell House."

6   HARDING, ROBERT. "Introduction," in Cranford. The Russell
Classics. London: P. R. Gawthorn, pp. v-vi.
Cranford "is a simple tale of simple lives" based on
actuality. Gaskell's "spirit sings to us" of this "little
country town...where the proprieties were so rigidly kept
and yet hearts were so human and understanding and kind."

7   JENKINS, ELIZABETH. "Introduction," in Cranford and Cousin
Phillis. The Chiltern Library. London: John Lehmann,
pp. v-xii.
Gaskell is not as great as our outstanding women novel-
ists--Jane Austen, the Brontës, and George Eliot--yet "no
other woman novelist" except them "can stand a comparison
with" Gaskell. All of her work shows talent, individual
charm, and even an "understanding of...economic problems,"
but her greatest works are Cranford, The Life of Charlotte
Brontë, and Wives and Daughters. A village such as Cranford "was obsolete to" Gaskell, just as it is "to us."
Cousin Phillis is next in "perfection" to Cranford but has
a "much smaller" scope. Both books show the encroachments
of the new world of machines upon village life. The

existence of Phillis and her family is noteworthy for its combination of "extreme simplicity" and "intellectual interest."

8 LANE, MARGARET. "Introduction," in The Life of Charlotte Brontë. The Chiltern Library. London: John Lehmann, pp. v-xii.
In spite of the vast amount written since on the Brontës, Gaskell's biography "remains a stirring and noble work." She faced enormous difficulties from the family relations and was extraordinarily brave in risking Mr. Brontë's anger by her unflattering portrait of him. Though supporters of the Rev. Carus Wilson attacked Gaskell ferociously for her description of the Cowan Bridge School, an examination of Wilson's sadistic "religious works for children" shows that she was actually "tender" with him. But her charges against Mrs. Robinson were reckless, and Gaskell was less than candid in dealing with Charlotte's relationship to M. Heger. Gaskell did not deal much with the juvenilia, which might not "have fitted her concept of Charlotte Brontë.... The harsh but satisfying tragedy of the" Brontës "thrust" Gaskell into a narrative which she would not have dared to use in a novel--as, for example, Charlotte's death after a brief time of married happiness.

9 MULGAN, JOHN, and D. M. DAVIN. An Introduction to English Literature. Oxford: Clarendon Press, pp. 120-21.
Mary Barton and North and South "show very close observation,...are packed with concrete details and at the same time full of pity for the working-class victims of financial self-seeking." Gaskell "also proved herself to be a tender, gentle, and amused humorist in Cranford"--a non-didactic novel.

10 TANSEY, GOERGE. "A Yank in Search of Merrie England.... Knutsford Keeps Old-World Fragrance," Daily Dispatch (Manchester) (23 March), p. 2.
"For the transatlantic appeal of Knutsford we...are indebted to" Gaskell, "authoress of 'Cranford'.... The charm of those slow-moving, delicately humoured pages still haunts the imagination of the richest, fastest...nation on earth.... The town librarian," Arthur Edwin Shard, showed "two new" Gaskell "relics"--her "paisley shawl and her favorite glass cake-stand."

11 WRAGG, ARTHUR. "The Illustrator on Cranford," in Cranford. Illustrated by Arthur Wragg. London: C. & J. Temple, pp. vi-viii.

1947

(WRAGG, ARTHUR)
"No book is more limited in its scope, more free from histrionics than is 'Cranford'. Yet it is enthralling, even exciting.... It is not a fairy story," for there is "hard, grinding poverty in it," though the "poverty is veneered by gentility.... And how conveniently...is Mary Smith called from Cranford when the inaction of the novel can continue more economically off-stage. For even Cranford would have been a bore had the author let it creep too close and allowed us to catch the characters momentarily off their guard."

12 ZANCO, AURELIO. Storia della letteratura inglese. II: Dalla Restaurazione ai giorni nostri. Turin: Chiantore, pp. 516, 543-44, 564, 573, 576, 597.
Gaskell's Mary Barton dealt with industrial conflicts. Her masterpiece was Cranford, though North and South, Sylvia's Lovers, and Wives and Daughters are worth reading, and her Life of Charlotte Brontë is an expression of sincere admiration.

1948 A BOOKS - NONE

1948 B SHORTER WRITINGS

1 ANON. "Anniversaries. An Exhibition of Books Published in 1648, 1748, 1848," BNYPL, LII (June), 294.
Gaskell "had not only beauty and charm but also a talent that made her novels on social problems powerful and popular." Her Mary Barton "attracted" immediate "wide attention, and though it was attacked as unfair to the manufacturers, it helped to alleviate the conditions it described."

2 ANON. "The Best of Mrs. Gaskell,..." TLS (28 February), p. 122.
These are reissues, by the Chiltern Library, of Gaskell's "best" works--The Life of Charlotte Brontë, Cranford, and Cousin Phillis--and her "best is regaining the place...held in the days of" Gaskell's "popularity." The Brontë biography is "in the high order of literature" and is also self-revealing about its courageous author. In Cousin Phillis and Cranford, Gaskell "was at home among the better habits and desires of humanity. They are charming pictures of a life that is gone" and show "a clear eye for oddities of behaviour and a disarming subtlety of manner."

1948

3   AYDELOTTE, WILLIAM O. "The England of Marx and Mill as Reflected in Fiction," <u>Journal of Economic History</u> (New York),
VIII, supplement, 42-58.
    Gaskell's essential political conservatism--similar to
that of Dickens, Kingsley, and Disraeli--limited her in
<u>Mary Barton</u> and <u>North and South</u> to preaching philanthropy
and mutual understanding out of her fear of both socialism
and democracy.

4   BAUGH, ALBERT C., ed. <u>A Literary History of England</u>.
New York: Appleton-Century-Crofts, pp. 1369-70.
    Gaskell's didactic fiction is allied to that of the more
serious George Eliot. Gaskell's provincial scene resembles
Trollope's, and her passion for social reform connects her
with Kingsley. "There are echoes of Charlotte Brontë in"
Gaskell's "books, and as a compensation for the lack of the
passion which her friend possessed abundantly," Gaskell has
"humorous aloofness." Her <u>Life of Charlotte Brontë</u> is a
"masterpiece."

5   BENÉT, WILLIAM ROSE. <u>The Reader's Encyclopedia: an Encyclopedia of World Literature and the Arts</u>. New York: Thomas Y.
Crowell Co. S.v. "Gaskell, Elizabeth Cleghorn; Jenkyns,
Deborah, Matty, and Peter; Brown, Captain"; plus summary
references under individual titles of Gaskell's books.
    Gaskell was "known for her pictures of English country
life and her studies of conflicts between capital and labor
in Victorian industrialism."

6   C.[OOLIDGE], T.[HERESA]. "Library Notes. Mrs. Gaskell to
Ruskin," <u>More Books. Bulletin of Boston Public Library</u>,
XXIII (June), 229-30.
    The Boston Public Library has acquired two "apparently
hitherto unpublished" letters by Gaskell: one to Geraldine
Jewsbury with humorous comments about the childhood friendship of Gaskell's great-grandmother and Robert Clive and
one to John Ruskin asking him to help Alfred Waterhouse to
enter an architectural competition.

7   CURL, JOAN. "Cranford Revisited," <u>Geographical Magazine</u>
(London), XXI (May), 4-7.
    "... The similarities between 19th-century Cranford and
20th-century Knutsford...amount to little more than the sur-
vival of certain identifiable buildings and of others which"
Gaskell "knew but did not introduce into her novel." Little
agriculture is left now, and there is heavy traffic in the
streets.

1948

8   DENT, J. C. "Exercises.... For General Study.... Vocabulary
     for Detailed Study," in Cranford. The Minister English
     Texts. London and Glasgow: Blackie & Son, pp. 235-47.
         The "satire" of the book is subtle and avoids moral
     condemnation. "Eccentricity," "verbal retaliation," and
     "good-will" "are three keys to...Cranford society."

9   DILLON, ALFRED E. "Centenary of 'Mary Barton" a Tale of
     Manchester Life'," ManR V (Autumn), 127-31.
         The Rev. William Gaskell had a great "influence on his
     wife's literary career," but "even" at "seventeen" her
     "favorite authors were Goldsmith, Cowper, Pope, and Scott,
     and the Bible was always a great...comfort to her." She
     learned "Latin, French, and Italian," but "mainly by self-
     study." Gaskell did not begin to write until thirty-five.
     Her Mary Barton is one of the great mid-Victorian novels
     that illuminated the miseries of the poor in a time of
     supposed "prosperity."

10   DIMNET, ERNEST. The Brontë Sisters. Translated by Louise
     Morgan Sill. New York: Harcourt Brace & Co., pp. 12-13,
     24, 68, 69, 88, 111, 163-64, 167, 186, 188, 190, 193-94,
     221, 251-52.
         Gaskell's Life of Charlotte Brontë "is one of the five
     or six books regarded as the masterpieces of English
     biography." In spite of Gaskell's reticences, indiscre-
     tions, occasional inaccuracies, her overly gloomy portrait
     of Charlotte, and a tendency to "uselessly" lengthen the
     narrative, the biography remains the essential work on
     Charlotte. "One of the delights of" Charlotte's "life"
     was her "friendship" with Gaskell.

11   HARRISON, G.[RACE] ELSIE. The Clue to the Brontës. London:
     Methuen & Co., pp. 10, 52, 159, 186, 192, 197, 198-203,
     204-10.
         Gaskell, as a Unitarian, missed, in her Brontë biography,
     the importance of Methodism as an influence on the Brontës
     and, specifically, on Patrick Brontë through the crucial
     personal influence of Thomas Tighe. Her biography
     was a "masterpiece," but it "was written as a woman writes
     history"--by using "intuition in a framework of fact." The
     apocryphal stories resulted from Gaskell's unsceptical trust
     in the literal truth of what Charlotte told her.

12   HOPKINS, ANNETTE B. "Mary Barton: A Victorian Best Seller,"
     Trollopian (Berkeley), III (June), 1-18.
         Mary Barton "was the first" of the Victorian "social"
     novels "to combine sincerity of purpose, convincing

portrayal of character, and a largely unprejudiced picture of...industrial life." John Barton "is a truly tragic figure," but Gaskell's yielding, halfway through the novel, to demands by the publishers that Mary become the center of interest contrasts sharply with Gaskell's resistence to such editorial pressures later in her career.

13 LEAVIS, F. R. The Great Tradition. London: Chatto & Windus. [Reprint. New York: New York University Press, 1964, pp. 1-2.]

Though Gaskell is a "minor novelist" not significantly different from almost a dozen other secondary figures, some critics would have us consider her major. Novelists "of the great tradition," such as Henry James and George Eliot, are far "above the ruck of Gaskells and Trollopes and Merediths."

14 LEHMANN, ROSAMUND. "Introduction," in Wives and Daughters. The Chiltern Library. London: John Lehmann, pp. 5-15. [First published as "A Neglected Victorian Classic," in Penguin New Writing, no. 32 (1947), 89-101.]

Wives and Daughters is "incomparably" Gaskell's "richest and most satisfying" novel, yet it is "comparatively neglected," in contrast to Cranford, which, after all, appeals primarily to women. Wives and Daughters reflects the "nature" of "an unusually fulfilled and integrated woman." Though Gaskell, in her working-class novels, does not wholly "succeed...in grasping industrial problems," she is, in Wives and Daughters, "completely at home" with the "stratified class pattern of the countryside." Gaskell is unique among the Victorians in the "tact," "simplicity," and "almost humorous...sympathy" that she displays in this novel. She is unsurpassed in the evocation of a "rural English landscape." Wives and Daughters is full of extraordinary characterizations, even including all the men except Osborne.

15 [LEWIS, NAOMI]. "Books in General [review of the Chiltern Library editions of Mary Barton, The Life of Charlotte Brontë, Cranford and Cousin Phillis, and Wives and Daughters]," New Statesman and Nation (London) (10 July), pp. 32-33. [Reprinted as Naomi Lewis. "Mrs. Gaskell," in A Visit to Mrs. Wilcox . London: Cresset Press, 1957, pp. 167-82.]

My Lady Ludlow is a "beautiful forgotten fragment of a tale." Gaskell could portray a "charming" rural scene but also the misery of Manchester in the 1830s. Her liking for deathbed scenes is understandable in view of the

1948

([LEWIS, NAOMI])

numerous deaths while she was growing up, yet her fiction contains "curiously little recollection of childhood." Gaskell was "impulsive and unpredictable," and her reformism was emotional, for "she had no conscious wish for violent change." The Life of Charlotte Brontë, in spite of the trouble it caused, has the virtue of its "recklessness," and Gaskell's style, usually undistinctive, "here takes on the colour and power of the subject." In Wives and Daughters "the captivating Cynthia must have taken" Gaskell "by surprise; can such charm be compatible with the highest principles? she seems to ask herself.... Wives and Daughters, and still more...Cranford suggest that" her "most individual gift was for comedy"--comedy based on "the social group in action." Gaskell's "place is not with the minor novelists," yet "she had curiously little critical sense, and even less literary vanity."

16   MARCHAND, LESLIE A. "The Symington Collection," JRUL, XIII (December), 11-12.

The Symington Collection includes two letters from Gaskell to John Stuart Mill and a reply, a letter to Gaskell from Dickens, one from Henry Chorley to her, Gaskell family correspondence with Miss Ellen Nussey, and also "a miscellaneous collection of notes and copies of letters gathered by C. K. Shorter toward a biography of" Gaskell "which was never written."

17   RAYMOND, ERNEST. In the Steps of the Brontës. London: Rich & Cowan, pp. 7, 8, 10, 16, 28-29, 36, 37, 39, 41, 51, 63, 72, 164, 179, 253, 259, 269, 289, 300, 304-7.

Gaskell "began" the tendency of Brontë biographers to be quarrelsome. "... She sacrificed Mr. Brontë...and Branwell...to make a sombre...background for the white figure of Charlotte." Gaskell's account, in a letter, of Patrick Brontë's kneeling down to pray with a pistol at his hip is as "delightful a picture" as she ever created. Gaskell "saw" Charlotte's letters to M. Heger but was "as discreet about her heroine, Charlotte, as she was unsparing with others."

1949 A   BOOKS

1   FFRENCH, YVONNE. Mrs. Gaskell. English Novelists Series. London: Home & Van Thal. Denver: Alan Swallow.

Two tendencies clash in Gaskell's work: a striving toward reform of the industrial present and an escapist yearning for the past, yet her "nature was fundamentally

happy." Mary Barton is more important for its social message than for its rather clumsy art. Gaskell showed "a
certain lack of integrity" in making her art secondary to
her domestic "duties." Her "plots" tend "to verge upon
bankruptcy," and her various works repeat the same situations obsessively. Cranford is a "minor English" classic
because of its "perfection" in presenting "former English
customs." Ruth, like Mary Barton, is "technically" inept
but shows an advance "in creative feeling and characterization." Gaskell's portrayal of man's evil remains limited,
in all her works, to "fraud, deception, and moral coward-
ice." North and South is the author's best social-reform
novel but also can be read for Margaret's love story. The
Life of Charlotte Brontë, in spite of the controversy it
aroused, "is remarkable purely as a story" and also as an
"inspired" "study of genius." The complex Philip in Sylvia's
Lovers is "psychologically" "one of" Gaskell's "most interesting creations," and this passionate novel has a far
"grander" scope than any of her previous works. The serene and perfect Cousin Phillis is as fine as Cranford.
Wives and Daughters was her "ablest work of fiction" and
her first "completely free from religious interest" or social messages, for it "is a straightforward love story."
"Throughout" Gaskell's "work the idea of understanding is
strong and pervasive."

[Reviews of Ffrench's book included the following: Anon.
"Mrs. Gaskell,..." Listener (London), XLII (4 August 1949),
203 (This book is too short to be of much use "for the
serious student of literature," but Miss Ffrench does make
some "penetrating and wise" comments that might help the
"general reader" of Gaskell's works.). Anon. "Mrs. Gaskell,..." N & Q, CXCIV (9 July 1949), 308 (Miss Ffrench,
who approves of Gaskell's "spirit" but not her prose, is
perhaps in no position to complain about style.). C. E.
Vulliamy. "Elizabeth Cleghorn Gaskell,..." Spectator
(London), CLXXXII (6 May 1949), 614-16 (Miss Ffrench tends
to make excessive claims for Gaskell's books yet does
achieve some excellent insights, as in analyzing Gaskell's
conflict between "'classic and romantic approaches to
society'.").]

1949 B   SHORTER WRITINGS

1   COOKE, JOHN D., and LIONEL STEVENSON. English Literature of
the Victorian Period. New York: Appleton-Century-Crofts,
pp. 105, 231, 270, 273-75, 277, 282, 368-69.
Gaskell's "style was the most lucid and natural of all
the Victorian novelists."

1949

2   CRUIKSHANK, R.[OBERT] J.[AMES]. <u>Charles Dickens and Early</u>
    <u>Victorian England</u>. London: Sir Isaac Pitman & Sons,
    pp. 55, 57, 58-59, 61.
        Gaskell, the author of <u>Mary Barton</u>, had none of the
    "simpering affectations" and sheltered "refinement" of the
    stereotyped Victorian woman. "... This grave, gentle,
    sensitive woman had the courage to look at the world around
    her, and the courage (and the skill) to tell what she had
    seen. In doing so, she was greatly abused, and one of her
    novels was cut off in its serial publication because it
    offended the taste of the magazine's subscribers."

3   HANSON, LAWRENCE and E. M. <u>The Four Brontës: The Lives and</u>
    <u>Works of Charlotte, Branwell, Emily, and Anne Brontë</u>.
    London: Geoffrey Cumberledge, Oxford University Press,
    pp. 37, 131, 297-99, 302-3, 311, 312, 326-29, 331.
        "Whatever" the "limitations" of the friendship of Char-
    lotte and Gaskell, it "provided Charlotte with much needed
    kindness, and future generations with a popular biography."
    Gaskell "had only a limited understanding of" Charlotte's
    acute shyness. "Even the quiet excitement" of Gaskell's
    "home depressed rather than stimulated" Charlotte by sug-
    gesting her unfitness for life outside Haworth.

4   HICKS, PHYLLIS D. <u>A Quest of Ladies: the Story of a Warwick-</u>
    <u>shire School</u>. Birmingham, England: the Press of Frank
    Juckes, unpaginated "Forward" and pp. 80-82.
        This book arose partly out of "the fervour of my admira-
    tion for" Gaskell's "works." She was the most famous pupil
    who attended the Byerley sisters' school at Stratford.
    Gaskell drew upon her memories of the school and the town
    in much of her fiction, so perhaps Knutsford has been
    stressed "too exclusively" as her model. Hollingford, in
    <u>Wives and Daughters</u>, has a church modeled on Stratford's,
    and the view of the Malvern hills from "outside" Holling-
    ford also suggests Stratford. Most notably, the distinc-
    tive structure of the Byerley school's building is clearly
    reflected in <u>My Lady Ludlow</u>, and the description of family
    prayers seems to echo the religious custom at the school.

5   PEARSON, HESKETH. <u>Dickens. His Character, Comedy, and</u>
    <u>Career</u>. London: Methuen & Co., pp. 179-80, 221.
        Gaskell, "whose <u>Cranford</u> was serialized in <u>Household</u>
    <u>Words</u>, was extremely vexed by the activity of" Dickens's
    "blue pencil on some of her stories, and wrote to complain.
    He was always impenitent; but as he was also prompt and
    generous with his payments, the rage of hurt pride was
    quickly transmuted into the relief of solvency."

6   WEIR, EDITH M., ed. "New Brontë Material Comes to Light. A
     Picture Attributed to Emily. Letters from the Hegers,"
     <u>Brontë Society Transactions</u> (Shipley), XI, part LIX, 249.
        [Unsigned letter, apparently to Louise Heger, daughter
     of M. Heger, from her aunt:] "Have you read" Gaskell's
     "wonderful, heart-rending book, the <u>Life</u> of C. B.? I do
     not know of anything which has moved me more.... I know
     that at one time" Gaskell "visited M. and Mme. Heger, but
     I doubt if she knew of the letters" of Charlotte to M.
     Heger. "... If you do not know" Gaskell's description of
     "C. B.'s unhappy youth, you are missing a great element of
     appreciation. Out of regard for the living," Gaskell "has
     left in the dark that which occupies us, but one finds
     everything in C. B.'s own books."

7   WEST, KATHERINE. <u>Chapter of Governesses: a Study of the
     Governess in English Fiction 1800-1949</u>. London: Cohen &
     West, pp. 115-22.
        Gaskell "was still at work on" the "delightful" <u>Wives
     and Daughters</u> "when she died,...and it is mellow with a
     life's experience of middle-class people," who are at the
     heart of this novel. Molly's governesss, Miss Eyre, is
     "sensitive," "conscientious," and good-tempered but, on
     Mr. Gibson's orders, tries to keep Molly from learning too
     much, either because she is a girl or to tease her into
     further studies. Mrs. Kilpatrick, however, is foolish and
     incompetent as a governess. Her daughter, the fascinating
     flirt Cynthia, threatens "to become a governess in Russia"
     merely in order to escape her romantic entanglements.

<u>1950 A BOOKS</u>

1   RUBENIUS, AINA. <u>The Woman Question in Mrs. Gaskell's Life and
     Works</u>. Essays and Studies on English Language and Litera-
     ture, edited by S. B. Liljegren, V. Upsala: A. B. Lunde-
     quistska Bokhandeln. Cambridge, Massachusetts: Harvard
     University Press.
        In spite of Gaskell's remark, in a letter, about the
     superiority of men's "judgment" to that of women, the women
     in her fiction tend to have more strength of character than
     her men. The generally expressed opinion that Gaskell's
     marriage was happy needs to be questioned. For all the
     genuine affection between Mr. and Mrs. Gaskell, she was
     disappointed by his overabsorption in his work, by the
     little time that he gave his family, and by his emotional
     reserve. She strove to maintain her independence, had
     many friends "who were interested in the women's" movement,

1950

(RUBENIUS, AINA)
and herself experienced "a conflict between home...duties"
and the requirements of her art. In her fiction Gaskell
moves from portraying submissive wives to representing
wives who are independent, and she explores such issues as
the "right" of women "to break" engagements, "dissolve"
marriages, and to pursue an intellectual life. Unusually
close to her own daughters, Gaskell rejected the assumption
that sons are "superior" to daughters, and she felt the importance of education for girls. On work for women, Gaskell, in her early novels in particular, stressed domestic
labor and used traditional arguments to oppose factory work
for women, yet her later fiction explores such female occu-
pations as nursing and teaching. On the issue of "fallen
women," the author moves from a conventional treatment of
Esther in Mary Barton to a courageous plea for Ruth's right
to self-respect in the novel by that name. Gaskell signed
the petition for a Married Women's Property Act but dis-
trusted positive legislative intervention in social issues
and also disliked campaigning in a cause that involved her
own self-interest.
[The following review of Rubenius's book is particularly
significant: Annette B. Hopkins. "The Women Question in
Mrs. Gaskell's Life and Works," NCF, VII (September 1952),
140-42 ("While wisely steering away from the hitherto idealized pictures of the Gaskell marital relation, Miss Rubenius
has swung too far to the other extreme." She takes completely seriously Mrs. Gaskell's humorous complaints and
overlooks how genuinely busy William Gaskell was with his
professional duties.).

1950 B   SHORTER WRITINGS

1   ALTICK, RICHARD D. The Scholar Adventurers. New York:
    Macmillan Co., pp. 312-13.
        When the Rev. Arthur Nicholls lent Gaskell a package of
    Brontë juvenilia in a tiny handwriting, she had "enough to
    do as it was" to prepare for her biography of Charlotte
    Brontë and so "did not try to find out in detail what these
    thousands of tiny pages contained. Instead," Gaskell
    "contented herself with making a note of their existence,
    and when she had finished her book she returned them to Mr.
    Nicholls."

2   ANON. "Charlotte Brontë and Harriet Martineau,..." TLS
    (9 June), p. 364.

288

Harriet Martineau's many letters complaining about the representation of her in Gaskell's <u>Life of Charlotte Brontë</u> have been lost, but their gist can be gathered from Miss Martineau's autobiography and her "marginal" comments in her copy of the <u>Life</u> and from Gaskell's changes in later editions. In sum, "Miss Martineau had only trifling charges to make against the biographer." Gaskell, who suppressed most of the letters to M. Heger for Charlotte's sake and who modestly omitted her own part in obtaining a pension for Charlotte's fiancé, "has never received praise for reticence, but she deserves it."

3   BLAND, D. S. "<u>Mary Barton</u> and Historical Accuracy," <u>RES</u>, n.s. I (January), 58-60.
      In contradiction of J. D. Kay (Sir James Kay-Shuttleworth), who in 1833 declared that the Manchester working classes did not "exercise in the open air," the more accurate Gaskell shows them doing so at the beginning of <u>Mary Barton</u>.

*4   BOGGS, W. ARTHUR. "Reflections of Unitarianism in Mrs. Gaskell's Novels." Ph.D. dissertation, University of California.
      Although Unitarianism harmed Gaskell's art by making it didactic, this "humanistic and undogmatic religion" did give her a "frame of reference" for judging "character and conduct." [Source: Marjorie Taylor Davis. "Annotated Bibliography of Criticism on Elizabeth Gaskell, 1848-1973." Ph.D. dissertation, University of Mississippi, 1974. <u>See</u> 1974.B6.]

5   BREDVOLD, LOUIS I. <u>The Literature of the Nineteenth and the Early Twentieth Centuries, 1798 to the First World War</u>. A History of English Literature, edited by Hardin Craig, IV. New York: Oxford University Press, pp. 507, 554.
      Gaskell, particularly in <u>Mary Barton</u> and <u>North and South</u>, was "by far the most serious literary artist" to attempt social-problem novels, "if we apply Trollope's criteria of clear-sightedness, accuracy, and moderation, and if we have in mind ability and honesty in the presentation of character and living conditions." Though <u>Cranford</u> is her "most famous" work, <u>Wives and Daughters</u>, a story of "motives and character development," "is considered" Gaskell's "masterpiece."

6   DRUMMOND, ANDREW L. <u>The Churches in English Fiction</u>. Leicester: Edgar Backus, pp. 141, 165-66, 254-56, 316.

1950

(DRUMMOND, ANDREW L.)
Though Gaskell was the wife of a distinguished Unitarian minister, her Mary Barton and North and South take a purely "humanitarian" and secular "approach" to the problems of the poor. She is too vague in North and South about Mr. Hale's theological reasons for leaving the ministry. In Ruth Gaskell "gives a delightful picture" of a Unitarian chapel and its "enlightened" minister but also portrays a hypocritic "pillar" of that chapel. Her minister-farmer Holman in Cousin Phillis "is a father, a master, and a cultivator and thus a true member of society."

7   HOPKINS, ANNETTE B. "A Uniquely Illustrated Cranford," NCF, IV (March), 299-314.
Most of the hand-painted water color illustrations by W.[illiam] H.[enry] Drake in the Huntington Library's copy of a cheap American edition of Cranford are actually copied from Hugh Thomson's illustrations for the 1891 British edition.

8   JACKSON, T.[HOMAS] A.[LFRED]. "The Realist-Romantics. Charles Reade.... Elizabeth Cleghorn Gaskell,..." in Old Friends to Keep: Studies of English Novels and Novelists. London: Lawrence & Wishart, pp. 70-73. [Reprinted from Daily Worker (London).]
In Mary Barton, Gaskell indicates "unconsciously...the source of Reade's and Dickens' misconceptions" by showing the difference between the paternalistic illusions of the southern worker and the "naked" exploitation of the worker in the north. Unlike Kingsley, she does not take atypical workers, such as tailors, but those who are exploited in "machine-equipped factories," and Gaskell avoids the demagogy of Disraeli, who could not understand working-class strength in the "class struggle." Gaskell was "the most accurate" of the "romantic-realist" school and "went a long way toward recognizing...that the exploited will be released from...suffering only through 'prolonged struggles transforming circumstances and men'."

9   LINDSAY, JACK. Charles Dickens. A Biographical and Critical Study. London: Andrew Dakers, pp. 307, 309-10, 445.
Gaskell had been "so affected" by Carlyle's message about "Chartist storm and stress" that "in North and South she even picks up his theme of Germanic blood, and her ruthless industrialist foreshadows the Nazi." There was mutual influence between Dickens and Gaskell, and her theme of "working-class bewilderment" in Mary Barton was echoed in his Hard Times and also in the works of many later novelists.

10 VINES, SHERARD. <u>One Hundred Years of English Literature</u>.
    London: Gerald Duckworth & Co., pp. 29, 69, 86, 100, 101,
    108.
        Gaskell's social-problem novels have resemblances to
    those of Dickens, with "sentimental deathbed scenes," "melo-
    dramatic situations," and "loving-kindness" as the solution
    to industrial difficulties, but <u>Cranford</u> is her best book.
    Gaskell "was kindly, with flashes of genius and strong emo-
    tional loyalties, but with neither the brain-power of George
    Eliot, nor the fiery prejudices of Charlotte Brontë."

11 WESTLAND, PETER. <u>The Teach Yourself History of English Litera-
    ture. V: The Victorian Age, 1830-1880</u>. London: English
    Universities Press, pp. 132, 139, 149-51, 233, 248.
    [Volumes II-V are "based on the original work of Arthur
    Compton-Rickett" but "edited throughout by Peter Westland,
    who wrote" volumes I and VI.]
        Gaskell's <u>Life of Charlotte Brontë</u> is essential "reading"
    for "anyone" curious about the Brontës. Yet Gaskell's
    other books lack "the intellectual equipment" and "artistic
    power of George Eliot," and, except for <u>Cranford</u>, Gaskell's
    novels are no more than "good, thoughtful, workmanlike fic-
    tion of the secondary order."

<u>1951 A BOOKS - NONE</u>

<u>1951 B SHORTER WRITINGS</u>

1   BOWEN, ELIZABETH. "Introduction," in <u>North and South</u>. The
    Chiltern Library. London: John Lehmann, pp. v-viii.
        Perhaps of all Gaskell's works, <u>North and South</u> most
    clearly "reflects" the tension in her "nature" between
    "sensuousness" and "wakeful morality." "Outdated...as a
    social document," the novel survives "nobly...as a work of
    feeling," a "love story" in which Margaret and Thornton
    "play their parts as embodiments of" the "wider forces" of
    north and south. Gaskell's "imagination was...sufficient"
    for her "vast" undertaking, "her intellect less so, and
    her technique" still less. One of the great qualities of
    <u>North and South</u> is the way in which "the characters not only
    face their destiny" but "in the end salute it."

2   CHURCH, RICHARD. <u>The Growth of the English Novel</u>. Home Study
    Books. London: Methuen & Co., pp. 174-75, 178.
        Gaskell, who was influenced by Dickens, wrote social-
    problem novels that were unsurpassed in the Victorian period,
    for "she controlled her imagination and her anger far more

1951

(CHURCH, RICHARD)
effectively than any other" critic of industrial "abuses."
Her <u>Cranford</u> served as an escape "from the horrors of Manchester <u>laissez-faire</u>," and it "has influenced a subsequent
genre of nostalgic fiction and semi-fiction" about
"vanished" rural life.

*3   GROSSO, AUGUSTA. "Introduzione," in <u>Cranford</u>. Translated by
Augusta Grosso. Turin: Utet, Unione t.p. & torinese.
[Source: Catherine Margaret Ellen Halls. "Bibliography
of Elizabeth C. Gaskell." Diploma in librarianship dissertation, University of London, 1957. <u>See</u> 1957.B5.]

4   HALE, LIONEL. "Producer's Note," in <u>Cranford. A Play in
Three Acts. Adapted by Martyn Coleman from the Novel by
Mrs. Gaskell</u>. London: Evans Brothers, pp. 5-6.
"At the opening of each of the three acts of this charming adaptation," Gaskell "herself appears...to introduce
the people of her novel, and to describe the scene of the
village of Cranford. Her appearance is not essential,...
but most will probably feel that she adds to the...cosiness
of the piece."

5   POPE-HENNESSY, JAMES. <u>Monckton Milnes. The Flight of Youth,
1851-1885</u>. London: Constable, pp. 65-66, 193, 196.
Milnes, "with" Gaskell's "connivance," appears to have
succeeded "in getting the Reverend Arthur Nicholls'
stipend so increased that he was able to" marry Charlotte
Brontë.

6   THIRKELL, ANGELA. "Introduction," in <u>Cranford</u>. The Novel
Library. London: Hamish Hamilton. New York: Pantheon
Books, pp. v-xxxi.
"So alive is" Gaskell "today that one hardly believes it
is nearly a hundred and fifty years since she was born and
more than eighty since she died." Aunt Lumb's house in
Knutsford, where Gaskell grew up, "must have been a good
comfortable middle-class home." Her husband was a
good man, whose advice that she relieve her grief over her
son's death by turning to the writing of a novel may be
echoed in Betty's advice to the heroine at the end of
<u>Cousin Phillis</u>. If Gaskell's contemporaries may have
valued her industrial novels the most, <u>Wives and Daughters</u>
is "delightful," though "largely unread today," and "will
sometime be rediscovered." The "delicate little...sketches"
of <u>Cranford</u>, with "the charm of the" English "past," have
"kept her reputation alive." <u>Cranford</u>'s characters, though
drawn from life, are probably composites, for she was

too much of "a lady" to depict an eccentric based on one recognizable person. Gaskell's fine use of comically irrelevant talk makes one wonder if she and Dickens "had any influence on one another's writing." She is "perceptive" about petty human "foibles." We are left too uninformed about the background of Mary Smith, the narrator, and wonder if she is Gaskell "in disguise" or "pure invention." It is too bad that such a "charming" young woman does not seem to have any prospects of getting married, "but perhaps in Cranford one did not talk of such things."

1952 A BOOKS

1   HOPKINS, A.[NNETTE] B. Elizabeth Gaskell: Her Life and Work.
London: John Lehmann.
Gaskell's best writing originated from her memories of her Knutsford childhood, which was essentially happy and "wholesome." Gaskell received a good schooling at Avonbank, in Stratford-upon-Avon. Her marriage to the Rev. William Gaskell was very happy, but his Manchester made her homesick for the country, though the city deepened her sympathy for the industrial poor. Though her husband encouraged her to write her first novel as a distraction from her grief over the death of their only male child, her works always remained preoccupied with death. Mary Barton was the first novel "to combine" effective characterization with a relatively "unprejudiced picture of" working-class life. "Lizzie Leigh," The Moorland Cottage, and the other works that appeared in the period after Mary Barton suffer from haste and the pressure of too many literary commitments. Cranford's humor made it, both at once and later, the most popular of Gaskell's writings. Ruth was controversial because Gaskell makes "illicit sex" a central theme and avoids simplistic judgments about the heroine, her seducer, and the minister and his sister who take Ruth in but lie about her past. North and South is "a Victorian Pride and Prejudice" that describes the wooing of a virtually Christian Socialist lady by a laissez-faire industrialist. In Gaskell's editorial quarrels with Dickens over the book's serialization, she showed herself to be "a sounder critic of her" own "work" than he was. The best thing about The Life of Charlotte Brontë is the writer's ability to use her materials "interpretatively" in depicting "the woman as distinct from the authoress." In spite of controversy over the book, Gaskell can be defended for everything except her sermonizing over Mrs. Robinson, and this great biography gives a portrayal of Charlotte that remains essentially

1952

(HOPKINS, A.[NETTE] B.)
    unchanged by subsequent scholarship. Gaskell's letters to
    George Smith are very vivacious, but those to Charles Eliot
    Norton probably express a "deeper" friendship. Her
    fiction from 1858 to 1862 shows the strain of a life di-
    vided between writing and an extremely active social life,
    though "Lois the Witch" is a powerful protest against "in-
    justice." Sylvia's Lovers would be a "faultless" master-
    piece except for the anticlimactic conclusion, and Cousin
    Phillis presents "a Wordsworthian figure in a Wordsworthian
    landscape" with "almost flawless" art. Wives and Daughters
    is Gaskell's one work equal to that of Jane Austen, but
    Gaskell's humor is gentler. Her life as household
    manageress, mother, minister's wife, and social hostess was
    full but wearing when combined with her work as a novelist.
    A reassessment of Gaskell's writing is "long overdue," for
    she was one of the great Victorian novelists.
    [Reviews of Miss Hopkins's book included the following:
    Anon. "Graces of Mind and Heart," TLS (28 March 1952),
    p. 220 (Gaskell, whose North and South has been appropri-
    ately reissued with an introduction by Elizabeth Bowen, is
    the subject of a good biography by A. B. Hopkins. Though
    the biography wisely avoids "psychological" analysis and
    lets Gaskell's letters "speak for" themselves, Miss Hopkins'
    prose is not "memorable," she overadmires "her subject,"
    and she overestimates Gaskell's fiction, which is "good"
    but not "great" because of an excessive dependence by Gas-
    kell on actual "experience."). Phyllis Bentley. "Mrs. Gas-
    kell," Brontë Society Transactions (Shipley), XII, part
    LXII (1952), 119-21 (Miss Hopkins makes skillful use of
    Gaskell's letters but overrates her novels, which are
    sentimental and fail in their portrayal of "physical pas-
    sion," though Miss Hopkins's praise of Gaskell's Brontë
    biography is justified.). (Lord) David Cecil. "A Neglected
    Author," Listener (London), XLVII (20 March 1952), 483
    (Miss Hopkins "is not of the first order of biographers,"
    for, although "conscientious," she fails to give us "an
    integrated portrait" and "has little gift for interpreta-
    tion." The quotations from Gaskell's letters do help us
    to understand a writer who combined satirical acuteness
    with a "genial" temperament.). Gordon S. Haight. "Annette
    B. Hopkins's Elizabeth Gaskell: Her Life and Work," NCF,
    VIII (June 1953), 73-76 (This does not supersede "the
    earlier biographies," whose accounts of Gaskell it leaves
    unaltered and unimproved. Miss Hopkins "fails to explore
    the anomalies of" Gaskell's "independent relationship with
    her husband" and also offers some "curious" "critical
    judgments," such as calling "Sylvia's Lovers 'a great

novel'." "Another biography will...have to be written"
when Gaskell's letters are fully collected.). T. W. Hill.
"For the Dickensian's Bookshelf.... Elizabeth Cleghorn
Gaskell,..." Dickensian (London), XLVIII (September 1952),
175-76 (This "extremely detailed" biography makes "excellent use" of new materials and "should become the standard
work of reference."). Margaret Lane. "Books in General,"
New Statesman and Nation (London), n.s. XLIII (15 March
1952), 323-24 (Gaskell, whose North and South has been reissued with an excellent introduction by Elizabeth Bowen,
is treated in a biography by A. B. Hopkins, which, though
"admirable," shows that the charming and "good" Gaskell
does not make an exciting subject.). Paul Le Moal. "A. B.
Hopkins--Elizabeth Gaskell. Her Life and Work,..." EA, IV
(February 1953), 60-61 (This is a study of the first order,
with justified judgments and careful documentation.).
Sylvia Norman. "Elizabeth Gaskell," Fortnightly (London),
n.s. CLXXI (May 1952), 355-56 (This is "the most fully
documented and correctly focussed" biography "that has yet
appeared" about Gaskell, who fell slightly "short of the
first rank" but is "well worth studying."). Sir John
Squire. "The Secret of the Author of Cranford," Illustrated
London News, CCXX (26 April 1952), 702 (In spite of a few
trifling and irrelevant details, this biography "will become standard." Gaskell "may yet get her due as a novelist,"
and "this book reveals her as somebody one would have liked
to have known,...sensitive, sensible, and amusing."). Kathleen Tillotson. "Elizabeth Gaskell: Her Life and Work,..."
RES, n.s. IV (April 1953), 90-91 ("As a biography this work
can hardly be superseded, though it is hoped that it may
one day be supplemented by a complete annotated edition of
the delightful letters." The criticism is good on the Life
and Ruth but unremarkable on the other works.). Lionel
Stevenson. "The Victorian Period," in Contemporary Literary
Scholarship. Edited by Lewis Leary for the Committee on
Literary Scholarship and the Teaching of English of the
National Council of Teachers of English. New York: Appleton-Century-Crofts, 1958, p. 148 (This biography "is a
thorough and sympathetic treatment of an unexciting subject.").]

1952 B SHORTER WRITINGS

1 ASCOLI, DAVID. "Introduction," in Cranford. London and Glasgow: Collins. [Reprint. London and Glasgow: Collins,
1965, pp. 9-14.]

1952

(ASCOLI, DAVID)
The Chartist riots of the early Victorian period were
"essentially...urban," for small towns "clung resolutely
to the old order," and "the only indication of progress"
in Cranford is the railway that kills Captain Brown. Yet
the narrator makes it clear that this society was old-
fashioned to her even then, and she is "a link" between un-
changing Cranford and the changing world of Drumble.

2 BRONTË, CHARLOTTE. "Two Letters from Charlotte Brontë to Mrs.
Gaskell," Brontë Society Transactions (Shipley), XII, part
LXII, 121-23.
[These letters are reprinted from Annette B. Hopkins's
Elizabeth Gaskell: Her Life and Work. See 1952.A1.]

*3 HÜFNER, WERNER. "Die Probleme der Arbeiterklasse bei Mrs.
Gaskell und George Gissing: eine vergleichende Studie zur
literarischen Darstellung der Arbeiterklasse im viktorinis-
chen England." Ph.D. dissertation, Graz.
[Source: Richard D. Altick and William R. Matthews.
Guide to Doctoral Dissertations in Victorian Literature
1886-1958. Urbana, Illinois: University of Illinois
Press, 1960. See 1960.B1.]

4 JOHNSON, EDGAR. Charles Dickens: His Tragedy and Triumph.
New York: Simon & Shuster. II, 666, 704, 707-8, 733,
749-51, 761, 797-98, 823, 956, 1131.
"Dickens suggested a few changes in narrative detail" in
"Lizzie Leigh," "a gloomy but impressive story," and Gas-
kell "accepted" them. Later he complained of the large
number of catastrophic physical accidents in her fiction.
Dickens and Gaskell quarreled over his proposed changes in
North and South, and in 1859, when he asked her to write a
serial for All the Year Round, she rejected his request.

5 LANE, MARGARET. "The Hazards of Biography," Cornhill Magazine
(London), CLXVI (Autumn), 154-79. [Revised slightly as
Margaret Lane. "Mr. Brontë's Request," in The Brontë Story.
London: Heinemann, 1953, pp. 1-10. See 1953.A1.]
The Life of Charlotte Brontë is Gaskell's "literary
masterpiece." Mr. Brontë insisted that the life be written,
in spite of the Rev. Nicholls's dislike of "private letters
being made public," and Ellen Nussey provided an ideal
biographic source. Gaskell tried to be accurate about Mr.
Brontë, but her portrayal of him "contains more of poetic
than of actual truth." Yet Mr. Brontë disapproved of William Dearden's defense of him in the Halifax Examiner because it attacked Gaskell. Her charge that Mr. Brontë

fed his children only potatoes seems based on Charlotte's own "vegetarian tendencies," but the story about Mr. Brontë's daily pistol firing is confirmed by Miss Nussey. Probably Mr. Brontë's character was a far more complex mixture of attractive and unattractive qualities than Gaskell suggests. She was essentially right on the Rev. Carus Wilson, who was a "deeply self-deceived Neurotic" with sadistic tendencies; she was wise to protect Charlotte's reputation by suppressing the letters to M. Heger; and, on Mrs. Robinson and Branwell, though Gaskell was too melodramatic, she was probably right in charging that there really "was a love affair."

6 LEHMANN, ROSAMUND. "Three Giants: Charlotte Brontë, Mrs. Gaskell and George Eliot," New York Times Book Review (21 December), p. 5.
   Charlotte Brontë, Gaskell, and George Eliot all were "giants" who succeeded as writers in a male-dominated world, and they all wrote out of a belief in the centrality of human "love," but only Gaskell was both "beautiful and fortunate" as a woman.

7 WOODRING, CARL R. Victorian Samplers: William and Mary Howitt. Lawrence, Kansas: University of Kansas Press, pp. 84, 89-90, 141-43, 150-52, 176-77.
   Mary Howitt's Little Coin, Much Care influenced Mary Barton, and, although William Howitt was rather vain in claiming full sponsorship of it, the Howitts did encourage Gaskell "during the formative period of" her "great telent" and helped to find a publisher for this, her first novel. Mary Barton was originally intended to be published under the name Cotton Mather Mills, the same pseudonym that Gaskell had used in her stories for the Howitts.

1953 A BOOKS

1 LANE, MARGARET. The Brontë Story. A Reconsideration of Mrs. Gaskell's Life of Charlotte Brontë. London: William Heinemann.
   "This book...is offered as a sort of footnote to" Gaskell's Life, "bringing the reader back at every point to her incomparable text, and at the same time putting him in possession of everything of importance that has come to light...since she wrote." As "a northerner herself," Gaskell "was not appalled by Haworth," but described it as "it was--a Yorkshire village in a manufacturing district." Her unsympathetic view of Patrick Brontë derived from

1953

(LANE, MARGARET)
the time when he blocked Charlotte's marriage, and Mary
Taylor agreed with Gaskell's view, though Martha Brown
could have given her an account of Mr. Brontë's more appealing side. The writer was essentially accurate on the
Cowan Bridge School. One of her reasons for shirking a
full examination of Charlotte's juvenilia was its "erotic
Byronic" nature. Gaskell suppressed all suggestions of
Charlotte's infatuation with M. Heger but decided that
Branwell's relationship with Mrs. Robinson was too widely
known to be hidden. Probably there "was a love affair"
between Branwell and Mrs. Robinson. Gaskell was forced to
give a discreet account of Charlotte's happiness in her
marriage with the Rev. Nicholls. "No great novelist has
ever devised a more tragically fitting, or more poignant,
ending than the famous, the almost unbearable, last passages of" Gaskell's "biography."
[Some of the most significant reviews of Miss Lane's
book included the following: Phyllis Bentley. "Mrs. Gaskell Reconsidered," Brontë Society Transactions (Shipley),
XII, part LXIII (1953), 206-8 (This is an illuminating
supplement to Gaskell's Brontë biography. Miss Lane's
fresh contributions are so intuitive and graceful that one
might confuse them with Gaskell's own prose.). Marghanita
Laski. "We Have Been So Happy,..." Spectator (London), CXC
(27 February 1953), 253-54 (Miss Lane takes Gaskell's
"superb biography and adds, with great sympathy, those
things that can now be talked about but couldn't be in"
Gaskell's "day."). Naomi Lewis. "Books in General," New
Statesman and Nation (London), XLV (7 March 1953), 266-67
(Gaskell's Brontë biography had "some ring of our modern
manner": "enthusiasm," "audacity," a "relentless eye," and
a "rapport" with her subject. The only flaw in Miss Lane's
reconsideration of Gaskell's Life is the omission of "some
of" Miss Lane's own "new material" that has been published
in various periodicals.).]

1953 B   SHORTER WRITINGS

1   ANON. "Cranford [Editorial]," Manchester Guardian (25 June),
    p. 6.
         Gaskell's "great novel," which is unsurpassed as a de-
    piction of a vanished world of rural security, "is a hundred
    years old this month and still going strong." Because the
    world described in Cranford in fact survived so long, one
    suspects that it may have been "as tough" as the Manchester
    world depicted in Mary Barton.

2   ANON. In <u>Dictionnaire des oeuvres de tous les temps et de tous</u>
    <u>les pays</u>. Paris: Sociéte d'édition de dictionnaires et
    encyclopedies. S.v. "<u>Cranford</u>" and "<u>Mary Barton</u>."
       Gaskell opened the way to a novelistic art that turned
    its back on romanticism.

3   ANON. "New Acquisitions. Letters from Emily, Anne and
    Patrick. Mrs. Gáskell's Annotations," <u>Brontë Society</u>
    <u>Transactions</u> (Shipley), XII, part LXIII, 193-204.
       [In addition to Gaskell's annotations on some Brontë
    letters, the article contains Mr. Brontë's letter to
    William Dearden regretting Dearden's attack on Gaskell.]

4   BOURRET, JEANNE. "Elizabeth Gaskell, écrivain intimiste,"
    <u>RGB</u>, 89th year (September), 789-94.
       Gaskell's best known work, <u>Cranford</u>, is not youthful,
    for she came to literature late. Gaskell excelled not at
    romanticism but at solid good taste.

5   COLLINS, H. P. "The Naked Sensibility: Elizabeth Gaskell,"
    <u>EIC</u>, III (January), 60-72.
       Annette B. Hopkins overestimates Gaskell as a novelist
    [1952.A1]. If the virtues of Gaskell's fiction come from
    her personal "sensibility," so do the limitations. She
    cannot go beyond the restrictions of the "<u>instinctive</u>
    feminine sympathies" of one with a limited "moral and in-
    tellectual scope" and with religious cravings thwarted by
    Unitarianism. She "never created an objective, drama-
    tized world in which men and women live without revealing
    the lineaments of their creator." In <u>Wives and Daughters</u>,
    however, Gaskell's womanly "sensibility" provides "the sus-
    tained delicacy and subtlety" of "the handling of Cynthia"
    and achieves "a masterpiece."

6   CURTIS, DAME MYRA. "Cowan Bridge School. An Old Prospectus
    Re-examined," <u>Brontë Society Transactions</u> (Shipley), XII,
    part LXIII, 187-92.
       The Cowan Bridge prospectus published in this journal
    [1946.B2] is not genuine, but the satirical poem published
    here [1946.B7] seems to come from the 1824-33 period.

7   HARDY, BARBARA. In <u>Cassell's Encyclopaedia of Literature</u>.
    London: Cassell & Co. S.v. "Gaskell, Elizabeth Cleghorn."
       <u>Mary Barton</u> and <u>North and South</u> are "critical rather
    than didactic" novels about industrial problems. Gaskell's
    "most popular work is <u>Cranford</u>, but the other novels, par-
    ticularly the unfinished <u>Wives and Daughters</u>, are more sus-
    tained and imaginative expressions of her humour and
    penetration."

1953

8   LAUTERBACK, EDWARD S. "A Note on 'A Uniquely Illustrated
     Cranford,'" NCF, VIII (December), 232-34.
         There were a number of minor errors in Annette B. Hop-
     kins's article in NCF on "A Uniquely Illustrated Cranford"
     [1950.B7].

9   LIDDELL, ROBERT. Some Principles of Fiction. London:
     Jonathan Cape, pp. 41-42. [Reprinted as Robert Liddell.
     Robert Liddell on the Novel. Chicago: University of
     Chicago Press, 1969.]
         Miss Jenkyn's argument, in Gaskell's Cranford, that
     Rasselas is superior to Pickwick Papers because Johnson
     wrote superb non-fiction would probably have been rejected
     by Johnson himself.

*10 OWENS, GRAHAM. "Town and Country in the Life and Work of Mrs.
     Gaskell and Mary Russell Mitford." M.A. thesis, University
     College of North Wales.
         [Source: Marjorie Taylor Davis. "An Annotated Bibliog-
     raphy of Criticism on Elizabeth Cleghorn Gaskell, 1848-
     1973." Ph.D. dissertation, University of Mississippi, 1974.
     See 1974.B6.]

11   RAYMOND, ERNEST. "The Brontë Legend, Its Cause and Treat-
     ment," EDH, n.s. XXVI, 127-41.
         Gaskell, in her Life of Charlotte Brontë, "was loyally
     discreet, far too discreet, about the dead Charlotte; and
     quite bewilderingly indiscreet about the living." Her
     denigration of both Mr. Brontë and Branwell has tended to
     be followed by subsequent biographers.

12   SPARK, MURIEL, and DEREK STANFORD. Emily Brontë: Her Life
     and Work. London: Peter Owen.
         [Part I: "Biographical," by Muriel Spark, 18, 38,
     97-99:] Gaskell adopts "some of Charlotte's fallacies
     about" Emily, "the principal being that which takes the
     last years...to represent the whole." Gaskell would "have
     her a silent morose orgulous genius at a time when Emily
     was patently the most buoyant and accommodating member of
     the family."
         [Part II: "Critical," by Derek Stanford, 112-14, 117,
     119:] Gaskell's Brontë biography is a hagiographic work
     that regards criticism of Charlotte as "destructive" and
     "denigrative" rather than the necessity that it actually
     is.

Elizabeth Gaskell: A Reference Guide

1954 A BOOKS

1   ASTALDI, MARIA LUISA. La Signora Gaskell. Rome: Fratelli
    Bocca.
        Gaskell was the best of wives and mothers. Her Uni-
    tarianism was significant, for that religion emphasized
    human solidarity and philanthropy. In an age of social and
    industrial transition, Gaskell's socialism was feminine,
    instinctive, and Christian. Although Mary Barton preaches
    reconciliation of masters and men, it shows the masters as
    intransigent in contrast to the more Christian workers.
    The admirable Cranford, though usually called a classic, is
    unclassical in its sentimental romanticism and nostalgia
    for a vanishing way of rural life. Gaskell obtained the
    advice of a woman friend about Ruth in order to eliminate
    anything too sentimental and to polish her prose, but the
    book is rather melodramatic though courageous. In North
    and South, which is more carefully thought through than
    Mary Barton, she shows herself to be the most concrete of
    the Victorian novelists who dealt with industrial unrest.
    Because her Brontë biography interprets Charlotte's life
    as one of suffering obedience and duty, the work is still
    another didactic book, though in fact Gaskell's last.
    Round the Sofa, in spite of structural flaws, gives an in-
    teresting portrayal of a rural lady aristocrat; the flawed
    Sylvia's Lovers has tragic power; but the Wordsworthian
    Cousin Phillis is Gaskell's finest story. The splendid
    Wives and Daughters gives a fascinating glimpse into early
    Victorian manners and mores. Her fiction remains alive
    today because of its simple spontaneity and its fidelity
    to the details of experience.

1954 B SHORTER WRITINGS

1   ALLEN, WALTER. The English Novel: a Short Critical History.
    New York: E. P. Dutton & Co., pp. 153, 169, 178, 193,
    208-14, 218-19, 229, 241-42.
        One is tempted "to overpraise" Gaskell because her fic-
    tion reveals the "personality of a wholly admirable woman
    in harmony with society." Of her two best works, Wives
    and Daughters is "less successful" than Cranford because
    Gaskell's men are not completely "convincing," (but) Cyn-
    thia is "one of the most striking young women in English
    fiction." We are fortunate that Gaskell did not know her
    own limitations, for her Mary Barton and North and South,
    though "very imperfect," remain important for their sym-
    pathetic "understanding" of the industrial poor.

1954

2   ANON. "The Letters of Prosper Mérimée," TLS (26 March),
     [special section on "French Writing To-day"], p. xiii.
          Mérimée, in a letter recording a meeting with Gaskell
     in April 1855, described her as always looking as though
     she "were just about to cry."

3   EVANS, MARY ANN [GEORGE ELIOT]. The George Eliot Letters.
     Edited by Gordon S. Haight. New Haven: Yale University
     Press. London: Geoffrey Cumberlege, Oxford University
     Press. II: 319-20; III: 198-99; and see index for
     numerous other references to Gaskell.
          [Letter from Mary Ann Evans to Sara Sophia Hennell,
     16 April (1857):] The Life of Charlotte Brontë is "deeply
     affecting throughout--in the early part romantic, poetic
     as one of her own novels; in the later years tragic."
     Gaskell "has done her work admirably, both in the industry
     and care with which she has gathered and selected her ma-
     terial, and in the feeling with which she has presented
     it," but she is mistaken in thinking that Branwell's be-
     havior was caused mainly by "remorse." [Letter from Mary
     Ann Evans to Gaskell, 11 November 1859:] Your "sweet"
     praise of Adam Bede particularly moved me because, as I
     was beginning to write fiction, I recognized "that my
     feeling towards Life and Art had some affinity with the
     feeling which had inspired 'Cranford' and the earlier
     chapters of 'Mary Barton'." I first read Cranford as "I
     was writing the 'Scenes of Clerical Life'," and I reread
     the "early chapters of 'Mary Barton'" as "I was writing
     'Adam Bede'."

4   HOPKINS, ANNETTE B. "A Letter of Advice from the Author of
     Cranford to an Aspiring Novelist," PULC, XV (Spring),
     142-50. [Reprinted in London Magazine, I (November 1954),
     73-75.]
          In reply to a letter from a young married woman, with
     children, who aspired to become a novelist, Gaskell advised
     sympathetically that she concentrate on untangling the
     muddle that she had made of her domestic duties. Gaskell
     warned the woman that it was difficult to succeed as a
     writer and told her to try to regain her health.

5   SPARK, MURIEL. "Introduction," in The Brontë Letters.
     London: Peter Nevill, pp. 19, 25, and see letter on
     p. 172 from Charlotte Brontë to W. S. Williams (20 November
     1849).
          Charlotte's account to Gaskell of Brontë troubles was
     even sadder than "the facts," for Charlotte knew "that her
     tale intrigued to the full, the popular novelist in"
     Gaskell.

6   SWINNERTON, FRANK. "Introduction," in Cranford. Everyman's
     Library. London: Dent. New York: Dutton, pp. vi-viii.
         When Everyman's Library first brought out Cranford in
     an edition in the early 1900s, "comfortable middle-class
     readers" preferred such quiet "classics" as it to Gaskell's
     "grander" novels and her great Brontë biography. Today a
     "new craze for documentation" has provided recognition for
     Mary Barton, North and South, and Sylvia's Lovers, yet "the
     art, taste, and the loving charity" with which Gaskell
     portrays shabby-genteel snobbery in a village makes
     Cranford still "unique."

7   TILLOTSON, KATHLEEN. "Mary Barton," in Novels of the Eighteen-
     Forties. Oxford: Clarendon Press, pp. 202-23, plus other
     references to Gaskell on pp. vii, 3, 7, 12, 24, 30-32, 50,
     58, 64-65, 78, 89, 92, 93, 98, 105, 107, 115, 118, 121,
     122, 124-25, 127, 135-36, 142, 144, 153, 156, 265-68, 270,
     278, 290-91, 299.
         Gaskell's Mary Barton showed "a wider impartiality" and
     a deeper "humanity" than other industrial novels, but she
     became "a great novelist" later in such works as Cousin
     Phillis and Wives and Daughters. Her Mary Barton takes an
     opportunistic advantage of a topical subject. John Barton
     has some of the same "tragic irrationality" as Hardy's
     Henchard, but Gaskell "holds the balance fairly between
     John Barton's bitter protest and Job Legh's acceptance of
     his bitter lot," and Gaskell condemns Carson's lack of
     Christian charity more than she condemns John Barton's
     moral failure. The label of "'novel with a purpose'" should
     be removed from Mary Barton, for, though the book had a
     powerful "social effect," Gaskell "wrote" it not for "ef-
     fect, but as one possessed and drenched in her subject."

1955 A BOOKS - NONE

1955 B SHORTER WRITINGS

1   BLONDEL, JACQUES. Emily Brontë: expérience spirituelle et cré-
     ation poétique. Clermont-Ferrand: Presses Universitaires
     de France, see index for numerous references to Gaskell.
         Although The Life of Charlotte Brontë was the authorita-
     tive work on the Brontës for the nineteenth century, Gas-
     kell showed little curiosity about the fiercely silent
     Emily.

2   CROMPTON, MARGARET. Passionate Search: a Life of Charlotte
     Brontë. London: Cassell & Co., pp. 5-6, 11, 33-34, 100,
     106-7, 131, 201-2, 219-20, 223-24, 227-29.

1955

(CROMPTON, MARGARET)
Gaskell was made "remorseful" by the courteousness of Mr. Brontë's request that "trifling" mistakes about him be corrected in the next edition of The Life of Charlotte Brontë, and she removed the "exaggerated stories." The Life, though a "masterpiece," is overly protective of Charlotte. About the Mrs. Robinson controversy, it "is unlikely that she took Branwell seriously," for "she was seventeen years older than" he was.

3   FORD, GEORGE H. Dickens and His Readers: Aspects of Novel-Criticism since 1836. Princeton, New Jersey: Princeton University Press, for the University of Cincinnati, pp. 9, 32, 111, 114, 182.
Gaskell's "retrospective" account of reading habits in Cranford shows Dickens's popularity "in the country villages."

4   HUDSON, WILLIAM HENRY. An Outline History of English Literature. London: G. Bell & Sons, p. 259.
We can include Gaskell among "humanitarian novelists" for such works as Mary Barton, but she is remembered today mainly for Cranford, a delightful story of village life.

5   LEE, AMICE. Laurels and Rosemary: the Life of William and Mary Howitt. London: Geoffrey Cumberlege, Oxford University Press, pp. 175, 189, 190, 211.
"... The Howitts had an almost possessive feeling" about Gaskell, "for it had been in their Journal that she published Libby Marsh's Three Eras--her first story."

6   PARROTT, THOMAS MARC, and ROBERT BERNARD MARTIN. A Companion to Victorian Literature. New York: Scribner, pp. 71, 118, 120.
Gaskell's Mary Barton and North and South "dealt with the shocking condition of the slums in a manufacturing city" and with "class warfare," but Gaskell's Cranford remains popular today, and her "unfinished" Wives and Daughters is a notable novel.

7   WARD, A.[LFRED] C. Illustrated History of English Literature. London: Longmans, Green & Co. III, 191, 196-97.
"Posterity has chosen to regard" Gaskell as the "one-book writer" of the "quaint" and "unique masterpiece" Cranford, though she was "Dickens's favorite contributor to his periodicals" and also wrote a great biography of Charlotte Brontë.

1956 A BOOKS - NONE

1956 B SHORTER WRITINGS

1 ALLOTT, KENNETH and MIRIAM, eds. "Gaskell, Elizabeth Cleg-
   horn," in Victorian Prose, 1830-1880. The Pelican Book of
   English Prose, edited by Kenneth Allot, V. Harmondsworth,
   Middlesex: Penguin Books, p. 306. [Gaskell's prose is
   represented, on pp. 220-22, by a selection from Wives and
   Daughters.]
      Gaskell wrote "social novels," including Mary Barton and
   North and South; "domestic novels," such as Cranford,
   Sylvia's Lovers, and Wives and Daughters; and a biography
   of Charlotte Brontë.

*2 BESWICK, THOMAS. "'Old Knutsford' Recalled on Author's
   Birthdate," Knutsford Guardian (28 September), p. 9.
      [Source: Marjorie Taylor Davis. "An Annotated Bibliog-
   raphy of Criticism on Elizabeth Cleghorn Gaskell, 1848-
   1973." Ph.D. dissertation, University of Mississippi, 1974.
   See 1974.B6.]

3 DAVIS, NUEL PHARR. The Life of Wilkie Collins. Urbana,
   Illinois: University of Illinois Press, pp. 71, 154, 176.
      Dickens wrote Collins that his Hide and Seek was "much
   beyond" Gaskell's fiction and complained to Collins about
   Gaskell's resistance to editorial changes in North and
   South. Collins, "who had let Dickens make all the changes
   he liked in 'Sister Rose', reassured him with jokes about"
   Gaskell's "foolish obstinacy."

4 HOPEWELL, DONALD. "Two Ladies: Mrs. Gaskell and Miss Brontë,"
   Brontë Society Transactions (Shipley), XIII, part LXVI,
   3-9.
      Gaskell "was never a woman of genius, though she had
   great talent." In spite of unconscious elements of radi-
   calism in the works of Gaskell and of Charlotte Brontë,
   both were "conventional women." Gaskell's "regional novels"
   are finer than Charlotte's Shirley. "Though less great
   than Miss Brontë," Gaskell "was infinitely more versatile."

*5 KATARSKY, I. M. "Forward [in Russian]," in Mary Barton.
   Commentary [in Russian] by Z. E. Alexandrova. Moscow:
   Foreign Languages Publishing House.
      [Source: Catalogue of the New York Public Library.]

6 TAYLOR, ROBERT H. "The Singular Anomalies," PULC, XVII
   (Winter), 71-76.

1956

(TAYLOR, ROBERT H.)
An "exemplary" Victorian lady in her life, Gaskell, as an author, had the opposite qualities of "a hard-hitting attacker of social injustice" in such works as Mary Barton and Ruth. The Parrish Collection has a first edition of Cranford in "splendid" condition and "inscribed" to "'Wm. Gaskell from his most affec^{te} wife'."

7   THOMSON, PATRICIA. The Victorian Heroine: a Changing Ideal, 1837-1873. London: Oxford University Press, pp. 32, 52, 70-72, 87, 107, 129, 132-35, 137, 154, 164-65.
Wives and Daughters, like many other well-known Victorian novels, is set in an "earlier" period "than the date of writing; so that,...while the thoughts and sentiments are unmistakably Victorian, the social conditions are those of another age." Among examples of the illumination provided by Gaskell's fictional treatment of the social condition of women are the "independence" of the heroine in Mary Barton, even though she wishes to marry Carson as an escape from factory work; the low social status of nurses in Ruth; and the sympathetic portrayal of "fallen women" in Mary Barton but particularly in Ruth. Gaskell was shocked by the "abuse hurled at her" over Ruth, though it was defended by a distinguished minority. Gaskell criticized the double sexual standard in the "dog-days of" men's "tolerance of their own shortcomings."

8   TREWIN, J. C. "Sound Broadcasting. Drama. Shadow and Substance," Listener (London), LV (22 March), 295.
"The new serial (Home) is 'Cranford', and few of us can complain that we do not know the book; Thea Holme's serial version keeps the proper winning gravity."

9   WAINWRIGHT, ALEXANDER D. "The Morris L. Parrish Collection of Victorian Novelists: a Summary Report and an Introduction," PULC, XVII (Winter), 60, 65.
Because the number of Gaskell's works was relatively small, the Parrish Collection of Gaskell was "nearly complete" at the beginning, and few additions have been needed.

1957 A BOOKS

*1   HARDACRE, KENNETH. Cranford. Notes on Chosen English Texts. London: Brodie.
[Source: Catalogue of the New York Public Library.]

1957 B   SHORTER WRITINGS

1   ANON. "A Brontë T.V. Programme," <u>Brontë Society Transactions</u>
    (Shipley), XIII, part LXVII, 153-56.
    "To celebrate the centenary of the publication of"
    Gaskell's <u>Life of Charlotte Brontë</u>, B.B.C. television on
    March 25th, 1957, devoted half of Women's Hour to a "pro-
    gramme on Haworth Parsonage," with Phyllis Bentley.

2   ARNOLD, HELEN H. "Annual Report of the Hon. American Repre-
    sentative," <u>Brontë Society Transactions</u> (Shipley), XIII,
    part LXVII, 165-67.
    Gaskell, in "a manuscript letter in my possession,...
    declines to" write for the <u>Atlantic Monthly</u> (Boston),
    clearly because she was at work on <u>The Life of Charlotte
    Brontë</u>.

3   DALZIEL, MARGARET. <u>Popular Fiction One Hundred Years Ago:
    an Unexplored Tract of Literary History</u>. London: Cohen &
    West. Philadelphia: Dufour editions, 1958, pp. 61, 83,
    96, 149-50.
    Gaskell was one of "the most popular authors" sold by
    the W. H. Smith bookstalls. She was one of the few popular
    novelists of the period who showed a merciful attitude
    toward "fallen" women, and her "stories about the poor"
    "are the outstanding" examples in Victorian fiction of a
    sympathetic portrayal of individual working-class men and
    women.

4   FORSTER, E. M. "The Charm and Strength of Mrs. Gaskell,"
    <u>Sunday Times</u> (London) (7 April), pp. 10-11.
    Gaskell is "assuredly...a great novelist" but not in
    the pleasant "twitterings" of <u>Cranford</u>, which has "tethered"
    "her reputation." The underrated <u>Wives and Daughters</u> is
    "her masterpiece." This "subtle, undulating," and "deli-
    cate" "comedy" has some resemblance to the novels of Ivy
    Compton-Burnett. Although Gaskell "was a good woman" who
    believed in human decency, she also describes a "villain"
    and a fool, the comic "scheming stepmother." I prefer the
    "heroine," Molly, to "any" other "fictional maiden of her
    century." Although "she expects the best from everyone
    she meets," she "learns from experience" more quickly than
    Jane Austen's heroines, and she is "brave." Her lacks--
    "affection, simplicity, straightforwardness"--are achieved
    by "the end." The "intelligent" but "underobservant" Dr.
    Gibson "is a triumph" of characterization, and Cynthia "is
    another triumph" because Gaskell leaves her "complex" and
    does not require "her to atone."

1957

5   HALLS, CATHERINE MARGARET ELLEN. "Bibliography of Elizabeth C.
     Gaskell." Diploma in Librarianship dissertation, University
     of London.
        [The bibliography supplements Northup (1929.B6) and
     Whitfield (1929.A3) by covering the years 1929-56, but it
     also contains sixty-two new items from the period 1848-
     1928, along with a list, deposited in the Manchester Central
     Library, of errata in Northup's bibliography noted by
     Annette B. Hopkins. Halls's annotations are sparse and
     brief.]

6   HOUGHTON, WALTER E. The Victorian Frame of Mind, 1830-1870.
     New Haven, Connecticut, and London: Yale University Press,
     for Wellesley College, pp. 6, 41, 60, 79, 114, 116, 174,
     185, 186, 191-92, 199-201, 215, 249-50, 275, 365, 402.
        North and South illustrates the "pressure of work" upon
     Victorian businessmen but also their "zest" for achievement,
     though the book echoes Carlyle's teaching that industrialism
     has destroyed feudal social relationships. The manufac-
     turing class in North and South associates learning with
     idleness, and Thornton believes that a successful business-
     man is "finer...than...a gentleman" and that men who fail
     do so out of weakness. Gaskell does seem to appreciate
     the "creative power" of both inventors and manufacturers.
     Thornton is proud of the "personal power" that he has
     gained, has a tendency to worship force, and believes that
     he is serving the "great cause" of progress.

7   PLUNKETT, LORRAINE. "Preface" and "Notes on Production," in
     Cranford: a Play, from the Novel by Mrs. Gaskell. Drama-
     tized by Lorraine Plunkett. Troubador Plays. London and
     Glasgow: Blackie & Son, unnumbered page and pp. 53-54.
        "The chief aim has been to retain the essence of the
     original with all its charm while at the same time making
     it theatrically effective." "... It is hoped that those
     who love the book will also enjoy bringing its delightful
     characters to life."

8   SHORT, CLARICE. "WHA Revaluations: 6--Studies in Gentleness,"
     WHR, XI (Autumn), 387-93.
        [On Gaskell's Cranford and Sarah Orne Jewett's The
     Country of the Pointed Firs (1896).] The two novels have
     much in common. Both are "delightful" in spite of an ab-
     sence of sex and violent excitement, depict old people
     tenderly mourning for "lost" "loves," are "episodic," have
     "respectable young women" as narrators, describe secluded
     villages, have fine styles, show heroism in commonplace
     people, and are mildly escapist.

9   SHUSTERMAN, DAVID. "William Rathbone Greg and Mrs. Gaskell,"
    PhQ, XXXVI (April), 268-72.
       North and South was written partly "to assuage the feel-
    ings of Greg," who produced the ablest of the attacks on
    Mary Barton's portrayal of industrial conflict. Though
    Mrs. Ellis H. Chadwick suggested that the model for the
    admirable industrialist Thornton was James Nasmyth, Greg
    himself could just as well have been Gaskell's model.

1958 A   BOOKS - NONE

1958 B   SHORTER WRITINGS

1   ARNOLD, HELEN H. "The Reminiscences of Emma Huldekoper
    Cortazzo. A Friend of Ellen Nussey," Brontë Society Trans-
    actions (Shipley), XIII, part LXVIII, 220-31.
       Emma Cortazzo wrote to her friend Ellen Nussey in 1867
    that "I read" Gaskell's Life of Charlotte Brontë "twice or
    three times a year, and enjoy it as much," or more, "as the
    first" not because of Charlotte's novels but rather the
    nobility of "her life."

2   ATTWOOD, E. M. "Note on Author. Note on Forms of Address,"
    in Cranford. Simplified by E. M. Attwood. Longmans' Sim-
    plified English Series. London: Longmans, Green & Co.,
    p. ix.
       Gaskell "wrote novels which faithfully reflected the
    middle and lower classes of her time. Her humour is gentle
    and her treatment of human nature is sympathetic."

3   BRIGHTFIELD, MYRON F. "Introduction," in Mary Barton. The
    Norton Library. New York: W. W. Norton & Co., pp. v-xiii.
       Social novels, such as Mary Barton, were justified by
    their being able to reach a wider audience than could
    "treatises" and "reports" on social issues. John Barton's
    tragedy is intermeshed with the actual social conditions of
    the period that is depicted, and, although Gaskell's
    Christian solution of a change of heart in master and men
    is often called "impractical," such an improvement in
    mutual feelings really did occur later, as North and South
    indicates. Mary Barton is one of the most successful of
    Victorian novels that combine traditional narrative with a
    social purpose. Gaskell was a skilled novelist, not equal
    to Dickens, Thackeray, and George Eliot but in their class.

4   FFRENCH, YVONNE. "Elizabeth Cleghorn Gaskell," in From Jane
    Austen to Joseph Conrad: Essays Collected in Memory of

1958

(FFRENCH, YVONNE)
James T. Hillhouse. Edited by Robert C. Rathburn and
Martin Steinmann, Jr. Minneapolis: University of Minne-
sota Press, pp. 133-45.
　　Gaskell was brought up in the "reforming" tradition of
liberal "Dissent," yet many of her works show a "nostalgia
for a vanished medieval heritage." During her lifetime
Gaskell was known for the reformist Mary Barton but after
her death for Cranford and in recent years for Wives and
Daughters, both of which reflect her nostalgic side. In
the charming world of Cranford, everyone, except intruders
from the city, knows his assigned place in "the social
hierarchy." Afterwards, she wrote better books than the
essentially minor Cranford, but they all echo its wistful
English regionalism. Sylvia's Lovers is first-rate historical reconstruction of a regional past; Cousin Phillis,
in its lyrical portrayal of "first love and deception" on
a farm, is as fine a story as Gaskell ever wrote; but Wives
and Daughters--with its technical mastery, lack of didacticism, and a cast of characters from a "cross section of
English country life"--is Gaskell's greatest full-length
novel. In contrast to the "sentimental figures from the
early reforming works," such great characterizations as
those of Clare and Cynthis reveal unidealized human beings
with faults, originality, and subtleties.

5　HOPKINS, ANNETTE B. The Father of the Brontës. Baltimore:
Johns Hopkins Press, pp. vii, viii-ix, 49, 50, 59, 124-36,
and also see index for numerous other references to Gaskell.
　　My work with Patrick Brontë's letters to Gaskell "revealed qualities in the man...overlooked" by "writers on
the Brontës." He had a genuine respect for the Rev.
William Gaskell's Unitarianism. Mr. Brontë also read and
enjoyed Mrs. Gaskell's works of fiction. She did not understand that some of his apparent eccentricities were the
result of Wesleyan principles of thriftiness, and, in portraying Mr. Brontë's temper, she underestimated his qualities of kindness.

6　KETTLE, ARNOLD. "The Early Victorian Social-Problem Novel,"
in From Dickens to Hardy. The Pelican Guide to English
Literature, edited by Boris Ford, VI. Baltimore: Penguin
Books, pp. 169, 170, 171, 173, 178-83, 186.
　　Gaskell's Mary Barton and North and South, like the fiction of Disraeli and Kingsley, ought to be called "social-
problem" novels, to distinguish them from Dickens's "social
novels," with their far greater universality. Her
"social-problem" novels, like those of Disraeli and

Kingsley, center around a specific topical situation, yet Gaskell is rare among Victorian novelists in dealing with the workers in the "factory towns" rather than rural labor or the London poor. Gaskell presents what she actually saw rather than something based on theory, and, like Disraeli and Kingsley, feels compelled to protest against the absence of "humane feeling" in "classical economics." Yet Gaskell's deep emotional involvement with "the lives of the working classes" is at variance with her conscious aim of Christian mediation between capital and labor. Still, Mary Barton gives a more "accurate and humane picture of" industrial "working-class life" than any other Victorian novel because of Gaskell's "respect for" the "decency" of her laboring characters. Her "Christian resignation" and her belief in the improving effect of suffering do weaken the novel, yet, other than Heathcliff, John Barton remains "the nearest approach to a tragic hero" in "the early Victorian novel." North and South, however, presents industrial problems "entirely from a middle-class point of view" and belongs to the tradition of Jane Austen.

7   KLINGOPULOS, D. G. "The Literary Scene," in From Dickens to Hardy. The Pelican Guide to English Literature, edited by Boris Ford, VI. Baltimore: Penguin Books, pp. 99, 106-7, 113.

Gaskell must be ranked among those ten Victorian "novelists who, whether great or not, are obviously" writers "of some genius" and contributors to the enlargement of "the scope of the novel." Gaskell "is rather underrated, being regarded merely as a writer of social criticism in novel form or at best as the author of Cranford," but, in her later, more freely "inventive" works--Sylvia's Lovers, Cousin Phillis, and Wives and Daughters--"she is able to use parts of her experience for which there had been little room in the" didactic "Manchester novels." Gaskell "is at her best in Wives and Daughters, which is one of the finest novels of the nineteenth century." In this story of contrasts "between different kinds of parental" relationships "and different kinds of" children, Gaskell's "consistent differentiation between examples of feminine mentality... becomes a varied and powerful moral analysis. The social and provincial setting is idealized without being faked, as it usually is in Dickens, Thackeray, and Meredith."

8   KOVALEV, Y. V. "The Literature of Chartism. Chartist Literature through Russian Eyes." Translated by J. C. Dumbreck and Michael Beresford. VS, II (December), 120, 127.
[First published in Russian as "The Literature of Chartism,"

1958

(KOVALEV, Y. V.)
in An Anthology of Chartist Literature. Moscow: Foreign
Language Publishing House, 1956.]
If Chartism had not "forced writers to see life from a
new point of view,...the inspired visions of such literary
masters as Dickens, Thackeray, and" Gaskell "would have
been unthinkable." Although Chartist critics often attacked Dickens and Thackeray, "often simply ignored...the
Brontës and" Gaskell, and often even attacked one another,
"all were attracted to the humanistic defense of personal
dignity." Gaskell's Mary Barton was one of the novels
that gave "a concentrated blow against anti-realistic and
anti-democratic art."

9   MacGILL, FRANK N., and DAYTON KOHLER, eds. Masterplots
Cyclopedia of World Authors. New York: Salem Press.
S.v. "Gaskell, Mrs. Elizabeth."
Following Mary Barton, Cranford, and Ruth, Gaskell's
distress over the harsh criticisms of The Life of Charlotte
Brontë made her give up authorship for a time, and when
"she turned to writing again in the early 1860s," she "had
ceased to write her best work."

10   WILLIAMS, RAYMOND. Culture and Society 1780-1950. New York:
Columbia University Press, pp. 87-92, 93, 163-4, 175.
[Reprinted in Garden City, New York: Doubleday & Co.,
Anchor Books, 1959.]
Mary Barton "is the most moving" literary treatment of
the sufferings of the industrial poor in the 1840s, because of the book's sympathetic evocation of "the feel of
everyday" working-class "life." Though some of the book
is mere reporting, at its best it foreshadows D. H. Lawrence's "intuitive" understanding of the working class,
particularly in Gaskell's descriptions of a tradition
among the poor of "sympathy" and help for one another.
Turning John Barton into a murderer is an artistic mistake,
for, after his crime, Gaskell can no longer portray him
sympathetically, and, in any case, "assassination" by the
working class was a hysterical middle-class fear with
little basis in reality. In spite of the deathbed reconciliation between Barton and the elder Carson, Gaskell
cannot make the surviving working-class characters happy
except by moving them all to the "New World." North and
South emphasizes "attitudes" toward "the working people"
rather than their own feelings.

1959 A BOOKS - NONE

1959 B SHORTER WRITINGS

1 ALLOTT, MIRIAM. <u>Novelists on the Novel</u>. London: Routledge &
 Kegan Paul, pp. 26-34.
 A novel such as Gaskell's <u>Ruth</u> "demonstrates the pitiful
 constriction on ethical grounds of the valuable Victorian
 impulse to stiffen the texture of the novel and extend its
 range of social reference."

2 ALTICK, RICHARD D. "Dion Boucicault Stages <u>Mary Barton</u>," NCF,
 XIV (September), 129-41.
 Boucicault's <u>The Long Strike</u> reworked Gaskell's <u>Mary
 Barton</u> "into a highly successful stage melodrama" by sim-
 plifying motives, characterization, and plot. "Boucicault
 subordinates John Barton to his daughter," thus eliminating
 "the didactic center of the novel." Unlike Dickens, Gaskell had "a certain feminine uneasiness" about "melodramatic
 situations," and Boucicault greatly improves Gaskell's
 story as melodrama. "<u>The Long Strike</u> is much more satisfying as a demonstration of the special art of the sensa-
 tional play than <u>Mary Barton</u> is an example of serious
 fiction."

3 GERIN, WINIFRED. <u>Anne Brontë</u>. London: Thomas Nelson & Sons,
 see index for numerous references to Gaskell.
 Gaskell's mistaken belief, in the <u>Life</u>, that Mrs. Brontë
 was miserable in her marriage is connected with a general
 distortion of Mr. Brontë's character.

4 HARRISON, ADA, and DEREK STANFORD. <u>Anne Brontë. Her Life and
 Work</u>. London: Methuen Co., see index for numerous references to Gaskell.
 Charlotte Brontë "was sincere when she told" Gaskell
 "that she was thankful for Miss Branwell's drilling, and"
 Gaskell "was right in observing that for the sisters' impulsive natures to have learnt obedience to external laws
 was positive repose. The Victorian woman's domestic rou-
 tine was normality and they did not question it."

5 HOLGATE, IVY. "The Brontës at Thornton, 1815-1820," <u>Brontë
 Society Transactions</u> (Shipley), XIII, part LXIX, 338.
 Gaskell, who describes Thornton briefly and unsympa-
 thetically in <u>The Life of Charlotte Brontë</u>, did not see
 the town as the Brontës saw it "in 1815." Gaskell "went
 there in 1856 when Thornton had lost much aesthetically,"
 and "she saw Nonconformity firmly established" in a town
 now dominated by mills.

1959

6   LALOU, RENÉ. La Littérature anglaise des origines à nos
    jours. "Que sais-je?" Le Point des connaissances ac-
    tuelles, no. 159. Paris: Presses Universitaires de France,
    pp. 95-96.
        Although she does not match Jane Austen's psychological
    insight, Gaskell achieves a fine satirical finesse in
    Cranford, a story of provincial life. She also wrote in-
    dustrial novels and a Life of Charlotte Brontë.

7   STANG, RICHARD. The Theory of the Novel in England 1850-1870.
    New York: Columbia University Press. London: Routledge &
    Kegan Paul, pp. 17, 22, 27, 47, 70, 71, 82, 164, 217, 219.
        Many critics and readers complained about Gaskell's un-
    happy endings and also about her choice of unpleasant sub-
    jects, such as "fallen women" and factory conditions.
    Mary Barton was attacked by W. R. Greg not for being didac-
    tic, but for reaching unacceptable conclusions. George
    Henry Lewes admired Ruth for its working out of a "moral
    problem" without obtrusive "didacticism," and he praised
    Cranford for its success at making ordinary life "interest-
    ing." When George Eliot attacked "silly" lady "novelists,"
    she exempted Gaskell, along with Charlotte Brontë and Jane
    Austen.

8   VANDERBILT, KERMIT. Charles Eliot Norton: Apostle of Culture
    in a Democracy. Cambridge, Massachusetts: Belknap Press
    of Harvard University Press, pp. 36, 63, 64, 68, 82, 103.
        English friends of Norton's such as John Kenyon, Crabb
    Robinson, Joanna Baillie, and Gaskell were "all minor
    figures but helpful in acquainting him with the atmosphere
    of literary life in London."

1960 A BOOKS

1   ALLOTT, MIRIAM. Elizabeth Gaskell. Writers and Their Work.
    Burnt Mill, Harlow, Essex: Published for the British
    Council by Longman Group.
        Gaskell was unlike most other Victorian writers in being
    "sanguine" and "uncomplicated." Four of her works are
    "English classics": Cranford, Cousin Phillis, Wives and
    Daughters, and The Life of Charlotte Brontë. Gaskell's
    social novels and also Sylvia's Lovers "show that if her
    heart was in the right place her intellectual equipment
    was amateurish." She did not understand economics, and
    she was class-bound in her morality. She has "an
    important secondary place...in the history of the English
    novel." In her "later" works, she became "better at

disguising her weaknesses of construction," yet her first books reveal her "characteristic qualities." The "great technical triumph" in Marty Barton is the sequence from the murder to the trial, somewhat reminiscent of The Heart of Midlothian. Gaskell's use in North and South of an outside observer who learns to understand the employers' viewpoint was an answer to charges of working-class bias, and the "bold presentation of the hero and heroine" makes the book "interesting" in spite of imperfections. The flawed Ruth is closer in theme to Sylvia's Lovers, with its story of a heroine who suffers for "a youthful passion," than it is to Gaskell's industrial novels. Sylvia's Lovers is marred by an inept conclusion, though its characterizations are complex and subtle. In the writer's works about "English country life," she avoids "missionary zeal," "exaggerated pathos," and "false heroics." Cranford "is a small master-piece achieved through emotional understatement," but the fine Cousin Phillis is subtler "in feeling." Wives and Daughters is Gaskell's "masterpiece" and her "only" full-scale "novel" that "a contemporary reader will feel at home with." Throughout the book, she sees "her subject from" the "inside," yet even in Wives and Daughters Gaskell's "comic scenes are...better than her serious ones."

[The following brief review noted the publication of Mrs. Allott's short book: Anon. "Elizabeth Gaskell,..." TLS (19 August), p. 534 ("Mrs. Allott...offers a well-written and sympathetic account of the minor Victorian novelist and her writings.").]

2 Gaskell Committee [of Knutsford], including J. R. T. and Alder-man Thomas Beswick. Knutsford and Mrs. Gaskell. Knutsford: Gaskell Committee of Urban District Council and voluntary bodies.

The Gaskell Committee, "which was set up...to supervise" the celebration of "the 150th anniversary of" Gaskell's "birth," has issued this pamphlet in order to give "a brief sketch of" her "character and achievement" and to describe "some...places and buildings with Gaskell associa-tions and other features of interest in the town today." [J. R. T. "Mrs. Gaskell. Her Life and Works," pp. 2-8:] For all her charm, Gaskell was a bit of a rebel, and not only did her Mary Barton outrage believers in laissez-faire, but even her humorous Cranford gently attacks "bar-riers of class and convention." Ruth also got Gaskell "into trouble" by describing the "redemption" of a "fallen" woman. In spite of faults of construction, North and South is "in many ways" Gaskell's "most interesting book," and her Life of Charlotte Brontë is "second only to Boswell's

1960

(Gaskell Committee...)
Johnson among...English biographies." Gaskell's most "ma-
ture" and "tranquil" works are <u>Sylvia's Lovers</u>, <u>Cousin</u>
<u>Phillis</u>, and particularly <u>Wives and Daughters</u>. [Alderman
Thomas Beswick. "Local Associations with Mrs. Gaskell,"
pp. 13-20:] Many details about Knutsford appear in
<u>Cranford</u>, <u>Wives and Daughters</u>, and other works of fiction
by Gaskell.

1960 B   SHORTER WRITINGS

1   ALTICK, RICHARD D., and WILLIAM R. MATTHEWS. <u>Guide to Doc-</u>
     <u>toral Dissertations in Victorian Literature 1886-1958</u>.
     Urbana, Illinois: University of Illinois Press. S.v.
     "Gaskell, Elizabeth."
        [This guide lists eight doctoral dissertations on
     Gaskell.]

2   ANON. [Note on the text and a biographical sketch], in <u>Lois</u>
     <u>the Witch</u>. London: Methuen & Co., unnumbered pages before
     and after text.
        Gaskell "has taken the bare record of historic" facts
     about "witch-hunting" in Salem "and woven it with deep in-
     sight into a tale in which we can recognize and understand
     the motives of its characters and see how mounting fear and
     superstition led to its tragic ending." Gaskell wrote many
     fine works, but her "greatest" is <u>Cranford.</u>

3   CONSTANDUROS, HILDA. "Mrs. Gaskell [Letter to the Editor],"
     <u>Listener and BBC Television Review</u> (London), LXIV
     (20 October), 697.
        <u>Wives and Daughters</u>, which was "adapted...for broad-
     casting" by "my late mother-in-law Mabel Constanduros," is
     "considered" by most critics to be Gaskell's "finest work,"
     yet the schools persist in teaching the far less enjoyable
     <u>Cranford</u>.

*4 GROSSMAN, L.[EONID]. "Mrs. Gaskell's Influence on Dostoevsky,"
     [translated] in <u>Anglo-Soviet Journal</u> (London), XXI.
     [First published in Russian in <u>Voprosi Literaturi</u> (Moscow),
     IV (1959).]
        [Source: Marjorie Taylor Davis. "An Annotated Bibliog-
     raphy of Criticism on Elizabeth Cleghorn Gaskell, 1848-
     1973." Ph.D. dissertation, University of Mississippi, 1974.
     <u>See</u> 1974.B6.]

5   STEVENSON, LIONEL. The English Novel: a Panorama. Boston:
     Houghton Mifflin, Riverside Press, pp. 279-80, 294, 304-5,
     312-13, 317, 320, 340, 358, 359.
        The flawed Mary Barton "survives because" of Gaskell's
     "power" of creating sympathetic characters, but Ruth is
     "inferior" because Gaskell "was writing about characters
     and events which she did not know at first hand." Cranford,
     though "episodic," lives through "its sympathetic...insight
     into everyday" existence, and North and South, though simi-
     lar in theme to Mary Barton, is better integrated and more
     impartial. Sylvia's Lovers develops the character of its
     heroine as truthfully "as anything in" the works of George
     Eliot, and Cousin Phillis is "a novelette of idyllic sweet-
     ness." Wives and Daughters, though "almost devoid of ac-
     tion," "comes closest to the quiet irony and tolerant in-
     sight of Trollope at his best" and "is certainly" Gaskell's
     "masterpiece."

6   STONE, DAVID. "Did You Hear That? The Author of Cranford,"
     Listener and BBB Television Review (London), LXIV
     (6 October), 553. [Delivered on the BBC "Women's Hour
     (Light) Programme," on September 29th, 1960, the 150th an-
     niversary of Gaskell's birth.]
        Gaskell's Mary Barton "was one of the first novels...to
     use fiction" successfully "as a platform for protest,"
     but Wives and Daughters is "generally regarded as her
     finest work. She was a prolific writer," yet "all the
     while running her Manchester home and bringing up four
     daughters."

1961 A BOOKS - NONE

1961 B SHORTER WRITINGS

1   ALLOTT, MIRIAM. "Mrs. Gaskell's 'The Old Nurse's Story': a
     Link between Wuthering Heights and 'The Turn of the Screw',"
     N & Q, n.s. VIII (January), 101-2.
        Gaskell's tale of a child haunted by an "exiled" ghost
     "child" struggling to get into the house resembles Lock-
     wood's dream in Wuthering Heights, which Gaskell had read
     and commented upon. Her tale, in turn, influenced
     James's "The Turn of the Screw," though in Gaskell the
     nurse saves the haunted child and in James the child is
     destroyed.

2   DU MAURIER, DAPHNE. The Infernal World of Branwell Brontë.
     Garden City, New York: Doubleday & Co., pp. 13-14, 37,
     49, 55-56, 65, 152, 225-26, 248, 295, 302.

1961

(DU MAURIER, DAPHNE)
Gaskell's portrayal of the Brontës in her Life of Charlotte Brontë is "so vivid...that every Brontë biography
written since has been based on it." But she did not understand the significance of the Brontë juvenilia and did not
realize that Branwell's "unhappiness" came, not from "the
abortive love affair, but" from "his inability to distinguish...reality from fantasy."

3 HOPKINS, A.[NNETTE] B. "Biographer's Postscript," Brontë
   Society Transactions (Shipley), XIV, part LXXI, 8-12.
   My study of twenty letters in manuscript from Patrick
   Brontë to Gaskell in the Arts Library of the University of
   Manchester led me to conclude that he had qualities of
   "courtesy, compassion and magnanimity" not conveyed in
   Gaskell's Brontë biography.

4 GÉRIN, WINIFRED. Branwell Brontë. London: Thomas Nelson &
   Sons, see index for numerous references to Gaskell.
   Gaskell, in her Life of Charlotte Brontë, is incorrect
   in saying that Aunt Branwell removed Branwell from her will,
   but the testimony of Dr. William Hall Ryott, Mr. Robinson's
   physician, seems to confirm Gaskell's charges against Mrs.
   Robinson.

5 GLOAN, PIERRE, ed. Histoire général des littératures. Paris:
   Librairie Aristide Quillet. II: 626; III: 65-68.
   Gaskell's Mary Barton and North and South give a sympathetic portrayal of working-class struggles in an industrial city. Cranford, a humorous portrayal of the foibles
   of a small provincial town, is Gaskell's most popular work
   in England.

6 LASKI, MARGHANITA. "Words from Mrs. Gaskell,..." N & Q, n.s.
   VIII (September and December), 339-41, 468-69.
   [From Gaskell's works, the article gives a long list of
   words that either have not appeared in the O. E. D. or were
   cited as first having been used by a later writer. See
   also 1962.B4.]

7 MAISON, MARGARET M. The Victorian Vision: Studies in the
   Religious Novel. New York: Sheed & Ward, pp. 202-5.
   "The success of" Uncle Tom's Cabin "doubtless inspired"
   Gaskell "to turn from the exquisite enchantments of Cran-
   ford to produce another explosive social novel...in Ruth,"
   which prominently features the conflict between the genuine
   Christian Benson and the "pharisaical" Nonconformist Brad-
   shaw. "The Sexton's Hero" contains elements of "Christian

pacifism." The Rev. Holman in Cousin Phillis rebukes his
"fellow ministers" for opposing the teachings of Christ by
their insistence that Phillis's illness was caused by his
"secret sins."

8   POLLARD, ARTHUR. "The Novels of Mrs. Gaskell," BJRL, XLIII
     (March), 403-25.
         Gaskell indicates the foibles of the "middle-class,"
     "elderly," and spinsterish characters in Cranford yet also
     tends to identify with these characters. Cranford is more
     profound than is generally thought, for it achieves insight
     about the lives of "apparently" "uninteresting" human be-
     ings. The artistically flawed Mary Barton retains vitality
     because of Gaskell's knowledge of deplorable working-class
     conditions and her "passion" to improve them. Though Ruth
     was attacked by some of Gaskell's contemporaries as im-
     moral, this reader finds "it tediously moral." North and
     South, in spite of its improvement in narrative technique
     over Mary Barton, lacks spontaneity and fails to make any
     of the southern characters seem alive, except Margaret.
     Sylvia's Lovers is too long and has a bad ending, yet it
     is the most "complex" and "controlled" of all of Gaskell's
     novels up to this point, with a strong sense of character
     development and interrelation. The characters in Wives and
     Daughters, and particularly Cynthia, Molly, and Clare, are
     Gaskell's richest and, in fact, rank with "the great in
     English fiction." "Although she may not be a major novel-
     ist," Gaskell "is certainly a major minor" one.

9   _____. "'Sooty Manchester' and the Social-Reform novel 1845-
     1855: an Examination of Sybil, Mary Barton, North and
     South, and Hard Times," British Journal of Industrial Medi-
     cine (London), XVIII (April), 85-92.
         Gaskell's portrayal of deplorable working-class living
     conditions in Manchester was based on actual observation
     and far more accurate than the descriptions in Sybil or in
     Hard Times. Gaskell's account of bad drainage and refuse
     in the streets is confirmed by the testimony of the Surgeon
     John Robertson before "the Committee on the Health of
     Towns" in 1840. Yet Gaskell, in contrast to both Disraeli
     and Dickens, was able to write sympathetically of manufac-
     turers as well as working men.

10   TIMINO, E. K. "A Great Fancy for Arms," Brontë Society Trans-
     actions (Shipley), XIV, part LXXI, 13-17.
         Gaskell's portrayal, in The Life of Charlotte Brontë,
     of Patrick Brontë's supposedly eccentric and aggressive
     interest in guns is corrected by his correspondence with

1961

(TIMINO, E. K.)
"the Ordinance Office, which suggests that his interest...
was more scientific than eccentric."

1962 A BOOKS - NONE

1962 B SHORTER WRITINGS

1   ANON. In <u>Grande Larousse encyclopédique</u>. S.v. "Gaskell,
     Elizabeth Cleghorn."
          Gaskell's <u>Mary Barton</u> shows the miseries of the working
     class, but <u>Cranford</u> is her best novel. Other works are
     <u>North and South</u>, <u>Sylvia's Lovers</u>, and <u>Wives and Daughters</u>.

2   COLLINS, PHILIP. <u>Dickens and Crime</u>. London: Macmillan & Co.
     New York: St. Martin's Press, pp. 94, 113, 330.
          In dealing with the theme of fallen women, Gaskell "em-
     ployed without scandal a vocabulary much blunter than
     Dickens's."

3   CURTIS, DAME MYRA, et al. "Further Thoughts on Branwell
     Brontë's Story. A Discussion," <u>Brontë Society Transactions</u>
     (Leeds), XIV, part LXXII, 3-16.
          [Dame Myra Curtis:] Gaskell's account of Branwell's
     downfall as a result of having been seduced and abandoned
     by Mrs. Robinson seems unsupported by the evidence.
     [Phyllis Bentley:] "I...think that Branwell's <u>affaire</u> with
     Mrs. Robinson was nearly all fiction." [Miss J. M. S.
     Tompkins:] Although Gaskell's account of Branwell's "liai-
     son" with Mrs. Robinson seems "very unlikely," it remains
     a possibility. [Miss M. Hope Dodds:] Gaskell's account of
     an affair between Branwell and Mrs. Robinson seems contra-
     dicted by the evidence. [Dr. Mildred G. Christian:] There
     seems sufficient evidence that Mrs. Robinson was devoted
     "to her husband" and that Gaskell's account is not accurate.
     [Daphne Du Maurier:] "Branwell's story of a liaison," re-
     corded by Gaskell, "was a fabrication from start to finish."

4   LASKI, MARGHANITA. "Words from Mrs. Gaskell,..." <u>N & Q</u>, n.s.
     IX (January), 27-28, 30.
          [A continuation of the earlier list of words in <u>N & Q</u>
     (1961.B6).]

5   SHAIN, CHARLES E. "The English Novelists and American Civil
     War," <u>AQ</u>, XIV (Fall), 399-400, 401, 406.
          In spite of her sympathy for the North in the Civil War,
     Gaskell had to be persuaded by Charles Eliot Norton that

the South did not have the right to secede from the Union.
Only then did "the Gaskell family become convinced supporters of the North."

6   STOLLARD, M. L.   "Members Visit Knutsford," Brontë Society
     Transactions (Leeds), XIV, part LXXIII, 34-35.
        On a visit to Knutsford, members of the Society heard
     "a short talk" by Donald Hopewell in which he said that
     Gaskell was "one of the most versatile" novelists "in
     literature": "a novelist of history, a regional novelist,
     and a novelist of manners and social life."

1963 A   BOOKS - NONE

1963 B   SHORTER WRITINGS

1   ANON.   In The Columbia Encyclopedia. 3rd ed. S.v. "Gaskell,
     Elizabeth Cleghorn."
        Cranford and Wives and Daughters describe "the joys and
     sorrows common to middle-class village life," but Mary
     Barton and North and South deal with the problems of the
     poor in an industrial city. The Life of Charlotte Brontë,
     though an "excellent" biography, shocked many Victorians
     by its candor.

2   ASTALDI, MARIA LUISA.   Il Poeta e la regina e altre letture
     inglesi. Florence: Sansoni, p. 197.
        Katherine Mansfields letters indicate that she was
     fascinated by Gaskell.

3   BRIGGS, ASA. Victorian Cities, London: Oldham's Press.
     [Reprint. New York and Evanston, Illinois: Harper & Row,
     1965, pp. 96, 97-98, 99-100, 101, 108, 327, 356, 366.]
        Gaskell's Mary Barton represents "not so much an anti-
     romantic reaction as a shift in romantic interest from high
     society to urban" and sometimes to "low society." Though
     such manufacturers as W. R. Greg attacked the novel as un-
     fair to them, they themselves "were not above emphasizing
     the romance of their own calling." The workers read Mary
     Barton "because it helped them to realize the heights as
     well as the depths of their nature." Although North and
     South was an attempt to make amends to the mill owners,
     the charge that Mary Barton showed "a grudge against 'the
     gentry and landed aristocracy'" may have led Cobden to
     admire even Gaskell's first book, as he did.

1963

4 BROUGH, MARY [JOHANNA HUTTON]. "Items from the Museum Cuttings Book," Brontë Society Transactions (Leeds), XIV, part
LXXIII, 30.
"The criticisms" of Gaskell's Life of Charlotte Brontë
for inaccuracies are put into a curious light by the following quotation from Mr. Brontë to Gaskell, before the book
was written, cited in the Dewsbury Reporter (4 December
1897): "... You will have plenty of material and if you
haven't enough, why you must invent some."

5 COLLINS, PHILIP. Dickens and Education. London: Macmillan &
Co. New York: St. Martin's Press, pp. 5, 21, 41, 97, 164,
232.
Gaskell "had told" Dickens "of the first English kinder-
garten, he was a frequent and fascinated visitor to it, and
Household Words contained" an "adulatory account of it and
of Froebel."

6 DODSWORTH, MARTIN. "Women without Men at Cranford," EIC, XIII
(April), 132-45.
Cranford expresses an unconscious feminine hostility and
envy toward males. Captain Brown is killed off because he
challenges Miss Jenkyns, but the later introduction of
Brunoni (Brown) unconsciously reintroduces the Captain's
masculine principle, and the women expiate their guilt by
attending on the ill Brunoni. At the end of the book, the
acknowledgement by the women of Hoggins's marriage and also
"the return of Peter Jenkyns" express male reascendancy.
Cranford's "wit and good humour" result from the "author's"
sane "adjustment to the masculine world around her."

7 GILBERTSON, RICHARD. "Haworth Parsonage [letter to the Edi-
tor]," TLS (28 June), p. 477.
A key passage describing Haworth Parsonage in "A Few
Words about Jane Eyre," Sharpe's London Magazine, n.s. VI
(1855), indicates that the article "must, surely, be by"
Gaskell, though her Life "did not appear until two years
later."

8 IZZO, CARLO. Storia della letteratura inglese. II: Dalla
Restaurazione ai nostri giorni. Milan: Nuova Accademia
Editrice, pp. 163, 208, 280, 460, 500-502, 504, 512.
Although Gaskell did admirable work in portraying sympathetically the privations of working-class life, she
ought not to be categorized by the simple formula of industrial novelist. Such non-industrial novels as Cranford
and Wives and Daughters are delightful, and Gaskell's Life
of Charlotte Brontë is a great biography.

9   SHARPS, J.[OHN] G.[EOFFREY]. "Charlotte Brontë and the Mysterious 'Miss H.': a Detail in Mrs. Gaskell's _Life_," _English_ (London), XIV (Autumn), 236.

        According to a letter that I have received from Mrs. Esmond Bryon, whose great-grandmother, Sarah (Hartley) Wade, helped Charlotte Brontë to find a job as governess, Gaskell became friends with Mrs. Wade while working on the _Life_ and intended to adopt John Wade when Sarah Wade died, but the boy died before the adoption took place. Gaskell's reference in the _Life_ to a "Miss H." seems to allude to Sarah (Hartley) Wade.

10   _____. "Mrs. E. C. Gaskell," _N & Q_, n.s. X (December), 466.

        I am trying to locate "Mss" and "other out-of-the-way material" for a "study" of Gaskell.

1964 A BOOKS - NONE

1964 B SHORTER WRITINGS

1   ANON. In _The Oxford Companion to English Literature_. Compiled by Sir Paul Harvey. 3rd ed. S.v. "Gaskell, Elizabeth Cleghorn"; "_Cranford_"; "Lois the Witch"; "_Mary Barton_"; "_North and South_"; "_Ruth_"; "_Sylvia's Lovers_"; "_Wives and Daughters_." [Abridged versions of the articles on "Gaskell, Elizabeth Cleghorn" and "_Cranford_" appear in _The Concise Oxford Dictionary of English Literature_. Edited by Dorothy Eage. 2nd ed. 1970.]

        Gaskell wrote impressive industrial novels, such as _Mary Barton_; fine studies of character, such as _Sylvia's Lovers_; and delightfully humorous studies of manners, such as _Cranford_ and _Wives and Daughters_.

2   BARRY, JAMES D. "Elizabeth Cleghorn Gaskell,..." in _Victorian Fiction: a Guide to Research_. Edited by Lionel Stevenson. Cambridge, Massachusetts: Harvard University Press, pp. 245-63.

        [This survey of Gaskell materials covers bibliography, editions, letters, biography, and other studies but omits most items that were already listed in Northup (1929.B6) or Whitfield (1929.A3).]

        Much less critical attention has been paid to Gaskell than "her contemporary fame would lead us to expect." Future critics should "search out the causes of James's high esteem for her." In spite of Naomi Lewis's perceptive remark in _A Visit to Mrs. Wilcox_ [1948.B15] that Gaskell's "distinctive gift" was comedy, her humor has never been formally studied. Another valuable area for study would be

1964

(BARRY, JAMES D.)

the differences between the serialized and book versions of Gaskell's fiction, and also worth studying is her tendency to reuse her own earlier materials. Richard D. Altick's comparison of Boucicault's The Long Strike with Mary Barton [1959.B2] suggests that a study of the stage adaptations of Cranford would be rewarding. Also needing examination are the history of Gaskell's reputation and the relationship of her work to that of other writers. Gaskell's place in the English novel needs to be reexamined.

3   CARNALL, GEOFFREY. "Dickens, Mrs. Gaskell, and the Preston Strike," VS VIII (September), 31-48.

Gaskell's North and South is far more accurate in dealing with the conflict between employees and employer than Dickens's Hard Times, which merely caricatures the union movement. Gaskell does at least bring in contemporary union ideas about "joint consultation" between workers and master, but even she is unable to accept the notion "that working people could be both radical and responsible," for she makes the union's "strike collapse in violence."

4   CHAPPLE, JOHN A. V. "The Letters of Mrs. Gaskell, the Novelist," Manuscripts (New York), XVI (Winter), 3-5.

Mr. Arthur Polland and I request "help in locating original letters" of Gaskell's "still unknown to us" for our forthcoming publication of her collected letters.

5   CHRISTIAN, MILDRED G. "The Brontës," in Victorian Fiction: a Guide to Research. Edited by Lionel Stevenson. Cambridge, Massachusetts: Harvard University Press, pp. 216, 218, 220, 221, 222-23, 225, 226.

Gaskell's Life of Charlotte Brontë is "basic to all later biographical studies of the Brontës and to most literary criticism" about them. Gaskell's book was done with both "thoroughness" and "art."

6   HOLLOWAY, S. W. F. "Medical Education in England, 1830-1858: a Sociological Analysis," History (London), XLIX (October), 310.

"Even as late as 1856 over 1500 persons were practising in England and Wales on the single qualification of the College of Surgeons. Mr. Gibson in" Gaskell's "novel Wives and Daughters, had a good general practice in the country yet only held a surgeon's diploma."

7   HULIN, JEAN-PAUL. "Les débuts littéraires de Mrs. Gaskell: réflexions sur un poème oublié," EA, XVII (April-June), 128-39.

"Rich and Poor," published in the North of England Magazine (Manchester) (May 1842), is almost certainly by Gaskell,
for it is signed "Lizzie" and deals with the same social
themes as Mary Barton. Other poems in the magazine may
also have been written by Gaskell.

8   NEILL, DIANA. A Short History of the English Novel. New,
rev. ed. New York: Collier Books. London: Collier-
Macmillan, pp. 181, 185, 200-1. [The first edition of this
work appeared in 1951.]
    Gaskell is "best-known" for Cranford and The Life of
Charlotte Brontë. Although her Mary Barton and North and
South are social-reform novels, even the "idyllic" Cranford
"shows the repercussions of Big Business on" small-town
innocents as a result of a bank failure.

9   POLLARD, ARTHUR. "Introduction," in Sylvia's Lovers. Everyman's Library. London: Dent. New York: Dutton, pp. v-ix.
    Sylvia's Lovers and Wives and Daughters "are built on a
bigger scale,...possess a finer control and...a more delicate perceptiveness than" Gaskell's earlier fiction, but
they are very different "from each other." If Wives and
Daughters is in the Jane Austen tradition, Sylvia's Lovers
is akin to the Brontës. Gaskell's historical novel is a
"tragedy of simple people" who cannot understand the forces
and relationships leading them to "disaster." In this work
of "pervasive irony," Sylvia's development from "lively
innocent girlhood to seared and suffering maturity" is im-
pressively portrayed, "the hated press-gang is" made "the
agent of" her "fate," and the major theme is "unwillingness
to forgive." Here, Gaskell "sought to deal more massively
with the passions than in any other of her works."

10   PRITCHETT, V. S. The Living Novel and Later Appreciations.
New York: Random House, pp. 75, 202, 205.
    The "heirs of" Utilitarianism--Gaskell, George Eliot,
Meredith, and Trollope--are unlike Disraeli in seeing
"politics as the indispensible but tedious regulator" of
society. Wives and Daughters is a "sound" and "accomplished"
novel because of Gaskell's strong sense of social reality.

1965 A BOOKS

1   POLLARD, ARTHUR. Mrs. Gaskell: Novelist and Biographer.
Manchester: Manchester University Press. [Chap. vii, on
The Life of Charlotte Brontë, was also published in BJRL
(1965.B12); chap. vi, on Gaskell's short stories, was also
published in Cambridge Review (1965.B13).]

1965

(POLLARD, ARTHUR)
Criticism since Gaskell's death has tended to underrate
her, for she was somewhat better than the "major minor
novelist" that I thought her in 1960. Because she was "a
simple writer," I have chosen the "simple" critical "method"
of examining her plots, characterization, and the "illusion
of reality" achieved in her novels. After 1859 Gaskell
"does not seem to have laboured under" her old "pressure to
produce," though the serialization of Wives and Daughters
did put a strain on her. Mary Barton, far from exaggerating
the degradation of working-class life, omitted some of its
worst aspects, and the book, though flawed, has "tragic"
power. Cranford is notable in its depiction of the connection between environment and character, is given structure
by its "progressive revelation" of Matty's character, and
is unified in tone by nostalgia. Ruth, with its "dominating moral intention," has a far too contrived plot. North
and South is a better constructed novel than Mary Barton
and achieves "a coalescence between personal and public
stories." Gaskell's late works show a "new realization and
grasp of the complexity" of "apparently simple lives" along
with superior technique. Sylvia's Lovers portrays the
tragic results of a conflict between "passion" and "pru-
dence," and, if the concluding section is "a disappointment," the final scene of mutual repentence is "surely the
greatest in all" of Gaskell's "work." Wives and Daughters
centers around the conflict between "responsibility and in-
clination," and the book is subtler in its analysis of
character and in its treatment of moral problems than any
other work of Gaskell's. Gaskell's view of life is neither
purely "comic" nor "tragic," for "she was too well-balanced"
for either view. Although she falls below George Eliot "as
a thinker and teacher," Gaskell remains "a considerable
artist of the moral imagination."
[Reviews of Pollard's book included the following:
K. J. Fielding. "Mrs. Gaskell, Novelist and Biographer,..."
N & Q, n.s. XIII (September 1966), 355-56 (Pollard's study
is "wise and informative,...if not exactly exciting." Gaskell "is unlucky in that almost everything she did has been
done better by someone else," yet Pollard "shows clearly
how much most of us have still to learn about her achievement."). Naomi Lewis. "Friends and Novelists," New York
Times Book Review (20 November 1966), pp. 36, 38 (A "great
but curiously unresolved" reputation is here "explored,"
for "no critical agreement has ever been reached about" the
"status" of Gaskell's impressive body of work. Pollard's
very high estimation of Sylvia's Lovers seems "a somewhat
personal quirk."). Arthur Minerof. "... Mrs. Gaskell:

Novelist and Biographer,..." LJ, XCI (1 September 1966),
3952 (This is a "useful" and "unpretentious" study, which
shows that Gaskell "is a neglected Victorian, deserving of
rereading today."). Lionel Stevenson. "Mrs. Gaskell,
Novelist and Biographer,..." ELN, IV (March 1967), 225-27
(Pollard's study of Gaskell's essentially "simple" works
"is likely to be definitive," and he "demonstrates the
steady diffident development of a novelist who came close
to greatness" in her last works.). Alexander Welsh. "The
Brontës and Mrs. Gaskell,..." YR, LVI (October 1966), 154-
56 (Pollard's book on Gaskell "is too simple and its criti-
cal vocabulary too limited." Still needed is a study of
the effect of literary "conventions" on Gaskell's fiction.).
For other reviews of Pollard's book, see under Edgar Wright.
Mrs. Gaskell: the Basis for Reassessment. London: Oxford
University Press, 1965 (1965.A2), and also see Margaret
Drabble. "Sense and Sensibility," Manchester Guardian
Weekly (1 December), p. 11 (1966.B5).]

2   WRIGHT, EDGAR. Mrs. Gaskell: the Basis for Reassessment.
London: Oxford University Press.
The needed "reassessment" of Gaskell's work must replace
the traditional praise of her charm, femininity, and truthfulness to her subjects by a more rigorously analytical
criticism. Gaskell's social-problem novels and her "non-
controversial" ones must be seen as a unity, for, in a
sense, they are all social, whether they deal with manufacturing life or stratified rural society, and all are based
on close social observation. Throughout her works, Gaskell
emphasizes "tradition, custom, tolerance, respect for the
affections," and "religion," but her late books show an
increasing ability to dispense with melodrama in order to
concentrate on the relationship of "character" to "social
background." She was more than merely "an intuitive novelist," but her technical artistry grew more refined in her
late novels. Gaskell's early works are less reformist than
religious--religious in the liberal and tolerant tradition
of Unitarianism. In Mary Barton she emphasizes faith in
general rather than any specific Christian doctrine, yet,
though explicit references to religion grow less frequent
in her late works, Gaskell's standard for "behavior" remains Christian. Her satire is limited by the fact that
"hypocrisy beyond a certain degree" ceases to be "comic"
for her, and the depiction of "good behavior comes more
naturally" to her "than to almost any other novelist."
Gaskell's novels deal obsessively with small, vulnerable
families; the loss of parents; and flawed upbringing as
factors contributing to weaknesses of character. Even The

1965

(WRIGHT, EDGAR)
Life of Charlotte Brontë fits into this framework, and,
similarly, Gaskell's fictional studies of fallen women must
be seen within the context of family responsibility and
motherhood. Another dominant theme in Gaskell's works is
the conflict between tradition and change, and, although
she portrayed industrial Manchester, her affections gravi-
tated toward the rural stability of her childhood in Knutsford, represented in her fiction by a somewhat idealized
Cranford, where "propriety and humanity govern action."
After Gaskell's last attempt, in North and South, "to do
justice to" an uncongenial "way of life," "My Lady Ludlow,
Sylvia's Lovers, Cousin Phillis, and Wives and Daughters
are expressions of...stages in her progress to the final
and full expression of the Cranford world." In My Lady
Ludlow change is finally accepted even by the aristocratic
central figure, in Sylvia's Lovers stability and family
are subverted by excessive passion, in Cousin Phillis an out-
sider upsets the traditional way of life, but in the "optimistic" Wives and Daughters the world of Cranford sur-
vives and flourishes in spite of changes in a now "industrialized country." Throughout her works, Gaskell's prose
style is comparable to Wordsworth's style in poetry--simple
and unpretentious but capable of rising to "surprising fit-
ness and effectiveness." Gaskell's use of dialect involves
an approximation rather than an exact transcription.
[Reviews of Wright's book included the following: Walter
Allen. "Mrs. Gaskell in Town and Country," Daily Telegraph
and Morning Post (London) (28 October 1965), p. 20 (I dis-
agree with Mr. Wright, who "prefers" Cousin Phillis and
Wives and Daughters, with their sure touch but modest aims,
to Gaskell's industrial novels. Gaskell, like many other
novelists, was at "her most interesting when" she strained
her "limits."). Anon. "Novelist of the Home,..." Economist (London), CCXVII (25 December 1965), 1425-26 (Wright
suggests that Gaskell has been patronized "just because she
was so womanly and so good and so lacking in eccentricity."
His survey of the novels is "thorough" but "somewhat pedestrian."). John Daniel. "The Perfect Wife,..." Spectator
(London), CCXV (21 October 1965), 518 (Dr. Wright's study
has the usual "forbidding" quality of the "academic" "monograph," and his one most important original point--that
Wives and Daughters is Gaskell's masterpiece--is not enough
to justify the whole book. A simple rereading of Cranford
will help one more than Wright does to appreciate just how
good Gaskell was.). U. Laredo. "Mrs. Gaskell: the Basis
for Reassessment,..." ESA, IX (September 1966), 217-19
(Wright, "while not claiming major status for" Gaskell,

shows that she "deserves" more and wider "attention" than
she has received, as a "regional novelist...of considerable
merit and sensitivity.... Admirably detached and carefully
documented as" this "study is, one could wish" that Wright
"had shown a little more enthusiasm for his subject."").
Jerome Thale. "Mrs. Gaskell, the Basis for Reassessment,
..." MP, LXV (November 1967), 170-71 (Gaskell, who has been
in "a critical limbo" because "most people know only Cranford and the social novels," is the subject of a "pedestrian" but "solid, thorough, sensible, and useful" study
by Wright. Gaskell's "peculiarly successful combination
of sensibility and intelligence demands of the critic much
in subtlety and judiciousness."). Gilbert Thomas. "Mrs.
Gaskell: the Basis for Reassessment,..." English (London),
XVI (Spring 1966), 23 (Wright's style "is heavy, but his
survey is comprehensive and sound."). Rudolf Vikloradter.
"... Mrs. Gaskell. The Basis for Reassessment,..." Anglia
(Tübingen), LXXXV (month unknown 1967), 229-31 (This study
attempts to trace a maturing process in Gaskell's art from
Mary Barton through Wives and Daughters.).]
    [Reviews that covered both Wright's book and Pollard's
Mrs. Gaskell: Novelist and Biographer (1965.A1) included
the following: Anon. "Family Fiction," TLS (13 January
1966), p. 26 (Wright's generalization about the unusualness
of the small families in Gaskell's fiction will not hold
up, his mingling of biography and criticism is unfortunate,
and he is best on Gaskell's style and use of dialect. Pollard's book "is on a higher level and much more useful,"
but perhaps he is wrong in thinking that Wives and Daughters is superior to North and South.). William F. Axton.
"Mrs. Gaskell in Apotheosis," MLQ, XXVIII (June 1967),
240-47 (Both studies underestimate "the rather high opinion
of" Gaskell's "achievement" already expressed by other
critics in order to emphasize their own "revaluation."
More attention should be paid to Gaskell's industrial novels
than either Wright or Pollard do, and a "deeper exploration" should be made of Gaskell's work as a whole.). James
D. Barry. (Review of Polland and Wright)," NCF, XXI (March
1967), 395-400 (Pollard's analyses have the high quality of
the best "Victorian reviews," and provide "the most exten-
sive critical" examination "of the novels to date." Wright
sometimes fails to provide enough analytical detail and
has too little to say about "plot," but is good at showing
how Gaskell's world view, which provides an underlying
"unity" to her apparently dissimilar works, was shaped by
her Unitarianism and her belief in "family and stability.").
Francoise Basch. (Review of Wright and Pollard), EA, XX
(January-March 1967), 93-95 (Wright's intelligent analyses

1965

(WRIGHT, EDGAR)

are weakened at times by his special pleading for a higher
evaluation of Gaskell than she deserves. Pollard's study
is well-balanced and lucid, and he is more willing than
Wright to admit Gaskell's faults.). H. Dombes. "Mrs.
Gaskell Now," EIC, XVI (October 1966), 473-79 (Although one
agrees with both Wright and Pollard that Wives and Daughters
is "loaded with excellences," one must still insist that it
is inferior to Middlemarch and that Gaskell's lack of "vivid
image and symbol" leaves her a prosaic novelist.). Graham
Handley. Review of Wright and Pollard, DUJ, n.s. XXVIII
(June 1966), 164-67 (In emphasizing "'the unity behind the
dissimilarity'" in Gaskell's works, Wright is "perceptive
and telling" about her "superb range" and has written "the
most valuable book on" her "so far published." Pollard's
study, though "sincere," is generally "pedestrian.").
Arnold Kettle. "Reviews and Comment," CritQ, VIII (Summer
1966), 185-87 (Gaskell, though not a major novelist, is a
better one than either Mary Barton or Cranford reveals--a
"really...serious" novelist. Pollard, though "sensible,"
tends, like most previous critics, "to damn" Gaskell "with
faint praise," but Wright is accurate in calling at least
Cousin Phillis an incontestable masterpiece.). Rosamond
Lehmann. "Current Books. Discarding the Cloak,..."
Listener (London), LXXV (20 January 1966), 107 (Wright's
study is "thorough," and he says "a number of...penetrating
things," but he "is an austere examiner," and his style "is
exceedingly dry." Pollard "has produced a straightforward,
sympathetic,...perceptive," and "invaluable" book on Gaskell, good for both general reader and "student."). John
Lucas. "Mrs. Gaskell Reconsidered.... Pollard....
.... The Letters of Mrs. Gaskell,..." VS, XI (June 1968),
528-33 (The edition of Gaskell's letters is "useful" and
"well edited" but reveals little about her as a writer.
Pollard's book is "simple-minded" and "blind to" Gaskell's
"finest qualities." Wright's is a much "better" study than
Pollard's and raises some relevant questions about such
larger issues as the effect of Gaskell's religion on her
fiction, and, although one disagrees with some of Wright's
specific judgments, his book "should be read by anybody
seriously interested in its subject."). V. S. Pritchett.
"Ourselves Included.... Wright.... Pollard.... The Novelist as Innovator" (see 1965.B9), New Statesman (London),
n.s. LXXI (7 January 1966), 16 (Wright emphasizes "social
and religious conscience" and Pollard "social history,"
but both claim currency for Gaskell's work and show how it
developed and improved. Gross, in his essay on Gaskell in
The Novelist as Innovator, places her with Peacock and

Forster as a "minor" novelist who refused to be great, and Gross finds her unique quality arising from the conflict between her rural preference and her life in Manchester.). Patricia Thomson (Review of Pollard and Wright), RES, n.s. XVIII (May 1967), 218-19 (Of the two studies, Wright's "is the more ambitious," but his "suggestion" that "as her art develops," Gaskell's "religious message" lessons is unconvincing. Pollard makes Gaskell look "simple" largely because "his own style" is simple. Neither study shows Gaskell's "unique" qualities, as displayed in North and South.). For other reviews of Pollard's book, see under Arthur Pollard. Mrs. Gaskell: Novelist and Biographer. Manchester: Manchester University Press, 1965 (1965.A1).]

1965 B SHORTER WRITINGS

1   BATESON, F. W. A Guide to English Literature. London: Longmans, Green & Co., p. 182.
   Clement Shorter's edition of Gaskell's works is "uncritical but complete." Annette B. Hopkins's biography of Gaskell "is thorough and sympathetic." "... There is a good essay on Mary Barton in Kathleen Tillotson's Novels of the Eighteen-Forties...."

2   BAYLEY, JOHN. "Why Read Mrs. Gaskell?" Sunday Telegraph (London) (14 November), p. 18.
   Gaskell's "excellence as a novelist is inseparable from her goodness as a woman" and her belief in human nobility. She lacked the egotistic single-mindedness of the dedicated "artist," and this lack gives her work both charm and "limitations." One hundred years after death, there is still no great working-class novel, though she wrote two of the "earliest." But Gaskell lacks analytical "pertinacity" in dealing with her subjects and her characters.

3   BEST, GEOFFREY. "The Scottish Victorian City," VS, XI (March), 355-56.
   It is puzzling that there "were no good novels written about Victorian Glasgow and Edinburgh.... Would not the North and South theme have made excellent sense in a Glasgow context?"

4   BRILL, BARBARA. "Getting to Know Elizabeth Gaskell," Library Review (Dunfermline), XX (Winter), 227-33.
   As one who first knew only Cranford among Gaskell's works, I was later startled to discover the range of her other writings, including novels of social reform, tragedy

1965

(BRILL, BARBARA)
"on the grand scale," and works with deep "insight" into character.

5   CARWELL, VIRGINIA A. "Serialization and the Fiction of Mrs. Gaskell," DA, XXVI (December), 3328. [Ph.D. dissertation, Northwestern University.]
     Under Dickens's editorship, Cranford was Gaskell's most successful serialization, and North and South was the most flawed. Her later serializations for the Cornhill show that she worked best when she could develop her story "slowly emphasizing character revelations and domestic details rather than exciting action."

6   EDWARDS, OLIVER. "The Story of a Lie," Times (London) (2 September), p. 5.
     My favorite of all of Gaskell's wide-ranging works is Sylvia's Lovers, which "foreshadows" Hardy's "masterpieces." Gaskell's ending, though improbable, is moving, and, in any case, is justified by "the conventions of the novel of her day." There is a basic "integrity" in all the characters of this tragedy: Philip's suffering comes from "one great lie," and Sylvia, though at times infuriating, "moves from petulance to dignity."

*7   EDWARDS, TUDOR. "Portrait of Knutsford: the Cranford of Mrs. Gaskell," Country Life (Garden City, New York), CXXXVIII, 1274-75.
     [Source: Marjorie Taylor Davis. "An Annotated Bibliography of Criticism on Elizabeth Cleghorn Gaskell, 1848-1973." Ph.D. dissertation, University of Mississippi, 1974. See 1974.B6.]

8   GASKELL, ELIZABETH. "A Letter from Mrs. Gaskell," Brontë Society Transactions (Keighley), XIV, part LXXV, 50.
     [The article prints a letter from Gaskell to R. S. Oldham of Glasgow, dated 1 June 1857, in which she says, among other things, that Emily Brontë "impressed" her "as something terrific."]

9   GROSS, JOHN. "Early-Victorian Writer with Charm," Listener (London), LXXIII (11 March), 361-63. [From a talk in the Third Programme.] [Reprinted as "Mrs. Gaskell," in The Novelist as Innovator. London: British Broadcasting Corporation, 1965, pp. 49-63. Walter Allen, in an "Introduction" on pp. xiv-xv, says that, before he read Gross's essay, he thought that Gaskell's only "significant" innovation was in writing about "the industrial scene" but is

now willing to concede that Gaskell's domestic novels may
be innovative too.]

Though not "a great writer," Gaskell was and is "under-
valued." Like Forster and Peacock, she refuses to be
great, and this "refusal" is part of her "strength" and
"charm." Unlike most critics, who emphasize either her
industrial or domestic novels, we "must take into account
both sides of her work," for her rural novels are just as
much a reaction to industrialism as are her novels about
Manchester. The innocent inhabitants of the worlds of
Cranford and Cousin Phillis are given a touching pathos
by the impending encroachment of industrial realities upon
their way of life.

10   HANDLEY, GRAHAM. "The Chronology of Sylvia's Lovers," N & Q,
      n.s. XII (August), 302-3.
         There are a number of inconsistencies of chronology in
      this otherwise fine novel.

11   LOCK, JOHN, and CANON W. T. DIXON. A Man of Sorrow: the
      Life, Letters and Times of the Rev. Patrick Brontë, 1777-
      1861. London: Nelson, pp. v, vii-viii, 114, 196, 204,
      227, 234, 258-59, 284, 401, 412, 462-65, 479, 494-517,
      519-22, 527, 537, 538.
         Mr. Brontë was "maligned" in The Life of Charlotte
      Brontë by Gaskell, who "met" him actually only "four times."
      Yet he generously told "a visiting Methodist minister"
      that Gaskell "'is a novelist, you know, and we must allow
      her a little romance, eh?... There are some queer things
      in it...about myself,...but the book is substantially
      true'."

12   POLLARD, ARTHUR. "Mrs. Gaskell's Life of Charlotte Brontë.
      With an Appendix by Albert H. Preston on Some New Gaskell
      Letters," BJRL, XLVII (March), 453-88.
         [Pollard's essay covers pp. 453-77:] Sensitive and
      sympathetic "observation" makes Gaskell's Life of Charlotte
      Brontë "one of the finest" of English biographies, but
      Gaskell was inhibited by a wish to put Charlotte "in the
      best possible light" and also not to offend Victorian
      standards of reticence. Gaskell creates a false impres-
      sion of Charlotte's relationship with M. Heger, ignores
      a possible "hereditary" connection between Mr. Brontë's
      strange moodiness and that of his children, fails to
      understand the Brontë juvenilia or the psychological ef-
      fect of the early deaths in the family, and does not re-
      alize that much of Charlotte's suffering may have been
      caused by her own neurotic expectations. [Preston's

1965

(POLLARD, ARTHUR)
appendix covers pp. 477-88:] Gaskell's letters to John
Greenwood, the Haworth stationer who helped her to compile
details about the Brontës, show "her desire for accuracy
and truth." [See 1965.A1.]

13 _____. "Mrs. Gaskell's Short Stories," Cambridge Review,
LXXXVI (8 May), 374-79.
Gaskell's short stories, including such significant
works as "Lois the Witch," tend to make moral points, but
this tendency is unassailable so long as "the moral arises"
naturally from the action, as it does in her best stories.
"Her strength" did not lay in plot but in "character,"
"mood," and "a sense of place." [See 1965.A1.]

14 SCHNEEWIND, JEROME B. "Moral Problems and Moral Philosophy
in the Victorian Period," VS, IX (September), Supplement
[English Institute Essays, 9-11 September 1964], 41-42, 43.
Gaskell, in North and South and through the character
of Margaret, shows us an "intuitionist conscience without
qualms," but Margaret is put into a dialectical relationship with the utilitarian Thornton. Ultimately, she helps
him to change his morality out of his feeling for her.

15 SCOTTON, JOHN. "Rev. John Jenkyns in Cranford," N & Q, n.s.
XII (May), 194.
"Who was" the "prototype" of Gaskell's Rector of Cran-
ford?

16 SHARPS, JOHN GEOFFREY. "Articles by Mrs. Gaskell in the
Pall Mall Gazette (1856)," N & Q, n.s. XII (August), 301-2.
There is firm evidence that Gaskell wrote the following
anonymous short pieces: "A Column of Gossip from Paris,"
Pall Mall Gazette (London) (25 and 28 March 1865); "A
Letter of Gossip from Paris," Pall Mall Gazette (25 April
1865); "A Parson's Holiday," Pall Mall Gazette (11, 15, 17,
21 August and 5 September 1865).

17 TILLOTSON, KATHLEEN. In Encyclopaedia Britannica, 14th ed.
S.v. "Gaskell, Elizabeth Cleghorn."
Gaskell "was a writer of courage and compassion with an
instinctive grasp of the story-teller's art." Though she
was best known during her lifetime for her industrial novels
and then later for Cranford, she wrote other works that are
finer. My Lady Ludlow is "an artfully linked chain of
retrospect"; Sylvia's Lovers is "one of the masterpieces of
Victorian fiction," comparable to the works of Scott and
Hardy; and Wives and Daughters shows Gaskell working with

her greatest artistic "freedom" and "insight" into character. She portrays the "forces that divide individuals and
classes," but she urges "reconciliation."

18   WRIGHT, EDGAR. "Mrs. Gaskell and the World of Cranford,"
Review of English Literature (Leeds), VI (January), 68-79.
[Expanded as chap. vii in Mrs. Gaskell: the Basis for Reassessment (1965.A2).]
      "... Cranford is a fiction, however much its components
are based on...reality...." Gaskell's "final achievement
in Cousin Phillis and Wives and Daughters is a reaffirma-
tion, in a far more complex and comprehensive way, of Cranford attitudes and standards alive in a changing society."
The episode in which the Cranford ladies rally round the
suddenly impoverished Miss Matty shows "that clear notions
of duty and behavior can achieve all that is necessary--if
everybody acts by them." "Religion," in Cranford, "is not
discussed" but is the basis for action. Many small
"touches" show that Cranford is subject to change from
outside influences, and the death of Captain Brown shows
that suffering can enter into this supposedly idealized
world.

1966 A   BOOKS - NONE

1966 B   SHORTER WRITINGS

1   ANON. "Wife and Mother,..." Economist (London), CCXXI
(24 December), 1331-32.
      One is impressed, in this edition of The Letters of
Mrs. Gaskell compiled by Chapple and Pollard, by Gaskell's
"healthy-minded outlook," which may have "militated against
fair appreciation of her works." The collection is well
edited, but at times necessary "footnotes are lacking."

2   CHAPPLE, J. A. V. "Letters to the Editor. Gaskell Letters,"
TLS (25 August), p. 770.
      J. G. Sharps has located "a number of almost completely
unknown" early letters to Gaskell--mostly from her brother
but also one from her father--and four of them are holo-
graphs.

3   _____, and ARTHUR POLLARD. "Introduction," in The Letters of
Mrs. Gaskell. Manchester: Manchester University Press.
Cambridge, Massachusetts: Harvard University Press, 1967,
pp. xi-xxix.
      Gaskell tried to have many of her letters destroyed be-
cause of her opposition to a biography about herself, but

335

1966

(CHAPPLE, J. A. V., and ARTHUR POLLARD)
her fame makes them public property. We have found roughly
six hundred and fifty letters, and they span the early
1830s through 1865, but we discovered none to her husband
or to Madame Mohl, for these may have been destroyed when
Meta Gaskell burned family papers. The letters provide no
evidence that Gaskell's marriage was unhappy, though it
was probably not based on passion. They do show her deep
love for her children along with her capacity to analyze
them objectively, and the letters also show her rare
social "charm." Above all, the letters reveal Gaskell's
spontaneity; her concern for others; and her "moral seri-
ousness," leavened by wit and "humour." They also show
how her wide-ranging interests led her to overtax herself.

4 DICK, KAY. "Introduction," in Mary Barton. London: Panther
Books, pp. 7-11.
Mary Barton is a propagandistic novel that combines
"charity"and "passion." It was "revolutionary" for Gaskell "to restrict her range of characters to Manchester's
working class." Although "she saw" that "social circumstances might provoke a man to" murder, her greatest
contribution was her awareness that even "harrassed" poor
people are "able to respond to their fellow" poor with
help and love. Gaskell is "one of the best, and most
underrated women novelists whose work certainly can take
its...place along with the Brontës and George Eliot."

5 DRABBLE, MARGARET. "Sense and Sensibility.... The Letters
of Mrs. Gaskell.... Mrs. Gaskell: Novelist and Biographer. By Arthur Pollard,..." Manchester Guardian Weekly
(1 December), p. 11.
Gaskell's "letters are" those "of a woman at home with
her age" and "well-balanced"--"a professional woman,...
yet oddly free from the neuroses of emancipation.... Only
such a nature could have produced Cranford...." Pollard's
study of Gaskell is characterized by "somewhat simple"
writing and "judgments" but is "very readable."

6 EWBANK, INGA-STINA. Their Proper Sphere: a Study of the
Brontë Sisters as Early-Victorian Female Novelists.
Göteborg: Akademiforlaget-Gumperts, pp. xii, xv, 2, 3,
10-11, 26-27, 37, 42-44, 46-48, 65, 157, 160-61, 178, 203.
"We no longer think of the Brontës, or, of George Eliot,
or even of" Gaskell "at her best, as 'female writers', but
as great individuals and major novelists." Gaskell understood from her own experience the difficulty of reconciling "domestic duties" and a writer's career. Her

excellence as a social novelist comes from her awareness
"that individuals are more important materials than a
social thesis."

7   JOHNSON, C. A. "Russian Gaskelliana," Review of English
    Literature (Leeds), VII (July), 39-51.
        Soviet scholars "suggest that" Gaskell's Mary Barton
    may have influenced the themes of mass poverty, Christian
    love, and "ideological" murder in Dostoevsky's Crime and
    Punishment. Dostoevsky's magazine published a translation
    of Mary Barton and began one of Ruth in the magazine's
    final issue. Gaskell's fiction was known in both Czarist
    and Soviet Russia. The Soviets play down Gaskell's "con-
    ciliatory message" in works such as Mary Barton in order
    to emphasize calls "to revolution."

8   LANE, MARGARET. "Introduction," in Wives and Daughters.
    Everyman's Library. London: Dent. New York: Dutton,
    pp. 7-11. [Reprinted in Margaret Lane. Purely for Pleas-
    ure. London: Hamilton, 1966, pp. 164-71.]
        In Wives and Daughters Gaskell shows herself to be "a
    sophisticated writer, humorous and ironic as well as ten-
    der," and "less sentimental by far than some of her con-
    temporaries." She understood both society and the human
    heart, "her style is...like good conversation," and the
    only thing old-fashioned about her book is her belief in
    goodness and "upright behavior." Cynthia is "one of the
    most delicious creations of any period of fiction," and
    the even finer Clare "is dissected slowly and delicately,
    without mercy." It is too bad that only Gaskell's Cranford
    is widely read today, for Wives and Daughters is a far
    richer work.

9   LUCAS, JOHN. "Mrs. Gaskell and Brotherhood," in Tradition
    and Tolerance in Nineteenth-Century Fiction: Critical
    Essays on Some English and American Novels. Edited by
    David Howard, John Lucas, and John Goode. London: Rout-
    ledge & Kegan Paul, pp. 141-205.
        "Even" Gaskell's failings "as a social-problem novelist"
    result from an integrity that gives her work far more value
    than that of Kingsley or Disraeli. If, in key places in
    Gaskell, a middle-class "ideology" of optimistic "progress"
    takes over, she never bends her characters to suit a
    "conscious thesis." Mary Barton portrays real working-
    class people in a real environment. Gaskell's depiction
    of John Barton's gradual embitterment as a result of so-
    cial injustice is "splendid," even though her moralizing
    comments occasionally jar and though the murder puts

1966

(LUCAS, JOHN)
Barton "beyond even her sympathy.... Mary Barton is a
remarkable novel because it so powerfully suggests the
guilt" of "liberalism" and of a "religion" that "may be
for the masters only," though Gaskell "finally turns away"
"from the shocked recognition of such possibilities."
North and South contains "the bones of a great" but uncompleted "tragedy" because, in spite of the writer's conscious
message of reconciliation, the book forces the reader into
an "awareness of how men" who feel sympathy for one another
"ought to be forced apart" by their overriding "class interests."

10   PRITCHETT, V. S. "Daily News,..." New Statesman (London),
n.s. LXXII (30 December), 967-68.
The Letters of Mrs. Gaskell show that she was naturally
gifted at writing them on account of her "feeling for
news." Gaskell's letters are "not as good as" those of
Lady Mary Wortley Montagu or Mrs. Carlyle, for Gaskell "is
sinless and her world is less lively than theirs," yet
Gaskell's letters have the attraction of being completely
impulsive and spontaneous. "... She has her principles
but does not flog them. She cannot have been all that
conventional. She knew the seamy side of Manchester...."

11   SEYMOUR-SMITH, MARTIN. "In Perspective,..." Spectator
(London), CCXVII (9 December), 760-61.
If Gaskell "had...not lived all her life in an atmosphere of Unitarian respectability,...she might have been
as good a novelist as George Eliot." But The Letters of
Mrs. Gaskell show that "Unitarian respectability was de-
cent in comparison to other kinds that throve in her
period," and Gaskell "never allowed it to inhibit her
better judgment." This well-edited collection "is an important book," for "it illuminates the works of a writer
who has not yet perhaps had her due," and it also reveals
her period through her "intelligent eyes."

12   [WHITFIELD, ARCHIE STANTON]. "Elizabeth Cleghorn Gaskell,..."
in The Cambridge Bibliography of English Literature.
Edited by F. W. Bateson. Cambridge: University Press.
III, 427-29.
[The bibliography contains a highly selective list of
secondary items, in addition to primary materials.]

Elizabeth Gaskell: A Reference Guide

1967 A BOOKS - NONE

1967 B SHORTER WRITINGS

1   ANON. "Reader's Guide. The Letters of Mrs. Gaskell,..." <u>YR</u>,
    LVI (June), xviii, xx.
        This is a "scrupulously edited" book, of interest to
    "biographers, literary historians," and "students of Mrs.
    Gaskell and her fiction." Unfortunately, "not a single
    letter to Mr. Gaskell has survived," and so "a whole di-
    mension of her life is missing.... The letters as a whole
    display the same steady good will" and restraint as do Mrs.
    Gaskell's novels.

2   ANON. "Yours Sincerely: Mrs. Gaskell in Full Flow,..." <u>TLS</u>
    (16 March), pp. 209-10.
        Gaskell, in <u>The Letters of Mrs. Gaskell</u>, is "an entranc-
    ing" correspondent, "enthusiastic, impetuous and quite in-
    defatigable," and she is free of all Victorian "pomposity."
    She liked to retail gossip about well-known Victorian
    figures and was unusually "perceptive" about their charac-
    ters, as in her remark that Florence Nightingale combined
    a lack "'of love for individuals' with 'intense love for
    the <u>race</u>'." Insight "of this kind...gives astringency to
    such a novel as <u>Wives and Daughters</u>." With Gaskell's "hec-
    tic family and social life," her literary achievement is
    all the more remarkable. "She might have been a better
    writer had she led a more soothing existence, yet this is
    questionable for she obviously needed a stimulus of ex-
    citement." This is an excellent scholarly edition of
    Gaskell's letters, but "a selected and less annotated"
    collection is needed to make these letters attractive to
    "the general reader" and "a delight for bed-time reading."

3   BLAKE, ROBERT. <u>Disraeli</u>. New York: St. Martin's Press,
    pp. 192, 218.
        Disraeli's <u>Sybil</u> "did not have the impact of" Gaskell's
    <u>Mary Barton</u>. "... He could not project himself into the
    lives of the poor as" Gaskell "did."

4   BUCKLER, WILLIAM E. [Introduction to] <u>Cranford</u>, in <u>Minor
    Classics of Nineteenth-Century Fiction</u>. Edited by William
    E. Buckler. Boston: Houghton Mifflin, Riverside Press.
    I: 363-64.
        "<u>Cranford</u> is perhaps the most consistent and modest and
    successful example of 'domestic' ruralism that the nine-
    teenth century produced," and Gaskell expresses a nostalgia
    for an already vanished way of life. <u>Cranford</u> was

1967

(BUCKLER, WILLIAM E.)
"reprinted nine times in" Gaskell's "lifetime, and more than 170 times" between 1853 and 1947. Martin Dodsworth's recent "Freudian reading" of Gaskell's book "is interesting but exaggerated" [See 1963.B6.]

5 CHAPPLE, J. A. V. "North and South: a Reassessment," EIC, XVII (October), 461-72.
Gaskell had a tendency toward leisurely story telling, but her North and South benefited from her being forced by Dickens to compress the ending. Details such as Margaret's reaction to the Thorntons' interior decorating or to the combination of "harshness" and "tenderness" in John Thornton fit into a pattern that illustrates Margaret's "inner progress towards the reconciliation of all conflicting claims." In spite of the inner tensions that it expresses, the novel has unusual unity and is Gaskell's "finest work."

6 COLBY, ROBERT A. Fiction with a Purpose. Major and Minor Nineteenth-Century Novels. Bloomington, Indiana: Indiana University Press, pp. 7, 10, 12, 14, 72, 179, 183, 222-23, 229-31, 249, 273, 337, 353-54.
Like other Victorian novelists from a religious family, Gaskell believed in the novel as "a moral force." Maggie Browne, in Gaskell's The Moorland Cottage, closely resembles George Eliot's Maggie Tulliver in The Mill on the Floss: both Maggies have a "brown complexion" and adored but teasing brothers. Gaskell "makes her sister and brother too much angel and devil, but then she...was writing a moral tale addressed principally to children."

7 DOBBIN, ANDRENA M. "Letters to the Editor. Mrs. Gaskell," TLS (20 April), p. 340.
Mrs. Lutyens, in her letters [1967.B19 and 1967.B20], does not realize that Gaskell, being part Scotch, would have been "aware of the patterns of Scottish courtship, whereby an engagement is something so slight, and delicate that no announcement is needed. One ought to be cautious in doubting" Gaskell's "words" about Effie Ruskin, for the portrait of Effie in The Order of Release shows her capable of spite.

8 ELLIS, J. B. "Mrs. Gaskell on the Continent," N & Q, n.s. XIV (October), 372-73.
The Tauchnitz edition of The Life of Charlotte Brontë, Leipzig, 1857, is not noted in any of the existing Gaskell bibliographies.

9   FURBANK, P. N. "Current Books. Behind Patrick Brontë's
    Door.... Charlotte Brontë: the Evolution of Genius. By
    Winifred Gérin,..." Listener and BBC Television Review
    (London), LXXVII (29 July), 86.
         "When one considers the flagrant dishonesty of North
    and South, the novel which" Gaskell "was writing at about
    the time of Villette, the veraciousness of Charlotte Brontë
    is striking. To" Gaskell's "shrewd, conventional mind,
    all muddled by taboos, it was laudable for a pure and high-
    principled girl, unjustly suspected of light behavior, to
    refuse to admit that she could have been suspected. North
    and South is a novel in praise of untruthfulness, and is
    therefore a thoroughly immoral work." Miss Gérin argues
    that Gaskell was completely unfair to Mr. Brontë, but one
    wonders whether there wasn't a good deal of truth in Gas-
    kell's portrayal of him in the Life.

10 GÉRIN, WINIFRED. Charlotte Brontë: the Evolution of Genius.
    Oxford: Clarendon Press, see index for numerous refer-
    ences to Gaskell.
         Mr. Brontë muddled the facts about Cowan Bridge in
    talking with Gaskell and gave her the impression that the
    sisters were sent back to the school even after the death
    of Elizabeth. Gaskell, unlike George Smith, did not
    recognize that Charlotte's "life" had been "blasted" by
    her frustrated "longing" both for "love" and "for physical
    beauty." Gaskell shows a weakness for novelistic "sensa-
    tionalism" in both the Life and her letters about Char-
    lotte. In the friendship of the two women, Gaskell's in-
    formality, "liveliness," "charm," and sincerity "cut
    through Charlotte's social inhibitions." Julia Gaskell
    seems to have been the model for Paulina in Villette.
    Gaskell's unsympathetic portrayal of Mr. Brontë was
    largely the result of her having observed him during the
    period when he was obstructing Charlotte's marriage. On
    the relationship of Charlotte with M. Heger, Gaskell
    wisely felt sure that "nothing dishonourable" had happened
    but also realized that the Victorian public would not
    understand.

11 HANDLEY, GRAHAM. "Mrs. Gaskell's Reading: Some Notes on
    Echoes and Epigraphs in Mary Barton," DUJ, n.s. XXVIII
    (June), 131-38.
         In Gaskell's novels, as in those of George Eliot, the
    use of epigraphs sets "up a reverberating relevance in
    the text which adds immensely to our enjoyment of the
    novel and to our critical appraisal of it." In Mary
    Barton Gaskell draws from Keats, Coleridge, and Ebenezer

1967

(HANDLEY, GRAHAM)
Eliot in ways that add "greatly to the imaginative experience of the reader."

12   H.[ARKIN], M.[ICHAEL] J.[OSEPH]. "'Lizzie Leigh': a Bibliographical Inquiry," ManR, XI (Spring-Summer), 132-33.
Northup's bibliography on Gaskell [1929.B6] cites an
undated edition of Lizzie Leigh and Other Tales, published
by Chapman & Hall, as appearing in 1854. Evidence indicates that the edition actually appeared in 1855 and was
identical to Chapman & Hall's dated edition of 1855.

13   HOPKINS, ANNETTE B. "The Letters of Mrs. Gaskell,..." Brontë
Society Transactions (Keighley), XV, part LXXVII, 151-57.
Gaskell's zestful "lively" letters to her wide circle
of friends reveal that she "loved people." Her letters
illustrate Gaskell's concern for the victims of society,
for religion, and for the Northern cause in the American
Civil War. The letters are non-literary, unself-conscious,
but "full of personality." The book is well edited but
needs a single index rather than the multiple ones used.

14   KAY, BRIAN, and JAMES KNOWLES. "Where Jane Eyre and Mary
Barton Were Born," Brontë Society Transactions (Keighley),
XV, part LXXVII, 145-48.
In 1846 Charlotte Brontë and Gaskell were each writing
their first published novels within walking distance of
one another. Charlotte was at what is now 59, Boundary
Street West, Manchester (then 83, Mount Pleasant), and
Gaskell was at what is now 95 Rumford Street, Manchester
(then no. 121).

15   KENNEDY, MALCOLM D. "Letters to the Editor. Mrs. Gaskell,"
TLS (30 March), p. 267.
Contrary to Mary Lutyens's assertion [1967.B19], Gaskell
was right in saying that "Effie was...engaged to someone
else at the time that she accepted Ruskin." My mother
told me that her father, Lieutenant-General William Kelty
McLeod, had been "unofficially engaged" to Effie but was
sent to India. Yet two of Ruskin's letters to Effie published in The Order of Release show that Gaskell was wrong,
in her letter, in thinking that he did not know of the
previous engagement.

16   _____. "Letters to the Editor. Mrs. Gaskell," TLS (13 April),
p. 309.
Notwithstanding Mary Lutyens's arguments [1967.B20],
Effie Gray's references to William McLeod in her letter

suggest spite rather than the absence of a previous engagement and tend to confirm Gaskell's assertions in her letter.

17 _____. "Letter to the Editor. Mrs. Gaskell," TLS (4 May),
p. 384.
Even the most recent extract quoted by Miss Lutyens from
a Ruskin letter to Effie Gray [1967.B21] seems to confirm
Gaskell's contention in her letter that Effie had already
been engaged to William McLeod.

18 LANE, MARGARET. "Introduction," in Ruth. Everyman's Library.
London: Dent. New York: Dutton, pp. v-xi.
Historical perspective allows us to see the pioneering
courage of the two major points that Gaskell makes in Ruth:
the need to include fallen women in the benefits of society
and the possibility that their illegitimate children could
bring them fulfillment rather than shame. Victorian antagonism to her ideas of forgiveness forced Gaskell to
make her heroine unusually innocent. Ruth's rejection of
her lover's belated offer of marriage is a central but
"costly victory." The violent attacks on Ruth by many
Victorians revolt us now, even though their "age" was, "in
many ways," far "less terrible...than our own."

19 LUTYENS, MARY. "Letters to the Editor. Mrs. Gaskell and
Effie," TLS (23 March), p. 243.
Contrary to the impression created by your review of
Gaskell's letters [1967.B2], she had no "first-hand knowledge of Effie" Gray "at school," for Gaskell "was eighteen
years older than Effie" and had long since left when Effie
went to Avon-bank. Gaskell was also wrong in thinking
that Effie "was engaged" to someone else when she accepted
Ruskin.

20 _____. "Letters to the Editor. Mrs. Gaskell," TLS (6 April),
p. 287.
Although Mr. Kennedy is right in saying that Effie Gray
was involved with William McLeod [1967.B15], Ruskin's
letter about William and a letter of Effie's to her mother
both tend to disprove that there was an engagement between
Effie and William.

21 _____. "Letters to the Editor. Mrs. Gaskell," TLS
(27 April), p. 368.
In spite of Miss Dobbin's comments about Gaskell's
knowledge of "the patterns of Scottish courtship" and in
spite of Miss Dobbin's low "opinion" of Effie Gray
[1967.B7], I remain unconvinced that Effie was ever

1967

(LUTYENS, MARY)
> engaged to William McLeod. Indeed, her letters show that
> she once considered marrying a Mr. Tasker.

22   MAURAT, CHARLOTTE. Le Secret des Brontës, ou Charlotte
     Brontë d'après les juvénilia, ses lettres et ceux qui
     l'ont connue. Paris: Buchet / Chastel, see index for
     numerous references to Gaskell. [Translated by Margaret
     Meldrum as The Brontës' Secret. London: Constable, 1969.]
     > Gaskell's Life of Charlotte Brontë is a great and in-
     > dispensable work but is limited by Gaskell's inadequate
     > understanding or use of the Brontë juvenilia.

23   MIDGAL, SEYMOUR. "The Social Novel in Victorian England,"
     DA, XXVII (January), 2536A. [Ph.D. dissertation, Univer-
     sity of California, Davis.]
     > Gaskell's industrial novels, like those of Disraeli,
     > Kingsley, Gissing, and Morris, are torn by a conflict be-
     > tween her belief in "Christian love" and her acceptance
     > of the basic assumptions of contemporary "political econ-
     > omy." Like the others, Gaskell finds it difficult to
     > believe that the good life can be lived anywhere except
     > in the country.

24   RAFF, ANTON DONALD. "Elizabeth Gaskell: a Critical Study,"
     DA, XXVIII (July), 201A-2A. [Ph.D. dissertation, Cornell
     University.]
     > Gaskell's "place clearly belongs with those who rank
     > just below the major figures," yet "too many readers"
     > have not given Gaskell due recognition.

25   SHAPIRO, CHARLES. "Mrs. Gaskell and 'The Severe Truth'," in
     Minor British Novelists. Edited by Charles Alva Hoyt.
     Carbondale, Illinois: Southern Illinois University Press,
     pp. 98-108. [Harry T. Moore, "Preface," p. v: Gaskell's
     Cranford "cannot be compared with the achievements of
     Shakespeare or...Dickens" yet is a "unique" portrayal of
     English rural life.]
     > Gaskell's polemical novels, as exemplified by Mary
     > Barton, are ridiculous and boring caricatures, effective
     > only in their occasionally humorous observation of social
     > habits. Cranford, her most humorous work, is very much
     > her "best." "I would hate to be an authority on" Gaskell;
     > "so much of her work is so bad.... Let us love Cranford
     > and forgive her the rest."

26   SYMONDS, JULIAN. "No Quailing. The Letters of Mrs. Gas-
     kell,..." Listener (London), LXXVII (2 March), 300.

Gaskell "has a secure small cosy place among the second order of Victorian novelists as a good industrial craftsman who dexterously blended sentiment and realism without ever looking outside the orthodoxies of her time and place.... Her letters are lively but trivial, good humoured yet never witty...." She gives one the feeling of a "wife" sometimes annoyed by the narrow intellectual and emotional range of her husband, a Unitarian minister, "but rarely" herself "able to express unconditionally" her "wider range of...sympathies." Only in The Life of Charlotte Brontë did Gaskell transcend "many of her usual limitations," "partly through ignorance of the laws of libel." The editors have done a "thorough job," but they might have indicated which of the letters are published here for the first time.

1968 A BOOKS

1 HANDLEY, GRAHAM. Sylvia's Lovers (Mrs. Gaskell). Notes on English Literature. Oxford: Basil Blackwell.
    The "conventional view" of Gaskell as the "charming" "dove" of Cranford overlooks the "uncompromising moral purpose" of her more ambitious novels, such as Wives and Daughters, which belongs in the "great" tradition of Mansfield Park and Middlemarch. Sylvia's Lovers is great for the first two volumes, the portion that owes the most to Gaskell's research about the press gang and Whitby. Gaskell wisely avoids playing out the scene of Daniel's last days before execution, but her later description of the battle of Acre is "unreal," though most of the book is convincing about "time and place." Gaskell's narrative "comments" in Sylvia's Lovers come "more naturally through her characters than in any of her other novels, unless it be Wives and Daughters," and the commentary shows "wisdom," "wit," compassion, and "irony." We are taken inside the mind of the sensitive Philip but not of the less sensitive Kinraid, though Gaskell leaves an attractive mystery about him. Although Hester is "good" and Sylvia is "wayward," our sympathies lie with Sylvia. Gaskell loves "her characters," and her fiction has "moral integrity." Though inferior to Middlemarch, Tess of the D'Urbervilles, and Wuthering Heights, Sylvia's Lovers "is much better" than Jane Eyre, "perhaps...better than Adam Bede," and "at least as good as The Return of the Native." Gaskell "remains... the most under-rated of the mid-Victorian novelists."

2   McVEAGH, JOHN. Elizabeth Gaskell. The Profiles in Literature
     Series. New York: Humanities Press. London: Routledge &
     Kegan Paul, 1969.
         Gaskell's novelistic portrayals of Victorian society are
     "worthy of study" because of their accurate representation
     of what life was really like. They seem ordinary as a re-
     sult of "rigorous self-discipline" rather than a lack of
     "imagination." Gaskell's Manchester novels "are...the
     first serious attempt in literature to present the un-
     adorned realities of the industrial age," but even her
     purely rural novels reflect certain "harsh realities" amid
     their tranquil settings. Her exploration of "human re-
     silience in the face of disappointment and disaster" avoids
     escapism. In order to appreciate her achievement, one must
     take her rural and industrial novels together. North and
     South "succeeds better" than Mary Barton in combining
     storytelling with social reporting about industrial condi-
     tions, largely through the use of Margaret as an outside
     observer. Gaskell's "avoidance of theoretical solutions
     to social problems" makes her novels "still readable when
     the problems have disappeared." In The Life of Charlotte
     Brontë, Gaskell first sets the physical and social scene
     of Yorkshire and then lets Charlotte speak for herself "as
     much as possible." By suppressing key facts about Char-
     lotte's neurosis, Gaskell produces a heroine "suspiciously
     like" those in Gaskell's own fiction, though there is an
     "essential rightness" to the portrait. In all her rural
     novels, "her sympathies are with the individuals involved
     in the" difficult change to new ways of life, as in Cousin
     Phillis or Wives and Daughters. Gaskell portrays human ad-
     versity in both her industrial and rural novels yet is es-
     sentially optimistic about the capacity "for survival" of
     honest, courageous, and tolerant people. Because she
     "was not compelled by failure to question her own talent,"
     her methods of construction remained the same throughout
     her career, though she may have refined them. She empha-
     sizes "crises," action, and external events yet is willing
     to slow up the plot for the sake of "local" color. All her
     novels could be subtitled "'an Every-day Story'." Her late
     work is "outstanding" for "its wit and zest of invention."
     Gaskell's work is weakest "when she tries to draw a moral
     or force a meaning,...for she lacks the mental stamina and
     ...rational power...needed for that kind of art." Her
     finest work is in her "discursive stories which make their
     point obliquely and at leisure."

1968 B SHORTER WRITINGS

1   BASCH, FRANÇOISE. "Études critiques. Mrs. Gaskell vue à
    travers ses lettres," EA, XXI (July-September), 257-71.
        The well-edited Letters of Mrs. Gaskell is invaluable
    for the light that it sheds on the Manchester citizen,
    mother, and wife. There is an odd lack of allusions to
    social problems in her letters before Mary Barton. One
    letter after her editorial troubles with Dickens expresses
    despair. The letters show that she placed more importance
    on her role of wife and mother than on her profession of
    writer. Compared to most of her female contemporaries,
    Gaskell lived a rich and diversified life, yet she some-
    times felt confined by her lack of privacy and by her
    domestic duties. Her attitude that literature was a
    pleasurable luxury may have prevented her from writing a
    great work, and, although she was imprisoned by the age's
    restrictions on women, she was a consenting prisoner.

2   BEACHCROFT, T. O. The Modest Art. A Survey of the Short
    Story in English. London: Oxford University Press, p. 103.
        Gaskell was a "novelist of considerable stature who con-
    tributed short stories to...many magazines and annuals."
    But in short fiction "she is apt to leave the quietly re-
    alistic vein of Cranford for rather melodramatic situa-
    tions," as in "The Squire's Story" or "The Old Nurse's
    Story."

3   BRIGHTFIELD, MYRON F. Victorian England in its Novels (1840-
    1870). Los Angeles: University of California Library in
    a Xeroxed edition of fifty copies, see index for numerous
    references to Gaskell.
        [The book uses many passages from Gaskell's Mary Barton,
    North and South, Wives and Daughters, Cranford, Cousin
    Phillis, Ruth, A Dark Night's Work, and The Moorland Cot-
    tage to illustrate Victorian manners and mores.]

4   CAMERINO, ALDO. "Il Paese delle nobili signore," in Scrittori
    di lingua inglese. Milan and Naples: Riccardo Ricciardi,
    pp. 62-64. [First published in 1951, apparently in
    Gazzettino (Venice).]
        In 1950, Cranford, a minor masterpiece, was belatedly
    translated into Italian. Apart from being a famous and
    worthy book, it has an importance beyond its intrinsic
    value in recreating the ambiance of English and Victorian
    provincial life and its attitudes. Although most of the
    important Victorian English writers are well known to us,
    Gaskell is not, in spite of such splendid works as North

1968

(CAMERINO, ALDO)
and South and, above all, Wives and Daughters. Some of
her books, such as Mary Barton, are dated by their subject,
but the still vital works deserve publication by some en-
terprising Italian publishers. Yet our readers might find
Gaskell's books not well enough constructed and too limited by the English attitudes of her time, and so they
would miss the chance to gain a deeper knowledge of nineteenth-century England. Like all of Gaskell's best work,
Cranford has a perfect lightness and amiability, but it
also has a uniquely adorable vitality.

5   CHAPMAN, RAYMOND. The Victorian Debate. English Literature
and Society 1832-1901. London: Wiedenfeld & Nicolson,
pp. 68, 78, 109, 127-29, 132-38, 144, 152, 163, 172,
174-75, 179, 183, 211.
The killing by a train of Captain Brown of Cranford, an
advocate of Dickens against Johnson, "is perhaps" a more
symbolically apt presentation of the conflict between "the
world of the stage-coach and the railway" than Gaskell
"herself realized." In a work such as Mary Barton, she
"combined social concern with talent." Though underrated
because of its excessively prolonged narrative, North and
South is Gaskell's best book and also the finest mid-
Victorian portrayal of conflicting social interests in the
day-to-day life of "an industrial town." "All" of Gaskell's "books" have the "calm innocence of the child who
utters profound truth in oversimplification."

6   CHAPPLE, J. A. V. "Introduction," in Life in Manchester:
Libby Marsh's Three Eras (1847). Manchester: Lancashire
& Cheshire Antiquarian Society, verso of front cover.
Gaskell's "first published piece of prose fiction" appeared in Howitt's Journal (5, 12, and 19 June 1847). The
story shows Gaskell's "sympathetic understanding of the
Manchester poor.... A preliminary sketch of Mary Barton"
includes the "Whitsun visit to Durham" actually used in
"Libby Marsh's Three Eras." Both the "humour" and the
observant details counteract the didacticism and the
"sentimentality," and the quality of "moderation" antici-
pates North and South.

7   ELLMANN, MARY. Thinking about Women. New York: Harcourt,
Brace & World, pp. 31-32, 214, 216.
The male critic's attitude toward female writers such
as Gaskell tends to be one of condescension, no matter
how benevolent, for the "caution" of the woman writer
makes him feel "devil-may-care" by comparison.

348

8 FIELDING, K. J. "... The Letters of Mrs. Gaskell," NCF, XXIII (September), 243-45.
   This is a well edited and "important work for Victorian studies," though the index and footnotes are somewhat too frugal. Also the editors might have indicated "how" Gaskell "had to contend with male prejudice, unhelpful editors, the realities of city life and so on." The letters show us that Gaskell was "even more like one of her own heroines than we thought."

9 GROSSO, AUGUSTA. In Grande dizionario enciclopedico. Turin: Unione Tipografico. S.v. "Gaskell, Elizabeth Cleghorn."
   Though Gaskell wrote social-problem novels, Wives and Daughters and Cranford are considered her finest works. Cranford almost ranks with Jane Austen.

10 HAIGHT, GORDON S. George Eliot: a Biography. New York and Oxford: Oxford University Press, pp. 97, 105, 128, 131-32, 209, 225, 231-34, 276, 285-87, 312-13.
   Blackwood's comments about George Eliot's "Janet's Repentence" disappointed her because he misunderstood "her aim" and "seems to have been hoping that she would write him another Cranford, which would 'puzzle' no one." She was infuriated by Swinburne's suggestion, in his Note on Charlotte Brontë [1877.B4], that The Mill on the Floss owed "things" to Gaskell's The Moorland Cottage. In spite of Yvonne Ffrench's reassertion of this indebtedness, George Eliot had, in fact, never read The Moorland Cottage.

11 HANDLEY, GRAHAM. "The Letters of Mrs. Gaskell,..." N & Q, n.s. XV (November), 438-39.
   Gaskell's letters convey a vivid sense of her time, as they range from "poignant" to "brilliant, racy," and "gossipy." They show wit but also great sensitivity. The letters reveal that Gaskell never became dull in her "domesticity" and that she was both "practical" and warmhearted. In spite of her own self-deprecation and the condescension of "critics and biographers," she, in fact, developed a wide "intellectual range."

12 HARRIS, JACK THOMAS. "The Factory Hand in the English Novel, 1840-1855," DA, XXVIII (March), 4176A. [Ph.D. dissertation, University of Texas.]
   Gaskell's deeply "sympathetic" "attitude" toward John Barton in Mary Barton makes him a more successful portrayal of a working-class figure than any in the works of Kingsley or Disraeli, even in spite of Gaskell's hostility toward Chartism. Working-class characters are less central in

1968

(HARRIS, JACK THOMAS)
North and South, which was written after Chartism had collapsed.

13   HARRIS, WENDELL V. "English Short Fiction in the 19th Century," Studies in Short Fiction (Newberry, South Carolina), VI (Fall), 3, 28, 32-33.

Gaskell's short fiction, like that of Dickens, Collins, and George Eliot, is "formless" by twentieth-century standards, yet it may be more valuable than "a number of widely acclaimed twentieth-century stories." Gaskell's Cranford, a tale of everyday life, is exceptional among her short fiction for depending upon "treatment" rather than "plot," because most of her short stories, in contrast to her novels, rely on the lurid actions of "violence, criminality, and the supernatural."

14   KOVAČEVIĆ, IVANKA ČUKOVIĆ. "Elizabeta Kleghorn Gaskell," in Romanopisac icartizam: prilozi sociologiji literature engleska socijalna knjizevnost u doba industrijske revolucije. Belgrade: Haucna Rnjiga, pp. 95-124, 178. [Expanded in English version as English Literature and the Industrial Scene, 1750-1850. Leicester: Leicester University Press. Belgrade: University of Belgrade, 1975.]

Gaskell had "authentic" "knowledge of the working class," and Mary Barton has the most originality of her works, though perhaps less "literary merit." Its uniquely sympathetic portrait of the workman John Barton makes the book "the most successful of the Chartist novels." Yet Gaskell's wavering between sympathy toward the working class and loyalty to her own may be responsible for the book's faults: melodrama, an unconvincing ending of reconciliation, and flaws of overall structure. North and South, an attempt to answer her middle-class critics, reflects "the slackening of the class struggle after...mid-century."

15   McVEAGH, J.[OHN]. "Notes on Mrs. Gaskell's Narrative Technique," EIC, XVIII (October), 461-70.

Chapple's argument that North and South was Gaskell's "masterpiece" because Dickens's editorial pressure forced her to be brief [1967.B5] denigrates the leisurely development of her finest work, Wives and Daughters. Perhaps North and South might have been still better without the compressed ending. When Gaskell is weak, the fault lies with the overall construction, but, at her best, in such works as Cousin Phillis, Cranford, and Wives and Daughters, an essentially "static" subject allows her to triumph through the leisurely use of "contrast, irony," vivid detail, and firm moral judgment.

16   MARTIN, HAZEL T. "Elizabeth Gaskell," in Petticoat Rebels:
     a Study of the Novels of Social Protest of George Eliot,
     Elizabeth Gaskell and Charlotte Brontë. New York: Helios
     Books, pp. 54-80.
          Gaskell "used the novel as a vehicle of protest" against
     the sexual "double standard"; inferior education for
     women; and, above all, bad working-class conditions. "Her
     novels are not as didactic as Eliot's, but the lesson"
     that Gaskell "strives to teach is just as clear." Cran-
     ford, though filled with "middle-class" female "stereo-
     types," has "survived" best of all her "works," for its
     portrayal of "an age and its people" shows the frustrations
     that result from an overly narrow Protestant Ethic particu-
     larly restrictive for women. "Part of" Gaskell's "purpose
     is to have women recognize...that they" are "themselves to
     a large extent, to blame for the inanities of their lives."

17   POLLARD, ARTHUR. Charlotte Brontë. New York: Humanities
     Press, pp. 1, 2.
          "There is a cult of the Brontës, and" Gaskell "was
     amongst its earliest devotees.... She was deeply moved by
     the harsh circumstances of Charlotte's life...." But
     Gaskell's biography "merely confirmed what" Charlotte's
     "novels first stated." Emily's "fearful intensity...was
     enough to frighten" Gaskell "even at second hand.

18   RILEY, MADELEINE. Brought to Bed. London: J. M. Dent &
     Sons. South Brunswick, New Jersey, and New York: A. S.
     Barnes & Co., pp. 21-24, 43, 76-78.
          Gaskell's Ruth violated the convention of the Victorian
     novel that illegitimate births were unmitigated disasters,
     yet Gaskell felt compelled to kill off Ruth at the end.
     Gaskell was "herself a mother" and wrote "eminently domes-
     tic novels...in all of" which "children are born," yet she
     avoided the impropriety of a direct description of child-
     birth. Even in her realistic description of "a fatal
     birth" in Mary Barton, "no close-ups are allowed." In
     Cranford Matty fails to recognize her maid's pregnancy
     and is surprised by the arrival of the child, "chastely
     wrapped in flannel."

19   ROBERTS, JOHN KIMBERLEY. "A Note on English Writers and
     Welsh Railways," AWR, XVII (Summer), 136-38.
          In an early short story of Gaskell's, she describes
     "the remote charm of Penmorfa," which appealed to her be-
     cause of its difference from the usual resort town in
     England.

1968

20 ROTNER, ARNOLD HERBERT. "Mrs. Gaskell's Art," DA, XXIX
(July), 272A. [Ph.D. dissertation, University of Colorado.]
The form of Gaskell's "art novels" is superior to that of
her "didactic novels." In the "art novels" she uses a
"central intelligence and an oblique form of interior mono-
logue," but in the "didactic novels" she damages immediacy
by "authorial intrusions." This study analyzes Mary Barton, Ruth, North and South, Sylvia's Lovers, and Wives and
Daughters.

21 SUSSMAN, HERBERT L. Victorians and the Machine: the Literary
Response to Technology. Cambridge, Massachusetts: Harvard
University Press, pp. 45, 50, 68, 70.
The comparison, by Mr. Hale in North and South, of the
steam-hammer to Arabian-Nights "genii" emphasizes the awe-
some "power of the machine rather than...its functional
beauty" and is typical of the nineteenth-century imagination when confronted by technology. One of the few descriptions "of a factory interior" in Mary Barton emphasizes its
hellishness. Rather than the "psychic harm" connected by
Gissing with "mechanization," Gaskell stresses "the simple
fact of starvation and disease." In North and South,
though, she "praises" the worker for matching the "endurance" of the machine.

22 TARRATT, MARGARET. "Cranford and 'the Strict Code of Gentility'," EIC, XVIII (April), 152-63.
Dodsworth's claim that Cranford is unified by an unconscious hostility toward men [1963.B6] ignores "the author's
conscious control of her material." He is wrong in thinking that Deborah Jenkyns is typical of Cranford's feminine
attitudes, for Deborah's "strict code of gentility" and
repression was originally imposed by a "patriarch," Parson
Jenkyns. Rebelling against this code, Miss Matty understands her parents' romantic love, Peter's adolescent revolt, and the sexual "relationship" of Martha and Jem. In
Cranford "it is not feminist assertiveness but feminine
subservience that is in question."

23 WOLFE, PATRICIA A. "Structure and Movement in Cranford," NCF,
XXIII (September), 161-76.
"The movement" of Cranford, epitomized by the shift from
Miss Deborah to Miss Matty, "can be explained as a progression from psychological abnormality to psychological
normality, from a perverted sense of feminism to a natural
application of femininity." The book's pattern "demonstrates the limitless strength of the female when she over-
comes her fear of male domination" and concentrates "on
giving tenderness and understanding to mankind."

1969 A BOOKS

1 GANZ, MARGARET. <u>Elizabeth Gaskell: the Artist in Conflict</u>.
   New York: Twayne Publishers.
   This study considers Gaskell's works thematically rather
   than chronologically. A basic "conflict between her instinctive impulses" and her social and religious conventionality "often prevented" Gaskell "from achieving the
   universality of the great artist." Only through "humor"
   does she "transcend" this conflict, and her only "masterpiece" is the comic <u>Cranford</u>. Evidence for Gaskell's ambivalence can be found in the contrast between the often
   serene tone of her fiction and her tendency toward "morbid...melodrama," between the "propriety" of her "wit" in
   her novels and its freedom in her letters, between the
   "sophistication" of her work and its "reticence." <u>Mary</u>
   <u>Barton</u> is a better working-class novel than any by Disraeli
   or Kingsley, yet Gaskell's impressive characterization of
   John Barton is marred by her judgment of him according
   to Christian standards of "resignation" and by her unwillingness "to establish the responsibility for social de-
   privation." <u>North and South</u> is artistically superior to
   <u>Mary Barton</u>, but the later novel, though largely about
   romantic love, portrays the working classes with a "pa-
   ternalism" inconsistent with Christian assumptions. <u>Ruth</u>
   reveals Gaskell's own conflict between a belief in divine
   mercy and in social retribution as an instrument of divine
   will. The comedy of <u>Cranford</u> allows Gaskell to deal with
   the conflict between "emotion" and social "convention" in
   an "amused" and non-reformist way. The less universal <u>My</u>
   <u>Lady Ludlow</u> does portray a comic ambivalence about conventional morality in a way that resembles <u>Cranford</u>. <u>Wives</u>
   <u>and Daughters</u> displays a new depth of psychological insight because of Gaskell's willingness to portray such im-
   perfect human beings as Clare and Cynthia without emphasizing an adverse "moral judgment," but the subtle characterization contrasts with the "unsubtle" plot. In <u>The Life</u>
   <u>of Charlotte Brontë</u>, impressive though it is, Gaskell's
   fear of the reading public's disapproval inhibits the
   lively frankness and "humorous sophistication" that she
   displays about the Brontës in her letters. "Lois the Witch"
   expresses Gaskell's condemnation of religious persecution
   but is confused by her own "susceptibility to" the "supernatural" and to "irrational feeling." The artistically
   "effective" <u>Cousin Phillis</u> "avoids melodrama at the end...
   by having Phillis recover" but does not make clear whether
   she will achieve "a final acceptance" of her troubles. The
   psychologically subtle tragedy of <u>Sylvia's Lovers</u> is flawed

1969

(GANZ, MARGARET)
by its framework of "conventional moral standards." [A
highly selective but useful bibliography, with brief annotations, appears on pp. 293-308.]
[Reviews of Mrs. Ganz's book included the following:
Keith Cushman. "... Elizabeth Gaskell: the Artist in Conflict," LJ, XCIV (15 June 1969), 2469 (Gaskell "does not
seem quite big enough to" justify Mrs. Ganz's thesis of
"an artist in conflict." The study shows that it is difficult to write "first-rate criticism about a resolutely
minor figure."). John McVeagh. "Elizabeth Gaskell: the
Artist in Conflict,..." MLR, LXV (October 1970), 887-88
(Mrs. Ganz's emphasis on a split within Gaskell between
"instincts" and conventionality is essentially inappropriate
because it stresses "what went wrong rather than what went
right" in a writer "so demonstrably free from neurotic in-
stability.") E.(dgar) Wright. "Elizabeth Gaskell: the
Artist in Conflict,..." VS, XIV (September 1970), 97-98
(It is hard to reconcile critically the split between Gaskell's social novels and her humorous ones of small-town
life, and this split causes a similar split in "Margaret
Ganz's otherwise sympathetic, interesting, and concise
study." She underestimates Wives and Daughters and ignores
the creative effect that can come from the tensions of a
culture.).]

1969 B   SHORTER WRITINGS

1   BENTLEY, PHYLLIS. The Brontës and Their World. New York:
Viking Press, a Studio Book, pp. 79, 104, 107-9, 113,
122-23.
Because Gaskell was a "Unitarian minister's wife in the
reign of Queen Victoria," it is no wonder that she was
horrified by Charlotte Brontë's letters to M. Heger and
"gave only two...decorous extracts from them" in The Life
of Charlotte Brontë. A friend of Charlotte's, Gaskell "was
one of the sweetest, kindest and most intelligent of women,
and a good novelist to boot." In spite of controversy
about it, Gaskell's Life is "one of the finest biographies
in English literature."

2   BRANTLINGER, PATRICK. "The Case Against Trade Unions in Early
Victorian Fiction," VS, XIII (September), 37-52.
Gaskell's Mary Barton depicts trade unions as violent
and irresponsible, just as Carlyle did in Chartism, yet,
actually, early-Victorian unions "had no monopoly on violence." In contrast to the vengeful portrayal of Luddism

in Shirley, Gaskell does allow John Barton to escape legal
retribution and be punished only by his own conscience.
But although she allows the union some justification and
shows that it "embodies the ideal of cooperation," she
criticizes it for setting "class against class." In North
and South, she allows Higgins no arguments against "the
iron law of wages," for, though she attacked "political
economy as unfeeling," she accepted many of its ideas.
Still, "North and South contains the most sympathetic account of trade union action in early Victorian fiction."

3   GROSS, JOHN. The Rise and Fall of the Man of Letters. A
    Study of the Idiosyncratic and the Humane in Modern Litera-
    ture. London: Wiedenfeld & Nicolson. U. S. A.: Mac-
    millan Co., pp. 275-76, 278-89.
        F. R. Leavis, in The Great Tradition [1948.B13], "in-
    discriminately" includes Trollope and Gaskell among "minor
    Victorian novelists" such as Charlotte M. Yonge, Charles
    and Henry Kingsley, and Shorthouse, and then robs these
    two important writers "of all individual distinction" by
    speaking of "'the ruck of Gaskells and Trollopes'." Leavis
    ignores the fact that George Eliot "learned" as much from
    Gaskell as from Jane Austen.

4   JOHNSON, WENDELL STACEY, comp. "Elizabeth Cleghorn Gaskell,"
    in Victorian Literature and American Literature. The
    Critical Temper: a Survey of Modern Criticism on English
    and American Literature from the Beginnings to the Twenti-
    eth Century, edited by Martin Tucker, III. New York:
    Frederick Ungar Publishing Co., pp. 99-101.
        [The item contains brief quotations from a few selected
    critical works on Gaskell.]

5   KNIES, EARL A. The Art of Charlotte Brontë. Athens, Ohio:
    Ohio University Press, pp. 4, 5, 15, 32, 34, 36, 38, 71,
    163, 167, 215-17.
        Gaskell's Life oversimplifies Mr. Brontë by emphasizing
    his selfishness and eccentricity yet remains the "best
    biography" of Charlotte. Evidence suggests that Charlotte
    may have begun Jane Eyre on March 16th, 1847, instead of,
    as Gaskell says, in August of 1846.

6   LERNER, LAURENCE. "Introduction," in Wives and Daughters.
    Harmondsworth, Middlesex: Penguin Books, pp. 7-27.
        Although Gaskell is usually dismissed as the author of
    the charmingly "feminine" but "limited" Cranford, her Wives
    and Daughters is "the most neglected novel of its century,"
    superior in "wit," "pathos," and "intelligence" "to Jane

1969

(LERNER, LAURENCE)
Eyre, Barchester Towers, or Pendennis," and comparable to
the works of Jane Austen and George Eliot. For all her
wide travels, Gaskell "was...a provincial at heart." Works
of hers that were attacked in their time now seem tame:
Mary Barton's criticism of "the bourgeosie" comes from an
unalienated member of it, Ruth is basically "conventional,"
and The Life of Charlotte Brontë appears more reticent than
indiscreet. Gaskell's second finest novel is North and
South because here an "ambivalence" about the conflicting
claims of opposing ways of life "keeps the writing tense
and" vital. Because Gaskell "was at home in her tradition"
of fictional "realism," "her fine but moderate gifts yielded
more than moderate results."

7 MEWS, HAZEL. Frail Vessels. Women's Role in Women's Novels
   from Fanny Burney to George Eliot. London: University of
   London, Athlone Press, pp. ix, 4, 6, 29, 81-97, 99, 126,
   140-44, 146, 161, 168-69, 183-84, 186-90, 196-97.
       Gaskell's "unmistakably feminine" novels "are an attrac-
   tive expression of the thought of an average woman of her
   time, not fully conservative and yet not radically advanced." Mary Barton accepts "contemporary standards"
   about women's behavior yet shows both the "difficulties"
   of the life of working girls and the need of women's gift
   for "human sympathy" in a harsh industrial world. The
   progression of the portrayal of fallen women from Mary
   Barton to Ruth shows Gaskell's increasing scepticism about
   Victorian moral standards, though Ruth is a commonplace
   heroine. North and South has a haughty heroine who medi-
   tates on the idea of women having the "freedom" to work,
   though she herself never neglects her traditional "feminine
   duties"; Cousin Phillis and Wives and Daughters both explore the problems involved in education for women; and
   Sylvia's Lovers hinges on a conflict between a woman's
   feelings and her duty to her husband. If The Life of Charlotte Brontë examines the difficulties of a woman with a
   career, Cranford exalts traditional female "virtues."

8 MORRISON, N. BRYSSON. Haworth Harvest. The Lives of the
   Brontës. London: J. M. Dent & Sons, pp. 232-33, 257,
   260-61, 263.
       Charlotte Brontë "was grateful for her friendship" with
   Gaskell, "a good, a great woman" with "cheerful, pleasing,
   cordial manners" and a "kind...heart."

9 SHORT, CLARICE. "The Letters of Mrs. Gaskell,..." MP, LXV
   (February), 284-85.

"... One may become addicted" to the "pleasant current" of Gaskell's letters, which are excellently edited. Her letters "reveal a character and that character's response to a stirring era," and they tend toward "a fine abandon" of style. This book sheds light both on social history and the English novel and should also revive interest in Gaskell's works.

10   TARR, ROGER LeROY. "Carlyle's Influence upon the Mid-Victorian Social Novels of Gaskell, Kingsley, and Dickens," DA, XXIX (January), 2285A. [Ph.D. dissertation, University of South Carolina.]
        Gaskell's Mary Barton and North and South conform to Carlyle's concept of what novels should be like: they propound a "message," contain "realistic portrayals," and express "fundamental truths." More specifically, Gaskell's two novels, like the social novels of Dickens and Kingsley, reassert Carlyle's "pronouncements" about society, morals, and politics.

1970 A   BOOKS

1   SHARPS, JOHN GEOFFREY. Mrs. Gaskell's Observation and Invention: a Study of Her Non-Biographic Works. With a forward by A.[rchie] Stanton Whitfield. Fontwell, Sussex: Linden Press.
        This study examines the element in Gaskell's work that derives from personal "observation" and that which derives from "invention" and art. The arrangement of the study is "chronological." Mary Barton is accurate in its descriptions of the working-class poor, but its art is not "altogether assured." Cranford draws so "heavily upon" Gaskell's "Knutsford childhood" that its success comes "as much from" her "skill in choosing as from her power of inventing." Ruth fails largely because Gaskell could not make up convincing particulars about her "heroine's seduction," which lay outside of the writer's own experience. She grew "artistically aware of herself" in North and South, a book in which observed details about industrial conditions become secondary to "the love theme." The structural weaknesses of My Lady Ludlow can be explained by Gaskell's having to invent "as she went along" for serialization in Household Words, and, as a result, the work is at its best in scattered passages. "Lois the Witch" affords one of the most structurally satisfying of" Gaskell's "plots, perhaps partly owing to the...historical framework." Some of the Whitby background for Sylvia's

(SHARPS, JOHN GEOFFREY)

Lovers was obtained by Gaskell through interviews with
local inhabitants, similar to those that she conducted in
researching The Life of Charlotte Brontë. Philip, in
Sylvia's Lovers, is "the most successful full-length male
character in all of" Gaskell's "fiction." Perhaps "arche-
typal" elements concerning a loss of Eden help explain why
Cousin Phillis achieves a universality and depth unusual
for Gaskell. Wives and Daughters exhibits a wider "social
panorama" than any of her other works, and the book
has a "Trollopean fidelity." "The slowness of the" book's
"action seems wholly in keeping with the gradual passing
of the years in a locality little touched by time." In
sum, Gaskell had fine powers of "observation" and invention but "possessed little architectonic power; nor did
she see into the life of things," yet "recent criticism
has done her less than justice."

[Reviews of Sharps's book included the following: Anon.
"Maximizing the Minor Writings of Mrs. Gaskell,..." TLS
(26 February 1971), p. 251 (The footnotes and scholarly
apparatus are excessively elaborate, and Sharps provides
far too much commentary on ephemeral lesser works. Though
he fails to indicate Gaskell's "final literary standing,"
one might very well decide that Gaskell is more important
than the "self-centered" Charlotte Brontë.). Anon. "Mrs.
Gaskell's Observation and Invention,..." British Books
News (London) (February 1971), p. 149 ("The literary criticism is not very profound," but the book will be a "useful" "quarry" of scholarly details for "advanced students.").
Stephen Gill. "Review. Mrs. Gaskell Belatedly Takes Her
Place on the Syllabus,..." Times Educational Supplement
(London) (August 1971), p. 13 (In her appreciation of the
"poetry" of humble life, Gaskell is closer to Wordsworth
than to "any other writer of her age," and she was "the
greatest Victorian novelist of sensibility." Sharps's
study of her is "definitive" in terms of "scholarship" but
fails to analyze the quality that makes Gaskell's fiction
"live."). Graham Handley. "Mrs. Gaskell's Observation
and Invention,..." N & Q, n.s. XIX (July 1972), 280 (This
book is "indispensible," because of its "exhaustive"
scholarship, to anyone interested in Gaskell. In spite
of its flatness, excessive footnotes, and absence of profound critical "insight," this is "the major work on"
Gaskell "so far published" and is unlikely to "be superseded."). D.[onald] [G.] H.[opewell]. "Reviews.... Mrs.
Gaskell's Observation and Invention,..." Brontë Society
Transactions (Keighley), XVI, part VIII (1971), 55-56
(Here is the outstanding work on Gaskell of the past twenty

years. This definitely scholarly study is "not easy to
read" but rewards one.). Lawrence Jones. "Mrs. Gaskell's
Observation and Invention,..." VS, XV (June 1972), 497-99
(The book's "main value lies in the wealth of detail that
Mr. Sharps has amassed." It provides "the raw materials
for criticism rather than criticism itself."). J.[ohn] R.
T.[ownsend]. "Mrs. Gaskell's World," Guardian (Manchester)
(9 December 1971), p. 8 (Sharps is an excellent "scholar"
through a "pedestrian" critic. "... There is still ample
room for perceptive criticism of" Gaskell's "novels.").]

1970 B SHORTER WRITINGS

1 BREUNINGER, MARGARETE. Funktion und Wertung des Romans im
   frühviktorianischen Roman. Tübingen: Max Niemeyer, pp. 7,
   9, 12, 14, 22, 27, 29, 114-16, 153.
       The literary quarrel in Cranford between Captain Brown
   and Miss Jenkyns over the relative merits of Dickens and
   Dr. Johnson as novelists is a quarrel between the moralistic novel of the eighteenth century and the work of the
   greatest comic genius of nineteenth-century English fiction.
   Gaskell strikes a blow here for the modern novel.

2 CHAPPLE, J. A. V. Documentary and Imaginative Literature,
   1880-1920. N.p.: Barnes & Noble, pp. 23, 55, 76-78, 80,
   99, 275, 361.
       Lawrence's The Rainbow presents some parallels to the
   way that Gaskell, in North and South, used "the industrial
   and the rural as the conflicting elements in a myth about
   ...England." But there are basic differences: Gaskell
   displays an unLaurentian optimism in believing that the
   old and the new can be reconciled and in her faith that
   "intelligence and good will" can save "the existing order."
   Gaskell sticks closer than Lawrence to historical facts.

3 DODSWORTH, MARTIN. "Introduction," in North and South. Edited
   by Dorothy Collin. Harmondsworth, Middlesex: Penguin
   Books, pp. 7-25.
       Some critics prefer Gaskell's non-didactic and rural
   novels for their art, but others prefer her industrial
   novels for their "cultural history." Neither critical approach is much help in analyzing North and South, for,
   though it describes an industrial "community," it emphasizes "the role of the individual." North and South is
   Gaskell's one work that tries to deal with the kind of
   powerful emotion portrayed in the novels of Charlotte
   Brontë, but Gaskell is far more aware than Charlotte that

1970

(DODSWORTH, MARTIN)
"passion" must express itself within "the social order."
The "courtship" of Margaret and Thornton develops through
their debate about industrial relations, yet the city's
"social problem" is not "the centre of interest." Even the
strike and the riot provide unconscious sexual comment
about the relationship of Margaret and Thornton, for, in
the violence of the men, Margaret perceives "for the first
time" the force of "aroused male passion." North and South
is not "a perfect novel," but it "has solid foundations."

4   EDDY, SPENCER L., JR. The Founding of the Cornhill Magazine.
Ball State Monograph, no. 10. Publications in English,
no. 13. Muncie, Indiana: Ball State University, pp. 3,
27-32.
Gaskell was a Cornhill contributor who "preferred to
deal directly with" publisher George Smith rather "than
with Thackeray," the editor. Her lack of a good relationship with Thackeray may have delayed her for a time in
agreeing to write for the Cornhill, and she also had reser-
vations about George Henry Lewes, a member of the staff.
Her first publication in the magazine was "Curious if True,"
but it also published her finest work, Wives and Daughters.

5   GILL, STEPHEN. "The Author," "Introduction," and "Prefatory
Note on the Background of Mary Barton," in Mary Barton.
Harmondsworth, Middlesex: Penguin Books, pp. 7, 9-28,
31-32.
Gaskell's "output was...wholly professional" in spite of
her commitment to being "a wife and mother." In writing of
the Manchester poor, she had the advantage over the more
imaginative Dickens and the more assertive Carlyle of
really knowing the scene. Mary Barton is a social document,
yet its portrayal of "the sufferings of the poor and innocent" touches "us with an appeal that is beyond time," for
Gaskell's "real strength is not fidelity to objects or
scenes, but fidelity to feelings." No novelist before
Hardy was as good as Gaskell at portraying the "sources of
tension in a society" through "human emotions." The novel
has flaws: the complex social portrayal of the first half
gives way to mere "moral tableau" and "romance," middle-
class attitudes intrude in narrative comments, and John
Barton's representative function is destroyed by making
him a murderer. Yet the fact that Gaskell even attempted
such a subject expresses a valuable "belief that the
imaginative artist" can both "interpret" and "change"
"society.

6 _____. "A Manuscript of Branwell Brontë with Letters of Mrs. Gaskell," Brontë Society Transactions (Keighley), XV, part LXXX, 408-11.

In the Wordsworth Library, Grasmere, are two letters of August 1850 to Jemima Quillinan, daughter of Wordsworth's son-in-law, asking and then thanking for her help in obtaining Branwell's letter to Wordsworth.

7 GOLDFARD, RUSSELL M. Sexual Repression and Victorian Literature. Lewisburg, Pennsylvania: Bucknell University Press, pp. 22, 34, 184.

Gaskell was one of the many Victorian writers who were "born and raised in an Evangelical era and in various ways affected by its repressive forces." Her Ruth shocked "the reading public" by portraying the troubles of a "lonely girl" who "is seduced by a minister [sic]."

8 HARDY, BARBARA. "Mrs. Gaskell and George Eliot," in The Victorians. Edited by Arthur Pollard. History of Literature in the English Language, VI. London: Barrie & Jenkins, pp. 169-83, 185, 186-87, 190.

Recent critics have "rightly" denied that Gaskell was merely "a minor, charming" writer and have "emphasized" her "sociological" strength and psychological perceptiveness. In her "six important novels, one fine nouvelle," and her great biography, Gaskell was, above all, a writer of "sensibility," free "from simplification and caricature." Mary Barton is rare in convincingly portraying the domestic "habits of the poor," yet Gaskell urges only "modest" demands for them. The saintliness of the heroine makes Ruth too "narrowly didactic." North and South is "the best of" Gaskell's "social novels" because of its range of characterization and its advance in the use of "fable." Apart from its famed "charm, pathos, and humour," Cranford achieves subtlety through the sympathetic irony of its narrator and a "cunning continuity" of plot. Both Cousin Phillis--with its "brillian creation" of a "beautiful," "bookish," and "vulnerable" heroine--and Wives and Daughters--with its complex portrayal of "Molly's passionate feelings"--reveal "almost unbearable sadness" and show "how human beings bear it." The powerful and "morally tolerant" Sylvia's Lovers is rare in having a heroine with a broad "range of passions" but not "high intelligence." "... One reason for the revival of interest in" Gaskell "may" be "her appealing lack of moral absolutism."

9 HUXLEY, ANN. "Preface," "Historical Appendix," "Chronology," "The Secret World of the Brontë Children," "Charlotte in

1970

(HUXLEY, ANN)
Love," "The Brontës and Their Books," "Why Did the Brontës
Die so Young?" in The Life of Charlotte Brontë. Geneva:
Edito-Service, published by an arrangement with J. M. Dent
& Sons, pp. xi-xiv, 406-30.
"Mr. Brontë expressly requested that" Gaskell "use her
own name when publishing the book," to insure its success
and immortality. And she, who had been upset by published
attacks on Charlotte, wrote the biography to vindicate her
friend. Gaskell would have been "shocked" by Charlotte's
"erotic fantasies," which are revealed in the juvenilia.
Probably Gaskell and M. Heger together decided that little
should be used from Charlotte's revealing letters to him.
Charlotte had made her publisher promise to prevent "any
French publication" of Villette, but the Hegers obtained
the pirated Brussels translation of 1855, and it was surely
the unflattering "portrait of Madame Heger...that led" to
her refusal "to see" Gaskell in 1856. Although there were
unsanitary conditions at Haworth, the principal cause of
the early deaths of the Brontës was medical ignorance of
the infectious nature of tuberculosis.

10   LANE, MARGARET. "Introduction," in Cousin Phillis. My Lady
Ludlow. Half a Life-time Ago. Right at Last. The Sexton's
Hero. Everyman's Library. London: Dent. New York:
Dutton, pp. v-xi.
Gaskell wrote Cousin Phillis to please herself and broke
with the "authoritarian" editor of Household Words, Dickens,
in offering it to the Cornhill instead. She left her
earlier subjects and wrote "a country love story of the
simplest and tenderest kind." With the possible "exception"
of Wives and Daughters, this is the best example of Gaskell's "feminine talent," "unforced prose," warm appreciation of "country life," and delicately humorous insight
about human nature.

11   LANSBURY, CORAL. Arcady in Australia: the Evocation of Australia in Nineteenth-Century English Literature. Carlton,
Victoria, Australia: Melbourne University Press, pp. 28,
38, 96, 99, 102.
In Mary Barton Gaskell shows "that John Barton's tragedy
lies in the essential futility of his work." In both Mary
Barton and Ruth, Gaskell displays a compassion for fallen
women that was rare among Victorians. She tried to help an
actual fallen woman by aiding Thomas Wright's scheme to get
her to emigrate to Australia.

12 McVEAGH, JOHN. "The Making of Sylvia's Lovers," MLR, LXV
   (April), 272-81.
   One can see "what went wrong" in the melodramatic conclusion of Sylvia's Lovers. Gaskell had planned to have
   the first volume concentrate on Sylvia and Kinraid, the
   second on Sylvia and Hepburn, and the third on the "tragic"
   complications in the relationship of the three. But the
   execution of Daniel Robson deprived Gaskell of the figure
   who linked various essential characters and themes, and
   the tragedy of Robson's death falsifies all her later attempts to restore some of the book's earlier gaiety. Gaskell's letters reveal that there were too many personal
   pressures and delays between the writing of the different
   volumes, and these pressures kept her from resolving "con-
   tradictions inherent in" her novel.

13 MELADA, IVAN. The Captain of Industry in English Fiction
   1821-1871. Albuquerque, New Mexico: University of New
   Mexico Press, pp. 18-19, 73-86, 88, 95, 101, 111, 147-52,
   180, 181.
   Gaskell was a Christian sentimentalist who preached
   "reconciliation" in Mary Barton, yet, "in writing the novel
   from the Chartist working man's point of view," she "un-
   wittingly" portrayed the manufacturer within the framework
   of three basic Radical assumptions: 1) that workers un-
   justly suffered more than their employers in hard times,
   2) that employers were "lascivious" with their female employees, 3) "that the newly-rich employer was full of ar-
   rogant pride." By contrast, North and South "ends on the
   note of social harmony with which the era of the 1830s and
   1840s ends: class antagonism is replaced by class association...."

14 WILLIAMS, RAYMOND. "Dickens and Social Ideas," in Dickens
   1970. Edited by Michael Slater. New York: Stein & Day,
   pp. 85-86.
   Gaskell comes much closer than Disraeli to equaling
   Dickens in his capacity to turn a social idea into a shaping
   vision rather than a mere illustration of a thesis. Mary
   Barton is Gaskell's "nearest" approach to Dickens's social
   "vision," but "she was driven back by external opposition,
   from her publisher and friends." Though North and South is
   technically better than Mary Barton, the later novel lacks
   the thematic richness of Gaskell's story of "the good man
   who is a murderer."

1971

1971 A BOOKS - NONE

1971 B SHORTER WRITINGS

1   BOYLE, PATRICIA M. "Elizabeth Gaskell: Her Development and
     Achievement," DAI, XXXI (April), 5352A. [Ph.D. disserta-
     tion, University of Pennsylvania.]
          The prevailing critical view of Gaskell as a minor
     novelist without "intellectual depth" or "development" is
     contradicted by the deepening of her "ideas" and her "art
     from Mary Barton to Wives and Daughters. Beginning with
     North and South and culminating in the later works, Gas-
     kell's faith in the efficacy of "Christian love" gives way
     to scepticism about human perfectability. If not one of
     the "greatest" of Victorian novelists, Gaskell deserves a
     higher reputation than she has.

2   COLLIN, DOROTHY W. "The Composition of Mrs. Gaskell's North
     and South," BJRL, LIV (Autumn), 67-93.
          The editorial quarrels between Dickens and Gaskell over
     the serialization of North and South stemmed largely from
     Dickens's original underestimation of how many printed pages
     would equal a manuscript page of Gaskell's and from his
     subsequent fear that the novel was getting too long.
     Dickens's suggestions for dividing her installments
     were aimed at achieving "suspense." Gaskell's later ex-
     pansion of the story for book form was aimed at clarifying
     themes.

3   EASSON, ANGUS. "Sources of the Following from Mrs. Gaskell's
     North and South (1854-5)," N & Q, n.s. xviii (July), 263-64.
          [The query requests the sources of seven literary allu-
     sions in North and South including the following:] "The
     story of the Eastern King," mentioned in chapter iii, who
     experienced an entire lifetime by dipping "his head into
     a basin of water, at" a "magician's command." [For reply,
     see 1971.B13.]

4   FABER, RICHARD. Proper Stations: Class in Victorian Fiction.
     London: Faber & Faber, pp. 13, 17, 18, 20, 22-24, 27, 29,
     31-33, 36-38, 42-50, 128, 135, 138-39, 149.
          North and South shows, "more clearly than any other
     novel," the dissimilarity between "traditional" English
     aristocrats and the new wealthy industrialists. Lady
     Harriet, in Wives and Daughters, combines a sense of aris-
     tocratic superiority with a belief in ultimate "equality
     in the sight of God." Gaskell's industrial novels achieve
     "rare insight into working-class life," but the subject she

loved most was rural Knutsford, with social ranks ranging
from the genteel poor to the aristocracy. In these rural
novels she urges humanization rather than radical change
of the existing "social structure."

5 FLEISHMAN, AVROM. The English Historical Novel: Walter Scott
   to Virginia Woolf. Baltimore & London: Johns Hopkins
   Press, p. 177.
        Gaskell "tried to win sympathy for the working class by
   realistically portraying, in Sylvia's Lovers,...a popular
   riot against the press gangs at Whitby during the Napoleonic
   Wars. The implication for her readers was undoubtedly that
   industrial strikes in the present age were similar demands
   for elementary justice, though misguided in their violence."

6 GÉRIN, WINIFRED. Emily Brontë: a Biography. Oxford: Clarendon Press, see index for numerous references to Gaskell.
        Charlotte's elegiac view of Emily, which was colored by
   recent loss, was the distorting basis of Gaskell's portrayal of Emily in the Life. Because Gaskell offended
   Emily's one-time employer, Miss Patchett, by repeating
   Charlotte's critical words, Miss Patchett "refused to give
   any information about Emily's life at Law Hill." It is
   strange to see the usually tolerant Gaskell condemning
   Emily's "'insular ideas of dress'."

7 _____. "Introduction," in The Life of Charlotte Brontë.
   Everyman's Library. London: Dent. New York: Dutton,
   pp. v-xii.
        Gaskell's sombre picture of Charlotte resulted from
   having known her only in her last grief-ridden years.
   Also, because of Charlotte's reticence, Gaskell received
   her first impression of her friend's life from a garbled
   version told to her by Lady Kay-Shuttleworth. Gaskell did
   not appreciate "the freedom and intensity" of the Brontës'
   childhood, which is "preserved...in the juvenilia." She
   wrote the Life as "an Apologia" in answer to charges
   that Charlotte was a naughty woman, but, in defending Charlotte, Gaskell was unjust to Mr. Brontë and also decorously
   omitted the key "experience" of her subject's life--her
   "frustrated love for M. Heger."

8 HANNAH, BARBARA. Striving towards Wholeness. New York:
   G. P. Putnam's Sons, for the C. G. Jung Foundation for
   Analytical Psychology, pp. 105, 107-8, 121-22, 125, 126,
   129-31, 137, 140-42, 146, 149, 153, 157, 176, 202, 204.
        Gaskell's Life greatly exaggerates Mr. Brontë's "wild-
   ness." He was a very broad-minded man and parent. Gaskell

1971

(HANNAH, BARBARA)
is just in emphasizing Charlotte's tendency to deprecate
herself, but Gaskell's portrayal of Branwell's decline reflects Charlotte's overly "moralistic" interpretation of
the facts. Branwell was dismissed from the Robinson house
just as likely in "protection" of the son as of the wife.

9   KEATING, P. J. The Working Classes in Victorian Fiction.
    London: Routledge & Kegan Paul, pp. 6, 7, 8, 27, 32, 33,
    35, 55-56, 136, 179, 225, 227-29, 237, 238, 246, 247, 269.
    Gaskell was one of the few English novelists to write
    about the industrial working class as opposed to the
    broader category of the urban poor, and she was the only
    "industrial" novelist who "knew the north of England at
    first hand." Unlike the often "petty" Gissing, who "in-
    spires...disgust at" the life "of the poor," the "idealis-
    tic" Gaskell achieves "sympathy" for them through careful
    selection of details. Her North and South is "the most
    subtle and complex" of all the Victorian industrial novels
    because of the focus provided by Margaret's changing
    attitudes.

10 McCREADY, H. W. "Elizabeth Gaskell and the Cotton Famine in
    Manchester: Some Unpublished Letters," Transactions of
    the Historic Society of Lancashire and Cheshire (Liver-
    pool), CXXIII, 144-50.
    These previously unpublished letters to the barrister
    Vernon Lushington "convey and...document" Gaskell's
    "assessment of the cotton famine" of the 1860s.

11 PAGE, NORMAN. "Ruth and Hard Times: a Dickens Source,"
    N & Q, n.s. XVIII (November), 413.
    Dickens's Gradgrind in Hard Times owes much to Gaskell's
    Bradford in Ruth, and Hard Times is also indebted to Gas-
    kell's use of Lancashire dialect and to her husband's
    lecture on the subject.

12 SCHWARTZ, STEPHEN LEE. "Elizabeth Gaskell: the Novelist as
    Artist," DAI, XXXII (December), 3269A. [Ph.D. disserta-
    tion, University of Rochester.]
    This study examines both "significant critical works
    on" Gaskell "since 1900" and Gaskell's "six novels" and
    concludes that her art has been overpraised.

13 SHIPPS, ANTHONY W. "Sources of the Following from Mrs. Gas-
    kell's North and South [reply to n.s. XVIII, 263]," N & Q,
    n.s. XVIII (November), 424.

1972

"The story of the eastern King" was told by Addison in the Spectator, no. 94 (18 June 1711) and "comes from 'The History of Chec Chahabeddin', in the Turkish Tales (1708)." [For query, see 1971.B3.]

14 SHOWALTER, ELAINE. "Women Writers and the Double Standard," in Woman in Sexist Society: Studies in Power and Power-lessness. Edited by Vivian Gornick and Barbara K. Moran. New York: Basic Books. [Reprint. New York and Scarborough, Ontario: New American Library, Mentor Book, 1972, pp. 452-58, 461-62, 463, 466, 467, 468-69, 470, 471, 475, 478, 479.]

Like other women writers of her "generation," Gaskell "did not wish" for special treatment from reviewers simply because she was a woman, so she at first wrote under a pseudonym or anonymously. Her resistence to Dickens's editorial changes of her work illustrates the increasing independence of women writers. Yet Gaskell's ideas about feminine independence were severely limited: she thought that women might be "aggressive" for "others" but not themselves, that women in general had low "capabilities," and that they should wait until their children had grown up before becoming writers.

1972 A BOOKS - NONE

1972 B SHORTER WRITINGS

1 ANON. "The Stiffening of Upper Lips," TLS (30 June), p. 741.
Cranford is a book read by school girls who generally have no "wish to reread it," but this reissue, edited by Elizabeth Porges Watson, "reveals how fully characteristic of its author's best work" it "is." Miss Watson's introduction is "perceptive" but too short. A possible influence on Cranford's use of "memory" might be Sterne's A Sentimental Journey. Gaskell's novel seems, at first glance, to be "class-ridden" but actually expresses her Christian socialism.

2 BREWSTER, JACK. "The Virtuous Heroes of the English Novel," DAI, XXXII (February), 4601A-2A. [Ph.D. dissertation, Indiana University.]
John Thornton, in Gaskell's North and South, is both "virtuous and heroic," yet he must "undergo a process of initiation," in order that his capitalist "beliefs" may be brought into line with the author's gentler "values of cooperation and sympathy."

1972

*3 BRILL, BARBARA. "Winter Reading. Self-Portrait of Mrs.
Gaskell," Stockport Advertiser (11 February).
North and South, out in a new Penguin edition, is "of
particular interest to anyone...in the Manchester area."
Even if you have already seen or heard the book adapted as
a "television and radio play," "you will enjoy both the
love affair" and Gaskell's portrayal of labor relations,
which is "more balanced" than that in Mary Barton.
"Margaret Hale is very much a self-portrait" of Gaskell.
[Unlocatable. Source: Gaskell Cuttings, Manchester
Central Library.]

4 BUTLER, MARILYN. Maria Edgeworth: a Literary Biography.
Oxford: Clarendon Press, pp. 144, 455, 478, 485.
Maria Edgeworth thought Mary Barton "well done...but...
not calculated to produce any good result." Gaskell's
Wives and Daughters is indebted to Maria Edgeworth's Helen.

5 _____. "The Uniqueness of Cynthia Kirkpatrick: Elizabeth
Gaskell's Wives and Daughters and Maria Edgeworth's Helen,"
RES, n.s. XXIII (August), 278-90.
Gaskell's Cynthia in Wives and Daughters is "substantially" derived from Cecilia in Maria Edgeworth's Helen
and is inferior to the original. The resemblances between
Cynthia and Cecilia are many: they both are charming but
"all things to all men," their speeches are impetuously
ambiguous, and they love the heroine in spite of their own
failings. Helen portrays a deeper relationship between
the two girls than does Wives and Daughters, and Maria
Edgeworth also develops dramatic complexity by having the
heroine involved in Cecilia's "errors." The one original
element that Gaskell has added to the Cecilia-Cynthia
character--the quality of "emotional detachment"--serves
a primarily didactic purpose in allowing Gaskell to make
a moralistic point about the avoidance of lies. If
Cynthia has the fascination of inscrutableness, Cecilia
is the more profound exploration of the moral problem of
lying.

6 COLLIN, [MRS.] DOROTHY W. "Cranford," N & Q, n.s. XIX
(January), 29.
In preparing for my forthcoming edition of Cranford, I
should like "locations of the editions published in" Gaskell's "lifetime," and I should also like to know "of any
contemporary manuscript references to Cranford and of any
advertisements, notices, or reviews."

7   FADER, DANIEL, and GEORGE BORNSTEIN. British Periodicals of
    the 18th and 19th Centuries. Ann Arbor, Michigan: Uni-
    versity Microfilms, pp. 73, 78.
        Gaskell was directly recruited by Dickens to write for
    his Household Words, and she contributed "more than seventy
    pieces," including "Cramford [sic]." She was also one "of
    the most important contributors to All the Year Round....
    It is not too much to say that Dickens, in his role as
    editor, trained" Gaskell "to write serially."

8   GANE, GILL, et al. "Bibliography.... Women Writers before
    the Twentieth Century," in Images of Women in Fiction:
    Feminist Perspectives. Edited by Susan Koppelman Cornil-
    lion. Bowling Green, Ohio: Bowling Green University
    Popular Press, p. 358.
        Gaskell "is particularly revealing of how women's lives
    changed with the changing economic situation of the early
    nineteenth century," and she "is also a good writer."
    Mary Barton, though "melodramatic," provides valuable
    "background" about "the lives of the poor" and particularly
    of "women"; Cranford has "sympathetic" insights into "the
    attitudes" of "spinsters"; and Sylvia'a Lovers deals with
    the "real problems" of a young woman's "relationships with
    men."

9   GORSKY, SUSAN. "The Gentle Doubters: Images of Women in
    Englishwomen's Novels 1840-1920," in Images of Women in
    Fiction: Feminist Perspectives. Edited by Susan Koppelman
    Cornillion. Bowling Green, Ohio: Bowling Green University
    Popular Press, pp. 29, 33, 41-42, 46-47, 49.
        Gaskell, along with George Eliot, Charlotte Brontë, and
    Virginia Woolf, was exceptional in portraying women with
    real individuality. In Wives and Daughters, for example,
    Cynthia's laughing admission that "she climbs...four steps
    at a time" in contrast to Molly's two is a blow for female
    unconventionality, and so is Molly's persistent striving
    for a genuine education over her father's opposition.
    Among Gaskell's numerous portrayals of "warm" and "realis-
    tic" women, Margaret Hale, in North and South, is most
    notable.

10 HARDWICK, ELIZABETH. "Working Girls: the Brontës. Charlotte
    Brontë: the Evolution of Genius. By Winifred Gérin....
    Emily Brontë. By Winifred Gérin,..." New York Review of
    Books, XVII (4 May), 14-15, 17. [Reprinted as Elizabeth
    Hardwick. Chap. i: "The Brontës," in Seduction and Be-
    trayal: Women and Literature. New York: Random House,
    1974, pp. 3-29.]

1972

(HARDWICK, ELIZABETH)
Gaskell's Life of Charlotte Brontë "is written with
perfect sympathy, an experienced and inspired feeling for
detail, and the purest assurance of style.... Out of the
withholdings on the one hand and the rash unfoldings on the
other," Gaskell "created some vexation for herself and
left room for the efforts of future scholars." Her great
biography is, in fact, about "the entire family" and
"records basic material: the anecdotes of home and school,
the deaths, the letters, the poignant gifts and hard work
of the sisters."

11 HOBSBAUM, PHILIP. A Reader's Guide to Charles Dickens.
London: Thames & Hudson, pp. 129, 144, 293.
Gaskell was "the only writer of real distinction" who
was a "regular contributor" to Household Words, "and she
was the only one whose work was free from the abridgment,
tightening, and brightening of Dickens's editorial hand."
The "scenes of poverty" in Dickens's "George Silverman's
Explanation" (1868) are "heavily influenced by" Gaskell's
Mary Barton "but with a raw drama of Dickens's own."

12 MURRAY, PHILIP. "Fantasia on a Theme by Mrs. Gaskell,"
Poetry (Chicago), CXX (July), 228-29.
[This is a poem about characters in Cranford, ending
with the following lines:] "But who can keep shiny boots
from lilac silk gowns? / There was a general chorus of
'indeed!' and then a pause. / That sound in the darkening
hallway? Talking; no, kissing."

13 SMITH, DAVID. "Mary Barton and Hard Times: Their Social
Insights," Mosaic (Winnipeg), V (Winter), 97-112.
Mary Barton gives a more realistic portrayal of working-
class life than does Hard Times, but Dickens's novel is
the more satisfying because "it distorts...minutiae" to
achieve an overall artistic comment about society. Gaskell's story is deformed by her "political and social
presuppositions" and, above all, by her insistence on
Christian "resignation." Because Gaskell's major concern
was "with reconciliation within the confines of society,"
she "was incapable of Dickens's" attack on "the heart" of
that society's very existence.

14 SPACKS, PATRICIA MEYER. "Taking Care: Some Women Novelists,"
Novel: a Forum on Fiction (Providence), VI (Fall), 36-41,
43, 51. [Expanded in Patricia Meyer Spacks. The Female
Imagination. New York: Alfred A. Knopf, 1975, pp. 88-95.]

1972

Gaskell--"a novelist seriously underrated in the twentieth century--wrote several novels dominated by a vivid,
although perhaps not entirely conscious awareness of the
plight of women." Both Mary Barton and North and South
suggest rather than state "hidden analogies between the
plight of women and...workmen," and North and South explores "the possibility of an individual female self-
assertion." In Wives and Daughters even the satiric comedy
about Hyacinth Kirkpatrick shows a sympathy for her inade-
quacies in view of the limited possibilities open to women,
Cynthia illustrates the "trap" of being a "charmer," Mrs.
Hamley is a "model of the woman who sacrifices everything
for" her "men," but Molly has too much "emotional vitality"
to accept such total "self-suppression." One suspects
that there are no happy marriages in Wives and Daughters,
not even the impending "one of Molly and Roger."

15 STEVENS, JOAN. Mary Taylor, Friend of Charlotte Brontë:
   Letters from New Zealand and Elsewhere. Dunedin, New
   Zealand: Auckland University Press, Oxford University
   Press, pp. 9-10, 57, 61, 72, 125, 126, 130, 132-34, 157-67,
   175.
       Gaskell recognized the literary "value" of Mary Taylor's
   letters to her about Charlotte Brontë and "incorporated
   them bodily into the Life."

16 WAGNER, GEOFFREY. Five for Freedom: a Study of Feminism in
   Fiction. London: George Allen & Unwin, pp. 105, 107.
       Gaskell "thought" that Emily Brontë was "like a man."

17 WATSON, ELIZABETH PORGES. "Introduction," in Cranford.
   Oxford English Novels. London: Oxford University Press,
   pp. vii-xii.
       "The structure of Cranford is based on the" interaction
   of the past with the present, and the climax of the work
   is Miss Matty's exchange of "the poor man's note for her
   five carefully saved sovereigns" after the bank failure,
   for her action affirms the positive "values" of the community. If Cranford is "not the greatest" of Gaskell's
   "works," it is certainly "the most...enjoyable."

18 WHEELER, MICHAEL D. "Mrs. Gaskell's Quotations and Allusions,"
   N & Q, n.s. XIX (July), 267.
       [This query asks the sources of five allusions in Mary
   Barton and six, including the following, in Ruth:]
   "Beauty is deceitful and favour a snare." [For reply,
   see 1973.B2.]

Elizabeth Gaskell: A Reference Guide

1973

1973 A   BOOKS - NONE

1973 B   SHORTER WRITINGS

1   ANON. "Between Cultures.... North and South. Edited...by
    Angus Easson,..." TLS (17 August), p. 950.
        As a result of her dissatisfaction with the serialized
    version of North and South produced under Dickens's edi-
    torial pressure, Gaskell made a number of "excellent"
    "additions" for the "book version," and, with more time,
    "might have...recast the whole" concluding "part" and im-
    proved the story's "balance." Even as it is, the book
    surpasses all other "early Victorian industrial" novels
    in "depth of observation and understanding of the struc-
    ture of social, class and personal relationships and how
    spiritual realities lie at their heart." Gaskell's use of
    her heroine as a mediator "between two cultures" reminds
    one of Scott. Gaskell's fiction reveals a "well-stored"
    and a "rich, deeply sane" personality.

2   BARR, D. J. "Mrs. Gaskell's Quotations and Allusions [reply
    to n.s. XIX, 267]," N & Q, n.s. XX (October), 394.
        The saying, in Ruth, that "beauty is deceitful and
    favour a snare" may be "a misquotation of Proverbs 31:30."
    [For query, see 1972.B18.]

3   BURKHART, CHARLES. Charlotte Brontë: a Psycho-sexual Study
    of Her Novels. London: Victor Gollancz, pp. 12, 13, 15,
    17, 19, 22, 28, 49, 50, 58, 88, 117-18, 147.
        Gaskell's concession in the Life about Charlotte Brontë's
    "coarseness" was a euphemism for sexuality. Charlotte
    lamented "that she lacked the wider life experience of" a
    writer such as Gaskell. "In tact, delicacy, and tone,"
    Gaskell's "life of her friend is one of the great biogra-
    phies."

4   De LAURA, DAVID J., ed. Victorian Prose: a Guide to Research.
    New York: Modern Language Association of America.
        [G. B. Tennyson, "The Carlyles," pp. 65, 71-72, 106:]
    Louis Cazamian [1904.B1] "claims a powerful social in-
    fluence for Carlyle on novelists" such as Gaskell and
    Kingsley. [Martin J. Svaglic, "John Henry Newman: Man
    and Humanist," p. 143:] Newman was fond of Gaskell's
    novels. [Richard Helmstadter, "The Victorian Churches,"
    p. 418:] Edgar Wright provides "a good discussion of the
    quality of" Gaskell's "Unitarianism" [1965.A2].

5   EASSON, ANGUS. "Introduction," in North and South. London: Oxford University Press, pp. ix-xviii.

Gaskell suffered from "headaches and dizziness" while writing North and South, partly because of her editorial quarrels with Dickens. The novel could have been made suitable for "serialization," but Gaskell either "could not, or would not" make the necessary changes. Yet North and South is superior to Dickens's Hard Times because Gaskell's book "works more consistently on" the "plane of psychological drama" and also because it avoids a "final solution."

6   EWBANK, INGA-STINA. In Encyclopedia Americana. S.v. "Gaskell, Elizabeth Cleghorn."

Gaskell is "best remembered for her biography of Charlotte Brontë and is not herself "in the first rank of Victorian novelists, but" Gaskell's "realistic and sympathetic rendering of life in various social strata gives her novels both a historical and human interest." The special quality of her fiction comes from her placing her domestic life ahead of her art.

7   FRANKO, PATRICIA. "The Emergence of Harmony: Development in the Novels of Mrs. Gaskell," DAI, XXXIV (August), 769A. [Ph.D. dissertation, Temple University.]

Gaskell "used her art as a way of reconciling the" following oppositions "in man and society": industrial "creativity and destructiveness," "self-hood and selflessness," "feminism and femininity," "permanence" and "change," "romance and reality," and "convention and the individual."

8   FURBANK, P. N. "Books and Writers. Mendacity in Mrs. Gaskell," Encounter (London), XL (June), 51-55.

Gaskell, like many Victorian novelists, had a tendency to put "day-dream" projections of herself into her novels, such as the overly noble heroine of Ruth and Margaret in North and South, about whose "good looks" the narrator shows an unseemly insistence. Also, the narrator of North and South shows no awareness that the self-conscious Margaret is constantly lying to herself about her pride in herself and about her moral attitudes. If deceit in Cranford is made the butt of comedy, the narrator of North and South is herself deceived about the characters that she describes.

9   GORSKY, SUSAN R. "Old Maids and New Women: Alternatives to Marriage in Englishwomen's Novels 1847-1915," JPC, VII (Summer), 68-85.

1973

(GORSKY, SUSAN R.)
Most women novelists in this era assume the necessity of marriage. Matty, in Cranford, illustrates the actual typical spinster: dependent, incapable, ill-educated. Ruth shows illicit love as an unacceptable alternative. The opposition of Molly's father, in Wives and Daughters, to her broad education was already anachronistic as Gaskell wrote the novel.

10 HARDWICK, MICHAEL. A Literary Atlas and Gazetteer of the British Isles. Newton Abbot, Devon: David & Charles (Holdings), pp. 24, 95, 113, 178.
"Knutsford is" Gaskell's Cranford, and her Hollingford in Wives and Daughters. She "lived at several addresses in Manchester," whose "working-class life is much featured in her books."

11 HEILBRUN, CAROLYN G. Toward a Recognition of Androgyny. New York: Alfred A. Knopf, pp. 57, 77.
Novelists such as Trollope, Gaskell, and Maugham, who are significant but not really great, "sport with the conventions in a new way, but never challenge them." "Coleridge was right; great minds do tend to be androgynous," but "in the novels of Trollope or, on the other hand," of Gaskell, "is there a passage which does not" betray the gender of its author?

12 ISAAC, JUDITH. "The Working Class in Early Victorian Novels," DAI, XXXIII (June), 6914A. [Ph.D. dissertation, City University of New York.]
Gaskell's Mary Barton, along with Kingsley's Alton Locke and George Eliot's Felix Holt, expresses ambivalence towards the working class. In these novels, sympathy for the workers is opposed by a "fear" of revolution and also by an inability to imagine an autonomous "working-class consciousness" or even autonomous working-class individuals.

13 PAGE, NORMAN. Speech in the English Novel. London: Longman, pp. 53, 64-65, 79, 91.
"In Mary Barton," Gaskell "put in footnotes from Chaucer and the Prayer Book to provide parallels to her serious" use of Lancashire dialect, "thus making a frontal attack on the...social prejudice" and "ignorance" of her readers. Gaskell's "distinctive achievement was to use" dialect "not as mere sources of comedy or curiosity, but for dramatic purposes in contexts which exploited the contrast with standard forms of speech."

14 SWINDEN, PATRICK. Unofficial Selves: Character in the Novel
    from Dickens to the Present Day. London and Basingstoke:
    Macmillan Press, pp. 42, 49-53, 55, 77, 146.
        Sometimes Gaskell's use of an omniscient narrator places
    a character "at an unfair disadvantage" by telling us
    more about the character's thoughts than he can know him-
    self. In Wives and Daughters Gaskell "is careful to re-
    lease the information she possesses at the most strategic
    points of her narrative," yet "she misses opportunities
    through unwillingness to disclose this information through
    a single dominant consciousness." The revelation of the
    novel's central secret--Cynthia's engagement to Preston--
    is weakened by Molly's "lack of a creative sensibility,"
    which has kept her from speculating about Cynthia's
    behavior.

15 WILLENS, SUSAN POPKIN. "The Novels of Elizabeth Gaskell: the
    Comic Vision," DAI, XXXIII (June), 6889A. [Ph.D. disser-
    tation, Catholic University of America.]
        The comedy in Gaskell's novels serves to resolve the
    conflict between "a stable society" and the changes caused
    by "industrialization," a "new" morality, and natural
    attrition.

16 WINNIFRITH, TOM. The Brontës and Their Background. London
    and Basingstoke: Macmillan Press, pp. 1-2, 8-14, 17, 19,
    30, 34, 46-47, 77-78, 82, 85, 107, 112, 131, 134, 199,
    202-3, 252, 256, 259.
        Gaskell's "classic" Life "immortalized" the Brontës
    but suffers from "faults of subjectivity, inaccuracy, con-
    troversy, and even prudery." Gaskell "was not a profes-
    sional scholar but a novelist" and blurred "fiction and
    fact." Also she tried to avoid "religious controversy"
    in the Life.

1974 A BOOKS - NONE

1974 B SHORTER WRITINGS

1   ALLOTT, MIRIAM. "Preface" and "Introduction," in The Brontës:
    the Critical Heritage. London and Boston: Routledge &
    Kegan Paul, pp. xv, 2-4, 9-10, 13-14, 16, 19, 23, 28-30,
    35-40, 41, 43, 46.
        Gaskell undertook the Life out of "pity, respect and
    admiration." Although Charlotte Brontë was paid only £500
    for each of her novels, Gaskell received £600 for North
    and South and £800 for the Life. Both Charlotte and

1974

(ALLOTT, MIRIAM)
Gaskell were mistaken in believing that Wuthering Heights received no positive recognition from the "early critics." Gaskell's talents as a novelist were wholly different from those of the Brontës, for she had a "generous but wholly conventional kind of insight." In dealing both with Charlotte's supposed "coarseness" and Emily's "supposed" "ruthlessness," Gaskell was limited by her own moral presuppositions. Her own literary "prestige" helped to make the Life popular, "but the fame of the Brontës" helped "still more."

2   ANON. In Micropaedia. The New Encyclopaedia Britannica. 15th edition. S.v. "Gaskell, Elizabeth Cleghorn."
Gaskell's working-class novel Mary Barton won her reputation, Cranford "has remained her most popular work," The Life of Charlotte Brontë is both "a work of art and a well-documented interpretation of its subject," but "many" consider Wives and Daughters Gaskell's "finest" work.

3   AXE, KATHRYN JANE. "Elizabeth Cleghorn Gaskell: a Critical Evaluation of Her Novels," DAI, XXXV (August), 1034A–1035A. [Ph.D. dissertation, University of Kansas.]
In both Gaskell's "social problem novels" and in her "art novels," there is a movement "towards the realization of a small perfect world, which, in turn, serves as a paradigm for society as a whole.... In all...the novels," Gaskell's "agent of reform...is a young woman." But only in Wives and Daughters does Gaskell achieve a thorough integration of "form and purpose."

4   BASCH, FRANÇOISE. Relative Creatures: Victorian Women in Society and the Novel. Translated by Anthony Rudolf. New York: Schocken Books, pp. 175–85, 243–51, and also see index for numerous other references to Gaskell.
Gaskell was sometimes annoyed at her husband's aloofness from family matters and sometimes felt the strain of being both a writer and a homemaker, but her marriage was essentially harmonious, and her relationship with her daughters was unusually fine. She gave her priority to "real" beings in her family as opposed to fictional creatures, yet in the Life she justified a woman's career as a writer by the parable of the talents. Right at Last, Wives and Daughters, and North and South employ the Victorian idea of the female "guide" who leads her men to higher moral goals, yet a character such as Molly shows realistic conflicts in attempting to achieve "altruism." Gaskell clearly does not exalt marriage in her fiction: in Sylvia's Lovers a

376

"loveless" marital relationship is described as a trial of "suffering" that only eventually leads to "maturity and generosity"; and Cranford explores the anomaly of those who remain spinsters because of "the girl's role in the family structure, the importance of money in the marriage-market and the rigidity of the class system." Gaskell's fiction does express a belief in useful education for women, and she is the only "major" Victorian writer of "the first half of the...era to have dealt fairly fully with female labour." Her treatment of the fallen woman in Ruth, for all Gaskell's philanthropic experience of the subject, reveals a "deep unease about sexuality, seduction, prostitution and adultery."

5   BEER, PATRICIA. Reader, I Married Him: a Study of the Women Characters of Jane Austen, Charlotte Brontë, Elizabeth Gaskell and George Eliot. London: Macmillan. New York: Barnes & Noble, Harper & Row, 1975, pp. 1, 9-11, 16-17, 21, 28, 33-38, 127, 129-74.

According to the conventions of her time, Gaskell, in contrast to Jane Austen and Charlotte Brontë, led "an entirely normal, feminine life." Though in many ways conservative on the women question, Gaskell was also capable of views and actions about women that were unorthodox for her time. Her fictional portrayals of religion ignore dogma and "formulae" and stress spontaneity and openness. Gaskell was a pioneer in portraying prostitutes and fallen women with compassion, but her insistence that the heroine of Ruth must suffer and die comes from her feeling that "sexual intercourse outside marriage" has the lingering effect of an incurable "disease," even though it may not be the victim's fault. "The seducers in" Gaskell's "novels are an unappetizing set of men," yet "near-seducers," such as Holdsworth and Kinraid are clearly presented as having a sexual attractiveness that is missing in her Paul Mannings and Philip Hepburns. Not "until Wives and Daughters did" Gaskell show "thorough interest in the eternal who-marries-whom." Within the general framework of sexual frustration in Cranford, she "presents her brightest portrait of sexual fulfillment in the unlikely form of the romance of Lady Glenmire and Mr. Hoggins." The quality that Gaskell admired most in women and heroines was "honesty," though she sometimes had troubles reconciling it with the Victorian ideal of "decorous behavior."

6   DAVIS, MARJORIE TAYLOR. "An Annotated Bibliography of Criticism on Elizabeth Cleghorn Gaskell, 1848-1973." Ph.D. dissertation, University of Mississippi.

1974

(DAVIS, MARJORIE TAYLOR)
[Two introductory chapters:] Gaskell's most important qualities as a writer were realism, the "balancing" of "pathos with humor," and humanitarianism. For a long period after her death, the major interest of critics was identifying models for her fiction from life, but her reputation began to rise in the 1950s, and recent criticism shows it "definitely improving." [The annotated bibliography contains 492 items, almost all of which were listed either in Northup (1929.B6), Whitfield (1929.A3), or in standard annual bibliographies. Fuller annotation is provided than in earlier bibliographies, but a large number of British items are merely listed as unavailable.]

7 EASSON, ANGUS. "Two Suppressed Opinions in Mrs. Gaskell's Life of Charlotte Brontë." Brontë Society Transactions (Keighley), XVI, part LXXXIV, 281-83.
In the manuscript of Gaskell's Life in John Rylands University Library of Manchester, there are two crossed-out "opinions" omitted from the published book. Gaskell called Emily Brontë's stoic behavior at the approach of death "'the very essence of stern selfishness'," but Gaskell may have decided that the comment was either "misleading" or distressing to Mr. Brontë. "She also crossed out a long passage explaining Charlotte's fierce hostility to Catholicism by a suppressed" attraction to it, yet Gaskell's insight was a "shrewd" one that may have been correct.

8 MONTOVANI, JUANITA MARIE. "The Feminine World View of Elizabeth Cleghorn Gaskell," DAI, XXXV (August), 1053A. [Ph.D. dissertation, University of Southern California.]
The strengths and weaknesses of Gaskell's novels result from her "incomplete identification with the Victorian feminine ideal and her preoccupation with womanly concerns." Her most successful characters are women who break out of the conventional female mold yet hold conventional views about the role of women. Although Gaskell's "intuitive" approach could not resolve feminine problems, she did depict them "with humor and...sympathy."

9 NICKEL, MARJORIE ANNE. "The Reconciliation of Opposites in the Work of Elizabeth Gaskell," DAI, XXXV (October), 2288A. [Ph.D. dissertation, University of Notre Dame.]
The central quality of Gaskell's work is a "tendency towards unification of all discordant elements."

10 TOMALIN, CLAIRE. "Books. Anger and Accommodation. Seduction and Betrayal. By Elizabeth Hardwick.... Reader, I Married

<u>Him</u>. By Patricia Beer,..." <u>Listener</u> (London), XCII
(28 November), 714-16.
    Gaskell, "in her great biography of Charlotte" Brontë,
"worries a little at" the Brontë family's "automatic assumption...that the girls should make sacrifices for their
infinitely less talented brother, but" she "does not question the appointed role of the son." Gaskell's attitude
may help to explain her "inconsolable grief upon the death
of her only son, little Willy....'" Though Gaskell was in
many ways enlightened in her portrayals of fallen women,
she never "entertained" "the idea" that they might desire
"sexual experience." [This piece was originally delivered
on B.B.C. Radio 3.]

11   WHEELER, MICHAEL D. "The Writer as Reader in <u>Mary Barton</u>,"
<u>DUJ</u>, n.s. XXXVI (December), 92-102.
    In spite of the widespread belief that Gaskell was a
merely intuitive and unintellectual writer, her reading was
wide and various, and her "novels teem with literary allusions." For example, though she denied any knowledge of
economics in her preface to <u>Mary Barton</u>, she had actually
read <u>The Wealth of Nations</u>.

Index

(Underlined entry numbers after subject headings indicate important items or important sequences of items. Authors of reviews of secondary books on Elizabeth Gaskell are indexed under the number of the item reviewed.)

Deardon, William, 1857.B87
Death of Miss Gaskell, The,"
    1913.B3
"Death of Miss Gaskell.
    Daughter of the Authoress
    of Cranford," 1913.B2
"Death of Miss M. E. Gaskell,"
    1913.B4
"Death of Mrs. Gaskell,"
    1865.B3-8
"Deaths. Gaskell," 1913.B5
"Deaths of Distinguished Per-
    sons. Mrs. Gaskell,"
    1865.B9
"Débuts littéraires de Mrs.
    Gaskell: réflexions sur
    un poème oublié, Les,"
    1964.B7
De Laura, David J., 1973.B4
"Delightful Friendship, A.
    Letters of Mrs. Gaskell
    and Charles Eliot Norton,"
    1932.B3
De Mouy, Charles, 1861.B1
Denison, Isabelle, 1924.B2
Dent, J. C., 1948.B8
Dent, J. M., 1904.B3
Descriptive List of British
    Novels, A, 1891.B4
De Sélincourt, Ernest, 1932.B14
Development of the English
    Novel, The, 1899.B7
Devonshire, Marion Gladys,
    1929.B2
Dialects, 1848.B2, B11;
    1854.B1-2; 1857.B18;
    1863.B8, B23, B25, B28;
    1877.B1; 1926.B2; 1929.A2;
    1941.B2, B6; 1965.A2;
    1973.B13
Diary, A (Bremer) as subject,
    1866.B24
Diary, Reminiscences and Cor-
    respondence, 1869.B2
Dicey, Edward, 1865.B33
Dick, Kay, 1966.B4
Dickens, Charles as letter
    writer, 1880.B3; 1892.B4;
    1912.B4; 1938.B2
--as subject, 1848.B1, B4, B8,
    B10, B13; 1853.B3; 1854.B3;

1855.B10; 1857.B76; 1866.B5,
    B22; 1874.B2; 1878.B7;
    1891.B2; 1893.B4; 1897.B15,
    B19-20; 1898.B10; 1906.B1,
    B11, B23, B33; 1907.B1, B16;
    1908.B15; 1909.B2; 1910.B17,
    B23, B73, B107, B122;
    1911.B17; 1913.B29-30,
    B38-39, B44; 1916.B4;
    1918.B1, B5; 1919.B5;
    1926.B3; 1927.B4; 1929.A2,
    B10; 1931.B10; 1932.B9;
    1933.B11; 1935.B2, B6;
    1936.B2, B9; 1937.B2;
    1941.B4; 1943.B4; 1945.B4-5;
    1946.B6; 1948.B3, B16;
    1949.B5; 1950.B8-10;
    1951.B2, B6; 1952.B4;
    1955.B3, B7; 1956.B3;
    1958.B3, B6-8; 1961.B9;
    1962.B2; 1963.B5; 1967.B5;
    1968.B1, B5, B13, B15;
    1969.B10; 1970.B1, B5, B14;
    1971.B2, B11, B14; 1972.B7,
    B11, B13; 1973.B1, B5
Dickens. His Character, Comedy,
    and Career, 1949.B5
"Dickens, Mrs. Gaskell, and the
    Preston Strike," 1964.B3
Dickens and Crime, 1962.B2
Dickens and Education, 1963.B5
Dickens and His Readers: aspects
    of Novel-Criticism since
    1836, 1955.B3
"Dickens and Mrs. Gaskell,"
    1946.B6
"Dickens and Social Ideas," in
    Dickens 1970, 1970.B14
"Dickens' Appreciation of Mrs.
    Gaskell," 1910.B23
Dickens Circle: a Narrative of
    the Novelist's Friendships,
    The, 1918.B5
"Dickens' Editorial Methods,"
    1943.B4
Dickens World, The, 1941.B4
Dictionary of English Authors:
    Biographical and Bibliog-
    raphical, A, 1898.B10
Dictionary of English Litera-
    ture, A, 1878.B1; 1945.B5

Emily Brontë, 1883.B4; 1929.B9
"Emily Brontë," 1919.B4
Emily Brontë: a Biography,
 1971.B6
Emily Brontë: expérience
 spirituelle et création
 poétique, 1955.B1
Emily Brontë: Her Life and
 Work, 1953.B12
Emotions in Literature, 1848.B9,
 B12; 1849.B5; 1853.B9, B23,
 B54, B57, B59; 1854.B4;
 1855.B2, B8-9, B11-12;
 1857.B8, B10, B24, B62;
 1858.B3, B6; 1860.B2;
 1863.B9, B15, B20, B23,
 B26, B30-31, B33; 1865.A1,
 B33, B35, B37; 1866.B26;
 1874.B3; 1894.B1; 1897.B6;
 1906.B36, B40-41; 1907.B2,
 B24, B29; 1910.B82;
 1911.A1, B11; 1912.B6;
 1916.B4; 1917.B2; 1920.B3;
 1924.A1, B3; 1930.A1;
 1934.B1; 1937.B1, B5-6;
 1941.B6; 1948.B4; 1949.A1;
 1950.B10; 1951.B1; 1960.A1,
 B2; 1964.B9; 1965.A1, B6;
 1966.B8; 1968.A1, B6;
 1969.A1, B6; 1970.B3, B5,
 B8; 1972.B14; 1974.B6
Enciclopedia italiana di
 scienze, lettere, ed arti,
 1932.B14
Enciclopedia universal ilustrada
 europeo-americana, 1930.B1
Encyclopedia Americana, 1973.B6
Encyclopaedia Britannica, The,
 1910.B125; 1965.B17
Encyclopaedia Britannica. A
 Dictionary of Arts, Sciences,
 and General Literature,
 1879.B6
"End of the Brontë Correspondence. A Suggestion. To
 the Editor," 1857.B100
"England," 1853.B9
"England of Marx and Mill as
 Reflected in Fiction, The,"
 1948.B3

Englische Literatur des 19 und
 20 Jahrhunderts, Die,
 1923.B7
Englische Literatur im Zeitalter
 der Königin Viktoria, Die,
 1909.B5
"English Autograph Letters in
 the John Rylands Library,"
 1941.B8
English Fiction from the Fifth
 to the Twentieth Century,
 1912.B8
English Historical Novel, The,
 1971.B5
English History in English
 Fiction, 1940.B5
English Literature, 1906.B25;
 1917.B7; 1918.B1
"English Literature. Biog-
 raphy. . . . The Life of
 Charlotte Brontë," 1857.B15
English Literature. An Intro-
 duction and Guide to the
 Best English Books, 1917.B6
English Literature in Account
 with Religion, 1800-1900,
 1910.B87
English Literature in Fact and
 Story: Being a Brief Ac-
 count of Its Writers and
 Their Backgrounds, 1929.B7
English Literature in the
 Nineteenth Century, 1909.B6
English Literature of the Vic-
 torian Period, 1949.B1
"English Memory, An," 1946.B8
"English Middle Class, The,"
 1854.B3
English Novel, The, 1913.B36;
 1931.B9
English Novel: a Panorama, The,
 1960.B5
English Novel: a Short Critical
 History, The, 1954.B1
English Novel in France, 1830-
 1870, The, 1929.B2
English Novelists, 1932.B9
"English Novelists and American
 Civil War, The," 1962.B5
English Regional Novel, The,
 1941.B2

"English Short Fiction in the 19th Century," 1968.B13
English Village: a Literary Study, 1750-1850, The, 1919.B7
Entwistle, William J., 1943.B2
E. P., 1897.B11
"Époque moderne et contemporaine (1660-1914)," in Histoire de la littérature anglaise, 1924.B3
"Erratum. Charlotte Brontë. To the Editor," 1857.B94
Erskine, Mrs. Steuart, 1915.B3
E. S., 1857.B88
Espinasse, Francis, 1863.B34
Études biographique et lit- téraires. Prosper Mérimée. Hugh Eliot, 1885.B2
"Études critiques. Mrs. Gaskell vue à travers ses lettres," 1968.B1
Evans, John, 1850.B9
Evans, Mary Ann [pseud. George Eliot] as critic, 1856.B3
--as letter writer, 1885.B1; 1953.B3
--as subject, 1866.B8, B22-23; 1867.B1; 1874.B3; 1877.B4; 1878.B7; 1879.B1; 1894.B1-3; 1897.B3, B15-16, B19-20; 1899.B7; 1901.B4, B6; 1902.B7; 1906.B7, B10-11, B20, B23, B31; 1907.B16, B32; 1909.B2; 1910.B47, B51, B103, B116, B122, B130; 1920.B4-5; 1924.A1, B3; 1927.B4; 1930.A1, B5; 1932.B9, B21; 1935.B6; 1936.B7; 1937.B1; 1944.B4; 1947.B2, B7; 1948.B4, B13; 1950.B10-11; 1952.B6; 1954.B3; 1958.B3; 1960.B5; 1964.B10; 1965.A1; 1966.B6, B11; 1967.B6, B11; 1968.A1, B10, B13, B16; 1969.B3, B6; 1972.B9; 1973.B12
E. V. T., 1891.B3
Ewbank, Inga-Stina, 1966.B6; 1973.B6

Excursion in Victorian Bibliog- raphy, 1922.B4
"Exercises. . . . For General Study. . . . Vocabulary for Detailed Study," in Cranford, 1948.B8
Extracts from the Letters and Journals of William Cory, Author of "Ionica," 1897.B8

Faber, Richard, 1971.B4
"Factory Hand in the English Novel, 1840-1855, The," 1968.B12
Facts of Fiction, The, 1932.B13
Fader, Daniel, 1972.B7
"False Morality of Lady Novelists, The," 1859.B6
"Family Life in Early Victorian Prose Fiction," 1941.B3
"Famous Knutsford Chapel, A. Next Month's Celebration of Its 250th Anniversary," 1939.B1
"Fantasia on a Theme by Mrs. Gaskell," 1972.B12
Faraday, F. J., 1904.B4
Father of the Brontës, The, 1958.B5
Fehr, Berhard, 1923.B7
"Feminine World View of Eliza- beth Cleghorn Gaskell, The," 1974.B8
Ffrench, Yvonne, 1932.B15; 1949.A1; 1958.B4
"Fiction. Mary Barton," 1848.B1
Fiction with a Purpose. Major and Minor Nineteenth- Century Novels, 1967.B6
Fielding, K. J., 1965.A1; 1968.B8
"Fifth Annual Meeting of the Brontë Society," 1899.B2
"Fireside Reading Circle, The. Cranford," 1911.B11
First Sketch of English Litera- ture, A, 1912.B12
Fitzgerald, Percy, 1913.B29

(Gaskell, Elizabeth Cleghorn)
--(humor)
    1866.B19, B23; 1867.B2-3;
    1885.B1; 1887.B2; 1890.B8;
    1893.B3; 1894.B1-2; 1895.B3;
    1869.B11; 1897.B6; 1899.B9;
    1902.B2, B5; 1904.B3;
    1905.B6; 1906.B11, B28, B36,
    B38, B41; 1907.B2, B16, B32,
    B38; 1908.B1; 1909.B3, B6;
    1910.B17, B28, B32, B78,
    B96, B135; 1911.B11, B13,
    B19; 1912.B6; 1913.B35, B46;
    1914.B41; 1920.B2-4;
    1923.B5; 1924.B3; 1925.B3,
    B9; 1926.B1; 1930.A1, B3;
    1931.B9; 1932.B14; 1934.B2;
    1935.B8; 1936.B5; 1937.B1-2,
    B6; 1938.B1, B3; 1945.B5;
    1947.B2, B4, B9; 1948.B4, B8,
    B14-15; 1951.B6; 1952.A1;
    1953.B7; 1958.B2; 1959.B6;
    1960.A1-2, B5; 1961.B5;
    1963.B6; 1964.B1; 1965.A1-2;
    1966.B3, B8; 1967.B25;
    1968.A1, B6, B11; 1969.A1,
    B6; 1970.B8, B10; 1972.B14;
    1973.B15; 1974.B6, B8
--as letter writer, 1965.B8
--memorials, 1899.B11; 1907.B5,
    B11-12, B14, B18, B20, B36;
    1910.B22, B53; 1913.B6-8,
    B12-14, B22-24, B47;
    1914.B1, B4-5, B7-23,
    B25-29, B34-40, B42, B44-49,
    B52-55; 1929.B8; 1931.B3-5
--plots, 1848.B8, B10-11;
    1851.B10; 1853.B25, B61;
    1855.B8; 1859.B4; 1863.B4-5,
    B8, B16, B26, B30, B32;
    1865.B37; 1866.B2, B8, B16;
    1890.B8; 1897.B12; 1906.B19,
    B28, B38-39, B41; 1910.B2,
    B82, B122; 1912.B14;
    1914.B32; 1928.B1; 1929.A2-3;
    1930.A1; 1933.B12; 1937.B1;
    1941.B6; 1946.B3; 1949.A1;
    1950.B10; 1954.A1; 1959.B2;
    1965.A1-2, B13; 1968.A2, B2,
    B13; 1969.A1; 1970.A1, B12;
    1972.B8

--style, 1853.B51; 1857.B26,
    B70; 1858.B6; 1863.B18;
    1865.B31, B33; 1866.B8;
    1885.B1; 1896.B11; 1906.B28;
    1908.B1; 1910.B42; 1911.B19;
    1912.B14; 1916.B4; 1934.B6;
    1943.B2; 1947.B2; 1948.B15;
    1949.B1; 1965.A2; 1966.B8;
    1970.B10; 1972.B10
"Gaskell, Elizabeth Cleghorn,"
    in Victorian Prose, 1830-
    1880, 1956.B1
"Gaskell, Gascoign," 1889.B1;
    1890.B1, B5-6
Gaskell, Julia (Daughter of
    Elizabeth) as subject,
    1908.B2-3, B6-7, B11-13,
    B16, B22-23, B29, B31;
    1967.B10
Gaskell, Margaret E. ("Meta,"
    Daughter of Elizabeth)
--as letter writer, 1910.A1
--as subject, 1910.B24, B66,
    B134; 1913.B1-5, B9-10,
    B15-21, B25-28, B30-31, B41;
    1914.B49, B51; 1917.B9;
    1918.B8; 1933.B1, B8;
    1945.B2; 1966.B3
Gaskell, Marianne (Daughter of
    Elizabeth) as subject,
    1922.B6; 1929.A1; 1935.B11
Gaskell, William (Husband of
    Elizabeth)
--as author, 1854.B2
--as subject, 1854.B1; 1880.B5;
    1884.B2-7; 1890.B4, B7;
    1892.B5; 1893.B5; 1903.B1-2;
    1904.B4; 1907.B36; 1910.A1,
    B17, B44, B81, B110;
    1911.B2; 1913.B5; 1914.B51,
    B55; 1925.B7; 1931.B10;
    1932.B4, B20; 1933.B6, B9,
    B11; 1937.B4; 1946.B3;
    1948.B9; 1950.A1; 1951.B6;
    1952.A1; 1956.B6; 1966.B3;
    1967.B1, B26; 1971.B11;
    1974.B4
"Gaskell Centenary, The,"
    1910.B26-32, B36, B88, B115
"Gaskell Centenary, The.
    Dickens's Admiration for the

"Little-Known Home of Mrs.
Gaskell, A," 1910.B129
Living Novel and Later Apprecia-
tions, The, 1964.B10
"'Lizzie Leigh': a Bibliog-
raphical Inquiry," 1967.B12
Lizzie Leigh and Other Tales
(Mrs. Gaskell) as subject,
1855.B1, B9; 1913.B39;
1967.B12
"'Lizzie Leigh' Sold as a
Dickens Item," 1911.B3
"Local Notes," 1910.B50
"Local Notes. Cranford,"
1910.B51
Lock, John, 1965.B11
"'Lois the Witch'," 1903.B11,
B14
Lois the Witch, 1960.B2
"Lois the Witch" (Mrs. Gaskell)
as subject, 1915.B5;
1930.A1; 1932.B21; 1952.A1;
1969.A1; 1970.A1
London County Council, 1914.B42
"London County Council. . . .
Mrs. Gaskell's Mary Barton,"
1907.B7
Long Strike, The (Boucicault)
as subject, 1866.B18;
1959.B2
"Lord Acton's List of the
Hundred Best Books," in
Immortal Memories, 1907.B34
Lorna, 1908.B22
Lover of Truth, A, 1857.B92
Lovett, Robert Morss, 1918.B6;
1932.B16
Low, Francis H., 1899.B9
"Lower Mosely-Street Schools,
Manchester, Annual Reunion.
A Link with Mary Barton,"
1910.B52
Lowndes, Marie Belloc,
1933.B9-10
Lucas, E. V., 1899.B10
Lucas, John, 1965.A2; 1966.B9
Ludlow, John Malcolm Forbes,
1853.B61
Lutyens, Mary, 1967.B19-21
Lyall, Edna. See Bayley, Ada
Ellen

Mabel Vaughan (Cummins) as
subject, 1857.B37
McCready, H. W., 1971.B10
MacDermid, Thomas Wright
1876.B2
Macdonald, Frederika, 1914.B43
MacGill, Frank N., 1958.B9
McLaughlin, Florence Catherine,
1932.B17
Macloed, Donald, 1895.B6
Macmillan, Frederick, 1910.B104
McNulty, J. H., 1917.B5
McVeagh, John, 1968.A2, B15;
1969.A1; 1970.B12
Macy, John, 1925.B4
"Madame Mohl, Her Salon and Her
Friends," 1885.B3
Madle, Herbert, 1938.B4
"Magazine Day. Cornhill,"
1863.B21; 1866.B12
"Magazines, The," 1866.B13
"Magazines for January, The,"
1866.B14
Magnus, Laurie, 1907.B26;
1909.B6
Maison, Margaret M., 1961.B7
"Making of Sylvia's Lovers,
The," 1970.B12
Malcolm-Hayes, Marian V.,
1945.B2
Man Charles Dickens: a Vic-
torian Portrait, The,
1929.B10
Manchester, 1848.B2, B7;
1853.B62; 1858.B3; 1865.B31,
B33; 1878.B2-4, B6, B8-9;
1891.B1; 1895.B4-5; 1896.B8;
1898.B13; 1899.B11; 1900.B18;
1902.B5; 1903.B2, B6;
1904.B2, B4; 1905.B2-4;
1906.B17; 1907.B36; 1908.B9,
B13, B31; 1910.B9-10,
B20-21, B25, B34-35, B38,
B51, B55-58, B74, B79, B81,
B84, B99, B102, B113-14,
B121, B124, B132, B134,
B138-39, B142; 1911.A2,
B1-2, B6, B15, B18; 1912.B1;
1913.B6-7, B10, B12-14, B16,
B28, B47; 1914.A1, B1, B4-7,